REFRIGERATION LICENSE EXAMINATIONS

A COMPLETE GUIDE TO THE WRITTEN AND PRACTICAL EXAMS

Antonio Mejias

Australia • Canada • Mexico • Singapore • Spain • United Kingdom • United States

An ARCO Book

ARCO is a registered trademark of Thomson Learning, Inc. and is used herein under license by Peterson's.

About The Thomson Corporation and Peterson's

With revenues approaching US$6 billion, The Thomson Corporation (www.thomson.com) is a leading global provider of integrated information solutions for business, education, and professional customers. Its Learning businesses and brands (www.thomsonlearning.com) serve the needs of individuals, learning institutions, and corporations with products and services for both traditional and distributed learning.

Peterson's, part of The Thomson Corporation, is one of the nation's most respected providers of lifelong learning online resources, software, reference guides, and books. The Education Supersite[SM] at www.petersons.com—the internet's most heavily traveled education resources—has searchable databases and interactive tools for contacting U.S.-accredited institutions and programs. In addition, Peterson's serves more that 105 million education consumers annually.

For more information, contact Peterson's, 2000 Lenox Drive, Lawrenceville, NJ 08648;
800-338-3282; or find us on the World Wide Web at: www.petersons.com/about

Second Edition

ISSN: International Standard Serial Number information available upon request.
ISBN: 0-7689-1019-6

Printed in the United States of America

10 9 8 7 6 5 4 3 2 04 03

ACKNOWLEDGMENTS

Grateful acknowledgment is extended to the following companies for their assistance and cooperation in the compilation of this material:

Prentice Hall/Simon & Schuster, Inc.
Carrier Corporation Inc.
The Trane Company
The Goodheart-Willcox Company, Inc.
Training Labs Inc.
AC & R, Components Inc.
Sportan Valve Company
Superior Valve Company
Delmar Publishers Inc.
Ketema Inc.
E.I. du Pont de Nemours & Company, Inc.
Johnson Controls, Inc.
Baltimore Aircoil Company
Robinair Division, Sealed Power Corporation
Tecumseh Products Company
Danfoss Inc.
Dunham-Bush Company
Grasso Refrigeration Equipment

Special thanks to Blanca Resto, Alice Corring, and colleagues of the following institutions, whose help and encouragement motivated me to do this project:

Thomas Shortman Training Center Local 32B-32J
Charles Breslin, Mike Spiteri and Steve Axel
Operating Engineers' Union Local 94
Joseph C. Camilleri
Jerry Peterson, New York Building Managers' Association

Steamfitters Local 638 Training Center:
Dr. Joe Kenner, John Cronin, Frank Panico, and Richard Green

The Trane Company:
Bruce Hampson

This manual is dedicated to the servicepeople and operating engineers who maintain refrigeration and air-conditioning equipment in the field. Your dedication, knowledge, and experience have made this career one of the most prestigious and rewarding in the industry.

TABLE OF CONTENTS

INTRODUCTION

This manual provides comprehensive coverage of both parts of the refrigeration machine operator's examination. It features study material, sample questions, and illustrations to prepare candidates for the written and practical exams. Refrigeration topics have been organized by category. At the end of each chapter are multiple-choice questions designed to help you review the chapter and to illustrate the kinds of questions you may be asked on your examination.

Each chapter contains the pictures, diagrams, and definitions needed to understand the contents of the lesson. The refrigeration cycle is described and compared with different systems in the field in order to give the reader a clear understanding of their similarities and differences. With the aid of pictures and diagrams, the instructor can develop a lesson plan for class discussion. The diagrams will give the student a visual understanding of the topic.

Refrigeration and air conditioning has its own terminology and codes. The written exam for refrigeration will test candidates on this terminology, ranging from the early ammonia systems to the present. The object of this test is to find out whether the candidate has the knowledge necessary to operate heavy-tonnage refrigeration equipment in a safe and professional manner.

Commercial and residential refrigeration systems expose the operator to potential hazards. Your knowledge of safety can *prevent* injury and illness to staff and residents. The license exam places great emphasis on safety.

One chapter has been specifically written for the Practical Exam. This oral examination tests the candidate in a refrigeration engine room. The candidate must answer questions and describe practical procedures used by operators in the field.

The questions and answers in this manual have been adapted from previous license exams given at the Thomas Shortman Training Center Local 32B-32J. The knowledge and dedication of the instructors at this trade school has been and continues to be a credit to the City of New York.

A bibliography at the end of the text lists all the sources used in this manual.

Chapter 1

REFRIGERATION THEORY

PRINCIPLES OF REFRIGERATION

The basic principle of refrigeration is the transfer of heat from a warm substance to a colder substance. Heat may be transferred by one or a combination of the following three methods.

conduction: the transfer of heat by direct contact between two objects at different temperatures. An example of conduction can be felt by holding a piece of metal on a fire. As the metal starts to warm up, heat will travel over the metal to your hand. If you hold the metal object long enough, it will burn your hand. Heat does not conduct equally well in all materials.

convection: the transfer of heat by movement through vapors, gases, or liquids. In convection, the gases and liquids move about due to changes in temperature and pressure. A furnace supplies heat by warming the air through the convectors (radiators). Most systems use either water or steam to warm the convectors in a home.

radiation: an invisible movement of heat. Heat transfer by radiation travels through space without heating the space. Heat is absorbed by the first solid object it encounters. For example, the sun warms the earth through electromagnetic heat radiation.

MATTER

Matter takes up space, has weight, and can take the form of a solid, liquid, or gas.

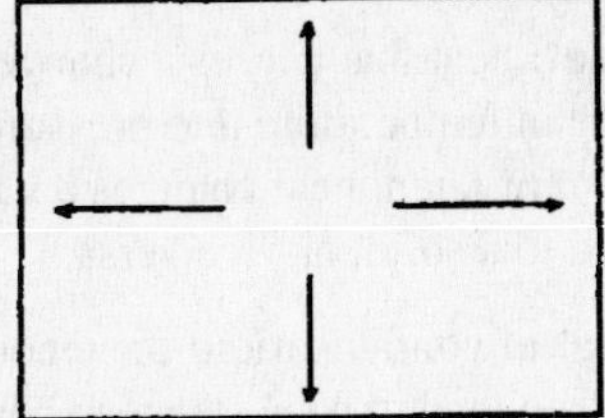

Fig. 1.1

solid: a substance with a definite size and shape. A solid exerts pressure in a downward direction.

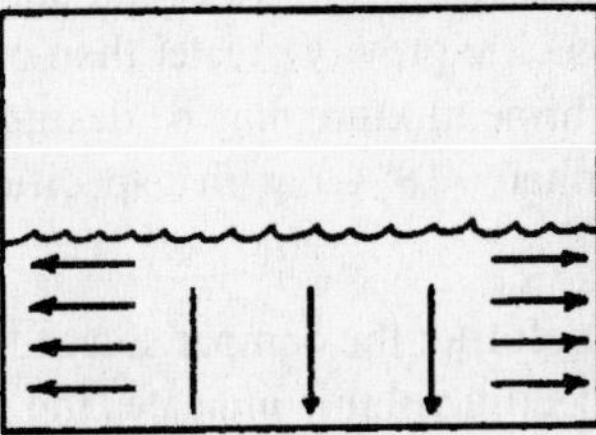

Fig. 1.2

liquid: a substance with no definite shape but a definite volume. A liquid will take the shape of its container. Pressure is exerted on all surfaces that contact the liquid.

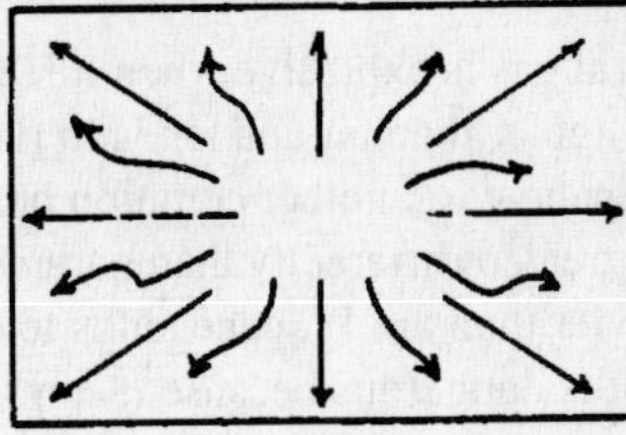

Fig. 1.3

gas: a substance that has no definite volume or shape. A gas must be enclosed in a container to prevent escape into the atmosphere. A gas exerts pressure on all sides of a container; it can also be compressed.

The state of a physical substance can be changed by changing its temperature or pressure. When a substance goes through a change of state, heat is transferred. Refrigeration uses these principles to transfer heat from a place where it is not wanted to a place where it does not matter.

density: a substance's mass per unit of volume. By knowing a refrigerant's density, we can determine what happens when a refrigerant leaks. The mass contained in a particular volume is the density of that substance. For example: Ammonia gas is lighter than air. If there is a leak of ammonia gas in a system, it will float to the highest point in the room.

Freon R-12 and R-22 are heavier than air. If there is a leak in an engine room, Freon will sink to the ground. It is important to compare the density and concentration of refrigerants in order to know where ventilation equipment should be located.

specific gravity: the ratio of a mass of a certain volume of a liquid or solid compared to the mass of an equal volume of water. Specific gravity compares the densities of various substances. For example: water has a specific gravity of one. Objects that float on water have a specific gravity of less than one; those that sink in water have a specific gravity greater than one. Mixtures of salt and water (brine) have a specific gravity greater than one. Calcium chloride brine mixture may be designed to freeze at 0° Fahrenheit (-18° C), with a specific gravity of 1.18.

specific volume: the comparison of the densities of gases. Specific volume indicates the space (volume) a certain weight of gas will occupy. One pound of clean, dry air has a volume of 13.33^3 ft. at standard conditions. Hydrogen has a density of 179 ft.^{3}/lb. under the same conditions. Because there are more cubic feet of hydrogen per pound, it is lighter than air. Although both are gases, hydrogen tends to rise when mixed with air.

Natural gas is explosive when mixed with air, but it is lighter than air and tends to rise like hydrogen. Propane gas, another common heating gas, must be treated differently than natural gas because it is heavier than air. Propane tends to collect in low places. It is dangerous because it can ignite and explode.

The specific volume of various gases used in refrigeration is invaluable information. It enables the engineer to choose the size of the compressor or vapor pump for a particular job. Note that the specific volume of a vapor varies according to the pressure on the vapor.

heat: energy that causes molecules to move and raises the temperature of a substance. Heat can be made to do work and is measured in btu.

temperature: a measure of the intensity of heat. Temperature is measured in degrees with a thermometer. The two common temperature scales are Fahrenheit and Centigrade. The calibration of these thermometers is determined by the boiling and freezing point of water. Below is a comparison of the Fahrenheit and Celsius scales.

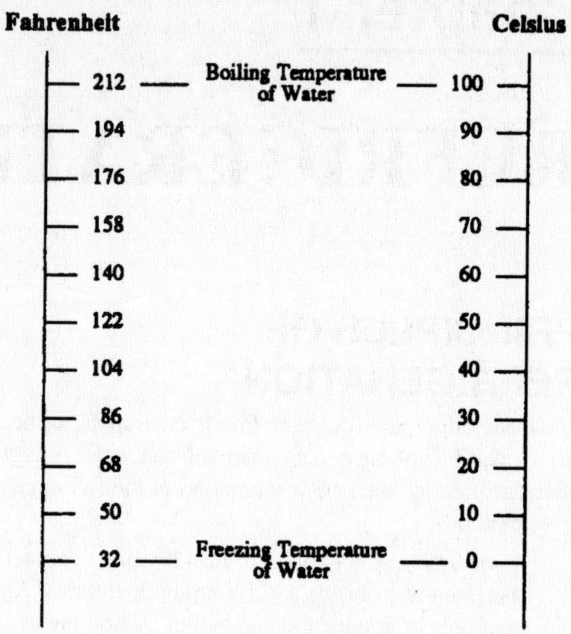

Fig. 1.4

The Fahrenheit scale is used in the United States. The freezing point of water is 32° Fahrenheit; the boiling point of water is 212°.

The Celsius scale, also called Centigrade, is the metric temperature system used throughout the world. The freezing point of water is 0° Celsius; the boiling point of water is 100°.

It is important to be able to convert between the two scales. The chapter "Air Conditioning and Refrigeration Mathematics" contains the formulas needed to solve the conversion problems on the written exam.

PRINCIPLES OF LATENT HEAT

One of the most important principles to understand in refrigeration is the theory of latent heat. Without latent heat, refrigeration and air conditioning could not exist.

British Thermal Unit (btu): the heat required to raise or lower the temperature of 1 pound of water by 1° Fahrenheit.

latent heat: heat that causes a change of state with no change in temperature and pressure. The removal or addition of latent heat changes a vapor to a liquid or a liquid to a solid, or vice versa.

latent heat of condensation: the amount of heat released by a pound of a substance to change its state from a vapor (gas) to a liquid. To change 1 pound of steam to water at 212° Fahrenheit, 970 btu must be removed. The greatest amount of heat is removed in a refrigeration system's condenser when the refrigerant changes state. As the refrigerant changes state, the heat is removed from the refrigerant.

latent heat of fusion: the amount of heat that must be added to change a solid to a liquid. It equals the heat that must be removed from a liquid to convert it to a solid at the same temperature. Using water as an example, water stays in the liquid state between 32° Fahrenheit and 212° Fahrenheit. 144 btu of heat energy must be removed from 1 pound of water at 32° F to change it to ice. During the change of state, the temperature stays the same. After ice has melted to water at 32° F, it will absorb another 180 btu before another change of state occurs.

sensible heat: heat change that can be measured by a thermometer. The 180 btu that warm water from 32° to 212° is sensible heat. This temperature change can be felt by hand.

latent heat of vaporization: the amount of heat required per pound of a substance to change its state from a liquid to a vapor. When water reaches the boiling point of 212° F, the temperature ceases to rise. At this temperature water starts to boil. 970 btu of heat are needed to change the state of 1 pound of water to vapor at 212° F. When a refrigerant reaches its latent heat of vaporization, its temperature remains the same while it changes state. During this stage, it has the greatest capacity to absorb heat. When a refrigerant's temperature increases, and its state does not change, it has a comparatively small heat-absorbing capacity.

latent heat of sublimation: the amount of heat that must be added to a substance to change its state from a solid to a vapor (gas), without any evidence of going through the liquid form. The latent heat of sublimation equals the sum of the latent heat of fusion and the latent heat of vaporization. Dry ice sublimates to carbon dioxide. Increase by adding 144 btu and 970 btu to equal the latent heat of sublimation.

The drawing below illustrates the temperature of 1 pound of ice being raised from 0° F to 32° F. The specific heat is .5. Sixteen btu are added. The 32° F ice melts into 32° F water with the addition of 144 btu. With no change in temperature, but a change in state, this is latent heat of fusion. The 32° F water rises in temperature to 212° F. This temperature rise is felt, or registered, so it is sensible heat. Because the specific heat of water is 1 btu, the total added is 180 btu.

At 212° F, more heat is added and the water changes to 212° F steam. Here again there is a change of state, with no temperature change, so the 970 btu added are latent heat of vaporization.

Super heat is the addition of sensible heat to the steam.

CYCLE OF REFRIGERATION

evaporator: the refrigeration component known as the cooling coil, chiller, and low side of the system. As heat is absorbed from the area to be cooled, the state of the refrigerant changes from a liquid to a gas.

As the liquid refrigerant enters the evaporator tubes or shell, its pressure drops to the pressure inside the evaporator. Once the liquid refrigerant reaches its latent heat of vaporization, it absorbs the greatest amount of heat while boiling into the vapor state. As the refrigerant passes through the evaporator coil, it continues to absorb heat and vaporize. The absorption of heat by the vaporizing refrigerant produces the cooling.

The refrigerant vapor leaves the evaporator through the suction line and flows into the compressor. There it is compressed into a hot, high-pressure gas.

The compressor inlet ends the low side of the system (see figure 1.6).

compressor: the component whose function is to draw the refrigerant vapor from the evaporator suction line and compress it from a low-pressure, low-temperature gas to a high-pressure, high-temperature gas.

The compressor lowers the pressure in the evaporator, making it colder than the surrounding air or water. Because evaporator pressure is below the saturation point, the refrigerant absorbs heat and vaporizes.

At the compressor outlet, high-pressure, high-temperature gas is discharged into the condenser. The outlet starts the high side of the system.

condenser: the component through which latent heat of vaporization is removed from the hot, high-pressure gas. As heat flows from the refrigerant, the vapor is cooled to saturation temperature. The vapor condenses to a hot liquid. The cooling medium of the condenser can be air, water, or a combination of the two. From the condenser the refrigerant leaves as a high-pressure, high-temperature liquid into the liquid line.

metering device: a major component located between the condenser and the evaporator; liquid refrigerant enters at the inlet and is controlled at the outlet. The metering device restricts the flow of refrigerant into the evaporator. The restriction in the metering device causes a sudden drop in refrigerant pressure, causing some refrigerant to boil and evaporate as it enters the evaporator. The metering device inlet ends the high side; the outlet starts the low side.

The refrigerant enters the evaporator, and the cycle is repeated.

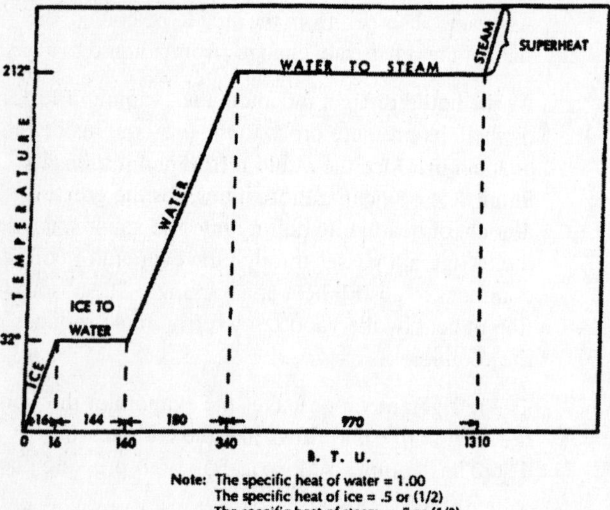

Fig. 1.5

CONTAMINANTS IN THE COOLING WATER SYSTEM

Sources of Bacteria

The bulk of bacteria found in open cooling water systems are scrubbed from the air that passes through the cooling tower or the evaporative cooling device. The slime developed from microorganisms also binds other suspended matter, such as air-borne dirt, corrosion products, and scale. This can cause a rapid accumulation of deposits where none would have formed without microbiological growth. Note that inorganic and organic scale in the water produce deposits, which retard heat transfer and/or restrict the flow of water.

In some industrial processes, such as aluminum extrusion, cooling water becomes contaminated with lubricants or other organic materials. Organic material may become dissolved in cooling water used to scrub air discharged from some industrial processes. Bacterial growth is frequently accelerated by the presence of such organic materials and can cause odors in the cooling tower. These odors or pollutants are offensive and possibly toxic to workers and building occupants.

Many problems can be prevented or corrected in the planning, design, construction, and operation of the cooling system. Shutdowns caused by contaminants can be minimized by providing convenient access, hose connections, and drains for physical removal of slime, bacteria, and scale.

System controls must be continually reevaluated. A certified cooling tower operator or a water treatment company should recommend the proper feeding program, with corrosion control chemicals, etc., at designated intervals. Without proper control, the water treatment program is of little value.

Operators test the cooling water system for its pH level. pH levels from 0 to 6.9 indicate that the water is acidic. pH levels decreasing from 7 to 0 indicate an increase in acidity. A pH level of 7 is neutral (neither acidic nor alkaline). Any pH level from 7 to 14 is considered alkaline, or increasing in alkalinity. Water distilled at 77° F is neither acidic nor alkaline, with a pH level of 7.

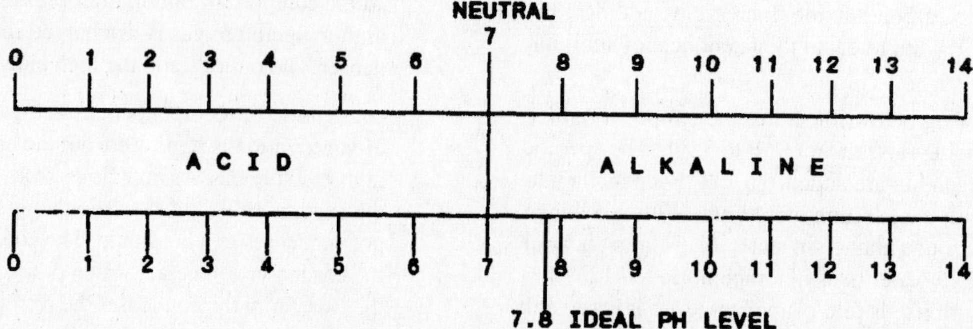

Fig. 1.7

TESTING CONDENSER AND EVAPORATOR COOLING WATER

The condenser cooling water system cools the condenser system and tower; the evaporator cooling water system does the refrigerating and air conditioning. Evaporator cooling water is normally called brine. Brine should be chemically neutral, because if it is too acidic it will corrode the pipes. If brine is too alkaline, bacteria or algae may grow in the water. Condenser water should also be chemically neutral for the same reasons.

Litmus Paper Test

Blue paper turns red in an acid solution; red paper turns blue in an alkaline solution. The degree of color change shows the relative acidity or alkalinity of the substance.

Comparator Test

Add a drop of indicator solution to a test tube containing a sample of brine or condenser water. Compare the result to tinted test tubes in a rack. Each color represents a standard degree of acidity or alkalinity.

Alkacid Paper Test

This test paper is similar to litmus paper, but it has a greater color range. This paper is dipped into a sample, and its color is compared to a reference color chart.

Rust Prevention

Brines are corrosive. A protective coating or film on the submerged surface of all the metal parts in the system will reduce rust and corrosion.

Corrosion inhibitors must be added to the brine solution. The most effective inhibitors are "chromates"—short for the true chemical name, sodium bichromate, also known as sodium dichromate.

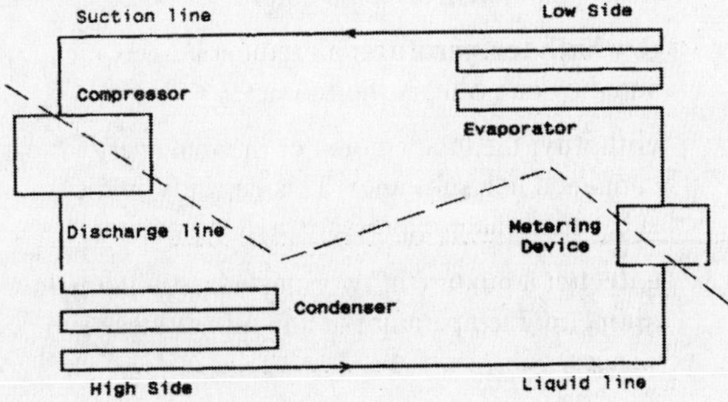

Fig. 1.6

REFRIGERATION DEFINITIONS

absolute pressure: the pressure exerted by the atmosphere, and indicated by a barometer. Gauge pressure plus atmospheric pressure (14.7 lbs. per sq. in.) equals absolute pressure. It is also defined as the pressure existing above a perfect vacuum.

absolute temperature: temperature above absolute zero.

absolute zero: the temperature at which all molecular motion ceases (-459° F, -273° C).

absorbent: a substance with the ability to take up or absorb another substance.

air conditioning: control of the temperature, humidity, movement, and cleanliness of air in a confined space.

ambient temperature: the temperature of fluid (usually air) that surrounds an object.

atmospheric pressure: the weight of a column of air at sea level. This column weighs 14.7 pounds per square inch and will lift a column of mercury to 30 inches. The actual weight is commonly rounded off to 15 pounds per square inch.

automatic control: valve action adjusted through self-operated or self-actuated means, not requiring manual adjustment.

azeotrope: a liquid mixture of refrigerant with a constant minimum and maximum boiling point.

barometer: an instrument used to measure atmospheric pressure.

back pressure: pressure in the low side of a refrigerating system; also called suction pressure or low-side pressure.

back seating: a position on a service valve. For example, in a suction service valve, the compression port and line port are open and the service port is closed. This is the normal position of the service valve when the system operates.

bellows: a corrugated cylindrical container that moves with pressure change or provides a seal when parts move.

boiling point: the boiling temperature of a liquid under a pressure of 14.7 psia. It is the boiling temperature of a liquid at a predetermined pressure.

boiling temperature: the temperature at which a fluid changes from a liquid to a gas. Any liquid may be made to boil at almost any temperature. When you have a liquid that boils at 30° F, and a room temperature at 70° F, the heat in the room will be great enough to boil the liquid. The resulting vapor will carry off heat; therefore, the room will get cooler. Another name for boiling temperature is boiling point.

brazed joint: a joint made with solder or brass alloy that melts at 1000° F or higher. The written exam uses the 1000° figure.

brazing: a method of joining metals with nonferrous (without iron) filler using heat between 800° F (427° C) and the melting point of the base metals.

brine: water mixed with a substance that will dissolve in it. The mixture is a fluid that can flow at temperatures below 32° F.

British thermal unit (btu): the heat required to raise the temperature of 1 pound of water by 1° F.

cascade system: the arrangement in which two or more refrigerating systems operate in series; the evaporator of one machine cools the condenser of another machine. The system produces ultra-low temperatures.

Celsius scale: the temperature scale used in the metric system. The freezing point of water in this scale is 0; the boiling point is 100° C.

change of state: the change from a solid to a liquid or a liquid to a gas caused by the addition of heat. Or the reverse, in which the removal of heat causes a substance to change from a gas to a liquid or a liquid to a solid.

cold: a term used to indicate the absence of heat.

compound gauge: an instrument for measuring pressures both above and below atmospheric pressure. On a manifold service assembly, it is the blue gauge used on the low side of the system.

compression ratio: the volume of the clearance space in a cylinder to the total volume of the cylinder.

compressor: one of the four main components of refrigeration. It draws a low pressure on the cooling side of the refrigeration cycle and squeezes or compresses the gases into the high-pressure or condensing side of the cycle.

condenser: one of the four main components of refrigeration. It receives high-pressure, high-temperature gas from the compressor and subcools it into a liquid state.

condensation: the process whereby a vapor changes to a liquid and loses the latent heat of condensation to the surroundings.

conduction: the transfer of heat by direct contact between two objects at different temperatures. It takes place in solids and also between two solids that are in direct contact with each other.

control: an automatic or manual device used to stop, start, and/or regulate the flow of gas, liquid, and/or electricity.

convection: the process by which gases and liquids move about and transfer heat, due to changes in temperature and pressure.

cooling tower: an accessory of the condenser used to cool water or brine by evaporation to the air's wet bulb temperature.

cycle: a series of events or operations that have a tendency to repeat in the same order.

dehydrate: to remove water from any form of matter. density: the weight per unit volume.

desiccant: a substance used to collect and hold moisture in a refrigerating system; a drying agent. Common desiccants are activated alumina and silica gel.

dew: condensed atmospheric moisture deposited in small drops on cool surfaces.

dew point: the temperature at which vapor (at 100 percent humidity) begins to condense.

direct expansion system: a dry system that does not store liquid refrigerant in the evaporator. It uses a predetermined amount of refrigerant.

drier: substance or device used to remove moisture from a refrigeration system.

dry bulb: an instrument with a sensing element to measure ambient air temperature.

dry bulb temperature: air temperature as measured by an ordinary thermometer.

enthalpy: the total amount of thermal energy (heat) contained in a substance. This depends on the substance's nature, pressure, and temperature.

eutectic: a mixture of two substances with the lowest melting temperature of any mix of those substances.

eutectic point: the freezing temperature for an eutectic solution.

evacuation: the removal of refrigerant or other gases from a refrigeration system.

evaporator: one of the four main components of a refrigeration system. It absorbs heat into the system while the liquid refrigerant evaporates.

Fahrenheit scale: the temperature scale in which the boiling point of water is 212° F and the freezing point is 32° F.

flash gas: the gas that forms immediately after refrigerant passes through a metering device.

front seating: a position on the service valve. In a suction service valve, the normal flow of refrigerant stops and the charging and compressor ports are open. The valve stem is all the way in. Only the line port is closed.

fusible plug: a device used to protect a pressure vessel from overheating. At a set temperature, the plug melts and the contents of the vessel escape.

head pressure: the pressure found on the condensing side of the system; also known as high-side pressure.

heat: thermal energy that causes molecules to move and raises the temperature of a substance. Heat can be made to do work and is measured in btu.

hermetic compressor: a compressor whose driving motor is sealed inside the compressor housing. The motor operates totally immersed in refrigerant vapor, which cools the windings.

high side: the high-pressure, high-temperature side of the system. It starts at the compressor outlet and extends to the metering device.

humidity: moisture in a gaseous form.

hydrometer: an instrument for measuring the specific gravity of a liquid using the flotation principle.

indirect system: a system in which the primary refrigerant never contacts the area to be cooled. A secondary refrigerant such as brine circulates through the area to be cooled to pick up heat. Then it returns to the flooded evaporator, where heat is absorbed. In the evaporator, the brine is in the tubes and the refrigerant is in the shell.

kinetic energy: the energy of a moving body.

latent heat: heat that causes a change of state with no change in temperature or pressure.

latent heat of condensation: the amount of heat in btu released by a pound of a substance to change its state from a vapor (gas) to a liquid.

latent heat of fusion: the amount of heat in btu that must be added to a solid to change it to a liquid. It is also equal to the heat that must be removed from a liquid to turn it back to a solid.

latent heat of sublimation: the amount of heat in btu that must be added to a substance to change it from a solid to a vapor, without any evidence of going through the liquid form. It equals the latent heat of fusion plus the latent heat of vaporization.

latent heat of vaporization: the amount of heat in btu required per pound of a substance to change it from a liquid to a vapor.

liquid line: the piping carrying high-pressure liquid refrigerant from the condenser to the metering device.

low side: the low-pressure, low-temperature side of the system. It starts at the outlet of the metering device and extends through the evaporator to the compressor inlet.

manifold service valve: a chamber equipped with gauges and manual valves used to service refrigeration systems.

manometer: an instrument for measuring pressure of gases and vapors.

metering device: one of the four main components of a refrigeration system. It controls the flow of refrigerant to the evaporator.

micron: a measurement equal to 1/1000 of a millimeter.

noncondensable gas: a gas that does not change into a liquid under normal operating conditions. Noncondensable gases in a system are usually moisture or air. Noncondensables cause undesirable high head pressure, increased evaporator pressure, or decreased vacuum pressure during compressor operation.

orifice: a hole or opening through which liquid refrigerant, brine, or air flows.

overload protection: a device in a compressor motor that shuts down the motor if excessive current, temperature, or pressure is drawn.

package unit: a refrigerating system with all major components located in one cabinet.

phosgene gas: a highly toxic gas produced whenever Freon refrigerant comes into contact with a heated object, such as a flame or a red-hot brazed metal.

potential energy: energy like that stored in a lake behind a dam. The water has great potential for doing work, but until it flows through a turbine, no work is produced.

pressure: force per unit area measured on either the absolute or atmospheric (gauge) scale. **PSIA** (pounds per square inch absolute) is the total pressure. Zero point is at absolutely no pressure. **PSIG** (pounds per square inch gauge) is the pressure compared to atmospheric pressure (14.8 psi). It registers in psi above atmospheric pressure and in inches of mercury below it.

pressure drop: the difference in pressure between two points.

psychometric chart: a chart showing the relationship of temperature, pressure, and humidity in the air.

pyrometer: an instrument used to measure high temperatures.

radiation: the transfer of heat by electromagnetic waves.

register: a device on an air distribution system that adjusts or directs airflow.

refrigerant: the fluid in a refrigeration system that picks up heat by evaporating at a low temperature and pressure and gives up heat by condensing at a higher temperature and pressure.

refrigeration: the transfer of heat from a place where it is not wanted to one where it is unobjectionable.

refrigeration effect: the useful cooling, or work, done by refrigeration, which equals the difference in enthalpy in the evaporator and the btu absorbed into the system. It can be figured by finding the heat content of the refrigerant entering the evaporator and the heat content of the gas leaving the evaporator. The difference is the actual work done.

relative humidity: the relationship of the actual humidity of moisture vapor in the atmosphere to the maximum that air could hold at that temperature and pressure.

rupture disk: a secondary safety found on the system's low side. It usually blows at 15 pounds psig.

saturated vapor: wet vapor holding the maximum gas. If pressure rises or temperature falls, the vapor will start to condense.

saturation: the amount of heat held in another substance at a particular pressure; e.g., the saturation point of R-22 at 60 psig is 38°F, or the saturation point of air at a given pressure/temperature. A condition existing when a substance contains the largest quantity of another substance it can hold for that temperature and pressure.

saturation temperature: another name for boiling point.

sensible heat: heat that changes the temperature of a substance. It can be sensed on a thermometer.

specific heat: the number of btu needed to raise the temperature of 1 pound of a substance by 1° F.

substance: any matter or material.

suction line: the line or piping between the evaporator and the compressor.

suction pressure: the low-side pressure between the compressor and the evaporator outlet. It is found on the low side of the refrigeration system.

superheat: a refrigerant vapor above its boiling point for its pressure. Each degree above the boiling-point temperature is 1 degree of superheat.

temperature: a measure of the intensity of heat. It is measured in degrees on a thermometer.

thermal energy: a form of heat energy contained in matter. A condition of the molecules or atoms in a substance, it exists in two forms: thermal kinetic energy and thermal potential energy. Thermal energy is sensible heat directly related to temperature and can be sensed through physical contact. Thermal potential energy is latent heat "stored" until a substance changes state.

thermocouple: a heat-sensing device made by joining two dissimilar metals by welding or soldering to form a thermocouple junction.

thermostat: an automatic device for regulating temperature in a system.

ton of refrigeration: the amount of cooling produced by melting 1 ton of ice in 24 hours.

volatile: the vapor state of any substance.

vibration arrestor: a soft or flexible substance or device that reduces the vibration tranmitted through a system; also known as a vibration eliminator.

wet bulb hygrometer: an instrument used to measure the relative humidity of air; also called a psychrometer.

wet bulb temperature: a measurement used to evaluate the humidity of air. Never above dry bulb temperature, it equals dry bulb temperature at 100 percent relative humidity.

REFRIGERATION THEORY QUESTIONS

1. The component that absorbs heat into the refrigerant is the

(A) metering device.
(B) condenser.
(C) compressor.
(D) evaporator.

2. The heat required to raise 1 pound of water 1° F is called

(A) British thermal unit.
(B) potential energy.
(C) kinetic energy.
(D) superheat.

3. The high side of the system includes a(n)

(A) metering device.
(B) evaporator.
(C) suction line.
(D) receiver.

4. Superheat is heat added

(A) with the aid of the automatic expansion valve.
(B) after all liquid has been changed to vapor.
(C) for the vaporization of the evaporator.
(D) to increase the heat of a substance.

5. In the Fahrenheit scale, boiling water at sea level has a temperature of

(A) 144
(B) 970
(C) 212
(D) 100

6. The low side of the system includes a(n)

(A) receiver.
(B) compressor.
(C) discharge line.
(D) evaporator.

7. The heat used to change a liquid to a gas or vapor is called latent heat of

(A) vaporization.
(B) fusion.
(C) condensation.
(D) superheat.

8. A thermometer is said to detect

(A) heat of vaporization.
(B) sensible heat.
(C) potential energy.
(D) hidden heat.

9. Hidden heat in refrigeration work is called

(A) superheat.
(B) kinetic heat.
(C) sensible heat.
(D) latent heat.

10. Latent heat of vaporization of water is

(A) 144 btu.
(B) 212° F.
(C) 970 btu.
(D) 270° C.

11. Which temperature scale uses 212° as the boiling point of water?

(A) Fahrenheit
(B) Celsius
(C) Kelvin
(D) Rankine

12. Zero gauge pressure equals an absolute pressure of

(A) 7.54
(B) 25.0
(C) 17.4
(D) 14.7

13. The heat required to melt 1 pound of ice at 32° to water at 32° is equal to

(A) 144 btu.
(B) 970 btu.
(C) 244 btu.
(D) 1114 btu.

14. The latent heat of fusion in water is

(A) 970 btu per lb.
(B) 470 btu per lb.
(C) 144 btu per lb.
(D) 244 btu per lb.

15. What is another word for latent heat?

(A) Hidden heat
(B) Absolute heat
(C) Sensible heat
(D) Specific heat

16. Heat added to a gas above the saturation temperature is called

(A) specific heat.
(B) potential energy.
(C) superheat.
(D) all of the above.

17. The latent heat used to change a liquid to a gas or vapor is called the latent heat of

(A) condensation.
(B) fusion.
(C) vaporization.
(D) temperature.

18. Convection is the process by which

(A) heat moves through gases and liquids.
(B) transfer of heat occurs by direct contact.
(C) heat gives up to the surrounding air.
(D) heat changes state.

19. Conduction is the transfer of

(A) heat by means of movement.
(B) heat by direct contact between two objects.
(C) heat by means of radiation of the sun.
(D) molecules in motion around a substance.

20. Saturated vapor is

(A) heat that can be sensed.
(B) the number of btu required to change the state of an object.
(C) a substance that has just turned into a vapor.
(D) all of the above.

Answers to Refrigeration Theory Questions

1. **The correct answer is (D).**
2. **The correct answer is (A).**
3. **The correct answer is (D).**
4. **The correct answer is (B).**
5. **The correct answer is (C).**
6. **The correct answer is (D).**
7. **The correct answer is (A).**
8. **The correct answer is (B).**
9. **The correct answer is (D).**
10. **The correct answer is (C).**
11. **The correct answer is (A).**
12. **The correct answer is (D).**
13. **The correct answer is (A).**
14. **The correct answer is (C).**
15. **The correct answer is (A).**
16. **The correct answer is (C).**
17. **The correct answer is (C).**
18. **The correct answer is (A).**
19. **The correct answer is (B).**
20. **The correct answer is (C).**

Chapter 2

EVAPORATORS

EVAPORATOR PRINCIPLES

The evaporator is the component that absorbs the unwanted heat into the refrigeration system. Evaporator temperature must always be lower than the temperature of the medium to be cooled. In other words, for the refrigerant to absorb heat, it must be colder than the area to be cooled. The heat gained by the evaporator equals the heat given up by the medium being cooled.

Refrigeration effect is the useful cooling done by the refrigerant. It is the amount of heat absorbed by the liquid refrigerant while it vaporizes. It equals the latent heat of vaporization.

The difference in enthalpy is between the heat carried in the liquid refrigerant entering the evaporator compared to the heat carried in the vapor refrigerant leaving the evaporator. This difference tells you how much work each pound of refrigerant is doing. Multiply the difference by the rate of refrigerant flow to find the capacity of the system.

To comprehend what happens in the evaporator, you must first understand how refrigerant absorbs heat. When a refrigerant reaches its boiling point, it has the greatest potential to absorb heat. The lower the boiling point of the refrigerant in the evaporator, the greater the amount of heat it will absorb. When a refrigerant changes state, from liquid to gas, the latent heat of vaporization of the refrigerant produces the cooling.

Note: When a refrigerant boils, it evaporates, absorbs heat, and produces cooling.

PROPERTIES OF AIR IN THE EVAPORATOR

dew point: the temperature at which moisture in the air will start to condense when air is cooled. Dew point is reached when there is 100 percent humidity.

relative humidity: the ratio of the actual amount of water in the air to the maximum amount of water that air could hold at the same temperature. The relative humidity figure greatly affects human comfort.

a. The higher the temperature, the more moisture air will absorb.

b. The higher the pressure of the air, the less moisture it will absorb.

DIRECT EXPANSION (DRY) EVAPORATOR

There are two basic types of evaporators, dry or direct expansion and flooded. The two types differ in the method of refrigerant circulation.

The direct expansion evaporator has a coil tubing between the metering device and the compressor. Refrigerant from the metering device is fed into one end and exits at the suction line. As the liquid enters the evaporator, a small percentage of liquid refrigerant boils off, creating flash gas. The remaining liquid refrigerant travels through the coil, absorbing heat from the medium being cooled. As a result, the refrigerant boils off, expanding into a low-pressure, low-temperature vapor. Because they use a pre- determined amount of liquid refrigerant, they are known as critical charged evaporators. The dry evaporator completely vaporizes the refrigerant before it reaches the suction line. Figures 2.1 and 2.2 show a dry evaporator.

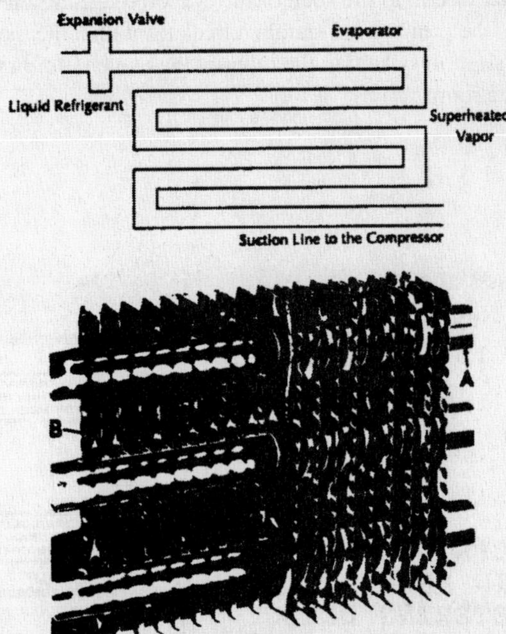

Figs. 2.1 and 2.2 No liquid refrigerant settles or is stored in the dry evaporator system. Section through tubes and fins of an evaporator. A—Tubing (primary surface). B—Fins (secondary surface).
Tube and corrugated evaporator, courtesy of Goodheart-Willcox.

TYPES OF DRY EVAPORATORS

bare pipe: the simplest type of evaporator; also called a prime surface evaporator. It uses bare pipes or tubing in the area to be cooled.

plate type: an evaporator that has sheets of metal welded to the tubes; it is normally found in refrigerators and freezers. The plate increases the surface area of this evaporator.

fin-tube type: an evaporator in direct contact with the substance to be cooled. Corrugated metal plates are machined onto the surface of the tubing. Fans circulate air around the evaporator. The corrugated fin plates increase the surface and increase the evaporator's heat-absorbing capacity. The fan also increases the cooling capacity. Common examples are found in household window air-conditioning units.

Figure 2.1 is an example of a shell-and-coil direct-expansion dry evaporator. In residential or commercial high-tonnage systems, this evaporator is normally called a chiller. In this evaporator, the refrigerant is in the coil and the brine or water is in the shell.

These evaporators are commonly found on indirect systems. Water, a secondary refrigerant, circulates through a water circuit to the shell of the evaporator. Liquid refrigerant, the primary refrigerant, circulates within the main refrigeration system to the tubes of the evaporator, in the engine room.

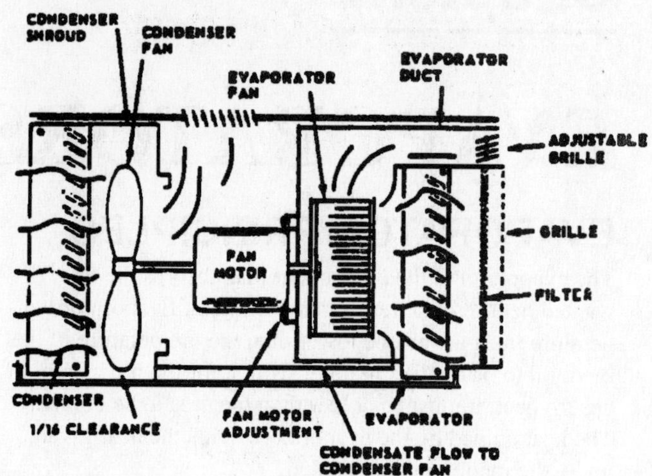

Fig. 2.3 Fin-Tube type
Drawing courtesy of Goodheart-Willcox.

When water or brine is circulated to coils in air handlers, convector units, or refrigeration ice fields, heat is picked up from the area to be cooled and absorbed at the evaporator. The heat from the water or brine that was absorbed is now known as your load, or chilled water return. Water or brine gives off its heat, to the lower-temperature primary refrigerant, in the evaporator coil.

The shell-and-coil direct-expansion evaporator uses either a thermostatic or automatic expansion valve to control the flow of refrigerant.

Warm brine from the chilled water line is pumped into the shell. Once the brine's heat reaches the refrigerant coil, the refrigerant inside boils and absorbs the heat.

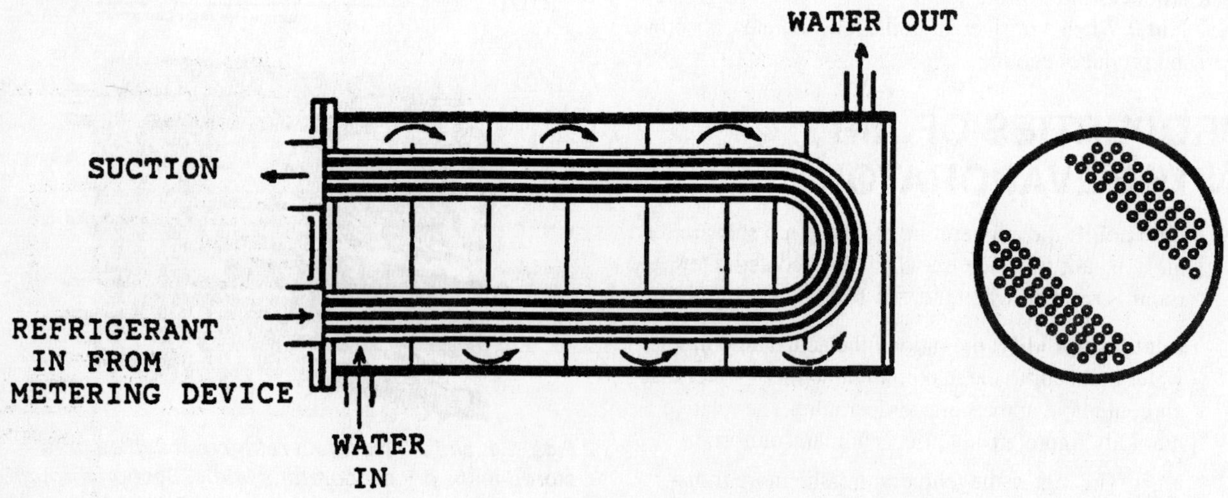

Fig. 2.4

AIR-COOLED EVAPORATORS: PROBLEMS, SYMPTOMS, CAUSES

1. **Problem:** Inadequate air flow through the coil
   a. Symptoms
      1. shortage of cooling capacity
      2. frosted or ice-caked coil
      3. low suction pressure
   b. Causes
      1. dirty air filters
      2. dirty evaporator coil
      3. fan belt slipping
      4. fan pulley improperly adjusted
      5. fan speed setting too low
      6. blockage in ductwork
      7. blockage at air supply or return grilles
      8. dampers improperly adjusted
      9. squirrel-cage fin fans dirty
      10. burned evaporator motor
2. **Problem:** Uneven air distribution over the coil
   a. Symptoms
      1. shortage of cooling capacity
      2. low suction pressure
      3. refrigerant floodback to compressor
   b. Causes
      1. bad duct design near coil
      2. improper coil placement
      3. air turbulence at coil
      4. lack of necessary air baffling near coil
3. **Problem:** Inadequate refrigerant supply to the coil
   a. Symptoms
      1. shortage of cooling capacity
      2. frosted or ice-caked coil
      3. low suction pressure or temperature
      4. flash gas or bubbles in liquid-line sight glass
      5. temperature drop in liquid line
      6. excess superheat
   b. Causes
      1. refrigerant charge low
      2. restriction in refrigerant line
      3. bad metering device
      4. blocked filter drier
4. **Problem:** Uneven refrigerant distribution to coil circuits
   a. Symptoms
      1. no condensation (sweating) on some circuits, while others have it
      2. combination of frost and dry spots on the evaporator coil
   b. Causes
      1. plugged distributor (feeder) tube(s)
      2. restricted distributor tube (external)
      3. distributor nozzle (orifice) improperly sized (TXV only)
      4. oil logging

FLOODED EVAPORATORS

When 80 percent of refrigerant is in the evaporator, it may be considered filled. Twenty percent is left for refrigerant expansion. Flooded evaporators are designed so brine, called secondary refrigerant, flows in the tubes, surrounded by liquid refrigerant in the shell. Since the shell is flooded with refrigerant, it boils and completely wets the interior walls. Flooded evaporators are more efficient than direct expansion evaporators of the same size. The flooded evaporator system is also known as an indirect system. One disadvantage of the flooded evaporator is that it is expensive to operate, due to the large amounts of refrigerant required.

Refrigerant absorbs heat from the secondary line, which contains brine. The refrigerant vaporizes and exits through the eliminators, then continues to the suction line.

The secondary refrigerant supply line is normally 45° F. The secondary return line should be 55° F, under normal operating conditions. The differential between return and supply lines should be 10°. Note that eliminators are located at the top of the evaporator to prevent liquid refrigerant from being drawn out the suction line to the compressor.

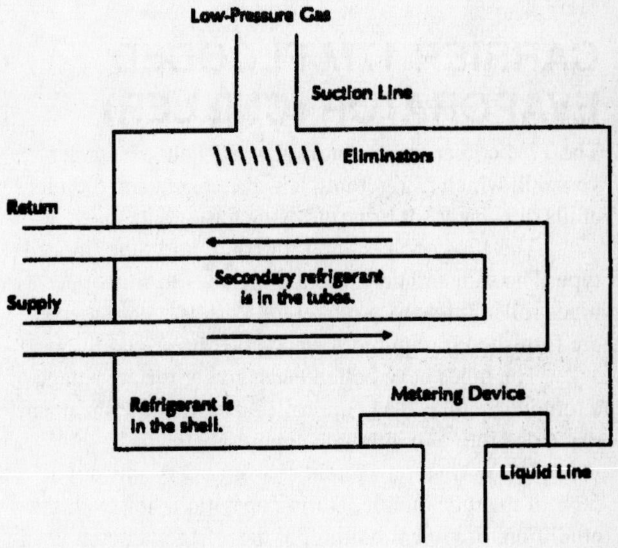

Fig. 2.5

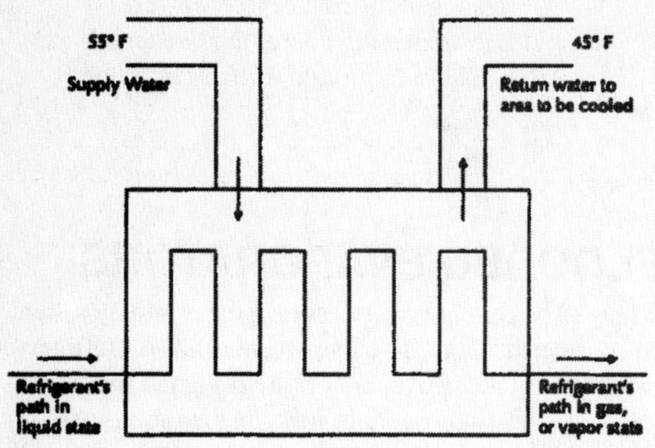

Fig. 2.6

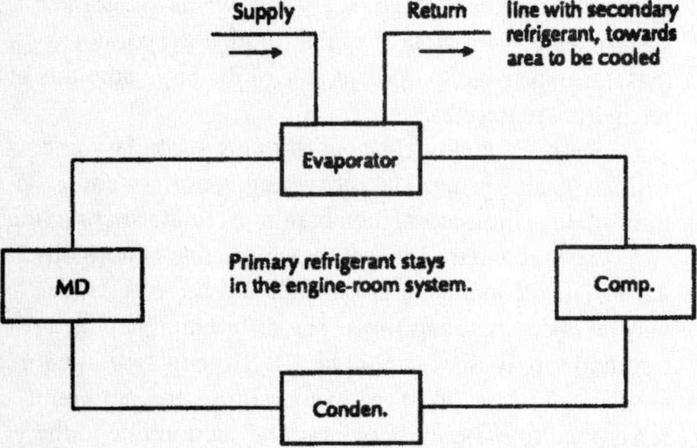

Fig. 2.7

CARRIER 17M FLOODED EVAPORATOR (CHILLER)

The 17M cooler (evaporator) acts as a heat exchanger vessel in which refrigerant picks heat from, and therefore chills, the water (or brine) flowing through its tubes.

The 17M coolers are of the shell-and-tube flooded type. The standard construction includes lo-fin copper tubes rolled into cupro-nickel tube sheets. Other metals are furnished if required for particular brine conditions.

The tubes have belled ends, giving the advantage of a removable tube. They are rolled into the tube sheet and expanded into two internal support sheets.

The normal refrigerant charge covers only about 50% of the tube bundle. During operation, however, the ebullition, or violent boiling, of the refrigerant completely covers the bundle. Above the bundles, eliminators prevent carry-over of liquid refrigerant particles into the compressor suction.

Inspection covers in the ends of the cooler permit access to the eliminators. A rupture valve with a 15-pound bursting disc is provided on the cooler.

The cooler water boxes are designed for maximum working pressure of 200 pounds per square inch and are tested in excess of this pressure. They have the necessary division plates to give the required flow. The water box covers may be removed without disturbing any refrigerant joint, since the tube sheets are welded into the cooler end flanges. Vent and drain openings are provided in the water circuit.

A refrigerant thermostat indicates the temperature within the cooler, during operation. A refrigerant sight glass is provided for observing the charging and operating refrigerant level.

A charging valve with connection on the side of the cooler allows for addition or removal of refrigerant. The connection is carried to the bottom of the cooler to allow complete drainage of the refrigerant.

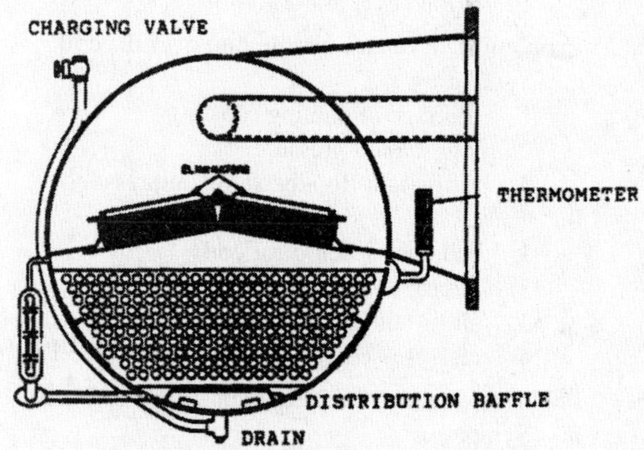

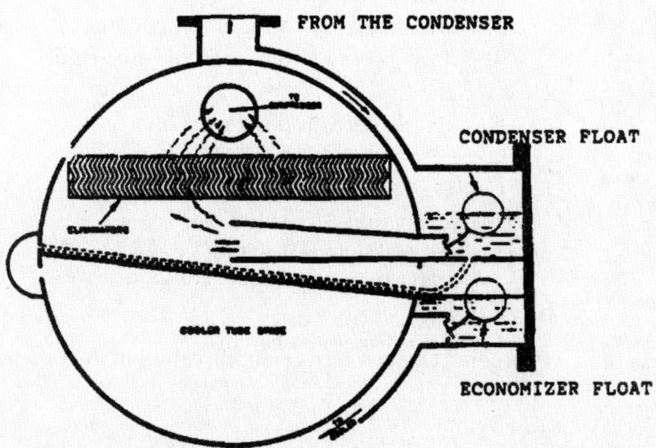

Figs. 2.8 and 2.9 Flooded Chiller Courtesy of Carrier Corporation.

WATER-COOLED EVAPORATORS (COOLERS): PROBLEMS, SYMPTOMS, CAUSES

1. **Problem:** Inadequate water flow through cooler (gallons per minute, or gpm)
   - **a.** Symptoms
     1. shortage of cooling capacity
     2. large temperature rise between supply and return water
     3. low suction pressure or temperature due to light load
     4. low leaving water temperature so safety thermostat shuts chiller down
   - **b.** Causes
     1. chilled water pump too small
     2. pump cavitation (air in chilled water system)
     3. obstructed water flow from
        - a. debris in cooler or piping or valve(s)
        - b. excessive water scaling (flooded cooler)
        - c. misplaced water baffles
     4. chilled water valve stuck
2. **Problem:** Uneven water distribution through cooler
   - **a.** Symptoms
     1. low chilled water temperature drop through cooler
     2. low suction pressure or temperature
   - **b.** Causes
     1. excess air in chilled water system
     2. plugged cooler water tube(s) (flooded coolers)
     3. baffles misplaced or broken
3. **Problem:** Inadequate refrigerant supply to cooler
   - **a.** Symptoms
     1. shortage of cooling capacity
     2. low chilled water temperature drop through cooler
     3. low suction pressure/temperature
     4. low leaving chilled water temperature; safety thermostat shuts chiller down
   - **b.** Causes
     1. low refrigerant charge
     2. plugged refrigerant filter-drier
     3. faulty thermostatic expansion valve
     4. restriction in refrigerant liquid line
     5. restriction in cooler tubes (direct expansion) caused by frost "pinching"

EVAPORATOR CAPACITY

To a certain extent, refrigeration system capacity floats with the load. In other words, the system automatically adjusts capacity upward as the load increases and downward as the load decreases.

First assume that a system has been running at peak load. As load decreases, less heat is absorbed by the evaporator. The amount of heat absorbed by the refrigerant decreases; the amount of liquid refrigerant boiled within the evaporator also decreases. However, the compressor continues to pump refrigerant vapor from the evaporator at the same rate as before. As a result, pressure within the evaporator is pulled below the level at which the system operated under full load. As refrigerant pressure drops in the evaporator, so too does its saturated temperature. In short, saturated evaporator temperature tends to drop with load reduction.

We know that fewer pounds of refrigerant are evaporated at partial load than at full load. However, each pound of refrigerant boiled in the evaporator takes up more volume as its pressure and saturated temperature become lower. At a lower pressure, the compressor pumps the same volume of gas per minute, but fewer pounds. Therefore, both the evaporator and compressor are delivering less cooling capacity. The cooling capacity is based primarily on pounds of refrigerant circulated per unit of time, not the volume.

The load reduction at the evaporator initiates a change that reduces the compressor inlet pressure and saturation temperature. This also reduces the compressor's discharge pressure and temperature, which reduces condenser pressure, saturation temperature, and capacity.

Review Question

As a mechanical refrigeration system operates with a load reduction, the evaporator pressure

(A) decreases, increasing the specific volume of the refrigerant, which decreases compressor capacity.

(B) increases, increasing the specific volume of the refrigerant, which decreases compressor capacity.

(C) decreases, decreasing the specific volume of the refrigerant, which decreases compressor capacity.

(D) none of the above.

The correct answer is (A).

EVAPORATOR TECHNICAL TIPS

1. The evaporator converts low-pressure liquid refrigerant to a low-pressure gas.

2. As the load on an evaporator decreases, suction pressure decreases.

3. The suction pressure of any refrigeration system is adjusted to a corresponding evaporator temperature below the material being cooled.

4. Insufficient cooling of a refrigeration system may be indicated by high suction pressure and low discharge pressure.

5. Short-cycling is the rapid cycling on and off of the compressor in response to pressure changes in a system. Low pressure can cause short-cycling. Abnormally low pressure may indicate that too little refrigerant is reaching the compressor. A restriction in the evaporator due to ice or oil logging may cause this problem.

6. Low pressure in a system can be caused by

a. low refrigerant charge
b. a malfunctioning metering device
c. restriction in the liquid line

7. As high-pressure refrigerant in the liquid line passes through the metering device and into the evaporator, it produces a sudden drop in pressure, causing flash gas. The sudden drop in pressure is caused by

a. the metering device restriction of refrigerant
b. low pressure of the evaporator

8. Approximately 15 to 20% of the refrigerant flashes to gas after it goes through the metering device and into the evaporator.

9. Flash gas is the evaporation of refrigerant immediately after it passes the metering device. It helps cool the liquid refrigerant due to the rapid evaporation.

10. Flash gas is a disadvantage because it decreases the capacity of a direct expansion (D-X) evaporator.

11. The capacity of the evaporator equals the amount of heat it absorbs over a given period of time. Factors that affect capacity are

a. the cleanliness of the evaporator
b. the physical size and shape of the evaporator
c. the thickness and material used in the evaporator
d. the velocity of refrigerant in the coil
e. the difference in temperature between the evaporator and the cooled medium

12. The superheat at the end of a direct expansion (D-X) evaporator is controlled by the metering device.

13. Superheat is designed into a refrigeration system to insure that the vapor returning to the compressor is 100 percent gas. Liquid vapor cannot be compressed. If liquid refrigerant enters the compressor, it can damage the compressor.

14. Secondary refrigerant is the brine or water that passes through the evaporator. Once the secondary refrigerant exits the evaporator, it goes to the area to be cooled, to absorb heat. The purpose of secondary refrigerant is to

a. absorb heat from the area to be cooled
b. release heat into the primary refrigerant

In an efficiently running system, brine or water may enter the evaporator at 55° F and exit at 45°. A 10° difference of heat loss is ideal.

15. Baffles in an evaporator coil redirect the flow of air or water in order to get the proper air flow or moisture carryover protection, or are used for condensation.

16. A hot-gas bypass system makes it possible to temporarily reduce the pumping capacity of smaller compressor systems. The bypass directs some hot discharge gas to the evaporator or directly to the suction line. The compressor capacity is reduced if needed and frost is removed from the evaporator coil.

17. Under normal conditions, a fin-tube direct-expansion evaporator has a wet surface. The wet surface indicates that the system is operating efficiently.

18. Frost accumulating at the beginning and end of an evaporator coil, but not at the center, indicates oil logging.

19. Prime surface evaporators operating below 32° F must be frequently defrosted.

20. Prime-surface evaporators are

a. plate-surface
b. plate-finned
c. bare-tube

21. Scale from water impurities will build up and must be removed periodically from the outside and inside of the tubes of a direct expansion (D-X) evaporator.

EVAPORATOR LICENSE QUESTIONS

1. The evaporator absorbs heat from the air or brine because the liquid refrigerant entering the evaporator
   (A) has a lower temperature than the air or brine.
   (B) has a higher temperature than the air or brine.
   (C) boils to a low-pressure gas.
   (D) boils to a high-pressure gas.

2. The evaporator
   (A) removes heat from the refrigerant.
   (B) absorbs heat into the refrigerant.
   (C) stores liquid refrigerant.
   (D) keeps the compressor busy.

3. As the load on an evaporator decreases, the
   (A) discharge pressure increases.
   (B) oil pressure increases.
   (C) suction pressure increases.
   (D) suction pressure decreases.

4. The heat picked up in the evaporator must equal the heat
   (A) gained by the condenser.
   (B) lost by the condenser.
   (C) of compression.
   (D) lost by the medium being cooled.

5. The disadvantage of a flooded system is that it
   (A) cannot be used on multiple systems.
   (B) needs a large charge of refrigerant.
   (C) cannot be used with a low-pressure motor control.
   (D) can be used only with ammonia.

6. Flooded feeds are different from direct expansion feeds because they
   (A) allow for regurgitation of liquid refrigerant.
   (B) use bigger and better evaporators for this purpose.
   (C) are not as effective in operation.
   (D) allow for recirculation of liquid refrigerant.

7. The suction pressure of any refrigeration system is adjusted
   (A) to a corresponding evaporator temperature below the material being cooled.
   (B) to a corresponding evaporator temperature equal to the material being cooled.
   (C) to a pressure above atmospheric at all times.
   (D) none of the above.

8. A direct expansion evaporator has frost on the upper and lower coils but not on center coils. This indicates
   (A) the evaporator is flooded.
   (B) the evaporator is starved.
   (C) the evaporator is short of refrigerant.
   (D) there is oil logging in the evaporator.

9. When the evaporator load increases, what happens to the suction pressure?
   (A) It decreases.
   (B) It increases.
   (C) It stays the same.
   (D) None of the above

10. Baffles in a gravity coil evaporator are used
    (A) for condensation.
    (B) for proper air flow.
    (C) to prevent moisture carry-over.
    (D) all of the above.

11. The temperature of the medium being cooled must be
    (A) below the freezing point of the area to be cooled.
    (B) above the evaporator temperature.
    (C) equal to the evaporator temperature.
    (D) below the evaporator temperature.

12. Assuming all other conditions are constant,
    (A) as low-side pressure falls, compressor capacity increases.
    (B) as load decreases, the low-side pressure decreases.
    (C) as head pressure increases, plant capacity increases.
    (D) as low-side pressure decreases, there is no change.

13. The two basic types of evaporators are
    (A) prime surface and finned.
    (B) finned and plate.
    (C) direct expansion feed and plate.
    (D) flooded and direct expansion feed.

14. A decrease in load on an evaporator causes
    (A) more refrigerant to be required.
    (B) pressure drop in the evaporator.
    (C) increase in evaporator capacity.
    (D) more heat to be absorbed.

15. Which of the following statements is most nearly correct?

(A) The efficiency of an evaporator coil decreases as the frost thickness increases.
(B) The efficiency of an absorber depends on and varies directly with the compressor speed.
(C) To lubricate the inside surfaces of an evaporator coil, 10 drops of machine oil per minute should be pumped into the coil.
(D) To lubricate the cylinder walls of an ammonia compressor, 10 drops of machine oil per minute should be drawn into the cylinder.

16. Prime surface evaporators operating below 32° F must frequently be

(A) purged.
(B) cleared.
(C) defrosted.
(D) painted.

17. Which of the following would not cause a starved evaporator?

(A) Improper bulb location
(B) Clogged distributor line
(C) Shortage of refrigerant
(D) Metering device stuck in open position

18. A Freon-12 refrigerating system in an air conditioning plant is equipped with a finned-tube evaporator. In operation, the outer surface of this evaporator is wet. Thus, the evaporator is

(A) not operating at highest efficiency.
(B) not receiving enough refrigerant.
(C) operating efficiently.
(D) operating with an oversized expansion valve.

19. The fastest way to remove frost from a direct expansion finned-tube evaporator is to

(A) shut it down and let the frost melt.
(B) run a hot gas line to the coil.
(C) wash frost off with warm water.
(D) scrape frost off.

20. A predetermined amount of refrigerant is used in what type of evaporator?

(A) Flooded evaporator
(B) Direct-expansion evaporator
(C) Indirect-type chiller
(D) Plate-type evaporator

21. The selection of the proper evaporator depends mainly on

(A) price.
(B) size.
(C) color.
(D) application.

22. What happens in an evaporator?

(A) High-pressure liquid converts to low-pressure liquid.
(B) Refrigerant in the gas state is saturated.
(C) Low-pressure liquid converts to low-pressure gas.
(D) High-pressure gas converts to low-pressure liquid.

23. Is the temperature outside the evaporator higher or lower than the inside temperature?

(A) Higher
(B) Stays the same
(C) Lower
(D) 10° lower

24. Secondary refrigerants are usually

(A) azeotrope.
(B) halocarbons.
(C) water or brine.
(D) trifluoromethane.

25. In a refrigeration system, where would you find superheat?

(A) After the metering device as refrigerant enters the evaporator
(B) In the middle of the evaporator coil, with no saturation
(C) After the evaporator so that no saturated vapor enters the compressor
(D) Superheat is a metering device calculation.

26. The disadvantage of the direct expansion system, compared to the flooded system, is that it

(A) requires a large refrigerant charge.
(B) frosts up much more quickly.
(C) passes flash gas through the evaporator.
(D) requires a larger compressor.

27. The refrigerant leaving a flooded evaporator is

(A) just like that leaving a D-X evaporator, slightly superheated.
(B) just like that leaving a D-X evaporator, saturated.
(C) saturated, while that leaving a D-X evaporator is slightly superheated.
(D) slightly superheated, and leaving a D-X evaporator saturated.

28. The flow of refrigerant into a flooded evaporator is controlled so it has

(A) mostly liquid refrigerant at the inlet but gas near the outlet.
(B) all its tubes wetted by liquid refrigerant from beginning to end.
(C) mostly liquid refrigerant at its outlet but gas at its inlet.
(D) a mixture of liquid and vapor refrigerant in its tubes from beginning to end.

29. As flash gas increases, evaporator capacity

(A) increases.
(B) decreases.
(C) stays the same.
(D) increases or decreases depending on the evaporator pressure.

30. Superheat is wanted at the outlet of a D-X evaporator mainly to

(A) improve evaporator efficiency.
(B) increase evaporator capacity.
(C) protect the compressor.
(D) increase system capacity.

31. An evaporator that fails to provide superheat at its outlet places which compressor in the most serious danger?

(A) Rotary
(B) Centrifugal
(C) Reciprocating
(D) Screw

32. Which of the following choices is INCORRECT in relation to prime surface evaporators?

(A) Has primer sprayed on it to protect it.
(B) Is either a plate-surface or plate-finned type.
(C) Is either a bare-tube or plate-surface type.
(D) Uses only the primary surface, without fins, to transfer heat.

33. Scale from water deposits will build up and need to be removed periodically from the

(A) outside and inside of the tubes of a D-X cooler.
(B) inside and outside of the tubes of a flooded cooler.
(C) inside of a tube-and-shell cooler only.
(D) outside of a tube-and-shell cooler only.

34. What is the difference between flooded and dry-expansion shell-and-tube evaporators?

(A) The flooded cooler has refrigerant in the shell and water in the tubes.
(B) The dry-expansion evaporator has refrigerant in the tubes and brine in the shell.
(C) The flooded cooler has refrigerant in the tubes and brine in the shell.
(D) The dry-expansion evaporator has refrigerant in the shell and brine in the tubes.

Answers to Evaporator License Questions

1. **The correct answer is (A).**
2. **The correct answer is (B).**
3. **The correct answer is (D).**
4. **The correct answer is (D).**
5. **The correct answer is (B).**
6. **The correct answer is (D).**
7. **The correct answer is (A).**
8. **The correct answer is (D).**
9. **The correct answer is (B).**
10. **The correct answer is (D).**
11. **The correct answer is (B).**
12. **The correct answer is (B).**
13. **The correct answer is (D).**
14. **The correct answer is (B).**
15. **The correct answer is (A).**
16. **The correct answer is (C).**
17. **The correct answer is (D).**
18. **The correct answer is (C).**
19. **The correct answer is (B).**
20. **The correct answer is (B).**
21. **The correct answer is (D).**
22. **The correct answer is (C).**
23. **The correct answer is (A).**
24. **The correct answer is (C).**
25. **The correct answer is (C).**
26. **The correct answer is (C).**
27. **The correct answer is (C).**
28. **The correct answer is (B).**
29. **The correct answer is (B).**
30. **The correct answer is (C).**
31. **The correct answer is (C).**
32. **The correct answer is (A).**
33. **The correct answer is (C).**
34. **The correct answer is either (A) or (B).**

Chapter 3

METERING DEVICES

This chapter describes the metering device function in a refrigeration or air conditioning system. The metering device controls the flow of refrigerant to the evaporator.

Six types of metering devices are commonly used in the field: the capillary tube, thermostatic expansion valve, automatic expansion valve, hand expansion valve, high-side float, and low-side float. Except for the hand expansion valve, these metering devices operate automatically.

It is important to thoroughly cover this chapter, because the written and practical exams have many metering device questions.

CAPILLARY TUBE

1. Four factors for effective operation:
   a. tube length
   b. inside diameter
   c. tightness of tube windings
   d. temperature of tubing
2. The capillary tube is a narrow, seamless tube with no moving parts.
3. Extreme load conditions can cause excessive floodback.
4. Systems with capillary tubes are considered critical charger systems and have limited control over the flow to the evaporator.
5. Capillary tubes are installed just before the evaporator. A strainer should be installed just before the tube.
6. After being shut down, the high-and-low pressure of the system eventually becomes balanced.

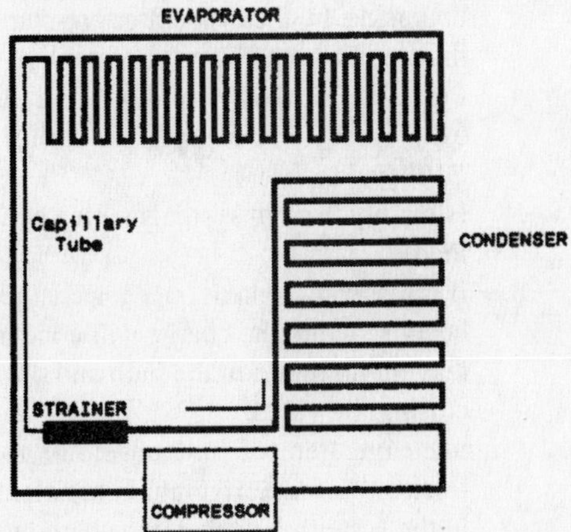

Fig. 3.1

THERMOSTATIC EXPANSION VALVE (TXV OR TEV)

1. The TXV is mainly used with the dry-expansion system. The TXV is controlled by the superheated gas coming from the evaporator. It meters (controls) the refrigerant to the evaporator with a thermal sensing bulb. Basically, TXV operation is determined by three fundamental pressures:
   a. Evaporator pressure on one side of the diaphragm (see #1 below) tends to close the valve.
   b. Bulb pressure on the other side of the diaphragm tends to open the valve (see #2 below). As evaporator pressure rises, the bulb's contents boil, pressing down on the diaphragm and opening the needle, and the valve opens.
   c. Spring pressure closes the valve (see #3 below) when evaporator pressure drops.

When the valve is modulating, bulb pressure is balanced by the evaporator plus the spring pressure.

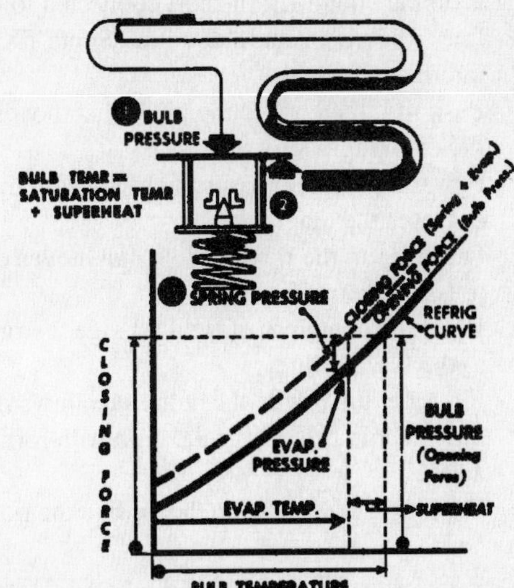

Fig. 3.2
Courtesy of Sporlan Valve Co.

2. The TXV meters refrigerant into the evaporator to meet changes in the refrigeration load. The valve meters the refrigerant by continuously increasing and decreasing the size of the orifice through which the refrigerant flows.

3. The TXV is rated in tons of refrigeration. For example, if you had a 20-ton system with a TXV, the TXV would be rated for 20 tons.
4. Internal parts/construction of the TXV
   a. Seal cap: a removable end piece for accessing adjustment stem.
   b. Stem adjustment: a screw mechanism used to increase or decrease spring tension.
      1. Clockwise turns increase spring tension by closing the orifice, reducing flow, and increasing superheat.
      2. Counterclockwise turns lower or decreases superheat.
   c. Spring guide: a connecting piece between spring and adjustment stem.
   d. Spring: the spring pushes upward, tending to close the valve.
   e. Plunger assembly: the mechanism connected to the spring that seats the valve.
   f. Inlet port: the entry for refrigerant from the liquid line.
   g. Outlet port: the line through which refrigerant exits the valve to the evaporator.
   h. Orifice: the small opening that changes in size according to the position of the plunger. The orifice opening is adjusted depending on spring pressure, evaporator pressure, and bulb pressure from the power element.
   i. External equalizer: the port connected to the line from the evaporator outlet. Some TXVs are internal equalizers.
   j. Push rod: the connecting piece that moves from the diaphragm's force.
   k. Power head: the pressure-tight housing that encloses the diaphragm.
   l. Diaphragm: the flexible disk that moves due to pressure from the bulb.
   m. Bulb: the container of fluid (charged) strapped to the suction line.
   n. Fill tube: the line to the bulb that allows the manufacturer to charge the bulb with refrigerant.
   o. Capillary: the line from the bulb to the power head.
5. The power element consists of the bulb, capillary tube, and power head. The power element contains the charge.

   If the bulb is warm, the pressurized gas or liquid within the sensing element will expand, increasing the pressure. This pressure is transmitted through the capillary tube to the TXV, where it expands a metal diaphragm. This diaphragm pushes on the needle, opening the valve and allowing more liquid refrigerant into the evaporator.

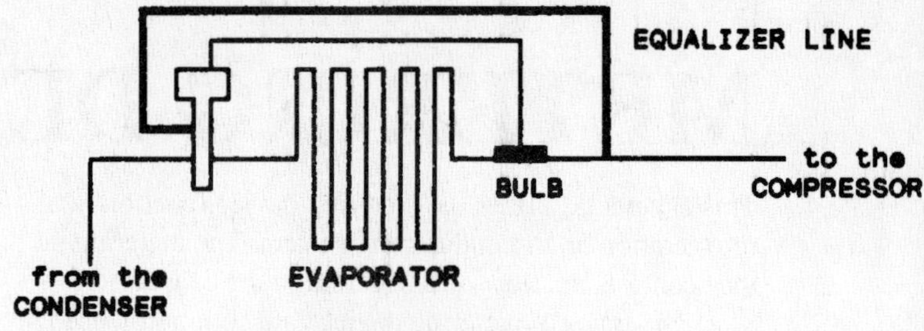

Valve with INTERNAL equalizer

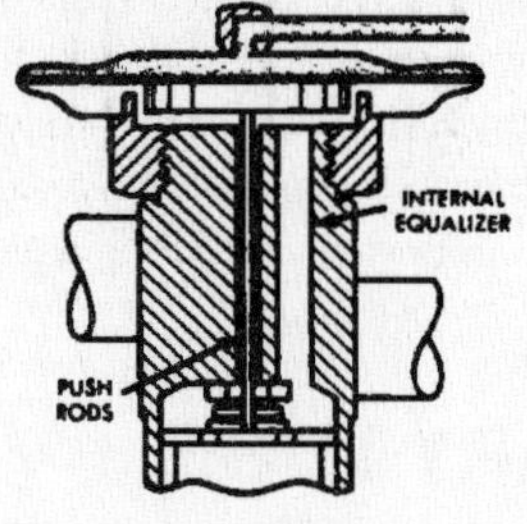

Figs. 3.3 and 3.4

6. Element charges can be gas charges, liquid charges, cross liquid charges, or cross vapor charges.
   a. Gas charge: (temperature range: 30° to 60° F)
      1. Uses the same refrigerant in the element as in the system.
      2. Is a limited charge that vaporizes at a specific temperature.
      3. Prevents the TXV valve from being controlled by the charge pressure above a predetermined temperature. When the charge reaches total vaporization, additional increases in evaporator superheat have little effect on the pressure of the bulb charge. Because the pressure of a gas charge bulb changes very slightly when it is fully vaporized, the valve is controlled on the underside, by the evaporator pressure, more than by the bulb charge pressure.
      4. Prevents floodback of liquid from the evaporator to the compressor during the OFF cycle.
      5. Is mainly used in systems with a constant load.
      6. If the power element on a gas charge bulb becomes cold, the charge will condense, leaving no liquid in the bulb and thereby closing the valve.
   b. Liquid charge: (temperature range: -20° to 40° F)
      1. Uses the same refrigerant in the element as in the system; however, the charge volume

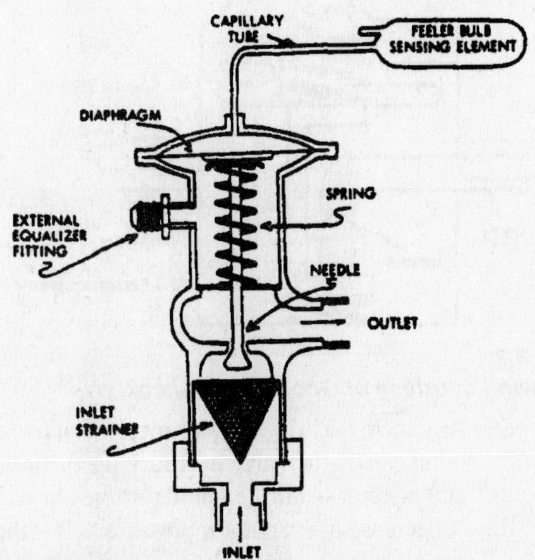

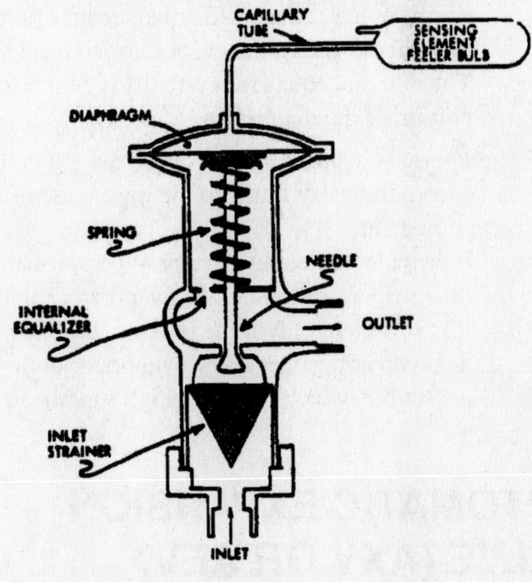

Figs. 3.5 and 3.6

is greater, because, there is always liquid in the bulb regardless of the amount of superheat on the suction line.

Disadvantages:

2. Liquid charge TXV bulbs should be avoided in low-temperature systems because they cause hunting.
3. Liquid charge bulbs contribute to floodback during start-up.

c. Cross liquid charge: (-40° to 40° F)
   1. Uses a different refrigerant in the bulb than in the system.
   2. The liquid refrigerant in the bulb is set to close the valve more quickly, with a rise in evaporator pressure. It is designed to close the TVX once the compressor shuts off, during the "off" cycle.
   3. Has such *advantages* as floodback protection during shutdown and start-up; suitability for low-temperature work; and greater responsiveness to changes in suction pressure than to changes in bulb temperature. This characteristic greatly reduces or eliminates system hunting.

d. Cross vapor charge:
   1. Uses a different gas refrigerant in the bulb than in the system.
   2. The bulb covers all applications and ranges.

7. TXV hunting is the alternate undermetering and overmetering of refrigerant to the evaporator until the valve settles at the correct setting. Contributing factors to TXV hunting are:

   a. oversized valves.
   b. improper size and arrangement of suction line piping.
   c. incorrect element charge.
   d. poor location of the bulb and/or external equalizer.

8. Bulb installation
   a. The bulb should be installed close to the evaporator outlet.
   b. The bulb should make good thermal contact with the pipe.
   c. When the evaporator suction line tubing is less than 7/8≤, the bulb is installed horizontally on top of the suction line.
   d. When the suction line tubing is greater than 7/8≤, the bulb installation should be horizontal with the suction line, at a 45° angle, in the 4 or 8 o'clock position.

9. The external equalizer enables the low-side pressure operating the TXV to equal the pressure of the sensing bulb. The external equalizer line gets pressure from the suction line downstream of the TXV bulb.
   a. The external equalizer line is physically connected into the system (directly). The TXV bulb is clamped on the suction-line piping (indirectly).
   b. The external equalizer provides a closing force based on the pressure of the refrigerant vapor at the evaporator outlet.
   c. The external equalizer should be used when the pressure drop across the evaporator is 2.5 psi.

   d. The external equalizer is usually a 1/2≤ capillary line, connected downstream of the bulb, at the end of the evaporator, to the TVX.
   e. The external equalizer exerts its pressure on the bottom of the diaphragm.

10. The internal equalizer consists of a passage in the valve from the valve outlet to the lower side of the power element.
   a. It provides a closing force based on pressure of the refrigerant vapor at the evaporator inlet.
   b. It is sufficient only if the pressure drop from the evaporator inlet to the evaporator outlet is negligible, which produces high superheat.

AUTOMATIC EXPANSION VALVE (AXV OR AEV)

The AXV is known as the backward or back-pressure metering device. This constant-pressure valve meters refrigerant to the evaporator according to evaporator pressure. The primary motivating forces are evaporator pressure balanced against spring pressure.

1. AXV parts include:
   a. inlet from the liquid line.
   b. outlet to the evaporator.
   c. valve assembly. Movement of the stem in seat adjusts orifice size.
   d. push rod, which connects the valve assembly to the diaphragm.
   e. diaphragm, which allows the stem to travel up and down.
   f. adjusting spring, which pushes down, tending to open the valve.

2. The AXV operates a spray nozzle, spraying refrigerant into the evaporator. The evaporator never fills with liquid; it contains a mist. Therefore, AXV systems are sometimes called dry systems.

3. As evaporator pressure increases, the valve closes.

4. As evaporator pressure decreases, the valve opens.

5. If the load decreases, evaporator pressure decreases, thus opening the valve.

6. AXV operation
   a. The AXV meters refrigerant to the evaporator based on the evaporator pressure and spring pressure. These two forces oppose each other. Evaporator pressure tends to close the valve, and spring pressure tends to open it.
   b. Spring tension can be adjusted to a desired point to determine how much evaporator pressure will be needed to overcome spring pressure.

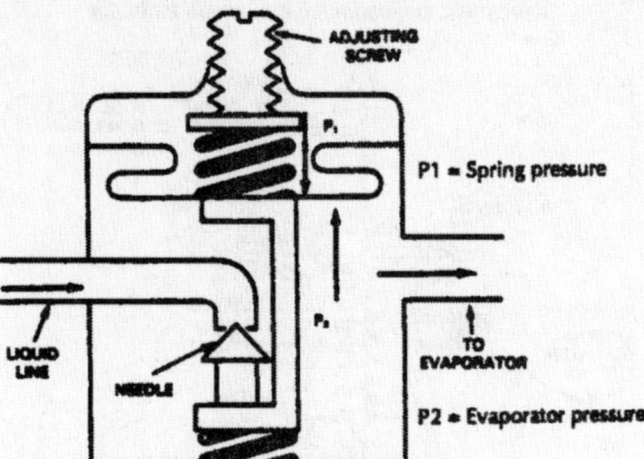

Fig. 3.7
Drawing courtesy of Goodheart-Willcox.

   c. Any increase in evaporator pressure above this point causes the valve to reduce the orifice size and meter less refrigerant; the valve closes.
   d. A decrease in evaporator pressure below the spring pressure opens the valve.
   e. The AXV maintains constant pressure at the evaporator inlet resulting in constant suction line pressure and constant load on the compressor, regardless of changes in the actual refrigeration load.
   f. The AXV is installed just before the evaporator.
   g. Systems with an AXV typically have a thermostat or low-pressure control to switch the compressor ON and OFF according to suction pressure or temperature.
   h. When the compressor stops, due to low suction temperature, pressure in the evaporator increases, closing the AXV. This prevents floodback to the compressor during the OFF cycle.
   i. Atmospheric pressure also acts in the same direction as spring pressure. For example: at higher altitudes, where atmospheric pressure is less, the spring adjusting screw should be turned to compensate for atmospheric pressure.
   j. The AXV settings also depend on refrigerant used, due to different evaporative pressures.
   k. The AXV is designed for a constant load system. It is *not* suitable for systems with variable loads.
   l. AXV capacity should equal the pump capacity. Undercapacity will starve the evaporator. Overcapacity will meter too much refrigerant, causing sweat-back or frost-back on the suction line.
   m. When the compressor stops in response to low pressure control, evaporator pressure rises and the AXV closes.
   n. A decrease in evaporator load opens the AXV.
   o. A decrease in evaporator load results in *no change of suction pressure.*

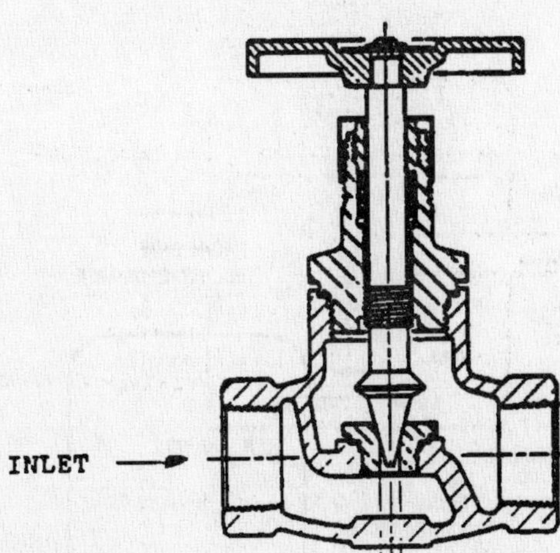

Fig. 3.8 Ductile Iron Globe Type 200E/300E. Drawing courtesy of Henry Valve Company.

HAND EXPANSION VALVE (HXV)

1. The HXV is a simple metering device used to separate the high and low sides of the system and feed refrigerant to the evaporator.
2. Parts of the HXV include the inlet, outlet, needle, and adjustment handle.
3. HXV operation:
   a. Turn the handle to lift the needle from the seat, enlarge the orifice, and feed more refrigerant to the evaporator.
   b. Turn the handle to lower the needle and close the valve, restricting refrigerant flow to the chiller.
4. The HXV does not adjust automatically. It is a manually operated device.
5. HXVs were popular in ice plants running ammonia.
6. An Ammonia HXV can be repacked under pressure in the backseated position.
7. HXVs today are used as bypass valves around an automatic valve. The HXV can meter the refrigerant while the automatic valve is being serviced.
8. Frost does not form on the last pipes in the evaporator if the HXV is closed too far. All the liquid evaporates before it reaches the coils, where it may warm to room temperature. Unless capacity operation of the evaporator is not desirable, open the hand expansion valve.

HIGH SIDE FLOAT (HSF)

This metering device is located on the liquid line, close to the condenser outlet. It separates the low side from the high side.

1. With this type, liquid refrigerant is stored in the evaporator. Note: the HSF requires a flooded evaporator.
2. Operation is controlled by the condenser receiver.
3. As the chamber fills with refrigerant from the condenser, the float rises and opens the valve, thus metering more refrigerant to the evaporator.
4. As the refrigerant level drops, the float drops, closing the valve.
5. When operating properly, the HSF maintains a constant pressure differential between the high and low sides of the system.
6. The HSF also maintains a constant refrigerant level on the high side.
7. In a critical charge system, the valve feeds the evaporator as fast as the liquid flows from the condenser.
   a. An overcharge does *not* allow the float to shut off. Too great a charge causes liquid flooding back to the compressor. Frost on the suction line is an indication of excessive refrigerant in the system, leading to compressor flooding.
   b. An undercharge prevents the float from opening. It starves the evaporator and reduces the system's capacity.
8. Parts of the high side float include:
   a. a float, usually made of copper or steel
   b. a needle valve connected directly to the float or with a simple lever
   c. an inlet from the condenser, receiver, or the liquid line
   d. an outlet to the evaporator
   e. a bleeder tube in some ammonia systems allows noncondensable gases to bleed off to the chiller.
9. HSFs generally require an oil return mechanism because oil binding can occur in the evaporator.
   a. At low temperature, oil is not miscible.
   b. At high temperature, oil is more miscible.
10. In an HSF system, the compressor motor is often cycled ON and OFF via a thermostatic or pressure control.
11. The amount of condensed refrigerant controls the liquid level, which in turn controls the rising or lowering of the float in the HSF. Note: condensation takes place in the condenser.

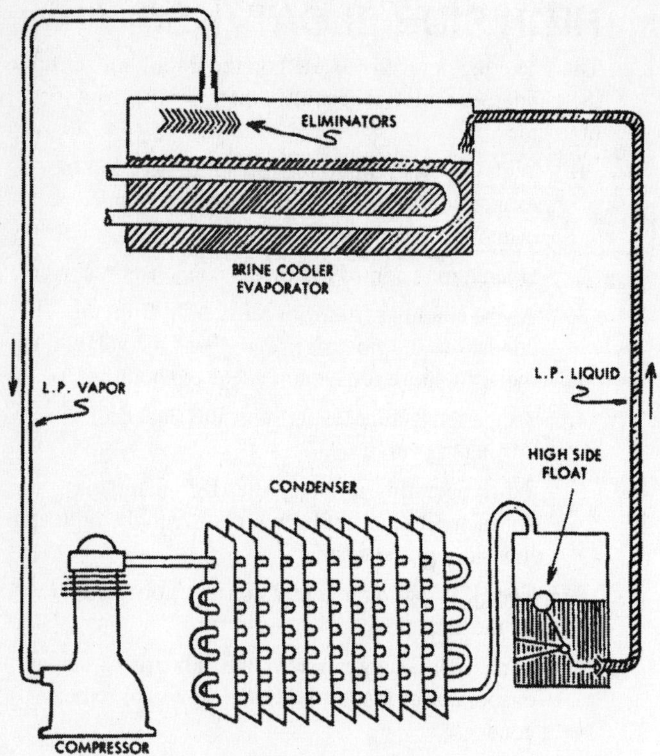

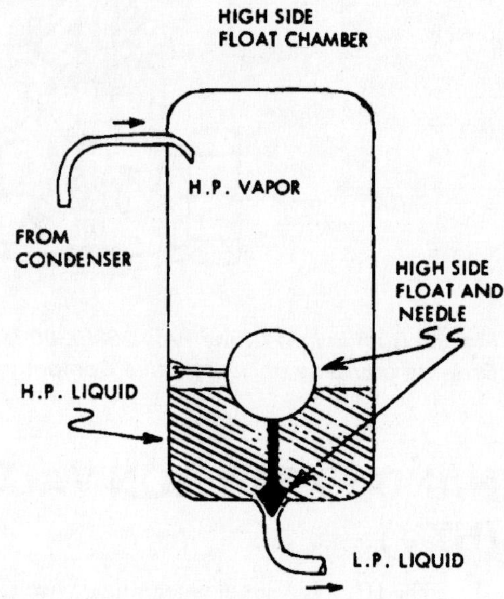

Fig. 3.9 Block Diagram of a Centrifugal System with a High-Side Float
Drawing courtesy of Goodheart-Willcox.

12. If the float develops a hole and sinks, the device will starve the system by causing low suction pressure.

LOW SIDE FLOAT (LSF)

This is a float-operated needle valve used to meter refrigerant to the evaporator. It separates the high and low sides of the system.

1. Basic parts of the LSF include:
   a. the float, which is a sealed ball, cylinder, or open pan
   b. the needle valve or ball valve
   c. the suction outlet to suction line
   d. the connection to the chiller
   e. the inlet from the liquid line
2. The float is located inside the evaporator or enclosed in a chamber connected directly to the evaporator. Flash gas resulting from the pressure drop at the valve is drawn through the suction line along with vapor from the evaporator. This is an advantage because LSFs eliminate flash gas in the evaporator.
3. The valve is calibrated so it is fully closed when the liquid reaches the proper level.
4. As the liquid level drops due to vaporization by the evaporator, the float drops and opens the valve, allowing more refrigerant from the liquid line.
5. The float rises to meter less refrigerant through the needle valve as the liquid level rises.
6. When the liquid level drops, the float drops and meters more refrigerant through the needle valve.
7. The amount of evaporation in the system, which controls the rising and lowering of the float, controls the refrigerant liquid level in the LSF.
8. The system will flood, causing high suction pressure, if the float in the LSF valve develops a hole and sinks.
9. A disadvantage of the LSF is that it requires a large amount of refrigerant.
10. LSFs come with fixed and adjustable float levels.
11. Float valves were popular metering devices in multiple-evaporator systems. This type of valve is also used, not as a metering device, but to control water level in cooling towers, evaporative condensers, and humidifiers. Today you may find the LSF in industrial systems and water cooling systems.

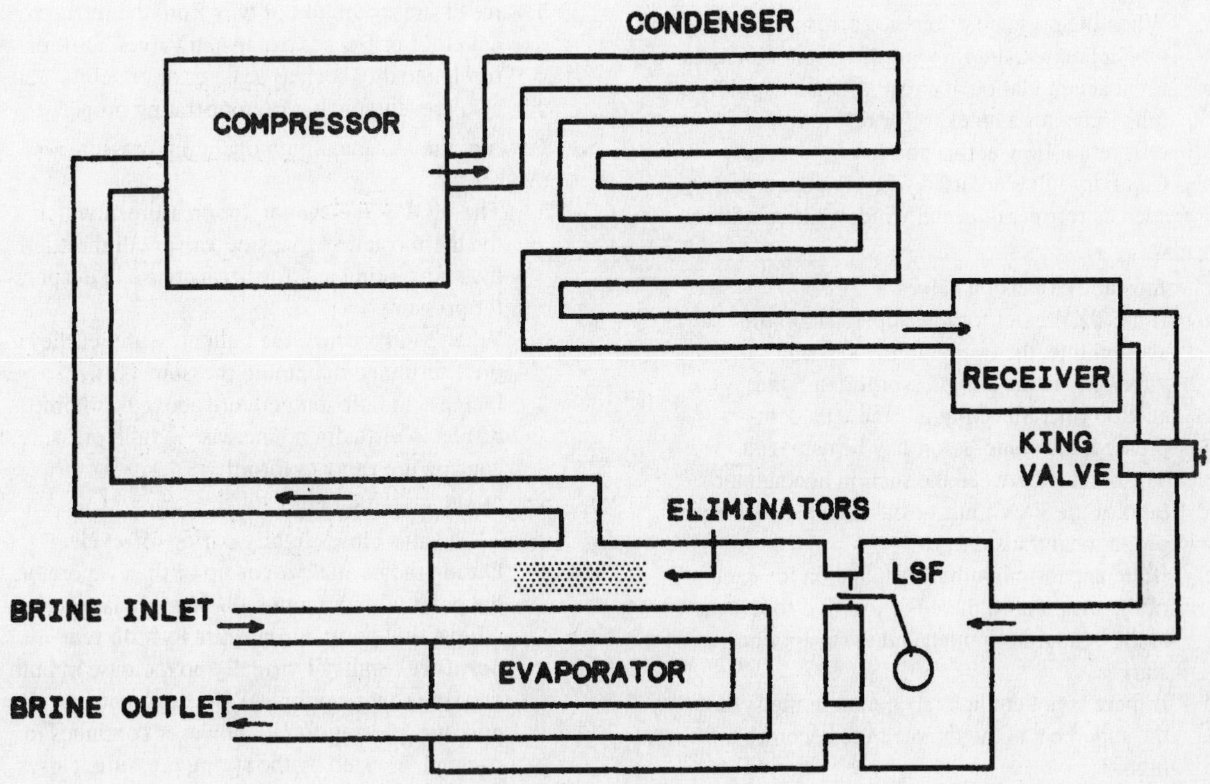

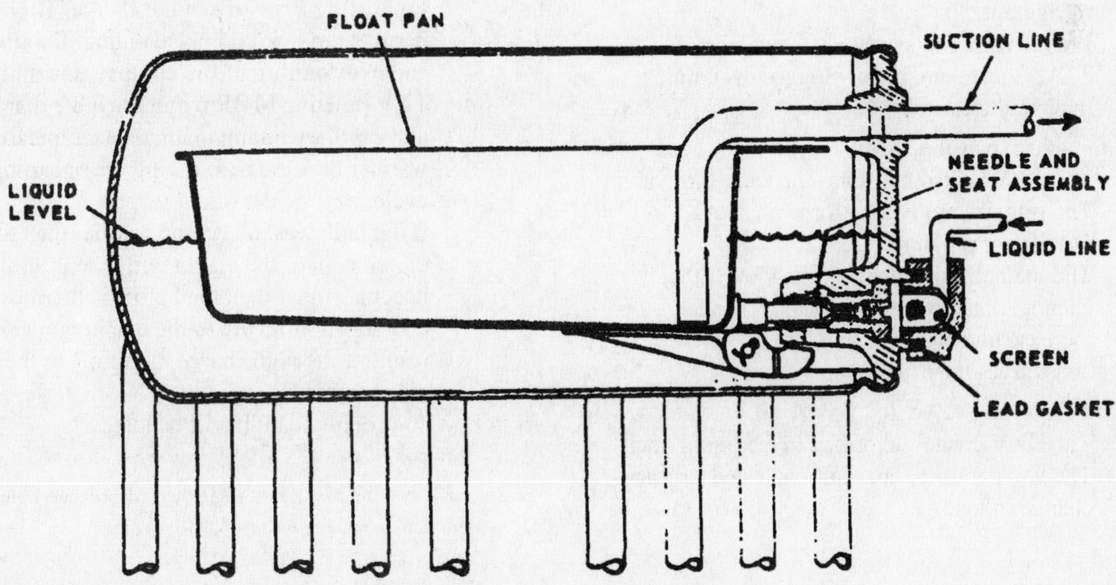

Fig. 3.10 Block Diagram of a Reciprocating System with a Low-Side Float
Drawing courtesy of Goodheart-Willcox.

METERING DEVICE TECHNICAL TIPS

1. Capillary tube
   a. When the pressure difference across a capillary tube increases, the flow of refrigerant increases.
   b. Frost accumulation at any point on a capillary tube indicates a blockage or restriction of refrigerant flow at that point.
   c. Capillary tubes are used with small equipment, such as refrigerators and window air conditioners.
2. Thermostatic expansion valve
   a. If the TXV is set for low superheat on the suction line, the evaporator floods and saturated vapor enters the compressor through the suction line. Since liquid cannot be compressed, the compressor may be damaged.
   b. The contact between the suction line and the bulb of the TXV must be clean and secure for proper heat transfer.
   c. If the expansion bulb is installed on the center of the evaporator, there is excessive superheat at the evaporator outlet, and the evaporator starves.
   d. If there is not enough refrigerant in the system, the superheat at the remote bulb becomes too high.
   e. A broken capillary tube on the remote bulb causes the valve to close and shuts down the system.
   f. If the equalizer line breaks, the system loses its refrigerant.
   g. If a refrigerating system does not react to a TXV adjustment, an oil-clogged evaporator may be the cause.
3. Automatic expansion valve
   a. The AXV is also known as the backward valve.
   b. The primary motivating force on an AXV is evaporator pressure.
   c. The main disadvantage of the AXV is that it cannot adjust to variable loads. A sudden increase of evaporator pressure closes the AXV and starves the evaporator.
4. Hand expansion valve
   a. The HXV creates an orifice in the liquid line.
   b. The valve must be manually adjusted for each change in load.
5. Expansion valves
   a. Refrigeration problems normally occur at the expansion valve, whether thermostatic, automatic, or hand.
   b. Ice or the separation of wax from the refrigerant clogs or freezes expansion valves. Dirt, or foreign matter such as scale or drier debris, can also prevent a valve from operating properly.
6. Pressure limit or maximum operating pressure (MOP)[1]
   a. The MOP is the evaporator pressure at which the thermostatic expansion valve will throttle, thus preventing any further increase in evaporator pressure.
   b. When MOP occurs, the bulb pressure reaches a predetermined maximum pressure. Any increase in bulb temperature above this point results in virtually no increase in bulb pressure, causing the valve to throttle.
7. TXV bulb operation
   a. TXV valve closes tightly during **off-cycle.** During the normal **warm-up** of the evaporator, the point of maximum bulb pressure is reached. **Above this point** an **increase in bulb temperature** results in virtually no increase in bulb pressure (opening force). The evaporator pressure (closing force), however continues to rise and, assisted by the spring pressure, closes the valve tightly.
   b. Valve remains closed during pulldown. While the evaporator temperature is relatively high, the valve remains closed until the **Maximum Operating Pressure** of the charge. This permits rapid pulldown, avoiding **floodback** and **overloading of the compressor motor.**
   c. TXV utilizing **MOP** require that the diaphragm and capillary tubing maintain a temperature warmer than the bulb during the operating cycle.

      If the bulb was to become warmer than the diaphragm, or the diaphragm case is allowed to become colder than the bulb, the thermostatic charge will **migrate** to the diaphragm case. The result of the bulb charge migrating to the diaphragm will cause the TXV to close, and control of the bulb will be lost.[2]

1 Sporlan Valve Company, Form 10-56: copyright January 1982

2 Modern Refrigeration & A/C, Goodheart-Willcox

METERING DEVICE LICENSE QUESTIONS

1. The TXV is controlled by

   (A) coil temperature.
   (B) the difference between gas temperature and the temperature corresponding to the gas pressure.
   (C) the difference between gas pressure and the pressure corresponding to the gas temperature.
   (D) coil pressure.

2. The feeler bulb of a TXV is located

   (A) before the evaporator.
   (B) after the evaporator.
   (C) midway along the evaporator.
   (D) on the suction line next to the compressor.

3. The three operating pressures of the TXV valve are

   (A) evaporator pressure, spring pressure, and suction pressure.
   (B) evaporator pressure, bulb pressure, and condenser pressure.
   (C) evaporator pressure, spring pressure, and discharge pressure.
   (D) evaporator pressure, spring pressure, and bulb pressure.

4. If a refrigerating system does NOT react to an adjustment of the TXV, it may be due to

   (A) noncondensable gases in the system.
   (B) insufficient condenser water flow.
   (C) an oil-logged coil or evaporator.
   (D) excessive motor speed.

5. In a compression refrigeration system, if the capillary line on the remote bulb of the TXV breaks and the charge is lost, the valve

   (A) remains open.
   (B) operates erratically.
   (C) shuts off completely; closes.
   (D) first closes, then opens.

6. Thermostatic expansion valves are rated in

   (A) superheat settings.
   (B) horsepower.
   (C) tons of refrigeration.
   (D) all the above.

7. TXV ratings are based on

   (A) slightly subcooled liquid entering the valve.
   (B) vapor-free saturated liquid entering the valve.
   (C) liquid with a small amount of vapor entering the valve.
   (D) 10° F subcooled liquid entering the valve.

8. If the feeler bulb of a TXV valve were moved to the center of the evaporator, you would get

   (A) more than 10° superheat.
   (B) less than 10° superheat.
   (C) no effect on superheat.
   (D) fluctuating superheat.

9. An external equalizer is used on an evaporator with a pressure drop of

   (A) less than 2 pounds.
   (B) more than 2 pounds.
   (C) less than 10 pounds.
   (D) more than 10 pounds.

10. A thermostatic expansion valve with a static setting of 7° superheat would have a field setting of

    (A) 7° superheat.
    (B) 0° superheat.
    (C) 4° F superheat.
    (D) 11° F superheat.

11. If the bulb of a TXV is installed right after the expansion valve, it is installed

    (A) correctly.
    (B) incorrectly.
    (C) in accordance with manufacture's requirements.
    (D) as an optional choice.

12. If you open the adjustment of a TXV, you

    (A) raise the suction pressure.
    (B) lower the suction pressure.
    (C) raise the superheat.
    (D) lower the superheat.

13. A thermostatic expansion valve was factory set at 0° superheat. How much was the field setting?

    (A) 0–3°
    (B) 3–5°
    (C) 4–8°
    (D) 10–15°

14. A TEV is attached to a finned evaporator coil with the bulb clamped to the suction line. In normal operation, the suction gas will leave this coil most nearly in the state of

(A) 0–5° superheat.
(B) 7–10° superheat.
(C) 10–15° superheat.
(D) 15–20° superheat.

15. A direct expansion cooling coil has a TXV. If the load variations are wide and subject to rapid change, the valve should be set for superheat from

(A) 1–3° F.
(B) 3–5° F.
(C) 7–9° F.
(D) 10–15° F.

16. In a refrigeration system, the bulb of the TEV is clamped in the middle of the evaporator coil. When operative the probability is that

(A) the vapor boiled off will be 100 percent saturated.
(B) the superheat in the evaporator will decrease.
(C) the superheat in the evaporator will increase.
(D) the liquid leaving the TEV will be hot.

17. A TEV shipped from the factory has a static superheat setting of

(A) 3° F.
(B) 5° F.
(C) 7° F.
(D) 10° F.

18. The static setting of a TXV is set

(A) in the factory.
(B) by the operator.
(C) in the field.
(D) all of the above.

19. What is the purpose of an external equalizer on a TEV?

(A) It lubricates the coil of the TEV.
(B) It equalizes the pressure in the evaporator.
(C) It eliminates the effect of the pressure drop across the evaporator.
(D) None of the above

20. Assume a TXV is set for 10° superheat. This means the gas passing the remote bulb is about 10°

(A) above the temperature of the evaporating refrigerant.
(B) below the temperature of the evaporating refrigerant.
(C) above the temperature of the ambient air temperature.
(D) below the temperature of the ambient air temperature.

21. In a particular air conditioning system using R-12, a refrigerant distributor is not necessary. In this case a TXV with an external equalizer should be used when the pressure drop through the evaporator is

(A) .5 psi.
(B) 1.00 psi.
(C) 1.5 psi.
(D) 2.5 psi.

22. A thermostatic expansion valve in a refrigeration system

(A) regulates the pressure in the evaporator.
(B) regulates the compressor pressure.
(C) regulates the flow of refrigerant to the pre-cooler.
(D) modulates and controls the flow of refrigerant to the evaporator.

23. If the external equalizer line of a TXV is disconnected from the evaporator, which of the following might result?

(A) No refrigeration
(B) Excess refrigeration
(C) Higher head pressure
(D) Higher suction pressure

24. What is the highest pressure that can be exerted on a Freon system's TXV bulb (vapor charge), with a saturated temperature of 60°, on the suction line?

(A) 55
(B) 70
(C) 100
(D) Higher

25. When using a TXV in a Freon system with the temperature range of +40 to –40, what type of charge would you use in a remote bulb?

(A) Gas charge
(B) Gas cross charge
(C) Liquid charge
(D) Liquid cross charge

26. Superheat is heat added

(A) to change liquid to vapor.
(B) to raise the temperature of water.
(C) after all liquid has been changed to vapor.
(D) to increase pressure.

27. An automatic expansion valve system on a variable loads causes

(A) a flooded evaporator on high loads.
(B) no apparent change in operation.
(C) an overloading of the compressor motor.
(D) a starved evaporator at high loads.

28. One main disadvantage of an automatic expansion valve is that it

(A) requires a critical charge of refrigerant.
(B) is only used on domestic refrigerators.
(C) cannot adapt to variable loads.
(D) all the above.

29. A high load affects the operation of a constant pressure expansion valve by

(A) causing overload.
(B) requiring an external equalizer.
(C) starving the evaporator.
(D) all the above.

30. Of the following, which component is found in a direct expansion valve system?

(A) Float valve
(B) Needle valve
(C) Globe valve
(D) Gate valve

31. An expansion valve is built most nearly like a

(A) shut-off valve.
(B) pressure-reducing valve.
(C) blow-off valve.
(D) double-seated globe valve.

32. What causes the drop in temperature and pressure as liquid refrigerant passes through the expansion valve?

(A) The superheat of the refrigerant
(B) The change in the rate of flow of the refrigerant
(C) The partial evaporation of refrigerant as it passes through the valve
(D) The temperature and pressure of the refrigerant in the liquid line

33. The subcooling effect of a liquid refrigerant just before the expansion valve would result in

(A) increased refrigeration effect.
(B) increased refrigerant density.
(C) increased miscibility of the oil.
(D) none of the above.

34. The automatic expansion valve maintains constant pressure at the

(A) condenser inlet.
(B) evaporator inlet.
(C) liquid line.
(D) condenser outlet.

35. Which of the following is also referred to as a backward operating valve?

(A) Thermal expansion valve
(B) Hand expansion valve
(C) Low side float
(D) Automatic expansion valve

36. What controls the operation of a high-side float?

(A) Accumulator
(B) Evaporator
(C) Condenser and receiver
(D) Evaporator and condenser

37. In a high-side float, frost on the suction line indicates

(A) recharging the refrigerant is necessary.
(B) an excessive amount of refrigerant is in the system.
(C) noncondensibles are in the system.
(D) there is a leak in the system.

38. On a refrigeration system with a high-side float metering device, what happens if the float fills with with liquid refrigerant and sinks?

(A) The evaporator starves.
(B) The evaporator floods.
(C) The compressor stalls.
(D) The condenser starves.

39. In a flooded evaporator using an accumulator and float valve, flash gas

(A) passes directly into the evaporator.
(B) passes directly into the suction line.
(C) does not occur.
(D) stays in the receiver.

40. A flooded system with a low-side float uses a thermostat that controls the liquid line solenoid valve. The thermostat is satisfied and the room continues to cool down due to

(A) a drop in head pressure.
(B) the pumping out of the low side.
(C) all the above.
(D) none of the above.

41. One advantage of a low-side float system is that it

(A) requires a large amount of refrigerant.
(B) can be used with a water cooled condenser.
(C) eliminates flash gas in the evaporator.
(D) can be used with a low starting torque motor.

42. One disadvantage of a low-side float valve is that it

(A) is nonadjustable.
(B) requires a large amount of refrigerant.
(C) is very expensive.
(D) cannot be used on multiple systems.

43. In a flooded system, a low-side float is used as a metering device. If the float fills with liquid refrigerant and sinks, this

(A) starves the evaporator.
(B) floods the evaporator.
(C) stalls the compressor.
(D) raises the evaporator temperature.

44. Flash gas forms in the

(A) compressor.
(B) condenser.
(C) evaporator.
(D) heat exchanger.

45. The flash gas loss at the expansion valve is approximately

(A) 2 percent.
(B) 5 percent.
(C) 22 percent.
(D) 12 percent.

46. What does a high superheat mean?

(A) Flooded evaporator
(B) Starved evaporator
(C) Pressure increase
(D) Motor speed too high

47. What does a low superheat indicate?

(A) Flooded evaporator
(B) Starved evaporator
(C) Pressure increase
(D) Motor speed too low

48. An R-12 refrigeration system has a gas-charged thermostatic expansion valve. The standard maximum operating pressure (MOP) for this valve at 60° F, saturated evaporator pressure, is

(A) 55 psig.
(B) 70 psig.
(C) 100 psig.
(D) 150 psig.

49. Which of the following distributors are not used with an external equalizer thermostatic expansion valve?

(A) Manifold type
(B) Venturi type
(C) Centrifugal type
(D) Pressure-drop type

50. Thermal expansion valves are generally rated at stated suction temperatures in

(A) tons of refrigeration effect.
(B) pounds per minute of refrigerant pumped.
(C) pounds per hour of refrigerant pumped.
(D) cubic feet per minute pf refrigerant pumped.

51. An electric expansion valve that operates with a heater motor and a thermistor has a control voltage of

(A) 6 volts.
(B) 12 volts.
(C) 24 volts.
(D) 110 volts.

52. On an operating electric expansion valve, if the thermistor senses superheat on the suction line, the result is

(A) it modulates to the closed position.
(B) it throttles to the open position.
(C) insulation at the thermistor stabilizes the valve.
(D) it increases the resistance to the heater motor.

Answers to Metering Device License Questions

1. **The correct answer is (B).**
2. **The correct answer is (B).**
3. **The correct answer is (D).**
4. **The correct answer is (C).**
5. **The correct answer is (C).**
6. **The correct answer is (C).**
7. **The correct answer is (B).**
8. **The correct answer is (A).**
9. **The correct answer is (B).** It's 2.5 lbs.
10. **The correct answer is (D).**
11. **The correct answer is (B).**
12. **The correct answer is (D).**
13. **The correct answer is (C).**
14. **The correct answer is (B).**
15. **The correct answer is (D).**
16. **The correct answer is (C).**
17. **The correct answer is (C).**
18. **The correct answer is (A).**
19. **The correct answer is (C).**
20. **The correct answer is (A).**
21. **The correct answer is (D).**
22. **The correct answer is (D).**
23. **The correct answer is either (A) or (D).** Higher suction pressure occurs first when the external equalizer line is disconnected. Since most systems use hundreds of pounds of refrigerant, a short period of time will pass before no refrigeration will occur.
24. **The correct answer is (A).**
25. **The correct answer is (D).**
26. **The correct answer is (C).**
27. **The correct answer is (D).**
28. **The correct answer is (C).**
29. **The correct answer is (C).**
30. **The correct answer is (B).**
31. **The correct answer is (B).**
32. **The correct answer is (C).**
33. **The correct answer is (A).**
34. **The correct answer is (B).**
35. **The correct answer is (D).**
36. **The correct answer is (C).**
37. **The correct answer is (B).**
38. **The correct answer is (A).**
39. **The correct answer is (B).**
40. **The correct answer is (B).**
41. **The correct answer is (C).**
42. **The correct answer is (B).**
43. **The correct answer is (B).**
44. **The correct answer is (C).**
45. **The correct answer is (D).**
46. **The correct answer is (B).**
47. **The correct answer is (A).**
48. **The correct answer is (A).**
49. **The correct answer is (A).**
50. **The correct answer is (A).**
51. **The correct answer is (C).**
52. **The correct answer is (B).**

Chapter 4

CONDENSERS

The condenser is the device that removes heat from the refrigerating system. It transfers heat from the refrigeration system to a medium that can absorb it and move it to an area where it will not cause a problem.

When refrigerant vapor leaves the compressor as a high-temperature gas, it is forced into the cooler condenser coil. The refrigerant loses its latent heat of condensation, giving up the greatest amount of heat as it changes state from a vapor to a liquid. The surrounding air or water passes over the condenser and absorbs heat. At the end of the condenser, the temperature of refrigerant falls below its condensing temperature and the liquid refrigerant is called subcooled.

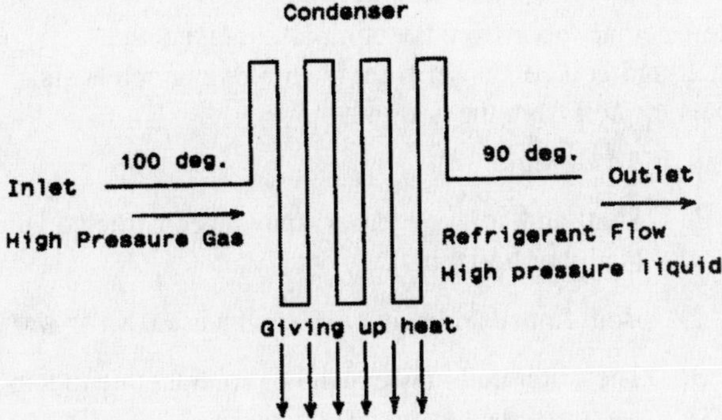

Fig. 4.1

Certain conditions must be met for a condenser to function properly:

1. The condensing medium must always be colder than the refrigerant it is condensing.
2. Heat given up by the refrigerant in a condenser equals the heat picked up by the condensing medium.
3. There must be nothing blocking heat transfer from the condenser to the outside air or water.
4. There should be a temperature differential of 10º between the inlet and outlet of the condenser.

The three types of condensers are the air-cooled, water-cooled, and evaporative.

AIR-COOLED CONDENSERS

Air-cooled condensers use air as the condensing medium. Their main advantage is that air is always available. Space is not needed for piping, cooling towers, or water pumps.

The three types of air-cooled condensers are the natural draft, forced-air, and inducted-air condensers. If a fan is used to increase the air flow, condenser capacity increases. Prevailing winds may affect the operation of an air-cooled condenser unit.

natural draft condenser: Ambient air is the condensing medium.

forced-air condenser: A fan pushes air through the condenser coil.

inducted-air condenser: A fan draws or pulls the air over the condenser coil.

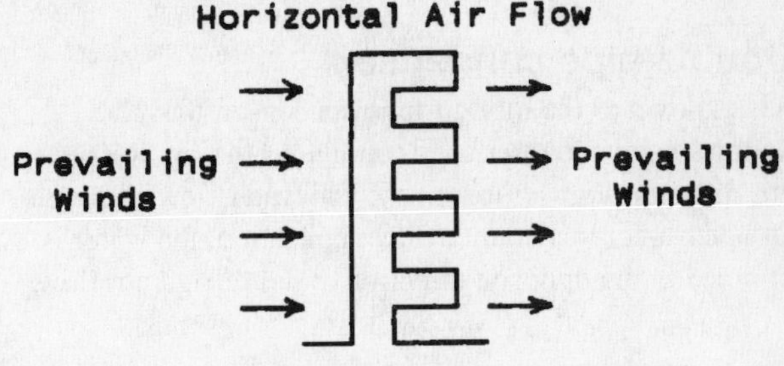

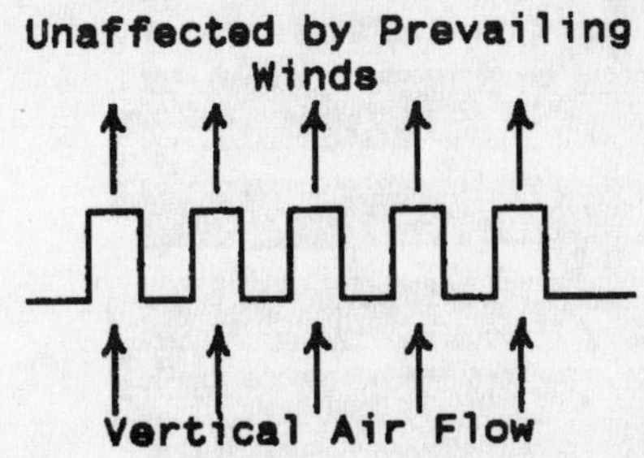

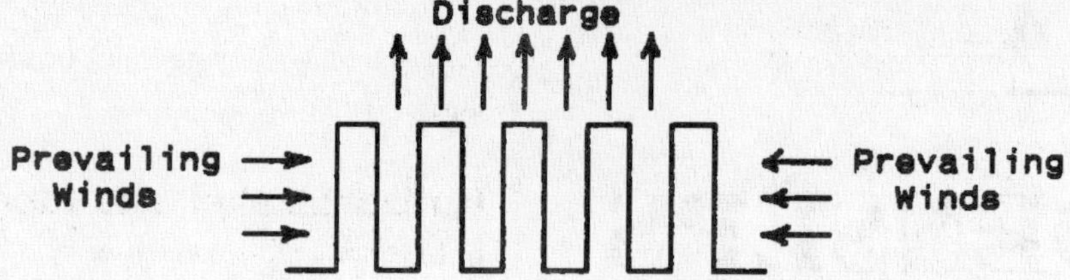

Fig. 4.2

Disadvantages Of Air-Cooled Condensers

1. Dirt or dust will insulate the tubes, preventing the rejection of heat from the system.
2. Condensing temperatures must be higher than with water-cooled condensers.
3. The condenser must be larger than a water-cooled condenser of the same capacity.

WATER-COOLED CONDENSERS

The water-cooled condenser uses water as the condensing medium. The four basic types of water-cooled condensers used are the double-pipe, shell-and-coil, vertical shell-and-tube, and horizontal shell-and-tube.

Double-pipe condenser

Also known as the tube-in-tube condenser, the double-pipe condenser uses continuous tubing. Refrigerant flows through an inner tube and water flows through an outer tube. In a counterflow application, the water is pumped in the opposite direction of the refrigerant flow.

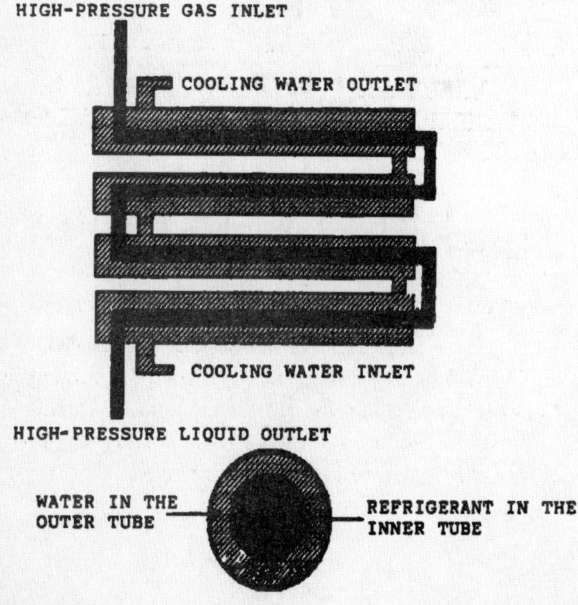

Fig. 4.3

Hot refrigerant vapor enters from the top, and cooling water enters from the bottom. The cooler water cools the liquid refrigerant, while the warmer water absorbs heat from the hotter refrigerant vapor. The refrigerant tube contacts ambient air, which also removes heat from the refrigerant.

Disadvantages

1. Double-pipe condensers must be cleaned with chemicals.
2. If there is a leak, the condenser must be replaced.

Shell-and-coil condenser

Refrigerant vapor from the compressor enters the shell-and-coil condenser from the top. Water enters and exits the coil from the bottom.

Advantages

1. Shell-and-coil condensers may be constructed vertically or horizontally.
2. Both finned and bare coils can be used.
3. The water coil may expand or contract due to temperature changes in the condenser.
4. As the refrigerant vapor changes state, liquid refrigerant can settle at the bottom of the condenser.

Disadvantages

1. The shell-and-coil condenser is designed for small-tonnage, low-pressure use.
2. It can only be chemically cleaned.
3. If the coil leaks, it must be replaced.
4. The heads are not removable.

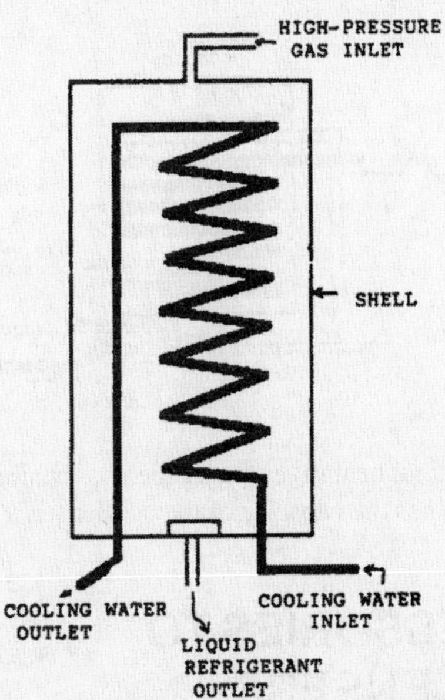

Fig. 4.4

Vertical shell-and-tube condenser

In this type of condenser, water from the supply line enters the water box at the top. The water feeds by gravity through a swirler into each tube. At the bottom of the condenser, the water flows into a sump.

Advantages

1. Vertical shell-and-tube condensers may be installed with limited floor space.
2. Tubes can be cleaned while the condenser is in service.
3. The swirler at the top of the water box forces water down the tubes, providing good heat transfer.
4. Under a heavy load, water pressure may be increased.

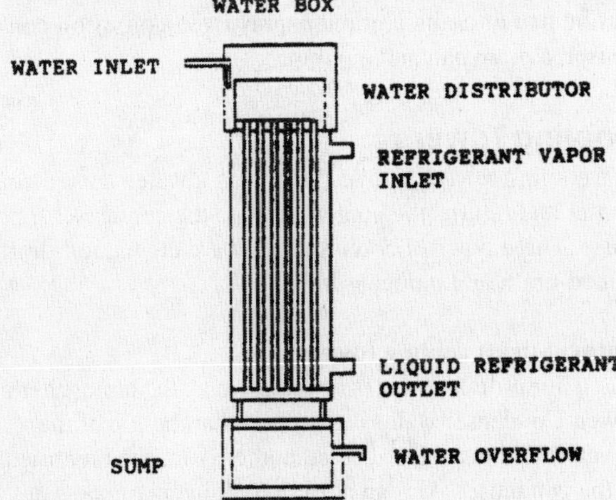

Fig. 4.5

Disadvantage

Large amounts of water must be used and drained down into the sump.

Horizontal shell-and-tube condenser

Refrigerant in this condenser is in the shell and water is in the tubes. The water box is bolted to the tubes at each end. Depending on the number of baffles inside the unit, water may pass several times.

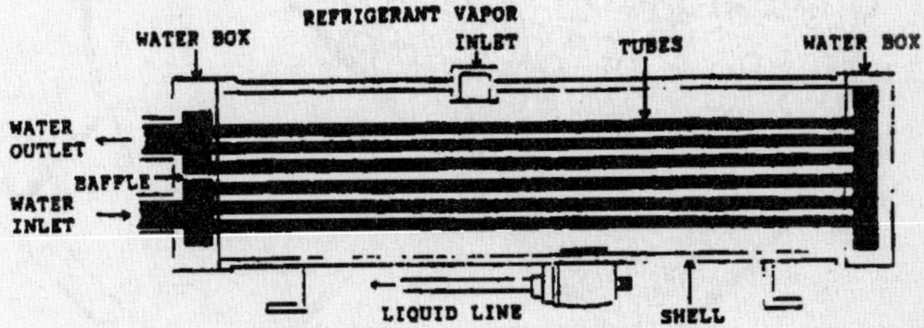

Fig. 4.6

Advantages

1. The more tubing in the condenser, the better the heat transfer.
2. The condenser can store refrigerant in the shell.

Disadvantage

During winter maintenance, the water-box heads must be removed so the tubes can be cleaned.

In the illustration below, an even-pass condenser is contrasted with an odd-pass condenser.

The condenser water inlet and outlet are on the same side on an even-pass condenser. Water enters from one end and exits at the opposite end on an odd-pass condenser.

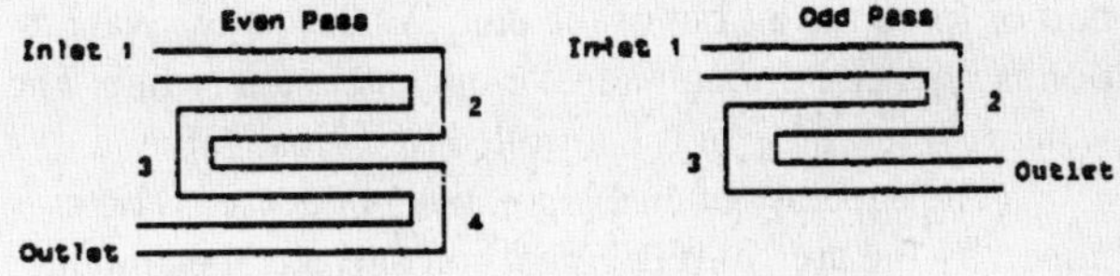

Fig. 4.7

On the practical exam, the Carrier 17M and the Trane unit use horizontal shell-and-tube condensers.

Disadvantages of water-cooled condensers

Mineral deposits and scale form on the condenser walls and tubes. These deposits insulate between the condenser and cooling water and must be cleaned with chemicals throughout the cooling season. Other deposits must also be mechanically cleaned during the off season.

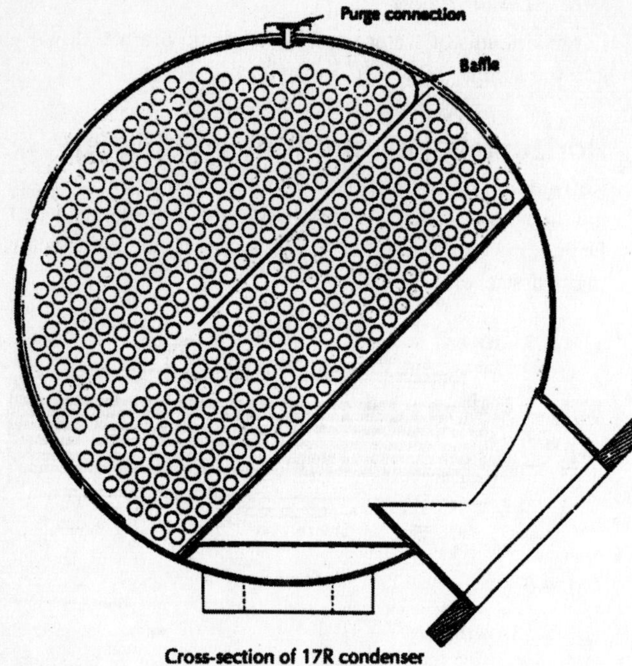

Fig. 4.8
Courtesy of Carrier Corporation.

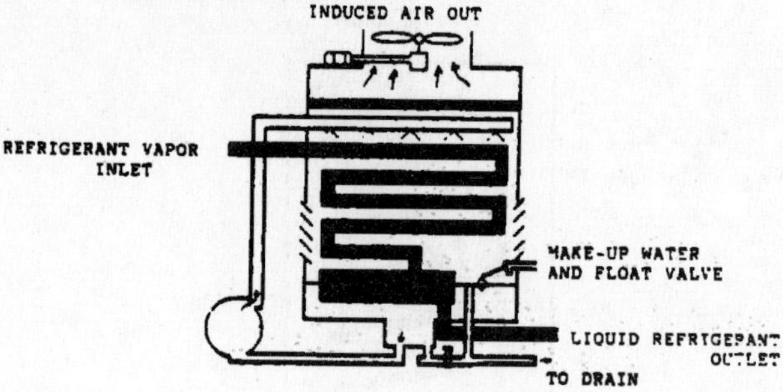

Fig. 4.9

The total heat given up by the condensing refrigerant determines the capacity of the condenser.

EVAPORATIVE CONDENSERS

In an evaporative condenser, heat is absorbed from the coil by the evaporation of water. The spray pump circulates water from the pan at the bottom to a series of spray nozzles over the refrigerant coil. Air enters through an inlet at the base and passes up through the coil and water spray, then through eliminators. The eliminators prevent water from being carried away with the air. Fans at the top pull or force the air out of the unit. Water lost by evaporation is replaced through a make-up water supply line. The water level in the pan is controlled by a float valve.

The capacity of an evaporative condenser is determined by the area of refrigerant coil surface, the amount of air flowing over the coil, and the amount of heat the entering air can absorb. The more heat the entering air contains, the lower the capacity. The lower the wet-bulb temperature of the entering air, the greater the condenser capacity. In other words, if the entering air is dry and carries less heat, the condenser will operate more efficiently.

ACCESSORIES TO CONDENSERS

Spray Pond

The spray pond is a water recirculating device that may be used in place of a water tower. It may be an artificial or a natural pond. For example, the United Nations plaza has a spray pond that cools the condenser water of the air-conditioning equipment in the UN building. The warm water is sprayed through a nozzle into the air as a decorative fountain. Some water evaporates in the air and the rest, now colder, falls back into the fountain basin. The water is picked up by the pump and recirculated through the machine.

A natural pond or lake in a rural area can be tapped for condenser water. By pumping the water from the lake, circulating it through a condenser, and spraying it back into the lake, the water is cooled. The spray increases the water's surface area and the rate of evaporation. Like a cooling tower, the spray pond reuses the cooling water.

An artificial spray pond has a spray tree and a collection pan or drain, a gravity spray over a pipe coil condenser, a drain pan and a pump.

Cooling Towers

The cooling tower removes heat from a water-cooled condenser and returns the cooler water to the condenser for reuse. Three types of cooling towers are the natural-draft, forced-draft, and induced-draft.

Natural-draft cooling tower

The natural-draft tower is also known as the atmospheric tower. Condenser water is distributed at the top of the tower, into the shell, collected at the basin, then returned to the condenser. Air enters through louvers on the sides. The louvers are slanted inward to prevent cooling water from blowing out. Tower cooling depends upon prevailing winds that blow across the falling water, causing some evaporation. The water falling to the basin pan is cooler. A float-controlled valve replaces water lost to evaporation.

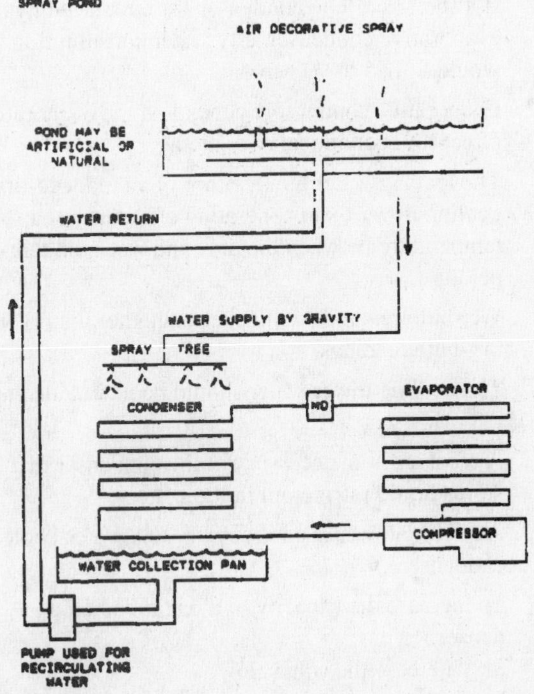

Fig. 4.10

Forced-draft cooling tower
The forced-draft tower also uses water evaporation for cooling. The difference is that a fan pushes the air into the shell. The air is pushed from the side of the tower, up through the wetted surface, and out the top.

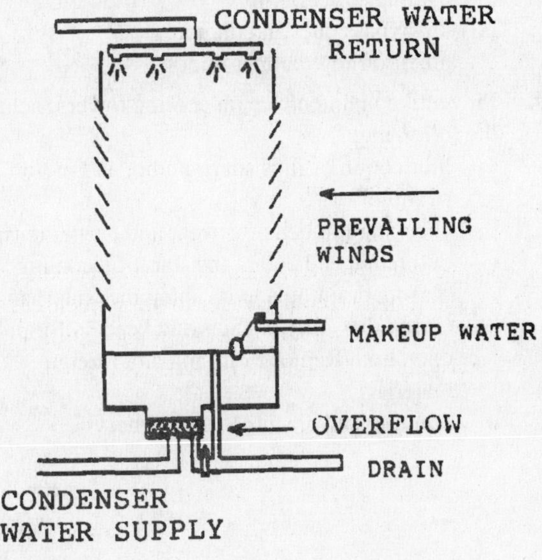

Fig. 4.11

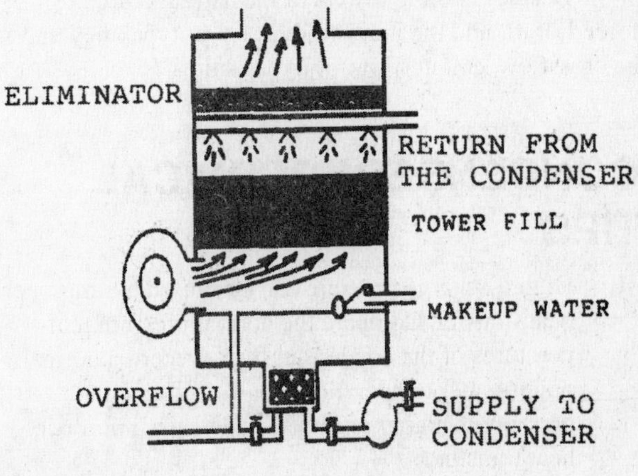

ELIMINATOR
RETURN FROM THE CONDENSER
TOWER FILL
MAKEUP WATER
OVERFLOW
SUPPLY TO CONDENSER

Fig. 4.12

Advantages

1. The forced-draft tower is smaller than the natural-draft tower.
2. It is not affected by prevailing winds.
3. It can be installed anywhere, even inside the building. Air can be ducted to the fan, into the tower, and out the top.

Induced-Draft Cooling Towers

The induced-draft cooling tower is one of the most popular towers used in cities. Two or more fans are installed on the top of the unit. The fans pull air out of the tower from the top. Air enters the tower from the sides, through the corrugated contact surface called fill, and is pulled out by the fans.

Condenser water is distributed over the top of the unit and sprayed onto the fill. The fill extends the contact surface and increases the unit's capacity to evaporate water. Cooling is done by the air drawn by the fans. As some water evaporates, the remaining water is cooled and recirculated to the condenser. Make-up water is supplied to the tower, controlled by a float valve.

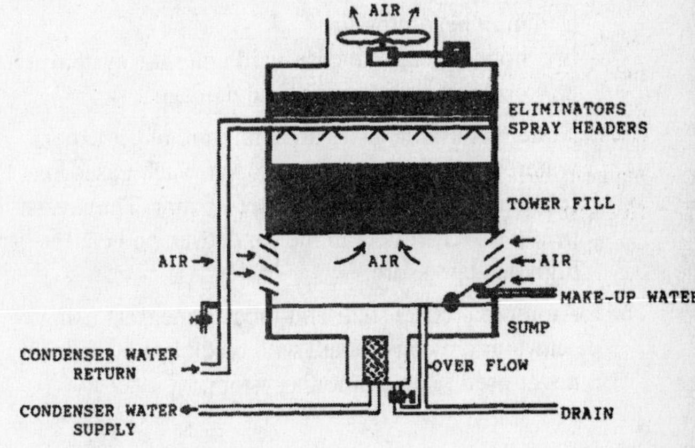

Fig. 4.13

Besides cooling towers of the natural draft, forced-draft, and the induced-draft tower type, they may be crossflow, counterflow, or hyperbolic.

CONDENSER TECHNICAL TIPS

1. High discharge pressure can be caused by improper heat transfer. Compare the normal pressure temperatures of the condenser. If you record a normal outlet-water temperature, but the refrigerant pressure is higher or lower, it indicates improper heat transfer.
2. Improper heat transfer is also caused by the buildup of scale and mineral deposits in the cooling system. Preventive maintenance with mechanical and/or chemical treatment should be conducted.
3. High head pressure can be caused by any of the following:
   a. undersized condenser
   b. insufficient condenser water or low condenser water flow
   c. improper heat transfer
   d. dirty coils
   e. noncondensable gases in the system (check the purger)
   f. overcharge of refrigerant
   g. condenser pump shutdown (check fuses or starter)
   h. cooling tower fan shutdown (check fuses or starter)
   i. tower makeup-water valve, float, or pump shutdown
   j. condenser pump strainer clog
4. If a system operates with the suction stop closed and the discharge stop valve opened, the following will occur:
   a. high head pressure
   b. noncondensable gases will enter the system
   c. possible compressor head damage
5. Noncondensable gases are a mixture of oil vapor, water, air, hydrogen, and nitrogen. Such gases in a refrigeration system do no useful work. They resist heat transfer, collect in the condenser, and cause high head pressure.
6. Ammonia (NH_3) shell-and-tube condensers using seawater are constructed with black iron. Copper is never used in an ammonia system.
7. The double-pipe condenser is also known as the anal tube condenser.
8. Natural-draft condensers are normally found in household refrigerators.
9. If a shell-and-tube condenser were replaced by an evaporative condenser, city water consumption would fall 85 to 90 percent.
10. Evaporative condensers depend on the evaporation effect for economical operation.
11. The leaving water temperature of an induced-draft cooling tower that is operating efficiently is a temperature between the dry- and wet-bulb temperature.
12. Wet-bulb readings will never be higher than dry-bulb readings.
13. The cooling tower water should be maintained at 7.8 pH.
14. A receiver is an accessory of the condenser that stores liquid refrigerant in the system.
15. A cooling tower is an accessory to a water-cooled condenser.
16. To increase the capacity of a water-cooled condenser:
    a. increase the water flow
    b. reduce the water temperature
17. The main advantage of the water-cooled condenser is that it enables lower head pressures on a system. This increases the capacity and reduces wear and tear on the moving parts.
18. The evaporative condenser controls condensing pressure by:
    a. cycling spray pump
    b. air-bypass duct and damper
    c. air-throttling damper inlet
19. Preventive maintenance on cooling towers includes the following:
    a. lubrication of fans shaft, pump, and motor bearings
    b. checking fan belts for wear and proper tension
    c. before the end and at the start of a cooling season, draining and cleaning the waterpan. Check the spray nozzles and headers for proper operation. Remove dirt and any foreign materials
    d. draining and cleaning tower filters

CONDENSER LICENSE QUESTIONS

1. The purpose of a condenser is to
   (A) remove water from the refrigeration system.
   (B) add heat to the refrigeration system.
   (C) remove heat from the refrigerant.
   (D) store liquid refrigerant.

2. An atmospheric condenser is generally
   (A) on the floor under the roof.
   (B) in the refrigeration room.
   (C) on the roof.
   (D) none of the above.

3. A condenser is
   (A) a good cost-saving accessory to a refrigeration system.
   (B) the exit for heat in a refrigeration system.
   (C) always mounted above the compressor.
   (D) always mounted below the compressor.

4. In an NH_3 shell-and-tube condenser using sea water, what would you use as the metal for the condenser?
   (A) Black iron
   (B) Galvanized steel
   (C) Muntz or admirality metal
   (D) Copper

5. The temperature at which moisture in the air starts to condense is known as
   (A) relative humidity.
   (B) dew point.
   (C) eutectic point.
   (D) wet-bulb temperature.

6. Condensing mediums must be
   (A) a liquid.
   (B) a gas.
   (C) noncorrosive.
   (D) in the right temperature range.

7. The capacity of an evaporative condenser will
   (A) increase as the entering air wet-bulb temperature decreases.
   (B) increase as the entering air wet-bulb temperature increases.
   (C) not change with changes in the entering air wet-bulb temperature.
   (D) decrease as the entering air wet-bulb temperature decreases.

8. Gas condenses in the anal or inner tube of a(n)
   (A) atmospheric condenser.
   (B) double-pipe condenser.
   (C) shell-and-tube condenser.
   (D) evaporative condenser.

9. Natural-draft condensers are most frequently found in
   (A) residential cooling.
   (B) room air conditioners.
   (C) household refrigerators.
   (D) large industrial plants.

10. The capacity of an evaporative condenser is greatest on a
    (A) warm day.
    (B) low-humidity day.
    (C) cool day.
    (D) rainy day.

11. The capacity of an evaporative condenser depends on
    (A) fan horsepower.
    (B) entering-air wet-bulb temperature.
    (C) the temperature of the entering air.
    (D) the amount of heat leaving air is capable of absorbing.

12. Which of the following does NOT increase the capacity of a water-cooled condenser?
    (A) Increasing the water flow
    (B) Reducing the water temperature
    (C) Decreasing the ambient temperature
    (D) None of the above

13. Open shell-and-tube condensers are mainly used with
    (A) a cooling tower or spray pond.
    (B) dirty water.
    (C) chemically treated water.
    (D) hard water.

14. If a shell-and-tube condenser were removed and an evaporative condenser were installed, city water consumption would
    (A) decrease 40 to 50 percent.
    (B) increase 40 to 50 percent.
    (C) increase 85 to 90 percent.
    (D) decrease 85 to 90 percent.

15. A cooling tower
   (A) is always used if water is scarce.
   (B) is an accessory to a condenser.
   (C) helps the operator maintain pressures.
   (D) must be in a location where the prevailing wind blows.

16. Of the many ways to control condensing pressure, which of the following methods is NOT used on an evaporative condenser?
   (A) Cycling spray pump motor
   (B) Coil flooding
   (C) Air-bypass duct and damper
   (D) Air-throttling damper inlet

17. If a system operated with the suction stop valve closed and the discharge stop valve open, what would happen?
   (A) The head would blow off.
   (B) High head pressure would occur.
   (C) Noncondensable gases would enter.
   (D) All of the above

18. At a given temperature, the relation of the actual pressure of a vapor in the atmosphere to the saturation pressure is called
   (A) relative humidity.
   (B) partial pressure.
   (C) humidifying effect.
   (D) refrigeration effect.

19. The capacity of a water-cooled condenser is least affected by the
   (A) amount of water circulated.
   (B) temperature of the water.
   (C) amount of gas circulated.
   (D) ambient temperature.

20. What effect would a refrigerant overcharge have on the system?
   (A) Head pressure would increase.
   (B) Head pressure would decrease.
   (C) Suction pressure would decrease.
   (D) Discharge pressure would decrease.

21. The leaving water temperature of an induced-draft cooling tower that is operating efficiently is
   (A) 10° F higher than entering water temperature.
   (B) some temperature between dry- and wet-bulb temperature.
   (C) at the dew-point temperature.
   (D) at the dry-bulb temperature.

22. The wet-bulb reading is higher than the dry-bulb reading when
   (A) relative humidity is 100 percent and temperature is above 32° F.
   (B) relative humidity is 100 percent and temperature is below 32° F.
   (C) relative humidity is above 100 percent.
   (D) This can never happen.

23. An evaporative condenser is constructed so that
   (A) refrigerant is sprayed over tubes.
   (B) refrigerant is in the tubes and air is over the tubes.
   (C) refrigerant is in the tubes while air and water are over the tubes.
   (D) noncondensables are easily removed.

24. Which statement concerning the evaporative condenser is correct?
   (A) An evaporative condenser and spray pond are most nearly alike.
   (B) Evaporative condensers depend on recirculation of bay water or ocean water.
   (C) A closed induced-draft evaporative condenser utilizes stack effect.
   (D) Evaporative condensers depend on evaporation effect for economical operation.

25. Cooling tower water should be maintained at a pH near
   (A) 4
   (B) 6
   (C) 8
   (D) 10

26. The discharge pressure in a condenser of an R-12 refrigerating system is 130 psig. What is that in psia?
   (A) 100
   (B) 115
   (C) 145
   (D) 160

27. One effect of noncondensable gas in a system is
   (A) high suction pressure.
   (B) low suction pressure.
   (C) high condenser pressure.
   (D) low condenser pressure.

28. Which would NOT cause high discharge pressure?

(A) An undersized condenser
(B) Insufficient condenser water
(C) Refrigerant undercharge
(D) None of the above

29. In a vertical open shell-and-tube condenser, where are the water boxes located?

(A) At the top
(B) At the bottom
(C) At the top and bottom
(D) There are none.

30. In a refrigeration system using a reciprocating compressor and a water-cooled condenser with a cooling tower, a decrease in the amount of cooling water will generally result in

(A) high head pressure.
(B) low suction pressure.
(C) no cooling.
(D) decrease in head pressure.

31. An evaporative condenser operates most efficiently when

(A) the dry-bulb temperature of the air is high.
(B) the wet-bulb temperature of the air is low.
(C) wet- and dry-bulb temperatures are high.
(D) the wet-bulb temperature is high.

32. The horizontal shell-and-tube condenser is more efficient than the vertical shell-and-tube condenser because

(A) it is mounted in a horizontal position.
(B) it is easier to clean.
(C) water passes through it more than once.
(D) it takes advantage of more air cooling.

33. Why have a receiver in a refrigeration system?

(A) It's a necessary component.
(B) It aids an expansion device.
(C) It's needed on the low side of the system.
(D) It's used as a storage tank.

34. In an air-cooled condenser,

(A) a fan is used.
(B) ambient air is the condensing medium.
(C) no water is used.
(D) all of the above.

35. In the condenser,

(A) heat is absorbed.
(B) heat is pressurized.
(C) heat is given up.
(D) all of the above.

Answers to Condenser License Questions

1. **The correct answer is (C).**
2. **The correct answer is (C).**
3. **The correct answer is (B).**
4. **The correct answer is (A).**
5. **The correct answer is (B).** This is the exact temperature at which moisture begins to form.
6. **The correct answer is (D).**
7. **The correct answer is (A).**
8. **The correct answer is (B).**
9. **The correct answer is (C).**
10. **The correct answer is (B).**
11. **The correct answer is (B).**
12. **The correct answer is (C).**
13. **The correct answer is (B).** It can use river or ocean water.
14. **The correct answer is (D).**
15. **The correct answer is (B).**
16. **The correct answer is (B).**
17. **The correct answer is (C).**
18. **The correct answer is (A).**
19. **The correct answer is (D).**
20. **The correct answer is (A).**
21. **The correct answer is (B).**
22. **The correct answer is (D).**
23. **The correct answer is (C).**
24. **The correct answer is (D).**
25. **The correct answer is (C).**
26. **The correct answer is (C).**
27. **The correct answer is (C).**
28. **The correct answer is (C).**
29. **The correct answer is (A).**
30. **The correct answer is (A).**
31. **The correct answer is (B).**
32. **The correct answer is (C).**
33. **The correct answer is (D).**
34. **The correct answer is (D).**
35. **The correct answer is (C).**

Chapter 5

COMPRESSORS

The compressor takes refrigerant vapor at a low temperature and pressure and raises it to a high temperature and pressure. It pumps refrigerant throughout the system. There are three main types of compressors: **reciprocating, centrifugal,** and **rotary.**

Compressor crankshaft seals are necessary to prevent refrigerant and oil from escaping the system. They also prevent air from entering a system and causing high head pressure. Four common types of seals are the packing gland, the stationary bellows, the diaphragm, and the rotary seal.

Compressors can be lubricated by the splash system, the pressure system, or a combination of both. Examples of the compressor lubrication systems will be illustrated.

The usual power source for a refrigeration compressor is an electric motor. Compressors may also be driven by a steam or internal combustion engine. This chapter will examine compressors by category, including the ammonia reciprocating type. The New York Refrigeration License Examination has many questions about the old ammonia system. In operation, it is similar to reciprocating refrigeration systems used today.

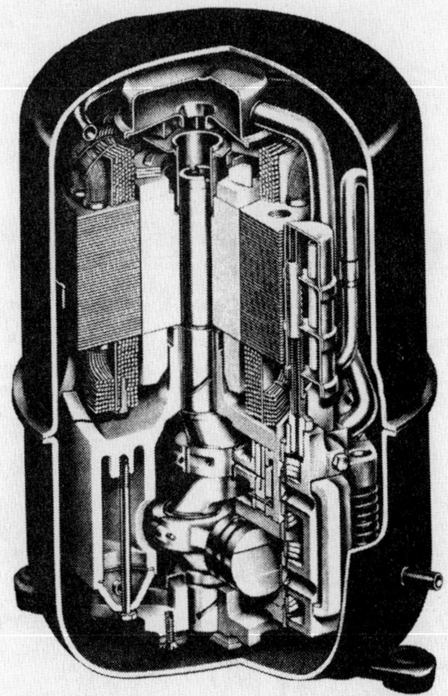

Cutaway model of a Tecumseh hermetic compressor

Fig. 5.1
Courtesy of Tecumseh Products Company.

RECIPROCATING COMPRESSORS

In the reciprocating compressor, a piston travels back and forth in a cylinder. A rod connects the piston to a crankshaft. As the motor turns, the crankshaft forces the piston up and down. A suction valve between the suction line and the cylinder lets refrigerant vapor enter the cylinder during the suction stroke. The discharge valve between the discharge line and the cylinder lets refrigerant vapor exit the condenser during the discharge (upward return) stroke.

The three types of reciprocating compressors are the hermetic, semi-hermetic, and open types.

Hermetic Compressor (Welded)

The electric motor in a hermetic compressor is factory-sealed (hermetically sealed) with the compressor inside a steel shell, which cannot be opened for servicing. The motor is generally cooled by suction gas passing through the windings. A common example is found in the household refrigerator. If the compressor malfunctions, it must be replaced.

Semi-Hermetic Compressor

This is a serviceable hermetic compressor. The motor and compressor are enclosed in one housing or shell. Usually the cylinder has plates that can be removed for servicing; some cylinders have bottom-removable plates. The motor can be cooled by suction gas passing through the windings, or it can be water cooled with a water jacket around the compressor.

Open-Type Compressor

In this compressor, one end of the crankshaft extends through the crankcase and is driven by an external power source. Also known as external-drive serviceable compressors, open-type compressors are bolted together. The two types of open compressors are the direct-drive and belt-drive.

In the direct drive compressor, the compressor shaft and motor shaft are connected by a coupling with little flexibility. The two shafts must be properly aligned.

In the belt-drive compressor, the crankshaft is driven by a flywheel (pulley) and V-belt. The mechanic can change the speed of the compressor by increasing or decreasing the pulley size. Because the pulleys must be in perfect alignment, the pulley shaft, motor, and compressor must be exactly aligned with each other. As the motor turns and spins the pulley, the belt turns the compressor shaft flywheel. In large-capacity installations, more than one V-belt may be used to transmit the required power.

A popular written exam question on the multi-V-belt drive is: If one belt snaps on a refrigeration compressor with a 5 V-belt drive, what should the watch engineer do? The answer is: Replace all five belts with a new set.

When changing a belt on an open-type compressor, make sure the belt isn't too tight. Test for proper belt ten-

Fig. 5.2 Grasso Reciprocating compressor, open type. Grasso RC11 refrigeration compressors, used for ammonia or halocarbon refrigerants.

Reciprocating open-type compressor

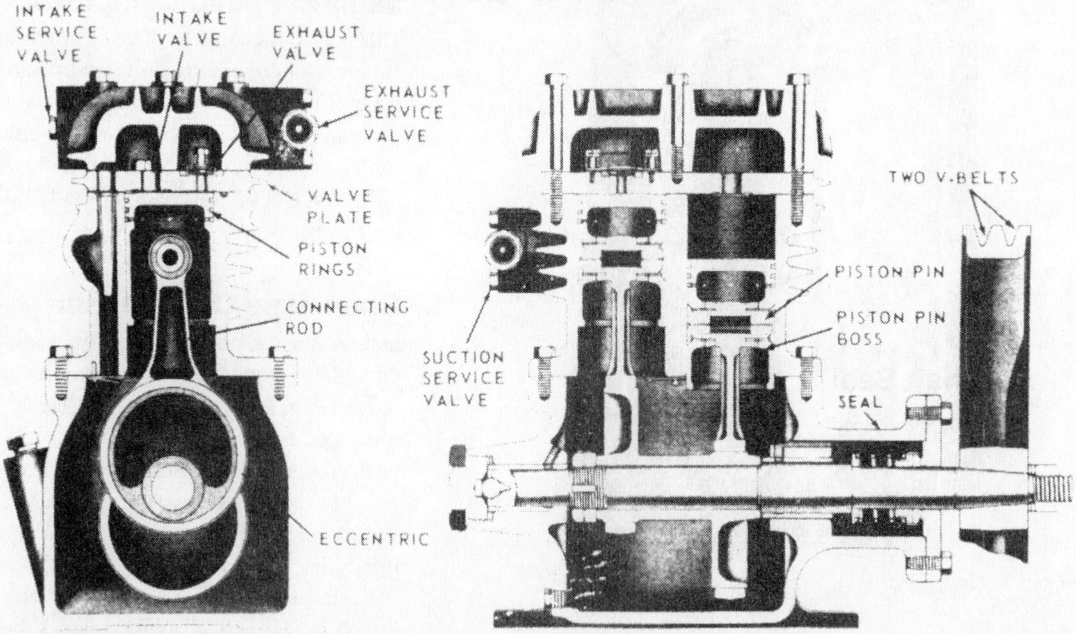

INTAKE SERVICE VALVE
INTAKE VALVE
EXHAUST VALVE
EXHAUST SERVICE VALVE
VALVE PLATE
PISTON RINGS
CONNECTING ROD
ECCENTRIC
TWO V-BELTS
PISTON PIN
PISTON PIN BOSS
SUCTION SERVICE VALVE
SEAL

Fig. 5.3
Drawing courtesy of Goodheart-Willcox.

sion by measuring the amperage on the three power lines (3-phase) to the compressor. If the belt is too tight, the motor will draw excess current.

TYPES OF RECIPROCATING COMPRESSOR SHAFTS

Crank-Throw

This is the conventional crankshaft. One end of the connecting rod is bolted to the crankshaft; the opposite end is attached to the piston with a pin. As the crankshaft revolves, the off-center throw guides the piston in a reciprocating motion (up and down).

Eccentric

This is similar to a cam lobe. It is constructed with a larger circular section, off-center from the shaft. The large hole of the connecting rod is mounted on the large eccentric section of the crankshaft; the opposite end of the connecting rod connects to the piston with a pin. As the eccentric revolves, the piston reciprocates.

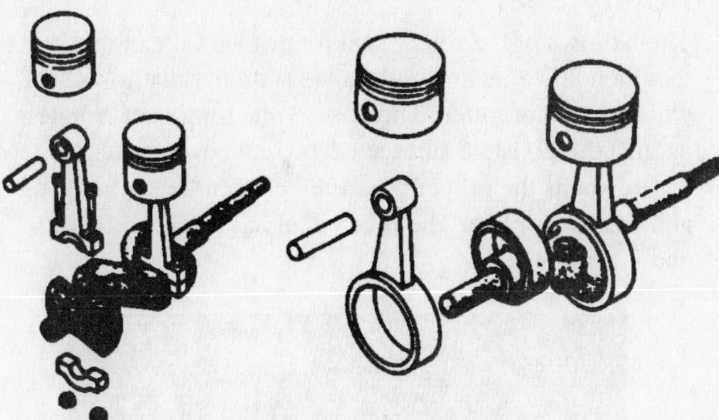

Fig. 5.4
Drawing courtesy of Carrier Corporation.

TYPES OF COMPRESSOR SEALS

Crank-Shaft Seal

A crankshaft seal is required at the point where the shaft enters the crankcase. The variable pressures and high temperatures of the crankshaft make the seal necessary. Crankshaft seals use two surfaces to prevent leaks. One surface turns with the crankshaft and is sealed to the shaft with an "O" ring; the other is stationary and is mounted on the housing with leakproof gaskets. The crankshaft seal must be lubricated during operation or it will wear and start to leak.

Packing Gland Or Stuffing Box

The packing gland prevents the leaking of pressurized refrigerant vapor from the compressor and from around the piston rod, which connects the piston to the crankshaft, as it moves in and out of the cylinder. The stuffing box contains rings of packing commonly used on vertical or horizontal ammonia compressors. This packing can be graphite asbestos, hemp, flax, or lead. A metal gland and packing nut keep the packing in place and compressed around the shaft. Sometimes a spring is installed between the nut and the gland to compensate for wear.

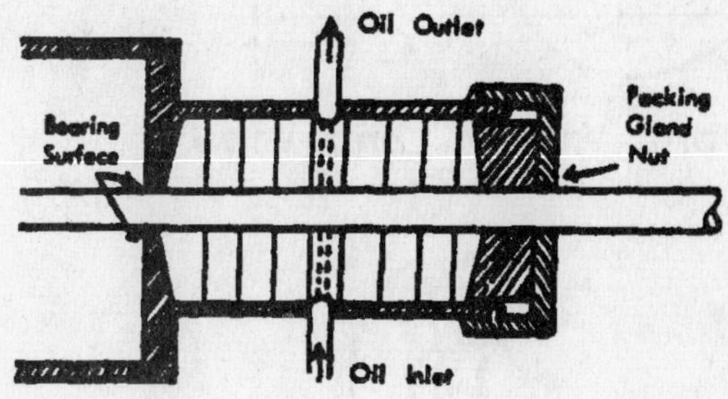

Fig. 5.5

Packing Gland And Lantern Ring

Lubrication is required between moving parts, such as compressor shafts, to prevent friction and wear. The shaft and the packing are lubricated by a lantern ring. This iron spacer ring separates the packing and allows oil into the gland for lubrication. The inner groove and outer grooves are connected by small drilled passages, as shown in the illustration below. The lantern ring is inserted in the middle of the stuffing box with rings of packing on either side of it.

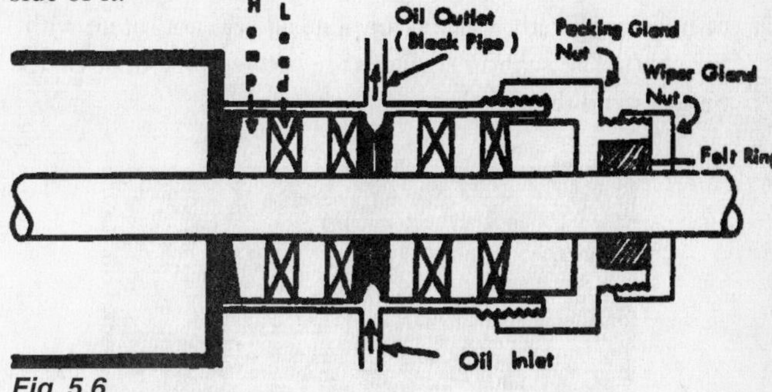

Fig. 5.6

Lantern Ring

Oil is pumped to the stuffing box and is fed into a pipe connected to the bottom of the gland. The oil goes to the outer groove of the lantern ring, through the hole to the inner groove, and lubricates the shaft and packing. Excess oil goes from the inner groove to the outer groove and out of the stuffing box. The oil inlet to the packing gland on an ammonia compressor is always on the bottom, with the oil outlet at the top. This maintains an oil level in the stuffing box at all times. The oil will trap any ammonia vapor that might leak from the compressor, along the shaft. Ammonia vapor, being lighter than air, will rise with the oil through the outlet oil pipe and will not leak into the engine-room space.

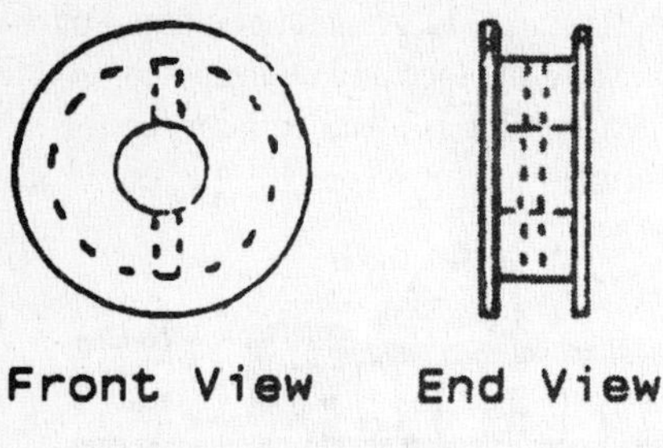

Fig. 5.7 Types of Compressor Seals: Lantern Ring

Stationary Gland Seal

A metallic bellows and ring or nose backed by a spring forces the compressor seal against a shoulder on the crankshaft. The shoulder is a separate part sealed to the crankshaft with a neoprene gasket. The bellows and ring or nose are fixed to the cover plate and do not rotate with the shaft. The sealing surfaces are between the nose on the bellows and the shoulder on the shaft.

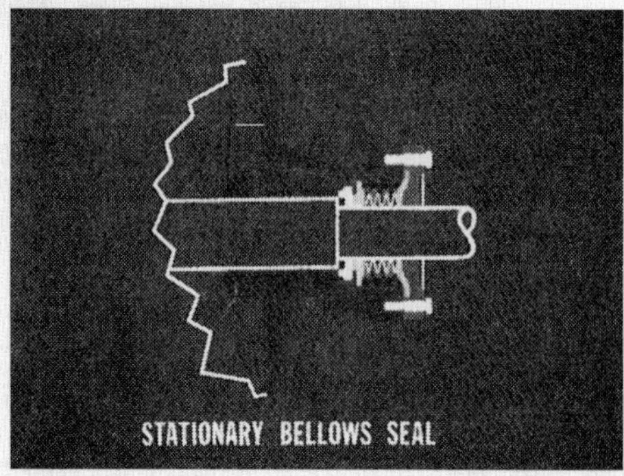

Fig. 5.8
Courtesy of Carrier Corporation.

Diaphragm Seal

In this type of seal, a stationary diaphragm with an attached nose presses against a shoulder or metal collar sealed to the crankshaft. The shoulder or collar on the crankshaft seals the nose of the diaphragm. The fulcrum forces the nose of the diaphragm against the crankshaft shoulder.

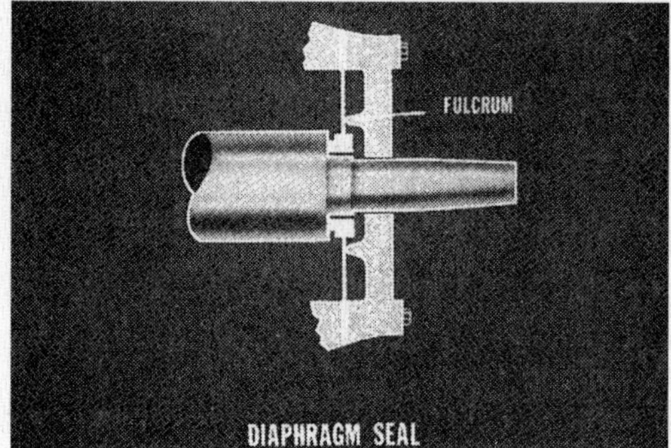

Fig. 5.9
Courtesy of Carrier Corporation.

Rotary Seal

The bellows of the rotary seal rotates with the crankshaft to which it is attached, unlike the stationary bellows seal, which does not rotate. The nose of the rotary seal rotates against the polished surface of the seal cover plate. A spring keeps the proper pressure between the carbon ring and the cover plate. The rotary seal has many variations and is widely used.

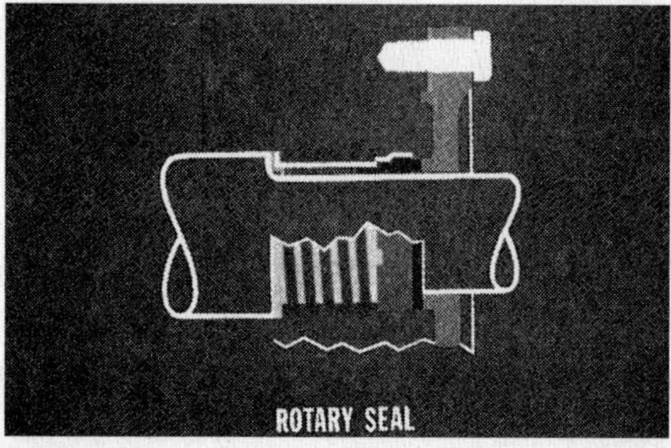

Fig. 5.10
Courtesy of Carrier Corporation.

LUBRICATION

Splash System

The splash system is normally used on older refrigeration systems. Oil is at the bottom of the crankcase. When the compressor operates, the crankcase oil is splashed by the eccentric or crankshaft to lubricate the cylinder walls, pistons, bearings, connecting rods, and shaft seal. The oil level must be maintained in the crankcase. A sight glass is normally installed to check this level. If it is low, the crankshaft won't dip enough into the oil, causing poor lubrication.

Fig. 5.11
Courtesy of Carrier Corporation.

Pressure Lubrication System/Force-Feed

In this system, a gear-driven pump at the end of the crankshaft turns when the compressor operates. Oil from the crankcase is pumped through a series of canals to lubricate the pistons, connecting rods, bearings, and seals. The gear-driven pump supplies a predetermined oil pressure to maintain proper system lubrication. If oil pressure is low during operation, safety cutout switches shut down the compressor.

The oil pressure regulator, located between the motor housing and the oil reservoir, has the following functions:

1. During normal operation, crankcase pressure and suction pressure are approximately equal. The oil pressure regulator valve is open.
2. During startup, the higher crankcase pressure resulting from the heated refrigerant/oil (due to crankcase heater) closes the valve.
3. The valve relieves excess refrigerant pressure from the oil reservoir, while keeping oil in the reservoir.

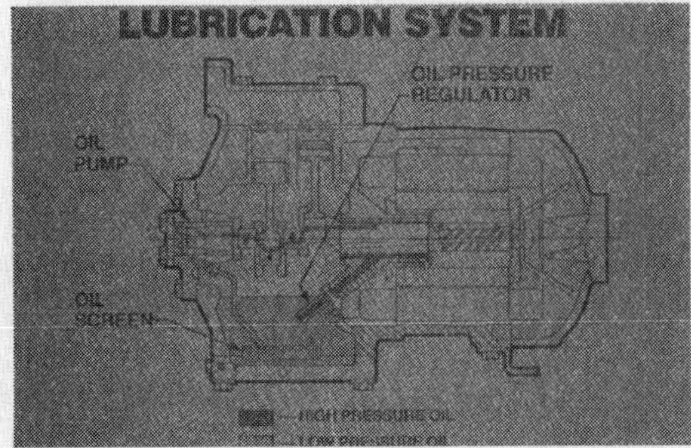

Fig. 5.12
Courtesy of Carrier Corporation.

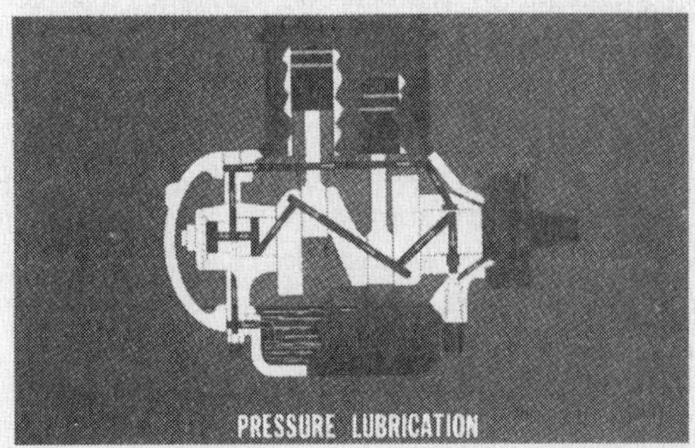

Fig. 5.13
Courtesy of Carrier Corporation.

VALVES AND VALVE PLATES

The usual valve assembly has a valve plate, an intake valve, an exhaust valve, and valve retainers. Valve plates are sometimes made of cast iron. However, hardened steel is also used; the plates can be made thinner with longer-wearing valve seats.

Compressor valves are usually made of high-carbon alloy steel. They are heat-treated to give them the properties of spring steel and are ground perfectly flat. The intake valve is kept in place by small pins or clamped between the compressor head and valve plate. Exhaust valves may be clamped the same way.

The valve disks or reed valves must be perfectly flat. A defect of only .0001 inch will cause the valve to leak. The intake valve gives less trouble because it is lubricated by oil circulating with the cool refrigerant vapor and operates at a relatively cool temperature.

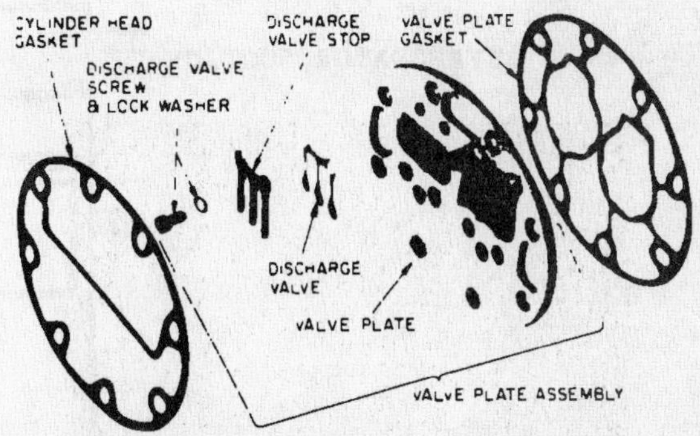

Fig. 5.14
Courtesy of Carrier Corporation.

The exhaust valve must be fitted with special care. It operates at high temperatures and must be leakproof against a relatively high-pressure difference. Due to high-vapor pressures and high temperatures, carbon (heavy molecules of hydrocarbon oils) tends to collect on the valve and valve seat.

Intake and exhaust valves open about .010 inch. Greater movement causes valve noise. If the movement is too little, not enough vapor can pass the valve. In small, high-speed hermetic compressors, the intake valves are very light and as large as possible. This allows great amounts of refrigerant vapor to enter the cylinder during the fraction of a second that the intake valve is open.

The compressor may be driven by belts from an electric motor or by a direct drive. Ammonia compressors run between 100 and 350 R.P.M. They do not need much oil pressure for lubrication due to the slow speed. The oil-pump discharge pressure must be 10 to 20 psi above compressor suction pressure.

Oil in the crankcase is picked up by the oil pump connected to the main compressor shaft. If the compressor runs, the pump runs, and the compressor gets lubricated.

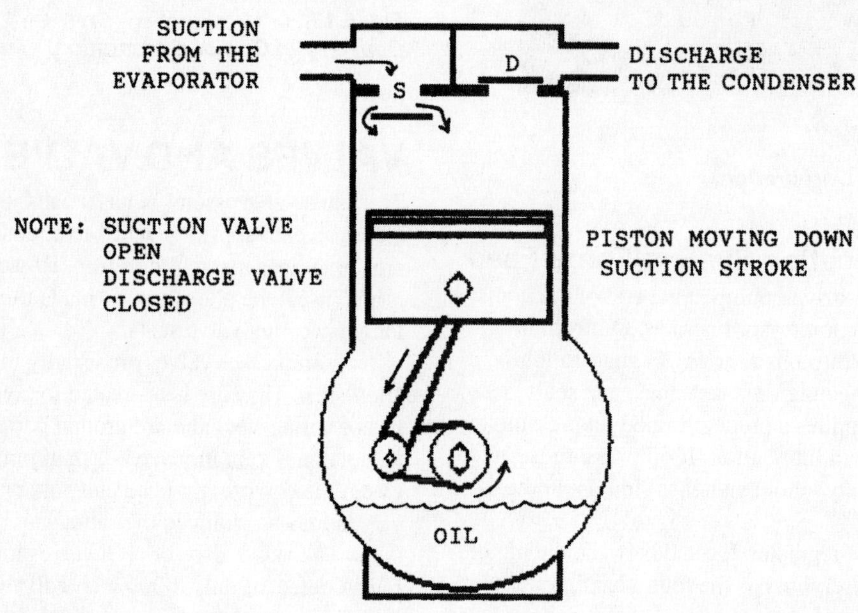

Fig. 5.15

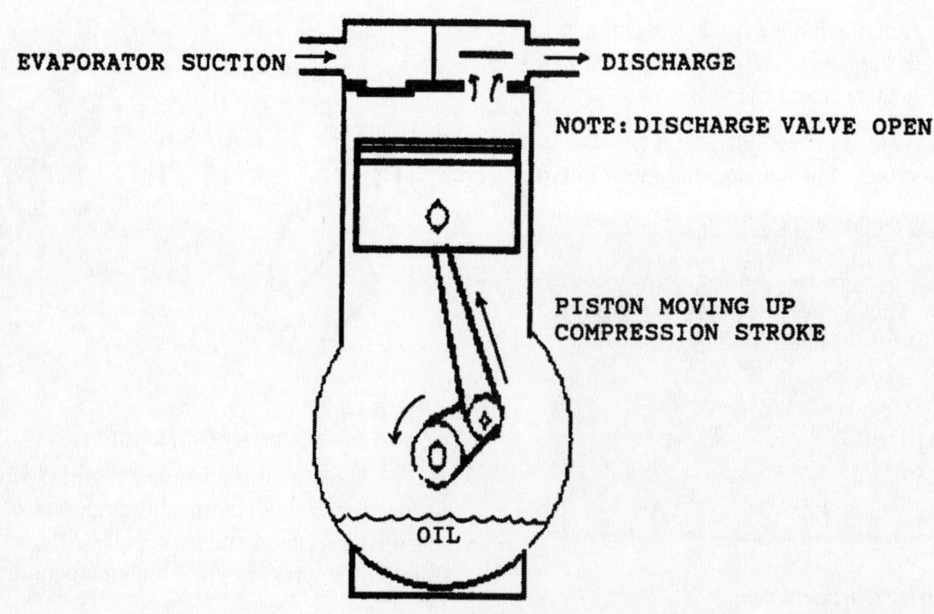

Fig. 5.16

Refrigeration oil, known as ammonia oil, is used. This vertical compressor may have an extended shaft, due to space requirements in an engine room. These conditions require an extended support or outboard bearing, sometimes called a pillow block bearing. With this bearing, the compressor contains two types of oil. Internally it uses ammonia oil. The pillow block bearing uses a good grade of lubricating oil.

The ammonia compression system used throughout the country is very efficient but is not allowed in new installations in New York City. Existing plants may be kept in repair. Parts and machines may be replaced, but new systems cannot be brought into the city.

The basic system consists of a compressor, condenser, metering device, and evaporator. The cycle is basically the one described in the chapter "Refrigeration Theory." However, there are many refinements to this system, so in practice a typical system consists of a compressor, oil separator, condenser, receiver, heat exchanger, expansion valve, accumulator, and scale trap. Other auxiliary equipment will be covered in the chapter on accessories.

Numerous types of compressors are in use. The vertical compressor type is the simplest: a piston travels up and down in a cylinder. On the down stroke, low-pressure vapor enters the cylinder through a valve above the piston and fills the cylinder. On the up stroke, the vapor is compressed and forced out at high pressure through the discharge valve in the compressor head. Pistons are of the double-trunk type with relieved, open central portion, which permits free inward flow of vapor from a suction port in the cylinder wall to the inside of the piston. Suction valves are mounted in the piston crown and may be either of plate or poppet type. A partition in the piston just above the pin prevents the direct access of suction vapor to the crankcase.[3] In late-model compressors, both suction and discharge valves are located in a valve plate on the compressor head, as shown below.

3 Refrigeration Compressors and their Lubrication, Socony Mobil Oil Company, Inc. Copyright 1955.

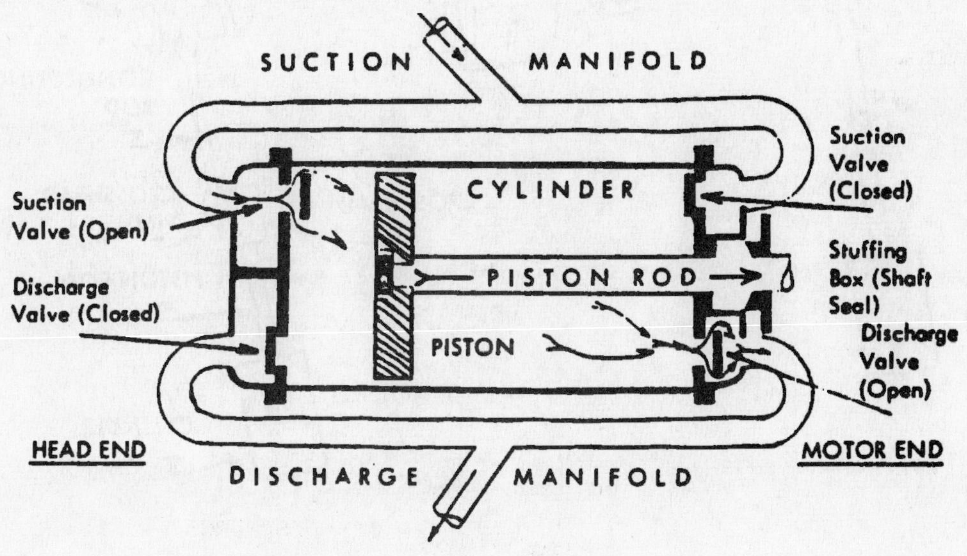

Fig. 5.17 **Horizontal double acting compressor (Top view cutaway)**

Another type of ammonia compressor is the horizontal compressor. The cylinder lies flat on a concrete bed and the motor is directly connected to the compressor; no belts are used. This compressor usually has one motor centered between two cylinders. The motor has a double end shaft and drives both compressors at once. This compressor does not have a crank case, and the lubrication is done with an external pumping system. The piston, cylinder, valves and shaft stuffing box are lubricated by a Manzel or Bowser force feed lubricator, containing ammonia oil. The external moving parts, which include the main bearings on the motor shafts, crank bearings, cross-head pins, cross-head guides, and slippers are lubricated with a good grade of lubricating oil, usually by a gravity feed tank. When two compressors are driven by one motor, this compressor is called a horizontal duplex.

Due to the arrangement of the valves within the ends of the cylinder, the horizontal duplex compressor will draw vapor in one side of the piston (suction) and, at the same time, compress vapor (discharge) in the cylinder on the other side. It has suction and discharge at each end of the stroke. This cylinder can do the work of two vertical compressor cylinders. Suction and discharge at each end of the stroke is called double acting. So the name of this compressor must be changed again, to horizontal double acting duplex compressor. As the piston moves to the right, toward the motor, the left-hand suction valve opens, allowing vapor to enter the cylinder. At the same time, the right-hand discharge valve is opening because the vapor on the right side of the piston is being compressed.

This high-pressure vapor goes through the discharge manifold to the condenser. At the right end of the stroke, the piston starts to return to the left. On the right side of the piston the right suction valve opens, the right discharge valve closes, and the refrigerant is sucked into the right side of the cylinder. On the left side, the low-pressure vapor that was sucked in before is now being compressed, the left suction valve is closing and the left discharge valve (the head end valve) is opening, allowing discharge vapor to enter the condenser.

The crank in the vertical compressor is similar to the crank in an automobile engine. It revolves and has offsets (or eccentrics). These eccentrics revolve in a larger circle than the shaft. The connecting rod drives the piston in an

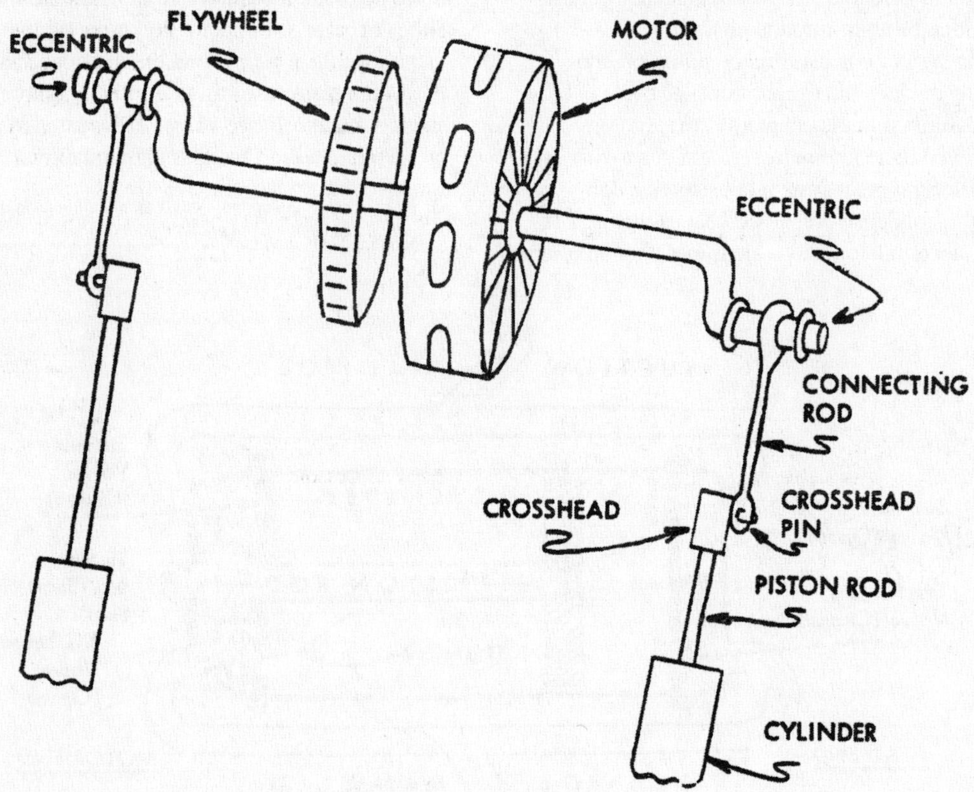

Fig. 5.18

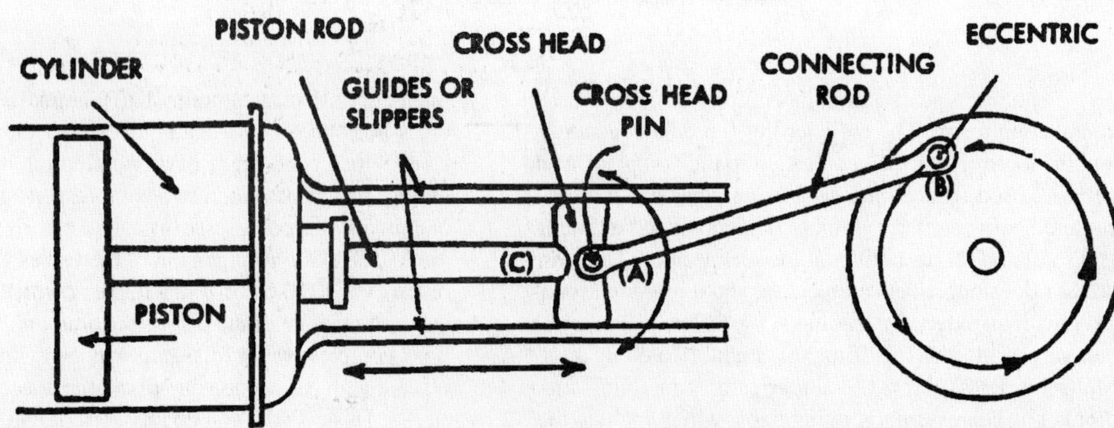

Fig. 5.19

up-and-down, or reciprocating, motion in the cylinder.

In the horizontal compressor, this reciprocating motion is obtained differently. The motor has an eccentric at each end of the shaft. These eccentrics, called cranks, are opposite each other. If one eccentric swings toward its compressor, the other eccentric swings away from its compressor. Each eccentric is connected to a connecting rod, which is connected to a metal block, called a crosshead.

The eccentric rotates, and is driven by the connecting rod. The block, or cross head, reciprocates. This change in motion from rotating to reciprocating motion is carried out through a cross head pin which connects the cross head to the rod. At one end, the connecting rod is rotating; at the other end, it is oscillating.

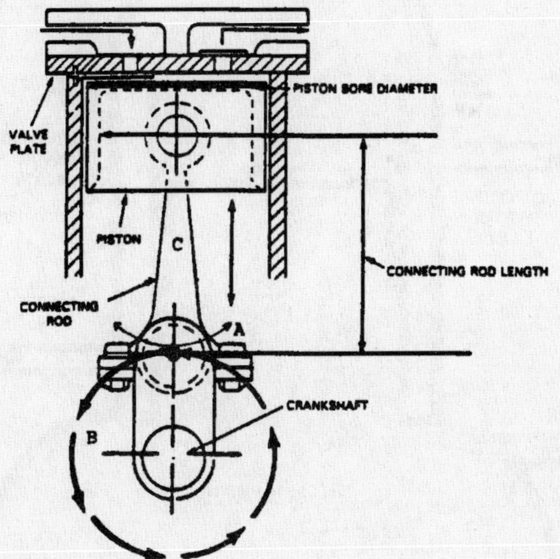

Fig. 5.20

To prevent damage to the piston rod, the cross head is placed between two metal plates called guides or slippers. All these external moving parts are lubricated by a gravity tank that feeds them a good grade of lubricating oil.

Liquid slugging can damage the compressor by washing oil out of the compressor crank case or entering the cylinder. Trying to compress liquid would blow the compressor head. To protect the compressor from liquid slugs, ammonia compressors have a **safety head.** The safety head has an internal discharge valve plate at the top of the cylinder, directly in front of the discharge pipe. This discharge valve plate lifts, making the full opening of the discharge pipe accessible to the cylinder. This movable valve plate will not open unless hydrostatic pressure builds up in the cylinder. It is held down by a heavy helical spring. If liquid is trapped in the cylinder and the piston starts its compression stroke, the liquid will push solidly against the safety head. Since liquids do not compress, the safety head allows any liquid that enters compressor to be expelled from the discharge, without physical damage to the compressor. As the piston starts to come down, the helical spring forces the safety head back into position.

The terms "wet compression" and "dry compression" relate only to the kind of suction vapor returning to the compressor.

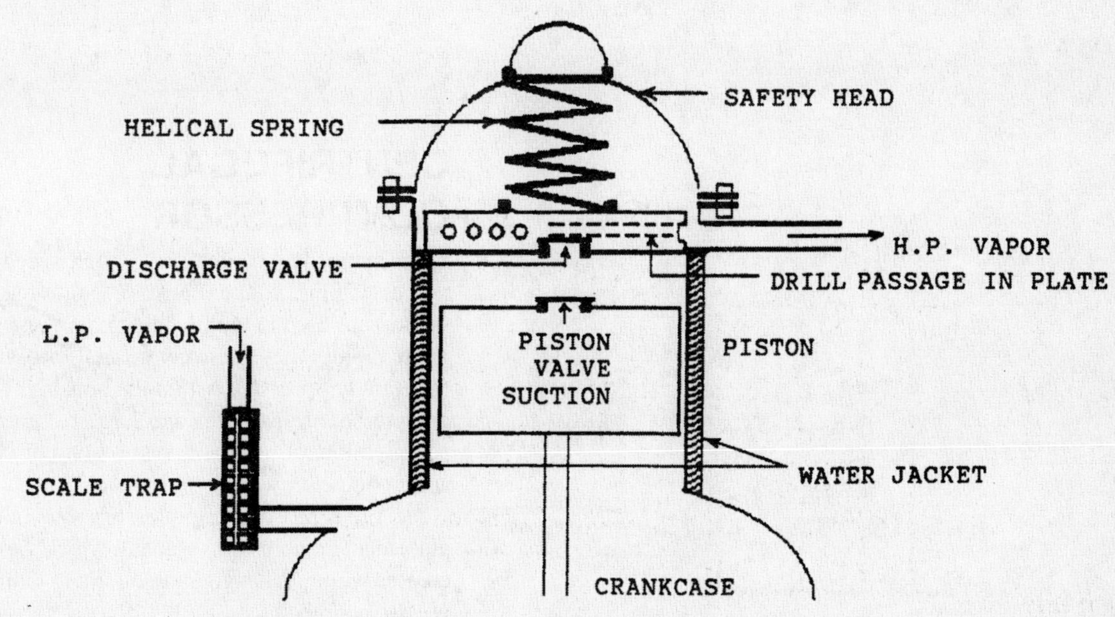

Fig. 5.21

WET COMPRESSION COMPRESSOR

A wet compression compressor draws in saturated vapor, compresses this vapor, and discharges it to the condenser. As the wet vapor enters the warm cylinder, droplets of liquid refrigerant vaporize and cool the cylinder. This compressor has fins around the outside of the cylinder for cooling. It is sometimes called an air-cooled compressor, but in reality it should be called a refrigerant cooled compressor.

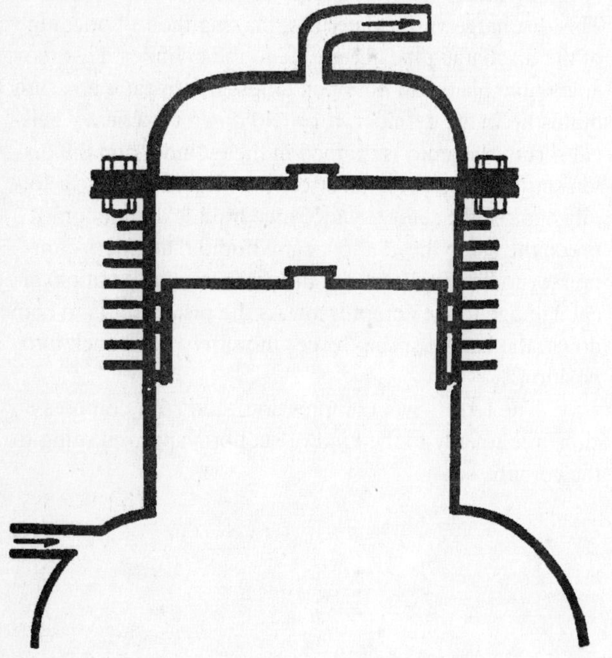

Fig. 5.22

DRY COMPRESSION COMPRESSOR

The dry compression compressor draws superheated refrigerant vapor into the cylinder. This vapor cannot cool the compressor, so there must be a cooling jacket around the cylinder. Water running through the jacket prevents the compressor from burning up. The dry compressor actually is a water-cooled compressor.

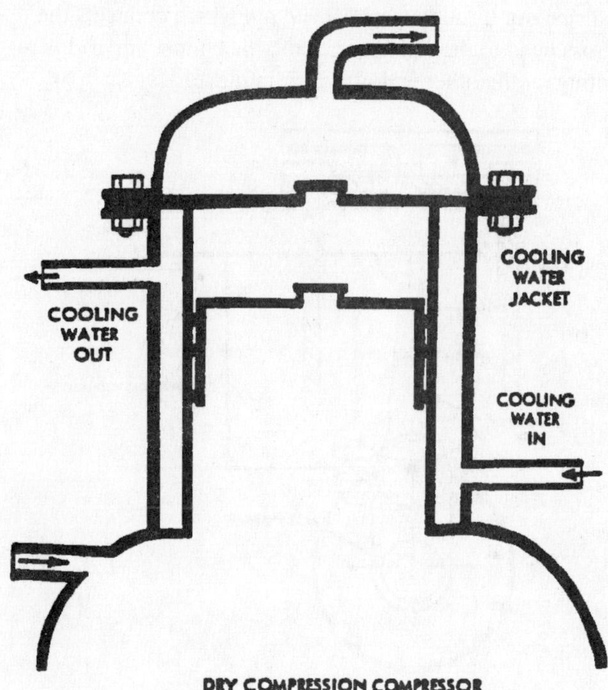

Fig. 5.23

CENTRIFUGAL COMPRESSOR

In the centrifugal compressor, a high-speed impeller blade rotates within a volute (housing). Additional impellers and volutes are used in multi-stafe compressors. As the blades rotate rapidly they cause centrifugal force to raise the refrigerant gas pressure within the housing. The centrifugal compressor normally handles large volumes of gas at low compression ratios. The compression ratio is increased by adding impeller wheels to the rotor.

The centrifugal compressor is a nonpositive displacement compressor, or one in which vapor pressure increases without changing the internal volume of the compressor chamber.

The drawing below shows a two-stage centrifugal compressor.

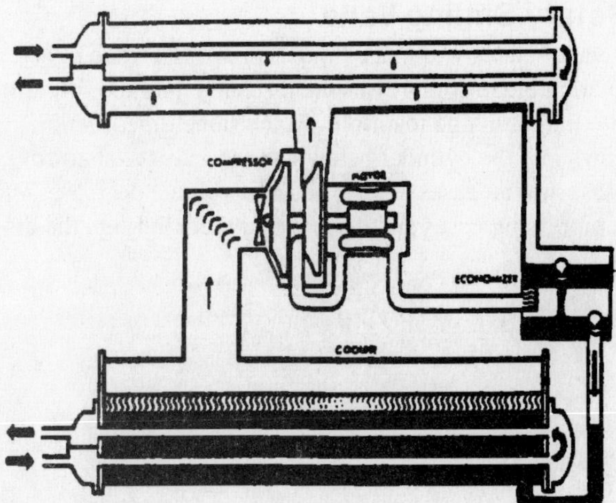

Fig. 5.24
Drawing courtesy of Carrier Corporation.

Low-pressure vapor is drawn into the suction of the first stage and is compressed. The vapor is discharged through fixed vanes in the housing of the second stage, where pressure again increases. At the compressor outlet, the compressed gas is discharged to the condenser. The major components of this system are closely connected to prevent pressure drops in long suction, discharge, and liquid lines.

The drawings below show the centrifugal compressor's suction and discharge lines. As the impeller rotates, a low-pressure area is created at its center. Note that the suction pipe is connected between the cooler and the compressor "eye." Because of the low pressure at the "eye" of the impeller, the refrigerant gases flow in that direction. This provides more area for vaporization of refrigerant in the cooler, and the cooling process continues.

As the impeller rotates rapidly, the gases are spun to the outside of the impeller by centrifugal force. The outer area of the impeller housing forms a passage for the gases to flow into the condenser. This is called the discharge volute. The gas leaves the impeller tip, moving nearly as fast as the impeller tip. As the gas flows into the discharge volute, this velocity changes to static pressure. When the gas pressure rises, temperature also increases. This high-temperature, high-pressure gas now enters the condenser.

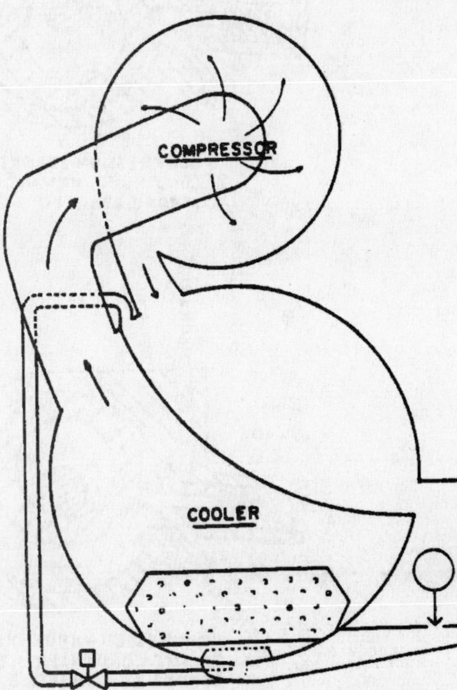

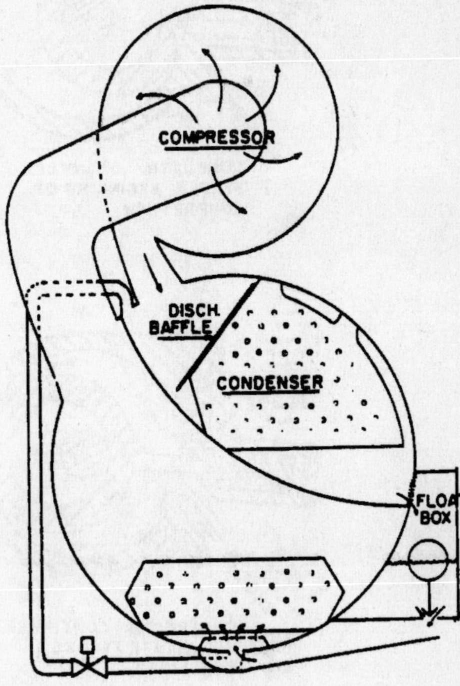

Fig. 5.25
Drawing courtesy of Carrier Corporation, 19D series.

ROTARY COMPRESSOR

In the rotary compressor, a vane rotates within a cylinder. In a single-vane model, a rotating blade compresses the gas and forces it into the discharge manifold. As the discharge gas is forced out, suction gas flows into the cylinder below the vane. As the shaft rotates, the vane moves in or out, always separating the suction and discharge gases. Rotary compressors normally range around 5-tons capacity. However, the helical rotary screw compressor ranges from 100- to 700-ton capacity.

A rotary compressor is a positive-displacement compressor. Two types are in common use.

Rotary Sliding Vane

A vane rotates within a cylinder. In a single vane rotary, a rotating blade compresses the discharge gas and forces it into the discharge manifold. At the same time, suction gas flows into the cylinder below the vane. As the shaft rotates, suction gases are trapped and volume decreases, compressing gases and discharging them through the dis-

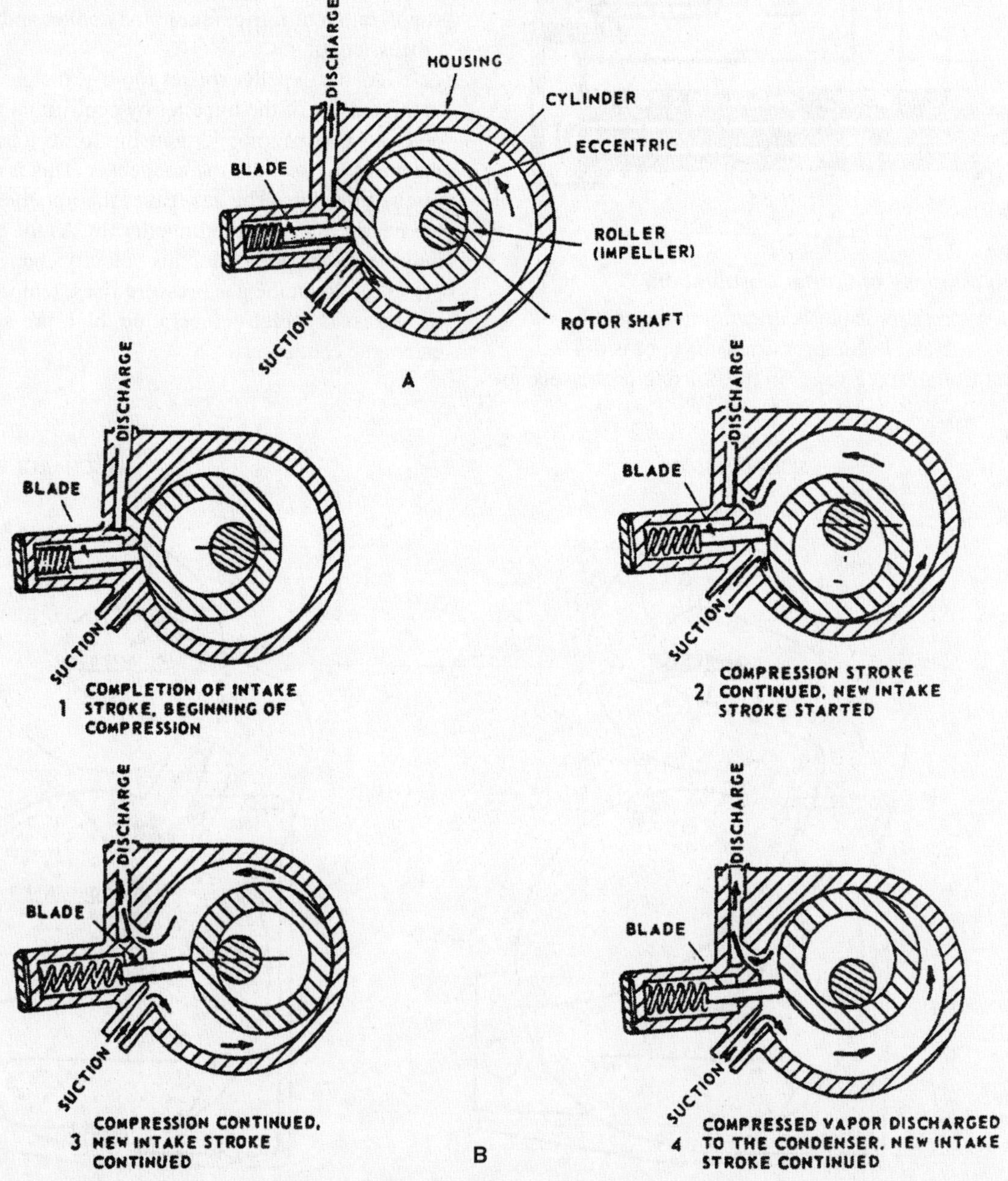

Fig. 5.26 Rotary Compressor
Drawing courtesy of Goodheart-Willcox.

charge line. The vane moves in or out, always separating suction gas and discharge gas.

Helical Rotary Screw Compressor

Meshing male and female helical rotors are in the housing with suction and discharge ports. The male rotor is called the lobe and the female rotor is the groove. The suction port is normally at the top of the compressor and the discharge port at the bottom. Suction enters the compressor port to the unmeshed rotors. As the rotors turn and start to mesh, they compress the suction gas. The volume area decreases, thus increasing the vapor pressure. The helical rotary screw compressor is popular in large industrial plants because of its smooth and quiet operation.

Fig. 5.27
Drawing courtesy of Dunham-Bush.

Cutaway screw compressor

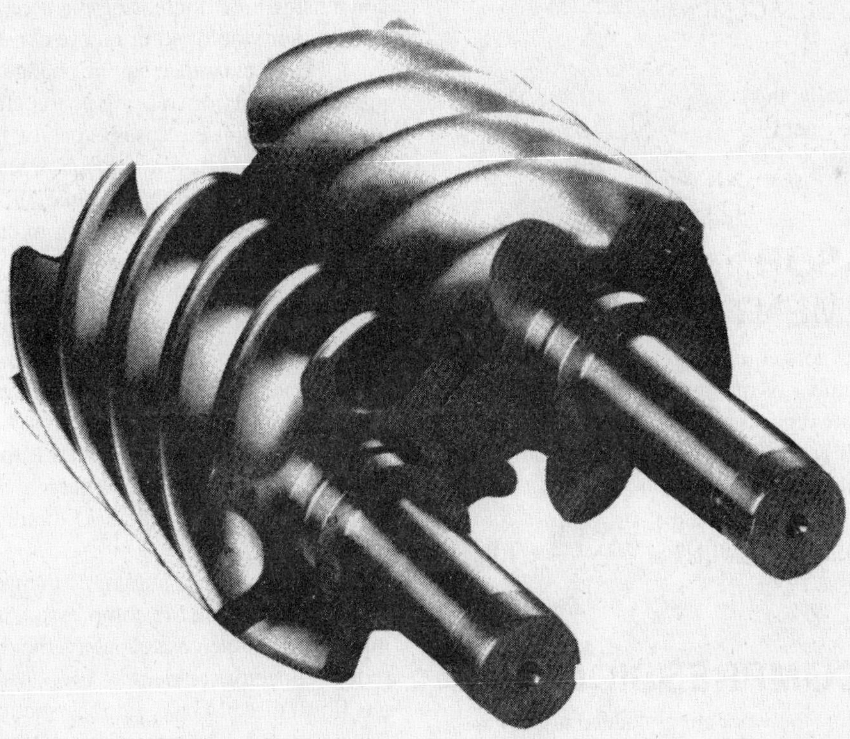

Helical rotary screw compressor, Trane Series R Centravac

Fig. 5.28
Drawing courtesy of the Trane Company.

COMPRESSION RATIO

The compression ratio is the amount of pressure change a compressor is required to create in a system. Compression ratios vary. If the ratio is 10 to 1 or less, single-stage compressors are used. The higher the compression ratio, the higher the head pressure, resulting in loss of efficiency. If the ratio is higher than 10 to 1, two-stage compressors must be used. To find the compression ratio, divide the absolute discharge pressure by the absolute suction pressure.

$$\text{COMPRESSION RATIO} = \frac{\text{ABSOLUTE DISCHARGE}}{\text{ABSOLUTE SUCTION PRESSURE}}$$

PISTON DISPLACEMENT

As low-pressure refrigerant fills the space between the top of the piston and the cylinder head, the piston begins its upward stroke. Piston displacement is the volume displaced by one piston as it moves from bottom dead center of the stroke to top dead center, multiplied by the number of cylinders. Use the following formula to find piston displacement:

$$\text{PISTON DISPLACEMENT} = \frac{\pi D^2 L n}{4}$$

$\pi = 3.14$
D = Cylinderdiameter(inches)
L = Length of stroke (inches)
n = Number of cylinders

COMPRESSOR DISPLACEMENT

Compressor displacement equals piston displacement multiplied by the number of revolutions per minute (RPM). Use the following formula to find compressor displacement. Note that D = cylinder diameter, L = length of stroke, and n = number of cylinders.

$$\text{COMPRESSOR DISPLACEMENT} = \frac{\pi D^2 L n}{4} \times \text{RPM}$$

HEAT OF COMPRESSION

Heat of compression is the work energy added to the vaporized gas during compression. As the piston moves to the top of the stroke, cylinder volume decreases and pressure increases. Due to the sudden decrease in volume, the vaporized refrigerant is compressed, increasing the speed of molecular movement and increasing its temperature. Some of the work energy (heat) that the compressor exerts is also transferred to the compressed vapor.

CAPACITY CONTROL

The capacity of a compressor may be controlled in several ways:

1. Vary the number of cylinders in use.
2. Vary the number of machines in use.
3. Increase or decrease clearance in the cylinder.
4. Vary compressor speed.
5. Use a bypass damper.

A cylinder may be unloaded in several ways:

1. Use a solenoid valve to by-pass discharge gas into the compressor suction.
2. Mechanically hold a flapper valve open.
3. Use a solenoid to lift or open the suction valve so the cylinder does no work.

Taking a compressor off-line decreases plant capacity. If a compressor is taken off-line, you must change the condensing area. Increasing plant capacity by adding a compressor would require more condensers.

Piston clearance can be changed to control compressor capacity. Increasing piston clearance cuts capacity; decreasing it increases capacity. If clearance increases, some high-pressure vapor stays behind and as the piston starts its downward stroke, the vapor re-expands. This prevents the compressor from taking in a full charge.

Clearance can be changed in a compressor with clearance pockets. To cut capacity, open the valve in the head to increase cylinder clearance and cut capacity.

Increasing or decreasing compressor speed is a popular method of controlling plant capacity or compressor capacity in centrifugal systems. A multispeed motor is used with a centrifugal machine. If the load increases, the motor speeds up. If the load decreases, the motor runs more slowly. The Carrier 17M motor uses this principle of capacity control.

The manual or automatic damper in a bypass line is connected between the compressor suction and discharge pipes. For 100 percent capacity, the damper is closed. To reduce capacity, the damper is opened so some discharge gas flows directly back into the suction port, rather than to the evaporator. This reduces capacity by bypassing the evaporator, even when the compressor runs at full speed. The more the dampers are opened, the greater the reduction in capacity.

On the newer centrifugal machines, prerotation vanes on the impeller blades are used to control the capacity of the system.

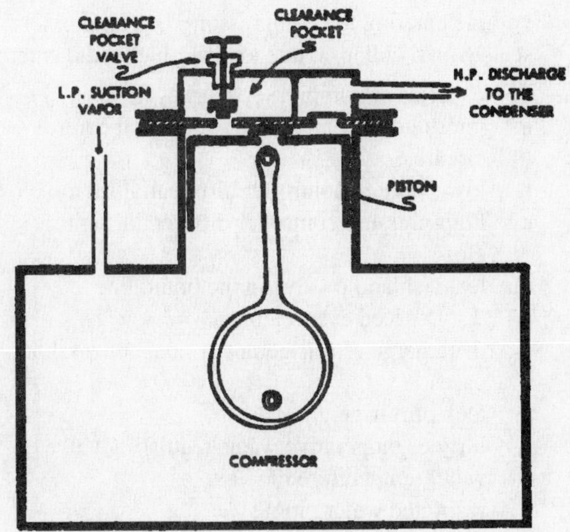

Fig. 5.29

INDICATORS AND INDICATOR DIAGRAMS

Indicator and indicator diagrams check compressor operation and efficiency. The indicator draws a diagram on a chart representing the pressure in the cylinder at all moments in one complete stroke.

The indicator is attached to the compressor through a threaded hole in the clearance space. The indicator has two parts joined by an arm. The part attached to the cylinder contains a small cylinder and a piston held down by a spring. The rod of this piston drives a pen mechanism. As pressure in the compressor changes, the piston and rod move, causing the pen mechanism to move up and down. The second part of the indicator is a drum to which an indicator card can be clipped. The drum is free to rotate. A spring wound around the base of the drum at one end and connected to the compressor crosshead at the other end moves the drum in one direction and at the same time winds a spring inside the drum. This spring returns the drum to its original position when the crosshead changes direction.

This combination of back-and-forth drum motion and the up-and-down motion of the indicator piston moved by cylinder pressure produces an indicator diagram that can be interpreted to show the compressor's operating efficiency.

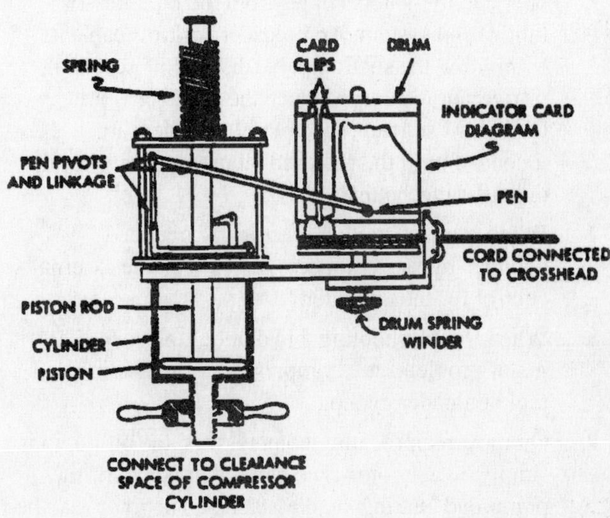

Fig. 5.30

COMPRESSOR TECHNICAL TIPS

1. Capacity control systems are designed to:
   a. allow the compressor to operate at partial capacity to meet cooling needs
   b. help reduce compressor cycling to increase compressor longevity
   c. reduce large temperature swings in the conditioned space
2. The bypass piston in the cylinder bypass unloader assembly separates the high and low side of the cylinder head when in the loaded position.
3. Pressure-operated unloaders use internal controls. The pressure control valve is operated by suction pressure. The two adjustments, the control setpoint and the pressure differential, determine when the cylinder loads and unloads.
4. Electrically operated unloaders use external controls. The electric control valve is energized from an external source such as a thermostat, pressurestat, or step controller. When the control valve is energized, the compressor cylinder bank unloads.
5. Suction cutoff unloaders differ from cylinder unloaders because:
   a. suction cutoff unloaders prevent suction vapor from entering the cylinder
   b. cylinder bypasses allow vapor to exit the cylinder, then recirculate to the suction part after passing through the cylinder

6. The primary operating power for hydraulically operated unloaders comes from the compressor lubrication system. An unloader controls capacity by holding the suction valve disc off its seat so no refrigerant is pumped when the cylinder is unloaded. At start-up, the control cylinders are unloaded until the required oil pressure reaches the unloader mechanism.
7. When troubleshooting electrically operated cylinder-bypass unloaders, first check the external control for the unloader.
8. When troubleshooting a hydraulic unloader, the major problems are compressor not unloading and rapid unloader cycling.
9. On most reciprocating compressors, the oil pump is simply a vane rotor-type pump that is part of the pump-end bearing head assembly. The rotor may be driven by a small drive segment attached to the end of the compressor crankshaft. It can be designed to supply pressurized oil to the compressor through internal passages in the crankshaft.
10. Some compressors have an internal pressure relief valve. This valve acts as a safety device to prevent excessive high-to-low side pressure differences.
11. The oil-pressure regulator keeps pressure constant throughout the compressor.
12. A noisy compressor may be caused by liquid in the compressor. Excessive bearing clearance can also cause compressor thumping. Liquid in the suction line frosts the line in large sets. If the unit is a small enclosed type, check the regulating valve before opening a noisy compressor.
13. The difference between a centrifugal and reciprocating compressor:
    a. In a centrifugal compressor (nonpositive displacement compressor), the volute spins and discharges vapor at high speeds without changing the size in the housing.
    b. A reciprocating compressor (positive displacement compressor) compresses or squeezes the vapor. The space changes size as the piston compresses the vapor against the cylinder head.
14. When vapor entering the compressor increases in temperature, this indicates a rise in suction pressure accompanied by increased load and higher temperature of the area surrounding the evaporator. No corrective action is needed here, although opening the expansion valve wider reduces the temperature to saturation for existing pressure.
15. The reciprocating compressor draws in refrigerant at the suction port. If the discharge valve were open and the suction port closed during operation, no vapor would be drawn into the compressor. The head pressure would not rise due to lack of vapor volume entering the compressor. The compressor seals would collapse; noncondensable would enter.
16. Some causes of compressor short cycles:
    a. intermittent contact in the electrical control circuit
    b. low-pressure controller differential set too close
    c. high-pressure controller differential set too close
    d. leaky solenoid valve in the liquid line
    e. dirty or iced evaporator
    f. overcharge of refrigerant or noncondensable gases
    g. lack of refrigerant
    h. dirty or inoperative water-regulating valve
    i. water temperature too high
    j. restricted water piping
    k. supply water pressure too low
    l. restricted strainer in the liquid line
    m. faulty motor
    n. faulty operation of an evaporative condenser
    o. thermal bulb on expansion valve has lost its charge
17. Some reasons why a compressor might run continuously:
    a. excessive load
    b. thermostat too low
    c. "welded" contacts on the electrical control in the motor starter circuit
    d. leaky discharge valve in the compressor
    e. solenoid stop valve stuck open or held open by manual lift stem or dirt
18. Some causes of low oil level in a compressor:
    a. dirty strainer, tubing, or valves
    b. liquid slugs in the suction line
    c. insufficient charge
    d. oil trapped by refrigerant suction line
    e. faulty oil separator or compressor leaks

COMPRESSOR LICENSE QUESTIONS

1. A compressor seal is a means of closing off the

(A) suction from the discharge side.
(B) condenser from the receiver leakage.
(C) crankcase, to prevent leakage from the compressor.
(D) crankcase, to prevent leakage from the evaporator.

2. As suction pressure in a reciprocating compressor increases and the horsepower decreases, compressor capacity

(A) decreases.
(B) increases.
(C) falls.
(D) stays the same.

3. When head pressure decreases in an ammonia compressor, horsepower

(A) capacity of compressor increases.
(B) decreases.
(C) increases.
(D) doesn't change.

4. When suction pressure decreases, compressor capacity

(A) increases.
(B) decreases.
(C) rises.
(D) slightly increases.

5. The most accurate of the following statements about compression ratio of a reciprocating compressor is

(A) it remains constant under all compressor operating conditions.
(B) it varies according to the conditions under which the compressor operates.
(C) it is the ratio of the suction pressure gauge to the discharge pressure gauge.
(D) it equals the saturated discharge temperature divided by the saturated suction temperature.

6. Compression ratio in a refrigeration compressor

(A) is the ratio of absolute suction pressure to absolute discharge pressure.
(B) is increasing due to advances in gasoline octane.
(C) is the ratio of absolute discharge pressure to the absolute suction pressure.
(D) is constant with each compressor.

7. A compressor capacity reduction device always reduces compressor capacity

(A) by using a hot-gas bypass.
(B) by reducing compressor speed.
(C) by reducing compressor horsepower proportionately.
(D) as the refrigerant load dictates.

8. On a wet-compression system, the discharge gas from the compressor is

(A) saturated.
(B) subcooled.
(C) superheated.
(D) supersaturated.

9. Which compressor gives the least side thrust when operating?

(A) Horizontal open
(B) Radial
(C) Vertical
(D) Y compressor

10. What causes oil to foam in the compressor crankcase?

(A) Pressure change
(B) Load change
(C) Temperature change
(D) All the above

11. Foaming in the compressor crankcase is caused by

(A) refrigerant overcharge.
(B) rise in discharge pressure.
(C) refrigerant undercharge.
(D) sudden drop in crankcase pressure.

12. Which of the following is NOT a design factor affecting compressor capacity?

(A) Compressor speed
(B) Clearance space
(C) Piston displacement
(D) Suction and discharge valve design

13. If refrigerant is to be changed to another type in an R-12 compressor system, which refrigerant will require the least changes to the system?

(A) CO2
(B) Methyl chloride
(C) NH3
(D) R-718

14. What will happen if the cut-in and cut-out settings are too close on an R-12 compressor?

(A) The compressor will not cycle off long enough to allow oil to return to the crankcase.
(B) The compressor will not start.
(C) The compressor will run continuously.
(D) The compressor will cut-out on high head-pressure.

15. A reciprocating compressor is operating with a matched set of five belts. One of the belts is worn out. What should you do?

(A) Replace the worn belt with a new one.
(B) Replace all five belts.
(C) Remove the worn belt and operate on four belts
(D) Replace the worn belt and add two belts.

16. Which of the following would not help determine compressor displacement?

(A) Length of piston
(B) Revolution per minute
(C) Diameter of piston
(D) Number of cylinders

17. A compressor may lose oil if

(A) there is air in the system.
(B) the velocity of refrigerant in the risers is too low.
(C) there are medium pressure drops in the evaporator.
(D) there are small load variations in the system.

18. A reciprocating refrigeration compressor is controlled by the temperature of water leaving the water chiller. If the thermostat used for compressor control did not have a wide enough differential, the probable result would be

(A) inadequate time for oil to return to the compressor.
(B) stop on low-pressure cut-out.
(C) stop on high-pressure cut-out.
(D) a very long operating cycle.

19. During the re-expansion portion of the compressor cycle,

(A) the suction valve is open.
(B) the suction valve is closed.
(C) the discharge valve is open.
(D) none of the above.

20. A liquid-line cooler is sometimes installed in a Freon compression system. The net result is generally a(n)

(A) decrease in liquid-line friction.
(B) decrease in suction-gas temperature.
(C) increase in compressor displacement.
(D) increase in refrigeration effect per pound pumped.

21. Liquid slugging is

(A) liquid in compressor clearance space.
(B) excessive liquid refrigerant in the receiver.
(C) the pounding of liquid refrigerant in the suction line at a point of refrigerant restriction.
(D) liquid in the condenser causing excessive noise.

22. In a single-acting compressor,

(A) piston speed can be automatically controlled.
(B) refrigerant gas is compressed alternately on one side, then the other side, of the same piston.
(C) piston speed can be manually controlled.
(D) refrigerant gas is compressed on only one side of the piston.

23. A vertical, multi-cylinder Freon reciprocating compressor has large capacity and trunk-type pistons. If the oil rings on these pistons started to leak badly, the compressor would probably

(A) pound on start-up.
(B) increase the compression.
(C) tend to scorch the cylinder walls on starting.
(D) start slowly, then run normally.

24. A refrigerating compressor is driven by a squirrel-cage induction motor. The operator can run this compressor at

(A) one speed.
(B) two speeds.
(C) three speeds.
(D) four speeds.

25. In a well-lubricated refrigeration compressor, the percentage of lubrication oil circulating with the refrigerant generally should not exceed

(A) 5 percent.
(B) 10 percent.
(C) 25 percent.
(D) 33 percent.

26. On a compression-type refrigeration plant, a synchronous motor

(A) can be used as a multi-speed compressor drive.
(B) can be used as a variable-speed compressor drive.
(C) can be used as a constant-speed compressor drive.
(D) cannot be used as a compressor drive.

27. If the compressor on a reciprocation system is V-belt driven and the belts are installed too tightly, after operating awhile,

(A) the motor runs normally.
(B) the motor overheats.
(C) compressor head pressure increases.
(D) compressor suction pressure increases.

28. The suction line back to the compressor is insulated to

(A) prevent condensation on the line.
(B) help efficiency.
(C) provide motor cooling.
(D) all of the above.

29. To lubricate a centrifugal compressor, the oiling should be

(A) only at the shaft end bearing.
(B) end bearing of shaft and rotor.
(C) end bearing of shaft and rotor and stage separator.
(D) end bearing of shaft and stage separator.

30. If the piston is at top dead center of the stroke, in what position are the valves?

(A) Suction valve open, discharge valve closed
(B) Suction valve closed, discharge valve open
(C) Suction and discharge valves open
(D) Suction and discharge valves closed

31. How many springs does a reed valve normally have?

(A) Four springs
(B) Two springs
(C) No springs
(D) The number of springs is determined by the valve size.

32. An atmospheric line on an indicator card from the head of a double-acting, single-stage horizontal ammonia compressor is used

(A) to record piston stroke.
(B) to record volumetric efficiency.
(C) to record compressor superheat.
(D) as a pressure reference or standard.

33. The engine indicator diagram would most likely indicate

(A) purity of refrigerant coming back to compressor.
(B) need for more refrigerant.
(C) condition of the valves.
(D) the compressor's need to change speed.

34. All refrigeration compressor valves are opened and closed by

(A) a camshaft.
(B) inherent spring tension.
(C) external springs.
(D) pressure difference.

35. A reciprocating compressor

(A) never has provision for an indicator card.
(B) operation can be checked with an indicator card.
(C) operates an indicator card by a cord running from the shaft.
(D) moves the indicator card from a telescopic oiler.

36. The opening and closing of suction and discharge valves on a reciprocating compressor is shown by

(A) a bailey meter.
(B) an indicator card.
(C) a mercury manometer.
(D) discharge and suction gauges.

37. Clearance volume

(A) affects compressor capacity.
(B) does not affect compressor capacity.
(C) varies depending on compressor speed.
(D) is the same on all compressors.

38. The most accurate statement about an R-12 reciprocating compressor that has been shut down is that oil is

(A) pumped into a service valve in the high-pressure liquid line.
(B) pumped into a service valve on the compressor crankcase.
(C) sucked into suction service valve on the compressor.
(D) pumped into the compressor discharge service valve.

39. As the horsepower of a compressor decreases,

(A) head pressure increases.
(B) compressor capacity decreases.
(C) compression ratio increases.
(D) volumetric efficiency increases.

40. When throttling the discharge on a centrifugal brine pump,

(A) pressure goes up and horsepower goes down.
(B) pressure goes down and horsepower goes up.
(C) pressure and horsepower go up.
(D) pressure and horsepower go down.

41. What would happen if you ran a reciprocating compressor with the suction valve closed and the discharge valve open?

(A) The plant capacity would increase.
(B) The compressor head would blow off.
(C) Noncondensable gases would enter the compressor.
(D) Head pressure would rise.

42. The item that should be engaged first when starting a centrifugal water chiller system is the

(A) centrifugal compressor.
(B) condenser water pump.
(C) cooling tower fan(s).
(D) chilled water pump.

43. A mechanical shaft seal is necessary in a(n)

(A) hermetic reciprocating compressor.
(B) semi-hermetic compressor.
(C) open-type compressor.
(D) hermetic rotary compressor.

44. Assume an ammonia wet-compression system is replaced by an ammonia dry-compression system in a particular process plant. If the capacity remains the same, the dry-compression system will

(A) use less cooling water in the condenser.
(B) reduce the danger of damage to the compressor unit.
(C) make lubrication of the compressor cylinder wall easier.
(D) have a lower compressor volumetric efficiency.

45. The compressor uses a set of valves to compress refrigerant gas. These valves are

(A) reed valves.
(B) flapper valves.
(C) Both (A) and (B)
(D) rex and hex valves.

46. The compressor produces heat in the gas it discharges. This work energy is known as

(A) heat of convection.
(B) heat of conduction.
(C) Both (A) and (B)
(D) heat of compression.

47. Flapper valves in the compressor operate

(A) on a pressure difference.
(B) on a temperature difference.
(C) Both (A) and (B)
(D) none of the above.

48. Which of the following seals is NOT a refrigeration compressor seal?

(A) Mechanical seal
(B) Packing gland
(C) Stationary bellows
(D) Rotary seal

49. The atmospheric line on the indicator card of a horizontal double-acting compressor is for

(A) pressure standard.
(B) compressor temperature.
(C) oil level.
(D) refrigerant charge.

50. An indicator card on a horizontal compressor indicates the

(A) control of water.
(B) tonnage capacity.
(C) valve efficiency.
(D) none of the above.

51. An engine indicator diagram for a reciprocating compressor would most likely show the

(A) purity of the refrigerant returning to the compressor.
(B) need for additional refrigerant.
(C) action of the compressor valve.
(D) need to change compressor speed.

52. Of the following, which is NOT a possible cause of a noisy compressor?

(A) Flash gas in the line after the expansion valve
(B) Lack of oil
(C) Loose compressor-drive coupling
(D) Dry or scored seal

53. What is the purpose of a stuffing box seal?

(A) It makes the unit start easily after lying idle overnight.
(B) It prevents air from entering the crankcase.
(C) It lubricates the bearings with cup grease.
(D) It prevents refrigerant leaks from the crankcase

54. Packing in the stuffing box is

(A) made of metal with oil passing through.
(B) made of metal with oil passing through, but not at each end.
(C) made of rubber with oil passing through.
(D) packed to prevent spreading.

55. As capacity decreases in a reciprocating compressor,

(A) suction pressure increases.
(B) suction pressure decreases.
(C) volumetric efficiency increases.
(D) head pressure decreases.

56. A superheated refrigerant, such as R-12, enters a reciprocating compressor. After being compressed it leaves as a

(A) superheated gas.
(B) 100 percent dry saturated gas.
(C) supercooled gas.
(D) supersaturated gas.

57. The main reason for insulating the suction piping of a compression-type refrigerating system is to

(A) absorb moisture condensation.
(B) prevent loss of refrigerating capacity.
(C) reduce compressor vibration.
(D) increase circulation of the lubricating oil.

Answers to Compressor License Questions

1. **The correct answer is (C).**
2. **The correct answer is (B).**
3. **The correct answer is (B).**
4. **The correct answer is (B).**
5. **The correct answer is (B).** Compression ratio is the absolute discharge pressure divided by the absolute suction pressure:

$$\text{Compression Ratio} = \frac{P2}{P1} = \frac{\text{discharge}}{\text{suction psia}}$$

6. **The correct answer is (C).**
7. **The correct answer is (D).**
8. **The correct answer is (A).**
9. **The correct answer is (C).**
10. **The correct answer is (A).**
11. **The correct answer is (D).**
12. **The correct answer is (A).**
13. **The correct answer is (B).** R-40
14. **The correct answer is (A).**
15. **The correct answer is (B).**
16. **The correct answer is (A).**
17. **The correct answer is (B).**
18. **The correct answer is (A).**
19. **The correct answer is (B).**
20. **The correct answer is (D).**
21. **The correct answer is (A).**
22. **The correct answer is (D).**
23. **The correct answer is (C).**
24. **The correct answer is (A).**
25. **The correct answer is (B).**
26. **The correct answer is (C).**
27. **The correct answer is (B).**
28. **The correct answer is (D).**
29. **The correct answer is (A).**
30. **The correct answer is (D).**
31. **The correct answer is (C).** They are flexible pieces of spring steel.
32. **The correct answer is (D).**
33. **The correct answer is (C).**
34. **The correct answer is (D).**
35. **The correct answer is (B).**
36. **The correct answer is (B).**
37. **The correct answer is (A).**
38. **The correct answer is (B).**
39. **The correct answer is (D).**
40. **The correct answer is (A).**
41. **The correct answer is (C).**
42. **The correct answer is (B).**
43. **The correct answer is (C).**
44. **The correct answer is (B).** The wet system is air-cooled. The dry system is water-cooled with a jacket to reduce the danger of compressor damage.
45. **The correct answers is (C).**
46. **The correct answer is (D).**
47. **The correct answer is (A).**
48. **The correct answer is (A).**
49. **The correct answer is (A).**
50. **The correct answer is (C).**
51. **The correct answer is (C).**
52. **The correct answer is (A).**
53. **The correct answer is (D).**
54. **The correct answer is (A).**
55. **The correct answer is (B).**
56. **The correct answer is (A).**
57. **The correct answer is (B).**

Chapter 6

ACCESSORIES

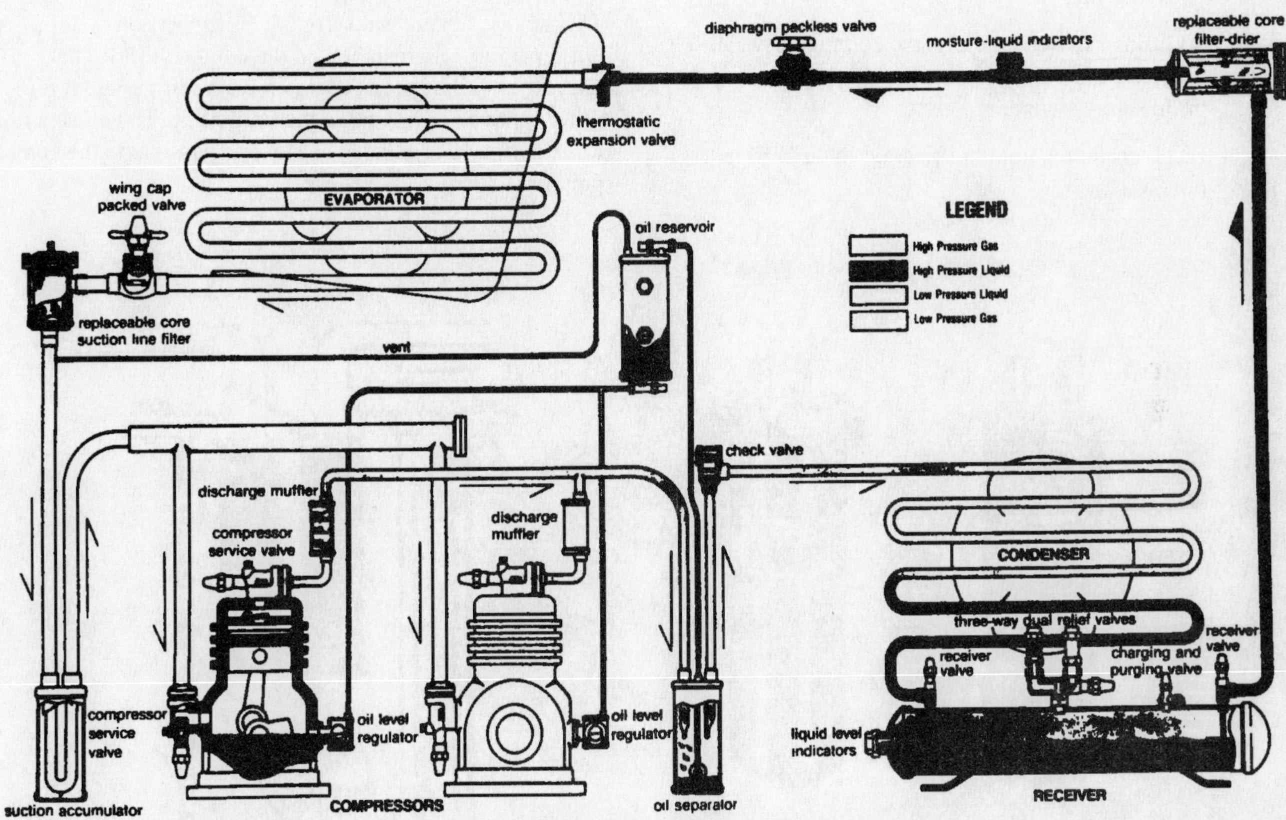

Fig. 6.1
Diagram courtesy of AC&R Components, Inc., Henry Valve Company.

A refrigeration accessory adds to the convenience or effectiveness of the system but is not essential. The essential components of a refrigeration system are the compressor, evaporator, metering device, and condenser. Accessories help the refrigeration system function better. The following are some of today's most common accessories and their functions.

oil separator: reduces oil flow through the system.

muffler: dampens or removes the hot-gas pulsations produced by a reciprocating compressor.

heat exchanger: transfers heat from liquid refrigerant to the suction gas.

sorbents: extract and hold other substances in a filter-drier, generating heat.

filter-drier: removes moisture and solid particles from a refrigeration system.

suction accumulator: prevents flooding of liquid refrigerant from the evaporator to the compressor.

crankcase heater: increases crankcase temperature during shutdown to minimize oil dilution, and separates oil from the refrigerant.

sight glass: helps check the condition of liquid refrigerant in the system.

moisture indicator: designed to warn the service person when moisture in dangerous quantities are present within the system.

water valve: controls head pressure by regulating the flow of water to the condenser.

solenoid valve: used as a stop-and-start valve of liquids or gases.

check valve: allows liquid or gas to flow only in one direction.

oil failure switch: protects the compressor against low oil pressure; also known as oil pressure switch or oil safety switch.

receiver: stores liquid refrigerant in the refrigeration system.

back pressure regulator: maintains constant pressure or temperature in the evaporator.

service valves: add or remove refrigerant (primary purpose). They are also used to monitor pressures in the system with the use of service gauges connected to the service valve.

OIL SEPARATOR

This device separates oil from the refrigeration system. Oil separators are installed on the compressor discharge line. After oil has been separated from refrigerant, it returns to the compressor via the return line. The oil separator is normally connected as close as possible to the compressor.

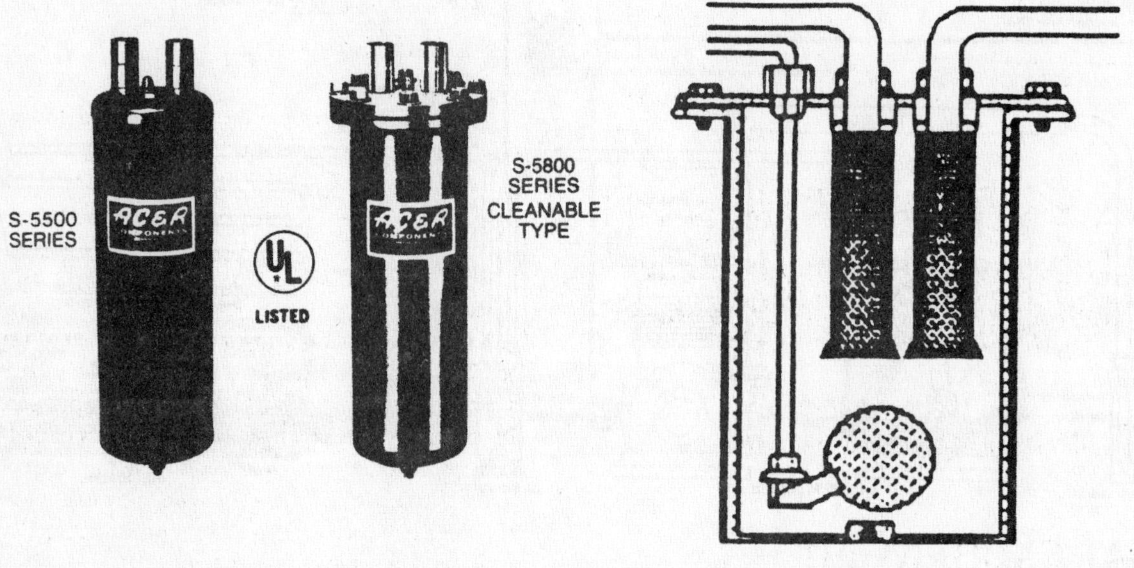

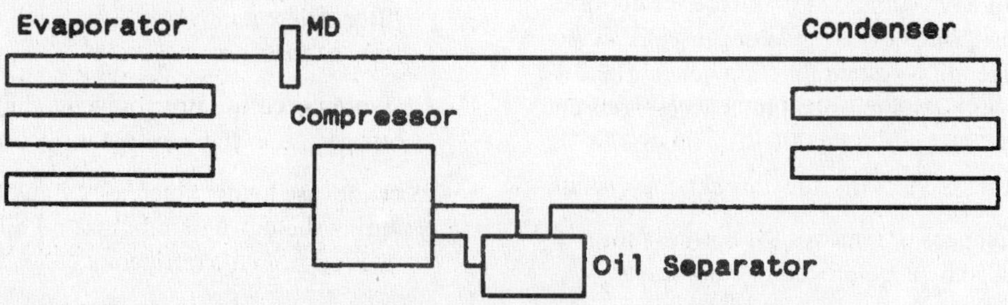

Fig. 6.2 Note 10 percent of the oil travels through the system.
Photo courtesy of Henry Valve Company, AC&R Components, Inc.

MUFFLER

Design purpose:

1. to eliminate noise
2. to eliminate vibrations that can result in line breakage

Mufflers eliminate pulsations in the compressor discharge line. They have internal baffles designed for minimum pressure drop that change the velocity of the discharge gases. This results in dampening the high-frequency sound waves in gases from high-speed compressors. Mufflers also iron out the pulsating waves in low-speed compressors. They can be installed vertically or horizontally depending on the application. They are sized according to the discharge line of the compressor.

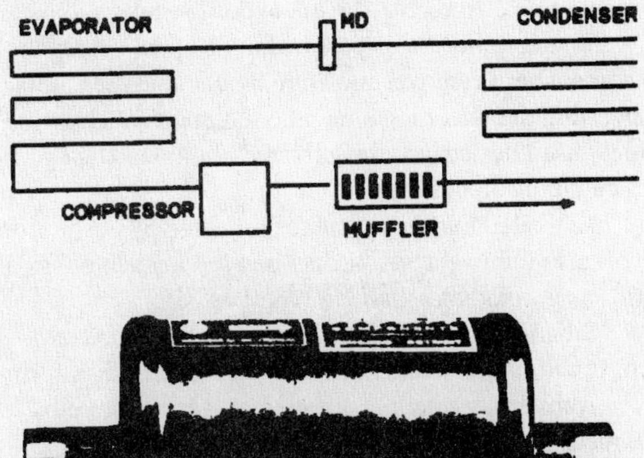

Fig. 6.3
Photo courtesy of AC&R Components, Inc.

HEAT EXCHANGER

This device transfers heat from the liquid line to the suction line. It evaporates excess liquid refrigerant in the suction line to keep it out of the compressor. This liquid refrigerant is also called "slop over refrigerant." The heat exchanger boosts system capacity by subcooling the liquid refrigerant in the liquid line.

When a heat exchanger is operating properly, it increases the temperature of the suction line and decreases the temperature of the liquid line.

Heat exchangers are not common with R-22 systems because of the high discharge-temperature of this refrigerant.

The evaporator and the condenser also function as heat exchangers.

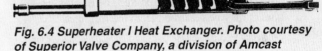

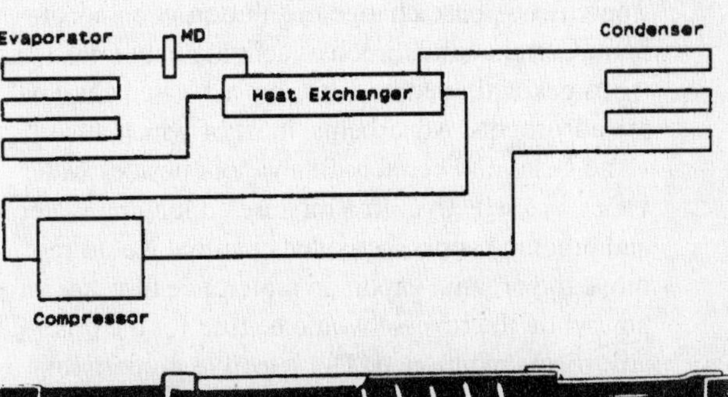

Fig. 6.4 Superheater / Heat Exchanger. Photo courtesy of Superior Valve Company, a division of Amcast Industrial Corporation.

SORBENTS AND DESICCANTS

Sorbents

Sorbents and desiccants are the materials or substances used in a filter-drier. In order to understand how a filter-drier works, it is important to cover sorbents and desiccants first. The New York City Exam will test the student on his knowledge of these substances.

Sorbents are solid or liquid materials that extract and hold other substances (usually gases or vapors, especially water vapor) they contact. The sorption process always generates heat, mainly from the condensation of water vapor. The weight of water held by a substance increases or decreases, depending on whether the vapor pressure of the water is less or greater, respectively, than its partial pressure in the surrounding atmosphere. All materials are sorbents to some degree. However, sorbent generally refers to materials with a large capacity to absorb moisture. Such materials are divided into two classifications:

absorbent: a sorbent that changes physically and/or chemically during the sorption process. Lithium chloride is one solid absorbent. When this material absorbs water, the lithium chloride converts to a hydrate and reaches a saturation point at $LiCl_{25}H_2O$. Additional moisture causes the material to lose its crystalline shape and dissolve in the water it absorbed. The phase changes from solid to liquid. Liquid absorbents include sulfuric acid, the ethylene glycols, and solutions of halogen salts such as lithium chloride, lithium bromide, and calcium chloride.

adsorbent: a sorbent that does not change physically or chemically during the sorption process.

There is no phase change or solution of an adsorbent. Certain solids, such as activated alumina, silica gel, activated bauxite, and activated charcoal are adsorbents. Adsorbents, most of which adsorb some gases and condensable vapors besides water vapor, are selective. In a mixture containing water and organic vapors, activated charcoal would remove the organic vapors in preference to water vapor, while the reverse would be true for the other adsorbents mentioned. The selective property of adsorbents can be used to remove contaminating vapors from an air or gas mixture. The desirable component may be adsorbed from the mixture.

When an active adsorbent contacts a gas of high humidity, the vapor pressure of water in the adsorbent tends to reach equilibrium with the partial pressure of the water in the surrounding gas; thus the adsorbent extracts water from the gas. This dehumidifies the gas stream or removes the moisture from air or gas.

FILTER-DRIER

The filter-drier removes moisture and solid particles from a refrigeration system.

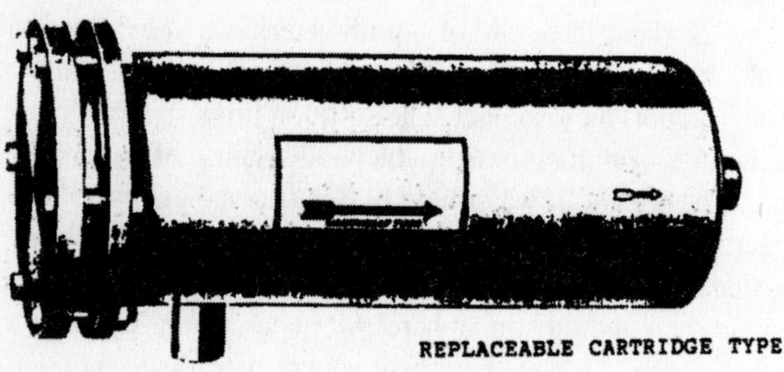

Fig. 6.5

Liquid line installation prevents moisture from entering the metering device. If moisture did enter, it could freeze and block refrigerant flow. In the art below, the arrow indicates the direction of refrigerant flow.

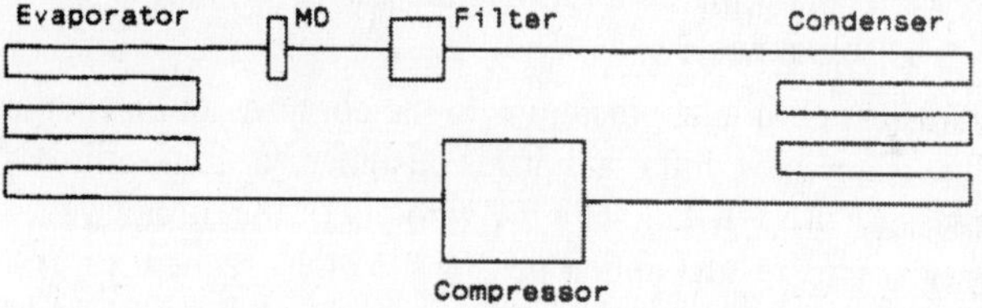

Liquid line filter drier

Fig. 6.6

The desiccant in the drier is normally either an adsorbent or an absorbent. The **adsorbent** removes moisture as water and holds it as water without a chemical reaction. The **absorbent** removes moisture by chemical reaction, converting the water to some other compound. Three widely used desiccants are activated alumina, silica gel, and calcium sulphate.

Activated alumina removes moisture by adsorption. It will also remove acids. It may be used in such physical forms as grain, tablet, ball, and molded core.

Silica gel removes moisture and acids by adsorption. It will not dust and is used in various physical forms.

Anhydrous calcium sulfate removes moisture by chemical action and forms dust.

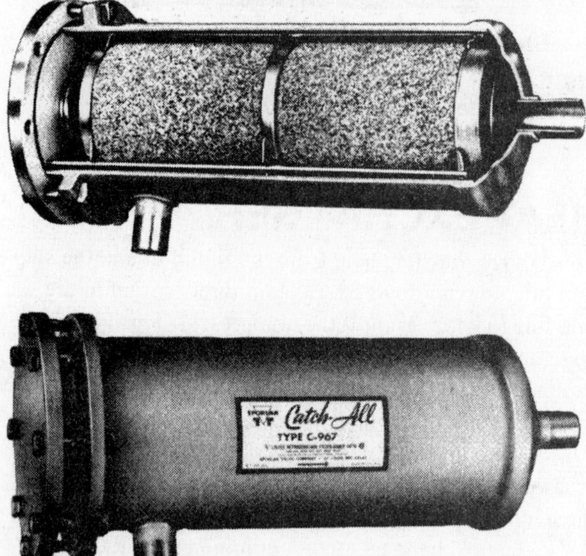

Fig. 6.7
Photo courtesy of Sporlan Valve Co.

Suction Line Filter Drier

The suction line filter drier is installed just before the compressor. It should be installed whenever the system is serviced. If the compressor is replaced, a drier is installed to prevent solid particles from entering the new compressor.

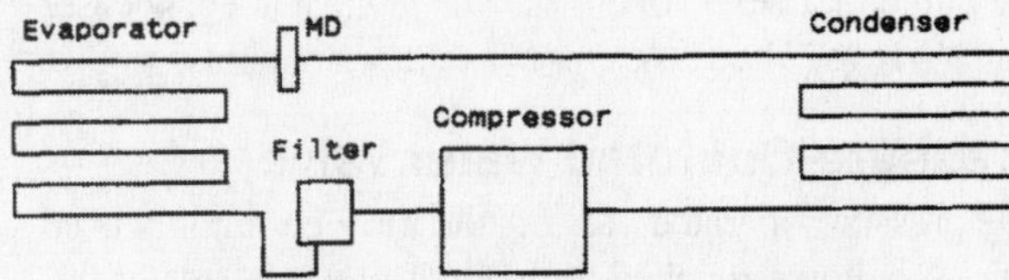

Fig. 6.8 Type CFA cartridge (cut-away) filter-drier. Photo courtesy of Superior Valve Company, a division of Amcast Industrial Corporation.

SUCTION ACCUMULATOR

A suction accumulator prevents the flooding of liquid refrigerant from entering the compressor.

Accumulators are normally found in hot-gas defrost units, in which liquid floodback from the evaporator can occur. The accumulator is basically a tank that traps liquid refrigerant coming from the evaporator. It insures that only superheated vapor can enter the compressor.

Liquid refrigerant entering the accumulator collects in the bottom of the tank, where some vaporizes and some is pulled into the suction line. The accumulator is designed so that neither the outlet nor the inlet is submerged in refrigerant.

CRANKCASE HEATER

In many condensing unit applications, the compressor crankcase must be heated to evaporate liquid refrigerant trapped in the oil. Most large compressors with commercial applications are fitted with a crankcase heater in the factory, especially if the compressor will be exposed to cold temperatures. Crankcase heaters may operate during the OFF cycle or may be thermostatically controlled.

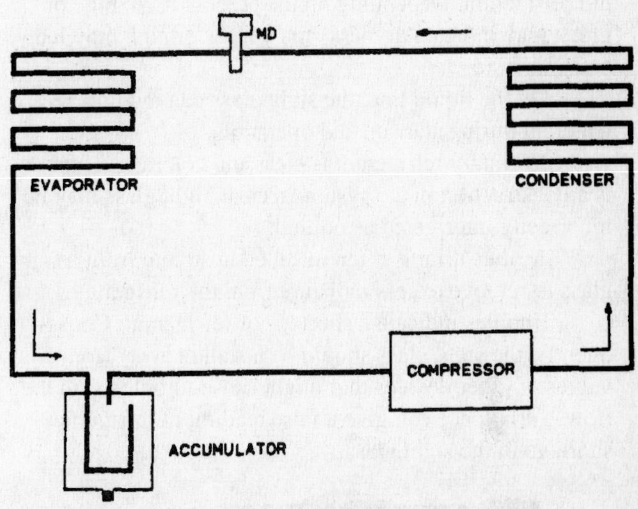

Fig. 6.9

For smaller installations without a built-in crankcase heater, an accessory heater may be attached to the crankcase. Crankcase heaters are generally required on remote installations if the compressor may operate at an ambient temperature below the evaporator temperature.

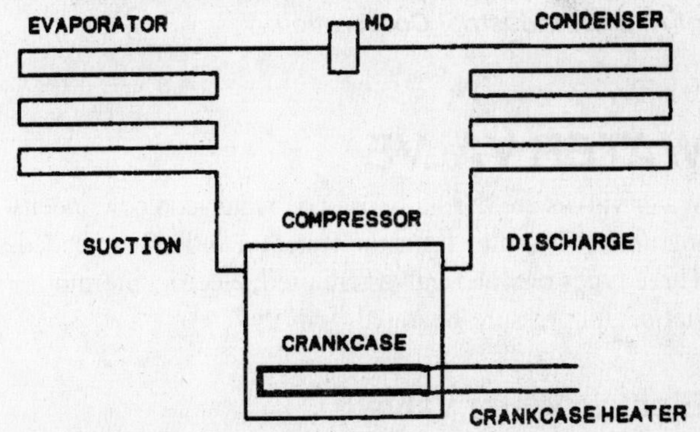

Fig. 6.10

SIGHT GLASS AND MOISTURE INDICATOR

A sight glass is a fixture that reveals the condition of liquid refrigerant in the system. The sight glass has a glass port for viewing the refrigerant; it is usually installed on the liquid line before the metering device.

A moisture indicator may be installed in the glass port. It will change color if moisture is present in the liquid refrigerant. Depending on the process used, blue or green may indicate dryness, and yellow or pink may indicate moisture.

On the liquid line, the sight glass can monitor refrigerant during start-up and operation.

Normally refrigerant is clear and colorless. If there is an obstruction in the system, a clear sight glass may be incorrectly interpreted as normal.

A filter-drier is often installed upstream from a sight glass to remove excess moisture from the refrigerant.

Bubbles indicate a shortage of refrigerant. Consequently, the sight glass should be installed away from any valves or other devices that might cause turbulence in the flow. Turbulence can give a false reading of refrigerant shortage in the sight glass.

Fig. 6.11
Photo courtesy of Superior Valve Company, a division of Amcast Industrial Corporation.

WATER VALVE

Water valves are normally used on water-cooled condensing units. The valve turns the water on and off as needed. Three types of water valves are used: electric, thermostatic, and pressure-operated.

Electric Water Valve

The electric water valve is solenoid activated or motor operated. It is usually located between the water supply and the condensing unit. The moment the motor starts, this valve opens, allowing water flow. When the motor circuit opens, the solenoid is de-energized, closing the valve and stopping water flow. An advantage is that the valve may be removed or replaced without disturbing the refrigeration system.

Thermostatic Water Valve

This valve is controlled by exhaust water temperature. It is similar to the pressure water valve but is operated by a thermostatic element connected to the bellows. The element is charged with a volatile liquid. The power bulb is mounted in the condenser water outlet line. Pressure from the volatile liquid in the bulb opens the valve when the condenser water warms. The valve closes as the water cools.

Pressure-Operated Water Valve

The pressure-operated valve is the most commonly used type. A bellows attached to the high-pressure side of the system, preferably to the cylinder head, operates the valve. As condenser pressure rises, the bellows contracts. When the valve opens, cooling water flows into the condenser. The valve opens the water circuit only when water is needed (when pressure rises). It will keep increasing the water flow as long as there is a tendency for pressure increase in the high side.

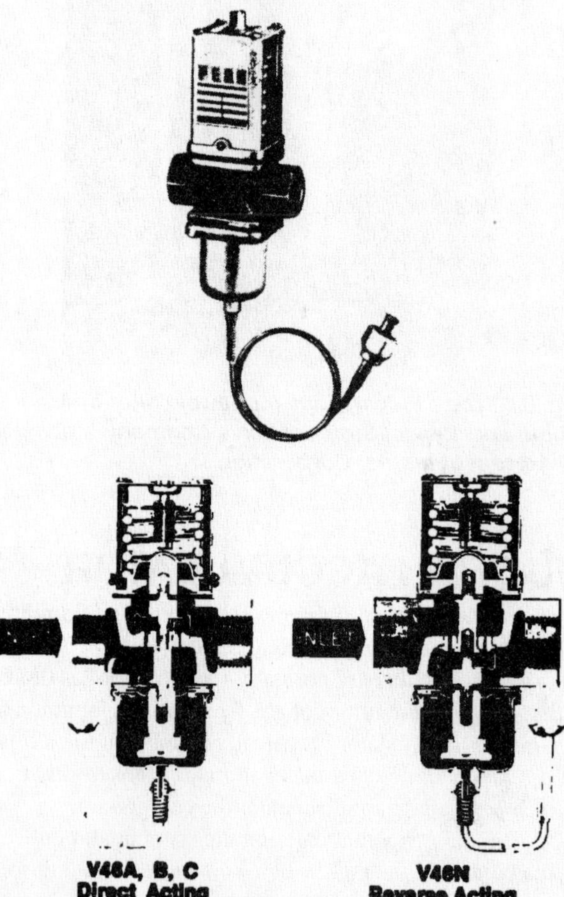

Fig. 6.12 Fig. 1—V46 All-Range Pressure Actuated Water Regulator.
Fig. 2—Typical cross-sections of threaded type valves. Interiors of flange models are similar.
Photographs courtesy of Johnson Controls, Inc.

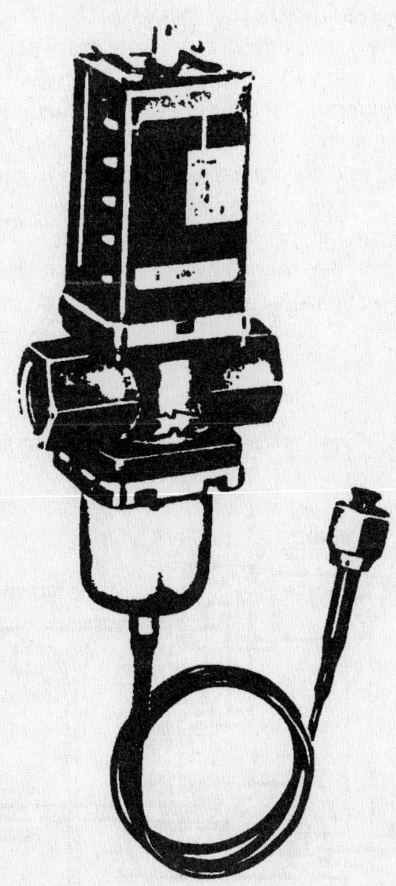

Penn Water Regulating Valve

Fig. 6.13

SOLENOID VALVE

An electrically operated solenoid valve automatically controls the flow of liquid or gas.

There are two basic types of solenoid valves. The more common is the normally closed (N.C.) type, in which the valve opens when the coil is energized and closes when the coil is de-energized. The normally open (N.O.) valve opens when the coil is de-energized and closes when the coil is energized.

Principles Of Operation

Solenoid valves are moved by electromagnets. The coil creates a magnetic field when electric current flows through it. If a magnetic metal, such as iron or steel, is introduced into the magnetic field, the field attracts the metal toward the hollow core of the coil. By attaching a stem to the magnetic metal (called plunger), the solenoid can open the valve port. When the electrical circuit is broken, the magnetic field collapses and the stem and plunger drop by gravity or are pushed down by the kick-off spring.

Some solenoid valves use a hammer-blow effect. When the coil is energized, the plunger starts upward before the stem. The plunger then picks up the stem by contacting a collar at the top. The momentum of the plunger helps open the valve against the unbalanced pressure across the port.

Pilot-Operated Normally Closed Solenoid Valves

In a pilot-operated valve, the stem and plunger open a pilot port. This releases pressure on top of the disc, piston, or diaphragm, which then moves upward and opens the main valve port. Note that the valve operation is the same whether the valve is a disc, piston, or diaphragm.

The following figure illustrates the four phases of the operating cycle of a typical pilot-operated valve.

Initially, the pilot port and main port are closed as shown in Figure A. Pressure at the valve inlet is present on top of the disc because of the equalizer hole in the disc.

When the coil is energized, the stem-and-plunger assembly lifts and the pilot port opens, as in Figure B.

The stem-and-plunger assembly is centered within the coil by the magnetic field. The pilot port, if properly sized for the fluid to be handled, relieves the pressure on top of the disc. Now the valve inlet pressure acts on part of the bottom of the disc, lifting the disc to open the main port, as in Figure C.

Once the port is open, the disc is held off the seat by the pressure difference across the port. When the coil is de-energized, the stem-and-plunger assembly drops due to gravity or the kick-off spring, closing the pilot port.

The pressure above the disc is no longer vented to the downstream side of the valve (see Figure D), so the disc drops, closing the main port. In some valves the plunger is spring-loaded and does not need gravity to close.

Fig. 6.14

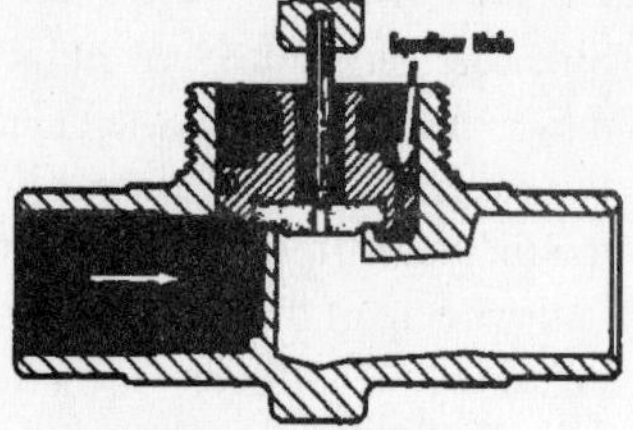

A *Coil De-Energized Pilot Port Closed Main Port Closed*

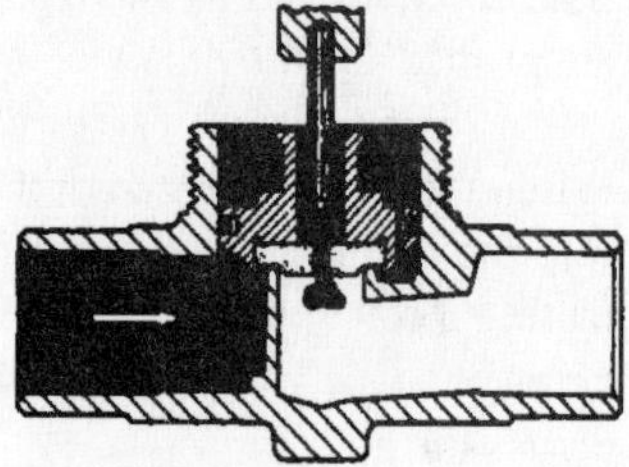

B *Coil Energized Pilot Port Open Main Port about to Open*

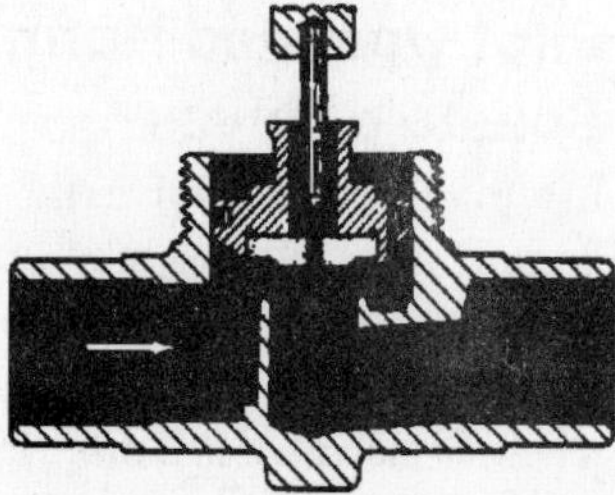

C *Coil Energized Pilot Port Opened Main Port Open*

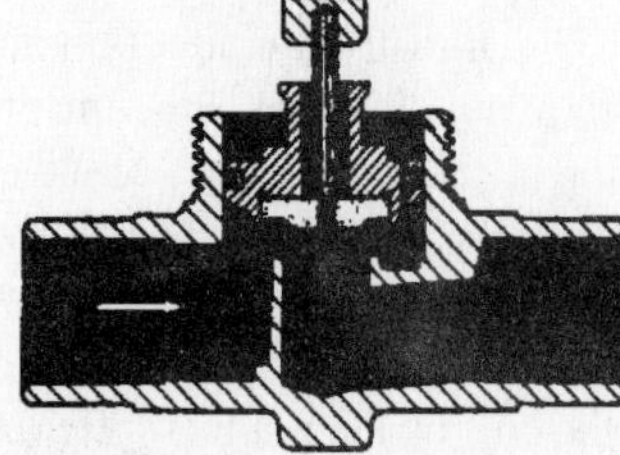

D *Coil De-Energized Pilot Port Closed Main Port Closing*

Normally Open Solenoid Valves

Normally open solenoid valves operate like normally closed valves. System pressure is used to open and close them. However, when the coil in the normally open valve is de-energized, a spring pushes the stem-and-plunger assembly upward to hold the pilot port open.

When the valve is de-energized or "OFF," it is open. When the coil is energized or "ON," the stem and plunger assembly is pulled down, closing the pilot port. Pressure on top of the disc then equalizes with the incoming pressure and the disc moves down, closing the main port. The valve remains closed as long as the coil is energized.

Application

A primary purpose of the solenoid valve is to prevent refrigerant from entering the evaporator during the off cycle. A liquid-line solenoid valve may be wired so it is energized only when the compressor runs. The source voltage for these valves ranges from 115 to 240 volts.

In a pump-down control system, a thermostat controls the solenoid. When the thermostat is satisfied, the valve closes and the compressor continues to run until a substantial portion of the refrigerant has been pumped from the evaporator. A low-pressure cutout stops the compressor at a predetermined evaporator pressure. When the thermostat again calls for refrigeration, the solenoid opens, causing the evaporator pressure to rise and the compressor to start.

OFF-CYCLE SOLENOID CIRCUIT

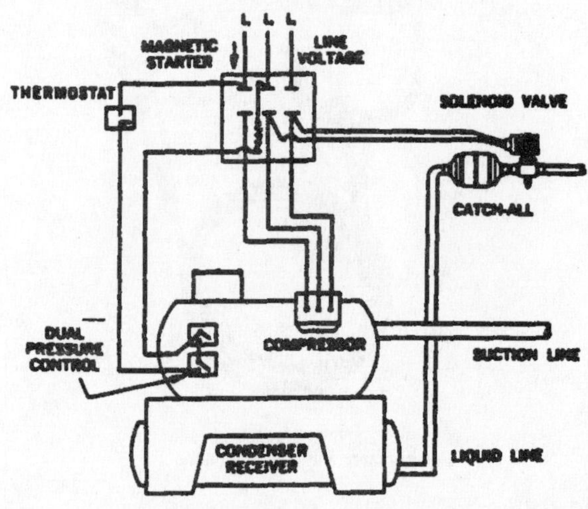

PUMP DOWN SOLENOID CIRCUIT

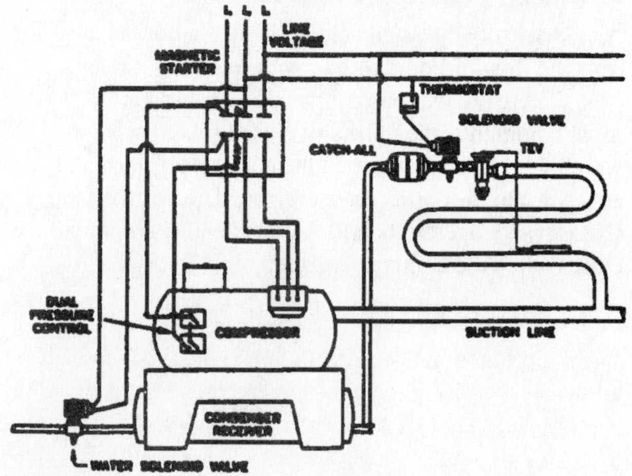

Fig. 6.15

CHECK VALVE

The check valve allows liquid or gas refrigerant to travel in one direction only. It also stops the refrigerant from migrating through the piping during the off cycle. The check valve creates a pressure drop, so it should be installed only when necessary.

Check Valve Operation

Refrigerant flowing through the inlet pushes the spring up and continues through the line. If refrigerant flows in the opposite direction, the valve plug is forced closed by the spring, preventing refrigerant from flowing backward. The check valve must be a tight seal in the opposite direction, to ensure stoppage of reverse flow.

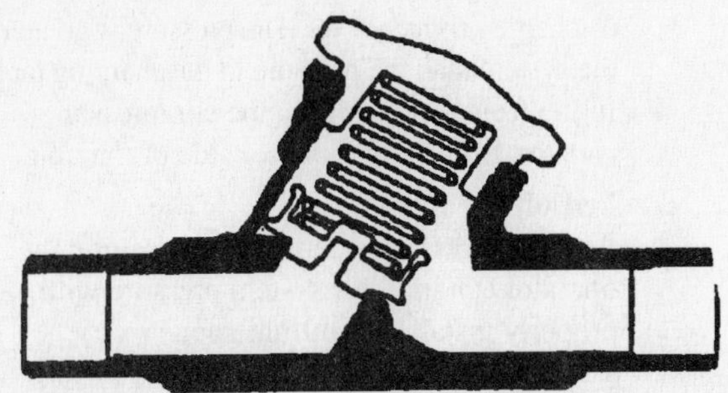

Fig. 6.16

Check Valve Application

A check valve is sometimes used in the discharge line to prevent refrigerant return to the compressor. A check is particularly useful in the discharge line of a system with an evaporative condenser, or an air-cooled condenser. An air-cooled condenser is outdoors, while the compressor is indoors. When the compressor shuts down, it becomes cooler than the condenser, so it attracts refrigerant. The check valve prevents this migration and avoids liquid slugging on startup. Check valves are also used in the heat pump system or the hot-gas defrost system. Check valves are useful with two temperature systems. In this application they prevent equalization of multitemperature evaporators during shutdown.

OIL FAILURE SWITCH

The main function of the oil failure switch, which is also known as the oil safety switch or the oil pressure switch, is to protect the compressor against low oil pressure in the lubrication system. The oil failure switch stops the compressor when the oil pump pressure is not sufficient enough to maintain proper compressor lubrication. It is wired into the compressor circuit, so a drop in oil pump pressure below its set point de-energizes the compressor.

The switch works on the differential pressure between the oil pump and the crankcase or suction pressure. If oil pressure is not at least 9 to 10 psig greater than crankcase pressure, the switch opens its contacts and stops the compressor.

The oil failure switch uses a heater-type time-delay circuit to allow 90 to 120 seconds' delay before cutoff. This allows the compressor to start while the oil pump builds to proper lubrication pressure.

The pressure differential switch in the oil failure switch measures the difference between suction pressure and oil-pump discharge pressure. It is a closed switch that opens when oil pressure exceeds crankcase (suction) pressure. Therefore, oil pressure is an opening force and crankcase pressure is a closing force. The pressure differential switch is wired in series with the heater of the time-delay circuit.

If oil pressure drops below a safe level, crankcase pressure closes the pressure differential switch and energizes the time delay heater. If oil pressure does not open the pressure differential switch within 90 to 120 seconds, the time-delay heater opens its normally closed contacts.

The oil failure switch is not a safety device, because low oil pressure causes no hazard to life or property. It is a **protective device** to guard the compressor from insufficient lubrication.

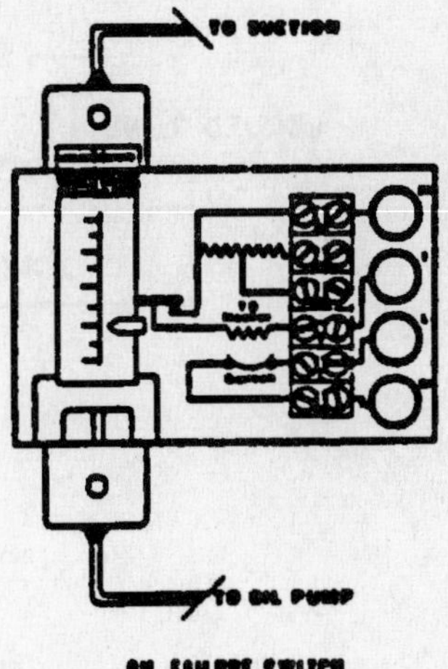

Fig. 6.17

RECEIVER

A receiver stores liquid refrigerant in the refrigeration system. Receivers are temporary storage tanks normally found in large systems. As storage tanks, they are useful during system shut-down.

The receiver is installed after and below the condenser so that the metering device has an adequate supply of refrigerant.

SERVICE VALVES

Suction Service Valve

A suction service valve allows addition or removal of gas refrigerant. It is located on the compressor suction inlet. On a reciprocating system, the suction gas cools the compressor motor windings. Oil can also be charged into the compressor through the suction service port of some compressors.

Suction Service Valve Positions

back-seated: Line port and compressor port are open; service port is closed (normal operating position).

front-seated: Service port and compressor port are open; line port is closed.

cracked-off the back seat position: All ports are open.

Discharge Service Valve

The discharge service valve is located between the compressor and condenser. Its three positions are similar to those of the suction service valve.

Discharge Service Valve Positions

back-seated:

a. Compressor port and discharge line ports are open.
b. Service port is closed.
c. This is the normal operating position of the valve.

front-seated:

a. Compressor port is closed.
b. Service port and discharge line ports are open.
c. On domestic refrigerators and window units, this position can be used to charge liquid refrigerant into the system with shrader valves.
d. On commercial central air conditioning units, you *never* charge the liquid refrigerant into the discharge service valve. The pressure is greater in the system than the pressure in the charging tank.
e. In the front seat position, the compressor is isolated from the condenser side of the unit.

cracked-off the front seat:

a. All three ports are open. In this position the operator can monitor system pressure with a properly installed manifold gauge.

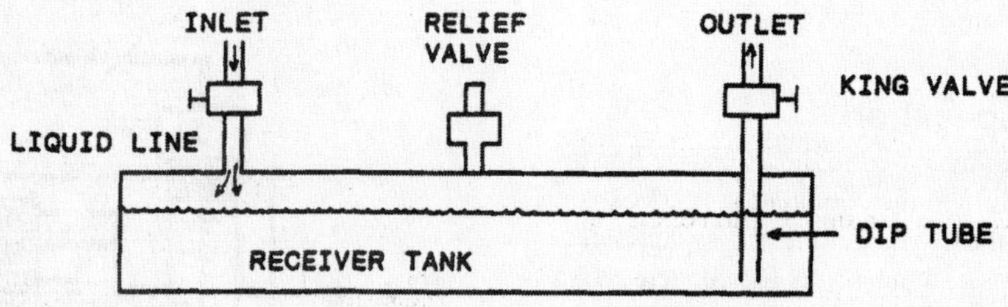

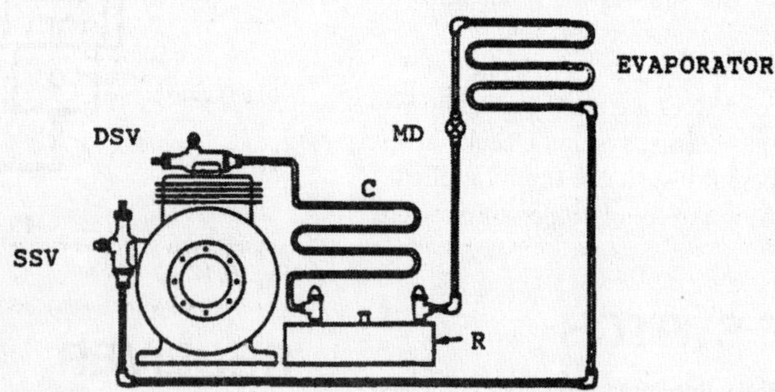

Fig. 6.18
Flow diagram courtesy of Goodheart-Willcox.

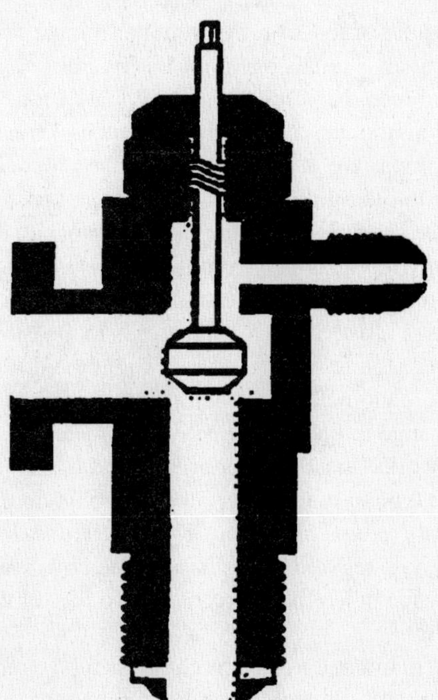

Fig. 6.19 Discharge Service valve

Liquid Line Service Valve

The liquid line service valve is located between the condenser and the metering device. Its' three positions are similar to the discharge service valve.

back-seated:

a. Condenser port and the liquid line port are open.
b. Service port is closed.
c. This is the normal operating position of the valve.

front-seated:

a. Condenser port is closed.
b. Service port and liquid line ports are open.
c. On commercial units, this position is used to charge liquid refrigerant into the system.
d. In this position, it can be used to manually pump down the system.

cracked-off the front seat:

a. All three seat ports are open. In this position, the operator can monitor system pressure with a properly installed manifold gauge.

King Valve

Like the liquid line service valve, the king valve is located between the condenser and the metering device. However, it is located right next to the condenser. Note that the king valve has only two positions.

back-seated:

a. Condenser port and liquid line port are open.
b. This is the normal operating position of the valve.
c. There is no service port on this valve.

front-seated:

a. Condenser port is closed.
b. Liquid line port is open.
c. This position is used to manually pump down the system.

NOTE: this valve is not crack-off the back seat since there is no service port.

BACK PRESSURE REGULATOR

Also called evaporator pressure regulators, back pressure regulators sense and control evaporator pressure. The primary function of this valve is to prevent evaporator pressure from falling below a predetermined value. When the evaporator is operating at design pressure, the valve is open. As the load is met and evaporator pressure drops, the valve automatically throttles or restricts vapor leaving the evaporator, maintaining the desired minimum evaporator pressure. When the load increases, the evaporator pressure rises above the valve setting and the valve opens further.

The back pressure regulator prevents freezing of water chillers that operate at excessively low suction temperatures. Another popular application is on multiple evaporators serviced by a common compressor. On a multitemperature evaporator system, the back pressure regulating valve is installed on the suction line of the higher-temperature evaporator.

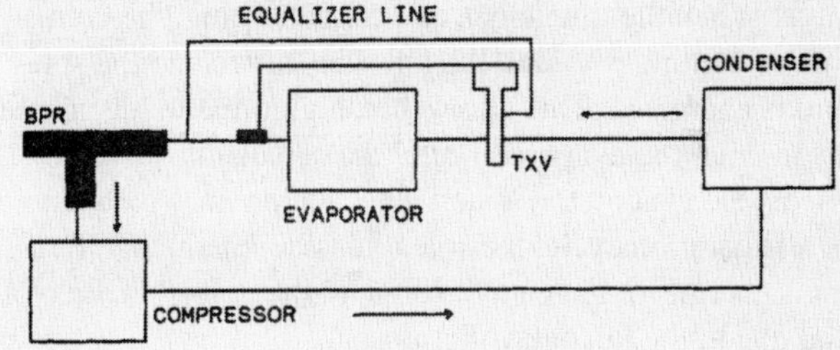

Fig. 6.20

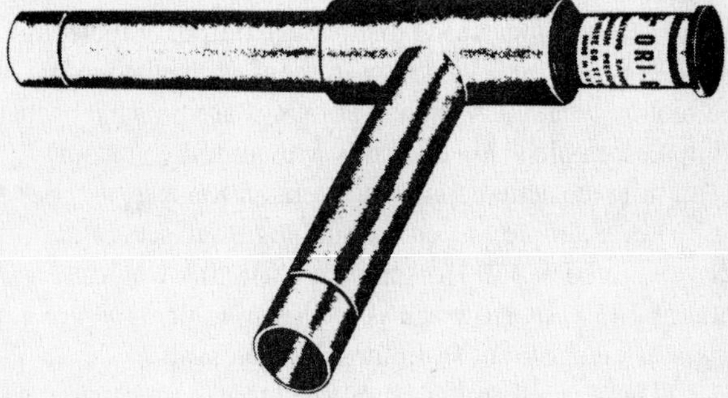

Fig. 6.21

ACCESSORIES

Automatic Defrosting

Automatic defrosting in Freon systems are primarily of two types, electric defrost or hot gas defrost. In the electric defrost system, at a predetermined time, a time clock will shut down the motor compressor and the fan on the evaporator, if one is used. At the same time it will energize resistance heaters built into the coil, in the drain pan, and wrapped around the drain pipe. After a given length of time the resistance heaters will shut down, the compressor will start to run, but the fan will stay off unit the coil has reached its normal operating temperature. The fan delay switch usually built into the coil will not allow the fan to run unless the coil is cold. This prevents warm air from being introduced into the refrigerated space. If the coil temperature should rise for any reason whatsoever, this fan delay thermostat built into the coil will shut down the fan. The drain pan and drain pipe resistance heaters are used to prevent freeze-up and overflow during the defrost cycle.

In the hot gas defrost system a tee fitting is cut into the discharge pipe between the compressor and condenser. Off the branch of this tee, in a simple hot gas defrosting system, a manual valve is installed. This shut-off valve is then connected to the evaporator immediately after the metering device. When this valve is opened with the machine in operation, hot discharge gas will enter the evaporator and defrost the coil. The automatic defrost version of this system requires the use of a time clock and a solenoid valve. When the time clock call for defrosting, the compressor continues to run, the fan shuts down and the solenoid is energized. This allows hot, high pressure discharge gas to enter the evaporator after the expansion valve, to defrost the evaporator. When the machine goes back into its refrigeration cycle, the solenoid is de-energized, the fan is energized, but cannot run until the coil is refrigerated due to the fan delay thermostat.

Manometer

In order to determine how efficiently the plant is operating, some means of measuring the tonnage output of the compressors is required. We know from the nameplate rating on the motors what the horsepower ratings are for each of the compressor units. However, this will not tell you at any given time the actual compressor output tonnage.

For example, if you are running three sets of compressors rated at 450 Horsepower each, this would be a total of 1350 HP. How can you determine that you are getting sufficient output from these compressors?

There is a formula established to use for refrigerants to determine the tonnage output capacities:

Number of lbs. of refrigerant per minute through the expansion valve equals one ton of refrigeration.

For Freon-12, 4 lbs. a minute equals 1 ton.

For ammonia, .5 lbs. a minute equals 1 ton.

Formulas are of no use to you unless there is a way to be able to measure the flow of refrigerant past a certain point in the system, so that the tonnage capacity can be calculated with the above formula. This is the purpose of the manometer and venturi installed in the system.

The purpose of the manometer is to measure a difference in pressure, no matter how slight the difference may be. A manometer is different from a pressure or vacuum gauge in that it is sensitive to any change in pressure and works on a different principle.

The type of manometer most common on the field is a mercury gauge, usually a "U" shaped tube. It is calibrated on both legs. Pressure is calibrated by measuring the difference in height between the two legs of the mercury column.

The manometer is a straight glass tube containing mercury and oil. The oil, being lighter than the mercury, floats on top of the mercury and fill the upper portion of the tube, while the mercury is in the lower portion of the tube. At each end of the manometer tube there is a cylinder and reservoir, one for the mercury and one for the oil.

Manometer

The pressure of the refrigerant acts on the bottom of the diaphragms and, in turn, moves the column of mercury and oil up and down in the manometer tube. The manometer is mounted on a plate that is calibrated in pounds per minute of refrigerant weight. It measures the flow rate of the refrigerant liquid passing one point in the system, to determine the capacity and efficiency that the plant is operating.

Venturi / Manometer

The venturi is used in conjunction with the manometer to measure the flow rate of the refrigerant in the system. The refrigerant flow must be accurately measured at one particular point in the system. This is done through the venturi, which is located in the liquid line after the receivers.

One type of venturi is the orifice plate. This type is commonly used today because it is simpler and cheaper to make. It is a metal disc, like a blank flange, that has a hole machined out in the center to a predetermined size. The venturi is uniquely built for particular systems or application.

It is similar to a spool piece, except that it has a slightly restricted opening at the center. This opening, or orifice is predetermined for the particular system. Because of the restricted opening, the high pressure liquid flowing past this point creates a pressure differential through the venturi.

It is this pressure difference that is measured by the **manometer**. This measurement is then converted to flow rate readings on the manometer. As the liquid refrigerant leaves the receivers and flows to the venturi, it encounters a slight restriction as it passes through the smaller opening in the venturi neck. This causes a slight pressure drop when the refrigerant squeezes through the neck of the venturi, while it causes the refrigerant to **increase in velocity.** If the flow rate through the expansion valves is **increased** by opening up more, then the flow rate through the venturi increases. This will cause the pressure on the outlet side of the venturi to drop more, while the velocity, or speed of the refrigerant increases more.

If the flow rate through the expansion valves **decreases**, then the pressure on the outlet side of the venturi increases and the velocity decreases, because there is less flow of refrigerant through the system.

This is a principle by which the refrigerant flow in the system can be measured. The line from the inlet side of the venturi is connected to the bottom cylinder on the manometer. The pressure in this line will exert itself against the diaphragm in the cylinder and will move the mercury column either up or down. The line from the outlet side of the venturi is connected to the top cylinder on the manometer, and its pressure will exert itself against the diaphragm, moving the oil column and counteracting the pressure exerted on the mercury. As the flow rate in the system varies, the pressure and velocity will vary through the venturi. These changes can now be measured on the manometer, which is calibrated to read in pounds of refrigerant per minute. Therefore, if you open the valves to the manometer, and get a reading of 100 lbs. per minute, the tonnage can then be calibrated.

To determine the tonnage, you would use the formula that was given, for example: 0.5 lbs. of ammonia per minute equals one ton of refrigeration. Therefore, 1 lb. of ammonia per minute equals 2 tons, multiplied by 100 lbs. equals 200 tons of refrigeration.

If the manometer reading was 250 lbs. per minute, the actual tonnage could be calculated as follows:

.5 lbs. of ammonia per minute = 1 ton of refrigeration

1 lb. of ammonia = 2 tons per minute

2 tons per minute × 250 lbs. per minute = 500 tons of refrigeration

The venturi converts flow rate into pressure differential, and the manometer converts this pressure differential into calibrated refrigerant rate per lb. per minute. From this, the efficiency of the plant is determined by comparing actual tonnage output to actual horsepower being used.

REFRIGERATION ACCESSORIES LICENSE QUESTIONS

1. The high-pressure relief valve is usually piped to
   (A) the low-pressure side and the atmosphere.
   (B) the mixer only.
   (C) atmosphere and a water tank.
   (D) fire department box and water.
2. Gauge glass connections on a horizontal liquid receiver should be
   (A) top and bottom with ball check valve.
   (B) top and slightly off bottom with ball check valve and tight packing.
   (C) top and slightly off bottom with ball check valve and free packing.
   (D) slightly off bottom with ball check valves and tight packing.
3. The pressure connection of an automatic water-regulating valve is connected to
   (A) discharge pressure.
   (B) city water pressure.
   (C) suction pressure.
   (D) the suction service valve.
4. Which of the following is NOT on the high side?
   (A) Oil trap
   (B) Liquid seal
   (C) Scale trap
   (D) King valve
5. A side-outlet drier is generally mounted
   (A) just after the expansion valve.
   (B) between the evaporator and the compressor.
   (C) liquid line, horizontally or vertically, with the flange on bottom.
   (D) suction line, with the flange on the top.
6. A drier is generally installed with other essential equipment. The recommended location is on the
   (A) high-pressure line between the condenser and the receiver.
   (B) suction line between the evaporator and the compressor.
   (C) discharge line between the compressor and the condenser.
   (D) liquid line between the receiver and the expansion valve.
7. What driers are used in R-12 systems?
   (A) Calcium chloride
   (B) Activated alumina
   (C) Sodium chloride
   (D) Soda lime
8. Of the following, which will NOT remove acid from refrigerant?
   (A) Calcium oxide
   (B) Calcium chloride
   (C) Activated alumina
   (D) Silica gel
9. The purpose of using activated alumina on the high side of a Freon refrigerating system is to
   (A) regenerate refrigerant.
   (B) remove noncondensables.
   (C) dry the refrigerant.
   (D) remove excess oil.
10. Which of the following is a drying agent?
    (A) Sulfur dioxide
    (B) Ethyl chloride
    (C) Hydrocarbons
    (D) Calcium sulfate
11. An air conditioning system with clogged filters will have which of the following conditions?
    (A) Low suction-pressure to the compressor
    (B) High head-pressure to the compressor
    (C) High suction-pressure to the compressor
    (D) Increased suction pressure
12. Which desiccant changes chemically or physically in a refrigeration system?
    (A) Activated alumina
    (B) Silica gel
    (C) Calcium chloride
    (D) Bauxite
13. If silica gel contained water before being installed in the system, at what temperature could you free the moisture?
    (A) 200° F
    (B) 500° F
    (C) 450° F
    (D) 850° F
14. Which of the following desiccants CANNOT be used with an R-40 system?
    (A) Drierite
    (B) Activated alumina
    (C) Calcium chloride
    (D) Silica gel
15. To operate two evaporators at different temperatures in a compression system with only one compressor, it would be necessary to install a back-pressure valve in the
    (A) suction line of the low-temperature evaporator.
    (B) suction line of the high-temperature evaporator.
    (C) common suction line in the system.
    (D) discharge line at the main booster unit.

16. A two-way pilot solenoid valve is NOT used for
(A) unloading a compressor for start-up.
(B) opening a spring-loaded metering device.
(C) a four-way heat-pump valve.
(D) a pressure-relief valve.

17. A valve that will not restrict the flow is the
(A) automatic-expansion valve.
(B) low-side float valve.
(C) solenoid valve.
(D) thermostatic expansion valve.

18. If you energize a solenoid valve and it closes, what kind of valve is it?
(A) Normally open
(B) Normally closed
(C) Direct-acting
(D) Pilot-operated

19. Which device automatically resets itself?
(A) Fusetron
(B) Circuit breaker
(C) Fusetat
(D) Thermal protector

20. A room thermostat controls a solenoid valve in a liquid line. The compressor ON and OFF is controlled by
(A) the high-pressure side of the system.
(B) the thermostatic cut-out switch.
(C) the high-pressure cut-out switch.
(D) the low-pressure control.

21. The most valid statement about a two-way solenoid valve in the liquid line between the receiver and the expansion valve is
(A) it is used as a liquid stop valve.
(B) it is closed when energized.
(C) it modulates the flow of refrigerant.
(D) it controls refrigerant vapor.

22. An oil separator with a float valve in a Freon-12 system is used to
(A) meter the amount of Freon.
(B) drain oil to the crankcase.
(C) keep a liquid level.
(D) keep the oil separator lubricated at all times.

23. The three types of water valves are
(A) electric, pressure, and thermostatic.
(B) pneumatic, electric, and pressure.
(C) hydraulic, pneumatic, and electric.
(D) automatic, pneumatic, and electric.

24. Which type of water valve will NOT vary water flow as the refrigeration load changes?
(A) Hydraulic
(B) Pneumatic
(C) Electric
(D) Pressure

25. How does an oil-pressure safety switch operate?
(A) It is a differential control using two bellows. Oil pressure must always be above the low-side pressure for oil to flow.
(B) It is a differential control using one bellows. Oil flows when oil pressure is above the high-side pressure.
(C) It is a thermostatic control with a bulb sensor. Oil flows when pressure is above suction pressure.
(D) None of the above

26. The material in a strainer-drier is called
(A) designate.
(B) filling.
(C) desiccant.
(D) desecrate.

27. Foaming in a compressor crankcase can
(A) indicate thickening of the oil.
(B) create liquid slugs.
(C) indicate excess oil in the refrigerant.
(D) indicate that the crankcase heater is not shutting off.

28. A sight glass in a full liquid line will be
(A) full of bubbles.
(B) cloudy.
(C) light green.
(D) clear.

29. A moisture indicator must
(A) bubble when filled with liquid.
(B) be yellow.
(C) change color when exposed to any moisture.
(D) be right-side-up.

30. A receiver
(A) is part of the condenser.
(B) stores liquid refrigerant.
(C) is an essential part of the system.
(D) stores refrigerant gas.

31. The check valve
(A) allows the flow of liquid and gas in both directions.
(B) is always spring-loaded.
(C) is always in horizontal lines.
(D) has a pressure drop.

32. An evaporator pressure regulator maintains constant pressure or temperature in the evaporator regardless of how

(A) high the compressor suction pressure goes.
(B) high the condenser pressure goes.
(C) low the compressor suction pressure goes.
(D) low the condenser pressure goes.

33. The oil separator is always installed

(A) to prevent oil clogging.
(B) in a cool spot.
(C) where it can be easily serviced.
(D) in the discharge line.

34. A suction accumulator always has a(n)

(A) oil return line.
(B) inlet and outlet.
(C) coil of liquid line around it.
(D) complex control system.

35. A refrigeration accessory is a device that

(A) adds to the convenience of a system.
(B) comes in many forms.
(C) is not essential in a refrigeration system.
(D) all of the above.

Answers to Refrigeration Accessories License Questions

1. **The correct answer is (A).**
2. **The correct answer is (B).**
3. **The correct answer is (A).**
4. **The correct answer is (C).**
5. **The correct answer is (C).**
6. **The correct answer is (D).**
7. **The correct answer is (B).** It removes acids.
8. **The correct answer is (B).** It is an absorbent.
9. **The correct answer is (C).**
10. **The correct answer is (D).** It removes moisture by chemical action.
11. **The correct answer is (A).**
12. **The correct answer is (C).**
13. **The correct answer is (C).**
14. **The correct answer is (C).**
15. **The correct answer is (B).**
16. **The correct answer is (D).**
17. **The correct answer is (C).** The solenoid valve is an open or closed valve. It does not regulate.
18. **The correct answer is (A).**
19. **The correct answer is (D).**
20. **The correct answer is (D).**
21. **The correct answer is (A).**
22. **The correct answer is (B).**
23. **The correct answer is (A).**
24. **The correct answer is (C).** Solenoid-operated
25. **The correct answer is (A).**
26. **The correct answer is (C).**
27. **The correct answer is (B).**
28. **The correct answer is (D).**
29. **The correct answer is (C).**
30. **The correct answer is (B).**
31. **The correct answer is (D).**
32. **The correct answer is (C).**
33. **The correct answer is (D).**
34. **The correct answer is (B).**
35. **The correct answer is (D).**

Chapter 7

PUMP-DOWN CYCLE

The pump-down cycle is used in a refrigeration or air-conditioning system for three main reasons.

1. The automatic pump-down cycle is used to start the machine unloaded. The driving motor draws less amperage because it is not doing much work.
2. The pump-down cycle prevents the spillover (carry-over or slugging) of liquid into the compressor on start-up.
3. Manual pump-down isolates the refrigerant in the condenser/receiver when the system is opened for maintenance, for repairs, or during winter shutdown.

Without the pump-down feature, pressure will equalize in the entire system on shut-down. The evaporator will tend to fill with liquid refrigerant. When the machine starts, this liquid will likely be pulled into the cylinder, causing oil to wash out of the crankcase and possible head valve breakage through liquid slugging. (Liquid cannot be compressed.)

On older systems, piston breakage and head blow-off was prevented by a **safety head.** This device had a moveable valve plate held in position by a heavy helical spring. If the cylinder held liquid during the compression stroke, the high pressure would push the valve plate enough to discharge the liquid without damaging the compressor. Once the intake stroke began, the helical spring would reseal the valve.

On modern compressors, liquid slugging is prevented by a crankcase heater, which boils off the liquid refrigerant before it can enter the cylinder.

The pump-down cycle system has a solenoid valve in the liquid line before the expansion valve. This system is controlled by a thermostat in the area to be cooled. When the desired temperature is reached, the thermostat points open, breaking the circuit to the solenoid. The machine continues to run, even though the valve has stopped the refrigerant flow, until all the refrigerant leaves the evaporator. Then the suction line pressure drops low enough for the low pressure control to stop the compressor motor.

A machine may operate from 1 to 5 minutes after the solenoid valve closes. The temperature in the area to be cooled may drop further, even though the thermostat has been satisfied. This drop in temperature is caused by pumping down the evaporator. When the room warms up enough for the thermostat to call for cooling, the solenoid energizes and opens. High-pressure liquid from the receiver flows through the valve to the expansion valve and into the evaporator. The pressure rises quickly and the machine starts with only a small amount of liquid in the evaporator.

MANUAL PUMP-DOWN

During the winter or service, a refrigeration system can be pumped down manually. The low-pressure control must be bypassed with a jumper switch. This allows the desired pump-down pressure to be reached. Next, the king valve is front-seated to stop the refrigerant flow. A manifold gauge should be installed on the suction and discharge service valves and cracked off the back seat to monitor system pressures. As the compressor runs, the solenoid valve stays open. This causes refrigerant to boil from the evaporator and pump down into the receiver for storage. If a system has no receiver, refrigerant will pump down into the condenser.

System low pressure must be equal to or above the pump-down pressure specified by the compressor manufacturer. If pump-down pressure is below atmospheric pressure, noncondensable gases can enter the system and the compressor can be damaged.

Once pump-down pressure is reached, the jumper switch is disconnected from the low-pressure control. Since the suction line is below cut-out pressure, the low-pressure control shuts down the compressor.

The manifold gauge should be carefully disconnected from the compressor. The manifold was cracked off the backseat, with its suction and discharge valves slightly open. If someone removes the gauges in this condition, refrigerant can leak, causing possible injury.

To remove the manifold gauge, front-seat the discharge service valve to prevent refrigerant from bleeding back into the system and isolating refrigerant in the condenser/receiver. Next, front-seat the suction service valve. Any refrigerant still in the manifold hoses can be withdrawn by a vacuum pump into a holding tank. Then, close the high- and low-side valves of the manifold gauge and disconnect the hoses. Refrigerant is not lost and the hoses can be removed safely.

Pump-down is complete when the circuit breakers are turned off and tagged to prevent someone from starting the system in the pump-down position.

Before restoring the system, back-seat the suction and discharge service valves. Open the king valve slowly until system pressure equalizes. Then leave the valve fully open (back-seated). Close the circuit breakers and remove the tag.

EXAM TIPS

1. Review automatic pump-down procedures for the written exam.

2. Review manual pump-down operations for the practical exam. You should be able to verbally describe each step without overlooking any safety procedure.

AUTOMATIC PUMP DOWN CYCLE

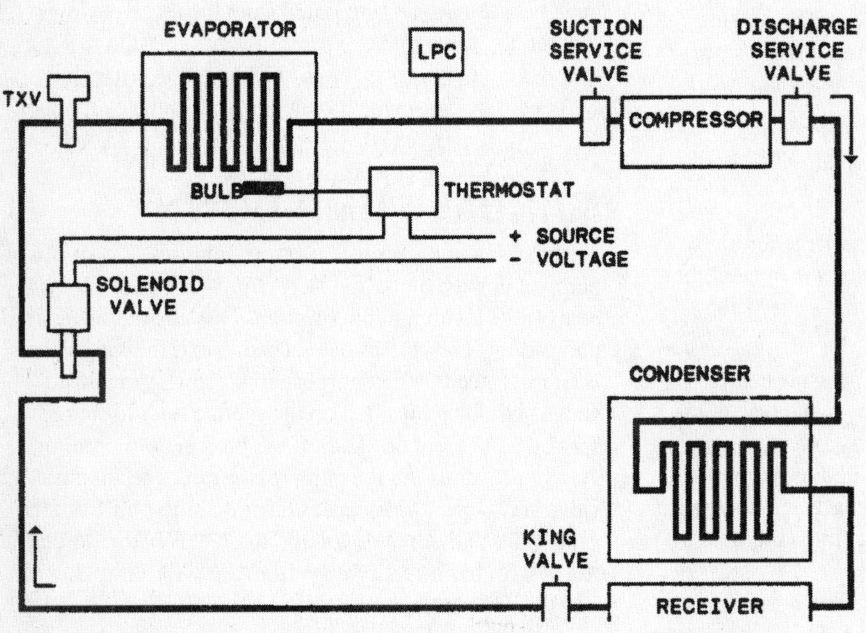

Fig. 7.1

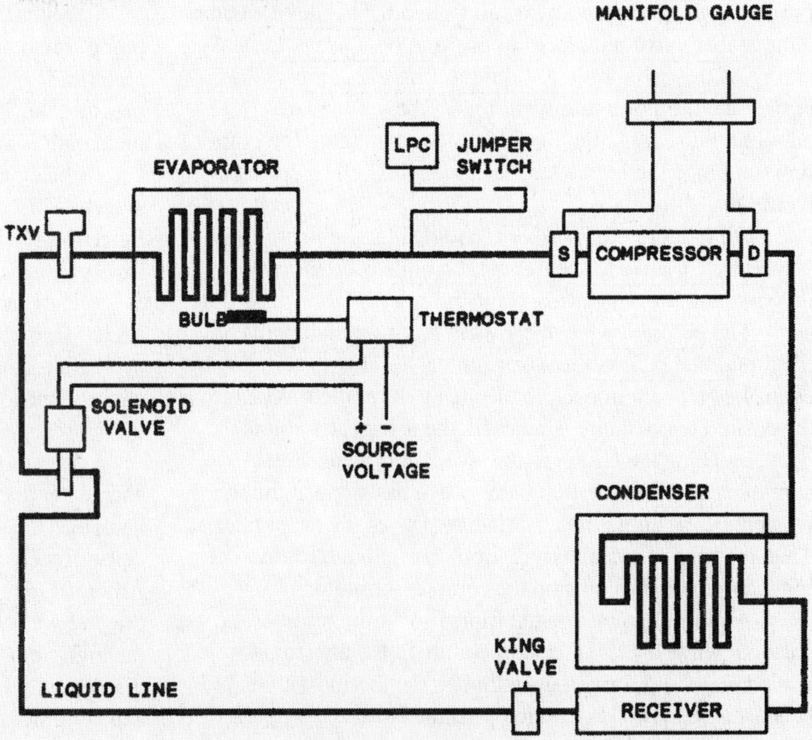

Fig. 7.2

PUMP-DOWN LICENSE QUESTIONS

1. What shuts down the compressor?

(A) Solenoid
(B) Low-pressure control
(C) Helical spring
(D) Safety head

2. How is the liquid-line solenoid valve used to pump down?

(A) When the evaporator thermostat is satisfied, the solenoid valve closes.
(B) The compressor continues to run until the solenoid valve stops the compressor.
(C) When the thermostat calls for cooling, the solenoid valve opens.
(D) As the suction pressure rises, it starts the compressor.

3. Where is the low-pressure control connected on a pump-down cycle?

(A) Discharge line
(C) Suction line
(B) Liquid line
(D) Low oil pressure line

4. What does it mean to say that the king valve is back-seated?

____
____
____
____

5. When taking high-pressure readings from a manifold gauge connected to the discharge service valve, in what position should the valve be?

____
____
____
____

6. Once the system is completely pumped down, why is it important to turn circuit breakers OFF and then tag?

____
____
____
____

7. If pump-down pressure is below atmospheric pressure, what can happen to the system?

____
____
____
____

8. Why is it important to bypass the low-pressure control with a jumper switch?

____
____
____
____

9. You see a technician improperly venting R-12 during pump-down. What should you do?

____
____
____
____

10. What else must be done besides pump-down when shutting a system down for the season?

____
____
____
____
____

Answers to Pump-Down License Questions

1. **The correct answer is (B).**
2. **The correct answer is (A).**
3. **The correct answer is (C).**
4. **The correct answer is the king valve is in the open position.**
5. **The correct answer is cracked off the back seat.**
6. **The correct answer is it prevents someone from accidently turning the system on and seriously damaging the compressor.**
7. **The correct answer is noncondensable gases can enter the condenser/receiver.** Normally pump-down pressure is slightly above atmospheric pressure, which prevents air or moisture from entering the system.
8. **The correct answer is the low-pressure control (LPC) is a safety feature that shuts down the compressor on low-suction pressure.** Unless a jumper switch bypasses the LPC, the desired pump-down pressure will not be reached.
9. **The correct answer is advise the technician to stop the illegal procedure or face fines and penalties under the Clean Air Act of 1990.**
10. **The correct answer is check the system for leaks, drain the cooling tower, loosen fan belts, clean condenser tubes and strainers, and replace system filter-driers and crankcase oil.**

Chapter 8

REFRIGERANTS

A refrigerant is a fluid in a refrigeration system that picks up heat by evaporating at a low temperature and pressure and gives up heat by condensing at a higher temperature and pressure. When a refrigerant changes state from liquid to gas, its latent heat of vaporization produces cooling. Heat from the material to be cooled vaporizes the liquid refrigerant, vaporizes the liquid, and is carried away by the vapor.

In the high side of the system, the reverse takes place. As high-temperature, high-pressure refrigerant vapor cools and gives up its latent heat of condensation, the greatest amount of heat is released. The refrigerant changes from a high-temperature, high-pressure gas to a high-temperature, high-pressure liquid.

Refrigerants can be classified by two major factors: thermodynamic properties and physical properties.

THERMODYNAMIC PROPERTIES

A thermodynamic property is any property with a direct bearing on heat movement. Examples include enthalpy and the relationship between entropy, pressure, volume, temperature, and density. Pressure, volume, temperature, and density relationships control the size, strength, and type of system.

Enthalpy

Enthalpy represents the total amount of thermal energy (heat) contained in a fluid. Enthalpy is expressed in btu/lb.

Enthalpy of evaporation is the amount of heat that must be added, at a given pressure, to evaporate a fluid from saturated liquid to saturated vapor. It is used to determine cubic feet flow per minute per ton.

Refrigeration effect is the useful cooling done by refrigeration, which is the difference in enthalpy between the refrigerant entering and leaving the evaporator. It is the amount of btu absorbed into the system that results in useful cooling.

Entropy is used in engineering calculations and research.

Pressure represents the energy impact a refrigerant has on a system. It determines the type of equipment used. Whenever a system is operating at negative pressures, noncondensable gases can enter the system.

When one pound of a substance rests on an area of one square inch, the pressure exerted downward is one pound per square inch (psi). Pressure can be expressed in psig or psia. All refrigeration systems depend on pressure-temperature differences. The relationship of vapor pressure and boiling point is called the pressure-temperature relationship.

1. When a system is under pressure, the boiling point increases. At 47.5 psia, R-22 boils at 10° F.
2. When system pressure decreases, the refrigerant's boiling point is reduced. At 25″ Hg psig, R-22 boils at –100° F.
3. A refrigerant with a low vapor pressure has gas molecules compressed closer together. The lower the vapor pressure, the higher the boiling point. At 14.7 psi, R-11 boils at 74° F.
4. A refrigerant with high vapor pressure has a low boiling point. At 14.7 psi, R-22 boils at –41° F.

R-22 Properties Chart

Temperature Degrees F	Pressure psia	Pressure psig	Vapor Volume ft³/lb$_m$	Density lb$_m$/ft³ Liquid
–130	0.68858	28.519*	59.170	96.313
–120	1.0725	27.738*	39.078	95.416
–110	1.6199	26.623*	26.578	94.509
–100	2.3802	25.075*	18.558	93.590
–90	3.4111	22.976*	13.268	92.660
–80	4.7793	20.191*	9.6902	91.717
–70	6.5603	16.564*	7.2139	90.761
–65	7.6317	14.383*	6.2655	90.278
–50	11.707	6.0851*	4.2039	88.807
–46	13.042	3.3666*	3.8007	88.408
–44	13.754	1.9186*	3.6168	88.208
–42	14.495	0.4090*	3.4437	88.007
–41.47	14.696	0.0	3.3997	87.954
–40	15.268	0.5717	3.2805	87.806
–38	16.072	1.3763	3.1267	87.604
–36	16.910	2.2138	2.9816	87.401
–34	17.781	3.0852	2.8446	87.197
–32	18.687	3.9914	2.7152	86.993
–30	19.629	4.9333	2.5930	86.788
–28	20.608	5.9119	2.4774	86.582
–26	21.624	6.9283	2.3680	86.375
–24	22.679	7.9832	2.2645	86.168
–22	23.774	9.0778	2.1664	85.960
–10	31.231	16.535	1.6757	84.695
0	38.726	24.030	1.3672	83.617
10	47.530	32.834	1.1253	82.516
50	98.758	84.062	0.55451	77.829
80	158.36	143.66	0.34497	73.926

* Inches mercury vacuum psig

Chart courtesy ASHRAE Handbook 1985 Fundamentals, Chapter 17.

Volume

Volume is the space (volume) a certain weight (amount) of gas occupies. Volume characteristics can determine the compressor type.

Specific volume compares the densities of gases. The specific volume of a vapor is the cubic feet of gas formed when one pound of it evaporates. For example, R-170 (ethane) produces only .53 cubic feet of gas when one pound is evaporated at 5° F. However one pound of R-717 (ammonia) will produce 8.15 cubic feet—almost fifteen times as much gas—under the same conditions. R-170 has the lowest specific volume of refrigerants listed below. Specific volume is important for sizing system components.

Specific volume at 5° F

Refrigerant Number	Vapor
R-11	12.27
R-12	1.49
R-22	1.25
R-30	49.9
R-40	4.47
R-170	.53
R-717	8.15
R-764	6.42

Low specific volume and vapor. If the refrigerant expands too much when vaporized, excessive demands are placed on the compressor. The size of the system will have a significant bearing on the scope of such demands.

High specific volume of liquid. The refrigerant should have a high enough volume for durable refrigerant control. A great difference between the volume of refrigerant in its liquid and vapor states will require a larger compressor.

Density

Density is the weight or mass per unit volume, normally expressed in pounds per cubic foot (lb./ft.). For example, R-40 (methyl chloride) weighs 56.3 pounds per cubic foot while R-170 (ethane) weighs 17.2 pounds per cubic foot. R-40 is almost three times as dense as R-170.

The chart below lists the liquid density of nine refrigerants at 86° F, saturation temperature. Note that some refrigerants are heavier than others.

Density at 86° F		Refrigerant boiling point	
Refrigerant Number	Liquid lb./cu.ft.	Fahrenheit at 0 psig	
R-11	91.4	R-11	74.7
R-12	80.7	R-12	–21.6
R-22	73.4	R-22	–41.4
R-30	81.7	R-30	105.2
R-40	56.3	R-40	–10.8
R-170	17.2	R-170	–127.5
R-717	37.2	R-717	–28.0
R-718	62.4	R-718	212.0
R-764	84.4	R-764	14.0

Temperature

Temperature measures the intensity of heat in degrees. It indicates the speed of molecular motion. Heat is the speed of atomic motion multiplied by the number of atoms affected. It is important not to use the words *heat* and *temperature* carelessly.

Boiling point is the temperature at which a fluid changes from liquid to gas. A refrigerant absorbs the greatest amount of heat while changing into the vapor state.

PHYSICAL PROPERTIES

Physical properties are those that have no direct bearing on the amount of heat a refrigerant can absorb or move. Some examples are stability, solubility, miscibility, flammability, toxicity, odor, leak detection, dielectric strength, and resistance to corrosion.

stability: a refrigerant's ability to remain in its original chemical form. A chemically stable refrigerant does not decompose during system operations. Chemical inertness also affects the stability of the refrigerant. A good refrigerant must not dissolve any part of the system, including seals, gaskets, and lubricants.

miscibility: a refrigerant's ability to mix with oil. Miscibility of oil and refrigerants has advantages and disadvantages. The principal advantages are ease of lubrication and returning oil to the compressor. Disadvantages include oil dilution in the compressor, poor heat transfer, and control problems.

solubility: a refrigerant's ability to mix with other substances. Refrigerant mixtures or blends can substitute, replace, and upgrade refrigerants. Unfortunately, moisture (water) is soluble in most refrigerants. Whenever moisture enters a system, refrigerant flow at the low side is usually restricted. If air, moisture, or water is detected in a system, it must be removed.

resistance to corrosion: a refrigerant's ability to resist the chemical reaction of corrosion. Nearly all refrigerants absorb moisture. Moisture in a system can develop corrosive acids, causing sludge, copper plating, and general deterioration of the system. Copper plating in a hermetic unit caused by corrosion could short-circuit the compressor motor windings.

leak detection: methods used to determine the presence of leaking refrigerant gas. An odor or hissing sound may alert the technician. The technician may use a halide torch, an electronic leak detector, a sulphur stick, soap solution, litmus paper, brom thymol blue, or dye added to find the leak on the system. Leaks can also be detected by pressurizing or evacuating a refrigeration system. A loss in pressure or vacuum indicates a leak in a system but not its location.

flammability: a refrigerant's ability to support combustion (fire or explosion). Highly combustible refrigerants are the hydrocarbons: propane, butane, isobutane, ethane, and ethylene.

toxicity: a term describing refrigerants that are injurious to human beings. In sufficient concentration, all refrigerants can create oxygen deficiency and cause suffocation, but some refrigerants are injurious even in small concentrations. The amount of injury depends on the refrigerant's concentration and nature plus length of exposure. Another toxicity factor is the refrigerant's reaction to flame. For example, the halogen refrigerants—R-11, R-12, and R-22—are decomposed by flame into highly toxic phosgene gas. When an open flame is used near any halogen refrigerant, ensure ample ventilation. See the chapter "Refrigeration Code" for the ANSI/ ASHRAE 15-1978 Safety Code and the Underwriters Laboratories Group Classifications for refrigerant toxicity values.

dielectric strength: a refrigerant's or oil's resistance to electric current. Refrigerant hermetic systems directly contact the compressor motor windings. If a refrigerant has a low dielectric strength, the motor windings of a hermetic compressor will short-circuit. A good refrigerant should be a nonconductor or highly resistant to electric current.

Electrical Properties of Liquid Refrigerants

Refrigerant	Temperature Degrees F	Dielectric Constant
R-11 Trichloromonofluoromethane	84–77	2.28–1.92
R-12 Dichlorodifluoromethane	84–77	2.13–1.74
R-13 Chlorotrifluoromethane	–22	2.3
R-21 Dichlorofluoromethane	82–77	5.34–4.88
R-22 Monochlorodifluoromethane	75–77	6.11–6.12
R-30 Methylene Chloride	77	9.1
R-113 Trichlorotrifluoroethane	86–77	2.44–1.68
R-114 Dichlorotetrafluoroethane	88–77	2.17–1.83
R-290 Propane	Ambient	1.27
R-500 Ambient	1.8	
R-717 Ammonia	69	15.5
R-744 Carbon Dioxide	32	1.59
R-764 Sulphur Dioxide	32	15.6

Chart courtesy E.I. DuPont De Nemours & Co., Inc.

REFRIGERANT LEAK DETECTION

Leaks in refrigeration equipment are major problems for manufacturers and service engineers. Several methods of leak detection are used.

Electronic Detector

Used in manufacture and assembly of equipment, this instrument detects a variation in current caused by the ionization of decomposed refrigerant between two opposite-charged platinum electrodes. It can detect any halogenated refrigerants except R-14. It is not recommended for use in atmospheres with explosive or flammable vapors. Vapors such as alcohol and carbon monoxide may interfere with the test.

Halide Torch

This is a fast and reliable method of detecting halogenated refrigerant leaks. Air is drawn over a copper element heated by a methyl alcohol or hydrocarbon flame. Any halogenated vapors present decompose, and the flame color changes to bluish-green.

Bubble Method

In this method, the object to be tested is pressurized with nitrogen. The object is immersed in water, where bubbles appear. A detergent is added to the water to decrease surface tension and forms a stream of bubbles. A solution of soap or detergent can be brushed or poured onto joints or other spots where leaks are suspected. Leaking gas forms soap bubbles that can easily be seen.

Pressurizing Or Evacuating

A manifold gauge can detect a leak by showing a drop in pressure. The gauge must be watched for at least 30 minutes. Never use air to pressurize the system. Nitrogen is recommended for the standing pressure test. This method indicates leaks but not their location.

Ammonia Leaks

To detect ammonia leaks, a sulfur candle is burned near the suspected leak or a solution of hydrochloric acid is brought near it. If ammonia vapor is present, a white cloud or smoke of ammonium sulfite or ammonium chloride forms. Ammonia can also be detected with indicating paper that changes color in the presence of a base.

Sulfur Dioxide Leaks

To detect these leaks, aqueous ammonia is brought near the suspected leak. White smoke forms if sulfur dioxide is present.

REFRIGERANT CHARACTERISTICS

The letter "R" plus a number was designated by the American Society of Heating, Refrigeration, and Air Conditioning Engineers (ASHRAE), to represent various refrigerants. The letters "CFC" represent chlorofluorocarbon, the generic term for most Freon refrigerants.

Trichloromonofluoromethane (CFC) R-11

1. Group 1: A low-temperature refrigerant that is nonflammable, nontoxic, and stable
2. Boiling point = 74° F at atmospheric pressure
3. Freezing point at atmospheric pressure = –168° F
4. Critical temperature = 338° F
5. Critical pressure = 639.5 psia
6. Gauge pressure at 5° F = 24 inches of Hg
7. Pressure at 86° F = 3.5 psig
8. High-side test pressure 30 psig
9. Low-side test pressure 30 psig
10. Leaks may be detected with soap solution, halide torch, or electronic detector.
11. A safe cleaning agent or solvent
12. Latent heat 5° F = 84 btu/lb.
13. Miscible in oil
14. Used in centrifugal and rotary compressors
15. Disadvantage: ozone depletion factor (ODF) = 1

Dichlorodifluoromethane (CFC) R-12

1. Group 1: Nonflammable, colorless, odorless, heavier than air, noncorrosive and nonirritating under normal conditions. Normally nontoxic; however, when exposed to open flame in the presence of copper, it forms phosgene, a poisonous gas.
2. Inert at ordinary temperatures
3. Boiling point = –21.7° F at atmospheric pressure
4. Freezing point at atmospheric pressure = –252° F
5. Critical temperature = 233° F
6. Critical pressure = 596.9 psia
7. Pressure at 86° F = 93 psig
8. Pressure at 5° F = 12 psig
9. High-side test pressure = 235 psig
10. Low-side test pressure = 140 psig
11. Low latent heat value, helpful in smaller machines

12. Leaks may be detected with soap solution, halide torch, electronic leak detector, or colored oil added to the system.
13. Latent heat of vaporization = –70 btu/lb.
14. Latent heat at 5° F = 68 btu/lb.
15. Miscible in oil
16. Used in reciprocating and rotary compressors
17. Disadvantage: ozone depletion factor (ODF) = 1

Monochlorodifluoromethane (CFC) R-22

1. Group 1: Stable, heavier than air, colorless, odorless, noncorrosive, nontoxic, nonflammable, and nonirritating under normal conditions
2. Boiling point at atmospheric pressure = –41° F
3. Freezing point at atmospheric pressure = –256° F
4. Critical temperature = 205° F
5. Critical pressure = 721.9 psia
6. Pressure at 86° F = 160 psig
7. Pressure at 5° F = 28.2 psig
8. High-side test pressure = 300 psig
9. Low-side test pressure = 150 psig
10. Leak may be detected with soap solution, halide torch, or electronic detector
11. Latent heat at 5° F = 93 btu/lb.
12. Miscible in oil
13. Used in reciprocating and centrifugal compressors
14. Disadvantage: Mixes well with water; ozone depletion factor (ODF) = .5

Methylene Chloride R-30

1. Group 1: Toxic and has a weak odor
2. Boiling point at atmospheric pressure = 105° F
3. Freezing point at atmospheric pressure = –142° F
4. Critical temperature = 480° F
5. Critical pressure = 882 psia
6. Gauge pressure at 5° F = 27.6 inches of Hg
7. Gauge pressure at 86° F = 9.5 inches of Hg
8. High-side test pressure = 30 psig
9. Low-side test pressure = 30 psig
10. Latent heat at 5° F = 162 btu/lb.
11. Miscible in oil
12. Used in centrifugal compressors

Methyl Chloride R-40

1. Group 2: Toxic, odorless, almost colorless, flammable, explosive, and irritating
2. Boiling point at atmospheric pressure = –10° F
3. Freezing point at atmospheric pressure = –144° F
4. Critical temperature = 290° F
5. Critical pressure = 968.7 psia
6. Pressure at 5° F = 6 psig
7. Pressure at 86° F = 80 psig
8. High-side test pressure = 210 psig
9. Low-side test pressure = 120 psig
10. Leaks may be detected with soap solution or halide torch
11. Latent heat at 5° F = 180 btu/lb.
12. Miscible in oil
13. Used in reciprocating and rotary compressors
14. Cannot be used in any system containing aluminum, magnesium, or zinc

Trichlorotrifluoroethane R-113

1. Group 1: Odorless
2. Boiling point at atmospheric pressure = 117.6° F
3. Freezing point = –31° F
4. Critical temperature = 417° F
5. Critical pressure = 489.9 psia
6. Gauge pressure at 5° F = 27.9 inches of Hg
7. Gauge pressure at 86° F = 13.9 inches of Hg
8. High-side test pressure = 30 psig
9. Low-side test pressure = 30 psig
10. Latent heat at 5° F = 70.6 btu/lb.
11. Miscible in oil
12. Used in centrifugal compressors
13. Operates at very low pressures and high gas volumes
14. Disadvantage: ozone depletion factor (ODF) = .8

Dichlorotetrafluoroethane R-114

1. Group 1: Odorless
2. Boiling point at atmospheric pressure = 38.4° F
3. Freezing point = –137° F
4. Critical temperature = 294° F
5. Critical pressure = 473 psia
6. Gauge pressure at 5° F = 16.1 inches of Hg
7. Pressure at 86° F = 22 psig
8. High-side test pressure = 50 psig
9. Low-side test pressure = 50 psig
10. Miscible in oil
11. Used in rotary compressors
12. Disadvantage: ozone depletion factor (ODF) = 1

R-500 Refrigerant (CFC)

1. Group 1: A nonflammable and nontoxic azeotropic mixture of R-12 and R-152a
2. Boiling point at atmospheric pressure = –28° F
3. Freezing point at atmospheric pressure = –254° F
4. Critical temperature = 221° F
5. Critical pressure = 641.9 psia
6. Pressure at 5° F = 16.4 psig
7. Pressure at 86° F = 113 psig
8. Leaks may be detected with soap solution, halide torch, electronic detector, or color tracing agent.
9. Latent heat at 5° F = 85 btu/lb.
10. Miscible in oil
11. Highly soluble in water
12. Used only in reciprocating compressors
13. Offers about 20 percent greater refrigerating capacity than R-12

R-502 Refrigerant (CFC)

1. Group 1: A stable, nontoxic, nonflammable, nonirritating, noncorrosive azeotropic mixture of R-22 and R-115
2. Boiling point at atmospheric pressure = –50° F
3. Critical pressure = 591 psia
4. Pressure at 5° F = 35.9 psig
5. Pressure at 86° F = 177 psig
6. Leaks may be detected by soap solution, halide torch, or electronic detector.
7. Latent heat at 5° F = 67.3 btu/lb.
8. Used only in reciprocating compressors

Ammonia (NH_3) R-717

1. Group 2: Flammable, toxic, irritating, pungent odor, lighter than air, and explosive when mixed with oil vapor or air in concentrations of 15 percent to 25 percent
2. Considered possible substitute for R-22 and R-502
3. Boiling point at atmospheric pressure = –28° F
4. Freezing point at atmospheric pressure = –107.9° F
5. Critical temperature = 271° F
6. Critical pressure = 1657 psia
7. High-side test pressure = 300 psig
8. Low-side test pressure = 150 psig
9. Latent heat of vaporization at 5° F = 565 btu/lb.
10. Leaks may be detected in several ways. Red or pink litmus paper turns blue; blue litmus paper does not change color; white litmus paper turns red. Nessler's solution in brine produces a rust-colored sediment. Sulphur stick or paper produces white smoke.
11. Ammonia may not be used in any system containing copper or its alloys, such as brass, muntz metal, admiralty brass, or bronze.
12. Not miscible in oil
13. High solubility in water
14. Used in reciprocating and absorption systems. In reciprocating systems, anhydrous ammonia is used; in absorption systems, aqua ammonia. The equation for refrigeration capacity is one-half pound of ammonia per minute equals one ton capacity.
15. Advantage: ozone depletion factor (ODF) = 0

Water R-718

1. Group 1: Odorless, nonflammable, nontoxic, and nonirritating
2. Boiling point = 212° F

3. Freezing point = 32° F
4. Critical temperature = 706° F
5. Gauge pressure at 86° F = 28.6 inches of Hg.
6. High-side test pressure = 0 lbs.
7. Low-side test pressure = 0 lbs.
8. Latent heat of vaporization = 970 btu/lb.
9. Not miscible in oil
10. Used in absorption systems, steam jet refrigeration, and pumps

Carbon Dioxide R-744

1. Group 1: Heavier than air. Concentration of 8% in the air is toxic.
2. Boiling point at atmospheric pressure = –109° F
3. Freezing point = –69.9° F
4. Critical temperature = 87.8° F
5. Critical pressure = 1070 psia
6. Operating head pressure from 1028 to 1500 psig
7. Pressure at 86° F = 1028 psig
8. Pressure at 5° F = 320 psig
9. High-side test pressure = 1500 psig
10. Low-side test pressure = 1000 psig
11. Latent heat at 5° F = 116 btu/lb.
12. Can be used as a fire extinguisher
13. Leaks may be detected by soap solution or brom thymol blue, which turns yellow in the presence of carbon dioxide.
14. Not miscible in oil
15. Used in reciprocating compressors

Sulphur Dioxide R-764

1. Group 2: Toxic and irritating
2. Boiling point at atmospheric pressure = 14° F
3. Freezing point at atmospheric pressure = –103.9° F
4. Critical temperature = 315° F
5. Critical pressure = 1143 psia
6. Pressure at 86° F = 51.8 psig
7. Gauge pressure at 5° F = 5.9 inches of Hg
8. High-side test pressure = 170 psig
9. Low-side test pressure = 85 psig
10. Latent heat at 5° F = 172.3 btu/lb.
11. Leaks may be detected by litmus paper and aqueous ammonia.
12. Not miscible in oil
13. Absorbs water, forming corrosive sulphurous acid
14. Used in reciprocating and rotary compressors

Ethane R-170

1. Group 3: Flammable and explosive
2. Boiling point at atmospheric pressure = –129°
3. Freezing point at atmospheric pressure = –297°
4. Critical temperature = 90° F
5. Critical pressure = 709.8 psia
6. Pressure at 86° F = 660 psig
7. Pressure at 5° F = 221 psig
8. High-side test pressure = 1200 psig
9. Low-side test pressure = 700 psig
10. Latent heat at 5° F = 150.5 btu/lb.

Propane R-290

1. Group 3: Flammable and explosive
2. Boiling point at atmospheric pressure = –43.7° F
3. Freezing point at atmospheric pressure = –305.8° F
4. Critical temperature = 202° F
5. Critical pressure = 617.4 psia
6. Pressure at 86° F = 140.5 psig
7. Pressure at 5° F = 27.2 psig
8. High-side test pressure = 300 psig
9. Low-side test pressure = 150 psig
10. Latent heat at 5° F = 170 btu/lb.
11. No longer used as a refrigerant

Butane R-600

1. Group 3: Flammable and explosive
2. Boiling point at atmospheric pressure = 31.3° F
3. Freezing point at atmospheric pressure = –211° F

4. Critical temperature = 306° F
5. Critical pressure = 550.7 psia
6. Pressure at 86° F = 26.9 psig
7. Gauge pressure at 5° F = 13.2 inches of Hg
8. High-side test pressure = 95 psig
9. Low-side test pressure = 50 psig

Ethylene R-1150

1. Group 3: Flammable and explosive
2. Boiling point at atmospheric pressure = –155° F
3. Freezing point at atmospheric pressure = –69.9° F
4. Critical temperature = 48.8° F
5. Critical pressure = 742.2 psia
6. Pressure at 86° F is above critical temperature
7. Pressure at 5° F = 400 psig
8. High-side test pressure = 1600 psig
9. Low-side test pressure = 1200 psig

ALTERNATIVES TO CHLOROFLUOROCARBONS

CFC Refrigerants

CFC is the abbreviation for a refrigerant containing chlorofluorocarbons. CFC refrigerants contain chlorine, fluorine, and carbon. They are known to reach the ozone layer and deplete it through a chemical reaction that replaces hydrogen atoms with chlorine or fluorine atoms.

HCFC And HFC Refrigerants

HCFC is the abbreviation for a refrigerant containing hydrochlorofluorocarbons. HCFC refrigerants contain hydrogen, chlorine, fluorine, and carbon. HFC is the abbreviation for hydrofluorocarbons, which contain hydrogen, fluorine, and carbon. All fluorocarbon-based refrigerants are heavier than air. They displace oxygen when confined in a space or engine room and can cause asphyxiation in humans. HCFCs and HFCs are CFC substitutes. It is believed that they harm the ozone layer less than CFCs.

New Refrigerants
Vapor Pressure/Temperature Chart

TEMP. ° F	HCFC 123	HCFC 124	HCFC 125	HCFC 34a
–100	29.9	29.2	24.4	27.8
–90	29.8	28.8	21.7	26.9
–80	29.7	28.2	18.1	25.6
–70	29.6	27.4	13.3	23.8
–60	29.5	26.3	7.1	21.5
–50	29.2	24.8	0.3	18.5
–40	28.9	22.8	4.9	14.7
–30	28.5	20.2	10.6	9.8
–20	27.8	16.9	17.4	3.8
–10	27.0	12.7	25.6	1.8
0	26.0	7.6	35.1	6.3
10	24.7	1.4	46.3	11.6
20	23.0	3.0	59.2	18.0
30	20.8	7.5	74.1	25.6
40	18.2	12.7	91.2	34.5
50	15.0	18.8	110.6	44.9
60	11.2	25.9	132.8	56.9
70	6.6	34.1	157.8	70.7
80	1.1	43.5	186.0	86.4
90	2.6	54.1	217.5	104.2
100	6.3	66.2	252.7	124.3
110	10.5	79.7	291.6	146.8
120	15.4	94.9	334.3	171.9
130	21.0	111.7	380.3	199.8
140	27.3	130.4	430.2	230.5
150	34.5	151.0	482.1	264.4
160	42.5	173.6	301.5	
170	51.5	198.4	342.0	
180	61.4	225.6	385.9	
190	72.5	255.1	433.6	
200	84.7	287.3	485.0	
210	98.1	322.1	540.3	
220	112.8	359.9		
230	128.9	400.6		
240	146.3	444.5		
250	165.3	491.8		
260	185.8			
270	207.9			
280	231.8			
290	257.5			
300	285.0			

Vapor pressure are shown in PSIG. Underline figures are shown as inches of Mercury vacuum.

* *Courtesy of DuPont SUVA Chemicals* *

Chemical Names & Formulars for SUVA Refrigerants

Registered Trademark	Chemical Name	Formular Point	Boiling
SUVA Centri-LP HCFC-123	ETHANE, 2,2-DICHLORO 1,1,1,TRIFLUORO	CHCL2CF3	82.2
SUVA Centri-LP HCFC-124	ETHANE, 2,CHLORO-1,1,1 2-TETRAFLUORO	CHCIFCF3	12.2
SUVA Freez-HP HFC-125	ETHANE, PENTAFLUORO	CHF2CF3	–56.3
SUVA Cold-MP HFC-134a	ETHANE, 1,1,1,2-TETRAFLUORO	CH2FCF3	–15.7

HOW THE OZONE LAYER PROTECTS THE EARTH

Approximately 20 to 30 miles above sea level is the ozone layer, part of the earth's stratosphere. Its height depends on latitude, season, and weather.

Ozone is formed in a chemical reaction that absorbs ultraviolet rays from the sun. The ozone layer shields the earth from much of the damage caused by ultraviolet rays.

Ozone molecules are destroyed by introducing chlorine-based refrigerants into the atmosphere. Ozone depletion allows ultraviolet rays to enter the earth's atmosphere and harm humans, animals, and plant life.

The most obvious way of reducing ozone depletion is to recover and recycle existing refrigerants. Whether we are manufacturers or users, whether we work in the commercial or private sector, we must conserve chlorine-based refrigerants, monitor their use, and find alternatives. Credit is due to companies such as DuPont and Allied for researching alternative refrigerants.

The following information is based on technical data that DuPont believes reliable. It provides an overview of HFC and HCFC applications. Since conditions of use are outside DuPont's control, no liability can be assumed for results obtained or damages incurred through the application of the data presented.

Dichlorotrifluoroethane HCFC-123

1. Substitute refrigerant for R-11 in centrifugal systems
2. Nonflammable, with low toxicity
3. Boiling point = 82° F
4. Estimated critical pressure = 523 psia
5. Vapor pressure at 77° F = 14 psia
6. Miscible in oil
7. Halocarbon global warming potential = 0.02
8. Molecular weight = 152.90
9. Heat of vaporization at boiling point = 73.3 btu/lb.
10. Ozone depletion factor (ODF) = .016
11. Disadvantage: An aggressive solvent for polymers and elastomers (seals that insure oil routing to the proper areas to maintain desired oil pressure). Alternate refrigerant oil required.

Refrigerant HCFC-124

1. Possible substitute for CFC-114 for medium temperature applications
2. Nonflammable
3. Boiling point = 12.2 F
4. Freezing point = –326° F
5. Critical temperature = 252° F
6. Estimated critical pressure = 514 psia
7. Vapor pressure at 77° F = 56 psia
8. Halocarbon global warming potential = 0.10
9. Molecular weight = 136.50
10. Heat of vaporization at boiling point = 83.2 btu/lb.
11. Ozone depletion factor (ODF) = .02

Refrigerant HFC-134A (Du Pont And Allied)

1. Substitute for R-12 and R-500 for centrifugal and reciprocating medium temperature applications. Developed for automotive air conditioning.
2. Nonflammable, with low toxicity
3. Boiling point = –15.08° F
4. Freezing point = –149.8° F
5. Latent heat at 40° F = 83.36 btu/lb.
6. Critical temperature = 214° F
7. Critical pressure = 589.8 psia
8. Vapor pressure at 77° F = 97 psia
9. Low miscibility. Current refrigerant oils cannot be used. Use polyalkaline glycol oil.

10. Ozone depletion factor (ODF) = 0
11. Halocarbon global warming potential = 0.26
12. Molecular weight = 102
13. Heat of vaporization at boiling point = 93.4 btu/lb.

Refrigerant HFC-152A

1. Possible substitute for R-12 for medium-temperature applications
2. Flammable and slightly toxic
3. Boiling point = –11.5° F
4. Freezing point = –178.6° F
5. Critical temperature = 236.3° F
6. Critical pressure 652 psia
7. Vapor pressure at 77° F = 87 psia
8. Low miscibility
9. Ozone depletion factor (ODF) = .02
10. Halocarbon global warming potential = 0.03
11. Molecular weight = 66
12. Heat of vaporization at boiling point = 141.5 btu/lb.

SAFETY IN HANDLING REFRIGERANTS

It has been said that safety is a state of mind. It is the attitude with which each individual approaches daily life, both at work and at home. In practicing safety, we are often our own worst enemies. Sometimes we overlook safety practices through ignorance, but more often we fail to practice what we know.

Safety Aids

Safety aids help keep a good safety record. Many potential tragedies have been avoided by wearing gloves, goggles, safety shoes, and proper clothing. Safety is also promoted by the right kind of tools, posted safety rules, and recognition of hazards. But the most important safety aid is mental attitude. As a student, apprentice, technician, or engineer, you must keep safety in mind during your day-to-day activities. Each job should be reviewed from the overall safety standpoint to see that all proper safeguards and procedures are being followed.

Freon Refrigerants

Freon is a trademarked name for fluorinated refrigerants, introduced by DuPont in 1931. Although the Freon refrigerant safety record is good, the hazards connected with using and handling them should be recognized.

Freon Refrigerants

Number	Year
12	1931
11	1932
114	1933
113	1934
22	1936
502	1961

The U.S. Department of Transportation regulates the shipment of explosives and other dangerous articles, including compressed gases. These regulations cover the metal that can be used for compressed gas cylinders, wall thickness, type of welding or other construction methods, and testing procedures.

Refrigerant cylinders should never be heated with an open flame or live steam. These cylinders are under pressure and should be treated with respect. The application of heat increases the pressure, possibly to dangerous levels. Pointing a torch at a cylinder concentrates heat in a small area, which can result in an explosion.

Cylinders designed for one-trip service (nonreturnable) are not built to the same standards as those designed to be returned and refilled. The 15-pound Dispos-A-Can™ type are service cylinders that are to be discarded when empty. Refilling risks an explosion.

Department of Transportation regulations require that cylinders never be heated above 125° F. To avoid hydrostatic pressure buildup, cylinders should not be liquid-full at 130° F. A maximum temperature of 125° F provides a small leeway below the 130° F on which regulations are based.

Safe-Handling Rules

Other rules recommended by the Compressed Gas Association for safe handling of cylinders include:

- **a.** Open valves slowly.
- **b.** Replace outlet caps when finished.
- **c.** Never force connections.
- **d.** Do not tamper with safety devices.
- **e.** Do not alter cylinders.
- **f.** Do not drop, dent, or abuse cylinders.
- **g.** Protect from rusting during storage.

These rules apply to both disposable and returnable cylinders.

Special Rules For Dispose-A-Can™ Containers

Attach hose connections carefully. Be sure threads are engaged properly so connections go on straight and the depresser is in the proper position to depress the plunger in the valve. The other end of the hose should be attached first, since refrigerant will start flowing as soon as the valve plunger is depressed. Loose connections can be made first to clear air from the hose; then tighten.

If a leak develops at one of the fittings while liquid refrigerant is flowing, do not try to tighten or remove the fitting with bare hands. Skin contact with liquid refrigerant can cause severe frostbite. Wear heavy leather gloves in this situation.

Pressure Relief

Refrigerant cylinders are protected against high pressure by a built-in relief device. This can be either a spring-loaded pressure relief valve or a rupture disc.

A **fusible metal plug** is used with some older cylinders, or for some special situations. The metal plug protects against overpressure from fire or another source of heat. It melts at about 160° F and vents the pressure.

Pressure relief devices protect against gradual increases of pressure from higher temperatures. They also protect against hydrostatic pressure that may develop if the container becomes full of liquid. But pressure relief devices **do not protect** against rapid pressure increases. This can happen if a cylinder is connected to a refrigeration system so that the compressor pumps directly into the cylinder. An enormous amount of pressure can develop quickly this way and cause considerable damage or injury.

Nitrogen Cylinders

Another hazard of overpressure is illustrated in the following drawing.

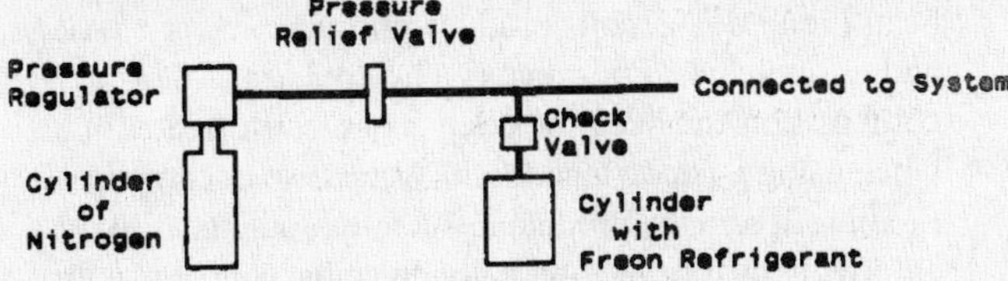

Fig. 8.1

Take special precautions when using nitrogen to purge lines. Nitrogen is shipped in cylinders at very high pressures, up to about 2200 psi. A pressure regulator should always be used with nitrogen. A **safety-relief valve** should be placed in the nitrogen line in case the reducing valve fails or is improperly adjusted. If nitrogen and refrigerant cylinders are connected to the same line, as they might be for leak-testing, another hazard exists. Refrigerant cylinders are designed for use up to 300 psi. It would be disastrous if the full nitrogen pressure were applied to the refrigerant cylinder. In addition to the other safeguards, place a check valve in the line from the refrigerant cylinder.

Liquid Density And Cylinder Volume

Liquid density differs for each refrigerant. Fluorinated refrigerants are heavier than water, while ammonia and methyl chloride are lighter. Refrigerant cylinders are filled by weight, and it is obvious that putting the same weight of different refrigerants in a cylinder gives different volumes. Thus, a given weight of one refrigerant might be safe and proper, while the same weight of another might cause dangerous overfilling.

Because Freon-12 is denser than Freon-22, more Freon-12 can be put in the same cylinder. For example, 60 pounds of R-12 can be put in a cylinder that holds 50 pounds of R-22.

Also remember that lubricating oil is light, about 80 percent as dense as water. A given weight has a larger volume. If a refrigerant is diluted with oil, it occupies a greater liquid volume than would pure refrigerant. In some cases, this leads to dangerous cylinder overfilling.

Cylinder Color Codes

The contents of any cylinder should be identified by the label, not the color. But over the years, certain colors have been associated with specific refrigerants.

Refrigerant	Color Code
R-11	Orange
R-12	White
R-22	Green
R-113	Purple
R-114	Blue
R-500	Yellow
R-502	Orchid

These colors are handy for identifying a refrigerant, but a cylinder should be used only after reading the label. Most refrigerant manufacturers use the same colors for the same refrigerants, although there is no standard code or official agreement on colors. In larger containers, such as tons or tank trucks, color is seldom used, except perhaps on the label. Reading the label to identify the contents is especially important with compressed gases such as nitrogen or oxygen, where the consequences of error can be extremely hazardous.

Fluorinated Refrigerants

One reason fluorinated products have largely replaced older refrigerants, such as sulfur dioxide, methyl chloride, and ammonia, is that they are nonflammable and low in toxicity. Most older refrigerants were flammable, explosive, or quite toxic. These properties greatly limited their use in refrigeration and air conditioning, especially in homes and public buildings.

Refrigerant Classifications

Refrigerants are classified by their properties. Those that are nontoxic, nonflammable, and nonirritating under normal conditions are in Group I; those that are somewhat flammable, toxic, or irritating are in Group II; and the hydrocarbons are in Group III. A hydrocarbon is a chemical compound containing hydrogen and carbon.

	Refrigerant number
Group I	
Trichloromonofluoromethane (CFC)	R-11
Dichlorodifluoromethane (CFC)	R-12
Tetrafluoromethane (CFC)	R-14
Dichloromonofluoromethane (CFC)	R-21
Monochlorodifluoromethane (CFC)	R-22
Trichlorotrifluoroethane (CFC)	R-113
Dichloroterafluoroethane (CFC)	R-114
Azeotropes (R-12 and R-152a) (CFC)	R-500
Azeotropes (R-22 and R-115) (CFC)	R-502
Carbon dioxide	R-744
Group II	
Methyl chloride	R-40
Ethyl chloride	R-160
Methyl formate	R-611
Sulphur dioxide (SO_2)	R-764
Ammonia (NH_3)	R-717
Dichloroethylene	R-1130
Group III	
Ethane	R-170
Propane	R-290
Butane	R-600
Isobutane	R-600a
Ethylene	R-1150

Chlorofluorocarbons (CFCs)

CFC chemicals are used in many refrigerants. In 1978, the United States became concerned that CFCs were depleting the atmosphere's ozone shield. The ozone layer around the earth protects us from the sun's ultraviolet light. If it is compromised, we can expect an increase in skin cancer, as well as harm to crops and marine life.

In 1978 the Environmental Protection Agency (EPA) banned CFCs in non-essential aerosols. The Montreal Protocol, signed in 1987, called for a halt to CFC production by the year 2000.

Effective January 1992, Chapter 294 of New York state law requires that no CFCs shall knowingly be vented into the atmosphere or otherwise be improperly disposed of during the repair or servicing of refrigeration systems. CFCs must be recycled to a uniform quality, such as that specified by the Air Conditioning and Refrigeration Institute's Standard 700 "Specification for Fluorocarbon Refrigerants."

In early 1992, scientists at the National Aeronautics and Space Administration reported that a satellite had detected exceptionally high levels of an ozone-killing chemical derived from CFCs over a wide area of the northern hemisphere. The chemical, **chlorine monoxide,** was noted in concentrations of one part per billion. The effect of chlorine monoxide in northern latitudes cannot be predicted with certainty.

Today the United States is urging the refrigeration industry to intensify efforts to conserve refrigerants now in use. Instead of venting used refrigerants into the atmosphere, the industry is encouraged to process and re-use it. Chemical companies, including DuPont, Allied-Signal, and the British firm ICI, are building plants to produce substitutes—the hydroclorofluorocarbons, or HCFCs, and the hydrofluorocarbons, or HFCs. These substitutes are believed to harm the ozone layer **less** than CFCs.

Effective July 1, 1992, the Clean Air Act prohibits the knowing release of CFCs or substitutes into the atmosphere. Further reduction in CFC production is scheduled to occur in 1993 and 1998 to phase out these ozone-depleting refrigerants. However, the problem has not been solved. Refrigerants that do not deplete the ozone layer are still under the development stage.

Refrigerant Decomposition

Fluorinated refrigerants are usually stabilized with organic compounds, but will decompose at high temperatures. Temperature limitations are different for each refrigerant and also depend on which other materials are present, such as metals, oils, or plastics. In the presence of heat, Freon refrigerants produce phosgene, a very toxic and unstable gas. Phosgene is a health hazard. This decomposition can occur near a gas or electric heater or when using an acetylene torch. Water also decomposes Freon refrigerants, producing such byproducts as hydrochloric, hydrofluoric, and halogen acids. Halogen acids are toxic and corrode metals. Hydrochloric acid attacks cotton clothing.

Warning: The presence of a strong, irritating odor signals that the refrigerant may have decomposed.

The vapors of fluorinated refrigerants are four to five times heavier than air. They tend to collect in low areas and high concentrations can build up. If a refrigerant is discharged in a confined unventilated area, high concentrations may cause suffocation. To reduce the hazard, provide good ventilation. Use an air mask when entering tanks or areas of high concentration.

Refrigerant Spills

Do not spill liquid refrigerant on the skin. Evaporation may cause freezing and frostbite. This warning applies particularly to the low-boiling refrigerants, such as R-12, R-22, and R-502. Use special care to avoid splashing liquid refrigerant in the eye, since freezing there can cause serious damage. The evaporation of higher-boiling refrigerants, such as R-11 and R-113, does not cause frostbite but may extract oils from the skin, drying and cracking it. Gloves, protective clothing, and goggles should be used whenever handling refrigerants.

Refrigerant Restrictions

Never use oxygen to purge lines or pressurize a system during leak testing. Oxygen is a dangerous gas that can spontaneously ignite in the presence of oil, grease, or plastic.

Ammonia should **not** be used with copper or brass. Methyl chloride should **not** be used with aluminum. Fluorinated refrigerants should **not** be used with magnesium or zinc unless completely anhydrous conditions can be maintained.

Ammonia Plant Fires

In case of fire in an ammonia plant, follow standard procedure. **Call the fire department first.** Push the remote stop button and shut down the plant as you exit. Proceed to control or extinguish the fire.

Regardless of the size of the fire—even if you just suspect fire—call the fire department immediately. Ammonia is highly explosive under certain conditions, as when mixed with the proper quantities of air or oil vapor. Never hesitate to notify the fire department.

It is standard procedure to call the fire department immediately whenever a fire is suspected in any refrigeration plant.

Ammonia First Aid

If liquid ammonia contacts the skin, strip the ammonia-saturated clothing from the body immediately Irrigate skin with water and then apply a saturated aqueous solution of **picric acid.**

If liquid ammonia contacts the eye, do not rub or irritate it. Irrigate the eye with clean water immediately. Next, irrigate the eye with a **2% boric acid** solution for 5 minutes. Lastly, allow two drops of **liquid petrolatum** to fall on the affected eyeball. The person suffering from an ammonia eye injury should be taken at once to an eye specialist.

For throat or nose irritation, sniff **boric acid solution** and rinse out the mouth thoroughly. A person with a throat or nose injury should be encouraged to drink large amounts of water.

Ammonia gas is lighter than air and therefore rises. Immediately move a person overcome by ammonia fumes to the open air, and get a physician. The patient should be kept warm and quiet. As an antidote, have the person drink one half gallon of equal parts of vinegar and olive oil. In case of an accident, keep an injured person as low as possible and place a wet sponge or cloth over the mouth and nostrils. Water will absorb the vapor and prevent it from being inhaled.

A first aid kit should contain **2% boric acid,** a saturated aqueous solution of **picric acid,** a seal package of absorbent cotton, **liquid petrolatum,** and a medicine dropper.

Brine

A brine is any liquid that can be cooled with refrigeration equipment and used to transfer heat. The brine flash point may not exceed 150° F.

Salt brine is used in indirect refrigeration systems with very cold coils. Salt is dissolved in fresh water to lower its freezing point.

Sodium chloride (common salt) brine or calcium chloride brine may be used. Calcium chloride brine has a lower freezing point than common salt brine (approximately –6° F) and is less corrosive. Due to these advantages, calcium chloride is used more widely, even though it is more expensive.

The freezing point of pure water is 32° F. Adding salt to water reduces the freezing point below 32° F. The stronger the brine solution is, the lower its freezing point. However, the brine should never be stronger than necessary, since the specific heat of brine falls as its saltiness increases. In other words, the more salt in the solution, the less heat it can hold.

At a certain point, adding more salt to water will **not** reduce the freezing point any further. This is called the **eutectic point.** In fact, if more salt is added, the freezing point will rise again.

A eutectic mixture, or eutectic brine, is a solution of 23 percent salt and 77 percent water, with a freezing point of about –6° F. If the salt percentage increases to 25 percent, the freezing point rises to 16° F above zero. In other words, by increasing the salt content of a eutectic brine by 2 percent, the freezing point rises about 22° F. Calcium brine is more commonly used for low-temperature work than common salt brine, because of its lower freezing point.

Brines	Specific gravity	Freezes at
Calcium chloride	1.29	–58° F
Sodium chloride	1.17	–6° F

A 25.5 percent solution of calcium chloride brine has a freezing point of –58° F. A 23 percent solution of sodium chloride (common salt) has a freezing point of –6° F.

The strength of a brine solution is measured by its density or specific gravity, which is the ratio of the weight of a given volume of brine to the weight of the same volume of water. The specific gravity of brine is measured with a hydrometer or salinometer, which is calibrated for different brine strengths.

Corrosion

Neutral brines are comparatively noncorrosive. However, contamination influences the brines' corrosivity. Air (oxygen) and carbon dioxide are contaminates. Whenever possible, prevent air or pollutants from mixing with the brine. **Sodium chromate** or **dichromate** is added to brine systems to inhibit corrosion. Periodic testing of the brine for inhibitor strength and pH is recommended. The pH for brines should be adjusted to an alkaline or pH between 7.0 and 8.5. Closed systems are the best types for avoiding contaminants.

Testing For Ammonia Leaks

water: Add a few drops of Nessler's solution to a sample of cooling water. If ammonia is present, the sample turns dark brown or rust-colored if the leak is large.

sodium chloride brine: Add Nessler's solution to a sample. If ammonia is present, the sample turns dark brown or rust-colored if the leak is large.

calcium chloride: Neutralize a sample by adding sodium carbonate. If ammonia is present, the sample turns yellow. If no ammonia is present, the sample turns white.

litmus paper: If ammonia is present, red or pink paper turns blue; blue paper does not change color; and white paper turns red.

REFRIGERANT LICENSE QUESTIONS

1. Undesirable refrigerant characteristics are

(A) nonflammable and nontoxic.
(B) high latent heat and low boiling point.
(C) high critical temperature and low freezing point.
(D) low critical temperature and high freezing point.

2. A desired chemical refrigerant characteristic is

(A) it mixes readily with oil.
(B) stability.
(C) it can easily change from a liquid to vapor and back.
(D) all of the above.

3. What refrigerant breaks down and forms phosgene in the presence of a carbon flame?

(A) R-718
(B) R-717
(C) R-764
(D) R-11

4. When heated, R-12 changes to

(A) hydrochloride.
(B) phosgene.
(C) carbon acid.
(D) chlorine gas.

5. Which choice would NOT help eliminate odors in vapors?

(A) Ozone lamps
(B) Charcoal fibers
(C) Water sprays
(D) Neutralization

6. Anhydrous ammonia is

(A) a mixture of ammonia and water.
(B) 29 percent aqua ammonia.
(C) ammonia without any water.
(D) none of the above.

7. Refrigerant is subcooled to

(A) increase the refrigeration effect.
(B) increase density.
(C) increase miscibility in oil.
(D) none of the above.

8. Aluminum CANNOT be used with

(A) R-12
(B) R-22
(C) R-718
(D) R-40

9. Any water in the refrigerant of a Freon system would cause a

(A) clogged oil trap.
(B) clogged scale trap.
(C) frozen discharge valve.
(D) frozen expansion valve.

10. Of the following refrigerants, which is the least flammable and the least toxic?

(A) Methyl chloride
(B) Ammonia
(C) Propane
(D) Freon-11

11. Calcium chloride freezes at

(A) –41° F.
(B) –32° F.
(C) 35° F.
(D) 20° F.

12. How do you know whether you have enough refrigerant charge in an ammonia system?

(A) By the head pressure
(B) By the suction pressure
(C) By the gauge glass on the receiver
(D) By the evaporator temperature

13. In a R-12 system with too much refrigerant, what will happen?

(A) High head pressure
(B) Low head pressure
(C) Low suction pressure
(D) Low motor current

14. Sodium chloride is NOT recommended for use in temperatures below

(A) 20° F.
(B) 5° F.
(C) 10° F.
(D) 0° F.

15. The instrument that measures the specific gravity of a brine is a(n)

(A) manometer.
(B) mercury barometer.
(C) anemometer.
(D) hydrometer.

16. The term toxicity means

(A) acidity or corrosiveness.
(B) poisonousness.
(C) diffusiveness.
(D) internal friction.

17. The term solubility means

(A) ability to mix with oil.
(B) ability of a refrigerant to mix with other substances.
(C) refrigerant weight per unit volume.
(D) the actual work done by the refrigerant in a system.

18. A calcium chloride brine with a specific gravity of 1.28 is used in an indirect low-side ammonia system. This brine will probably

(A) freeze when back pressure in the cooler is 20 psi gauge.
(B) freeze when back pressure in the cooler is 15 psi absolute.
(C) freeze when back pressure in the cooler is 15 psi gauge.
(D) not freeze when back pressure in the cooler stays above 0 psi gauge.

19. Of the following temperatures, which is the lowest recommended for use with calcium chloride brine?

(A) 0
(B) –35.7
(C) –41.8
(D) –61.2

20. When charging, the best way to determine the quantity of refrigerant is the system is to

(A) open the petcock on the liquid receiver.
(B) weigh the cylinder charge of refrigerant.
(C) feel the temperature change of the receiver shell.
(D) put a gas meter on the liquid line.

21. Which chemical derived from CFC depletes the ozone layer in the atmosphere?

(A) Carbon dioxide
(B) Chlorine monoxide
(C) Carbon monoxide
(D) Calcium chloride

22. Of the following thermal properties of a refrigerant, the undesirable ones are

(A) high viscosity and low pour point.
(B) high latent heat of evaporation.
(C) low critical and high freezing temperature.
(D) high viscosity and high film heat conductivity.

23. The main reason for purging a Freon centrifugal refrigerating system is to remove

(A) Freon.
(B) gaseous lubricating oil.
(C) water.
(D) noncondensable gases.

24. Refrigerant 744 belongs to

(A) Group 1.
(B) Group 2.
(C) Group 3.
(D) Group 4.

25. Which of the following refrigerants are in Group 1?

(A) R-12, R-22, and R-717
(B) R-11, R-502, and R-744
(C) R-12, R-40, and R-502
(D) R-11, R-13, and R-717

26. R-718 is

(A) methyl chloride.
(B) dichlorodifluoromethane.
(C) carbon dioxide.
(D) water.

27. Which of the following refrigerants are in Group 3?

(A) Ethyl chloride, ethane, and propane
(B) Methyl chloride, propane, and butane
(C) Butane, ethane, and propane
(D) Ethyl chloride, butane, and propane

28. Which refrigerant is most miscible in oil?

(A) R-113
(B) R-40
(C) R-718
(D) NH_3

29. Which of the following refrigerants are in Group 3?

(A) Propane, butane, ethylene, and isobutane
(B) Propane, butane, ethylene, and methyl chloride
(C) Ammonia, propane, ethylene, and isobutane
(D) Propane, butane, methyl formate, and isobutane

30. Which refrigerant is in Group 2?

(A) Methyl chloride
(B) Dichlorodifluoromethane (F-12)
(C) Isobutane
(D) Ethane

31. Refrigerant cylinders should never be heated to temperatures above

(A) 100° F.
(B) 125° F.
(C) 150° F.
(D) 170° F.

32. Containers should NOT be completely filled with liquid refrigerant because

(A) they would be too heavy to carry.
(B) if the temperature goes up, hydrostatic pressures could rupture the container.
(C) there wouldn't be any vapor present.
(D) moisture in the liquid can cause phosgene.

33. If the specific gravity of calcium brine increased from 1.29 to 1.30, the freezing point would

(A) not be affected.
(B) fluctuate up and down.
(C) drop.
(D) rise.

34. Sodium chloride cannot be used for a brine solution below

(A) –15° F.
(B) 15° F.
(C) 30° F.
(D) none of the above.

35. If a salt brine were too alkaline, you would

(A) add sodium hydroxide.
(B) dump it and make a new batch.
(C) add muriatic acid.
(D) add sulfuric acid.

36. The leaving water temperature of an efficiently operating induced-draft cooling tower is

(A) 85° F.
(B) between the dry- and wet-bulb temperatures.
(C) at the dew-point temperature.
(D) at the dry-bulb temperature.

37. If the specific gravity of a calcium brine is 0.9725,

(A) the brine needs more water.
(B) the brine needs more salt.
(C) it is pure water.
(D) This can never happen.

38. A brine solution to be used at –25° F may NOT contain

(A) calcium chloride.
(B) sodium chloride.
(C) ethylene glycol.
(D) alcohol.

39. The amount of chromate required to make 1,000 cubic feet of brine is

(A) 50 lbs.
(B) 75 lbs.
(C) 100 lbs.
(D) 200 lbs.

40. Brine should

(A) not be corrosive with zinc.
(B) be as close to neutral as possible.
(C) not be acidic with bronze.
(D) be neutralizable by CO_2 if acidic.

41. One characteristic of brine is

(A) it is not corrosive when treated with carbon dioxide.
(B) acid brine will not corrode zinc piping.
(C) alkaline brine will not corrode bronze piping.
(D) it should be neutral.

42. The freezing point of brine should be:

(A) 32° F.
(B) 0° F.
(C) 10 to 15° F below the lowest refrigerant saturation temperature.
(D) –59° F.

43. A compressor in a refrigerating system may lose oil if

(A) air is in the system.
(B) refrigerant velocity in the risers is too low.
(C) there are medium pressure drops in the evaporator.
(D) there are small load variations in the system.

44. The evaporator absorbs heat from air or brine because liquid refrigerant entering it

(A) has a lower temperature than the air or brine.
(B) has a higher temperature than the air or brine.
(C) boils to a low-pressure gas.
(D) boils to a high-pressure gas.

45. The refrigerant used in a stream jet system is

(A) R-22.
(B) methyl chloride.
(C) anhydrous ammonia.
(D) water.

46. The eutectic point of calcium chloride brine is:

(A) –59.8° F with a hydrometer reading of 1.29
(B) –59.8° F with a hydrometer reading of 1.17
(C) –6° F with a hydrometer reading of 1.29
(D) –6° F with a hydrometer reading of 1.17

47. The specific gravity of a brine with 10 pounds of calcium chloride per 100 pounds is about

(A) 0.84
(B) 0.92
(C) 1.00
(D) 1.29

48. A brine solution having a pH value of 10 is compared to a similar brine solution with a pH of 8; it is said to be
(A) 10 times as acidic.
(B) 10 times as alkaline.
(C) 100 times as alkaline.
(D) 100 times as acidic.

49. Cooling tower water should be maintained at a pH value near
(A) 4
(B) 6
(C) 7.8
(D) 10

50. Carbonate deposits from brine on ice cans can be controlled to a great extent by
(A) adding sodium dichromate to the brine.
(B) increasing the pH to 8 for a period of time.
(C) adding calcium chloride to the brine solution.
(D) decreasing the pH to slightly under 7 for a period of time.

51. For best corrosion control, the pH of a cooling tower should be kept at
(A) 6.0
(B) 8.0
(C) 1.0
(D) 14.0

52. A sample of water taken from a cooling tower is found to have a pH of 7.8. It can be said that it is
(A) slightly acid.
(B) slightly alkaline.
(C) neither acid or alkaline.
(D) highly alkaline.

53. The specific test for CO_2 in condenser water is brom thymol blue. If CO_2 is present, the test sample will turn
(A) green.
(B) purple.
(C) white.
(D) yellow.

54. A halide torch is used in a refrigeration plant to
(A) solder piping.
(B) light the equipment.
(C) test for ammonia leaks.
(D) test for Freon leaks.

55. The minimum testing time for pressure on a Freon system is
(A) 30 minutes.
(B) 1 hour.
(C) 2 hours.
(D) 3 hours.

56. The minimum field leak-test pressures for methyl chloride are
(A) 300 high side, 150 low side.
(B) 210 high side, 120 low side.
(C) 235 high side, 140 low side.
(D) 170 high side, 85 low side.

57. When a strong leak of Freon vapor is detected by an alcohol-fired leak detector, the color of the flame is
(A) green.
(B) blue.
(C) yellow.
(D) orange.

58. When testing a newly repaired refrigeration circuit for leaks, which substance should NOT be used to develop pressure in the circuit?
(A) Nitrogen
(B) Carbon dioxide
(C) Oxygen
(D) Refrigerant

59. When you find a leak in a Freon system, the leak-detector flame will
(A) triple in size.
(B) change color.
(C) extinguish itself.
(D) go out completely.

60. Which would be true of a leaking ammonia refrigerant cylinder?
(A) Frost around the hole
(B) A hissing sound
(C) A fog or mist in the vicinity
(D) None of the above

61. Calcium chloride brine is used in an ammonia compression system as the cooling medium for an ice field. A leak is discovered in the evaporator and the ammonia has mixed with the brine. After fixing the leak, you, as operating engineer, would
(A) test the brine with Nessler's solution.
(B) pump out the brine and run it through a condenser until all ammonia is gone.
(C) dump the brine and make a new batch.
(D) use a sulphur solution.

62. The purpose of the stuffing box seal is to
(A) make the unit start up easily after lying idle overnight.
(B) ensure air will not be drawn into the crankcase.
(C) lubricate the bearings with cup grease.
(D) prevent refrigerant from leaking out of the crankcase.

Refrigerant Characteristics Questions

TRUE or FALSE

63. It is difficult to find enthalpy data on most refrigerants. _______

64. R-22 can be practically poured from a bucket under normal room conditions. _______

65. The enthalpy of the saturated liquid less the enthalpy of the gas equals the latent heat. _______

66. Latent heat and refrigeration effect can be the same for a refrigerant. _______

67. Refrigerant entropy is used in engineering calculations. _______

68. Alcohol and water are miscible. _______

69. R-22 is always a miscible refrigerant. _______

70. From an odor standpoint, R-30 is a desirable refrigerant. _______

71. R-12 is not toxic; therefore, it is never dangerous. _______

72. R-22 will support combustion under certain conditions. _______

Fill in the blanks with the proper words.

73. Refrigerant properties can be classified as _______________ and _______________.

74. In a refrigeration cycle, the medium that picks up and carries heat is the _______________.

75. _______________ properties of a refrigerant deal with the movement of heat.

76. The CFM per ton of a refrigerant affects the _______________ and _______________ of the compressor.

77. A toxic refrigerant should have a _______________ odor.

78. A _______________ solution for leaks can be used with any refrigerants.

79. A halide flame will burn a _______________ color in the presence of halogenated hydrocarbons.

80. When moisture is present in a system, _______________ and _______________ normally occur.

81. When a moisture-saturated refrigerant is _______________, water is released.

82.

	Refrigerant number	Common name
(A)	R-30	_______________
(B)	R-718	_______________
(C)	R-764	_______________
(D)	R-717	_______________
(E)	R-40	_______________
(F)	R-12	_______________
(G)	R-22	_______________

83. Hydrochlorofluorocarbons may be classified as
(A) high ozone depletion potential.
(B) very low ozone depletion potential.
(C) high global warming potential.
(D) threshold limit valve refrigerant.

84. The chemicals that *deplete* the *ozone* layer are
(A) methane and ethylene.
(B) chlorine and bromine.
(C) dioxide and fluoride.
(D) ethylene and chloride.

85. Hydrochlorofluorocarbon are refrigerants containing
(A) carbon, hydrogen, fluorine, and chlorine.
(B) hydrogen, chlorine, methane, and carbon.
(C) ethane, methane, hydrogen, and carbon.
(D) hydrogen, oxygen, chlorine, and carbon.

86. What does CFC stand for?
(A) Halogenated Chlorofluorocarbons
(B) Chlorine, fluorine, hydrogen, carbon
(C) Partially halogenated
(D) Hydrofluorocarbons

87. What is Blend Fractionation?
(A) A refrigerant mixture having a constant maximum and minimum boiling points. Azeotrope
(B) A refrigerant mixture that does not combine chemically
(C) Where one of the refrigerants in a blend may leak at a faster rate than the other refrigerants in the same blend.
(D) When a blend will evaporate or condense at a range of temperature for a given pressure.

Answers to Refrigerant License Questions

1. **The correct answer is (D).**
2. **The correct answer is (B).**
3. **The correct answer is (D).**
4. **The correct answer is (B).**
5. **The correct answer is (D).**
6. **The correct answer is (C).**
7. **The correct answer is (A).**
8. **The correct answer is (D).**
9. **The correct answer is (D).**
10. **The correct answer is (D).**
11. **The correct answer is (A).**
12. **The correct answer is (C).**
13. **The correct answer is (A).**
14. **The correct answer is (D).**
15. **The correct answer is (D).**
16. **The correct answer is (B).**
17. **The correct answer is (B).**
18. **The correct answer is (D).**
19. **The correct answer is (C).**
20. **The correct answer is (B).**
21. **The correct answer is (B).**
22. **The correct answer is (C).**
23. **The correct answer is (D).**
24. **The correct answer is (A).**
25. **The correct answer is (B).**
26. **The correct answer is (D).**
27. **The correct answer is (C).**
28. **The correct answer is (A).**
29. **The correct answer is (A).**
30. **The correct answer is (A).**
31. **The correct answer is (B).**
32. **The correct answer is (B).**
33. **The correct answer is (D).**
34. **The correct answer is (D).** Sodium chloride cannot be used for a brine system below –6° F.
35. **The correct answer is (C).** You could also add hydrochloric acid.
36. **The correct answer is (B).**
37. **The correct answer is (D).** It cannot be a brine or a calcium brine with a reading of .97.
38. The correct answer is (B).
39. **The correct answer is (C).**
40. **The correct answer is (B).**
41. **The correct answer is (D).**
42. **The correct answer is (C).**
43. **The correct answer is (B).**
44. **The correct answer is (A).**
45. **The correct answer is (D).**
46. **The correct answer is (A).**
47. **The correct answer is (D).**
48. **The correct answer is (C).**
49. **The correct answer is (C).** The exam may not have 7.8 as an answer choice. Instead it may give another number, such as 8. The closest number to 7.8 is the correct answer.
50. **The correct answer is (D).** Making it slightly acidic would break up the carbonate deposit. Add sodium dichromate to lower the pH of acidic brine.
51. **The correct answer is (B).**
52. **The correct answer is (B).** The ideal ph of brine is 7.8.
53. **The correct answer is (D).** It will turn brownish-yellow.
54. **The correct answer is (D).**
55. **The correct answer is (A).**
56. **The correct answer is (B).**
57. **The correct answer is (A).**
58. **The correct answer is (C).**
59. **The correct answer is (B).**
60. **The correct answer is (B).**
61. **The correct answer is (C).**

62. **The correct answer is (D).**

63. **The correct answer is false.**

64. **The correct answer is false.**

65. **The correct answer is false.**

66. **The correct answer is true.**

67. **The correct answer is true.**

68. **The correct answer is true.**

69. **The correct answer is false.**

70. **The correct answer is true.**

71. **The correct answer is false.**

72. **The correct answer is false.**

73. **The correct answer is thermodynamic; physical.**

74. **The correct answer is refrigerant.**

75. **The correct answer is thermodynamic.**

76. **The correct answer is type; size.**

77. **The correct answer is irritating; pungent; bad.**

78. **The correct answer is soap.**

79. **The correct answer is green.**

80. **The correct answer is free water will freeze and corrosive acids will form.**

81. **The correct answer is cooled.**

82. **The correct answers are as follows:**

Refrigerant	Common Name
A. R-30:	Methylene Chloride
B. R-718:	Water
C. R-764:	Sulphur Dioxide
D. R-717:	Ammonia
E. R-40:	Methyl Chloride
F. R-12:	Dichlorodifluoromethane
G. R-22:	Chlorodifluoromethane

83. **The correct answer is (B).** Potential Ozone Depletion (POD) is expressed as a ratio classification of the ozone depletion rate for CFC refrigerants.

84. **The correct answer is (B).**

85. **The correct answer is (A).**

86. **The correct answer is (A).** Refrigerant classified CFC are members of the chlorofluorocarbon family. Each has chlorine, fluorine, and carbon as part of its structure. Chlorine-containing CFC refrigerants are a source by which the ozone layer is diminished, depleted, and destroyed. Example: CFC-22, which is the same as R-22.

87. **The correct answer is (C).**

Chapter 9

REFRIGERANT OILS

Refrigerant oils lubricate the internal parts of system components. They have low-temperature properties suitable to the application. The oils form a friction-reducing film between rubbing surfaces and seal critical clearances. Note: 10 percent of oil normally travels through the system.

GENERAL CLASSIFICATION OF MINERAL OILS

paraffin base: a petroleum lubricating oil fraction in which straight or branched chain hydrocarbon structures predominate. Paraffin oils undergo a waxy-type pour brought about by a crystalline structure of wax particles.

naphthene base: a petroleum lubricating oil fraction in which naphthenic ring-type hydrocarbon structures predominate. Experience has shown that the naphthene-base oils are better suited for refrigeration work because they flow better and deposit less wax at low temperatures. Carbon deposits from these oils are "soft" and can be easily removed.

mixed base: a mixture of the above two bases. Properly refined and treated paraffin, naphthene, and mixed-base mineral oils can be used in refrigeration.

OIL CHARACTERISTICS

viscosity: the coefficient of internal friction. Viscosity is of prime importance in selecting oil for compressors. Excessive viscosity leads to increased power consumption. Too low a viscosity can result in gas leakage past critical clearances and increased component wear due to a lack of lubricant film.

floc point: the temperature at which wax first separates from oil. Wax can clog the evaporator and metering device. Low floc point or wax-free oils are generally required for refrigeration.

dry and moisture free: Water and oil do not mix. Moisture can cause sludging of lubricants and clog refrigerant flow due to ice forming on the low side.

noncorrosive/low neutralization: Corrosion occurs when a combination of water, air, oil, and heat causes acid and sludge. Oil should have low acid content. A low neutralization number indicates very little acid in the oil—a desired characteristic of refrigerant oils.

carbonization: the decomposition of oil by hot surfaces in the refrigeration system. The remaining carbon is hard and adhesive in paraffin-base oils, forming sludge with all its resultant problems. Naphthene-base oils form a light, fluffy carbon that, though a contaminant, is not as damaging as hard carbon. However, neither type of carbon residue is desirable, as there is some indication of a relationship between oil breakdown carbonization, and copper plating. A good oil should not carbonize when it contacts hot surfaces during normal operation.

pour point: the lowest temperature at which an oil will flow under prescribed conditions. A refrigerant oil should have a low pour point—the lower, the better. According to the ASTM D97-85 test method for pour point of petroleum oil, pressure, diluents, and container size and shape will affect minimum flow temperatures. In general, naphthenic oils have a viscous pour, while paraffinic oils have a waxy pour due to the crystalline structure of wax particles.

flash point: the temperature at which an oil vapor will flash when exposed to a flame. A refrigerant oil has a high flash point., preferably over 300° F.

miscibility: the ability of oil to mix with refrigerants.

dielectric strength: a measure of resistance to the passage of electric current. It is measured in KV (thousandths of a volt). The dielectric of a good refrigerant oil is normally 25 KV.

fire point: the temperature at which an oil will continue to burn.

color: the appearance of an oil when viewed by transmitted light. Oil color is compared to a numbered series of color standards ranging from pale to very dark red. The color that best matches the oil is the oil's number. Color is useful in identifying oils and can reflect the degree of processing. Light colors usually indicate more severe processing, which removes color bodies (ASTM D1500-82).

phase separation: the separation of oil at low temperatures. Oil should resist separation at low temperatures. At very low temperatures it will separate and float on top of refrigerant (CO_2). Some miscible refrigerants (R-22) separate from oil at certain conditions.

The compressor manufacturer recommends the oil to be used in a refrigeration system. Most refrigerant oils are naphthene base.

CHARACTERISTICS OF IDEAL REFRIGERANT OIL

1. Lubricates at high temperatures and flows at low temperature.
2. Has a low enough pour point to allow it to flow anywhere in the system.
3. Does not carbonize when touching hot surfaces in the system during normal operations.
4. Does not deposit wax when exposed to the lowest temperatures normally found in the system.
5. Contains little or no corrosive acid.
6. Has high resistance to the flow of electricity.
7. Has a high flash and fire point to indicate proper blending.
8. Is stable in the presence of oxygen.
9. Contains no sulphur compound. Sulphur alone is a deadly enemy of the refrigeration system. In the presence of moisture, it forms sulphurous acid, one of the most corrosive compounds in existence. Refrigerant oils should never contain any sulphur.
10. Does not separate from miscible refrigerants at normal operating temperatures.
11. Does not contain moisture.
12. Is light in color, indicating proper refining.

In general, there is no "best" oil. The manufacturer recommends the oil that is most suitable for each compressor under rated conditions.

REFRIGERANT OIL LICENSE QUESTIONS

1. A desirable property of ammonia refrigerant oil is

(A) high paraffin content.
(B) being free of water.
(C) very low flash point.
(D) all of the above.

2. The solubility of refrigerant oil is lowest in

(A) CO_2.
(B) R-22.
(C) NH_3.
(D) R-12.

3. How would you determine whether oil is present in other parts of the system?

(A) By using carbon paper at the receiver
(B) By measuring oil in the compressor
(C) By discharging entire system and weighing the oil
(D) By using a halide leak detector

4. An oil system in an R-11 centrifugal system must have

(A) oil separator, reservoir, and distributor lines.
(B) reservoir, pump, and pump motor.
(C) pump, pump motor, and centrifuge.
(D) reservoir, pump, and distributor lines.

5. What percentage of oil travels with the refrigerant?

(A) 10 percent
(B) 20 percent
(C) 25 percent
(D) 33 percent

6. Which refrigerant separates from oil in the evaporator?

(A) R-12
(B) R-764
(C) R-717
(D) R-22

7. What causes oil to foam in the compressor crankcase?

(A) Pressure change
(B) Load change
(C) Temperature change
(D) All of the above

8. Which substance separates from the lubricating oil in an operating evaporator, leaving the oil floating on top of the liquid refrigerant?

(A) Ammonia
(B) CO_2
(C) Sulphur dioxide
(D) Freon-12

9. Oil foaming in the compressor indicates

(A) high flash point of oil.
(B) low pour point of oil.
(C) low oil acidity.
(D) high solubility of refrigerant in oil.

10. Carron oil, used for burns, is a mixture of

(A) lanolin and vinegar.
(B) sulphur dioxide and water.
(C) linseed oil and lime water.
(D) vaseline and picric acid.

11. In a Freon-12 compressor with a splash scoop lubrication system, what causes the oil to foam?

(A) Sudden drop in crankcase pressure
(B) Shortage of refrigerant
(C) Not enough oil in the crankcase
(D) Overcharge of refrigerant

12. Carron oil is generally recommended for use in first aid of ammonia burns. It is made of equal parts of linseed oil and

(A) lanolin.
(B) nitric acid.
(C) vaseline.
(D) lime water.

13. Refrigerating oils in an ammonia plant should

(A) not have a low pour point.
(B) not have a high pour point.
(C) not have high viscosity.
(D) be free of moisture.

14. Freon-12 is most like methyl chloride because

(A) the chemical composition is similar.
(B) the cost is approximately the same.
(C) the vapor densities are the same.
(D) both are miscible in oil.

15. In an ammonia compression system, the evaporator becomes oil-logged. The result is

(A) low suction pressure.
(B) loss of refrigerant.
(C) increase in suction pressure.
(D) increase in discharge pressure.

16. As the temperature of an oil decreases,

(A) the oil's viscosity increases.
(B) the oil's viscosity decreases.
(C) the hydrocarbons will darken the oil.
(D) wax deposits are unlikely to occur.

17. A most desirable quality of Freon refrigerants is

(A) complete miscibility in mineral lube oil.
(B) good surface-wetting characteristics.
(C) relatively higher coefficient of performance than R-717.
(D) they don't break down when exposed to gas flame in a temperature range of 1100 to 1300° F.

18. Which approximates the definition of flash point for refrigerant oils?

(A) The temperature at which an oil vapor will ignite when exposed to flame
(B) The temperature at which an oil will continue to burn
(C) The temperature of a good refrigerant oil that can operate over 300° F
(D) The temperature at which oil resists separation

19. What is the purpose of oil in a refrigeration system?

(A) To cool the refrigerant
(B) To reduce wear and friction
(C) To seal the system at packings
(D) To eliminate flash gas

20. Of the following properties of refrigerant system lubricating oil, the one that is a chemical property of the oil is

(A) refrigerant resistance.
(B) volatility.
(C) solubility of water in oil.
(D) wax separation.

21. Which of the following statements is most correct about the lubrication of a centrifugal compressor (without regard for the drive) ?

(A) The only parts requiring lubrication are the rotor bearings and the thrust bearing.
(B) No auxiliary oil pump is used.
(C) Leakage of refrigerant to the oiling system is common.
(D) Auxiliary oil pumps are manually operated.

22. Where should the oil trap be installed on a refrigeration system?

(A) In the liquid line as far from the compressor as possible
(B) In the suction line after the accumulator
(C) In the suction line as far from the compressor as possible
(D) In the discharge line as far from the compressor as possible

23. Oil in a refrigeration system should

(A) have a high pour point.
(B) have high viscosity.
(C) have a low flash point.
(D) not contain moisture.

24. Indiscriminate use of paraffin-base oil will most seriously affect the

(A) compressor.
(B) condenser.
(C) evaporator.
(D) liquid receiver.

25. To add oil to an R-12 reciprocating compressor that has been shut down for this purpose, the oil is

(A) pumped into the service valve in the high-pressure liquid line.
(B) pumped into the service valve on the compressor crankcase.
(C) sucked into the service valve on the suction side of the compressor.
(D) pumped into the service valve on the discharge side of the compressor.

26. Of the many ways to lubricate a Freon-12 compressor, which of the following is NOT used?

(A) Splash
(B) Pump
(C) Chain and loop
(D) Drop cup

27. A circulating oil system in a centrifugal compressor system must have at least

(A) a reservoir, a filter, and distribution lines.
(B) a reservoir, a pump, and distribution lines.
(C) a heater, a filter, and distribution lines.
(D) a filter, a centrifuge, and a reservoir.

28. Which of the following is incorrect?

(A) Refrigerant oils have a low flash point and fire point.
(B) Refrigerant oils should have a high resistance to the flow of electricity.
(C) Refrigerant oils should have a pour point low enough to flow at low temperatures.
(D) Refrigerant oils should not contain sulphur components.

29. A refrigerant oil is electronically tested to have a low neutralization number. A low neutralization number indicates

(A) an unstable oil with corrosive acids present.
(B) a stable oil with few corrosive acids present.
(C) undesirable refrigerant oil.
(D) uncertain composition of organic acids.

30. The flash point of refrigerant oil is

(A) the temperature at which oil vapor will flash when exposed to a flame.
(B) the temperature at which oil will continue to burn.
(C) the temperature in which an oil will burn below 100°.
(D) all of the above.

31. The fire point of a refrigerant oil is the temperature at which

(A) oil vapor will flash when exposed to a flame.
(B) oil will continue to burn.
(C) oil will burn below 100°.
(D) wax first separates from the oil.

32. Viscosity is

(A) a coefficient of internal friction.
(B) a coefficient of external friction.
(C) the temperature at which wax first separates from the oil.
(D) none of the above.

33. Floc point is the temperature at which

(A) oil vapor will flash when exposed to a flame.
(B) wax first is noticed separating from the oil.
(C) oil is carbonized when it contacts hot surfaces.
(D) oil ceases to flow.

34. Pour point is the

(A) temperature at which oil vapor will flash when exposed to a flame.
(B) lowest temperature that oil will flow.
(C) temperature at which oil should resist separation.
(D) temperature at which an oil will continue to burn.

35. The dielectric property of an oil is

(A) the amount of moisture in a refrigerant oil, which may be measured by its resistance to the flow of electric current.
(B) compounds in the oil that can absorb or release heat with little or no change in temperature.
(C) the highest temperature at which free water is liberated, on the cooling of the oil.
(D) the temperature at which an oil will continue to burn.

36. Which of the following is true?

(A) Ammonia does not mix with oil, and floats on top of oil.
(B) Carbon dioxide will not mix with oil, and will float on top of oil.
(C) Oil floats on top of sulphur dioxide, and the two do not mix.
(D) All of the above

Answers to Refrigerant Oil License Questions

1. **The correct answer is (B).**
2. **The correct answer is (A).**
3. **The correct answer is (A).**
4. **The correct answer is (D).**
5. **The correct answer is (A).**
6. **The correct answer is (D).**
7. **The correct answer is (A).**
8. **The correct answer is (B).**
9. **The correct answer is (D).**
10. **The correct answer is (C).**
11. **The correct answer is (A).**
12. **The correct answer is (D).**
13. **The correct answer is (D).**
14. **The correct answer is (C).**
15. **The correct answer is (A).**
16. **The correct answer is (A).**
17. **The correct answer is (A).**
18. **The correct answer is (A).**
19. **The correct answer is (B).**
20. **The correct answer is (B).**
21. **The correct answer is (C).**
22. **The correct answer is (D).**
23. **The correct answer is (D).**
24. **The correct answer is (C).**
25. **The correct answer is (B).**
26. **The correct answer is (D).**
27. **The correct answer is (B).**
28. **The correct answer is (A).**
29. **The correct answer is (B).**
30. **The correct answer is (A).**
31. **The correct answer is (B).**
32. **The correct answer is (A).**
33. **The correct answer is (B).**
34. **The correct answer is (B).**
35. **The correct answer is (A).** A good refrigerant oil will normally run 25 KB dielectric strength. More than 25 KB suggests impurities in the oil. Dielectric readings measure oil impurities. An oil free of foreign matter has a high resistance to current; an oil with impurities has a low resistance to current.
36. **The correct answer is (D).**

Chapter 10

OPERATING PRESSURES AND TEMPERATURES

In refrigeration and air conditioning, the operating engineer must maintain system pressures and temperatures. This chapter consists of pressure/temperature exercises designed to help you in the written and practical examinations.

The chapter explains the relationship of pressure and temperature in a refrigeration system. It briefly discusses dry-bulb temperature, wet-bulb temperature, psychrometric properties of air, the psychrometric chart, and superheat conversions. In the section on the refrigerant vapor pressure chart, you will learn to find the pressure of a refrigerant from its temperature. A series of pressure conversion exercises drill you for the written exam. It is important that you learn how to calculate the pressure conversions problems and not memorize the questions and answers.

Finally, a practical review describes operating pressures and temperatures for the high and low side of the ACME and Carrier 17M refrigeration machines.

DRY-BULB TEMPERATURE

Human comfort and health depend a great deal on air temperature. In air conditioning, dry-bulb temperature is the temperature measured by an ordinary thermometer.

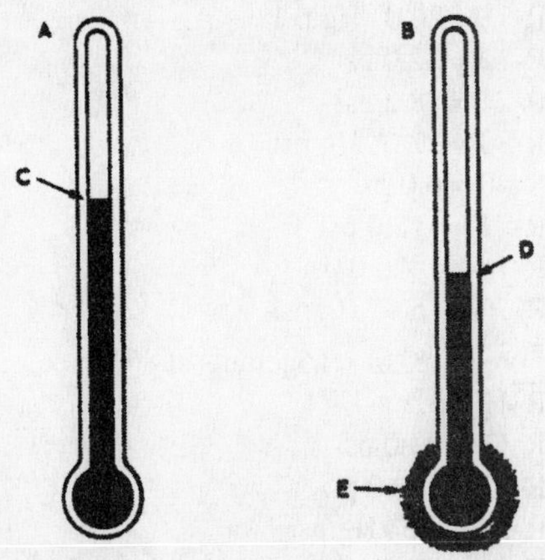

Dry bulb and wet bulb thermometers. A—Dry bulb thermometer. B—Wet bulb thermometer. C—Dry bulb temperature. D—Wet bulb temperature. E—Wick surrounding wet bulb. Note that the temperature shown on the wet bulb thermometer is considerably lower than the dry bulb thermometer.

Fig. 10.1

WET-BULB TEMPERATURE

If a moist wick is placed over a thermometer bulb, the evaporation of water from the wick will lower the thermometer reading. This is the wet-bulb temperature. If the air surrounding a wet-bulb thermometer is dry, evaporation will be faster than if the air is moist. The drawing below compares dry-bulb and wet-bulb temperatures taken at the same place and time.

When the air is saturated with moisture, no water will evaporate from the wick, and the temperature on the wet-bulb thermometer will equal the dry-bulb thermometer reading. However, if the air is not saturated, water will evaporate and lower the wick temperature. Heat will flow from the mercury to the wet wick and the reading will fall. The accuracy of the reading depends on how fast air passes over the wick.

PSYCHROMETRIC PROPERTIES OF AIR

Psychrometrics is the science and practice of air mixtures and control, especially with mixes of dry air and water vapor.

Psychrometry deals with the specific heat of dry air and its volume. It also deals with the heat of water, the heat of vaporization or condensation, and the specific heat of steam in reference to moisture mixed with dry air.

Psychrometric tables show the pressure, temperature, heat content (enthalpy), moisture content, and volume of air. The tables are based on one pound water of dry air, plus the water vapor to produce the air conditions being studied. A pressure of 29.92″ Hg of mercury is the standard atmospheric pressure.

PSYCHROMETRIC CHART

On the psychrometric chart, the horizontal scale reads temperature, while the vertical side reads water vapor pressure. A psychrometric chart is shown in Figure 10.2. To use it, remember that the warmer the air, the more moisture it will hold. Also, as pressure is reduced, air absorbs more moisture.

To determine the amount of moisture in a pound of air at 67° F, locate the temperature at the bottom of the chart. Then move upward to the saturation curve. This indicates that, at this temperature, a pound of air will hold approximately .014 pound of water.

Most people are comfortable in a relative humidity between 30 and 70 percent, and temperatures between 70 and 85° F. Locate these points on the psychrometric chart; they all fall within the area outlined.

PRESSURE/TEMPERATURE OUTLINE

atmospheric pressure: the weight of a column of air at sea level, equal to 14.7 pounds per square inch. It will lift a column of mercury 30 inches. Atmospheric pressure is commonly rounded to 15 pounds.

psig (pounds per square inch, gauge): a zero gauge reading at atmospheric pressure. The gauge registers pounds above atmospheric pressure and inches of mercury vacuum below atmospheric pressure.

psia (pounds per square inch, absolute): a gauge reading of 14.7 pounds at atmospheric pressure, and zero at 30 inches of mercury vacuum. These readings are known as absolute pressure readings.

relative humidity: the ratio of the weight of water vapor in an air sample to the weight of water vapor that the same air sample contains when saturated. Note that if an air sample is fully saturated, its relative humidity is 100 percent. You can determine relative humidity if you know the dew point and dry-bulb temperatures.

dew point: the temperature at which air begins to condense.

boiling temperature: a measurement determined by pressure on the liquid. Any liquid may be boiled at almost any temperature. If a liquid that boils at 30° F is placed in a room heated to 70° F, the liquid will evaporate (boil). The resulting vapor will carry off heat, cooling the liquid.

Water may be boiled at almost any temperature above 32° F. At atmospheric pressure, water boils at 212° F. If water is placed in a pressurized vessel, the boiling temperature may rise to 300° F, 500° F, or even higher. If a vacuum pump or a compressor suction is placed on the vessel, the water may boil at 100° F, 50° F, or as low as 32° F, depending on the amount of vacuum. Therefore, any change in pressure will affect boiling temperature. An increase in pressure raises boiling temperature, and a decrease in pressure lowers it.

The following refrigerant pressures and boiling temperatures show the effect of a change in pressure on evaporating temperatures.

Refrigerant	Pressure	Boiling temperature
R-12	0 # psig	–21 Degrees F
R-12	32 # psig	+35 Degrees F
R-717	0 # psig	–28 Degrees F
R-717	15 # psig	–0 Degrees F
R-744	0 # psig	–109 Degrees F
R-744	320 # psig	–5 Degrees F

Refrigerants are liquids that pick up heat by evaporating at a low temperature and low pressure, and give up heat by condensing or liquefying at a high temperature and high pressure. The latent heat of vaporization of the refrigerant produces the cooling, due to the change in state from liquid to gas, and from gas back to liquid. Heat is transmitted from the material to be cooled to the liquid refrigerant, vaporizes the liquid, and then is carried away by the vapor.

REFRIGERANT PRESSURE/ TEMPERATURE EQUIVALENTS

1. Suction pressures of refrigerants at 5° F. These pressures often appear in exam questions.
   a. R-11 = 24.0″ Hg psi
   b. R-12 = 12.0 psi
   c. R-22 = 28.2 psi
   d. R-30 = 27.6″ Hg psi
   e. R-40 = 6.0 psi
   f. R-717 = 12.0 psi
   g. R-744 = 320.0 psi
   h. R-764 = 5.9″ Hg psi
2. Head pressures of refrigerants at 86° F:
   a. R-11 = 3.5 psi
   b. R-12 = 93.0 psi
   c. R-22 = 160.0 psi
   d. R-30 = 9.5″ Hg psi
   e. R-40 = 80.0 psi
   f. R-717 = 92.0 psi
   g. R-744 = 1028.0 psi
   h. R-764 = 51.8 psi

3. Low/high test pressures of refrigerants in psi:
   a. R-11:30/30
   b. R-12: 140/235
   c. R-22: 150/300
   d. R-30: 30/30
   e. R-40: 120/210
   f. R-717: 150/300
   g. R-744: 1000/1500
   h. R-764: 85/170
4. Boiling points of refrigerants:
   a. R-11 = +74° F
   b. R-12 = –21° F
   c. R-22 = –41° F
   d. R-30 = +105° F
   e. R-40 = –10° F
   f. R-717 = –28° F
   g. R-744 = –109° F
   h. R-764 = +14° F

Examiners may ask a variety of questions based on the above data:

1. Which refrigerant has the highest boiling point?
2. Which refrigerants have the same low-side test pressure of 30 lbs.?
3. Excluding carbon dioxide, which refrigerant has the highest high-side test pressure?
4. Which refrigerants have the same high-side test pressure of 300 lbs.?

SUPERHEAT

Superheat is the temperature of a refrigerant vapor above its boiling point. Each degree above the boiling point temperature is a degree of superheat. (The TXV is often called the superheat valve.)

To measure superheat, measure suction pressure and determine the saturation temperature. Refer to the pressure-temperature chart below for the refrigerant. Then, measure the suction-line temperature at the evaporator outlet. Subtract the saturation temperature from the suction-line temperature. The result is superheat.

Suction-line temperature is relatively easy to measure. Just clamp a thermometer to the suction line at the TXV bulb location.

To get suction-line pressure, connect a pressure gauge to the external equalizer line. Suction-line pressure can also be taken at the suction service valve on the compressor.

Suction pressure readings at the compressor should be corrected upward of about 2 psi to account for pressure drop in the suction line between the evaporator and compressor.

Pressure-temperature chart

Temperature (Fahrenheit)	R-12 psig	R-22 psig	R-502 psig
0	9.2	24.0	31.2
2	10.2	25.6	33.1
4	11.2	27.3	35.0
6	12.3	29.1	37.0
8	13.5	30.9	39.0
10	14.6	32.8	41.1
12	15.8	34.7	43.2
14	17.1	36.7	45.5
16	18.4	38.7	47.7
18	19.7	40.9	50.1
20	21.0	43.0	52.5
22	22.4	45.3	54.9
24	23.9	47.6	57.4
26	25.4	49.0	60.0
28	26.9	52.4	62.7
30	28.5	54.9	65.4

TXV SUPERHEAT CALCULATIONS

When calculating these sample problems, keep in mind that saturation temperature is listed in the pressure-temperature chart under Fahrenheit.

1. Given R-12, suction pressure of 27 psig at the equalizer, and suction-line temperature of 30° F, use the pressure-temperature chart to find the saturation temperature.

   27 psig on chart = 26.9 psig = 28° saturation temperature
2. Given R-12, suction pressure of 21 psig, and suction-line temperature of 28° F, find the superheat.
   a. Find the saturation temperature at 21 psig. It is 20° F.
   b. Subtract the saturation temperature from the suction-line temperature:
      28 – 20 = 8° superheat
3. Given R-22, suction-line temperature of 38° F, and superheat temperature of 8° F, find the suction pressure.
   a. Subtract the superheat temperature from the suction-line temperature to get the saturation temperature: 38° F – 8° F = 30° F.

b. Use the pressure-temperature chart to find suction pressure: 30° F = 54.9 psig.
c. Round up 54.9 to 55 psig suction pressure.

4. Given R-502, determine the suction-line temperature if the superheat is 10° F and the saturation pressure is 50 psia.
a. Convert 50 psia to psig: 50 psia – 15 = 35 psig.
b. Find the saturation temperature on the pressure-temperature chart: 35 psig = 4° F.
c. Add superheat and saturation temperature to find the suction-line temperature:

10° F	superheat
+ 4° F	saturation temperature
14°	suction - line temperature

5. Given R-22, an evaporator outlet temperature of 39° F, and suction pressure of 55 psig, find the superheat.
a. Convert 55 psig to saturation temperature: 55 psig = 30° F saturation temperature.
b. Subtract saturation temperature from evaporator outlet suction temperature.

39° F evaporator outlet temperature
−30° F saturation temperature
9° F superheat

PRESSURE

Pressure is the force per unit area measured as:

a. psia: pounds per square inch absolute, measured on the absolute scale. The zero point is at zero absolute pressure.
b. psig: pounds per square inch gauge, measured on the gauge scale. The zero point is 14.7 psia, or atmospheric pressure.

The mercury absolute scale is similar to the barometer. At 70° F, sea level pressure is 29.92 inches of mercury.

Pressure Scales

psig	psia	Hg absolute
4	19 lbs. psia	
3	18	
2	17	
1	16	
0	15	30″ Hg absolute
1″ Hg gauge	14.5	29
2	14	28
3	13.5	27
4	13	26
5	12.5	25
6	12	24
7	11.5	23
8	11	22
9	10.5	21
10	10	20
11	9.5	19
12	9	18
13	8.5	17
14	8	16
15	7.5	15
16	7	14
17	6.5	13
18	6	12
19	5.5	11
20	5	10
21	4.5	9
22	4	8
23	3.5	7
24	3	6
25	2.5	5
26	2	4
27	1.5	3
28	1	2
29	.5	1
30″ Hg gauge	0 pounds psia	0″ Hg absolute

Conversions

The following problems will deal with conversions between psig and psia. Absolute pressure conversions are given from inches mercury absolute to absolute psi. These exercises are designed to give you confidence in pressure problem-solving. It is very important to learn to solve these problems and not memorize them. The above chart can be used to check your answers.

1. What is the equivalent of 25 inches of mercury vacuum in psia? (Note: Hg = mercury.)

$$\text{PSIA} = \frac{\text{30 minus Hg}}{2} = \frac{\text{30 minus 25}}{2} = \frac{5}{2} = 2.5 \text{ psia}$$

2. If the pressure gauge reads 15 inches, what would be the absolute pressure in pounds psi ?

Solution: 15 + 2 = 7.5 psia

3. Convert 15 psig to inches of mercury absolute.

   15 lbs.

   −30

   15 inches Hg absolute

4. Convert 35 psia to psig:

   35 lbs.

   −15

   20 lbs. psig

5. Convert 8 lbs. psia to psig:

   8 lbs.

   −15

   $-7 \times 2 = 14''$ Hg (gauge) psig

   Note: The negative number was multiplied by 2, and the solution was positive.

6. Convert 17″ Hg psia to psig:

   17

   −30

   13 divided by 2 = 6.5 psia

7. A gauge reading of 9 inches vacuum is close to what absolute pressure? Given 9″ psig, find psia.

   $$\frac{30 \text{ minus Hg}}{2} = \frac{30 \text{ minus } 9'' \text{ Hg}}{2} = \frac{21}{2} 10.5 \text{ psia}$$

8. Convert 44.7 psia to psig:

   44.7

   −14.7

   30 psig

9. What is the equivalent of 30 ″ Hg in psia?

   $$\text{psia} = \frac{30 \text{ minus Hg}}{2} = \frac{30 \text{ minus } 30}{2} = 0 \text{ psia}$$

10. Convert 13 lbs. psia to Hg absolute:

    $13 \times 2 = 26''$ Hg absolute

11. Convert 2 lbs. psig to psia:

    2 + 15 = 17 lbs. psia

    In this question, the pressure is above 0 psig. Add the atmospheric pressure of 14.7 (rounded up to 15) to the psig to obtain the psia.

12. A R-12 DOT-39 cylinder has a room temperature of 75° F. What is the corresponding pressure? **See chart:** Note if the pressure was between 70.2 and 84.2. You must pick out of the choices an approximate figure to get the correct corresponding pressure. Answer: 75 psi

13. If the pressure for HFC-134z was 14.7 psia, what is the corresponding temperature? **See chart:** Note that the 0 psig pressure is between +1.8 psig and 3.8" Hg psig. Those figures are between -20 and –10 degrees. You must pick out of the choices an approximate figure to get the correct corresponding temperature. Answer: -15°

Vapor Pressure Chart In Psig, Color Coded

Temp. (F)	Orange 11	White 12	Green 22	Purple 113	Blue 114	Yellow 500	Orchid 502
−50	28.9	15.4			27.2		0
−45	28.7	13.3			26.7		2.0
−40	28.4	11.0	.5		26.1	7.9	4.3
−35	28.1	8.4	2.5		25.5	4.8	6.7
−30	27.8	5.5	4.8	29.3	24.7	1.4	9.4
−25	27.4	2.3	7.3	29.2	23.9	1.1	12.3
−20	27.0	.6	10.1	29.1	22.9	3.1	15.5
−15	26.5	2.4	13.1	28.9	21.8	5.4	19.0
−10	26.0	4.5	16.4	28.7	20.6	7.8	22.8
−5	25.4	6.7	20.0	28.5	19.3	10.4	26.9
0	24.7	9.2	23.9	28.2	17.8	13.3	31.2
5	24.0	11.8	28.1	27.9	16.1	16.4	36.0
10	23.1	14.6	32.7	27.6	14.3	19.8	41.1
15	22.1	17.7	37.7	27.2	12.3	23.4	46.6
20	21.1	21.0	43.0	26.8	10.1	27.3	52.4
25	19.9	24.6	48.7	26.3	7.6	31.6	58.7
30	18.6	28.5	54.8	25.8	5.0	36.1	65.4
35	17.2	32.6	61.4	25.2	2.1	41.0	72.6
40	15.6	37.0	68.5	24.5	.5	46.2	80.2
45	13.9	41.7	76.0	23.8	2.2	51.8	87.7
50	12.0	46.7	84.0	22.9	4.0	57.8	96.9
55	10.0	52.0	92.5	22.1	6.0	64.1	109.7
60	7.7	57.7	101.6	21.0	8.1	71.0	115.6
65	5.3	63.8	111.2	19.9	10.4	78.1	125.8
70	2.6	70.2	121.4	18.7	12.9	85.8	136.6
75	0.1	77.0	132.2	17.3	15.5	93.9	147.9
80	1.6	84.2	143.6	15.9	18.3	102.5	159.9
85	3.2	91.8	155.6	14.3	21.4	111.5	172.5
90	5.0	99.8	168.4	12.5	24.6	121.2	185.8
95	6.8	108.3	181.8	10.6	28.0	131.3	199.7
100	8.9	117.2	195.9	8.6	31.7	141.9	214.4
105	11.1	126.6	210.7	6.4	35.6	153.1	229.7
110	13.4	136.4	226.3	4.0	39.7	164.9	245.8
115	15.9	146.8	242.7	1.4	44.1	177.4	266.1
120	18.5	157.7	259.9	0.7	48.7	190.3	280.3
125	21.3	169.1	277.9	2.2	53.7	204.0	298.7
130	24.3	181.0	296.8	3.7	58.8	218.2	318.0
135	27.4	193.5	316.5	5.4	64.3	233.2	338.1
140	30.8	206.6	337.2	7.2	70.1	248.8	359.2
145	34.4	220.3	358.8	9.2	76.3		381.1
150	38.2	234.6	381.5	11.2	82.6		404.0

Underlined numbers = inches mercury, below 1 ATM

Refrigerant vapor pressure chart courtesy Kaiser Chemical, 300 Lakeside Dr., Oakland, CA 94604.

Vapor Pressure Chart In Psig, Color Coded

Temp. (F)	Gray 123-HCFC	Green 124-HCFC	Tan 125-HFC	Sky Blue HFC-134A
–100	29.9	29.2	24.4	27.8
–90	29.8	28.8	21.7	26.9
–80	29.7	28.2	18.1	25.6
–70	29.6	27.4	13.3	23.8
–60	29.5	26.3	7.1	21.5
–50	29.2	24.8	0.3	18.5
–40	28.9	22.8	4.9	14.7
–30	28.5	20.2	10.6	9.8
–20	27.8	16.9	17.4	3.8
–10	27.0	12.7	25.6	1.8
0	26.0	7.6	35.1	6.3
10	24.7	1.4	46.3	11.6
20	23.0	3.0	59.2	18.0
30	20.8	7.5	74.1	25.6
40	18.2	12.7	91.2	34.5
50	15.0	18.8	110.6	44.9
60	11.2	25.9	132.8	56.9
70	6.6	34.1	157.8	70.7
80	1.1	43.5	186.0	86.4
90	2.6	54.1	217.5	104.2
100	6.3	66.2	252.7	124.3
110	10.5	79.7	291.6	146.8
120	15.4	94.9	334.3	171.9
130	21.0	111.7	380.3	199.8
140	27.3	130.4	430.2	230.5
150	34.5	151.0	482.1	264.4
160	42.5	173.6		301.5
170	51.5	198.4		342.0
180	61.4	225.6		385.9
190	72.5	255.1		433.6
200	84.7	287.3		485.0
210	96.1	322.1		540.3
220	112.8	359.9		
230	128.9	400.6		
240	146.3	444.5		
250	165.3	491.8		
260	185.8			
270	207.9			
280	231.8			
290	257.5			
300	285.0			

Underlined numbers = inches of mercury vacuum

Chart courtesy DuPont Chemicals: Suva Refrigerants.

The following pressure/temperature questions cover high and low head pressure for the Carrier 17M centrifugal and ACME refrigeration systems. Give special attention to these questions because they are the kind used in the practical exam.

Low Head Pressure

Reducing suction pressure lowers evaporator temperature. When evaporator temperature is lowered, more power is needed per ton of refrigeration. The compressor capacity falls off because vapor is lighter and the piston displaces less weight per stroke.

Low head pressure may be the result of:

a. restriction at the expansion valve, liquid line, or suction strainers
b. insufficient refrigerant in the system
c. too much oil circulating in the system
d. TEV bulb may have lost its charge
e. expansion valve adjustment too wide
f. evaporator clogged by frost

Low Head Pressure Questions

1. Your brine pressure just dropped from 100 psi to 50 psi. What should you do first?

   Answer: Put another pump on the line to prevent brine coolers from freezing due to the pressure drop. Then investigate why the pressure dropped.

2. In the ACME refrigeration system, if the temperature on the return line is 40° F, what should you do? What will happen?

   Answer: You do nothing but watch the controls.

   a. The thermostat signals the unloader to unload the compressor
   b. The three-step thermostat starts its shut-down sequence

3. In the Carrier 17M centrifugal machine, what would cause suction pressure to go to 25″ Hg?

   Possible answers:

   a. The refrigerant charge is low.
   b. The chiller water is getting cold; the load has dropped.

4. What would you do to correct this condition?

   Possible answers:

   a. Charge the machine with more refrigerant.
   b. Slow down the machine, and check the temperature-regulating controls.

   Note: A clogged strainer or filter-drier may cause a change in the suction pressure.

5. If the brine temperature were abnormally low, what safety device would stop the compressor?

   Answer: The chill-water temperature control.

6. If the refrigerant temperature became too low, what safety device would shut down the compressor?

   Answer: The refrigerant temperature control, Frezzestat.

7. Low refrigerant or brine temperature causes what kind of damage?

   Answer: The evaporator tubes might freeze and burst.

High Head Pressure

More power is needed per ton of refrigeration when head pressure and discharge temperature rise. Head pressure should be kept as low as possible, and suction pressure as high as necessary, to produce the needed evaporator temperature.

High head pressure may be the result of:

a. noncondensables in the system
b. overfeeding expansion valve
c. leaky suction valve
d. system overcharged with refrigerant
e. clogged condenser tubes

High Head Pressure Questions

1. You notice condenser pressure is too high. How should you troubleshoot?

   Answers:

   a. Check the condenser water pump and purger operation.
   b. Check for a closed valve in the cooling water circuit. Someone may have closed it by mistake.
   c. Check the cooling tower fan for proper operation.
   d. Check the tower make-up water valve—ensure it is not stuck closed.
   e. Determine whether water box division plates are damaged, causing water bypass.

2. Your machine has high head pressure. What do you do?

   Answers:

   a. Most of the time, lower the head pressure simply by cleaning the condenser strainer.
   b. If the strainer is clean and head pressure continues to rise, check the cooling tower motor, fans, and related fuses.

Questions 3 through 5 relate to the Carrier 17M centrifugal machine.

3. If head pressure continues to rise, what could happen?

   Answers:

   a. The high-pressure cutout could shut down the machine.
   b. If the high-pressure cutout does not work, the rupture disc could blow the refrigerant out when it reaches 15 psi in the chiller.

4. If the high-side operating pressure is from 3 to 5 lbs., what could cause the high side to go to 9 lbs.?

   Answer: Air in the system.

5. If you run the system with high condenser pressure, what may result?

   Answer: If the safeties do not function, high condenser pressure will cause overloading of the compressor, gear, or motor. Damage to the condenser could result.

Pressure	Tonnage	Horsepower
Head pressure increases	decreases	increases
Head pressure decreases	increases	decreases
Suction pressure increases	increases	decreases
Suction pressure decreases	decreases	increases
Volumetric efficiency increases	increases	decreases
Volumetric efficiency decreases	decreases	increases
Compression ratio increases	decreases	increases
Compression ration decreases	increases	decreases

In an effort to teach pressure, tonnage, and horsepower, the Refrigeration License instructors of the Thomas Shortman Training Center came up with the following chart, read from left to right:

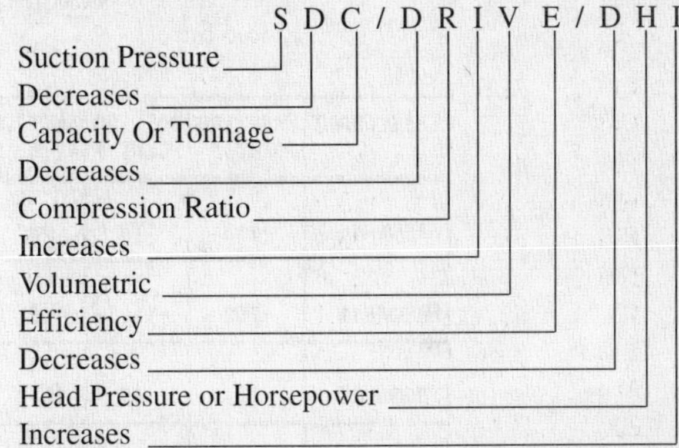

The chart above is read like this: as the suction pressure decreases, the capacity or tonnage decreases. Compression ratio increases as the volumetric decreases, and therefore, the head pressure or horsepower increases.

By reading the chart from left to right, a student can figure out when pressure increases or decreases in relation to tonnage, horsepower, compression ratio, or volumetric efficiency. The chart above even can be reversed (**S I C / I R D V E / I H D**), and the opposite of tonnage, horsepower, compression ratio, or volumetric efficiency (increase or decrease) also applies. For example, to read the chart in reverse, it is read like this: as the suction pressure increases, the capacity or tonnage increases. Compression ratio decreases as the volumetric efficiency increases, and therefore, the head pressure or horsepower increases.

volumetric efficiency: the relationship between the actual performance of a compressor and its calculated performance, based on its displacement.

ton of refrigeration: the cooling effect equal to that produced by a ton of ice melting in 24 hours.

1 ton of refrigeration = 288,000 btu/per day
12,000 btu/per hour
200 btu/per minute
3.3 btu/per second

compression ratio: the amount of pressure change a compressor is required to create in a system. The higher the compression ratio, the higher the head pressure, resulting in a loss of efficiency.

horsepower: a unit of power equal to 33,000 ft./lb. of work per minute.

1 horsepower = 33,000 ft./lb./minute
550 ft./lb./second
46 watts or .746 kw
2545.6 btu/hour
42.42 btu/minute

1 horsepower hour = 746 watt hours
.746 kilowatt hours
(1 kw = 1.341 Hp)
2545.6 btu

PRESSURE/TEMPERATURE TECHNICAL TIPS

1. The total heat to be carried away is a function of the **wet bulb** temperature. It represents sensible heat plus the latent heat in the air.
2. **Wet-bulb** readings are always cooler than dry-bulb readings due to evaporation of the moist water in the wick.
3. **Wet bulb** temperature is never higher than **dry bulb** temperature.
4. The warmer the air, the more moisture it holds.
5. The cooler the air, the less moisture it holds.
6. As the pressure is reduced, more moisture is absorbed by the air.
7. As the pressure is increased, less moisture is absorbed by the air.
8. The **hygrometer** uses both the amount of moisture in the air. The hygrometer utilizes both the Dry/Wet Bulb thermometers. The readings are interpreted with a **psychrometric chart** to find relative humidity or dew point.

REFRIGERANT	FREEZING POINT F	BOILING POINT F	SUCTION AT 5 F	DISCHGE AT 86 F	LATENT HEAT 5 F	REFRIGERAT EFFECT	CRITICAL TEMP. F	TEST PRESS HIGH	LOW	CIRC/LB MIN/TON
FREON-11	-168	74	24"	3.5	84	67.5	388	30	30	2.96
FREON-12	-252	-21.7	12	93	69.5	51.1	233	235	140	3.9
FREON-21	-211	48	19.2"	16.5	109.3	89.4	353	70	40	2
FREON-22	-256	-41	28.2	160	93	69.3	205	300	150	2.9
METHYL R40 CHLORIDE	-144	-10	6	80	180	150.2	290	210	120	1.3
FREON-113	-31	117.6	27.9"	13.9"	70.6	53.7	417	30	30	3.7
R-500	-254	-28	16.4	113	85	82.5	221	285	150	2.42
R-717 AMMONIA	-107.9	-28	20	154	565	474.4	271	300	150	.42
R-718 WATER	32	212	(40 F) 29.67"	28.6"	970	1025.3	706	0	0	.19
CARBON DIOXIDE	-69.9	-109	320	1028	116	55.5	87.8	1500	1000	3.6
SULPHUR DIOXIDE	-103.9	14	5.9"	51.8	172.3	141.4	315	170	85	1.4

Fig. 10.2

9. A psychrometric chart is a graph of the temperature/pressure relationship of steam.
10. Relative humidity is the amount of moisture contained in the as compared to the amount the air can hold at that temperature.
11. A **sling psychrometer** is used to measure relative humidity readings quickly. It also utilizes both the Dry/Wet Bulb thermometers. This device spins these devices, giving the Wet Bulb thermometer a lower temperature reading. The difference in temperature depends on the humidity in the air. The drier the air, the greater the temperature difference.
12. A **micron** is a unit of length equal to .001 of a millimeter.
13. A **micron gauge** measures pressure close to perfect vacuum.
14. **A U-tube** manometer measures low vapor pressure. Vapor pressure may be checked against a column of mercury or water.
15. **Coefficient of performance** is the ratio of usable *output* energy divided by *input* energy. The output is the amount of heat absorbed; the input is the amount of heat needed to produce the output.

OPERATING PRESSURE/ TEMPERATURE LICENSE QUESTIONS

1. Reducing suction pressure lowers evaporator temperature, but
   (A) more power is needed per ton of refrigeration and compression capacity falls because vapor is lighter and piston displaces less weight per stroke.
   (B) less power is needed per ton of refrigeration, because vapor is lighter and the piston displaces less weight per stroke.
   (C) power is not a factor when reducing evaporator temperature.
   (D) none of the above.

2. Raising head pressure raises discharge temperature and
   (A) more power is needed per ton of refrigeration.
   (B) less power is needed per ton of refrigeration.
   (C) suction temperature is decreased.
   (D) none of the above.

3. To reduce power input and conserve capacity, keep head pressure as low as possible and keep
   (A) suction pressure as high as needed to produce the desired evaporator temperature.
   (B) suction pressure as low as needed to produce the desired evaporator temperature.
   (C) suction pressure stable at low evaporator temperature.
   (D) none of the above (pressure and temperature have no effect on system capacity).

4. An ammonia compressor is running at 20 psi suction and 165 psi head pressure. If the suction pressure drops to 0 psi and everything else remains the same, then the tonnage
   (A) decreases and horsepower decreases.
   (B) increases and horsepower increases.
   (C) increases and horsepower decreases.
   (D) decreases and horsepower increases.

5. Assuming all other conditions remain constant, the horsepower per ton of refrigeration
   (A) decreases as the head pressure increases.
   (B) increases as the head pressure decreases.
   (C) decreases as the suction pressure increases.
   (D) increases as the suction pressure increases.

6. Assuming all other conditions remain constant in a refrigerating plant, the statement about operating characteristics that is most correct is
   (A) as load decreases, low-side pressure falls.
   (B) as head pressure rises, plant capacity increases.
   (C) as low-side pressure falls, compressor capacity increases.
   (D) none of the above (low-side pressure is not affected by the load change).

7. If the suction pressure were raised from 0 to 25 psig, the horsepower per ton of refrigeration would
   (A) increase.
   (B) decrease.
   (C) remain the same.
   (D) increase, then decrease.

8. When suction pressure is decreased, horsepower
   (A) increases.
   (B) decreases.
   (C) remains the same.
   (D) decreases due to evaporator load.

9. As suction pressure drops in a Freon 22 system, compressor capacity
   (A) increases.
   (B) decreases.
   (C) remains the same.
   (D) increases, then decreases.

10. If a compressor is running at 20 psi suction and 175 psi head, and the suction pressure drops, tonnage
    (A) increases.
    (B) decreases.
    (C) remains the same.
    (D) increases, then decreases.

11. If tonnage increased as the suction pressure increased, horsepower would
    (A) increase.
    (B) decrease.
    (C) remain the same.
    (D) increase, then decrease.

12. Assuming all other conditions remain the same, the horsepower per ton of refrigeration
    (A) increases as the suction pressure decreases.
    (B) increases as the suction pressure increases.
    (C) decreases as the suction pressure increases.
    (D) Both (A) and (C)

13. In an ACME compressor, the suction pressure is 60 psig and head pressure is 200 psig. If the suction pressure drops to 35 psig and everything else remains the same, then tonnage
(A) decreases and horsepower decreases.
(B) increases and horsepower increases.
(C) increases and horsepower decreases.
(D) decreases and horsepower increases.

14. On a Carrier M17 compressor, the suction pressure is 15" Hg and head pressure is 5 psi. If the suction pressure changes to 19" Hg, and everything else remains the same, then tonnage
(A) decreases and horsepower decreases.
(B) increases and horsepower increases.
(C) increases and horsepower decreases.
(D) decreases and horsepower increases.

15. To produce the desired evaporator temperature, power input is reduced, conserving capacity by keeping head pressure
(A) as low as possible and suction pressure as low as needed.
(B) as high as possible and suction pressure as high as needed.
(C) as low as possible and suction pressure as high as needed.
(D) as high as possible and suction pressure as low as needed.

16. The temperature on a wet-bulb thermometer equals the dry-bulb temperature when
(A) the air is below freezing.
(B) the air is saturated with moisture.
(C) the air has no moisture.
(D) this can never happen.

17. Relative humidity refers to the total moisture content of air. This statement
(A) is true.
(B) is false.
(C) is partly true.
(D) defines absolute humidity.

18. The difference between dry-bulb and wet-bulb temperature is
(A) dry-bulb refers to the air temperature of evaporation.
(B) wet-bulb refers to ambient temperature of a thermometer.
(C) wet- and dry-bulb temperatures are directly proportional to the gauge pressure below atmospheric.
(D) dry-bulb refers to the ambient temperature. Wet-bulb refers to the air temperature of evaporation.

19. What are the physical properties of air?
(A) Weight, density, temperature, specific heat, and heat conductivity
(B) Enthalpy, entropy, pressure, specific heat, and density
(C) Weight, temperature, enthalpy, and conductivity
(D) Weight, enthalpy, density, specific heat, temperature, and conductivity

20. A refrigerating system is operating at 100 psi in the high side. This high-side pressure gauge should have a minimum full-scale reading of
(A) 100 psi.
(B) 110 psi.
(C) 115 psi.
(D) 120 psi.

21. The index of performance of a refrigeration system is the
(A) refrigerant performance factor.
(B) coefficient of performance.
(C) efficiency.
(D) pressure ratio.

22. If compression ratio and horsepower increase, tonnage
(A) increases.
(B) decreases.
(C) does not change.
(D) none of the above.

23. The capacity of a refrigeration reciprocating compressor increases as
(A) suction pressure decreases.
(B) volumetric efficiency decreases.
(C) discharge pressure decreases.
(D) compression ratio decreases.

24. The capacity of a refrigeration rotary compressor decreases as
(A) volumetric efficiency decreases.
(B) horsepower decreases.
(C) compression ratio decreases.
(D) suction pressure increases.

25. If the capacity of a refrigeration system increases and horsepower decreases,
(A) head pressure increases.
(B) volumetric efficiency decreases.
(C) the head pressure decreases.
(D) none of the above.

26. What can happen on a centrifugal compressor if suction pressure decreases to 30" Hg or lower?

(A) Capacity can increase
(B) Rupture disc can burst
(C) Tubes can freeze
(D) All of the above

27. Volumetric efficiency is defined as

(A) the amount of pressure change a compressor is required to create in a system.
(B) the relationship between the actual performance of a compressor and its calculated performance.
(C) transfer of heat that occurs by direct contact between two objects at different temperature.
(D) none of the above.

28. An overcharge of refrigerant would result in

(A) increase in capacity with an increase in head pressure.
(B) increase in capacity with an increase in suction pressure.
(C) decrease in capacity with an increase in head pressure.
(D) increase in horsepower with an increase in capacity.

29. A sling psychrometer is read in units of

(A) relative humidity.
(B) absolute humidity.
(C) temperature.
(D) inches of mercury absolute.

30. Pressure relief valves installed on a reciprocating compressor handling R-12 refrigerant are normally set at

(A) the same pressure as the high-pressure cut-off device.
(B) higher pressure than the high-pressure cut-off device.
(C) a pressure equal to twice the oil pressure.
(D) lower pressure than the high-pressure cut-off device.

31. The vacuum-indicating instrument used to measure pressures of 1,000 microns or less is

(A) electronic vacuum gauge.
(B) compound gauge.
(C) wet-bulb vacuum indicator.
(D) U-tube manometer.

32. On a compound pressure gauge, units of vacuum are read in inches of

(A) ammonia.
(B) water.
(C) mercury.
(D) air pressure.

33. The readings of a sling psychrometer are in units of

(A) relative humidity.
(B) absolute humidity.
(C) temperature.
(D) inches of mercury absolute.

34. Pressure relief valves that are installed on a reciprocating compressor handling R-12 refrigerant are normally set at

(A) the same pressure as used in the high-pressure cut-off device.
(B) a higher pressure than that of the high pressure cut-off device.
(C) a pressure equal to twice the oil pressure.
(D) a lower pressure than that of the high pressure cut-off device.

35. Of the following types of vacuum indicating instruments, the one that is recommended to be used when measuring pressures in the range of 1000 microns or less is the

(A) electronic vacuum gauge.
(B) compound gauge.
(C) wet-bulb vacuum indicator.
(D) U-tube manometer.

36. The units of vacuum on a compound pressure gauge are read in inches of

(A) ammonia.
(B) water.
(C) mercury.
(D) air pressure.

37. Where is the **ozone** layer found around the earth?

(A) Troposphere
(B) Stratosphere
(C) Lower atmosphere
(D) Ionosphere

Answers to Operating Pressure/ Temperature Licensing Questions

1. **The correct answer is (A).** Horsepower increases.
2. **The correct answer is (A).**
3. **The correct answer is (A).**
4. **The correct answer is (D).**
5. **The correct answer is (C).**
6. **The correct answer is (A).**
7. **The correct answer is (B).**
8. **The correct answer is (A).**
9. **The correct answer is (B).** More power is needed per ton of refrigeration. Compression capacity falls due to lighter cylinder charge; thus, the piston displaces less weight per stroke. Rule: If tonnage increases, suction increases and horsepower decreases; if suction decreases, tonnage decreases and horsepower increases.
10. **The correct answer is (B).**
11. **The correct answer is (B).**
12. **The correct answer is (D).**
13. **The correct answer is (D).**
14. **The correct answer is (D).**
15. **The correct answer is (C).**
16. **The correct answer is (A).**
17. **The correct answer is (A).**
18. **The correct answer is (D).**
19. **The correct answer is (A).**
20. **The correct answer is (D).**
21. **The correct answer is (B).** This is the ratio divided by the output. The output is the amount of heat absorbed by the system; the input is the amount of energy required to produce this output.
22. **The correct answer is (B).**
23. **The correct answer is (D).**
24. **The correct answer is (A).**
25. **The correct answer is (C).**
26. **The correct answer is (C).**
27. **The correct answer is (B).**
28. **The correct answer is (C).**
29. **The correct answer is (C).**
30. **The correct answer is (B).**
31. **The correct answer is (A).**
32. **The correct answer is (C).**
33. **The correct answer is (C).**
34. **The correct answer is (B).**
35. **The correct answer is (A).**
36. **The correct answer is (C).**
37. **The correct answer is (B).**

Chapter 11

AIR-CONDITIONING AND REFRIGERATION MATH

This chapter provides a sample of the math questions on the written refrigeration exam. Each question contains the calculation and solution to the problem. Whenever possible, an explanation is given with definitions for the mathematical calculation or formula. A symbols section with related questions is included to teach you how to identify various air-conditioning and refrigeration components in drawings.

The questions in this chapter are related to finding the tons of refrigeration, temperature conversions, btu concepts, motor horsepower, frequency, efficiency, rpm calculations, and symbol identification.

TONS OF REFRIGERATION PROBLEMS

A ton of refrigeration is equal to 288,000 btu per day, 12,000 btu per hour, 200 btu per minute, or 3.3 btu per second.

1. Which of the following equals one ton of refrigeration?

(A) 200 btu per hour
(B) 200 btu per minute
(C) 200 btu per second
(D) 200 btu per day

The correct answer is (B).

2. A 10-ton refrigeration unit has a capacity of

(A) 12,000 btu per hour.
(B) 2,000 btu per minute.
(C) 20,000 btu per minute.
(D) 144,000 btu per day.

Solution to question 2:

$$\begin{array}{r l} 200 & \text{btu per minute} \\ \times\ 10 & \text{ton unit} \\ \hline 2000 & \text{btu per minute} \end{array}$$

The correct answer is (B).

3. A machine with 600,000 btu capacity per hour produces how many tons of refrigeration?

(A) 300
(B) 3,000
(C) 500
(D) 50

Solution to question 3:

600,000 btu per hour ÷ 12,000 = 50 tons of refrigeration

The correct answer is (D).

Fahrenheit to Celsius Conversions

Formula: $C = \dfrac{F - 32}{1.8}$

4. Convert –13° Fahrenheit to Celsius.

$$\frac{-13 - 32}{1.8} = -25° \text{ Celsius}$$

Celsius to Fahrenheit Conversions

Formula: $F = (C \times 1.8) + 32$

5. Convert 47° Celsius to Fahrenheit:

$$F = (47 \times 1.8) + 32$$
$$F = (84.6) + 32$$
$$F = 84.6 + 32$$
$$F = 116.6° \text{ F}$$

DEFINITIONS FOR AIR-CONDITIONING MATH PROBLEMS

specific heat: the heat needed to raise or lower the temperature of 1 pound of a substance by 1° Fahrenheit. The term "specific heat" may be abbreviated "SH."

The specific heat of ice is .5; that is, .5 btu is required to raise or lower the temperature of 1 pound of ice at 32° F by 1° F. The specific heat of steam is .5. The specific heat of water is 1.

latent heat of fusion: hidden heat that fuses molecules of a substance changing from liquid to solid or solid to liquid. To change 1 pound of water at 32° F to ice at 32° F, remove 144 btu; to change one pound of ice at 32° F to water at 32° F, add 144 btu.

latent heat of vaporization: heat required per pound of a substance to change its state from liquid to vapor. Add 970 btu of heat to change 1 pound of water at 212° F to vapor at 212° F.

latent heat of condensation: the amount of heat released (lost) by a pound of a substance as it changes state from vapor to liquid. Subtract 970 btu of heat to change water vapor to liquid.

BTU CONCEPTS

6. How many btu are needed to change 1 pound of water at 0° F to 212° F steam?

(A) 0° F ice to 32° F ice = 32 × .5 SH = 16 btu
(B) 32 F ice to 32 F water = latent heat of fusion = 144 btu
(C) 32 F water to 212 F water = 180 × 1 SH = 180 btu
(D) 212 F water to 212 F steam = latent heat of vaporization = 970 btu

Answer: 1310 btu

Explanation:

(A) Subtract difference of temperature from 32° ice.
(B) Add 144 btu to account for latent heat of fusion as the pound of ice at 32° F changes to a pound of water at 32° F.
(C) There is a 180° temperature difference between the 32° F water and the 212° F steam. Multiply this by the specific heat of water, which is 1 SH.
(D) Add 970 btu to account for latent heat of vaporization as a pound of water at 212° F changes to a pound of steam at 212° F.

In some problems, steam may be at a temperature higher than 212° F. In these cases you subtract 212 to find the difference. For example, if the above problem had used 220° F steam, you would have subtracted 212 from 220 to get a difference of 8. Then you would have multiplied 8 by .5, the specific heat of steam, to get an answer of 4 btu.

Some problems might use a greater amount of mass than 1 pound. In these cases, solve for 1 pound, then multiply your answer by the total mass. For example, if the above problem related to 2 pounds of water, you would multiply 1310 btu by 2 to get the answer. Problem 8, below, is solved like this.

7. If a 10-ton refrigeration plant ran at full load for 1 day, it would absorb how many btu?

288,000 btu = 1 ton of refrigeration per day
× 10 tons
28,800,000 btu a ten-ton plant would absorb in one day

Rules For Multiplying Negatives And Positives

a. $(-) \times (-) = (+)$
b. $(-) \times (+) = (-)$
c. $(+) \times (+) = (+)$

8. How many btu are needed to warm 2 pounds of water from –12.22° Celsius to 110° Celsius? Give answers in tons of refrigeration per day, per hour, per minute, and per second.

(A) Convert from Celsius to Fahrenheit with this formula:

$C = -12.22°$
$F = (C \times 1.8) + 32$
$F = (-12.22 \times 1.8) + 32 = 10°\ F$
$F = (110 \times 1.8) + 32 = 230°$

(B) Given:
Specific heat of ice = .5 btu/lb.
Specific heat of steam = .5 btu/lb.
Specific heat of water = 1 btu/lb.
Latent heat of fusion = 144 btu/lb.
Latent heat of vaporization = 970 btu/lb.

(C) Use 10° F as the low point and 230° F as the high point:
10° F ice to 32° F ice = 22 × .5 SH = 11 btu
32° F ice to 32° F water = Fusion = 144 btu
32° F water to 212° F water = 180° F × 1 SH = 180 btu
212° F water to 212° F steam = Vaporization = 970 btu
212° F steam to 230° F steam = 18° F × .5 SH = 9 btu
1314 btu

(D) 2 pounds of water × 1314 btu = 2628 btu
(E) 2,628 ÷ 288,000 = .009125 btu per ton per day
(F) 2,628 ÷ 12,000 = .219 btu per ton per hour
(G) 2,628 ÷ 200 = 13.14 btu per ton per minute
(H) 2,628 ÷ 3.3 = 796.36 btu per ton per second

Formula for Quantity of btu If There is No Change of State

$Q = MSH (T_h - T_l)$
Q = quantity of btu
M = mass
Sh = specific heat
T_h = temperature high
T_l = temperature low

9. Six bars of iron are heated from 34° F to 75° F. Each bar weighs 5 pounds, and the specific heat of iron is .118 btu/lb. How many btu are needed?

$Q = MSH (T_h - T_l)$
$Q = 5(6) \times .118 (75–34)$
$Q = 30 \times .118 (41)$
$Q = 3.54 \times 41 = 145.14$ btu

HORSEPOWER, FREQUENCY, AND RPM CALCULATIONS

10. How many poles are in the field of a synchronous motor at 1800 rpm, with a frequency of 60 cycles?

$$\text{rpm} = \frac{120 \times \text{cycles}}{\text{number of poles}} = \frac{\text{frequency} \times \text{cycles}}{\text{number of poles}}$$

$$1800 \text{ rpm} = \frac{7200}{X}$$

Now solve the equation:

Multiply both sides by X. The X cancels out in the fraction. Next, divide both sides by 1800.

$$\frac{1800\ (X)}{X} = 7200(X)$$

$$1800\ X = 7200$$

$$\frac{1800\ X}{1800} \times \frac{7200}{1800}$$

$$X = \frac{7200}{1800} = 4 \text{ poles}$$

11. A Freon system rated at 4 horsepower per ton will absorb how many btu per hour in the evaporator?

$$\frac{12{,}000 \text{ btu / hr}}{4 \text{ hp / ton}} = 3{,}000 \text{ btu / hour}$$

12. How much does a 10-hp motor cost to run for 1 hour at 2 cents per kilowatt hour?

.746 kw
× 10 hp
7.460 kw per hour
× .02 cents per kw
.14920 = 15 cents (at 100% efficiency)

13. Referring to question 12, what does it cost to run the motor at 80% efficiency?

80% = .8
.15000 ÷ .8

Move the decimal points one place to the right.

1.5000 ÷ 8 = .1875 = 18 cents

14. Find the rpm of an 8-pole synchronous motor rated at 40 hp, 440 volts, and 60 hertz:

40 hp and 440 volts are not used in the solution.
120v × HZ = 120 × 60 = 900 rpm
No. of poles: 8

15. Convert 16″ Hg absolute to psig gauge:

30 – 16 = 14″ Hg psig

To convert from psig to Hg absolute subtract psig from 30. Example:

Convert 9″ Hg psig to inches of mercury absolute.
30 – 9 = 21″ Hg absolute

You can check your answer by looking at the pressure scale chart illustrating psig, psia, and Hg absolute.

16. How much refrigerant may be stored in a machine room if the system has 150 pounds in it?

You are allowed to store 20% of the entire charge of the system refrigerant in the machine room.

150 × .20 = 30 pounds

17. Five pounds of water must be warmed two degrees at sea level. How many btu are required?

5 pounds × 2 = 10 btu

18. Plants A and B have evaporator temperatures of 5° F and 28° F, respectively. Plant A absorbs 600 btu per minute and Plant B, 6,000 btu per hour. What is their tonnage?

600 ÷ 200 = btu/minute = 3 tons

6,000 ÷ 12,000 = btu/hour = $\frac{1}{2}$ tons

Plant A operates at 3 tons; Plant B operates at $\frac{1}{2}$ ton.

19. If an air-conditioning compressor weighing 300 pounds had to be lifted 4 ft. to be mounted on a base, how many ft./pounds of work are needed?

Formula: Work = Force × Distance
Work = 300 pounds × 4 ft. = 1,200 ft./pounds

20. The volume of air passing through a duct 35 inches by 24 inches has a velocity of 1,200 feet per minute. Find the cubic feet per minute (cfm):

(A) 5,000 cfm
(B) 7,200 cfm
(C) 12,000 cfm
(D) 1,500 cfm

First, convert 35" x 24" into feet = $\frac{35}{12}$ = 2.9' and $\frac{24}{12}$ = 2'
Solution: 3' × 2' × 1,200 = 7,200 cfm
The correct answer is (B).

21. Find the area of a piston 12 inches in diameter:

Formula: $A = \pi R^2$
3.14×6^2
$3.14 \times 36 = 113.04$ square inches

22. An air-conditioning system has three compressors, each of which may operate at either 50 percent or 100 percent capacity. The maximum number of operating capacities allowed is:

(A) three
(B) four
(C) six
(D) eight
The correct answer is (C).

Multiply the number of compressors by the number of capacities:

$3 \times 2 = 6$
Note that this solution only applies when the capacities are 50 percent and 100 percent.

23. If the pressure gauge reads 8" Hg, what is the absolute pressure in inches of mercury?

(A) 22
(B) 28
(C) 30
(D) 24
The correct answer is (A).
30 – 8 = 22″ Hg absolute

24. If the factory setting of a TXV is 2° of superheat, what is the field setting?

2É + 4 (low field setting) + 4 (high field setting) = 10É

25. Find the volume of a cylinder 8 inches in diameter with a 10 inch stroke:

Formula: $V = \pi R^2 \times$ length
$3.14 \times 4^2 \times 10$
$3.14 \times 16 \times 10$
$50.24 \times 10 = 502.4$ cubic inches

How much water can you put in this cylinder?
Note: 1 gallon = 231 cubic inches.
502.4 cubic inches ÷ 231 cubic inches = 2.17 gallons

26. Find the surface of a pipe 3 inches in diameter and 100 feet in length:

First convert length and diameter to either feet or inches.
100 ft. × 12 = 1,200 inches
Formula: $\pi \times D$ = Circumference
$3.14 \times 3 = 9.42$ inches
Length × Circumference = Surface
$1200 \times 9.42 = 11,304$ square inches

27. What is the total force exerted on a piston 3 inches in diameter if pressure in the cylinder is 100 psig?

Formula: $A = \pi R^2 \times$ pressure
$A = 3.14 \times 1.5^2$
$A = 3.14 \times 2.25 = 7.065$ inches
100 psig (pressure) × 7.065 = 706.5 pounds

28. Compute the rated discharge capacity of a rupture member in pounds of air per minute.

Formula: $C = .8\ PD^2$
If C = 1.2 and P = 24 psia, what does D equal?

$C = .8\ PD^2$

$1.2 = .8(24)D^2$

$1.2 = 19.2\ D^2$

$\frac{1.2}{19.2} = \frac{\cancel{19.2}}{\cancel{19.2}} D^2$

$D^2 = \frac{1.2}{19.2} = .0625$

$.0625 = D^2$

$\sqrt{.0625} = D$

$.25 = D$

SQUARE ROOTS

A square root is a number that is multiplied by itself.
$2^2 = 2 \times 2$.
Examples:

Square root of $4 = 2 = (2 \times 2 = 4)$ or $2\sqrt{4}$

Square root of $25 = 5 = (5 \times 5 = 25)$ or $2\sqrt{25}$

Use the formula $C = .8\ PD^2$ to find the square root of a number once the equation has been simplified.

Simplify the above formula:

$$\frac{C}{.8P} = D^2$$

Now, find one equal factor of D^2 (the square root of D^2).

On the exam, you will be given four answer choices for the square root. The easiest way to pick the correct answer is to multiply each choice by itself. Then check each choice with the solution to the given equation. The correct answer equals the solution. See the example below.

29. $C = .8PD^2$

Given that C = 1.2 and P = 24, find D.

Answer choices:

(A) .165

(B) .195

(C) .250

(D) .220

First, solve the equation:

$1.2 = .8(24)D^2$

$1.2 = 19.2D^2$

$\frac{1.2}{19.2} = D^2$

$.0625 = D^2$

Now, multiple each answer choice by itself:

(A) $.165 \times .165 = .027225$

(B) $.195 \times .195 = 038025$

(C) $.250 \times .250 = .0625$

(D) $.220 \times .220 = .0484$

When multiplied by itself, choice (C) equals .0625—the solution to the above equation. .0625 equals D squared, and .250 equals D. Therefore, choice (C) is correct.

RISERS

You may need to estimate the amount of water in a riser. Do this by figuring the volume of the pipe through its entire length and converting this into gallons of water.

Formula:

$\pi R^2 \times$ length (either cubic inches or cubic feet) π 1728 (number of cubic inches in a cubic foot)

$\pi = 3.1417$

R = radius of the pipe in either inches or feet

L = length in either inches or feet

Note: Always use *either* inches or feet in a problem—never combine them.

Multiply the numerator first. Then divide that number by the denominator. 1728 is the number of cubic inches per cubic foot. Finally, convert cubic feet into gallons of water.

A simple way to do this problem is to multiply the constant, 2.04, by the diameter squared.

$$2.04 \times D^2 = \frac{G}{50 \text{ ft.}}$$

The answer gives the gallons in a 50-foot section of a riser. Then multiply by the number of times the pipe is longer than 50 feet. See sample problems below.

30. A 3-inch riser that is 150 feet long contains how many gallons of water?

$D^2 = 3 \times 3 = 9$

$\frac{150}{50} = 3$

$2.04 \times 9 = 18.36$ gallons per 50 - foot length

$3 \times 18.36 = 55.08$gallons

31. A 5-inch riser that is 200 feet long contains how many gallons of water?

$D^2 = 5 \times 5 = 25$

$\frac{200}{50} = 4$

$2.04 \times 25 = 51$ gallons per 50 - foot length

$51 \times 4 = 204$ gallons

32. A $\frac{1}{2}$-inch riser that is 100 feet long contains how many gallons of water?

$D^2 = .5 \times .5 = .25$

$\frac{100}{50} = 2$

$2.04 \times .25 = .51$ gallons per 50 - foot length

$.51 \times 2 = 1.02$ gallons

It is important to square the diameter on paper. Do not square it mentally, because there may be a fractional-inch pipe, as in the problem above. The square of a $\frac{1}{2}$-inch-diameter pipe is .25. The square of $\frac{1}{2}$ inch ($\frac{1}{2} \times \frac{1}{2}$, or $.5 \times .5$) is .25, or $\frac{1}{4}$ inch.

33. A $\frac{3}{4}$-inch riser that is 100 feet long contains how many gallons of water?

$.75 \times .75 = .5625$

$\frac{100}{50} = 2$

$2.04 \times .5625 = 1.15$ gallons per 50 - foot length

$1.15 \times 2 = 2.30$ gallons

Use the following formula to find the weight of water in a pipe. It gives the pounds of water per 50-foot length.

17 × D2

17 × D2 = lb./50 ft.

34. A 3-inch riser that is 150 feet long contains how many pounds of water?

Multiply your answer by 3 to find the weight of water in a 150-foot length of pipe.

$3 \times 3 = 9$
$17 \times 9 = 153$ pounds per 50-foot length
$150 \div 50 = 3$
$153 \times 3 = 459$ pounds

35. A $\frac{3}{4}$-inch riser that is 100 feet long contains how many pounds of water?

$.75 \times .75 = .5625$
$17 \times .5625 = 9.56$ pounds per 50-foot length
$100 \div 50 = 2$
$9.56 \times 2 = 19.12$ pounds

36. A cooler is 45 inches in diameter and 75 feet long. The dry weight of the cooler is 2,000 pounds. What is the cooler's gross volume in cubic feet when it is full of water?

Formula: $\pi R^2 L$ when $\pi = 3.14$, R = radius, and L = length.

45″ diameter ÷ 2 = 22.5″ radius
22.5″ radius ÷ 12″ = 1.875 ft. radius
$V = 3.14 \times (1.875^2) \times 75$ ft.
$V = 3.14 \times 3.515625 \times 75$ ft.
$V = 11.039 \times 75$ ft.
V = 827.93 = gross volume of cooler in cubic feet
827.93 cu. ft. × 7.5 (gallons of water in 1 cubic foot) = 6,209.475 cu. ft. of water
6,209.475 cu. ft. of water × 8.34 pounds (weight of 1 gallon of water) = 51,787 pounds of water in cooler
51,787 pounds + 2,000 pounds of cooler dry weight = 53,787 pounds, the gross volume weight of the cooler, in cubic feet, when full of water.

37. A shell-and-tube condenser normally has a 1° temperature increase per 25 gpm (gallons per minute) per ton. If a 60-ton machine with 8 gpm has 80° F water entering, what should be the outgoing temperature?

Every 1° temperature rise = 25 gpm/ton
60-ton machine × 8 gpm = 480 total system gpm

$\frac{480}{25 \text{ gpm}} = \frac{19.2 \text{ temperature increase}}{\text{through the condenser}}$

80 temperature at the inlet
+19.2 temperature increase
99.2 temperature at the outlet

Answer: 99.2° F outgoing temperature

38. Compute the rpm of a single-acting air compressor, given S (stroke) = 8 inches and piston speed = 400 feet per minute.

Formula:

$$\text{Piston speed in ft./min.} = \frac{2 \times S \times \text{rpm}}{12}$$

$$400 \text{ ft./min.} = \frac{2 \times 8 \times \text{rpm}}{12} = 12\ (400) = 2 \times 8 \times \text{rpm}$$

$$12(400) = 16 \times \text{rpm}$$

$$4{,}800 = 16 \times \text{rpm}$$

$$\frac{4{,}800}{16} = \text{rpm}$$

$$300 = \text{rpm}$$

KILOPASCALS / PSIA / PSIG

Many of today's refrigeration gauges use the black line pressure readings to show PSIG scale and the red line to show the Kilopascal (kpa) scale. Therefore, it is important that operating engineers learn how to convert between Kilopascals, PSIG and PSIG.

39. What is the equivalent of 1,584kpa in psia?

(A) 215 psia
(B) 792.35 psia
(C) 763.605 psia
(D) 230 psia

Solution: you have to divide by 6.89
The correct answer is (D).
1,584 ÷ 6.89 = 229.898 psia

40. Convert 137.8 kpa to psia:

Solution: 137.8 kpa ÷ 6.89 = 20 psia

41. Convert 11" Hg Absolute to Kilopascals:

(A) 37.895 kpa
(B) 75.70 kpa
(C) 141.245 kpa
(D) 179.14 kpa

Solution: you have to divide by 2 then multiply by 6.89

The correct answer is (A). 11" Hg psia ÷ 2 = 5.5 × 6.89 = 37.895 kpa

42. What is the equivalent of 29" Hg Absolute in Kilopascals?

Solution: 29 ÷ 2 = 14.5 × 6.89 = 99.905 kpa

43. 26" Hg psig equals how many kpa?

Solution: first subtract 30, then divide by 2, then multiple your answer by 6.89

Solution: 30 - 26 = 4" Hg Absolute ÷ 2 = 2 × 6.89 = 13.78 kpa

44. Find the equivalent of 5" Hg psig in Kilopascals:

Solution: 30 - 5 = 25" Hg Absolute ÷2 = 12.5 × 6.89 = 86.125 kpa

45. Convert a R-22 system from psig to kpa if the suction is 62 psig and the discharge is 270 psig:

Solution: 62 psig + 15 = 77 psia x 6.89 = (suction) 530.53 kpa and 270 psig + 15 = 285 psia × 6.89 = (discharge) 1,963.65 kpa

46. Convert a R-123 system from psig to kpa if the suction is 18" Hg psig and the discharge is 7 psig:

Solution: 30 - 18" hg psig = 12" Hg Absolute ÷ 2 = 6 × 6.89 = 41.34 kpa and 7 psig +15 = 22 psia × 6.89 = 151.58 kpa

In reverse: Convert 41.34 kpa and 151.58 kpa in psig

Solution: If the kpa is above 41.34 kpa ÷6.89 = 6 × 2 = 12 -30 = 18" Hg psig 151.58 kpa÷ 6.89 = 22 -15 = 7 psig

47. Convert 103.37 kpa to psig:

Solution: 103.37 ÷ 6.89 = 15 psia - 15 = 0 psig

48. Convert 99.905 kpa to psig:

Solution: When any kpa is under 103.97, you must use the following solution to find psig: 99.905 ÷ 6.89 = 14.5 psia × 2 = 29 -30 = 1" Hg psig

GENERAL INFORMATION

1 ton of refrigeration = 288,000 btu per day
1 ton of refrigeration = 12,000 btu per hour
1 ton of refrigeration = 200 btu per minute
1 ton of refrigeration = 3.3 btu per second
1 gallon of water = 8.33 pounds.
1 gallon of water = 231 cubic inches
1 cubic inch of water = .0361 pounds
1 cubic foot of water = 7.48 gallons
1 cubic foot of water = 62.4 pounds

The unit of power is the watt. Power is the rate at which work is done, or the rate at which energy is expended.

Formula: watts = volts × amperes (P = E × I)

Electricity is supplied in various voltages. Voltage is the electrical pressure between any two points in a circuit. One volt is the amount of pressure needed to force one ampere of current through a resistance of one ohm.

The ohm is the unit of electrical resistance. Resistance in an electrical circuit is the opposition to current flow.

Ohm's Law: $E = I \times R$ or $I = \frac{E}{R}$ or $R = \frac{E}{I}$

E = volts or electromotive force
I = amps or current
R = ohms or resistance
Horsepower equals 33,000 foot-pounds per minute.
746 watts = 1 horsepower
1 horsepower = 2,545 btu per hour
Work = force × distance
1,000 watts = 1 kilowatt
1 kilowatt = 1.341 horsepower
1 kilowatt = 3,415 btu
144 square inches = 1 square foot
1,728 cubic inches = 1 cubic foot

Atmospheric pressure is the pressure exerted by the atmosphere. It is indicated by a barometer reading of 14.7 pounds psi or 29.92 inches of mercury.

Absolute zero is the temperature at which molecular motion stops. This is –460° F, or –273° C.

PSIG	PSIA	Hg ABSOLUTE	KILOPASCALS
50 Pounds	65 Pounds	447.85	
40	55	378.95	
35	50	344.5	
30	45	310.05	
25	40	275.6	
20	35	241.15	
15	30	206.7	
10	25	172.25	
5	20	137.8	
1	16		
0	15	30"Hg Absolute	103.35 kpa
0	14.696 psia	29.921	101.255
1"Hg Gauge	14.5	29	99.905
2	14	28	96.46
3	13.5	27	93.015
4	13	26	89.57
5	12.5	25	86.125
6	12	24	82.68
7	11.5	23	79.235
8	11	22	75.79
9	10.5	21	72.345
10	10	20	68.9
11	9.5	19	65.455
12	9	18	62.01
13	8.5	17	58.565
14	8	16	55.12
15	7.5	15	51.675
16	7	14	48.23
17	6.5	13	44.785
18	6	12	41.34
19	5.5	11	37.895
20	5	10	34.45
21	4.5	9	31.005
22	4	8	27.56
23	3.5	7	24.115
24	3	6	20.67
25	2.5	5	17.225
26	2	4	13.78
27	1.5	3	10.335
28	1	2	6.89
29	.5	1	3.445
30"HG Gauge	0 Pounds PSIA	0"Hg Absolute	0

SYMBOLS

In the HVAC industry, symbols are used to identify various components on drawings and blueprints. They help the operator or service mechanic to plan a job on paper. The following are some of the most common symbols used.

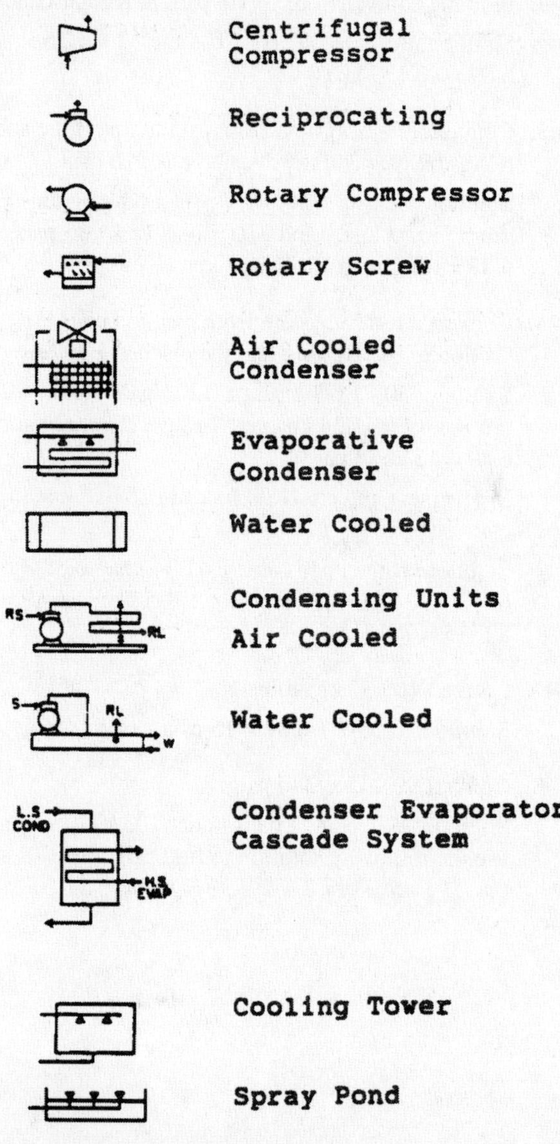

Fig. 11.1
Symbols chart courtesy of ASHRAE Handbook 1985, "Fundamentals," Chapter 36.

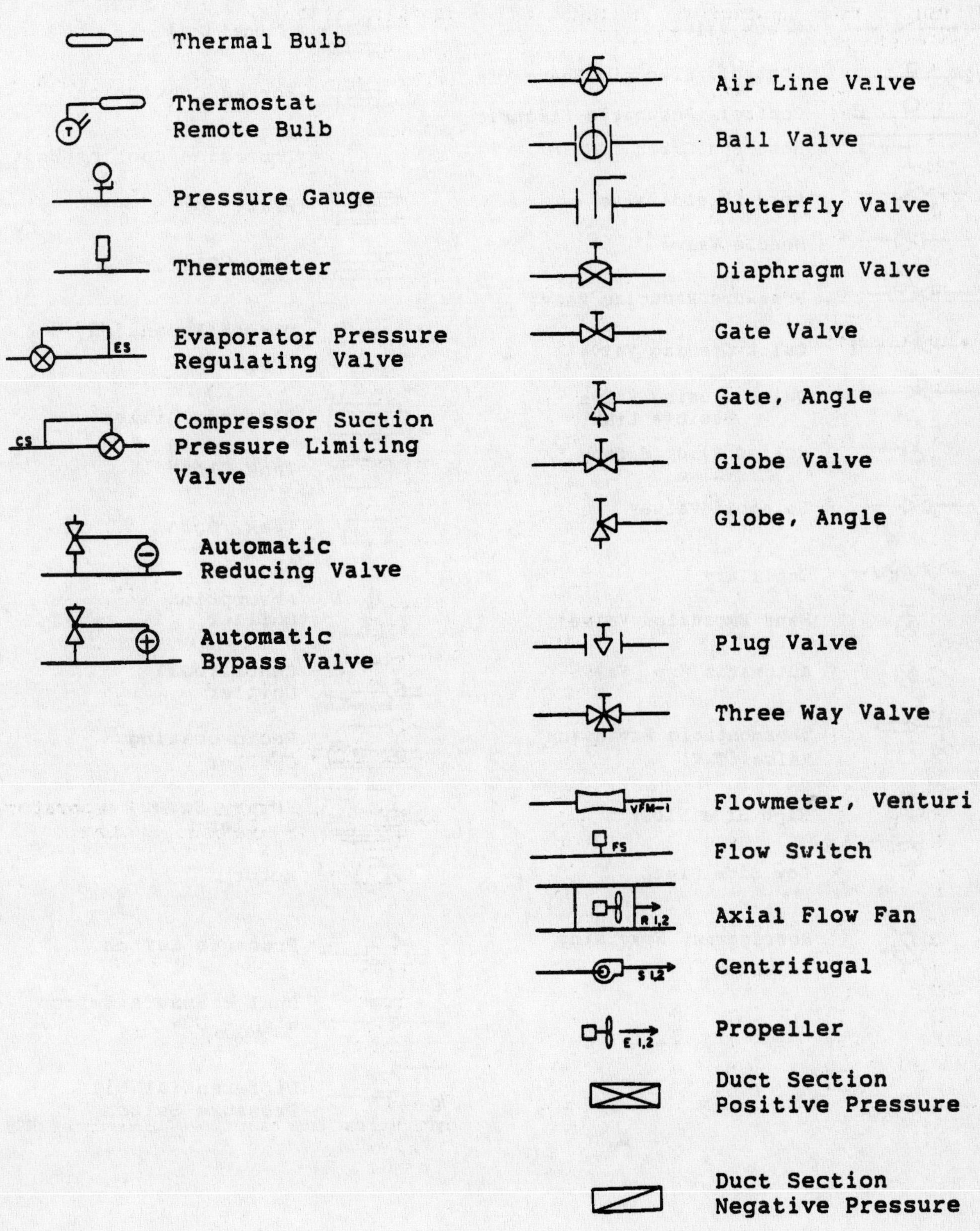
Thermal Bulb
Thermostat Remote Bulb
Pressure Gauge
Thermometer
ES
Evaporator Pressure Regulating Valve
CS
Compressor Suction Pressure Limiting Valve
Automatic Reducing Valve
Automatic Bypass Valve
Air Line Valve
Ball Valve
Butterfly Valve
Diaphragm Valve
Gate Valve
Gate, Angle
Globe Valve
Globe, Angle
Plug Valve
Three Way Valve
VFM-1
Flowmeter, Venturi
FS
Flow Switch
R 1,2
Axial Flow Fan
S 1,2
Centrifugal
E 1,2
Propeller
Duct Section Positive Pressure
Duct Section Negative Pressure

Fig. 11.1 (continued)

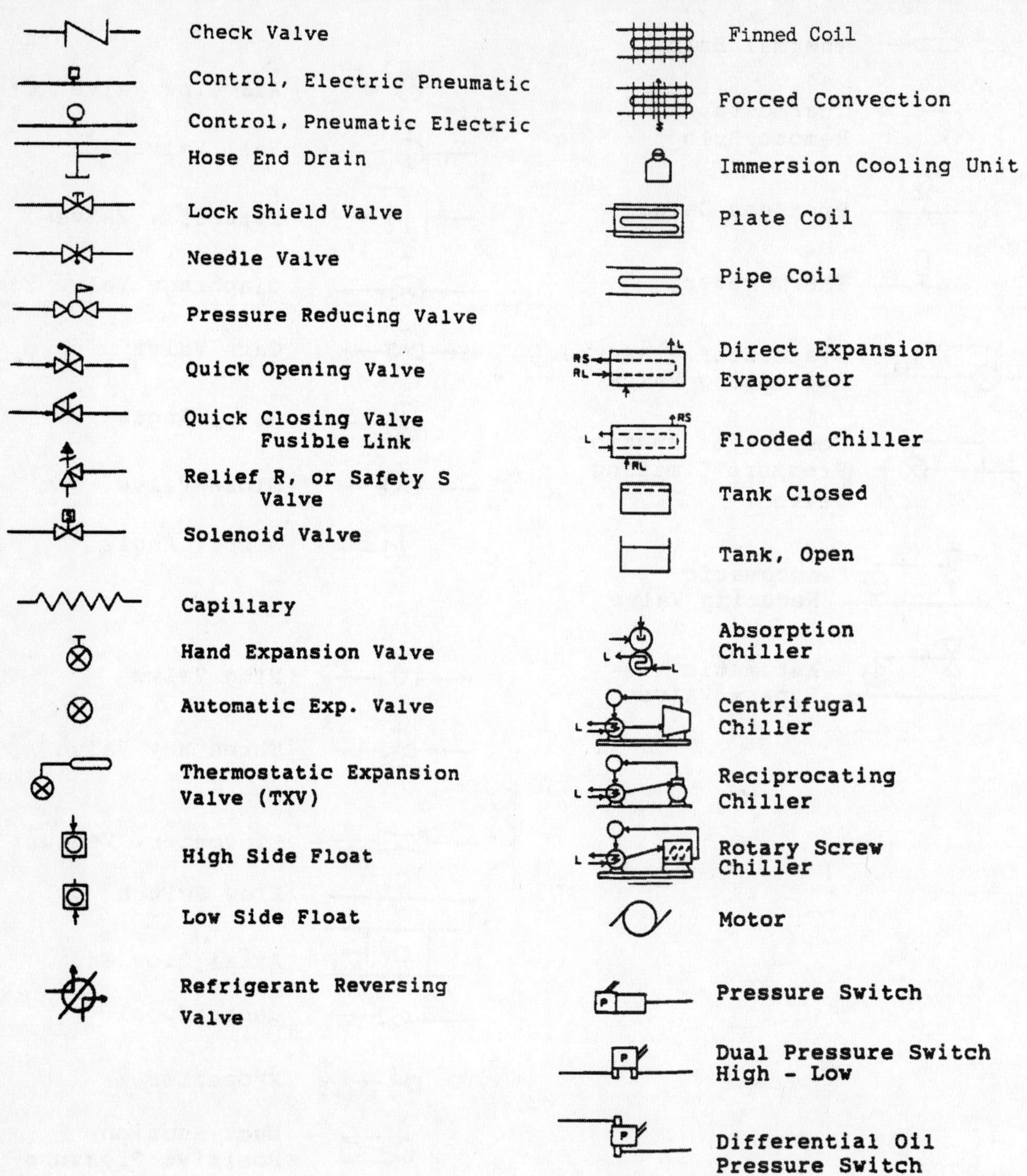
Check Valve
Control, Electric Pneumatic
Control, Pneumatic Electric
Hose End Drain
Lock Shield Valve
Needle Valve
Pressure Reducing Valve
Quick Opening Valve
Quick Closing Valve Fusible Link
Relief R, or Safety S Valve
Solenoid Valve
Capillary
Hand Expansion Valve
Automatic Exp. Valve
Thermostatic Expansion Valve (TXV)
High Side Float
Low Side Float
Refrigerant Reversing Valve
Finned Coil
Forced Convection
Immersion Cooling Unit
Plate Coil
Pipe Coil
RS
RL
L
Direct Expansion Evaporator
RS
L
RL
Flooded Chiller
Tank Closed
Tank, Open
L
L
Absorption Chiller
L
Centrifugal Chiller
L
Reciprocating Chiller
L
Rotary Screw Chiller
Motor
P
Pressure Switch
P
Dual Pressure Switch High - Low
P
Differential Oil Pressure Switch

Fig. 11.1 (continued)

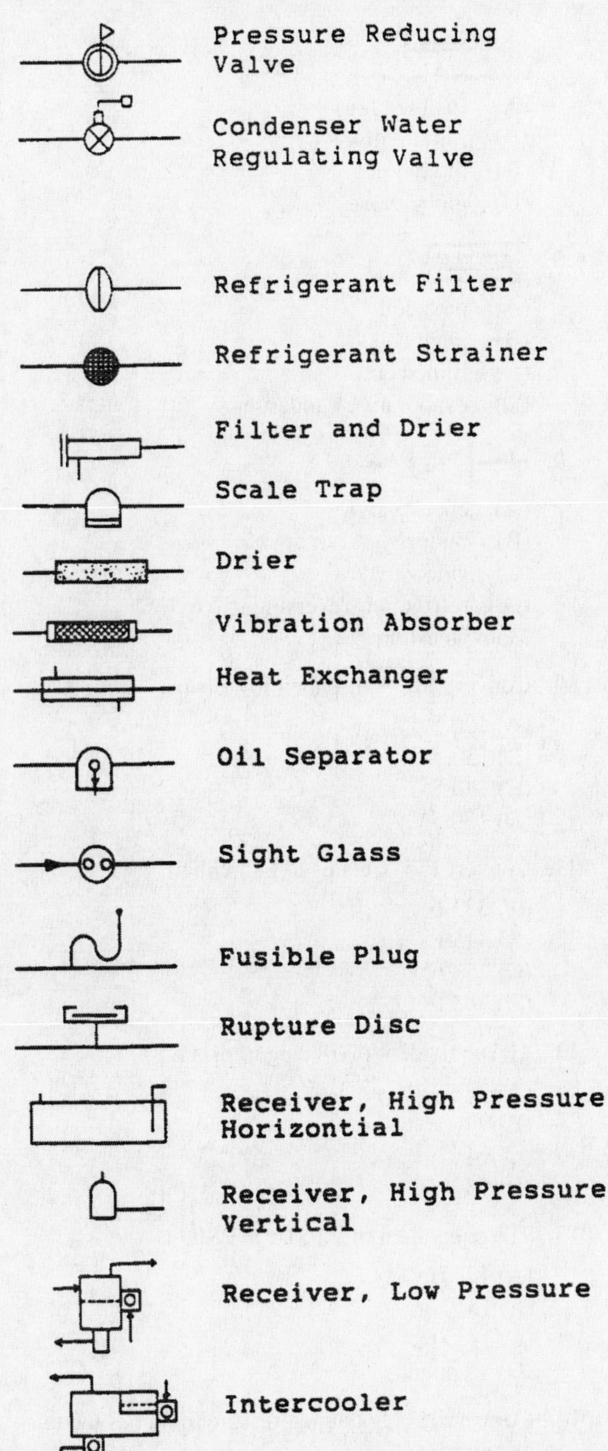
Pressure Reducing
Valve
Condenser Water
Regulating Valve
Refrigerant Filter
Refrigerant Strainer
Filter and Drier
Scale Trap
Drier
Vibration Absorber
Heat Exchanger
Oil Separator
Sight Glass
Fusible Plug
Rupture Disc
Receiver, High Pressure
Horizontial
Receiver, High Pressure
Vertical
Receiver, Low Pressure
Intercooler

Fig. 11.1 (continued)

SYMBOL AND MATH QUESTIONS

Identify the following symbols on a refrigeration plant drawing:

1. 

   (A) low-side float
   (B) charging valve
   (C) oil separator
   (D) high-side float

2. 

   (A) gate valve
   (B) float valve
   (C) AEV
   (D) TXV

3. 

   (A) thermal bulb
   (B) rupture disc
   (C) fusible plug
   (D) display counter

4. 

   (A) thermal bulb
   (B) AXV
   (C) pressure switch
   (D) high-side float

5. 

   (A) filter drier
   (B) scale trap
   (C) fuse
   (D) sight glass

6. 

   (A) gate valve
   (B) hand expansion valve
   (C) AXV
   (D) refrigerant-reversing valve

7. (A) fusible plug
   (B) rupture disc
   (C) intercooler
   (D) globe valve

8. (A) pipe coil
   (B) plate coil
   (C) finned coil
   (D) evaporative condenser

9. 

   (A) check valve
   (B) butterfly valve
   (C) gate valve
   (D) refrigerant-reversing valve

Math Questions

10. Convert 285° Fahrenheit to Celsius.

    (A) 120.5 C
    (B) 130.5 C
    (C) 140.5 C
    (D) 150.5 C

11. Convert 185° Celsius to Fahrenheit.

    (A) 333 F
    (B) 345 F
    (C) 353 F
    (D) 365 F

12. The equivalent of 78 psig in psia is

    (A) 92
    (B) 93
    (C) 94
    (D) 95

13. The equivalent of 9 PSIA in PSIG is

    (A) 12″ Hg.
    (B) 13″ Hg.
    (C) 14″ Hg.
    (D) 15 pounds.

14. Convert 22″ Hg gauge pressure to inches mercury absolute.

    (A) 10″
    (B) 9″
    (C) 8″
    (D) 7″

15. The specific heat of copper is .094. If 10 copper pipes are heated from 65° F to 100° F, and each pipe weighs 3 pounds, how many btu are exerted?

(A) 92.7
(B) 94.7
(C) 96.7
(D) 98.7

16. At how many rpm does a four-pole motor run if it is rated at 100 horsepower, 120 volts, and 60 cycles?

(A) 900 rpm
(B) 1,000 rpm
(C) 1,800 rpm
(D) 2,000 rpm

17. To compute the rated discharge capacity of a rupture disc in pounds of air per minute, use the refrigeration code formula $C = 0.8\ PD^2$. If $P = 28$ psia and $D = .48$, what is C?

(A) 4.17
(B) 5.16
(C) 4.16
(D) 5.18

18. A Freon system rated at 1.75 horsepower per ton will absorb how many btu per hour in the evaporator?

(A) 6857
(B) 6957
(C) 7052
(D) 7257

19. Find the air velocity in a duct with a free opening of 5.5 square feet and an air volume of 500 cfm. Use the formula $V = Q + A$.

(A) 100.8 ft./min.
(B) 90.9 ft./min.
(C) 109.8 ft./min.
(D) 98.5 ft./min.

20. A shell and tube condenser normally has a 1° temperature increase per 44 gpm/ton. If a 75-ton machine with 10 gpm has 75° water entering, what should be the outgoing termperature?

(A) 81°
(B) 86°
(C) 92°
(D) 96°

Answers to Air-Conditioning and Refrigeration Symbol and Math Questions

1. **The correct answer is (A).**
2. **The correct answer is (D).**
3. **The correct answer is (C).**
4. **The correct answer is (D).**
5. **The correct answer is (D).**
6. **The correct answer is (D).**
7. **The correct answer is (B).**
8. **The correct answer is (A).**
9. **The correct answer is (A).**
10. **The correct answer is (C).**

    $$C = \frac{E-32}{1.8} = \frac{285-32}{1.8} = \frac{253}{1.8} = 140.5$$

11. **The correct answer is (D).**

    F = (C × 1.8) + 32

    F = (185 × 1.8 + 32

    F = 333 + 32 = 365

12. **The correct answer is (B).** Above zero atmospheric pressure:

    78 + 15 = 93 psia

13. **The correct answer is (A).** Below 15 lbs. psia: (9 – 15) × 2

    –6 × 2 = 12″ Hg psig

14. **The correct answer is (C).** Gauge pressure is the same as psig.

    22 – 30 = 8″ Hg absolute

15. **The correct answer is (D).**

    Q = msh (Th – T1)

    Q = 10(.94) (100 – 65)

    .94(35)

    32.9 × 3 pounds = 98.7 btu

16. **The correct answer is (C).**

    $$\text{rpm} = \frac{120 \times \text{Hz}}{\text{poles}} = \frac{120 \times 60}{4} = \frac{7{,}200}{4} = 1{,}800 \text{ rpm}$$

17. **The correct answer is (B).**

    $$C = .8(28)\,(48^2)$$
    $$22.4\,(.48 \times .48)$$
    $$C = 22.4(.2304) = 5.16096 = 5.16$$

18. **The correct answer is (A).** 12,000 btu/hr.

    (1 ton) divided by 1.75 horsepower/ton = 6857.2

19. **The correct answer is (B).**

    $$90.9 = \frac{500}{505}$$

    V = velocity, Q = CFM, A = square foot area

20. **The correct answer is (C).**

    Every 1° temperature rise = 44 gpm/ton

    75-ton machine × 10gpm = 750 total system gpm

    750 ÷ 44 gpm = 17.045° temperature increase through the condenser

    75° + 17.04 = 92.04° temperature at the outlet of the condenser

Chapter 12

MULTITEMPERATURE SYSTEMS

Multitemperature systems normally use two or more evaporators operating at different temperatures, connected to one compressor and one condenser. The following illustration shows one example of a multitemperature system:

Multitemperature systems utilize the EPR (evaporator pressure regulator) valve to control the pressure of the warmer evaporator. The EPR valve maintains the pressure above a minimum value and prevents the evaporator from freezing.

EPR OPERATION

In a system with an evaporator pressure set for 30 lbs., the EPR valve must also be set for 30 lbs. As the metering device meters liquid refrigerant into the evaporator, with the EPR valve closed, the pressure rises. When the pressure in the evaporator reaches 30 to 30 $\frac{1}{2}$ lbs., the EPR valve opens slightly, allowing the excess pressure to be dumped into the suction line. As evaporator pressure rises above its set point, the EPR valve bleeds excessive evaporator pressure into the suction line. As the pressure drops, the valve closes.

As the metering device allows more liquid refrigerant into the evaporator, the EPR valve continues to open and close to maintain 30 lbs. of pressure in the evaporator.

The EPR valve is known in the field as the constant-pressure valve, back-pressure valve, or back-pressure regulating valve.

On a multitemperature system, a check valve is installed on the suction line of the colder evaporator. The check valve prevents high-pressure gas from the warmer evaporator from entering the colder evaporator.

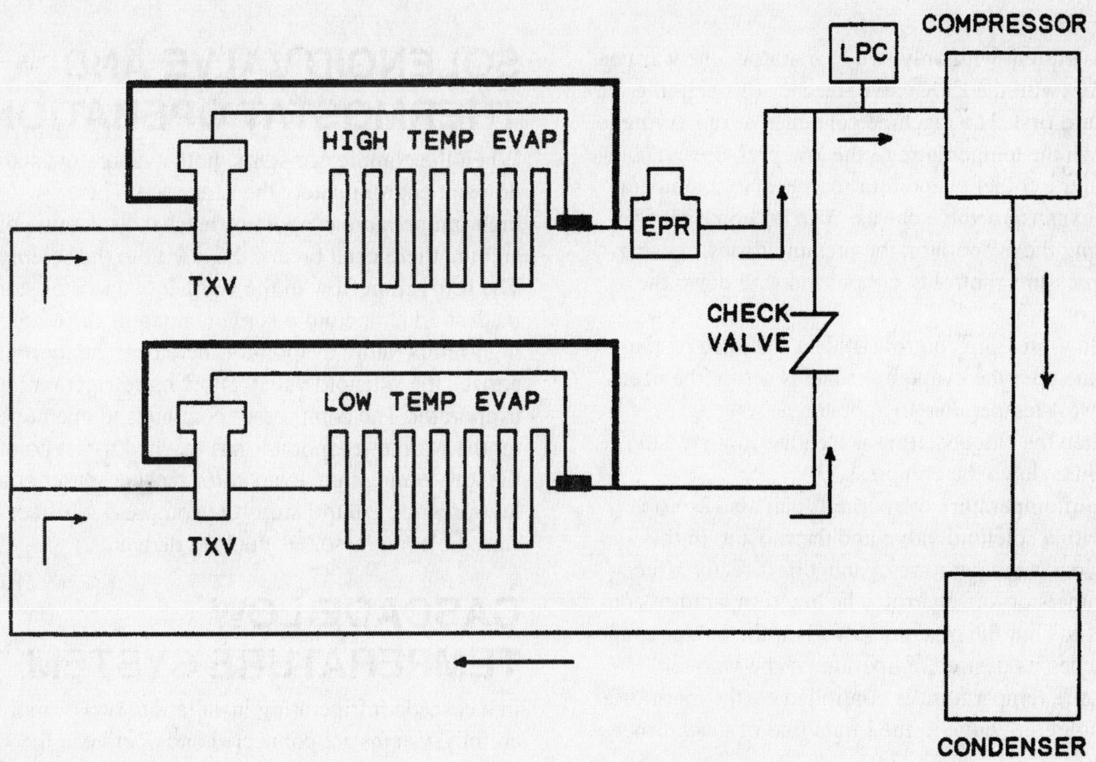

Fig. 12.1

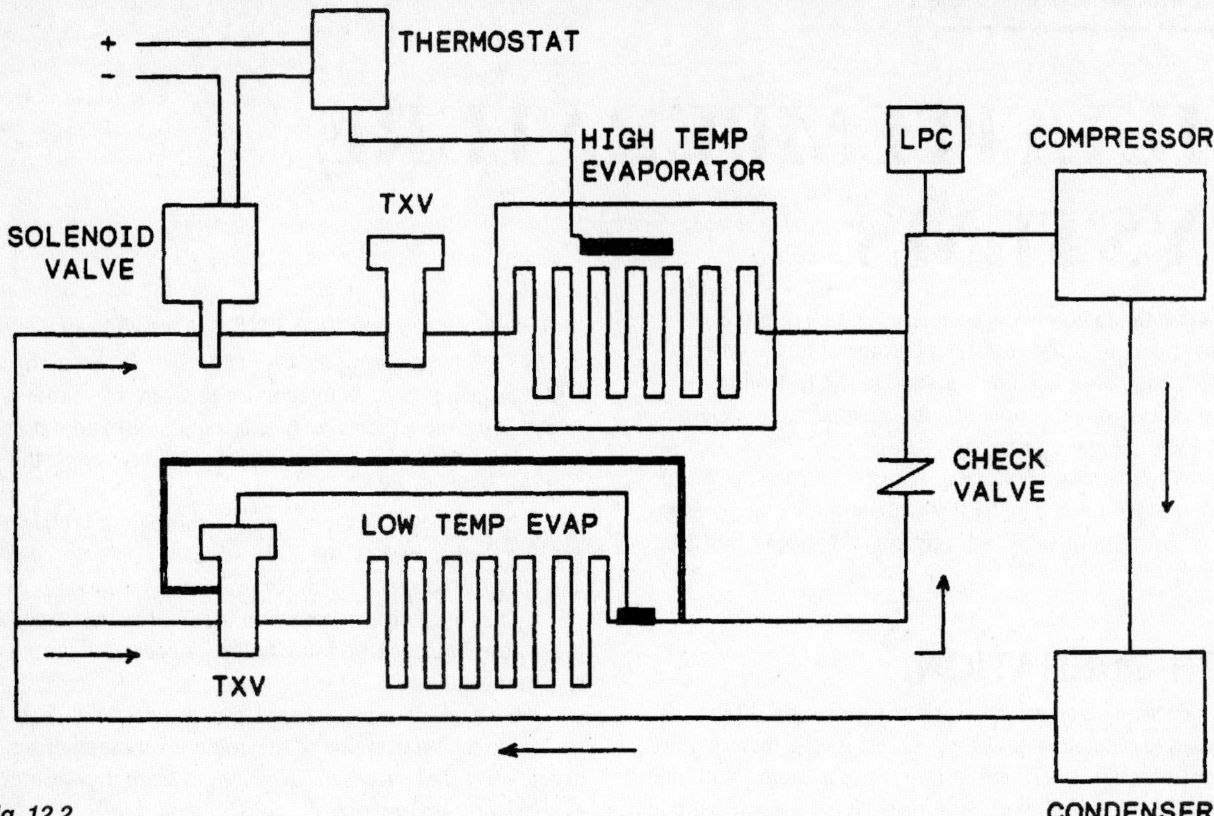

Fig. 12.2

In a system with only two evaporators, the warmer evaporator (with the EPR valve) reaches its operating temperature first. The machine continues to run, trying to bring down the temperature of the low-pressure evaporator. When the colder evaporator reaches its set temperature, the expansion valve closes. With no liquid refrigerant entering the evaporator, the pressure drops, causing the low-pressure control to cut out and shut down the compressor.

A low-pressure control (LPC) is installed on the suction line after the evaporators and is set for the needs of the lowest-temperature evaporator.

When the cutout setting is met, the low-pressure control shuts down the compressor.

Multitemperature evaporators can also be controlled with a solenoid valve and thermostat. In this system, the lower-temperature evaporator directly affects the machine's on-off control. The low-temperature control is set to shut the machine off when the colder evaporator reaches its desired temperature. The warmer evaporator's temperature is controlled by the thermostat and the solenoid valve in the liquid line of the warmer evaporator.

SOLENOID VALVE AND THERMOSTAT OPERATION

When the compressor starts, both evaporators start to pull down at approximately the same rate. The high-temperature evaporator reaches its cutout point first, and the thermostat breaks the circuit to the solenoid valve. The refrigerant flow in the warmer evaporator stops and its desired temperature is maintained. If the load on the high-temperature evaporator increases, the thermostat energizes the solenoid valve, allowing refrigerant into the evaporator. The compressor continues to operate even after the warmer evaporator has reached its set point. When the low-temperature evaporator reaches its set point, the low-pressure control stops the compressor. Either coil can start the compressor, as the load demands.

CASCADE LOW TEMPERATURE SYSTEM

In a cascade refrigerating installation, two or more refrigerating systems are connected and operate at the same time. The evaporator of System A (on the right in figure

12.3) cools condenser B. The evaporator of System B supplies the desired cooling effect. The low-pressure liquid of System A cools the high-pressure vapor of System B. Each system has a thermostatic expansion valve for refrigerant control. In figure 12.3, one motor control is used for both motors. It is connected to a temperature-sensing bulb on evaporator B.

Cascade systems are often used in industrial processes for cooling below –50° F. Motors must be able to start under a load. With thermostatic expansion valves, pressures do not balance on the off-cycle. Evaporator A is usually combined with condenser B in a shell-and-tube flooded device.

Since these systems operate very low temperatures, the refrigerant must be very dry. Any moisture could condense at the needle-seat of the TXV and stop the refrigerant flow. System B must have a special refrigerant oil that is wax-free, moisture-free, and flowable at extra-low temperatures. Oil separators should be installed in the discharge lines of Systems A and B to help keep oil in the compressor.

The following illustration shows how a cascade system may employ two or three different refrigeration systems using different refrigerants. These are interconnected to produce very low temperatures. The first, highest-temperature system might be an R-12 system. All parts of this

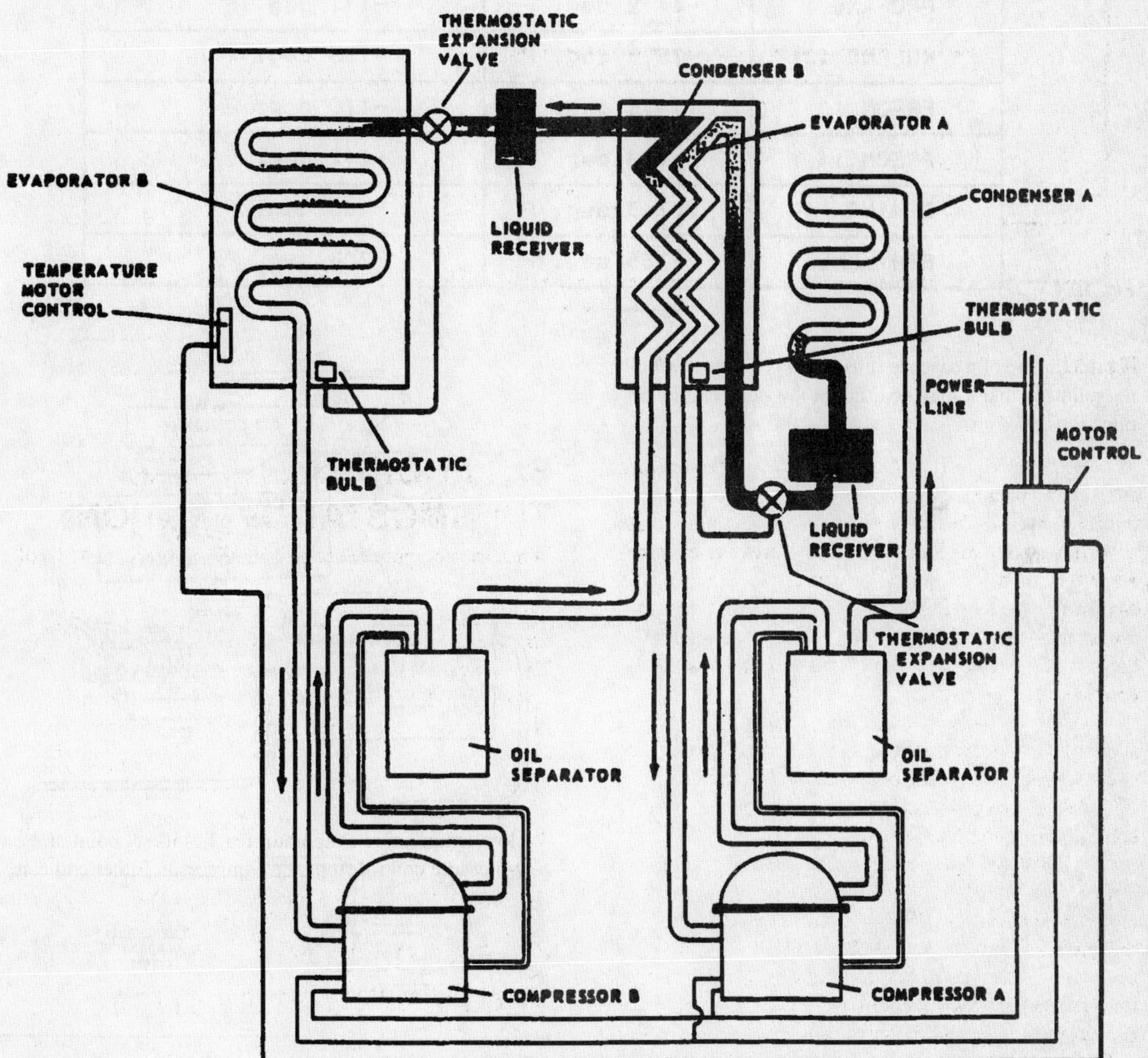

Fig. 12.3

system would comprise a simple compression plant, except for the evaporator; this would be similar in construction to a shell-and-coil condenser. It would cool the condenser of the second, lower-temperature machine. The second machine might use another refrigerant such as R-22. It would resemble any other R-22 system, except that its condenser, being part of the R-12 system, would be refrigerant-cooled. The evaporator of the R-22 system is in turn part of the third, lowest-temperature system. One side of the R-22 evaporator cools this system's Kulene 131 condenser. If the Kulene 131 condenser is refrigerated, the pressures become lower on both the discharge and suction sides of the machine. This enables the Kulene 131 system to lower the temperature to –135° F. The three refrigerants cited here are not the only ones used in cascade systems; some use exotic refrigerants, as shown in the figure below.

REFRIGERANT	BOILING POINT AT 14.7# PSIA	SATURATED TEMPERATURE AT 2# PSIA
PROPANE	-44.2 deg. F	-111 deg. F
KULENE 131	-73.6 deg. F	-135 deg. F
FREON 13	-114.5 deg. F	-170 deg. F
FREON 14	-198 deg. F	-242 deg. F
ETHANE	-127.5 deg. F	-183 deg. F
ETHYLENE	-155 deg. F	-208 deg. F

Fig. 12.4

A prerequisite of a cascade refrigerant is a very low boiling point, so that it may be used for low-temperature applications.

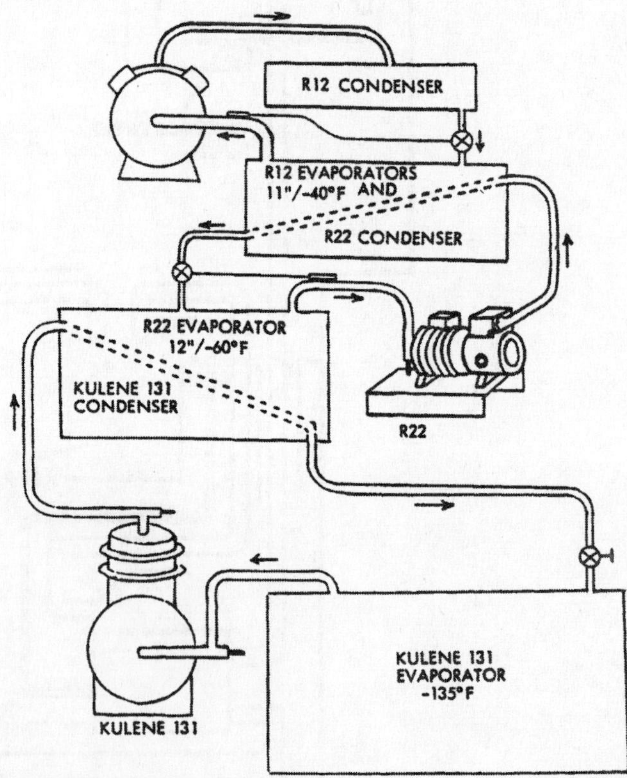

Fig. 12.5

CASCADE SYSTEM

MULTITEMPERATURE SYSTEMS LICENSE QUESTIONS

1. If the EPR valve froze open in a two-temperature system,

(A) both evaporators would warm up.
(B) the warmer evaporator would get colder.
(C) the colder evaporator would get too cold.
(D) none of the above.

2. In a multitemperature system, the two-temperature valve is located

(A) in the suction line of the warmer evaporator.
(B) in the suction line of the colder evaporator.
(C) in the common suction line.
(D) none of the above.

3. If a two-temperature valve froze open,

(A) the system would overload and cut out.
(B) the warmer evaporator would cool to the temperature of the colder evaporator.
(C) the temperature in the warmer evaporator would rise.
(D) it would have no effect on the system.

4. To operate two evaporators at different temperatures in a system with one compressor, it is necessary to install a back-pressure valve in the

(A) suction line of the low-temperature evaporator.
(B) suction line of the high-temperature evaporator.
(C) common suction line.
(D) common discharge line.

5. The check valve of a two-temperature system is located on

(A) the suction line of the high-temperature evaporator.
(B) the liquid line of the high-temperature evaporator.
(C) the suction line of the low-temperature evaporator.
(D) the liquid line of the low-temperature evaporator.

6. Where is the low-pressure control connected on a two-temperature system?

(A) In the discharge line
(B) In the liquid line
(C) In the suction line
(D) In the pressure line

7. Cascade systems are sometimes necessary for

(A) low-temperature applications in hospitals.
(B) industrial processes requiring cooling below –50 F.
(C) cooling two or more compartments that are at the same or different temperatures.
(D) all of the above.

8. What is the main advantage of a cascade system?

(A) It is capable of reaching very low temperatures.
(B) It does not deplete the ozone layer.
(C) Low cost and low maintenance
(D) All of the above

Answers to Multitemperature System License Questions

1. **The correct answer is (B).**
2. **The correct answer is (A).**
3. **The correct answer is (B).**
4. **The correct answer is (B).**
5. **The correct answer is (C).**
6. **The correct answer is (C).**
7. **The correct answer is (D).**
8. **The correct answer is (A).**

Chapter 13

OTHER REFRIGERATION SYSTEMS

STEAM JET SYSTEM

The steam jet system uses water as a refrigerant. It operates on the principle that reduction of pressure lowers the boiling point of water. This is an efficient system used for air-conditioning or high-temperature refrigeration. It consists of a steam nozzle, venturi, evaporator, condenser, condensate pump, and secondary condenser.

Steam forced through the nozzle and through the venturi pulls a vacuum from behind the venturi, removing most of the air from the system. The jet stream pressure should be approximately 55 psig to 85 psig. The venturi is connected to a large water tank, or evaporator. The flow of steam continues through the piping into a water-cooled condenser. The jet stream pressure produces a high vacuum above the surface of the evaporator, producing chilled water approximately 40° F.

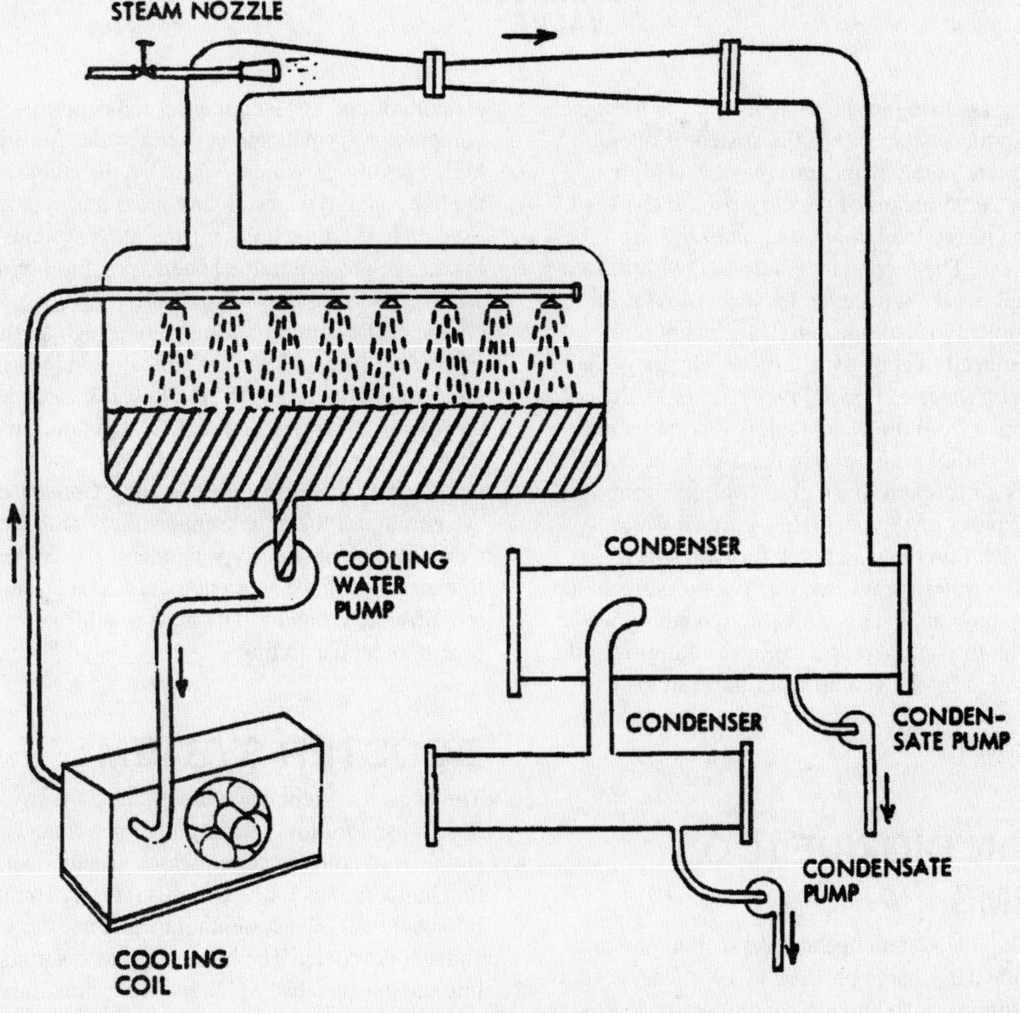

Fig. 13.1

STEAM JET SYSTEM

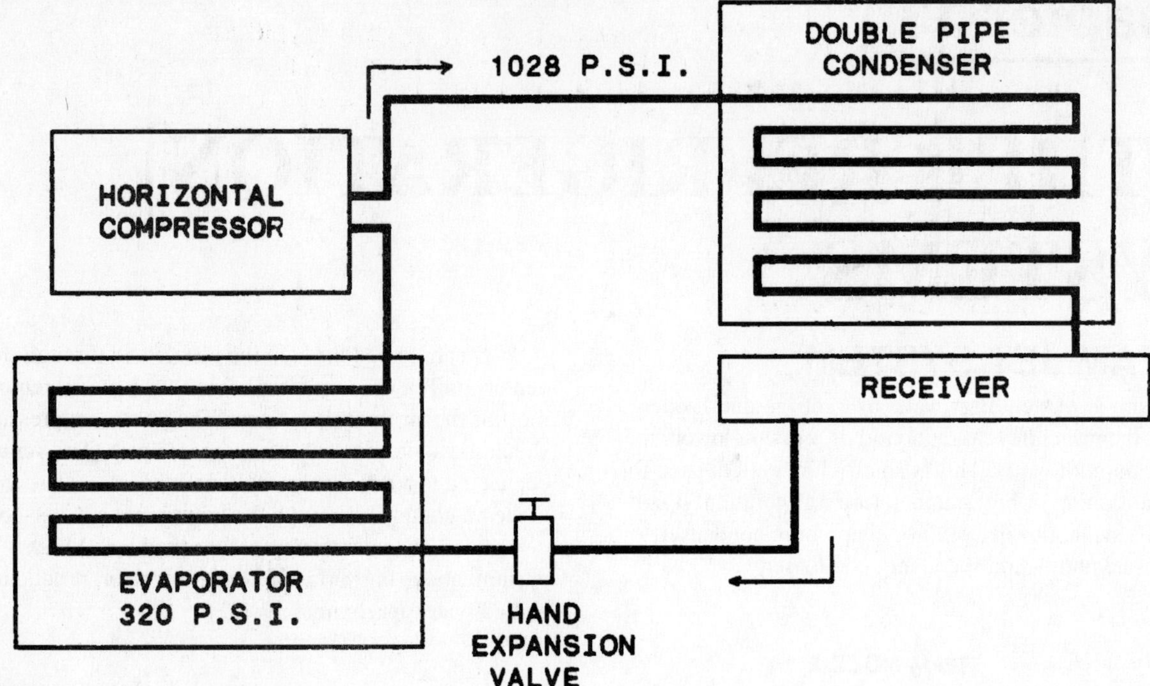

Fig. 13.2

Steam condensing in the condenser helps increase the vacuum in the system. When the system is operating properly, vacuum in the evaporator may be as high as 29.8, 29.9, or 29.95 inches of mercury psig. If the system is under a heavy load, more steam nozzles are brought into use. The secondary condenser, with its condensate pump, is used whenever the steam flow is increased to prevent loss of vacuum. If the evaporator pressure is reduced to approximately 30″ Hg. psig, the boiling point of water can be as low as 32° F. As the cold water is pumped from the water tank (evaporator) into and through a chiller-water coil in the area to be cooled, the fan blows air through this coil to cool the room. The chilled water picks up the heat. This warmed water is transferred back into the water tank through spray nozzles. As the water sprays into the low-pressure area, some flashes into vapor. This chills the remaining water for re-use. The low-temperature vapor resulting from the flashing is pulled by the venturi from the system. This additional condensing helps maintain the high vacuum on the water tank.

CARBON DIOXIDE (CO_2) SYSTEMS

The carbon dioxide system operates on suction pressure of 320 psig and a discharge pressure of 1028 psig, at standard ton conditions. Standard ton conditions are 5° F evaporator and 86° F condenser temperatures. The CO_2 compressor is small and very heavy due to its extremely high working pressures. Normally, the compressor is of the horizontal type. For many years this system has been used on low-temperature refrigeration systems. CO_2 at 0 lbs. gauge pressure (atmospheric pressure) will boil at 109° below zero. In warm climates the high-pressure discharge of the compressor may go as high as 1500 lbs. One of the few drawbacks to the CO_2 system is the low critical temperature of CO_2: 87.8° F. Thus, if the condensing water rises to 87.8° F or above, CO_2 will not liquefy. No matter how high the pressure, the 87.8° F vapor cannot liquefy, and this reduces the efficiency. Condensers on CO_2 systems are of the double-pipe variety. It is not safe to use CO_2 in a tank or shell-type condenser, because its wall thickness would be so great that the condenser would be too difficult to handle. The mass would also reduce the heat-transfer capability.

BOOSTER SYSTEM

The booster system, sometimes called the two-stage system, is used for low-temperature operation. The slow-speed ammonia compressor usually operates at suction temperatures for 0° F to 40° F brine. To refrigerate brine below 0° F, a system requires a booster compressor and an intercooler. The booster compressor discharges into the inter-cooler, which gives the ammonia vapor to the primary compressor. The primary compressor then

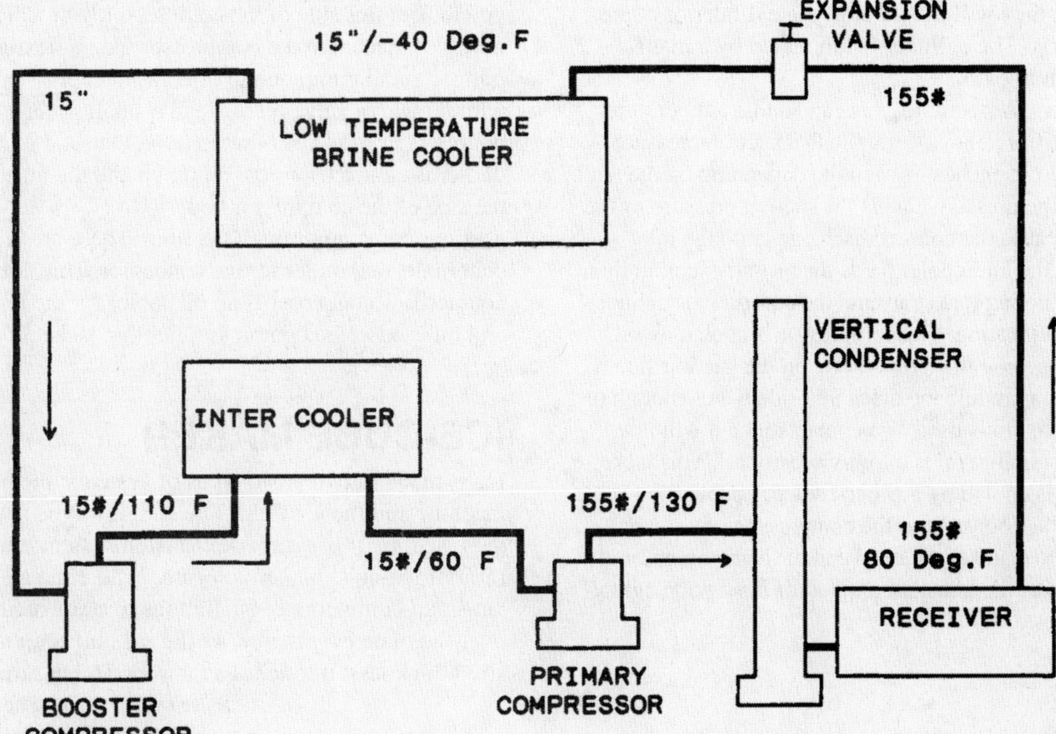

Fig. 13.3 Booster System

compresses the vapor and sends it to the condenser. The cycle from here on is the same as in other ammonia compression systems.

The booster compressor has either a higher speed or a greater bore and stroke than the primary compressor. If the speed is the same, the booster compressor is larger than the primary compressor. The reason for this difference in speed or size is that the suction of the booster compressor may be anywhere from 5 psig down to 15 inches vacuum. The slow-speed primary compressor usually operates between 5 and 20 psig of suction pressure. The booster compressor must take this very low-pressure refrigerant gas and compress enough not to starve the primary compressor, which operates with denser, higher-pressure suction gas. The booster compressor takes low-pressure vapor at any pressure from 5 pounds to 15 inches of vacuum, compresses it to approximately 15 psig, and feeds it to an intercooler. The intercooler removes some heat without affecting pressure or changing the state. This cooled, compressed vapor enters the primary compressor without harming it. The primary compressor will compress the vapor 155 psig and send it to the condenser. The primary compressor is designed to handle 15 pounds of pressure refrigerant in the suction side, but not if this refrigerant is too hot, as the compressor may be scorched. To avoid damaging the primary compressor, some heat of compression must be removed in the inter-cooler.

Refrigerant in the booster system enters the first, or booster, compressor as a low-pressure vapor. It is compressed and sent to the intercooler and then the second compressor, which is called the primary compressor because it is the first compressor to start when the system is put into operation. This gives the booster discharge someplace to go. If the booster were started with no outlet for this discharge gas, pressure would build and damage might occur.

BOOSTER COMPRESSORS

The booster compressors are F.E.S. (Freezing Equipment Sales) Fuller Rotary Booster Compressors. They are made in Pennsylvania and sold out of Philadelphia.

The rotary compressor is a high-speed, positive-displacement unit with a minimum of moving parts. It consists of a jacketed casing, or cylinder, containing a smaller-diameter rotor that rotates on an offset axis.

The steel rotor is fitted with fiber vanes that glide in and out of their slots. As the rotor turns, the vanes, or blades, are thrown outward to the cylinder wall by centrifugal force. This forms as many cells as there are vanes. Each cell traps vapor. As the rotor turns and the blades move toward the discharge port, the cells become smaller, compressing the vapor and discharging it at higher pressure. The blades are made of fiber so that if they break, they will not damage the cylinder or other internal parts. The cylinder is lubricated by a manzel force feed lubricator.

The booster compressors can handle temperatures as low as –50° F. They operate with a suction pressure from 5 psi to 15 inches of vacuum, depending on the load. The discharge pressure equals the suction pressure of the primary because the booster discharges into the intercooler, and the intercooler feeds the primary suction line.

The cooling jacket around the compressor cylinder prevents overheating. The compressor is cooled by oil, not water, because the temperature on the suction side is below freezing, while the discharge side is hot enough to need cooling. Oil is used as a coolant since it will not freeze. The cooling oil is a low-viscosity oil. This jacket-cooling oil is cooled by a water-cooled, double-pipe condenser on the floor next to the compressor.

As you stand at the head end of the compressor, the suction side of the booster compressor is on your right. If you look at this side of the compressor, you will see the motor connected to the compressor with a flexible coupling, a small pump on the floor, a small glass tank filled with oil with a valve on top, and a small water-cooled, double-pipe condenser on the floor. One end of this condenser is connected to the oil pump and the other end to the side of the compressor body. Two city water-line connections come up through the floor. These are the cooling water inlet and outlet for the condenser. This double-pipe, counterflow condenser is an oil cooler for the light mineral oil used in the compressor cooling jacket.

ICE-CUBE MAKER

Ice is made in two basic types of systems: the plate ice machine and the ice field. The simplest type is the plate ice machine. It is a direct-expansion system; the evaporator or ice-cube maker is located where the ice is made. On small commercial installations, water usually flows over the plate evaporator. As the ice builds up to the desired thickness, it touches a thermostat that turns on the defrost mechanism. The plate evaporator is tilted to allow the sheet of ice to slide off onto a metal grid that cuts the ice into cubes. This is an efficient direct-expansion machine.

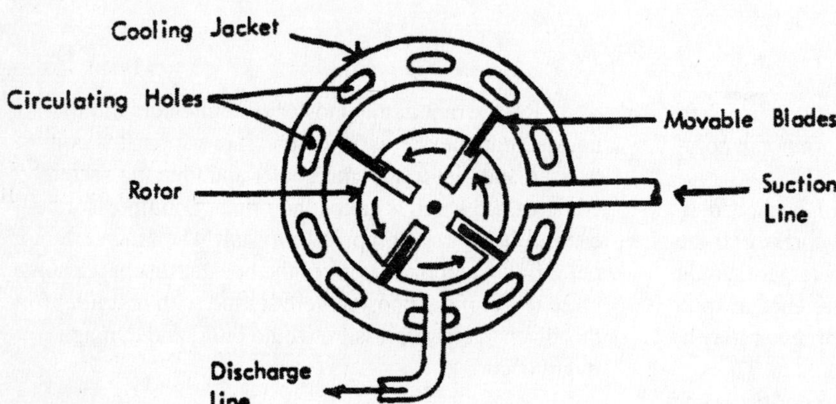

Fig. 13.4

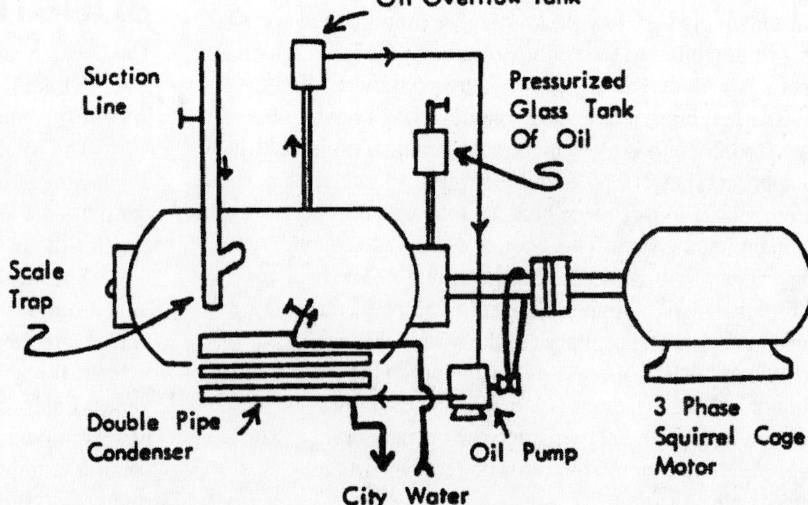

Fig. 13.5

PLATE ICE SYSTEM

The industrial plate ice machine is usually found in rural areas. A pit may be dug approximately 12 feet square and 12 feet deep that is lined with metal, with the cooling coils on the outside facing the earth. This 1,728-cubic-foot pit is then filled with water. When low-pressure refrigerant is sent through the coils, the water starts to freeze. Mechanical beaters and/or paddles stir the surface of the water to prevent distortion of the pit from expansion and to prevent freezing from taking place at the top. This means that the 12-foot cube must freeze from the bottom and sides inward, allowing for expansion upward. This agitation of the water also results in clear ice. When the cube is almost completely frozen, the beaters/paddles are removed and total freezing takes place. The system is then defrosted, and the 12-foot cube is hoisted out and cut to size. This is a very efficient direct-expansion machine. Since it cannot produce large quantities at a time, it is not commonly used in cities.

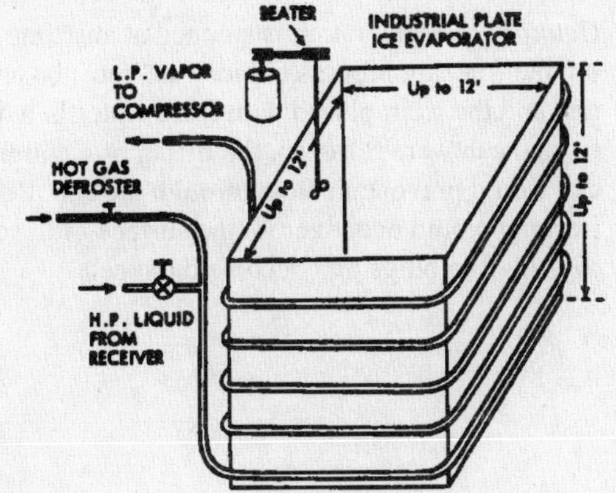

Fig. 13.6

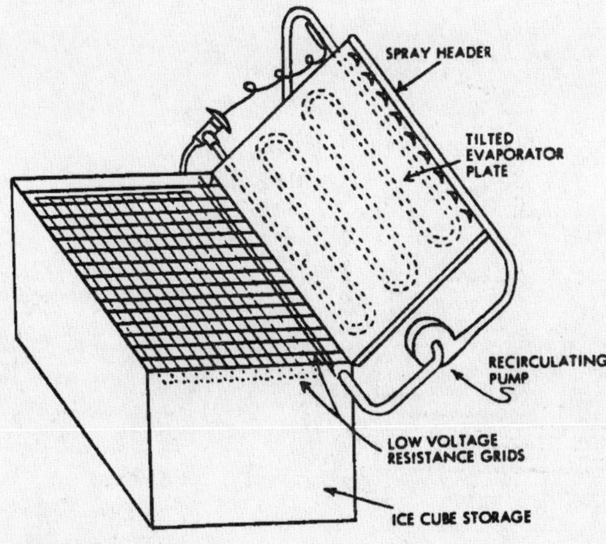

Fig. 13.7

ICE FIELD

The ice field, a less efficient but more productive system, is used in New York. It is an indirect system. Brine is refrigerated in the machine and pumped into a large tank, whose size varies with the tonnage of the plant. Individual blocks of ice made in the ice field weigh approximately 300 pounds. These blocks are frozen in stainless-steel cans averaging 11″ × 22″ × 44″. A pipe welded to the outside of the can runs vertically from about 2 inches above the top to the bottom, then bends 180° to run horizontally across the bottom, ending inside the bottom center. Air is bubbled up through the water from this pipe, primarily to make clear ice, secondarily to agitate the water sufficiently to prevent surface freezing. Freezing takes place from the sides inward. This allows the freezing water to expand and prevents the can from buckling.

Brine is refrigerated to a temperature between 14 and 21° F. If the temperature were below 14° F, ice would be made faster but would be brittle and hard to handle. If the temperature were above 21° F, the ice would be wet and would melt too quickly to be sold commercially. The ideal ice-making temperature is 14 to 21° F.

Cold brine is pumped into the ice field tank and is circulated around the ice cans, then sent back to the brine cooler to lose heat. When ice in a can is almost completely frozen, a vacuum hose is used to remove the small quantity of water left, along with any impurities. If the ice were removed now, it would have a funnel-shaped hole down the center. This hole must be washed out and filled with fresh water. The air hose is disconnected and the hole frozen solid. When the 300-pound cube is removed from the can, it has a funnel-shaped center of cloudy ice. Cloudy ice, sometimes mistakenly called ammonia ice, is caused by a lack of air and agitation during freezing.

When the ice is completely frozen, the can is lifted from the ice field and sent to a dip tank filled with warm water. The can is removed from the dip tank and turned upside down. After the ice slides out, the can is returned to the ice field and refrozen. The ice field may hold from one to 300 cans or more. Equipment tonnage determines can number and field size.

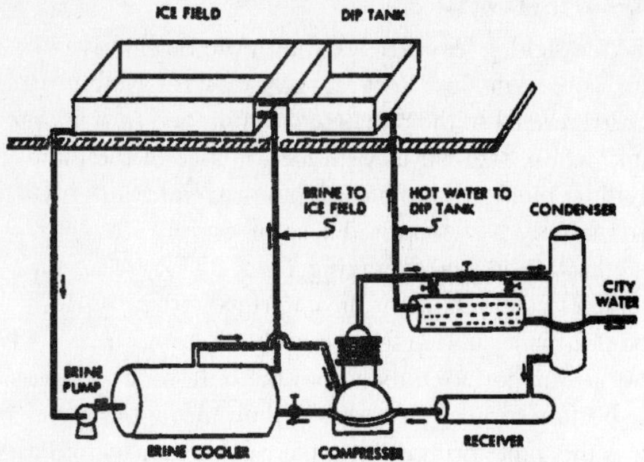

Fig. 13.8

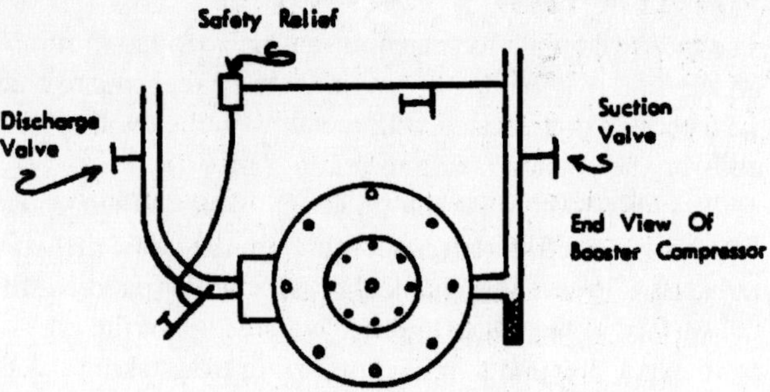

Fig. 13.9

The basic equipment for the ice field system was covered under ammmonia compression systems. The new equipment is the ice field, the dip tank, and the heat exchanger for hot water in the dip tank.

ice field: a large, waterproof pit into which refrigerated brine is pumped, usually in one end and out the other. Air hoses hang from the ceiling for each ice can. Ice cans are suspended in racks or rows in the brine. When frozen, they may be lifted out a rack at a time.

dip tank: a smaller, waterproof pit with a continual flow of hot water. A rack of cans is dipped into the tank to free the ice, which goes to a storage room. The cans are refilled in the dip tank, then sent to the ice field for refreezing.

hot-water heat exchanger: a heat exchanger placed in the discharge line between the compressor and the condenser. The hot discharge gas goes through the outer pipe to the condenser. Fresh city water goes through the inner pipe to the dip tank. The city water picks up heat from the discharge gas. This heat defrosts the ice cans.

Caution: If refrigeration is stopped at any time during the freezing process, all ice cans must be emptied and the ice replaced with fresh water. If a defrosted can were refrozen, the lifting of ice in the can would prevent air flow through the can. Refreezing would occur across the surface of the can, causing it to bulge and become damaged.

OTHER REFRIGERATION SYSTEMS LICENSE QUESTIONS

1. Cascade and two-stage booster refrigeration systems are used for

(A) low-temperature applications.
(B) air-conditioning operation.
(C) any application.
(D) ice-making only.

2. The booster compressor of a two-stage refrigeration system is located between the

(A) main compressor and condenser.
(B) intercooler and main compressor.
(C) condenser and metering device.
(D) evaporator and intercooler.

3. A water-cooled condenser with one or more assemblies of two tubes, one inside the other, is called

(A) atmospheric.
(B) shell-and-tube.
(C) shell-and-coil.
(D) double-pipe.

4. What is the pressure at the intercooler outlet?

(A) The same as the evaporator
(B) The same as the main compressor suction line
(C) 86° F
(D) 120° F

5. In a booster system, the booster compressor should be

(A) at the high side.
(B) at the low side.
(C) for Freon-11 only.
(D) for CO_2 only.

6. Which refrigerant usually has a condenser pressure of 1050 pounds?

(A) NH_3
(B) Butane
(C) Methyl chloride
(D) CO_2

7. Which of the following could be termed a cascade system?

(A) An ammonia system cooling the condenser of a carbon dioxide system
(B) An ammonia system cooling the brine tank ready to be circulated
(C) A Freon system cooling brine for a brine spray
(D) A methyl chloride system used as a heat pump

8. In a carbon dioxide system, the oil system is usually

(A) a splash system for vertical compressors.
(B) a high-pressure system for horizontal compressors.
(C) a low-pressure system for horizontal compressors.
(D) Both (A) and (B)

9. What is the main refrigeration principle used in the steam jet system?

(A) If you reduce the pressure of water, the boiling point will be lowered.
(B) Heat always flows from a warmer to a cooler substance.
(C) Heated surfaces lose heat to cooler surrounding surfaces.
(D) The total pressure of a confined mixture of gases is the sum of the pressures of each gas in the mixture.

10. The industrial plate ice machine uses mechanical beaters to stir the water surface during the freezing cycle. The main reason is to

(A) provide greater freezing during agitation.
(B) prevent freezing from starting at the surface and to make clear ice.
(C) produce large quantities of ice during the agitation period.
(D) none of the above.

11. What are some components of an ice field?

(A) Separator tank, ice field, heat exchanger, condenser
(B) Brine cooler, analyzer, ice field, heat exchanger
(C) Brine cooler, dip tank, heat exchanger, separator tank
(D) Condenser, ice field, heat exchanger, dip tank

12. Where is the hot-water heat exchanger in the ice field system?

(A) Between the evaporator and the condenser
(B) Between the discharge line of the compressor and the condenser
(C) Between the liquid line of the condenser and the metering device
(D) Between the suction line of the evaporator and the condenser

13. If an ice field is stopped during the freezing process, what should the operator do?
    (A) Send the defrosted ice to a holding room and return the cans to the dip tank
    (B) Agitate the defrosted ice and reuse it immediately
    (C) Reset the thermostat, turn on the defrost mechanism, and return the water to the brine cooler
    (D) Empty all ice cans and refill with fresh water

14. If a defrosted can were refrozen,
    (A) initial refreezing would occur across the top of the can, causing bulging and damage to the can.
    (B) lifting of ice in the can would prevent air flow through the can.
    (C) initial refreezing would make the ice brittle and hard to handle.
    (D) none of the above.

15. Ideal ice-making temperature is
    (A) between 14 and 21° F.
    (B) between 4 and 14° F.
    (C) between 14 and 29° F.
    (D) anywhere below 32° F.

16. What factor causes cloudy ice, mistakenly called ammonia ice, to form?
    (A) Impurities in the ice
    (B) The inability to filter out NH_3
    (C) Lack of air and agitation while the hollow center freezes
    (D) Water was frozen too quickly

17. Why isn't water used to cool booster compressors?

____

18. If the compressor is cold enough to freeze water, why is it necessary to use a cooling jacket?

____

19. In the booster system's double-pipe condenser, where is the oil and where is the water? What is in the inside pipe, and what is in the outside pipe?

____

20. What is located at the bottom of the booster-compressor suction line?

____

21. What kind of motor drives the booster compressor?

____

22. On the end of the compressor are two flanged covers. What would you see if you removed the smaller one?

____

23. What would you see if you removed the booster's larger flanged cover?

____

24. Relief lines of booster compressors are insulated. A valve wheel and a plug stick out of the insulation, off the side of the relief line. There is also a line that goes to the relief valve coming out of the insulation at this point. What would happen if someone closed the discharge valve while the booster was running?

____

25. What would happen if the relief valve did not lift?

____

26. Would this damage the compressor?

____

27. Can you affect the relief line by opening or closing the exposed valve wheel?

____

28. Could you pipe the valve from the discharge line into the hot-gas defrost line?

____

29. If this valve is not for defrosting, what is it for?

____

30. How would you check for a leak on the suction side of the booster compressor?

____

31. What is the purpose of the pressurized glass tank of oil on top of the booster compressor?

____

Answers to Other Refrigeration Systems License Questions

1. **The correct answer is (A).**
2. **The correct answer is (D).**
3. **The correct answer is (D).**
4. **The correct answer is (B).**
5. **The correct answer is (B).**
6. **The correct answer is (D).**
7. **The correct answer is (A).**
8. **The correct answer is (D).**
9. **The correct answer is (A).**
10. **The correct answer is (B).**
11. **The correct answer is (D).**
12. **The correct answer is (B).**
13. **The correct answer is (D).**
14. **The correct answer is (A) and (B).**
15. **The correct answer is (A).**
16. **The correct answer is (C).**
17. **The correct answer is it would freeze due to the low temperature of the suction gas.**
18. **The correct answer is even though the suction side of the compressor is below freezing, the discharge side is quite hot and requires cooling.**
19. **The correct answer is water is in the inside pipe and oil is in the outside pipe.** This is so the water side of the cooler may be cleaned when the tubes get dirty.
20. **The correct answer is a scale trap, a basket-type strainer to catch scale in the suction line.** The trap prevents scale or foreign objects from entering the compressor and damaging the cylinder walls, rotor, and blades.
21. **The correct answer is "It is a three-phase AC induction motor. Push a button to start and stop."**
22. **The correct answer is the rotor shaft and the bearing.**
23. **The correct answer is the rotor, the rotor blades, and the end parts of the compressor cooling jacket.**
24. **The correct answer is the relief valve would lift and dump back to the suction line.**
25. **The correct answer is the rotor blades would break.**
26. **The correct answer is not seriously.** The blades are made of fiber, so if they break they will not damage the internal compressor.
27. **The correct answer is no.** The valve is plugged on one side, so it obviously is not connected to the relief valve. This valve is off a nipple on a "T" coming off the side of the discharge line. The other part of the "T" is for the relief line connection." It is against the law to have a shut-off valve between a relief valve and the unit it is protecting. There is also another valve on a "T" between the relief valve and the suction line. So now there are two valves whose purpose we haven't discussed yet.
28. **The correct answer is no.** Although the discharge line is hot enough for defrosting, the booster discharge pressure is the same as the primary suction pressure. It does not have enough push to reach the evaporators.
29. **The correct answer is it is used for evacuating the ammonia compressor for repairs or maintenance.** Connect a piece of pipe from this valve, close the suction and discharge valves, and open this valve and vent ammonia from the compressor into a pail of water. If the doorway is only ten feet away, you can vent to the atmosphere. This is possible since ammonia vapor is lighter than air and would rise into the atmosphere. The valve could also be used as a gauge connection to check the booster discharge or the primary suction gauges on the panel. Since the booster discharge pressure equals the primary suction pressure, the valve in the relief line to the suction side of the booster compressor can check the booster suction gauge on the panel.
30. **The correct answer is shut down the compressor, since the suction side is under a vacuum.** After shutdown, the pressure rises, at which point you can use a sulphur stick to test for leaks.
31. **The correct answer is this tank of oil feeds the mechanical seal on the compressor.** It assures that no air will be sucked into the compressor along the shaft. Since a portion of the cylinder (the suction) is under a vacuum, air can be sucked in along the shaft if the seal leaked. Because oil is

under slight pressure, it seeps into the cylinder instead and maintains an airtight seal. The oil tank is pressurized from a connection to the discharge side of the booster compressor.

Chapter 14

MOTORS

A knowledge of the basic fundamentals of electricity is necessary to understand operating principles of motors.

DEFINITIONS

electricity: an invisible force known by its effect on material things. Electron theory explains the nature of electricity. The electron is the smallest quantity of negative electricity moving between atoms. The atom consists of a central nucleus with a positive charge and orbiting electrons with a negative charge. Free electrons migrating among the atoms are responsible for electricity. When an electromagnetic force from a battery or motor exists, electrons move from negative to positive.

current: as illustrated below, the flow of electrons through the conductor.

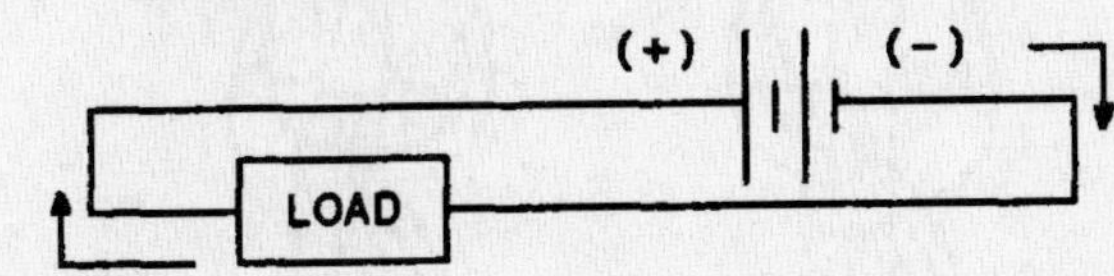

Fig. 14.1

voltage: the electromagnetic force, or potential difference, between the terminals of an electric source.

low voltage: 24 volts control circuits in A/C systems called low-voltage circuits. These systems use a step-down transformer and low-voltage relays. In a low-voltage circuit, one live and one neutral wire come from the secondary side of the transformer. The circuit may have any number of wires, but the 24-volt feed will be one (+) and one (–).

115 volts—60 cycle: A/C circuits are either two-wire or three-wire circuits. The two-wire circuit has one positive and one neutral line. The three-wire, or grounded, 115-volt circuit has one positive wire, one neutral wire, and one ground wire. The receptacles are usually two parallel flat blades and a round grounding blade. The positive wire carries 115-volt current.

117 volts: The usual line voltage in wall outlets in the United States. The actual voltage may vary from 115 to 120 volts, depending on the distance from the distribution transformer and the size of the branch circuit wire. This voltage is often mistakenly called 110-volt current.

220 volts—single-phase current: the common name for the 208-volt current found in private homes in New York City. Within the city limits, Consolidated Edison supplies only 208 volts. In the New York counties of Nassau and Westchester, 230 volts is supplied; in New Jersey, 240 volts. This circuit may be either two- or three-wire. The wall outlet is normally a tandem blade type. Each live wire carries 115 volts. In the two-wire circuit, both wires are live and the third wire is grounded. There is no neutral unless 115 volts will be tapped from the circuit.

THREE-PHASE ELECTRICITY

Single-phase current is used in homes to produce light and turn simple motors. There are other electrical tasks that can best be performed by three-phase electricity.

The word "phase" is related to the time relationships of voltage and current and whether or not they are reaching their peaks at the same time. A three-phase current is one in which three separate alternating currents are generated, one after the other, and separated by equal time intervals. Since a given period of time can be conveniently plotted as 360 degrees of rotation, time is often expressed in electricity as degrees of rotation. In a three-phase system, the voltage of phase A is generated in one set of coils. Another set of coils for phase B is 120 electrical degrees away; a third set for phase C is 240 degrees away. The combined voltage waves form an interlaced pattern.

These three-phase alternators use a three-wire electrical system with a grounded neutral. There are three separate phase buses. Single-phase circuits may operate off one system and ground. Three-phase motors are connected to three phases to give greater torque per pound.

In 208/220/230-volt, 60-cycle, three-phase current, all three wires are live. There is no neutral wire. In the 208-volt, 60 cycle, four-wire circuit, one wire is grounded and the other three wires are live.

If a lighting circuit is needed, it can be tapped between any one of the three live legs and a neutral wire. The accepted term for 208-volt current supplied in New York City, and usually found in commercial establishments, is 220-volt, three-phase current.

TYPES OF POWER

Within New York City limits, the primary wires at the top of electric poles carry distribution voltages up to 4,800. They may go to 12,000 volts in some long-distance transmission lines.

In single-phase power, one or two primary wires are at the top of the poles. With three-phase power, all three wires on the poles are primaries.

On the domestic pole, two primaries supply the transformer. The secondary transformer output gives single-phase, 120/240-volt current through three wires, two hot and one neutral. These three secondaries may supply as many houses as the transformer rating allows.

In three-phase service for commercial and industrial applications, three primaries are tied into two transformers. The secondary of the two transformers, a four-wire circuit, supplies 120 volts and 240 volts in either single- or three-phase. These secondaries can supply as many consumers as the transformers can handle.

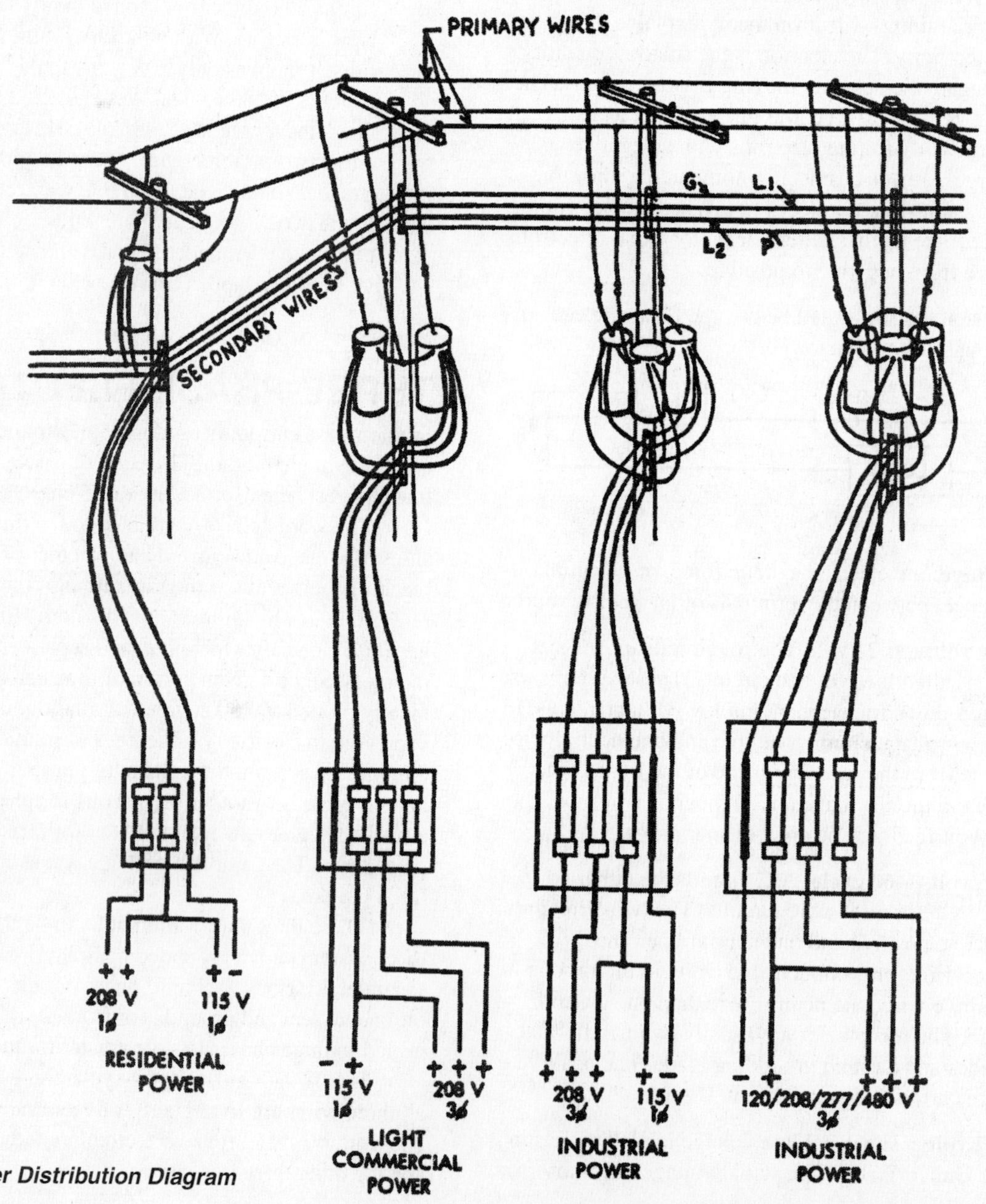

Fig. 14.2 Power Distribution Diagram

Other transformer configurations can supply 277- or 480-volt current.

DIRECT CURRENT

Direct current is defined as a current of uniform value in a single direction. Direct current reaches its maximum value very quickly after the circuit is completed. This maximum value, once reached, stays at a given value unless the circuit constant is changed.

The basic DC motor consists of a pair of poles that produce a magnetic field, an armature made up of a single-turn loop, a commutator, and a brush assembly. Each coil side of the loop lies within the magnetic field.

When a DC voltage is applied to the brushes, the current around the loop creates a magnetic field through the conductor coils. The magnetic field produced by the current in the conductors interacts with that produced by the poles of the magnets. The resultant magnetic field is represented by lines of force as shown in the figure. The loop rotates under the influence of the resultant magnetic field.

The amount of torque (turning power) developed is determined by the strength of the field poles and the amount of current in the armature.

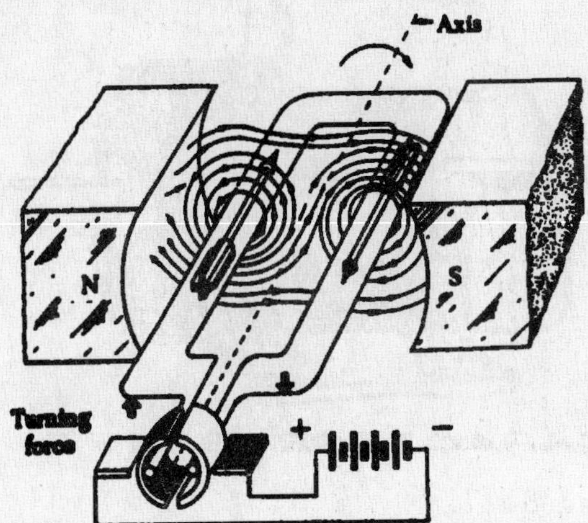

Fig. 14.4

Classification Of DC Motors

Motors are rated by voltage, average current draw, RPM, horsepower developed, and duty. They are also classified by the type of enclosure used. Open-type motors have ventilating holes in the motor frame or covers that permit circulation of air over motor windings. A fan is used with some motors to speed up circulation of cooling air across the windings. Totally enclosed motors have no ventilation openings and are thus protected from dirt, oil, and foreign matter.

Direct current is used for cordless applications, electronic low-voltage circuits, and charging batteries. It can be produced by batteries.

ALTERNATING CURRENT

Alternating current is another kind of electricity in motion. It implies that current (electron flow) reverses its direction of movement. Unlike direct current, which remains at a fixed value once it reaches its full magnitude, alternating current is continually changing value. It builds from zero value to maximum in a positive direction, then back to zero. In the opposite direction, it reaches a maximum value before the AC sine wave returns to zero. One complete cycle consists of two alternations.

To understand the principle of alternating current, you must know the definition of frequency. Frequency is the number of times an event happens in a given period of time, as expressed by the number of cycles occurring per second. In the United States, ordinary current has a frequency of 60 cycles per second (cps). A frequency of 60 means the current completely halts 120 times per second (twice per cycle).

Alternating current at operating frequencies does not cause lights to blink, even though the current drops to zero when it reverses. The period of time without current is so short that the human eye cannot discern it.

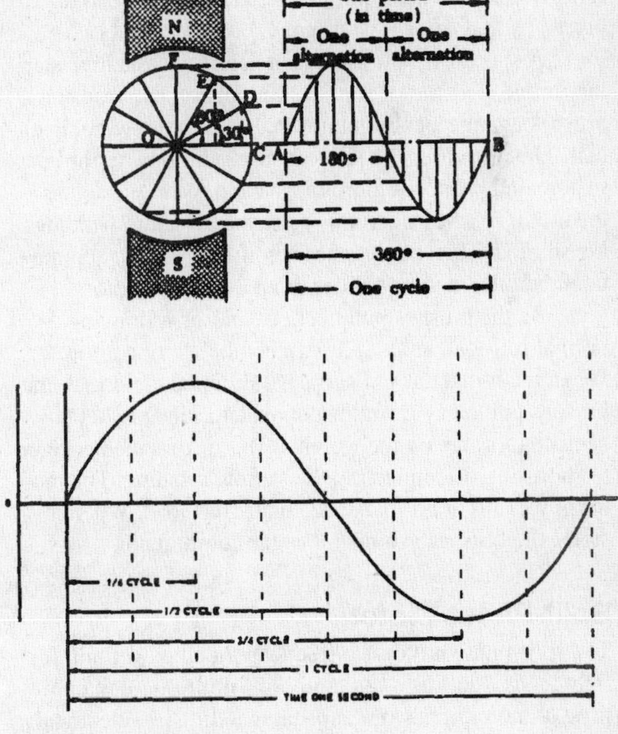

Figs. 14.5 and 14.6

INDUCTION MOTORS

Induction motors have no windings on the armature (rotor). Instead, the rotor has copper bars or other conducting material on its outer surface, parallel to the shaft. When current is induced (made to flow) in them, turning power or torque is produced by the magnetism the current creates.

One or more field windings are mounted in the stator. Alternating current passing through these windings creates an alternating magnetic field. This magnetism passes through the rotor, inducing (building up) current in the rotor bars. The induced current creates an opposite magnetic field in the rotor, causing it to revolve as it tries to keep up with the changing polarity in the field.

All hermetic machines use induction motors. Most induction motors use two field windings: a starting winding and a running winding.

Hermetic motors often need a starting relay, always located outside of the housing, or dome.

The starting relay temporarily supplies current to the starting winding. As soon as the motor reaches about 75 percent of operating speed, the relay opens the circuit and disconnects this winding from the power.

Repulsion-Start Induction Motor

Repulsion-start induction motors were once widely used for starting under a heavy load when torque power was needed at once. They were typically used in external-drive refrigerators and air compressors. Many have been replaced by capacitor-type motors.

A special winding in the armature gives a high starting torque. The motor starts as a repulsion motor, using brushes against a commutator in the armature winding circuit. This increases the induced electrical flow to the armature and produces more magnetic power. As soon as the motor reaches a certain speed, the armature windings are shorted. Then the brushes are lifted from the commutator, and the motor operates as an induction motor.

As the brushes pull back, the motor is drawing its normal full-load amps (F.L.A.), not the starting amps. When the initial current surge has dropped to normal, the brushes pull away from the commutator and are held by centrifugal force on the weights. This allows the necklace to short-out, disconnecting the starting winding. The motor nows runs at normal speed under full load. When it stops, the brushes again contact the commutator.

Split-Phase Motor

The split-phase motor is a fractional-horsepower unit for light loads. Ideal as a fan motor or a domestic-unit compressor motor, it has run and start windings 90 electrical degrees apart. At 80 percent of speed, a centrifugal switch cuts out the start winding. This motor has a low starting torque and runs on single-phase AC.

SPLIT PHASE MOTOR

Fig. 14.3a
Courtesy of Dayton Electric Manufacturing Company.

Capacitor Induction Motor

The open-capacitor motor, also called capacitor-start induction-run motor, is popular. The name indicates that a capacitor—a device for storing electrical energy—is in the starting winding. The motor operates as a two-phase motor at start-up for greater torque. At about 75 percent of its full speed it operates as a single-phase motor.

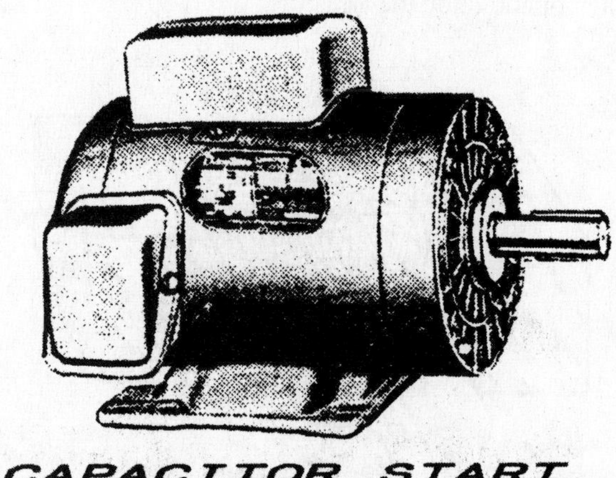

CAPACITOR START

Fig. 14.3b
Courtesy of Dayton Electric Manufacturing Company.

During start-up, the capacitor changes the phase of the starting winding current to produce two-phase electrical characteristics. The capacitor motor is built like the repulsion start-induction motor. The exterior, mountings, and bearings are similar. However, it has a capacitor, not a starting winding, in the armature. The capacitor is connected to a centrifugal switch and the starting winding in the stator. A centrifugal switch whirls around with the shaft and opens its contacts when centrifugal force overpowers its spring.

Operation is simple. When the motor starts, the centrifugal switch (closed when the motor is idle) passes current to both the starting and running windings. The starting winding is connected in series with the capacitor. The capacitor makes electrical current in the starting winding out of phase with current in the running winding. The motor then acts temporarily as a two-phase motor and has a very high starting torque.

At about 75 percent of the motor's rated speed, the centrifugal switch opens, disconnecting the starting winding. The unit continues to run as an induction motor.

The capacitor is usually mounted on top of the motor in a metal or plastic cylinder. It has two terminals, one connected to the centrifugal switch terminal and the other to the common running and starting winding terminal.

A capacitor in an alternating current line is charged during the buildup of the voltage and current by the surge of power. During the decrease in current flow in the power line, as the AC reverses, the capacitor discharges. This causes another power surge in the starting windings.

The motor also has a running capacitor. This capacitor operates the same way, except it continues operating when the motor reaches full speed. This capacitor is usually smaller and provides better heat removal, as it operates full-time.

Squirrel-Cage Motor

Motors in large systems are often the single-speed squirrel-cage type. A squirrel-cage motor is often a three-phase induction motor, running at either 208, 220, 230, 277, or 440 volts. This motor has three live AC circuits.

THREE PHASE MOTOR

Fig. 14.3c
Courtesy of Dayton Electric Manufacturing Company.

The motor speed cannot be altered. The rotation may be reversed by swapping any two of the three feed wires. The squirrel-cage motor has a stator, a rotor, and two end bells containing the bearings for the rotor shaft. The stator is a three-phase winding, or three single-phase windings spaced 120 degrees apart. When energized, they generate a revolving magnetic field.

The rotor is a laminated cylinder, with heavy copper bars for windings. The copper bars are connected at each end by a copper or brass ring. The rotating magnetic field generated by the stator cuts through the copper bars in the rotor, and it induces or generates current and magnetic fields in the rotor. The rotor magnetic fields try to catch up to the revolving magnetic fields of the stator, so the rotor turns.

The speed of a three-phase squirrel-cage motor may be approximated with this formula:

$$\text{RPM} = \frac{120 \times \text{cycles}}{\text{\# of poles}}$$

The formula is approximate, because there is always some slippage in an induction motor. The motor always turns slightly more slowly than the revolving field.

Squirrel-Cage Motor With External Resistance Brought Out

The squirrel-cage motor with external resistance is a multispeed, three-phase induction motor. It has a handle similar to an old-fashioned trolley car handle and normally has four positions (stop, first, second, and third speed). The motor is started in the first position, and as load requirements vary, brought to higher speeds. It is the only multispeed squirrel-cage motor.

Resistance in the rotor circuit can reduce speed by as much as 50 percent. The starting torque of the motor is increased by high resistance. When all resistance is removed, the motor runs at full, rated speed. Increasing the resistance slows down the rotor; decreasing the resistance increases the speed of the rotor.

This type of motor was used in large centrifugal systems. The motor speed was one way of controlling system capacity.

SYNCHRONOUS MOTORS

Important characteristics

1. Always runs at a constant speed.
2. Power factor is controlled by the operator at all times, and therefore helps control the plant power factor.
3. With adjustment of its DC field, a synchronous motor can draw AC that is leading.
4. Rotor fields are wound for direct current excitation. A starting winding with short-circuited copper bars starts the rotor when AC is fed into the stator.

The synchronous motor operates like a squirrel-cage motor (induction motor) until direct current is sent to the rotor fields. On start-up, when the motor reaches 90 percent of full speed, the rotor receives its excitation and the motor comes into step with the revolving field of the stator. A synchronous motor operating at unity power factor will operate under conditions up to 175 percent of full-load torque. When starting, the AC is fed with a manual switch and the DC usually follows automatically through mechanical relays.

Fig. 14.7

Synchronous motors should be installed at the end of the power line parallel to the squirrel-cage motors. The power factor can be controlled by changing the DC amperage to the rotor. At unity power factor, AC amperage is lowest for the work to be done. If the DC amperage is reduced to the rotor, AC amperage will lag behind its voltage to the stator. Increasing the DC amperage to the rotor above unity for the load causes the AC amperage to lead its voltage and give a lead power factor.

The motor acts as a condenser when it has a lead power factor. When the DC amperage is adjusted to bring AC amperage and voltage into phase, the power factor is unity. When the DC amperage is reduced, the field is underexcited (rotor) and there is a lagging power factor. When the DC amperage is increased, the rotor field is overexcited and there is a leading power factor. Power factor is important in large plants, as it affects the cost of operation.

Power is the result of current and voltage. The maximum power is delivered when the voltage and amperage are in phase, or in step. When they are out of phase, less power is delivered. When they are 90 degrees out of phase, no power is delivered.

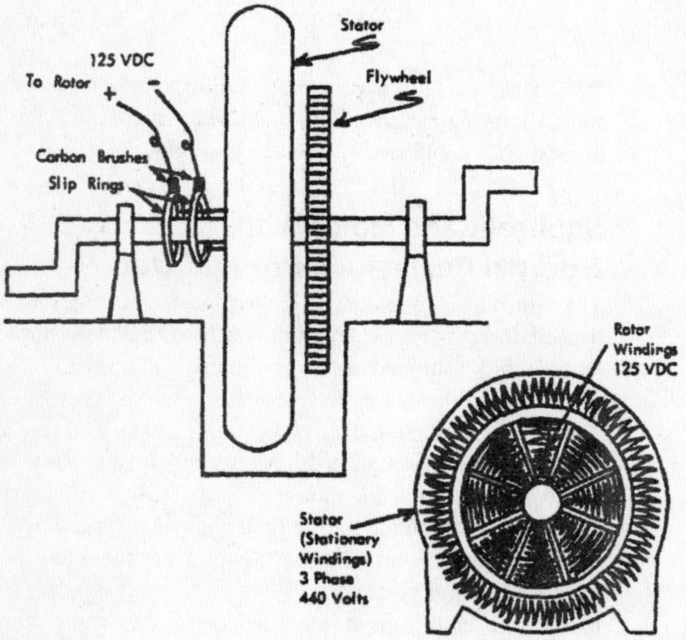

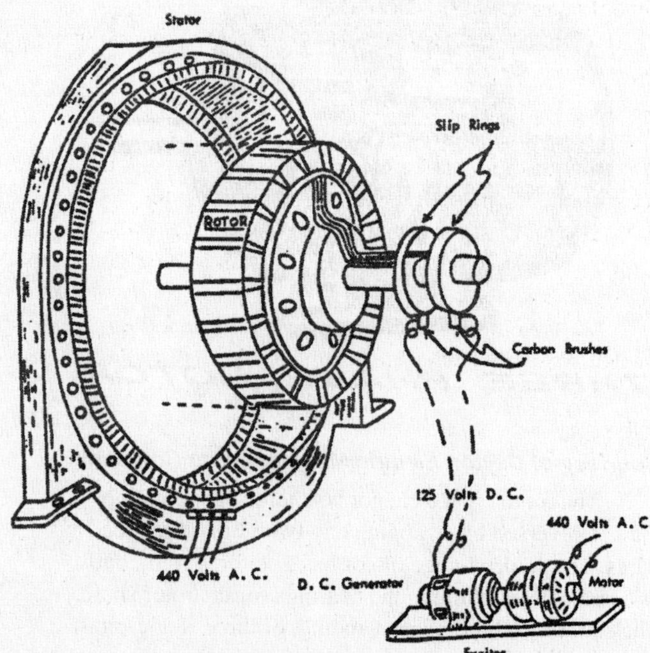

Fig. 14.8

A synchronous motor consists of a shaft with an opposed crank, or eccentric, at each end. The shaft and motor are supported by two main bearings. The motor windings are of two types: stator windings (or stationary windings) in the outer housing and rotor windings (or moving windings) that are on the shaft and rotate with it.

Two bronze slip-rings are attached to the shaft but insulated from it. They revolve with the shaft. A carbon brush rides on each slip ring to supply DC voltage to the rotor windings. The stator windings are supplied with three-phase, 440-volt current.

The synchronous motor is a constant/single speed motor. It can start on AC, but it runs on AC and DC. If AC and DC are not both fed to the synchronous motor, it cannot operate.

The AC is fed into the stator, or the stationary windings of the motor. When the AC switch is thrown, these windings are energized and the motor starts turning as an induction motor. When the motor is at about 90 percent of full speed, the DC switch is thrown. This feeds DC to the rotor through the slip ring. This DC field provides the excitation to bring the motor into step; that is, the magnetic fields of the stator and rotor windings are locked in and the motor is ready to do work.

Synchronous motors cannot start up under a load because they have very little starting torque, or pulling power. They are started as induction motors when AC is supplied to the stator windings. They start up doing no work.

A motor can't start with the compressor discharge stop valve open, because it can't handle the load. Once the motor is up to speed, and DC is supplied to the rotor windings, a synchronous motor can handle up to 175 percent of its rated full-load capacity.

When you throw in the AC to the motor, the motor starts to run. After about 30 to 40 seconds, the motor reaches about 90 percent of full speed. It has reached full speed when the whining sound of the motor levels off. At this point the automatic time-delay DC switch pulls in. It locks in the magnetic fields of the stator and rotor windings. The motor is now ready to work at full capacity. In fact, it can handle from 140 to 170 percent of the rated full-load capacity.

At the bottom of each compressor panel a dog switch, or safety latch switch, supplies AC to the stator windings. Above the dog switch is a DC rheostat. This variable resistor adjusts DC voltage to the motor by setting up a resistance. As voltage increases, DC amperage decreases; as voltage decreases, amperage increases. DC amperage can be read on the DC ammeter at the top of the compressor panel. The other ammeter reads AC supplied to the motor. As the rheostat is adjusted and the DC amps increase, AC amps decrease; as DC amps decrease, AC amps increase.

Power Factor

The two ammeters and the rheostat adjust the power-setting factor of the compressor motor. The power factor meter is the third meter on the panel.

The power factor is the electrical balance of the plant. Current should be drawn equally on all three phases of the electrical system. Synchronous motors can help balance the system in this way.

The power factor meter is marked off from a center point of 100. To the left of the 100 mark the scale reads lag, and to the right, lead. The first two digits to the right and left are scaled in tenths, to 98, and from there on the meter is scaled in units of one, as shown in the following figure.

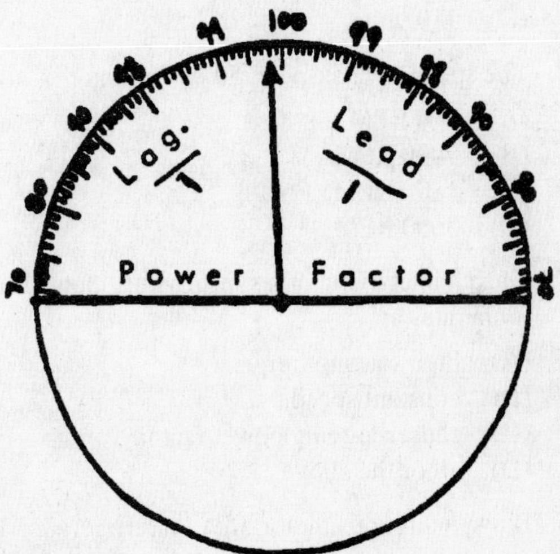

Fig. 14.9

Thermal Overload Protector

Thermal overload protectors guard against overheating. The overload protector consists of a thermally controlled switch connected to the electrical circuit. When the current of the motor becomes higher than normal, due to overloading, a movable diaphragm opens a pair of contacts and cuts off the power. When the motor cools, the contacts close and power is supplied again to the motor.

MOTOR LICENSE QUESTIONS

1. With proper frequency, motor operating limitations are
   (A) 10 percent plus or minus voltage.
   (B) 15 percent plus or minus voltage.
   (C) 5 percent plus or minus voltage.
   (D) none of the above.

2. On a 220-volt, three-phase, 4-wire electric service, any line to neutral will read
   (A) 220 volts.
   (B) 440 volts.
   (C) 70 volts.
   (D) 110 volts.

3. The speed of a six-pole, 50-cycle motor is
   (A) 600 RPM.
   (B) 1000 RPM.
   (C) 1800 RPM.
   (D) 3600 RPM.

4. One characteristic of a synchronous motor is that it operates at
   (A) high starting torque.
   (B) constant speed.
   (C) causes lagging power factor.
   (D) all of the above.

5. If a synchronous motor drives a refrigeration compressor,
   (A) the speed of the compressor will change the load.
   (B) DC is required.
   (C) the compressor will run at constant speed.
   (D) the refrigerant must be SO^2.

6. The compressor in a refrigerating system is V-belt driven from an electric motor. If the unit were operated with belts installed too tightly, in a short time the
   (A) motor would run normally.
   (B) motor would overheat.
   (C) compressor and motor would run at reduced speed.
   (D) compressor would be driven at a higher speed.

7. A large refrigeration plant has three compressors with synchronous motor drives and seven compressors with squirrel-cage induction motors. One important reason for this arrangement is to
   (A) provide some refrigeration capacity in the event of an AC power failure.
   (B) allow some variation in capacity, since synchronous motors can easily be run at various speeds.
   (C) correct the overall power factor.
   (D) stabilize the overall plant demand factor.

8. A system using a squirrel-cage induction motor can operate at
   (A) one speed only.
   (B) either of two speeds.
   (C) any of three speeds.
   (D) variable speeds.

9. Since the synchronous motor is used for constant speed, the rheostat is used for
   (A) adjusting the AC to the exciter.
   (B) varying the power factor to load conditions.
   (C) shutting off AC to the fields.
   (D) shutting down the motor.

10. A synchronous motor
    (A) can vary its speed.
    (B) starts on DC, operates on AC and DC.
    (C) starts on AC, operates on AC and DC.
    (D) starts on AC, operates on DC.

11. A wound-rotor induction motor with external resistance is a
    (A) multispeed motor.
    (B) constant-speed motor.
    (C) single-speed motor.
    (D) waterproof cover.

12. What does the motor drive mechanism do?
    (A) Transfer the motor's power to the driven device, pump, compressor, or fan
    (B) Transfer the motor's power to the heat of compression
    (C) Convert the motor's power to an electrical source
    (D) None of the above

13. What causes an overload protection device to function?
    (A) Excessive heat or amperage
    (B) High head pressure in the condenser
    (C) An activated rupture disk
    (D) An overloaded fusible plug

14. A 200-ton air-conditioning plant is set up with two Freon compressors. Neither compressor is equipped with bypass solenoids. To get at least four steps of capacity with these machines, you would drive them by

(A) synchronous motor.
(B) capacitor start-run motor.
(C) repulsion-induction motor.
(D) wound-rotor induction motor.

15. Reversing (changing the rotation of) a three-phase, 60-cycle induction motor should be done by

(A) switching any two leads to the rotor.
(B) reversing the field connections.
(C) reversing the connections to the starting winding.
(D) interchanging two of the power leads.

16. A common fan motor used for condenser and evaporator blower motors is the

(A) repulsion-start, induction run.
(B) squirrel cage.
(C) capacitor-start, induction run.
(D) synchronous.

17. What cools the motor in a semihermetic reciprocating compressor?

(A) The squirrel-cage fan
(B) The water cooling-jacket
(C) The refrigerant suction gas
(D) The cooling tower

18. Why does a hermetic compressor need special materials?

(A) Its construction requires a start capacitor due to the high starting torque.
(B) It is an open type system.
(C) The compressor is connected to the shaft, and the motor requires high torque.
(D) The motor runs in a refrigerant atmosphere.

19. What two methods are used to cool most hermetic compressors?

(A) Water cooled and pressure cooled
(B) Air cooled and subcooled
(C) Refrigerant cooled by absorption
(D) Refrigerant cooled and air cooled

20. As the DC amperage goes up on a synchronous motor, what happens to the AC amperage?

(A) It rises.
(B) It has no effect on AC amperage, because they are separate.
(C) It goes down.
(D) None of the above

21. Fuses and circuit breakers are safety devices for electric motors. But they will not protect motors against

(A) short circuit.
(B) heavy overload.
(C) burnout.
(D) overheating.

Answers to Motor License Questions

1. **The correct answer is (A).**
2. **The correct answer is (D).**
3. **The correct answer is (B).**
4. **The correct answer is (B).**
5. **The correct answer is (C).**
6. **The correct answer is (B).**
7. **The correct answer is (C).**
8. **The correct answer is (A).**
9. **The correct answer is (B).**
10. **The correct answer is (C).**
11. **The correct answer is (A).**
12. **The correct answer is (A).**
13. **The correct answer is (A).**
14. **The correct answer is (D).**
15. **The correct answer is (D).**
16. **The correct answer is (B).**
17. **The correct answer is (C).**
18. **The correct answer is (D).**
19. **The correct answer is (D).**
20. **The correct answer is (C).**
21. **The correct answer is (D).**

Chapter 15

PURGERS

AMMONIA SYSTEM PURGER

As a refrigerant, ammonia has a unique characteristic: its vapor is lighter than air. This creates a problem when purging a system, because any air entering the system eventually collects in the condenser. While the system operates, the bottom portion of the condenser contains liquid ammonia and the upper portion contains a mix of ammonia vapor and air. Because the two are intermingled, the air cannot be vented without losing ammonia vapor as well. On the other hand, if the condenser is shut down, a certain amount of ammonia vapor is always present in the condenser. This vapor, being lighter than air, rises above the air in the condenser, creating layers of ammonia vapor, air, and liquid ammonia. To purge air from the condenser, an external unit must be used to cool the mixture of ammonia vapor and air. The ammonia condenses and the remaining air can be expelled. This is done with a purger (see Figure 15.1).

On an ammonia system, you cannot effectively purge a condenser with the unit shut down. A mixture of ammonia vapor and air is pulled from the condenser and separated in the purge unit.

Air vapor is noncondensable and cannot be liquefied at any reasonable pressure and temperature. Ammonia vapor is condensable under pressure, if it is cooled. Once the ammonia vapor is condensed, the remaining noncondensable gases can be expelled from the system in the purger unit.

The purger is a small tank about 9 inches in diameter and about 18 to 24 inches high. It contains an evaporator coil to condense the ammonia. The evaporator coil chills the liquid in the purger, causing the ammonia vapor from the condenser or receiver to condense more rapidly. One end of this coil has an expansion valve and the other connects to the primary suction line. The purger line runs from the top of the condenser and receiver to the bottom of the purger. A level of chilled liquid ammonia always is maintained in the bottom of the purger. The entering air and ammonia vapor bubble up through it, enabling the ammonia vapor to condense more rapidly and separate from the air vapor.

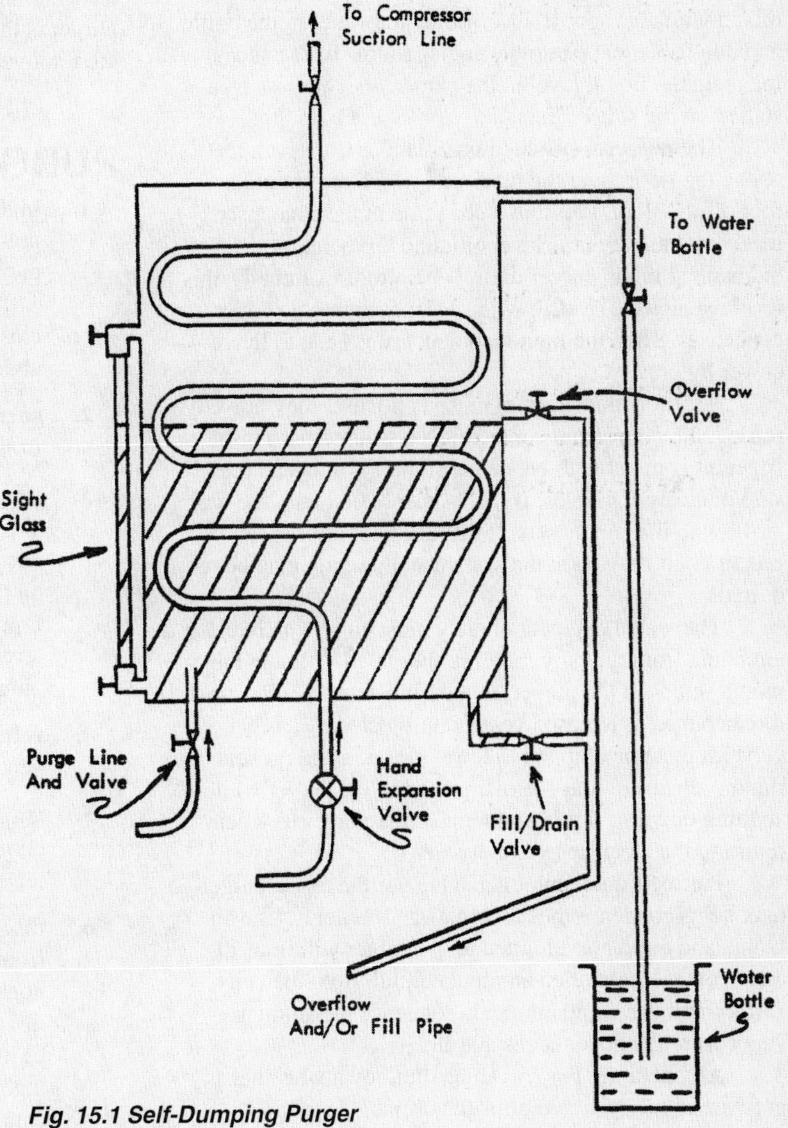

Fig. 15.1 Self-Dumping Purger

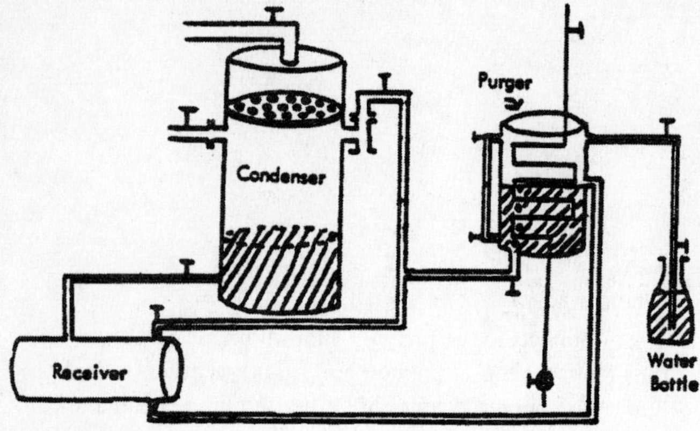

Fig. 15.2

The air vapor rises to the top of the purger and is removed through the bleed line.The end of the bleed line is immersed in a bottle of water, so any ammonia vapor still mixed with air vapor is absorbed by the water in the bottle and does not escape into the engine room. To see and maintain the liquid level in the purger, a sight glass is installed on the side of the tank.

The purger is installed on a stand six or seven feet above the floor, over the receivers, which are about one foot off the floor. Pressure is the same in the condenser, receiver, and purger. A level of liquid ammonia is always maintained in the purger during operation. Eventually, this level reaches the overflow line as more ammonia vapor condenses. Then the liquid ammonia runs back to the receiver by gravity.

Air (noncondensable) in the condenser may prevent refrigerant vapor from contacting the water tube. This refrigerant is not able to condense properly, and head pressure in the system rises. If this happens, first increase water flow to the condensers. If this does not lower head pressure, air may be in the system and purging may be required.

The watch engineer on duty must empty the liquid ammonia from the purger before shutdown. If liquid ammonia settles in the purger, it boils and expands. The ammonia purger is a closed vessel unprotected by a relief valve. It must be emptied to lower pressure and prevent rupture. Pressure must be maintained in the purger while shutting down so liquid ammonia in the purger tank can return to the receiver by gravity.

Putting liquid ammonia in the bottom of the purger tank helps condense the ammonia vapor quickly. The ammonia and air vapor admitted to the purger will immediately contact the chilled ammonia liquid. Both the coil surface and the liquid ammonia condense the ammonia vapor from the noncondensable air.

An operating purger can be shut down when head pressure in the system returns to normal (155 psig).

CARRIER 17M CENTRIFUGAL SYSTEM TYPE L PURGER

Pressure in a portion of the centrifugal refrigeration system is below atmospheric pressure, so it is possible for air to enter the system. Since air contains water vapor, a small amount of water enters with the air. Even a small amount of water in a refrigeration unit can cause excessive corrosion of various components.

The presence of air or noncondensable gases can be detected by the air indicator above the gauge panel on the 17M machine. An increase in head pressure may indicate that air has entered the system.

The purge system removes water vapor and air from the system. It also removes refrigerant that has mixed with these gases. The air is automatically purged to the atmosphere. Remaining refrigerant is automatically returned to the cooler as a liquid. Water trapped in the purger is then manually drained. Noncondensable gases are removed from the top of the condenser.

PURGER COMPONENTS

1. **high-pressure cutout switch:** connected to compressor discharge. It is adjusted to stop the compressor if condenser pressure increases to about 110 lbs., due to an abnormal condition. The switch closes automatically on reduction of pressure to about 75 psig.

2. **suction pressure gauge:** the purger component in front of the casing.

3. **evacuator chamber:** the chamber that separates air, water, and refrigerant; also called the separation chamber or separation tank. Two sight glasses on the lower compartment (see number 20 on type L purger illustration) are for inspecting refrigerant level. A third sight glass (see number 10 on type L purger illustration) is used to check for water.

4. **refrigerant weir:** the purger component that prevents liquid refrigerant from draining.

5. **trap:** the component that traps water in the upper compartment. R-11 is 1.5 times heavier than water, so it settles into the lower compartment.

6. **discharge pressure gauge:** the gauge located in front of the casing. Once the purger draws in noncondensable gases and refrigerant, watch the discharge gauge (see number 6 in figure 15.3) until it reaches 80 psig. This reading indicates that high-pressure gases are in the purger's air-cooled condenser (see number 18 in the same).

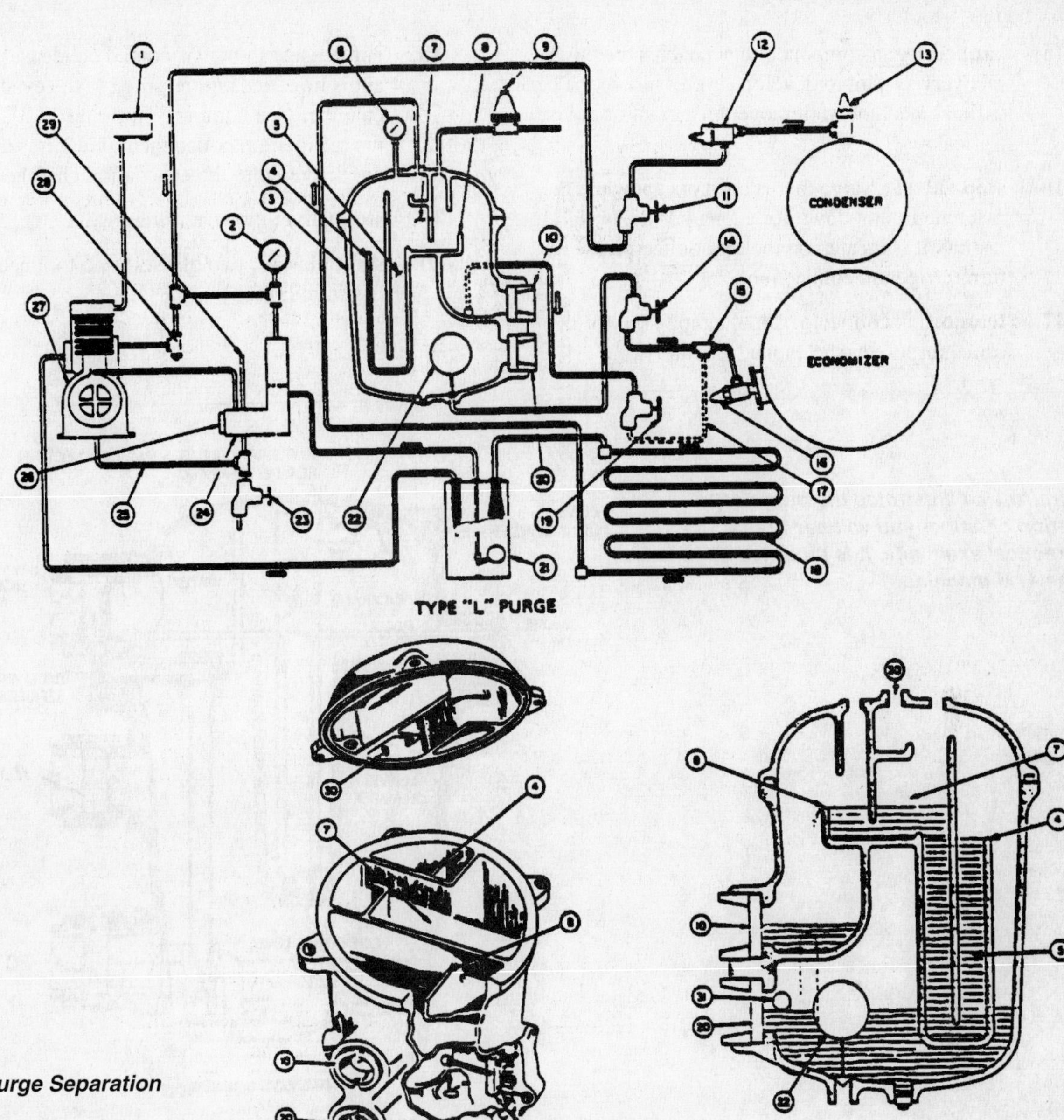

Fig. 15.3 Purge Separation Chamber

7. **settling compartment:** the area where the water and refrigerant separate.

8. **water weir:** the component that prevents water from dropping into the lower refrigerant chamber after separation.

9. **automatic relief valve:** the valve that automatically purges air into the atmosphere.

10. **water-level sight glass:** the upper chamber inspection eye used to check for water.

11. **suction line stop valve:** the valve that opens when the purge unit operates; it is closed at all other times. The valve is marked with the words "FROM THE CONDENSER."

12. **pressure-reducing valve:** the valve that regulates compression suction pressure. It is located on the suction line.

13. **stop valve on main condenser:** a valve that is open except during repairs. Before starting the purge unit, this stop valve (see number 13 in figure 15.3) must be opened and kept open whenever the system runs.

14. **stop valve:** a valve that is open only when the purger operates. It is located on the refrigerant return line at the end of the casing.

15. **capped tee:** a component that enables the purge recovery system to develop air pressure in the centrifugal machine, to remove refrigerant or to test for leaks.

16. **stop valve:** a valve that is open except when the machine is shut down for a long period, or during testing. It is located on the economizer in the return refrigerant connection.

17. **temporary connector pipe:** a pipe used for the same purpose as the capped tee (above).

18. **condenser:** in the air-cooled condenser, refrigerant is liquefied and returned to the evacuation chamber (see number 3 in figure 15.3). Along with the refrigerant, noncondensable gases and water are delivered to the evacuation chamber.

19. **stop valve:** the water drain valve.

20. **sight glasses:** two glasses used for checking refrigerant level.

Figure 15.4 illustrates the purge separation chamber you will see at the practical exam site. It is mounted on the 17M machine.

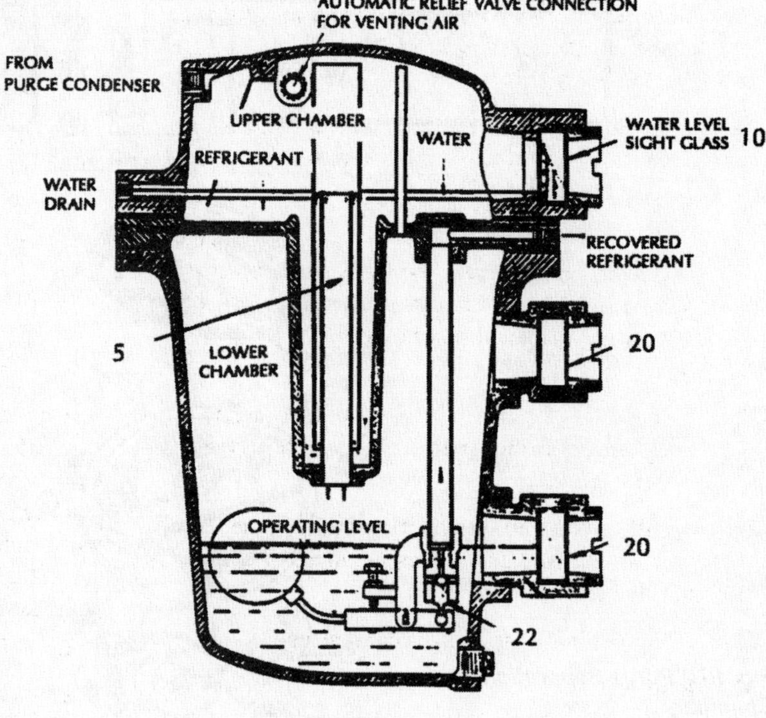

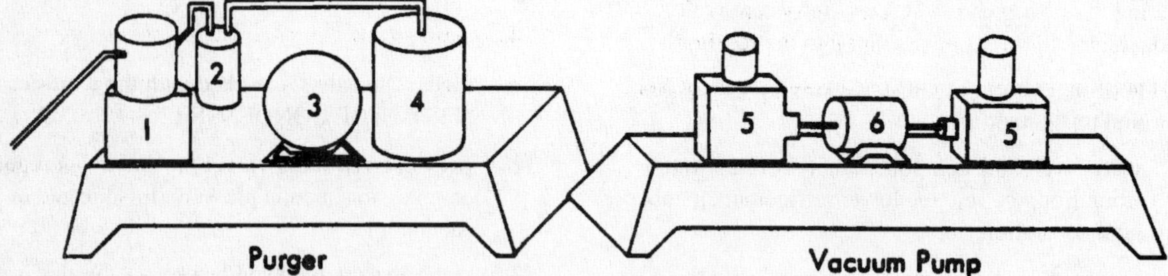

Figure 15.5 illustrates the purger unit at the practical exam site. It is removed from the unit and mounted on the wall.

1. Vacuum pump compressor
2. Oil separator trap
3. Motor
4. Purger tank (settling tank)
5. Beach Russ vacuum pump compressor
6. Motor

21. **oil separator:** a component that separates oil from refrigerant and returns it to the compressor crankcase.
22. **high-pressure float valve:** a valve that opens when the liquid level rises, allowing gas pressure to force liquid refrigerant into the condenser.
23. **oil drain valve:** a drain for the auxiliary oil reservoir (see below).
24. **auxiliary oil reservoir:** a chamber that relieves the refrigerant from the compressor crankcase to the suction line, without loss of oil. It also contains extra oil for the compressor.
25. **oil tubing between compressor and tee to drain:** a tube that connects the auxiliary reservoir and the crankcase.
26. **sight glass:** a glass that checks the oil level in the compressor and auxiliary oil reservoir, located in front of the casing.
27. **purger compressor:** a compressor that should be operated continuously when the centrifugal compressor is operating and before starting the system, as required by the presence of air (noncondensables).
28. **plugged tee:** a component used for leak-testing operations or for removing refrigerant from the system.
29. **oil fill connection (plugged):** a fitting in the reservoir. In order to add oil, pressure in the system must be balanced.
30. **inlet opening from purger condenser**
31. **loop seal**

The purger is used whenever the entire charge must be stored in the receiver. It pressurizes the system with 5 pounds of air and forces refrigerant into the receiver.

CAUTION: When the purger is pressurizing the system, do not exceed 8 pounds.

LEAK TESTING

The purge recovery unit can be used to develop air pressure in the centrifugal machine for the purpose of removing refrigerant or testing for leaks.

For this purpose, plugged tees 28 and 15, together with a separate connector pipe 17, are provided. To build up pressure in the machine with both the centrifugal machine and the purge recovery unit shut down, proceed as follows:

1. Block the compressor bellows seal.
2. Open valve 19 to drain any water in the evacuation chamber; leave the valve open.
3. Close valves 11 and 14.
4. Remove the plug from 15, allowing air to the machine and breaking the vacuum.
5. Connect pipe 17 to 15 and to the water drain connections at the bottom of the cabinet, as shown by the dotted line in the diagram.
6. Remove the plug from 28.
7. Turn on the purge recovery unit and operate until required pressure is reached (usually 5 psig and not more than 8 psig).
8. Remove the compressor block seal on the bellows.

Machine pressure may be raised to 25 psig maximum with dry air or nitrogen, provided the rupture disc is blanked off or pressure equalized. Be sure the oil reservoir is full of oil.

Added air should always be evacuated through the purge system to conserve refrigerant. Proceed as follows:

1. With the purge unit off, close valves 19 and 16.
2. Remove pipe 17 and replace plugs in 15 and 28.
3. Open valves 11, 14, and 16.
4. Start the purge unit and evacuate the air.
5. Return the purge to normal operating conditions.

TRANE "PURIFIER" PURGE

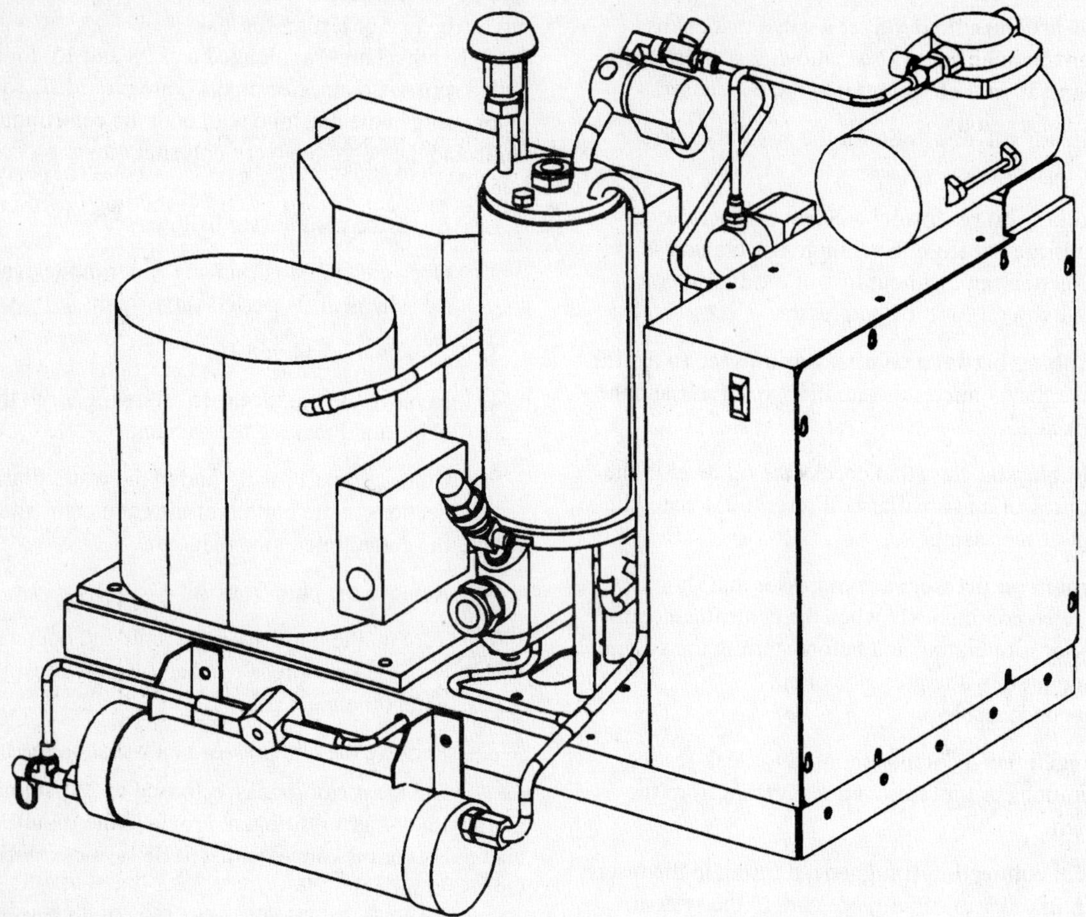

Fig. 15.6

Specifications

Electrical Power Requirements
103-127 VAC, 60 Hz. 1-Phase, 8 Amps.
99-121 VAC, 50 Hz, 1-Phase, 8 Amps.

Fault Relay Output Rating
120 VAC, 1 Amp

Operating Environment
40° F to 120° F; 5 percent to 95 percent relative humidity, non-condensing.

Storage Environment
-40° F to 150° F; 5 percent to 95 percent relative humidity, non-condensing.

Mounting
Direct-mounted on condenser shell above liquid level of highest condenser.

Dimensions (approx.)
25 1/2″ high × 24 3/4″ wide × 18 3/4″ deep, with filter drier.

Weight
115 pounds with filter drier.

Model Number Description

The operating components and options for any Trane Purifier Purge are assigned a multiple-character alphanumeric model number that precisely identifies each unit. An explanation of the identification code that appears on the unit nameplate is shown here.

Use of the service model number will enable the owner/operator, installing contractors, and service technicians to define the operation, components, and options for any specific unit.

Sample Model Number

Model No.	P	R	G	C	A	0	0	1	A	A0	A
Digit No.	1,	2,	3	4	5	6	7	8	9	10,11	12

Digits 1,2,3
Unit Type
PRG = Purifier Purge

Digit 4
Development Sequence
A = First Generation
B = Second Generation
C = Third Generation

Digit 5
Controls Type
A = Standard
B = NEMA-4
S = Special

Digit 6
Digit Not Used

Digit 7
Human Interface Type
0 = UCP2 Based Display
1 = Purge Based Display

Digit 8
Electrical Characteristics
1 = 115/60/1, 110/50/1
S = Special

Digit 9
Refrigerant Type
A = CFC-11/HCFC-123
B = CFC-113
S = Special

Digits 10, 11
Design Sequence
A0 = First (original) Design Sequence

Digit 12
Agency Approval
A = UL and CSA
B = None

Operating the Purge

The basic purpose of the Purifier Purge is to remove non-condensibles from the chiller. The available ADAPTIVE mode allows this to be accomplished in the most efficient manner. The AUTO and ON modes are available to allow alternate operating modes better suited to certain applications and in chiller service environments.

The ability to monitor current and historical purge activity via the purge reports allows the operator to monitor chiller leakage, resulting in an effective means to protect the chiller's refrigerant charge.

Purge pumpout minutes are used to

- Allow the operator to determine and set appropriate PURGE MAXIMUM PUMPOUT RATE setting
- Allow the ADAPTIVE mode to determine the most effective pumpout schedule for the individual chiller
- Determine if the chiller leak rate has increased

The microprocessor monitors the pumpout activity of the purge system and alerts the operator if an unexpectedly high level of activity is present by shutting down the purge via a diagnostic.

The pumpout timer is used to sense and accumulate pumpout time within a 24-hour sliding window. It does this by determining the length of each pumpout cycle and adding that time increment to an accumulation buffer. In order to accumulate time within the 24-hour constraint, the pumpout time measured 24 hours previously is erased from the buffer. When the accumulated time in the buffer exceeds the PURGE MAXIMUM PUMPOUT RATE setting as specified at the purge human interface, a purge latching fault is generated and the purge is disabled. The 24-hour buffer is cleared, and the purge is allowed to resume operation after the operator clears the MAX PUMPOUT RATE EXCEEDED diagnostic. The PURGE MAXIMUM PUMPOUT RATE setting is selectable at the human interface. The selectable range is from 1 to 100 minutes per 24 hours. The factory setting is 20 minutes. Since individual chillers operate at differing temperature conditions, run schedules, and air-leak rates, the chiller operator may need to set a rate more appropriate for his particular system.

At initial startup, the operator should log the purge pumpout activity to develop a short history for his machine. After gathering this pumpout data, the operator should set a PURGE MAXIMUM PUMPOUT RATE that will protect the chiller from any sudden increases of pumpout activity but will not result in nuisance trips under what is normal pumpout activity for his machine.

Note: Be certain that any normal increases in pumpout activity due to extended chiller off cycles (normal duty rotation or weekends) are taken into account.

The MAX PUMPOUT RATE EXCEEDED diagnostic may be disabled when known large quantities of air must be removed from the chiller (such as after major chiller servicing). The PURGE DISABLE PUMPOUT ALARM FOR XX HRS setting is programmable from the purge human interface. The disable interval may be selected from 1 to 72 hours. The remaining time for the disable mode may be determined by monitoring the human interface. The displayed interval will decrease as time elapses. The set point for the disable mode may be modified at any time by modifying the disable time and entering the new value.

Note: Since the purge has no fault protection in the disable alarm mode, it is recommended that this mode be used sparingly and only when the purge and controls are known to be operating properly.

Purge Start-Up

Before the Purifier Purge is operated for the first time, be sure to perform the following procedures:

If the purge unit is equipped with a replaceable filter drier core, perform the following steps, beginning with step 1. If the purge unit is equipped with a replaceable filter drier assembly, begin with step 3.

1. Remove the cover from the filter-drier canister and install the two filter-drier cores that shipped with the purge. Refer to "Filter-Drier Core Replacement" in "Service Procedures" section.

   Note: The drier cores adsorb moisture from ambient air, so they are shipped in sealed containers. Keep the cores sealed prior to installation.

2. Replace the filter-drier canister cover, positioning the drain at the bottom of the canister, and tighten the bolts evenly.

   Note: Be sure all internal components are in the proper position when replacing the canister cover (see Figure 10).

3. Perform the "Purge Pumpout and Fault Check" as described in the "Service Procedures" section.
4. Open the purge tank isolation valves on the purge tank inlet and liquid return lines.
5. Program the purge control mode to AUTO or ADAPTIVE for normal operation.
6. Check maximum pumpout rate setting. Factory setting is 20 minutes/24 hours. Adjust setting as needed later, based on purge system pumpout requirements.
7. If there is an excessive amount of air in the chiller:
   a. Temporarily bypass the pumpout restrictor (see "Bypassing Pumpout Restrictor")
   b. Program the PURGE DISABLE PUMPOUT ALARM for 24 hours.

Data Logging

One of the most valuable features of the microprocessor-based purge is the ability to use stored purging data to monitor the condition of the chiller. It is strongly recommended that the operator maintain a log on a daily or weekly basis, recording at least the following data:

- Purge pumpout last 24 hours
- 30 Day purge pumpout average
- 30 Day purge pumpout average, chiller running
- Last 5 cycle pumpout average, interval from shutdown to three hours after shutdown
- 30 Day pumpout average, interval from three hours after shutdown to next start.

A sudden change in the trend of this data, which cannot be accounted for by a change in chiller operational patterns, may indicate the need for a chiller leak check and repair. See the example chart below.

A graphical data log will be easier to interpret than a tabular log.

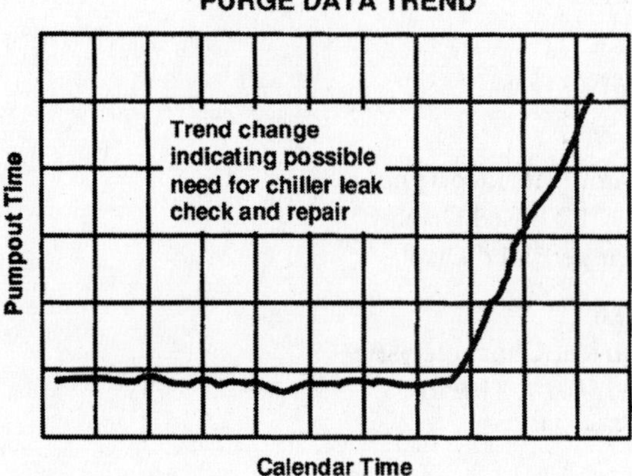

Fig. 15.7

Purge-Based Human Interface

Purifier Purge units supplied as purge-based display purges have a different human interface than UCP2-based display purges on Trane Cen TraVac chillers.

UCP2-based display purges have access to the chiller main panel for input and report screen display. In general, purge-based display purges will not have a compatible main panel display available. For this reason, purge-based display purges are supplied with their own interface. The interface ships attached to the microprocessor panel as shown in Figure 4 but may be easily separated and mounted in any convenient location on or near the chiller.

There are two primary differences between the UCP2 human interface and the purge-based human interface:

1. Because of a smaller screen display area, the messages outlined in the preceding sections "Setup" and "Reports" are somewhat abbreviated for display on the purge-based human interface.
2. Because the purge-based human interface is a free-standing unit not linked to the main chiller panel, its function is wholly dedicated to control and operation of the purge. Since the screens do not form a subset of a larger group of screens, the menu structure is simpler and more direct.

The following sections explain the menu concept and slightly modified command set of the purge-based human interface.

Display Overview

The purge-based human interface contains 8 keys and a 2 × 16 character display on the front panel. A display backlight will illuminate when the display keys are pressed. The information displayed on the purge-based human interface is constantly updated from the purge control module inside the purge control box.

The keys on the human interface are functionally grouped to start and stop the purge, "change" the purge setpoints, and "view" the contents of the purge menus.

- The "view" keys include the <Next> and <Previous> keys. These keys will display the next or previous menu entry.
- The "change" keys include a <+> and <–> key to change the operator setpoints in the SETTINGS report and an <Enter> and <Cancel> key to either accept or reject the changed setting.
- The <Stop> key is used to stop the purge. The <Auto/On> key is used to return the purge to an active state after the stop key is pressed. The <Auto/On> key will place the purge into the mode set up in the SETTINGS report for "Purge Control Mode."

Purge Based Display

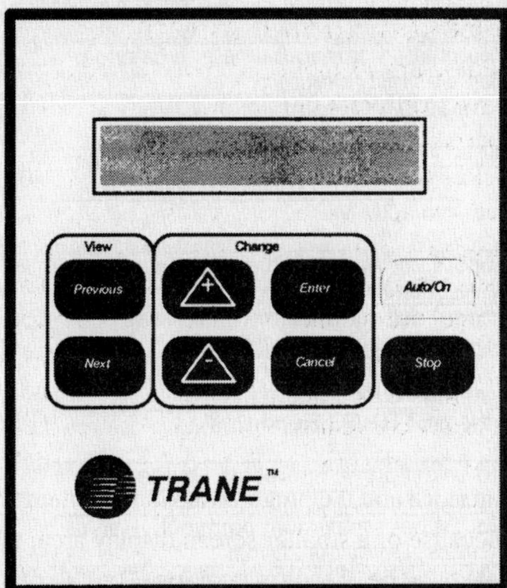

Fig. 15.8

Menu Overview

The purge-based human interface uses a major menu structure with entry points into side menus (see the following chart entitled "Purge Based Human Interface Menu Structure"). The <NEXT>, <PREVIOUS> keys are used to navigate vertically through the menus. If the side menus are not accessed, only the major menu entries are displayed (those shown on the left column of the chart entitled "Purge Based Human Interface Menu Structure"). The side menus are accessed by pressing the <ENTER> key at the entry points into the side reports. Once a side menu is accessed, the <NEXT>, <PREVIOUS> keys are used to navigate vertically through the screens. The <NEXT>, <PREVIOUS> keys will return to the major menu loop once the side menu is exhausted.

A brief description is given in the chart for each menu entry. Additional explanation may be found in the referenced UCP2 human interface section.

Alarm Messages

If an alarm is active, an alarm message will display alternately with the alarm heading. The list of alarm messages that may be displayed for the purge-based human interface are

> Suction Temp Sensor Fail

> Liquid Temp Sensor Fail

> Liquid Level Too High

> NOVRAM Error 1

> NOVRAM Error 2

> NOVRAM Error 3

> Lost Communication

> Max Pumpout Rate Exceeded

> Max Pumpout Rate Exceeded–Service

A further explanation of these alarm diagnostics may be found in the "Diagnostics" section for the UCP2 human interface.

As indicated in the above referenced section, some diagnostics are latching—that is, they force the purge to the STOP state—and some are non-latching. Non-latching diagnostics are cleared when the fault causing the diagnostic is corrected. No reset is required, and purge operation resumes automatically. Latching diagnostics are cleared by pressing the <+> key after appropriate corrective action has been taken. The purge will then restart.

Status Messages

Valid status messages for the purge-based human interface are

> IDLE - Condensing unit is off

> RUNNING - Condensing unit is on

> PUMPOUT - Temperature initiated pumpout is active

> SVC-PUMP - Pumpout initiated by the service switch

> LOW TEMP - Pumpout inhibited by a low liquid temperature

> SVC-OVRD - Max pumpout rate alarm is disabled

A further explanation of the status displays may be found in the "Status of Operation" section for the UCP2 human interface.

Default Displays

After 20 minutes of inactivity, a default screen is displayed. The default screen consists of either an alternating status display or an alternating alarm display if an alarm is currently active. The alternating status display consists of the Mode/Status screen and the Last 24 hour pumpout rate

Purge Based Human Interface Menu Structure

Major Menu	Side Menus	Description/Ranges
Mode: ADAPTIVE Status: RUNNING		Purge operating mode [STOP, ON, AUTO, ADAPT] Purge Status See "STATUS MESSAGES"
Last 24 Hr Pump Rate: XXXX.X Min		Current purge pumpout rate for the last 24 hours
**** ALARM! **** Press + to Reset		Alarm status - Backlight will flash when in alarm (See "ALARM MESSAGES"
1 TEMP Report <Enter> to View		Entry point into the **TEMPERATURE** Report
	Prg SUCTION Temp = XXX.X F	Purge refrigerant compressor suction temperature
	Prg LIQUID Temp = XXX.X F	System refrigerant liquid temperature returned to the chiller from the purge
2 RUNTIME Report <Enter> to View		Entry point into the **RUNTIME** Report
	PUMP Time Last 24 hr=XXXX.X min	Current purge pumpout rate for the last 24 hours
	PUMP Time Total = XXXXX.X min	Log of total purge pumpout time since installation
	PURGE Run Time Ttl= XXXXX.X hrs	Log of total purge run time since installation
	ADAPT Cycle Time w/CHLR ON= XXhrs	Adaptive mode "off-interval" - for use when chiller is running (varies from 0 to 4 hrs).
	ADAPT Cycle Time w/CHLR OFF=xxxhr	Adaptive mode "off-interval" - for use when chiller is off (varies from 1 to 14 days, displayed in hours).
	Time until Purge Runs: =XXX.X hrs	Amount of time left on the adaptive cycle timer until the purge runs
	LOG <+> to Reset XXXXmin XXXXdays	Service log - accumulated pumpout time and calendar days since the log was last reset.
3 30 Day Report <Enter> to View		Entry point into the **30 DAY** Report
	Avg 30 Day Pump = XXXX.X min/day	Last 30 day pumpout activity - indicative of total chiller leak picture
	Avg 30 Day Chlr Run=XX.X hrs/day	Last 30 day chiller run activity
	Avg Pmp;CHLR RUN = XXXX.X min/day	Last 30 day pumpout activity while the chiller was running - indicative of chiller low side leakage
	Avg Pmp;CHLR OFF = XXXX.X min/day	Last 30 day pumpout activity while the chiller was off - indicative of low and high side leakage
	Avg Pmp;CHLR DWN =XXX.Xmin/Shtdwn	Pumpout activity during 3 hours after chiller shutdown - indicative of air storage during operation
4 SETTINGS Reprt <Enter> to View		Entry point into the **SETTINGS** Report
	Purge Control Mode = ADAPTIVE	Operator entry to select purge operational mode. Mode may be set to [ON, AUTO, ADAPTIVE]
	Max Pump Rate = XXX min/24 hr	Operator entry for 24 hour maximum pumpout. Range from 1 to 100 minutes, Default is 20 min.
	Disable Pump Alarm for XX hrs	Max pumpout rate override. Range is from 0 to 72 hours. Display will count down as time elapses.
	Low Liquid Temp Protect= DISABLE	Enable / disable for low liquid temp limit (next setpoint)
	Low Liquid Temp Limit = XX F	Pumpout is disabled when liquid temperature falls belo this setting (range is 32 to 50 F when enabled).
	Display Units = ENGLISH	Select units display "English" or "SI".
	Language Setting ENGLISH	Select language (entries are - English = Standard
	Prg Control/Type 01-Micropurge	01-Micropurge = standard

screen. The alarm display consists of an alarm screen and an alarm message. The backlight will flash when the alarm screen is displayed and an alarm is active.

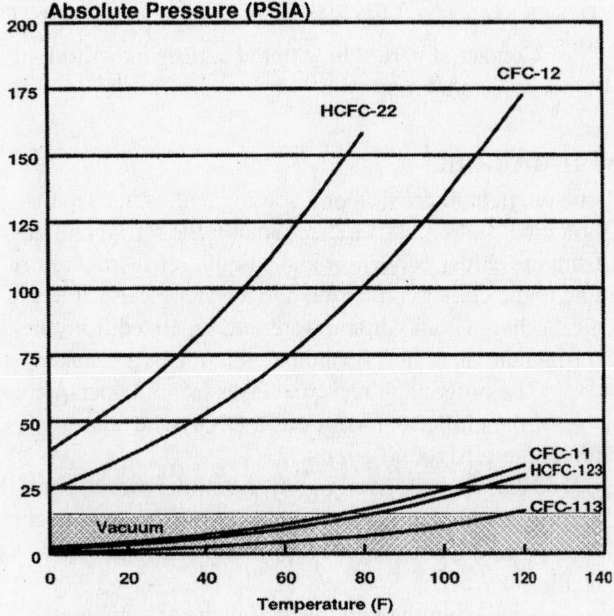

Fig. 15.9 Temperature/Pressure Relationship for Common Refrigerants

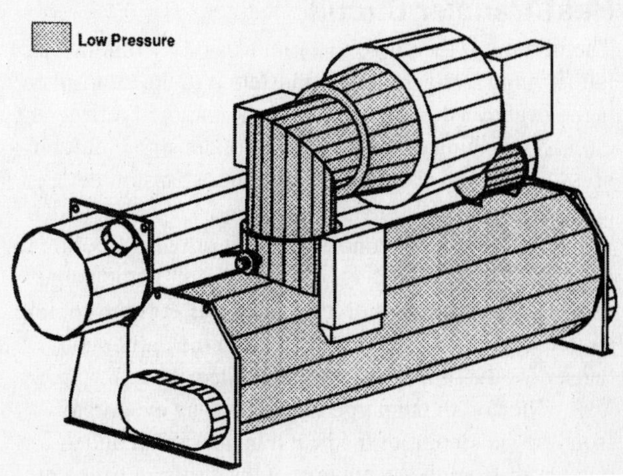

Fig. 15.10 Low Pressure Areas of Operating CVHE Unit

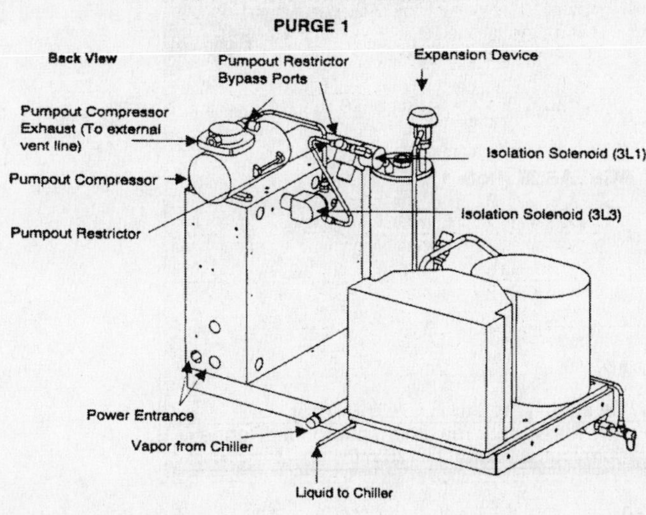

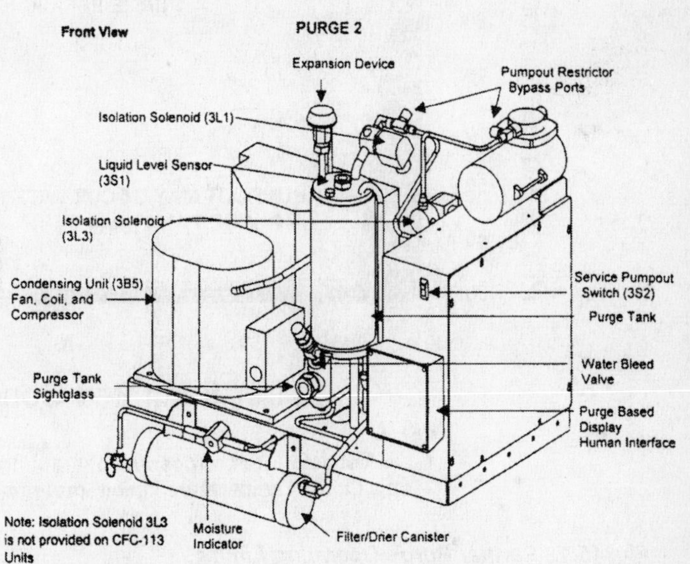

Fig. 15.11 Purifier Purge Component Layout

Heat Transfer Circuit

The portion of the purge that removes heat from the circulating purge refrigerant and transfers it to the atmosphere is the heat transfer circuit. This is an enclosed refrigerant circuit consisting of an air-cooled condensing unit (compressor, fan, and condensing coil), an expansion device, and a coil in the purge tank (evaporator).

The air-cooled condensing unit provides cooling for the purge coil (3/8-inch copper tubing coil in the purge tank). In conjunction with the purge coil, it is the cooling source that draws the refrigerant from the chiller condenser for the separation of non-condensibles.

The coil in the purge tank acts as an evaporator from the standpoint of the heat transfer circuit and as a condenser from the standpoint of the chiller refrigerant.

The condensing unit operates effectively over an ambient temperature range of 40°–120° F. As ambient temperature increases, condensing unit capacity decreases, reducing the rate at which the purge will remove air from the chiller (Fig. 15.12).

Note: Because the Purifier Purge utilizes an air-cooled condenser, it is operable whether the chiller is running or not. No additional cooling source is required (e.g. ,water hookup).

IMPORTANT: No water connections are required to the Purifier Purge.

WARNING: HOT SURFACES. SURFACE TEMPERATURES MAY EXCEED 150° F ON CONDENSING UNIT.

Contact of bare skin with hot surface may result in minor to severe burns.

Purge Tank

The purge tank consists of a cooling coil, water separation tube, sight glass, connections for the refrigerant gas from the chiller condenser and a liquid refrigerant return line to the chiller condenser, and a water bleed valve and air discharge port. Air and water are separated from the refrigerant vapor and accumulated in the purge tank.

The purge tank is a condenser from the perspective of the chiller but serves as a DX-type evaporator in the purge refrigerant circuit.

Heat is transferred out of the chiller vapor, condensing it, and is transferred into the colder refrigerant of the purge circuit, first evaporating and then superheating it.

Air within the tank decreases the effectiveness of this heat transfer, decreasing the exit superheat of the

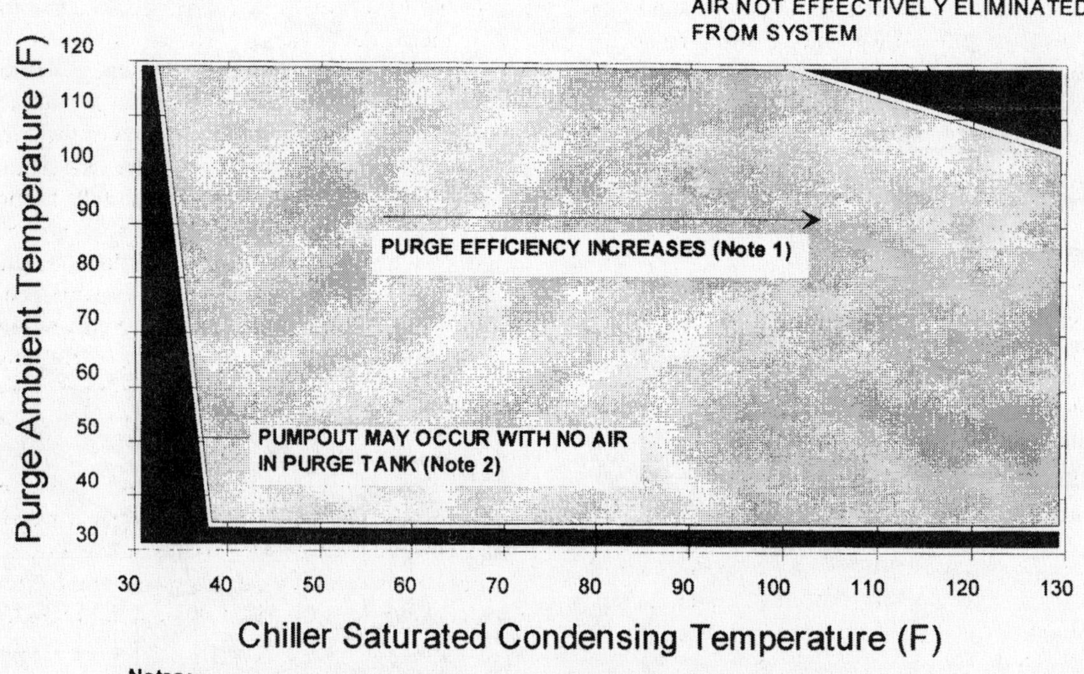

Fig. 15.12 Purifier Purge Operating Limits

purge refrigeration circuit. When the superheat decreases to 18° F, enough air is deemed to be present to initiate a pumpout cycle.

The water separation tube assembly (Fig.15.13) serves as both a trap to prevent the "short circuiting" of chilled vapor through the purge tank and also as a means to separate excessive quantities of water that may be present. This trapped water may be removed via the water bleed valve in the sump. Dissolved water remaining in the liquid refrigerant is removed in the filter-drier.

Pumpout System

The pumpout system consists of a small pumpout compressor, two isolation solenoids, and a restriction device located at the pumpout compressor suction connection. When the purge control system detects the presence of air in the purge tank, the isolation solenoids are opened and the pumpout compressor is turned on. The compressor and a restriction device cause the purged air to be removed slowly. This slow air removal process enhances the efficiency of the purge system. The standard pumpout compressor is compatible with both CFC-11 and HCFC-123. An alternate pumpout compressor and restrictor are available for CFC-113 applications.

Note: Trane recommends using 3/8-inch copper tubing to connect the purge pumpout compressor exhaust to the chiller rupture disc vent line. If the optional Purifier Plus is installed, 3/8-inch copper tubing should be used to connect the purge pumpout compressor exhaust to the Purifier Plus, with 3/8-inch copper tubing from the Purifier Plus to the chiller rupture disc vent line.

Purge Control System

The purge control system is comprised of a microprocessor control module mounted in the purge control box and a human interface. For purges operating with UCP2 controls, purge information is displayed on the UCP2 human interface. For purge-based display installations, a separable purge display panel is provided. This purge-based display human interface may be remotely mounted from the purge in any convenient operating location.

A service switch is mounted on the purge control box. This manual switch will start the pumpout system. All other control functions and data access are controlled through the purge human interface.

Purge operating controls located inside the purge control panel are

- Microprocessor module
- Transformer
- Terminal strip

Purge operating controls not located inside the purge control panel are

- Service switch 3S2 for manual operation of pumpout system
- Isolation solenoid valves 3L1 and 3L3
- Purge-based display human interface
- Liquid level sensor 3S1
- Temperature sensors 3RT2

Note: Solenoid valve 3L3 is not used on CFC-113 Purifier Purge units.

Operating Principles

General

The purge is active when the purge condensing unit is powered. The condensing unit is used to condense refrigerant vapor in the purge tank. The condensing refrigerant lowers the pressure in the tank, drawing vapor from the chiller condenser. The vapor carries non-condensibles and moisture into the purge tank.

Refrigerant vapor enters the purge tank through a 5/8-inch line connected at the bottom of the purge tank (Fig.15.13). Once inside the tank, the refrigerant vapor condenses on the purge tank coil and falls to the bottom of the tank. Non-condensibles accumulate in the purge tank only when there is air in the chiller condenser.

A layer of liquid refrigerant is maintained in the bottom of the purge tank during purge operation. The refrigerant liquid level is determined by the height of the liquid refrigerant standpipe in the purge tank. When the purge is running, the liquid level is visible in the purge sump sight glass.

Note: Free water in the purge sump is an uncommon occurrence. Liquid water is less dense than liquid refrigerant and will "float" on top of the liquid refrigerant. It may be seen during purge start-up, if major leaks occur, or if the filter drier is saturated.

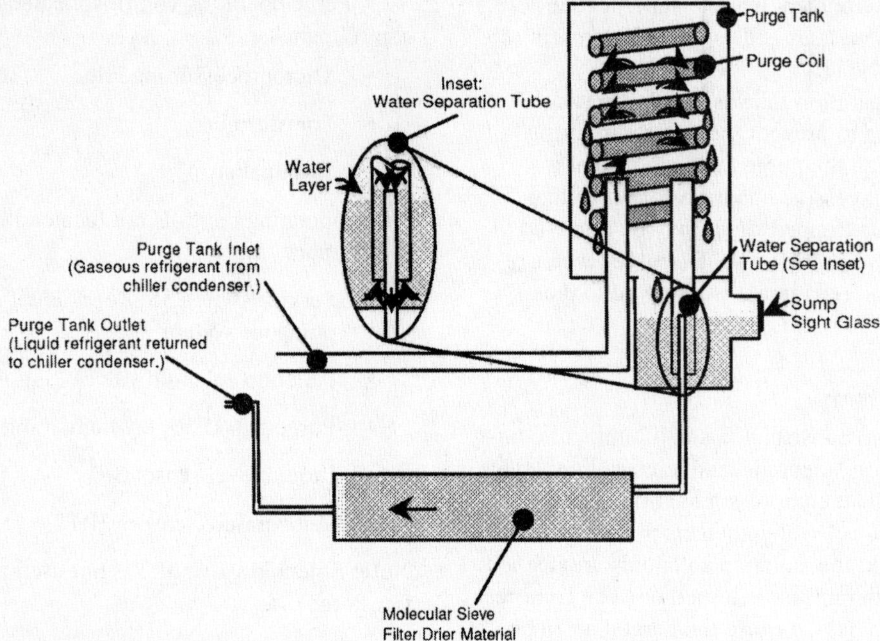

Fig. 15.13 Purge Tank Refrigerant Flow

Operating Cycle

The following discussion describes the Purifier Purge unit operating cycle at typical conditions (70° F ambient, 8 psig chiller condensing pressure). Fig. 15.14 illustrates the cycle of the active purge (condensing unit compressor running). The conditions that should exist at points 1 through 5 in Fig. 15.14 are

- Point 1 = 0° F
- Point 2 = greater than 22° F
- Point 3 = 140° F
- Point 4 = 85° F
- Point 5 = 75° F

The purge condensing unit compressor suction temperature varies with the amount of air in the purge tank. When the amount of air present in the purge tank limits the available condensing surface in the tank, the condensing unit compressor suction temperature will fall. The purge module will initiate a pumpout cycle when the suction temperature reaches 18° F. The air in the purge tank is then vented from the purge tank. As air is removed from the purge tank, condensing unit compressor suction temperature increases to terminate the pumpout cycle.

Operating Limits

Purge efficiency is dependent upon the chiller condenser pressure. Purge efficiency increases as the chiller con-

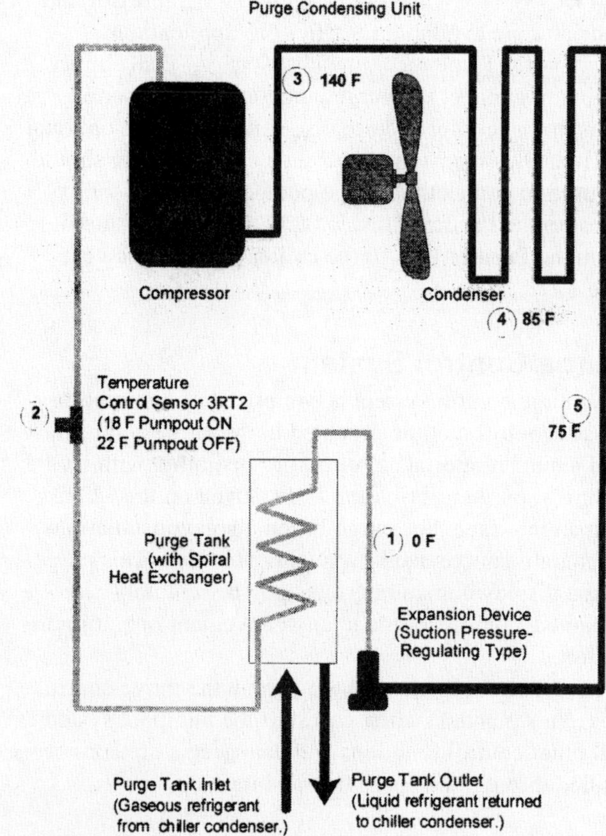

Fig. 15.14 Purifier Purge Refrigerant Circuit Schematic

denser pressure increases. Fig. 15.12 illustrates the purge operating limits and relative efficiency.

The Trane Purifier Purge can operate with a chiller saturated condensing temperature between 40–130 F (Fig. 15.12).

Higher saturation temperatures and corresponding higher chiller condensing pressures result in less refrigerant lost to the atmosphere when air is purged.

Lower saturation temperatures result in more refrigerant loss when air is purged, decreased suction superheat to the condensing unit compressor, and increased pressure ratio on the pumpout compressor.

In the AUTO mode, the purge will run whenever the chiller is running. Continuous purge operation (mode set to ON) is intended for use primarily during service procedures as described in "Maintenance." The ADAPTIVE operating mode will run the purge at various times when the chiller is both operational and off. The purpose of the ADAPTIVE control is

- Limit how often the purge is run (to save energy)
- Run the purge during chiller shutdown to insure air is removed from the chiller
- Keep pumpout statistics to help diagnose chiller leak patterns

IMPORTANT: Do not operate the purge when saturation temperatures are less than 40° F, as seen when ice storage units are turned off or when a chiller is operating in free-cooling mode. The low liquid temperature setting provides automatic lockout based upon saturated condensing temperature.

Air Removal

When there is no air in the purge tank, the refrigerant returning to the purge condensing unit compressor suction has a high superheat. As air accumulates in the tank, displacing the refrigerant vapor, the effective coil surface exposed to vapor decreases, reducing available superheat at the purge condensing unit compressor suction.

When condensing unit compressor suction temperature reaches 18° F, the purge control activates the isolation solenoids and the pumpout compressor to remove the accumulated non-condensibles. As air is removed from the purge tank, the coil is once again exposed to refrigerant vapor. The purge condensing unit compressor suction temperature rises and turns off the pumpout system. Pumpout cycle duration is typically 40 to 60 seconds.

Moisture Monitoring and Removal

A moisture indicator is provided in the liquid return line from the purge tank to the chiller condenser. This allows the machine operator to monitor the quality of the liquid refrigerant in the chiller.

Inspect the moisture indicator periodically. The indicator will show "wet" whenever the chiller moisture level exceeds the levels shown in Table 1. Notice that the indicator becomes more sensitive as the temperature decreases. (The moisture indicator normally operates at equipment room ambient temperatures.) A "wet" indication for more than 72 hours typically indicates that the filter drier is saturated and should be replaced.

Consult the moisture indicator only under these conditions:

1. The chiller is operating
2. The purge unit is operating and has been allowed sufficient time to remove system moisture property (minimum of 72 hours after replacing filter-drier cores).

The filter drier dehydrates the refrigerant passing through the purge and prevents moisture from re-entering the chiller. The nominal life of the filter drier is one year and should be replaced once the cores become saturated; refer to the "Drier Core Replacement" and "Filter-Drier Assembly Replacement" sections of this manual. If the filter drier becomes saturated and the moisture indicator shows "wet" refrigerant, water will accumulate in the purge sump. Due to the small volume of the purge tank sump, free water will typically form a visible layer on top of the refrigerant and be visible in the purge tank sump sight glass. This free water must be removed to avoid corrosive conditions in both the purge and the chiller. To remove moisture from the purge sump, refer to the "Service Procedures" section of this manual.

Table 1 Refrigerant Moisture Content As Determined By Moisture Indicator

Refrigerant		CFC-11			HCFC-123	
Moisture Level	75° F	100° F	125° F	75° F	100° F	125° F
Dry	Below 5	Below 10	Below 20	Below 20	Below 30	Below 35
Caution	5-15	10-30	20-50	20-50	30-80	35-100
Wet	Above 15	Above 30	Above 50	Above 50	Above 80	Above 100

Note: Refrigerant Moisture content given in parts per million (ppm)

PURGER LICENSE EXAM QUESTIONS

1. If purging does not occur in a refrigerating system, what is the result?

(A) High-head pressure
(B) Low-condenser pressure
(C) Low-head pressure
(D) None of the above

2. The purger has a refrigerated coil in it. This coil

(A) prevents operator injury.
(B) reclaims refrigerant usually lost.
(C) saves the operator from manually purging.
(D) removes the water.

3. The main reason for purging a Freon centrifugal refrigerating system is to remove

(A) water lubricating oil.
(B) gaseous lubricating oil.
(C) noncondensable gas.
(D) water vapor.

4. What reclaims refrigerant after it is condensed in an automatic purger?

(A) Aqua ammonia
(B) Anhydrous ammonia
(C) Cold brine
(D) None of the above

5. In some ammonia plants, purged gases are refrigerated before they are bled into a water bottle. This refrigerating is done to

(A) increase the purging rate.
(B) condense and recover any ammonia gases that may be mixed in with the gases being purged.
(C) save the operator the trouble of manually purging the plant.
(D) none of the above.

6. The best time to purge an ammonia plant with 250 pounds of ammonia is

(A) during shut-down, because you will lose ammonia.
(B) while charging the plant.
(C) during operation.
(D) none of the above.

7. When an automatic purger unit operates in an ammonia compression system, the ammonia carried along with the noncondensables is generally condensed and recovered by

(A) chilled air.
(B) cold brine.
(C) aqueous ammonia.
(D) ammonia.

8. Purging a double-pipe condenser should be done from the

(A) bottom, near the liquid refrigerant outlet.
(B) middle, on one of the bands.
(C) top, near the gas inlet.
(D) relief valve by the outlet of the liquid line.

9. The liquid in the bottle of an ammonia purger is

(A) water.
(B) weak liquor.
(C) anhydrous ammonia.
(D) strong liquor.

Answers to Purger License Questions

1. **The correct answer is (A).**
2. **The correct answer is (B).**
3. **The correct answer is (C).**
4. **The correct answer is (B).**
5. **The correct answer is (B).**
6. **The correct answer is (C).**
7. **The correct answer is (D).**
8. **The correct answer is (C).**
9. **The correct answer is (A).**

Chapter 16

ABSORPTION SYSTEMS

THE AMMONIA ABSORPTION SYSTEM

Intermittent Cycle

The intermittent refrigeration cycle in the ammonia absorption machine was used many years ago in rural areas that did not have illuminating gas or natural gas. In the intermittent cycle, a kerosene burner boils ammonia vapor in the generator.

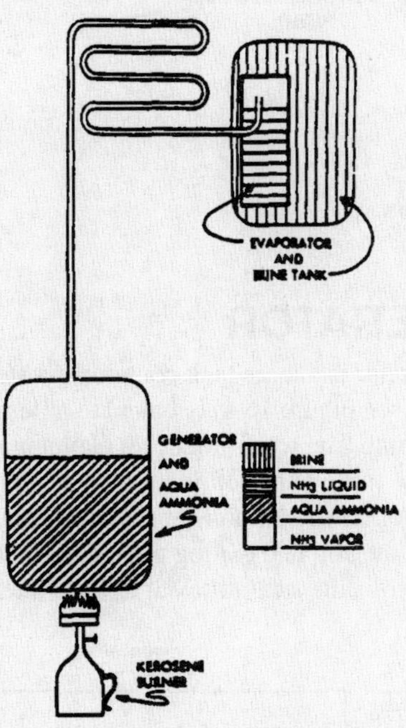

Fig. 16.1 Intermittent Absorption System

This system has a generator, condenser, evaporator, and kerosene burner. The system is charged with aqua ammonia, a mixture of ammonia and water. The ammonia mixture is placed in the generator. When the kerosene burner ignites, the heat warms the mixture and boils the ammonia. This ammonia rises into the condenser, where it cools and liquefies, and collects in the evaporator as liquid ammonia. The kerosene burner burns long enough to boil all the ammonia. After a few hours the burner stops and pressure in the system drops. The weak solution left in the generator cools and acts as a sponge, absorbing ammonia vapor from the evaporator. The liquid in the evaporator continues evaporating and picking up heat from the refrigerated space. This heat is carried to the weak solution with the low-pressure vapor.

This is an intermittent cycle because refrigeration takes place during the evaporation period, not while the burner is heating the generator. The box stays cold during the condensing time because the evaporator is immersed in a brine tank.

CONTINUOUS AMMONIA ABSORPTION SYSTEM

This system includes a steam-heated generator, analyzer, rectifier, condenser, receiver, metering device, brine cooler or evaporator, absorber, strong-liquor pump, and heat exchanger. The refrigerant is aqua ammonia. The solutions are 28 percent of strong liquor, 21 percent of weak liquor, and 100 percent of anhydrous ammonia.

Ammonia has a lower boiling temperature than water. When boiled from water, it forms "weak liquor." The terms "liquor" and "solution" mean the same thing.

Operation

1. The strong solution in the generator is heated by a steam coil running through the generator tank. The generator takes the place of the compressor discharge.
2. The ammonia vapor boiled from the solution rises and goes through the analyzer, which removes moisture, from the vapor.
3. The vapor continues through the rectifier (if the system has one) to remove any remaining moisture.
4. This dry (anhydrous) high-pressure ammonia vapor enters the condenser, where it is cooled and liquefied.

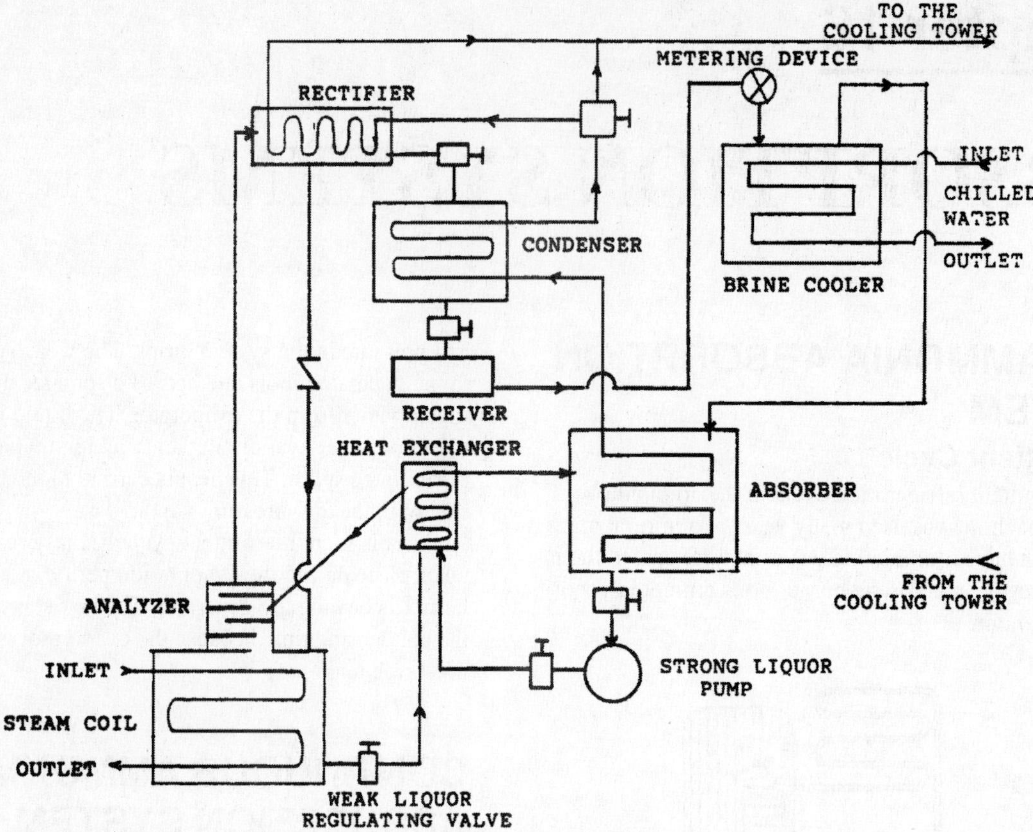

Fig. 16.2 **Continuous Ammonia System**

5. The high-pressure liquid ammonia then moves into the receiver for storage.
6. The high-pressure liquid in the receiver flows through the metering device as refrigerant is needed. This device controls the refrigerant flow and reduces pressure through the hand expansion valve.
7. The low-pressure liquid flows into the brine cooler. Heat from the brine is transferred to the low-pressure liquid, boiling it.
8. The low-pressure vapor resulting from this heat transfer flows from the brine cooler back to the absorber, carrying heat from the brine. In the absorber, the ammonia is absorbed into the weak solution. The absorber replaces the compressor suction by drawing the low-pressure vapor from the brine cooler into the absorber.
9. When the solution becomes strong enough, the strong-liquor pump pulls it from the absorber through the heat exchanger to the generator.
10. The weak solution left in the generator is then sent through the weak-liquor regulating valve, through the heat exchanger, and into the absorber.

GENERATOR

The generator is a large tank containing a steam coil. The analyzer (see Figure 16.4) is bolted to a flange on top of the generator. The weak-liquor regulating valve may be attached to the side or bottom of the generator to remove weak liquor. The solution is heated by steam feeding into the top of the coil and exiting out the bottom. A regulating valve controls the steam flow at the coil inlet.

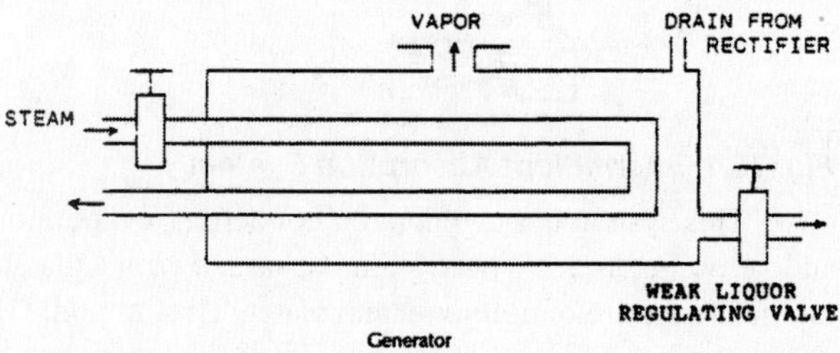

Fig. 16.3

ANALYZER

The analyzer, bolted to the generator flange, is usually a vertical tank with a series of baffles inside. Vapor from the generator flows up through the analyzer and around the baffles. The returning strong liquor flows into the opening on the side of the analyzer. Strong liquor flows down over the baffles into the generator, where it is heated by the steam coil.

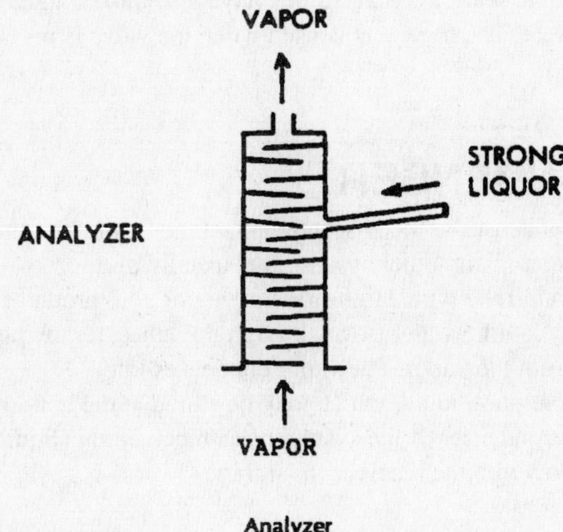

Fig, 16.4

RECTIFIER

The rectifier is a water-cooled dehydrator unit with a small tank, water coil, vapor inlet and outlet, and condensate drain. If the ammonia vapor contains some water vapor, the cooling water coil condenses this water from the ammonia. The water falls to the bottom of the rectifier and drains into the generator through a line and check valve. The rectifier is a closed-type heat exchanger.

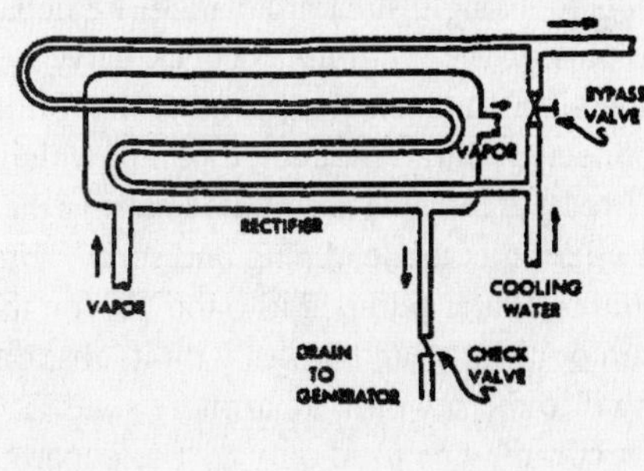

Fig. 16.5

WEAK-LIQUOR REGULATING VALVE

This is the most important valve in the system. It controls the balance of the system by controlling the flow of weak liquor to the absorber. If the valve is opened, the flow increases, increasing the suction and drawing more low-pressure vapor out of the brine. This either raises system tonnage or lowers brine temperature. If the valve is partially closed, the flow to the absorber is reduced and capacity decreases. As the weak-liquor valve is adjusted, adjustments must also be made to the strong-liquor pump outlet, to the generator's steam supply, and to the flow of high-pressure liquid through the metering device. It is most important to adjust the outlet valve of the strong-liquor pump. It must be adjusted to balance the change in the weak-liquor regulating valve to prevent fluctuation of generator or absorber levels. The regulating valve and the pump discharge must balance each other.

ABSORBER

Ammonia vapor coming out of the brine cooler is drawn back into the absorber by the cool, weak solution it contains. The absorber is a tank with flanged pipe connections and a cooling coil. Near the top are weak-solution and ammonia-vapor pipes. The weak-solution flange connects to the generator by way of the heat exchanger. The hot solution from the generator goes through the weak-liquor regulating valve and is partially cooled in the heat exchanger. It is then dumped into the absorber, where it is cooled further by a water coil.

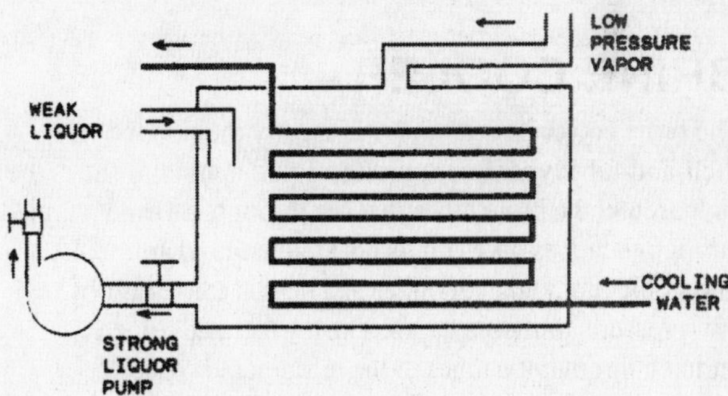

Fig. 16.6 Absorber

This cool, weak solution has a great affinity for ammonia. It draws ammonia as a sponge absorbs water or a blotter absorbs ink.

The weak solution in the absorber draws ammonia vapor out of the brine cooler and returns it to the generator to be reheated (cooked) and reused. The cooler the weak solution, the more ammonia it can absorb, so a water coil in the absorber cools the weak solution. This water coil also cools the high-pressure vapor in the condenser.

Part of the weak solution goes through the rectifier to condense and remove moisture.

The strong solution leaves the bottom of the absorber through a strong-liquor pump. This is a centrifugal pump built for ammonia service with extra-heavy black iron. Brass or bronze parts are not allowed in ammonia systems.

HEAT EXCHANGER

The heat exchanger in the absorption system makes the machine more efficient. The cool, strong solution leaving the absorber is warmed in the heat exchanger on its way to the generator. The hot, weak solution leaving the generator is cooled in the heat exchanger before reaching the absorber. The heat exchanger saves steam and cooling water. If it were removed, more steam would be required by the generator, and more cooling water by the absorber.

Whether the strong solution is in the coil and the weak solution in the shell or vice versa is unimportant; the machine works equally well either way. The piping is determined by the steamfitter or plumber who installs the equipment.

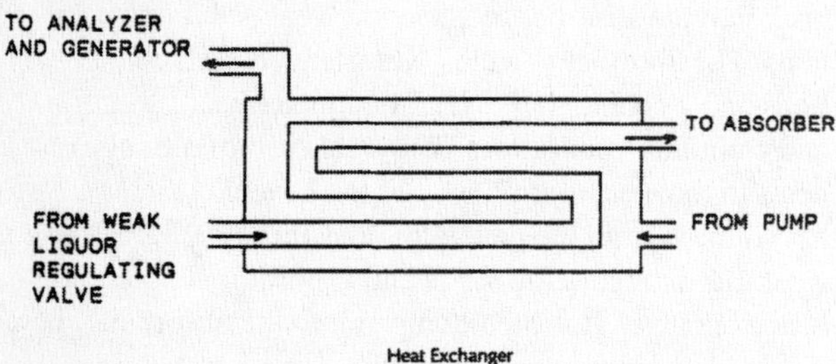

Fig. 16.7

BRINE COOLER

The brine cooler or evaporator is usually the flooded shell-and-tube type. Low-pressure liquid ammonia enters the tank around the brine tubes that run through it. Brine pumped through the tubes gives up its heat to the liquid ammonia. The liquid ammonia vaporizes and heat is carried off by the low-pressure ammonia vapor. The refrigerated brine is pumped through the tubes to the refrigerated spaces.

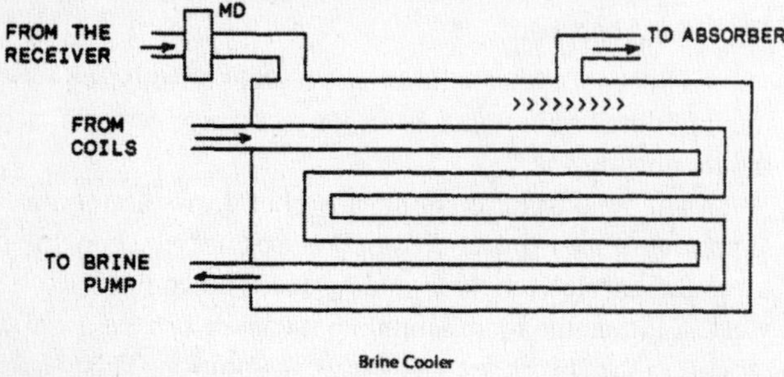

Fig. 16.8

METERING DEVICE OR HAND EXPANSION VALVE

The metering device in the ammonia absorption machine is usually a hand valve controlled or adjusted by the watch engineer. Like all metering devices, this is a needle valve. The valve, a double-seating type, is made of extra-heavy black iron. By law, all ammonia valves must be double seating—that is, they have a front seat and a back seat. The back seat is used when the valve is repacked.

CONDENSER

The condenser in the absorption machine is no different from that in any other system. It is usually of the shell-and-tube type. High-pressure vapor goes around the tubes. Cooling water flows through the tubes, removing heat from the vapor. The vapor condenses into high-pressure liquid, which may be stored at the bottom of the condenser. If the system has a receiver, this liquid will flow into the receiver for storage.

AMMONIA MIXER

The ammonia mixer is a safety device required by the New York City Code. It is a large-diameter pipe connected to the sewer. A hole is drilled at its upper end and another piece of piping is welded on at a sharp angle, forming a "Y." At the upper end of the outer pipe, a flange with a hole through the center, or a coupling, connects to a length of perforated lead piping inside the mixer body. The holes in this lead pipe are each 3/32 inch in diameter. The bottom of the pipe is sealed with a lead diverging plug to impede refrigerant flow by forcing refrigerant to spray through the 3/32-inch holes. The pipe welded to the side connects to a single standard 3-inch fire department connection outside the building. A check valve is installed in this connection. In an emergency, the inlet of this check valve is connected to the fire engine pump, which is supplied by a fire hydrant. The ammonia entering the lead pipe in the mixer hits the lead plug and sprays through the 3/32-inch holes. Water pumped into the "Y" on the mixer hits this ammonia spray and mixes with it, absorbing it and sending it to the sewer in a harmless state.

The mixer may be used only by fire departments. (See Figures 16.9 and 16.10.) The valve for the low-pressure ammonia to the mixer is in a locked box in the outer wall of the engine room. The engineer on watch cannot unlock the box to touch this valve. The mixer is used by the fire department to dump the entire charge of refrigerant in the system.

The test pressure for the mixer is 50 psig. For systems with up to 27,000 pounds of refrigerant, one mixer is required. An additional mixer is required for each additional 27,000 pounds or any fraction of this amount.

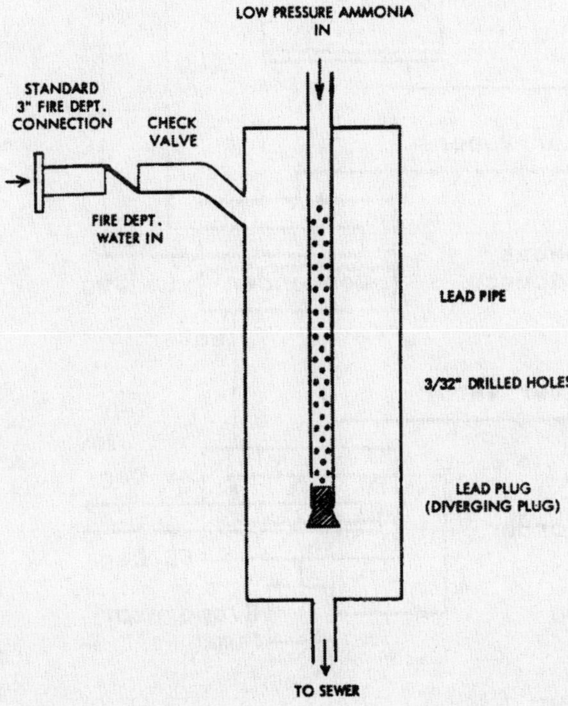

Fig. 16.9

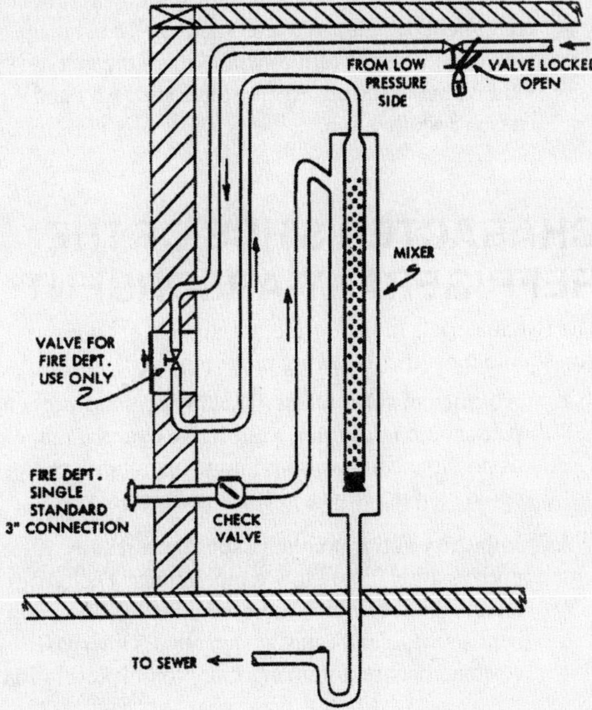

Fig. 16.10

LITHIUM BROMIDE ABSORPTION SYSTEM

Lithium Bromide Absorption Cycle

1. Water vapor is drawn from the evaporator to the absorber due to lithium bromide's strong affinity for water.
2. At the absorber, water vapor condenses and gives up its latent heat of vaporization to the absorbent.
3. The 59 percent solution, at 105° F, is pumped from the absorber to the heat exchanger.
4. As the solution goes through the heat exchanger, it picks up heat and enters the generator at 175° F.
5. In the generator, 12 pounds of steam pressure is added to the solution, increasing its heat to 195°. The solution's water (the refrigerant) vaporizes and flows to the condenser. The strong 64.5 percent solution flows by gravity to the heat exchanger, then back to the absorber. The solution's temperature is reduced to 135° F in the heat exchanger.
6. In the condenser, refrigerant vapor condenses at 122° F. Refrigerant condenses in the condenser and absorber.
7. As the refrigerant leaves the condenser through the orifice, some flashes, dropping to 40° F.
8. In the evaporator, the refrigerant absorbs heat from the chilled water coil and vaporizes.
9. In the evaporator, the remaining refrigerant (water) is in a vacuum and boils at 40° F. After the refrigerant vapor boils off, it is drawn out by the absorber, and the cycle is repeated.
10. A thermostat senses the temperature of chilled water leaving the evaporator to operate the steam valve or hot-water valve at the generator. If the leaving chilled-water temperature drops, the thermostat throttles the control valve to reduce heat input to the generator. This lessens the cooling effect in the evaporator. If the load increases, the thermostat opens the control valve, increasing the heat to the generator.
11. Another name for the generator is concentrator. At 12 pounds of steam pressure, it produces a temperature of 277° F. This produces enough btu to boil water from the lithium bromide solution.
12. The lowest pressure component is the absorber. Solution from the heat exchanger is 64.5 percent

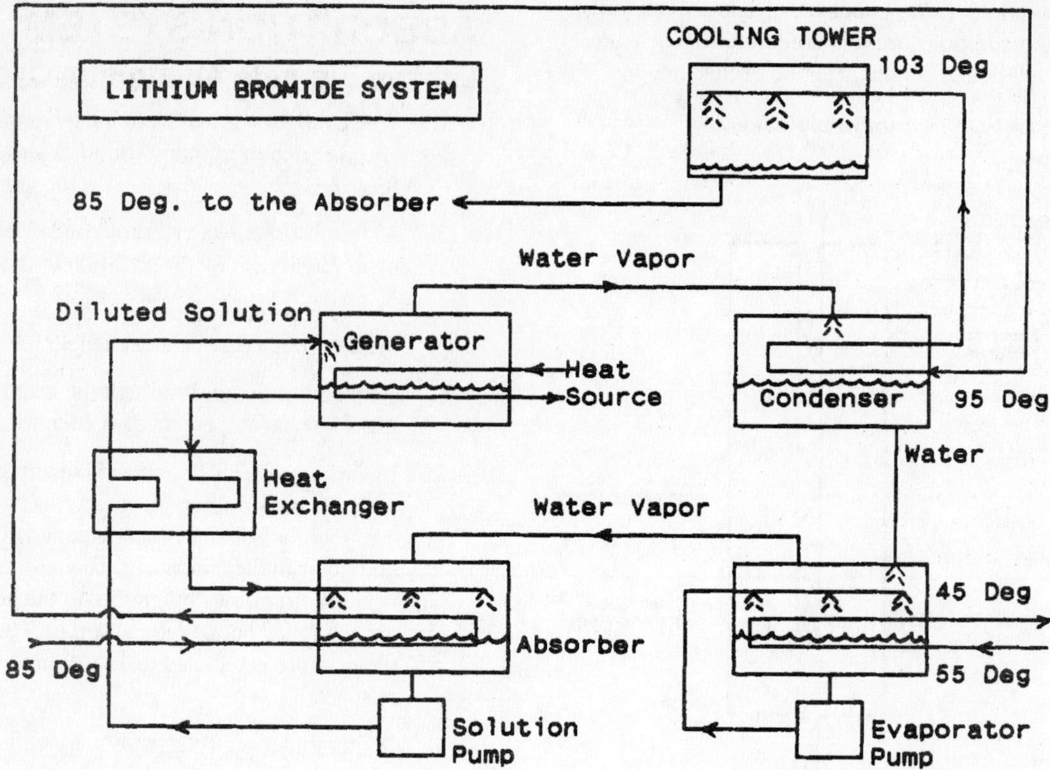

Fig. 16.11

of lithium bromide at 135° F. The spray headers increase the surface area of the strong solution in the absorber, increasing efficiency and reducing pressure.

Two Principles of Absorption Refrigeration

1. Lithium bromide or water (absorbent) absorbs the primary refrigerant (water/ammonia) that was vaporized in the evaporator. In these cases, both lithium bromide and water are only absorbents and not secondary refrigerants. The water in a lithium bromide system and ammonia in an ammonia/water system are the primary refrigerants.
2. Water boils at low temperatures in a vacuum.

Lithium Bromide and Water Solution

Advantages: High safety, high volatility ratio, high affinity, high stability, and high latent heat.

Disadvantages: When the absorbent solution cools below its saturation temperature, it causes lithium bromide to precipitate. If cooled too fast, the lithium bromide crystallizes into a solid. These salt crystals block the flow, causing a system shutdown. Proper equipment design can overcome this disadvantage. However, a power failure while operating at a heavy load will cool the absorbent solution rapidly and cause crystallization.

CHARACTERISTICS OF THE REFRIGERANT-ABSORBENT

The two materials in the refrigerant-absorbent combination should meet the following requirements:

1. **Absence of solid phase.** The refrigerant-absorbent pair should not form a solid phase over the range of possible compositions and temperatures. Solids could stop the flow and cause shutdown.
2. **Volatility ratio.** A volatile substance readily vaporizes at relatively low temperatures. The refrigerant should be much more volatile than the absorbent so they can be easily separated. Otherwise, cost and heat requirements can prohibit separation.
3. **Affinity.** The absorbent should have a strong affinity for the refrigerant under conditions in the sys-

tem. Affinity is the attractive force between substances or particles that cause them to enter into and remain a chemical combination.

4. **Pressure.** Operating pressures, established by physical properties of the refrigerant, should be moderate. High pressures necessitate use of heavy-wall equipment, and significant electrical power may be required to pump the fluids from the low side to the high side. Low pressures (vacuum) necessitate use of high-volume equipment and special means of reducing pressure drop in refrigerant vapor flow.

5. **Stability.** Almost absolute chemical stability is required, because fluids are subject to rather severe conditions over many years of service. Instability could cause undesirable formation of gases, solids, or corrosives. Stability is the resistance to chemical change or physical disintegration.

6. **Corrosion.** Since fluids or substances can corrode equipment, corrosion inhibitors should be used.

7. **Safety.** Fluids must be nontoxic and nonflammable if used in an occupied dwelling. Industrial process refrigeration is less critical in this respect.

8. **Transport properties.** Viscosity, surface tension, thermal diffusivity, and mass diffusivity are important characteristics of the pair. For example, low viscosity of fluid promotes heat and mass transfer, and to some extent reduces pumping problems.

9. **Latent heat.** The refrigerant's latent heat should be high to keep the circulation rate of the refrigerant and absorbent at a minimum.

ABSORPTION SYSTEM LICENSE QUESTIONS

1. In an NH_3 absorption system, ammonia goes directly from
   (A) evaporator to absorber.
   (B) condenser to rectifier.
   (C) absorber to analyzer.
   (D) analyzer to generator.

2. The rectifier is between the
   (A) generator and expansion valve.
   (B) weak-liquor cooler and generator.
   (C) analyzer and generator.
   (D) condenser and analyzer.

3. In an NH_3 absorption system, the ammonia pump drives
   (A) strong liquor to generator.
   (B) weak liquor to heat exchanger.
   (C) weak liquor to absorber.
   (D) heat exchanger to absorber.

4. To pack an angle valve in an NH_3 system,
   (A) open valve all the way and pack.
   (B) close valve and pack.
   (C) shut down and pack.
   (D) none of the above.

5. A lantern on an ammonia compressor should be
   (A) placed in the center of the gland between the packing.
   (B) directly under the oil line to the gland.
   (C) eliminated if the system is changed to Freon.
   (D) lighted while the compressor is running.

6. In an NH_3 absorption system, the mixing chamber has a lead pipe. Inside the pipe's end should be
   (A) diverging nozzles.
   (B) a strainer.
   (C) an open end.
   (D) a lead plug.

7. An oil intercepter is placed in a 300-ton ammonia plant
   (A) so it returns to the sump.
   (B) on the discharge line between the compressor and condenser.
   (C) as an oil strainer before the pump.
   (D) none of the above.

8. The intercooler in an ammonia booster system would be
   (A) placed after the high-pressure compressor.
   (B) placed after the condenser.
   (C) installed to cool booster discharge gas.
   (D) installed for cooling the jacket water.

9. The flow of weak liquor to the absorber is controlled by
   (A) gas pressure.
   (B) throttling device.
   (C) float valve.
   (D) pressure of the strong-liquor pump.

10. What will make the strong liquor in the absorber decrease?
    (A) Expansion valve open too much
    (B) A decrease in evaporator load
    (C) An increase in evaporator load
    (D) Too much steam on the generator

11. In an ammonia absorption system, the analyzer can be best described as a(n)
    (A) closed-type heat exchanger.
    (B) open-type heat exchanger.
    (C) bubbling-type heat exchanger.
    (D) device different from a heat exchanger.

12. Anhydrous ammonia is
    (A) a mixture of ammonia and water.
    (B) 29 percent aqua ammonia.
    (C) ammonia without any water present.
    (D) none of the above.

13. Assume an ammonia wet-compression system is replaced by an ammonia dry-compression system in a processing plant. If the capacity of the plant remains the same, the dry-compression system will
    (A) use less cooling water in the condenser.
    (B) reduce the danger of damage to the compressor unit.
    (C) make lubrication of the compressor cylinder walls easier.
    (D) have a lower compressor volumetric efficiency.

14. The best way of detecting ammonia brine is by using
    (A) CO_2 gas.
    (B) potassium of lime.
    (C) Nessler reagent.
    (D) carbonate of soda.

15. For ammonia burns, linseed oil is mixed with carrene oil and
    (A) lanolin.
    (B) nicotine.
    (C) Vaseline.
    (D) lime water.

16. What refrigerant has the same test pressures of an ammonia system?
    (A) R-11
    (B) R-12
    (C) R-22
    (D) R-30

17. If brine becomes saturated with ammonia in a small compression plant, the proper thing to do is
    (A) run the brine through the cooling tower and treat it with lime.
    (B) treat the brine with lime.
    (C) run it to the sewer and make a new batch.
    (D) pay no attention to the problem since it will correct itself.

18. In case of an accident with an ammonia absorption system, the
    (A) ammonia pump should immediately be shut down.
    (B) water supply to the condenser should be increased.
    (C) steam to the generator should be shut off.
    (D) absorber pressure should be removed or reduced by discharging it to the sewer.

19. The balance in an absorption system is maintained by the
    (A) governor on the ammonia pump.
    (B) steam pressure to the generator.
    (C) liquid regulating valve on the weak-liquor line to the absorber.
    (D) temperature on the heat exchanger.

20. The ammonia gauges commonly used on the low side of an ammonia compression refrigerating system are of the compound type. They are usually calibrated to read from
    (A) 90″ vacuum to 0 psig to 90 psig.
    (B) 30″ vacuum to 300 psig.
    (C) 0 psig to 500 psig.
    (D) 15 psig to 250 psig.

21. In an ammonia plant, a manometer measuring the amount of refrigerant circulating would normally be located between the
    (A) compressor and the condenser.
    (B) condenser and the receiver.
    (C) expansion valve and the evaporator.
    (D) receiver and the expansion valve.

22. In order to vary the capacity of an absorption refrigerating plant, an operating engineer should regulate the
    (A) flow of steam to the generator, and adjust the expansion valve.
    (B) relief valves on the generator, and the speed of the NH_3 pump.
    (C) speed of the absorber pump.
    (D) flow of water to the condenser.

23. The flash gas loss at the expansion valve of an ammonia system is approximately:
    (A) 2 percent.
    (B) 5 percent.
    (C) 22 percent.
    (D) 12 percent.

24. On a bare-pipe ammonia system with evaporator coils in the 28-to-33° F range, you notice that the lower two coils are not frosted. This indicates
    (A) the compressor is inefficient.
    (B) the evaporator is starved.
    (C) the evaporator is flooded.
    (D) none of the above.

25. Where is the strong liquor, and where is the weak liquor in an ammonia absorption system?
    (A) Strong liquor is in the rectifier, and weak liquor is in the receiver.
    (B) Strong liquor is in the compressor, and weak liquor is in the heat exchanger.
    (C) Strong liquor is in the generator, and weak liquor is in the analyzer.
    (D) Strong liquor is in the generator, and weak liquor is in the absorber.

26. What is the absorbent in an ammonia absorption system?
    (A) Lithium bromide
    (B) Water
    (C) Aqua ammonia
    (D) 10 percent oil solution

27. In an ammonia absorption system, the
- (A) weak liquor heats the strong liquor.
- (B) strong liquor heats the weak liquor.
- (C) anhydrous ammonia is in the shell.
- (D) anhydrous ammonia is in the tubes.

28. The scale trap of an ammonia system is located
- (A) in the liquid line between the receiver and the expansion valve.
- (B) in the discharge line between the compressor and the condenser.
- (C) in the suction line between the compressor and the chiller.
- (D) none of the above.

29. Anhydrous ammonia is
- (A) 28 percent ammonia.
- (B) 100 percent ammonia.
- (C) aqua ammonia.
- (D) strong liquor.

30. In an aqua ammonia system,
- (A) refrigerant is the ammonia, absorbent is the water.
- (B) lithium bromide is the absorber, refrigerant is the water.
- (C) anhydrous ammonia is 100 percent, aqua solution is the refrigerant.
- (D) none of the above.

31. Of the following parts of a conventional absorption system, the one that may be an auxiliary apparatus is the
- (A) generator.
- (B) absorber.
- (C) analyzer.
- (D) evaporator.

32. The strength of the strong liquor in the absorber of an absorption system decreases as the
- (A) expansion valve opens.
- (B) evaporator load increases.
- (C) condenser pressure decreases.
- (D) evaporator load decreases.

33. An ammonia compressor is pumping gas from two pipes, one at 15 psig and the other at 35 psig. Under these conditions, a back pressure valve should be installed in the
- (A) suction line.
- (B) line with the highest pressure.
- (C) lowest-pressure line.
- (D) none of the above.

34. The first sign that a drum of ammonia refrigerant is almost empty is
- (A) the appearance of frost on the lower end of the drum.
- (B) the appearance of fog in the vicinity of the drum.
- (C) a hissing or whistling noise in the drum.
- (D) a gurgling noise.

35. In an NH_3 dry expansion evaporator with TXV and bulb clamped properly on the outlet of the evaporator, the superheat is
- (A) 7 to 10° F.
- (B) 5 to 9° F.
- (C) 20 to 30° F.
- (D) 1 to 2° F.

36. An ammonia system using 30,000 pounds of refrigerant requires
- (A) an ammonia mixer connected to the sewer.
- (B) more than one ammonia mixer for Fire Department use.
- (C) low side to discharge into a water tank.
- (D) no water tank or mixer if vented to the atmosphere.

37. The ammonia mixer should be made to withstand which one of these pressures?
- (A) 90 psi
- (B) 50 psi
- (C) 180 psi
- (D) 160 psi

38. Which of the following is a cascade system?
- (A) An ammonia system cooling the condenser of a carbon dioxide system
- (B) An ammonia system cooling the brine tank ready to be circulated
- (C) A Freon system cooling brine for a brine spray
- (D) None of the above

39. In an ammonia refrigeration system running at 20 psig suction with 155 psig head pressure, how much NH_3 passes the expansion valve per ton per minute?
- (A) 2 lbs.
- (B) 1/2 lbs.
- (C) 20 lbs.
- (D) 200 lbs.

40. What metal would you use in an NH_3 shell-and-tube condenser using sea water?

(A) Black iron
(B) Galvanized steel
(C) Muntz or admiralty metal
(D) Copper

41. You are using sulphur tapers to find a leak in an NH_3 plant. When the ammonia leak is found, the color of the smoke will be

(A) light yellow.
(B) brilliant green.
(C) dull gray.
(D) white.

42. In an ammonia system, a two-bolt oval flange would be

(A) flat flange.
(B) serrated.
(C) tongue and groove.
(D) raised flange.

43. In a lithium bromide absorption system producing chilled water, the lowest possible temperature leaving the evaporator is

(A) 31° F.
(B) 33° F.
(C) 35° F.
(D) 38° F.

44. Refrigerating oil for an ammonia plant

(A) should not have a low pour point.
(B) should not have a high pour point.
(C) should not have high viscosity.
(D) should be free of moisture.

45. In an ammonia refrigeration plant, a ground-joint, screw-type union is part of the

(A) purger.
(B) bypass line around the expansion valve.
(C) compressor-starting apparatus.
(D) discharge side of the relief valve.

46. What auxiliary device in an ammonia system prevents excessive oil circulation?

(A) The heat exchanger
(B) The rectifier
(C) The receiver
(D) The oil separator

47. In an absorption system, refrigerant boils in the

(A) absorber.
(B) evaporator.
(C) condenser.
(D) generator.

48. A large ammonia plant has a purger with a refrigerant coil. The coil

(A) prevents loss of suction pressure.
(B) saves the operator from purging manually.
(C) reclaims refrigerant that might be lost with foul gases.
(D) prevents operator injury.

49. In an absorption system, which absorbent draws more refrigerant from the evaporator?

(A) Strong liquor
(B) Weak liquor
(C) Ammonia
(D) All of the above

50. In a brine cooler system, the suction pressure and brine pressure drop at the same time. To correct this

(A) readjust the X valve and check the brine temperature indicator.
(B) readjust the brine temperature indicator and watch the brine temperature.
(C) purge the system and watch the indicator.
(D) throttle the suction valve and watch the brine indicator.

51. A vertical, double-cylinder, single-acting ammonia compressor is lubricated by a rear-connected pump. Which pressure is best?

(A) Twice the condenser discharge pressure
(B) 10 to 20 pounds above suction pressure
(C) 50 pounds above discharge pressure
(D) 40 to 60 pounds above suction pressure

52. In an NH_3 system, it is common to use a double-seated valve to

(A) shut off the system in case a pipe leaks.
(B) increase the efficiency of the plant.
(C) decrease the efficiency of the plant.
(D) pack the valves while the system operates.

53. The ideal cooling tower temperature of a lithium bromide absorption system should be 85° F. What could result if the cooling tower temperature dropped to 78° F?

(A) High head pressure in the system
(B) Low head pressure in the absorber
(C) No load in the system, causing activation of the unloader
(D) Crystallization in the system

54. An ammonia plant rated at 10 tons would produce

(A) slightly more than 10 tons of ice.
(B) slightly less than 10 tons of ice.
(C) 20 tons of ice.
(D) exactly 10 tons of ice.

55. An ammonia brine cooler of the shell-and-tube design is to be used as a flooded evaporator. What kind of metering device should be used?

(A) Capillary tube
(B) Low-pressure float
(C) Thermostatic expansion valve
(D) High-pressure side float

56. The amount of ammonia permitted in a Class T machinery room for a commercial building is

(A) 300 pounds.
(B) 500 pounds.
(C) 1,000 pounds.
(D) unlimited.

57. The suction gauge of an ammonia system reads 15 pounds. This is equivalent to

(A) –28°.
(B) 28° F.
(C) 15° F.
(D) 0° F.

58. In a lithium bromide system, the evaporator's refrigerant is boiling at 40° F. What is its corresponding pressure?

(A) 0 psig
(B) 29.7 inches of vacuum
(C) 5.5 inches of mercury
(D) 5.5 psia

59. To pack an ammonia globe valve,

(A) back-seat the valve.
(B) remove the refrigerant and pack the valve.
(C) front-seat the valve.
(D) the valve must be replaced, not packed.

60. The bypass valve for a large ammonia compressor

(A) regulates compressor capacity.
(B) relieves motor load at start-up.
(C) pumps out the high side.
(D) all of the above.

61. What device reclaims the ammonia in an ammonia purger?

(A) The ammonia bottle
(B) The low-side float valve
(C) A refrigeration coil
(D) A water-cooled heat exchanger

62. The suction temperature of an ammonia system reads 50° F. This is equivalent to

(A) 40 psi.
(B) 75 psi.
(C) 150 psi.
(D) 200 psi.

63. Gas condenses in the anal or inner tube of a(n)

(A) double-pipe condenser.
(B) shell-and-tube condenser.
(C) atmospheric condenser.
(D) evaporative condenser.

64. When we say a refrigerant is anhydrous, we mean

(A) water is present.
(B) water is absent.
(C) it is aqua ammonia.
(D) it has ammonia.

65. In an ammonia compression system designed for standard conditions (86° F condensing temperature and 5° F evaporator temperature), with 24.27 psig suction pressure and 169.2 psig head pressure, what is the compression ratio?

(A) 17.2 to 1
(B) 4.94 to 1
(C) 2.5 to 1
(D) 202 to 1

66. Lithium bromide is ideal for absorption systems. Which statement about lithium bromide is false?

(A) It is nontoxic.
(B) It has a high affinity for water.
(C) It has a high boiling point.
(D) It is noncorrosive.

67. The counterflow heat exchanger in an absorption system is normally located between the

(A) condenser and liquid cooler.
(B) absorber and rectifier.
(C) generator and absorber.
(D) absorber and pump.

68. In an ammonia compression system, the evaporator becomes oil-logged. The direct result would be

(A) low suction pressure.
(B) increase in discharge pressure.
(C) increase in suction pressure.
(D) loss of refrigeration.

69. The strength of strong liquor in an absorption system decreases as the

(A) expansion valve is opened.
(B) condenser pressure decreases.
(C) evaporator load increases.
(D) evaporator load decreases.

70. What is refrigerant R-718?

(A) Propane
(B) Ammonia
(C) Methyl chloride
(D) Water

71. The freezing point of brine is

(A) 2° F.
(B) 0° F.
(C) –59° F.
(D) 10 to 15° F below the lowest prevailing refrigerant saturation temperature.

72. In a horizontal ammonia liquid receiver equipped with a liquid seal, the receiver

(A) does not have a safety valve.
(B) usually does not have a gauge glass.
(C) will pass only liquid ammonia into the liquid line.
(D) is never large enough to store the entire ammonia charge.

73. The principal operating difference between a lithium bromide water absorption cycle and an ammonia water absorption cycle is the

(A) thermodynamic cycle.
(B) pressure range of the cycle.
(C) type of evaporator used.
(D) control of the generator and absorber.

74. The evaporator absorbs heat from the air or brine because the liquid refrigerant entering it

(A) has a lower temperature than the air or brine.
(B) has a higher temperature than the air or brine.
(C) boils to a low-pressure gas.
(D) boils to a high-pressure gas.

75. Which statement is most accurate?

(A) The efficiency of an evaporator coil decreases as frost thickness increases.
(B) The efficiency of an absorber depends on and varies directly with the compressor speed.
(C) To lubricate the inside of an evaporator coil, 10 drops of machine oil per minute should be pumped into it.
(D) None of the above

76. What is the fastest way to defrost an old ammonia direct-expansion coil in a cold-storage room?

(A) Spray water on the frost.
(B) Turn the coil off and let the frost melt.
(C) Chop and scrape the frost off.
(D) Run a hot-gas line to the coil.

77. The ammonia in a shell-and-tube condenser is in

(A) the shell (water is in the tubes).
(B) the tubes (water is in the shell).
(C) both the shell and the tubes.
(D) neither the shell nor the tubes.

78. In an ammonia compression system, calcium chloride brine is the cooling medium for an ice field. The evaporator leaks and ammonia mixes with the brine. As operating engineer, you should

(A) test the brine with Nessler solution.
(B) pump out the brine and run it through a condenser until test samples show all ammonia is gone.
(C) dump the brine and make a new batch.
(D) use sulphur solution.

79. The generator in an absorption system receives

(A) strong liquor.
(B) weak liquor.
(C) pure water.
(D) pure ammonia.

80. In the evaporator chilling brine, the greatest cooling effect is caused by

(A) low temperature refrigerant entering the expansion valve.
(B) transfer of heat to the low pressure gas.
(C) heat absorption of the flash gas.
(D) effect of boiling a low-pressure liquid.

81. In an ammonia absorption system, a rectifier is a device used to

(A) transfer heat and remove water.
(B) transfer heat and remove ammonia.
(C) change strong liquor into weak liquor and remove water.
(D) remove water condensation.

82. In a refrigeration system, the refrigerant is cooled before it reaches the evaporator to

(A) remove the refrigerant gas.
(B) remove moisture from the refrigerant.
(C) improve the refrigeration effect.
(D) help return the coil to the compressor.

83. If the strong- and weak-liquor heat exchanger were disconnected in an absorption system, it would be wise to

(A) close the weak-liquor valve.
(B) shut down the strong-liquor pump.
(C) increase the steam pressure.
(D) none of the above.

84. To pack ammonia flanges, the gaskets should be made of

(A) rubber.
(B) asbestos sheet.
(C) neopine.
(D) lead.

85. The primary function of the heat exchanger in an absorption system is to allow the

(A) steam condensate from the generator to heat the strong liquor from the absorber.
(B) weak liquor to heat the strong liquor.
(C) steam condensate from the generator to heat the weak liquor from the absorber.
(D) strong liquor to heat the weak liquor.

86. What is used to make a tightly threaded connection in an NH_3 system?

(A) Mixture of lead and oil
(B) Pipe compound
(C) Litharge and glycerine
(D) Lampwick and white lead

87. Ammonia vapor is

(A) nontoxic.
(B) lighter than air.
(C) heavier than air.
(D) nonpoisonous.

88. On a vertical ammonia compressor with poppet-type valves, the valves are opened by

(A) an eccentric and a rod.
(B) a valve linkage.
(C) the piston rod.
(D) a pressure differential.

89. With the same compressor displacement, discharge pressure, and suction pressure, which refrigerant will give the most effect per pound?

(A) Ammonia
(B) Sulphur dioxide
(C) Methyl chloride
(D) F-12

90. The flow of refrigerant in an ammonia compressor system is from

(A) compressor to evaporator to condenser.
(B) compressor to evaporator to metering device.
(C) compressor to condenser to metering device.
(D) compressor to evaporator to receiver.

91. What is the correct flow of NH_3 through the compression cycle?

(A) Compressor, oil trap, analyzer
(B) Compressor, oil trap, receiver
(C) Compressor, oil trap, condenser
(D) Compressor, absorber, generator

92. Swirls in the Bronx ammonia plant are found on what type of condenser?

(A) Vertical open shell-and-tube
(B) Double-pipe
(C) Horizontal shell-and-tube
(D) Fin-and-coil

93. In a double-coil, direct-system shell-and-tube condenser, water is in the ammonia. How would you remove it?

(A) Regenerate
(B) Drain from the high-pressure side
(C) Pump it out
(D) None of the above

94. Oil in an ammonia compressor should

(A) not have a viscosity over 150.
(B) be dehydrated.
(C) not have a flash point over 330° F.
(D) not have a pH under 8.

95. You can ventilate an old ammonia machine room by deluge cooling, which is

(A) venting to the atmosphere.
(B) using a fire department mixer.
(C) spraying water over equipment.
(D) none of the above.

96. During winter operation, an ammonia plant with an atmospheric condenser should have its

(A) water supply increased.
(B) water heated by stream to prevent freezing.
(C) water pressure reduced.
(D) water shut off.

97. A lantern ring used on an ammonia compressor is

(A) placed in the center of the gland between the packing.
(B) directly under the oil line to the gland.
(C) eliminated if the system is changed to Freon.
(D) lighted while the compressor is running.

98. On an ammonia system, which of the following are the test pressures?

(A) High 250, low 150
(B) High 300, low 225
(C) High 250, low 180
(D) High 300, low 150

99. The primary function of an absoption system is to

(A) absorb the low-pressure refrigerant in the evaporator.
(B) generate strong liquor in the system.
(C) pump strong liquor to the generator.
(D) force weak liquor under pressure to the absorber.

100. What are the working fluids in the absorption cycle for ammonia and for lithium bromide?

____

____

101. Name the two major components of the high- and low-pressure sides of the absorption machine.

High-pressure: ______________________________

Low-pressure: ______________________________

102. What causes the reduced vapor pressure condition on the low side of the absorption machine?

____

____

103. Describe the content of the following solutions.

Dilution solution: ______________________________

Concentrated solution: ______________________________

Intermediate solution: ______________________________

104. Where is intermediate solution used in the absorption machine?

____

____

105. Name the components in the absorption cycle in correct order, starting with the low side:

____

____

106. Why is refrigerant easily separated from the solution?

____

____

107. What is the purpose of the heat exchanger?

____

____

108. An increase in solution concentration at a constant temperature results in what?

____

____

109. List six things that occur when load increases in an absorption system.

1. ______________________________
2. ______________________________
3. ______________________________
4. ______________________________
5. ______________________________
6. ______________________________

110. What is the purpose of the part-load economizer?

____

____

111. Define crystallization:

____

____

112. What is the most common cause of crystallization in a modern absorption machine?

____

____

113. Why must chilled water flow be maintained at all times, even during the dilution cycle?

____

____

114. How does the absorption cycle benefit by reduced-temperature cooling water?

____

____

115. Why is the steam-control valve throttled when the cooling water is at a reduced temperature?

____

____

116. What is the function of the demand limiting system?

____

____

117. How often should the purge system be operated?

____

____

118. What is the best preventive maintenance for heat transfer surfaces?

____

____

119. What is the maximum suggested steam pressure used for an absorption machine?

____

____

120. What refrigerant is in the absorption machine?

____

____

121. What is the secondary refrigerant?

____

____

122. Give six reasons for using lithium bromide (LiBr) in an absorption machine:

1. ______________________
2. ______________________
3. ______________________
4. ______________________
5. ______________________
6. ______________________

123. At what pressure will water boil at 40° in an absorption system?

____

____

124. What are the temperatures and concentrations in the following parts of a Trane or Carrier *absorption* machine?

Condenser: ______________________
Evaporator: ______________________
Absorber: ______________________
Generator: ______________________

125. What is the ideal temperature of the cooling tower of the Trane or Carrier absorption machine?

____

____

Answers to Absorption System License Questions

1. **The correct answer is (A).**
2. **The correct answer is (D).**
3. **The correct answer is (A).**
4. **The correct answer is (A).**
5. **The correct answer is (A).**
6. **The correct answer is (D).**
7. **The correct answer is (B).**
8. **The correct answer is (C).**
9. **The correct answer is (B).**
10. **The correct answer is (B).**
11. **The correct answer is (B).**
12. **The correct answer is (C).**
13. **The correct answer is (B).**
14. **The correct answer is (C).**
15. **The correct answer is (D).**
16. **The correct answer is (C).**
17. **The correct answer is (C).**
18. **The correct answer is (C).**
19. **The correct answer is (C).**
20. **The correct answer is (B).**
21. **The correct answer is (D).**
22. **The correct answer is (A).**
23. **The correct answer is (D).**
24. **The correct answer is (B).**
25. **The correct answer is (D).**
26. **The correct answer is (B).**
27. **The correct answer is (A).**
28. **The correct answer is (C).**
29. **The correct answer is (B).**
30. **The correct answer is (A).**
31. **The correct answer is (C).**
32. **The correct answer is (D).**
33. **The correct answer is (B).**
34. **The correct answer is (B).**
35. **The correct answer is (A).**
36. **The correct answer is (B).**
37. **The correct answer is (B).**
38. **The correct answer is (A).**
39. **The correct answer is (B).**
40. **The correct answer is (B).**
41. **The correct answer is (B).**
42. **The correct answer is (C).**
43. **The correct answer is (D).**
44. **The correct answer is (D).**
45. **The correct answer is (D).**
46. **The correct answer is (D).**
47. **The correct answer is (B).**
48. **The correct answer is (C).**
49. **The correct answer is (B).**
50. **The correct answer is (D).** Suction damper
51. **The correct answer is (B).**
52. **The correct answer is (D).**
53. **The correct answer is (D).**
54. **The correct answer is (B).**
55. **The correct answer is (B).**
56. **The correct answer is (D).**
57. **The correct answer is (D).**
58. **The correct answer is (D).**
59. **The correct answer is (A).**
60. **The correct answer is (B).**
61. **The correct answer is (C).**
62. **The correct answer is (B).**
63. **The correct answer is (A).**
64. **The correct answer is (B).**
65. **The correct answer is (B).**
66. **The correct answer is (D).**
67. **The correct answer is (C).**
68. **The correct answer is (D).**

69. **The correct answer is (D).**
70. **The correct answer is (D).**
71. **The correct answer is (D).**
72. **The correct answer is (C).**
73. **The correct answer is (B).**
74. **The correct answer is (A).**
75. **The correct answer is (A).**
76. **The correct answer is (D).**
77. **The correct answer is (A).**
78. **The correct answer is (C).**
79. **The correct answer is (A).**
80. **The correct answer is (D).**
81. **The correct answer is (A).**
82. **The correct answer is (C).**
83. **The correct answer is (C).**
84. **The correct answer is (D).**
85. **The correct answer is (B).**
86. **The correct answer is (C).**
87. **The correct answer is (B).**
88. **The correct answer is (D).**
89. **The correct answer is (A).**
90. **The correct answer is (C).**
91. **The correct answer is (C).**
92. **The correct answer is (A).**
93. **The correct answer is (A).**
94. **The correct answer is (B).**
95. **The correct answer is (C).**
96. **The correct answer is (D).**
97. **The correct answer is (A).**
98. **The correct answer is (D).**
99. **The correct answer is (A).**
100. **The correct answer is refrigerant: water and lithium bromide solution.**
101. **The correct answer is high pressure: concentrator, condenser; low pressure: evaporator, absorber.**
102. **The correct answer is an absorbent solution with a high affinity for refrigerant vapor causes reduced vapor pressure on the low side.**
103. **The correct answer is dilution solution: high refrigerant content and low lithium bromide content. Concentrated solution: low refrigerant content and high lithium bromide content. Intermediate solution: mixture of diluted and concentrated solutions.**
104. **The correct answer is it is used in the absorber sprays.**
105. **The correct answer is evaporator, absorber, heat exchanger, concentrator, condenser, and orifice.**
106. **The correct answer is the boiling temperature of the refrigerant is lower than that of the lithium bromide.**
107. **The correct answer is its purpose is to reduce both the amount of heat energy required in the concentrator and the cooling water required in the absorber.**
108. **The correct answer is an increase in solution concentration at a constant temperature results in a decrease in vapor pressure.**
109. **The correct answer is when the operational load increases in an absorption system:**
    a. leaving chilled water temperature rises
    b. the steam valve opens
    c. concentrator steam pressure increases
    d. absorber solution concentration increases
    e. evaporator pressure decreases
    f. heat transfer increases
110. **The correct answer is it modulates the flow of diluted solution to the concentrator in direct porportion to the load.** Therefore, at part load, less heat energy is required to boil the solution.
111. **The correct answer is when absorbent solution is cooled below its saturation temperature, it causes lithium bromide to precipitate from the solution.** At this point, lithium bromide has turned into a solid, blocking the flow in the absorption machine.

112. **The correct answer is crystallization is commonly caused by air in the machine.** Routine purging can avoid this condition. Improper shutdown is another cause of crystallization.

113. **The correct answer is chilled water flow is required to prevent evaporator freeze-up.**

114. **The correct answer is reduced-temperature cooling water increases the efficiency of both the absorber and the condenser.**

115. **The correct answer is less heat energy is required to liberate refrigerant from the highly diluted solution entering the concentrator.** Also, reduced heat input prevents violent boiling of the diluted solution, which would result in carry-over of salt into the condenser.

116. **The correct answer is it slows the opening of the steam control valve, preventing overloading of the boiler.**

117. **The correct answer is once a week for approximately one hour.**

118. **The correct answer is by using properly treated water.**

119. **The correct answer is 12 pounds, or 12 psi steam = 277° F.** Note that the high side is 10 times higher than the low side. These pressures and temperatures may be different on newer systems.

120. **The correct answer is water.**

121. **The correct answer is chilled water, brine.**

122. **The correct answer is stable, nontoxic, affinity, high boiling point, ability to operate at very low temperatures (vacuum), and inexpensive.**

123. **The correct answer is 29.7 inches of mercury, vacuum.**

124. **The correct answers are as follows:**

    Condenser: 103-95° F, 0% concentration at 122° F

    Evaporator: 55-45° F, 0% concentration at 42° F

    Absorber: 85-95° F, 59% concentration at 105° F

    Generator: 200° F, 64% concentration

125. **The correct answer is the ideal tower temperature is 85° F.** Below 78° F, crystallization occurs in the system.

Chapter 17

THE REFRIGERATION CODE

The first section of this chapter contains the complete ASHRAE Standard ANSI/ASHRAE 15–1992, "Safety Code for Mechanical Refrigeration," which is used nationwide. The second section contains selected portions of the 1975 New York City Refrigeration Code, edited by the author. It also contains information about safety group classifications of refrigerants, reprinted from ASHRAE Standard ANSI/ASHRAE 34–1992. Both sections promote safety practices for the construction, installation, and operation of refrigeration systems.

Lastly, this chapter discusses proposed regulations on Section 608 of the Clean Air Act concerning refrigerant recycling and the prohibition on venting. At the end of the chapter are refrigeration code questions for review.

The following organizations are acknowledged for the information appearing in this chapter:

ASHRAE Standard ANSI/ASHRAE 15–1992
ASHRAE Standard ANSI/ASHRAE 34–1978
ASHRAE Handbook *Fundamentals,* 1985
Goodheart-Willcox
Underwriters Laboratories, Inc.

SECTION I: SAFETY CODE FOR MECHANICAL REFRIGERATION ASHRAE STANDARD 15-1992[1]

Contents

(This foreword is not part of this standard but is included for information purposes only.)

Foreword

The industry response to the CFC issue has accelerated the introduction of alternative refrigerants. The entry of new refrigerants and blends in the market and the introduction of new safety classifications prompted the early revision of this standard. Requests for interpretation or proposals for revision of this standard may be addressed to the ASHRAE Manager of Standards.

This standard is directed to the safety of persons and property on or near the premises where refrigeration facilities are located. It includes specifications for fabricating a tight system. It does not address the effect of refrigerant emissions on the environment. For information on the relative potential environmental effects of halocarbon refrigerants, see *ASHRAE Guideline 3–1990, Reducing Emission of Fully Halogenated Chlorofluorocarbon (CFC) Refrigerants in Refrigeration and Air-Conditioning Equipment and Applications.*

The principal changes in this revision include the following:

Section 5—Addition of new refrigerants.
Section 6—Adoption of new refrigerant classification.
Section 7—Refrigerant use in listed equipment.
Section 8—New design pressures.
Section 11—New machinery room requirements.

The hazards of refrigerants are related to their physical and chemical characteristics as well as to the pressures and temperatures occurring in refrigerating systems. Personal injury and property damage from inadequate precautions may occur from

- rupture of a part or an explosion with risk from flying pieces of metal or from structural collapse;
- release of refrigerant from a fracture, from a leaking seal, or from incorrect operation; and
- fire resulting from or intensified by burning or deflagration of escaping lubricant or refrigerant.

Personal injury from accidental release of refrigerants may occur from

- suffocation from heavier-than-air refrigerants in unventilated spaces;
- narcotic and cardiac sensitization effects;
- toxic effects of vapor or the decomposition products due to vapor contact with flames or hot surfaces;
- corrosive attack on the eyes, skin, and other tissue; and
- freezing of tissue by contact with liquid.

New safety classifications for refrigerants are adopted from *ASHRAE 34–1992, Designation and Safety Classification of Refrigerants*. To assess the risks, the commonly used refrigerants are classified according to increasing toxic effects and increasing flammability characteristics. (See Section 6.)

Table 1 shows the amount of refrigerant in a given space that, when exceeded, requires a machinery room. When a refrigerant is neither classified in *ASHRAE 34–1992* nor shown in Table 1, it is the responsibility of the owner of a refrigerating system to make this judgment. For blends, Appendix A is offered to aid in determining allowable concentrations.

All commonly used refrigerants except ammonia (R-717) are heavier than air. Care should be taken to avoid stagnant pockets of heavy refrigerant vapors by proper location of ventilation inlet and exhaust openings. All machinery rooms are now required to have mechanical ventilation and oxygen deficiency alarms or refrigerant vapor alarms.

During public review of this standard, extensive comments were received from those interested in the use of ammonia as a refrigerant. The Society has established an ASHRAE Position Statement, *Ammonia as a Refrigerant*, to which the reader is referred for positions in this regard. For more information on equipment, design, and installation on ammonia refrigeration systems, see *ANSI/IIAR-2*, published by the International Institute of Ammonia Refrigeration, Washington, DC 20036.

A short publishing history of this code traces the origins of these safety provisions. In 1919, the American Society of Refrigerating Engineers (ASRE) proposed a Tentative Code for the Regulation of Refrigerating Machines and Refrigerants. Over the next 11 years, representatives from the American Gas Association, American Institute of Electrical Engineers, American Institute of Refrigeration, American Chemical Society, American Society of Heating and Ventilating Engineers, American Society of Mechanical Engineers, National Electrical Refrigerator Manufacturers Association, National Fire Protection Association, and ASRE met to expand the code to address all of the issues raised on the use of refrigeration equipment. The first Safety Code for Mechanical Refrigeration, recognized as American Standard B9 in October 1930, appeared in the first edition, 1932–1933, of the ASRE Refrigerating Handbook and Catalog. ASRE revisions designated ASA B9 appeared in 1933 and 1939. ASRE revisions designated ASA B9.1 appeared in 1950, 1953, and 1958. After the formation of ASHRAE, editions appeared as ASA B9.1–1964, ANSI B9.1–1971, ANSI/ASHRAE 15–1978, and ANSI/ASHRAE 15–1989.

1. Purpose

The purpose of this standard is to promote the safe design, construction, installation, and operation of refrigerating systems.

2. Scope

2.1 This code establishes reasonable safeguards of life, limb, health, and property; defines practices that are consistent with safety; and prescribes safety standards.

2.2 This code applies

(a) to mechanical refrigerating systems and heat pumps used in the occupancies defined in Section 4 and installed subsequent to adoption of this code and

(b) to parts replaced and components added after adoption of this code.

2.3 This code does not apply where water is the primary refrigerant.

2.4 Equipment listed by an approved, nationally recognized testing laboratory is deemed to meet the design, manufacturing, and factory test requirements section of this code for the refrigerant or refrigerants for which the equipment is designed.

2.5 In cases of practical difficulty or unnecessary hardship, the authority having jurisdiction may grant exceptions from the literal requirements of this code or permit the use of other devices, materials, or methods but only when it is clearly evident that equivalent protection is thereby secured.

3. Definitions

approved: acceptable to the authorities having jurisdiction.

approved, nationally recognized laboratory: one acceptable to the authorities having jurisdiction, which provides uniform testing and examination procedures and standards for meeting the design, manufacturing, and factory testing requirements of this code; is properly organized, equipped, and qualified for testing; and has a follow-up inspection service of the current production of the listed products.

blends: refrigerants consisting of mixtures of two or more different chemical compounds, often used individually as refrigerants for other applications.

brazed joint: a gas-tight joint formed by joining metal parts with alloys that melt at temperatures higher than 800ºF (426.5ºC) but less than the melting temperatures of the joined parts.

companion or block valves: pairs of mating stop valves that allow sections of a system to be joined before opening these valves or separated after closing them.

compressor: a machine used to compress refrigerant vapor.

compressor unit: a compressor with its prime mover and accessories.

condenser: that part of the refrigerating system where refrigerant is liquefied by the removal of heat.

condenser coil: a condenser constructed of pipe or tubing, not enclosed in a pressure vessel.

condensing unit: a combination of one or more power-driven compressors, condensers, liquid receivers (when required), and regularly furnished accessories.

container: a cylinder for the transportation of refrigerant.[1*]

critical pressure, critical temperature, and critical volume: a point on the saturation curve where the refrigerant liquid and vapor have identical volume, density, and enthalpy, and there is no latent heat.

department store: a public assembly occupancy (see 4.1.2) where large numbers of people congregate to purchase personal merchandise.

design pressure: the maximum pressure for which a specific part of a refrigerating system is designed.

dual pressure-relief device: two pressure-relief devices, each sized per 10.4.5, mounted on a three-way valve.

duct: a tube or conduit used to convey or encase as specified: (a) ***air duct*** is a tube or conduit used to convey air (air passages in self-contained systems are not air ducts). (b) ***pipe duct*** is a tube or conduit used to encase pipe or tubing.

entrance: a confined passageway, immediately adjacent to the door, through which people enter a building.

evaporator: the part of the refrigerating system that is designed to vaporize liquid refrigerant to produce refrigeration.

evaporator coil: an evaporator constructed of pipe or tubing, not enclosed in a pressure vessel.

exit: a confined passageway, adjacent to the door, through which people leave a building.

fusible plug: a plug containing an alloy that will melt, at a specified temperature, and relieve pressure.

hallway: a corridor for the passage of people.

* Superscript numbers denote references listed in Section 14.

header: a pipe or tube (extruded, cast, or fabricated) to which a number of other pipes or tubes are connected.

heat pump: a refrigerating system used to transfer heat into a space or substance.

highside: those portions of the refrigerating system that are subject to approximate condensing pressure.

IDLH (Immediately Dangerous to Life or Health): the maximum concentration from which one could escape within 30 minutes without any escape-impairing symptoms or any irreversible health effects.[2]

inside dimension: inside diameter, width, height, or cross-sectional diagonal.

internal gross volume: the volume as determined from internal dimensions of the container with no allowance for the volume of internal parts.

limited charge system: a system in which, with the compressor idle, the design pressure will not be exceeded when the refrigerant charge has completely evaporated.

liquid receiver: a vessel, permanently connected to a refrigerating system by inlet and outlet pipes, for storage of liquid refrigerant.

listed: equipment that has been tested and is identified as acceptable by an approved, nationally recognized testing laboratory.

lobby: a waiting room or large hallway serving as a waiting room.

lower flammability limit (LFL): the minimum concentration of the refrigerant that is capable of propagating a flame through a homogeneous mixture of refrigerant and air.[3]

lowside: the portion of a refrigerating system that is subjected to approximate evaporator pressure.

machinery: the refrigerating equipment forming a part of the refrigerating system, including, but not limited to, any or all of the following: compressor, condenser, liquid receiver, evaporator, and connecting piping.

machinery room: a space that is designed to safely house compressors and pressure vessels (see 11.13).

manufacturer: the company or organization that evidences its responsibility by affixing its name, trademark, or trade name to refrigerating equipment.

mechanical joint: a gas-tight joint obtained by joining metal parts with a positive-holding mechanical construction, such as a flanged, screwed, or flared joint.

nationally recognized testing laboratory: see approved, nationally recognized laboratory.

nonpositive displacement compressor: a compressor in which the increase in vapor pressure is attained without changing the internal volume of the compression chamber.

occupied space: that portion of the premises normally frequented or occupied by people, excluding machinery rooms.

piping: the pipe or tube mains for interconnecting the various parts of a refrigerating system. Piping includes pipe; flanges; bolting; gaskets; valves; fittings; the pressure-containing parts of other components, such as expansion joints or strainers; and devices that serve such purposes as mixing, separating, muffling, snubbing, distributing, metering or controlling flow, pipe support, and structural attachment.

positive displacement compressor: a compressor in which the increase in pressure is attained by changing the internal volume of the compression chamber.

premises: a tract of land and the buildings thereon.

pressure-imposing element: any device or portion of the equipment used to increase refrigerant pressure.

pressure-limiting device: a pressure-responsive electronic or mechanical control designed to automatically stop the operation of the pressure-imposing element at a predetermined pressure.

pressure-relief device: a pressure-, not temperature-, actuated valve or rupture member designed to automatically relieve excessive pressure.

pressure-relief valve: a pressure-actuated valve held closed by a spring or other means and designed to automatically relieve pressure at and in excess of its setting.

pressure vessel: any refrigerant-containing receptacle in a refrigerating system. This does not include evaporators where each separate section does not exceed 0.5 ft^3 (0.014 m^3) of refrigerant-containing volume, regardless of the maximum inside dimension, evaporator coils, compressors, condenser coils, controls, headers, pumps, and piping.

pumpdown charge: the quantity of refrigerant stored at some point in the refrigeration system for operational, service, or standby purposes. *Note:* The pumpdown charge is not necessarily equal to the total system charge.

refrigerant: the fluid used for heat transfer in a refrigerating system; the refrigerant absorbs heat and transfers it at a higher temperature and a higher pressure, usually with a change of state.

refrigerating system: a combination of interconnected parts forming a closed circuit in which refrigerant is circulated for the purpose of extracting, then rejecting, heat. (See Section 4 for classification of refrigerating systems by type.)

refrigerating system, direct: (see 5.1.1).

refrigerating system, indirect: (see 5.1.2).

rupture member: a device that will rupture at a predetermined pressure.

saturation pressure: the pressure at which vapor and liquid can exist in equilibrium at a given temperature.

sealed absorption system: an absorption system in which all refrigerant-containing parts are made permanently tight by welding or brazing.

secondary coolant: any liquid used for the transmission of heat, without a change of state, and having no flash point or a flash point above 150°F (65.5°C) as determined by the American Society for Testing and Materials D93.[4]

self-contained system: a complete, factory-assembled and tested system that is shipped in one or more sections and has no refrigerant-containing parts that are joined in the field by other than companion or block valves.

set pressure: the pressure at which a pressure-relief device or pressure control is set to operate.

shall (shall not): used where the provision is mandatory.

should: used where the provision is not mandatory but is recommended good practice.

soldered joint: a gas-tight joint formed by joining metal parts with alloys that melt at temperatures not exceeding 800°F (426.5°C) and above 400°F (204.5°C).

specified: explicitly stated in detail. Specified limits or prescriptions are mandatory.

stop valve: a device used to shut off the flow of refrigerant.

tenant: a person or organization having the legal right to occupy a premises.

three-way valve: a service valve for dual pressure-relief devices that allows using one device while isolating the other from the system.

TLV-TWA (Threshold Limit Value-Time Weighted Average): the refrigerant concentration in air for a normal 8-hour workday and a 40-hour workweek to which nearly all workers may be repeatedly exposed, day after day, without adverse effect. See reference 5 and ASHRAE Standard 34 for more detail. (TLV is a registered trademark of ACGIH.)[5]

ultimate strength: the highest stress that a component can tolerate without rupturing.

unprotected tubing: tubing that is unenclosed and therefore exposed to crushing, abrasion, puncture, or similar damage after installation.

unit system: (see self-contained system).

zeotropic: refers to blends comprising multiple components of different volatilities that, when used in refrigeration cycles, change volumetric composition and saturation temperatures as they evaporate (boil) or condense at constant pressure. The word is derived from the Greek words *zein* (to boil) and *tropos* (to change).

4. Occupancy Classification

4.1 Locations of refrigerating systems are described by occupancy classifications that consider the ability of people to respond to potential exposure to refrigerant as follows:

4.1.1 *Institutional occupancy* is that portion of the premises from which, because they are disabled, debilitated, or confined, occupants cannot readily leave without the assistance of others. Institutional occupancies include, among others, hospitals, nursing homes, asylums, and spaces containing locked cells.

4.1.2 *Public assembly occupancy* is that portion of the premises where large numbers of people congregate and from which all occupants cannot quickly vacate the space. Public assembly occupancies include, among others, auditoriums, ballrooms, department stores, and passenger depots.

4.1.3 *Residential occupancy* is that portion of the premises in which occupants, because they are sleeping, may be unaware of a hazard. Residential occupancies include, among others, dormitories, hotels, multi-unit apartments, and private residences.

4.1.4 *Commercial occupancy* is that portion of the premises where people transact business, receive personal service, or purchase food and other goods. Commercial occupancies include, among others, office and professional buildings, restaurants, and markets but not department stores. Other commercial occupancies are work or storage areas that do not qualify as an industrial occupancy.

4.1.5 *Industrial occupancy* is that portion of the premises where only authorized persons have access, which is used to manufacture, process, or store goods, including, among others, chemicals, food, ice, meat, and petroleum.

4.1.6 *Mixed occupancy* is where two or more classes of occupancies share the same building. When each occupancy is isolated from the rest of the building by tight walls, floors, and ceilings and by self-closing doors, the requirements for each occupancy shall apply to that portion of the building. For example: cold storage spaces in a hotel might be classified as an industrial occupancy while the rest of the building would remain a residential occupancy. When the various occupancies are not so isolated, the occupancy having the most stringent requirements shall be the governing occupancy.

4.2 Adjacent Locations. Equipment other than piping, located less than 20 ft (6.1 m) from any building opening, shall be governed by the occupancy classification of the building.

5. Refrigerating System Classification

5.1 Refrigerating systems are defined by the method employed for extracting or delivering heat as follows (see Figure 1):

5.1.1 A ***direct system*** is one in which the evaporator or condenser of the refrigerating system is in direct contact with the air or other substances to be cooled or heated.

5.1.2 An ***indirect system*** is one in which a secondary coolant cooled or heated by the refrigerating system is circulated to the air or other substance to be cooled or heated. Indirect systems are distinguished by the method of application given below.

5.1.2.1 An ***indirect open spray system*** is one in which a secondary coolant is in direct contact with the air or other substance to be cooled or heated.

5.1.2.2 A ***double indirect open spray system*** is one in which the secondary substance for an indirect open spray system (5.1.2.1) is heated or cooled by the secondary coolant circulated from a second enclosure.

5.1.2.3 An ***indirect closed system*** is one in which a secondary coolant passes through a closed circuit in the air or other substance to be cooled or heated.

5.1.2.4 An ***indirect vented closed system*** is one in which a secondary coolant passes through a closed circuit in the air or other substance to be cooled or heated, except that the evaporator or condenser is placed in an open or appropriately vented tank.

5.2 Refrigeration System Classification. For the purpose of applying Tables 1 and 2, the refrigerating system shall be classified according to the degree of probability that a leakage of refrigerant could enter an occupancy-classified area as follows:

5.2.1 High-Probability Systems. Any system in which the basic design, or the location of components, is such that a leakage of refrigerant from a failed connection, seal, or component could enter the area under consideration. Typical high-probability systems are (a) any direct or indirect open spray system or (b) any arrangement in which refrigerant-containing parts in the refrigerant circuit are located in such a way that refrigerant leakage could enter the area.

5.2.2 Low-Probability System. Any system that cannot be considered as a high-probability system. This class includes indirect closed and double indirect systems but only on condition that all joints and connections in the refrigerant circuit are effectively isolated from the classified area.

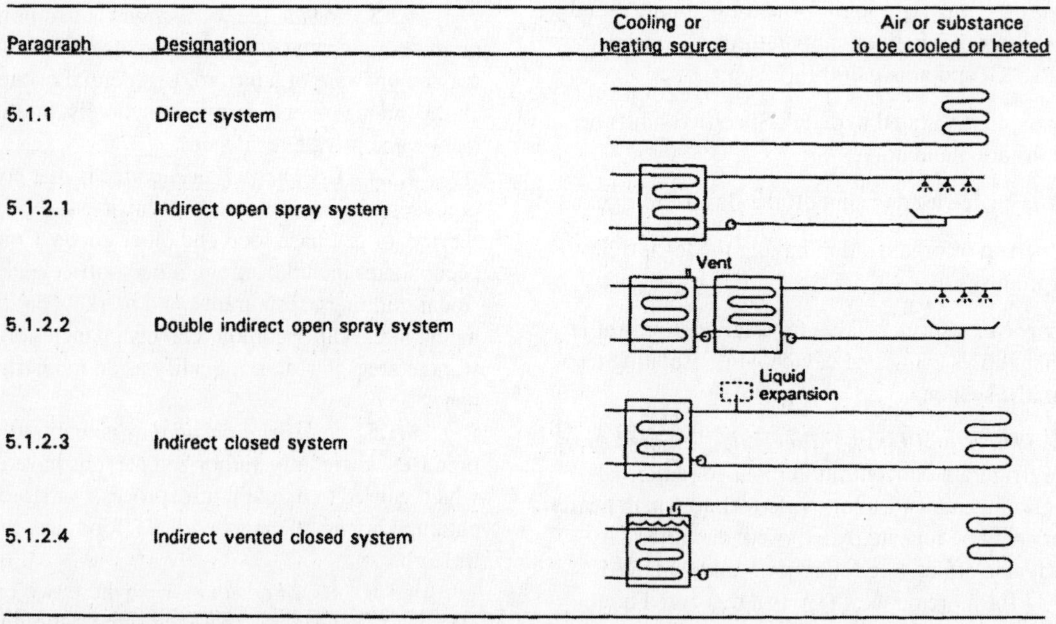

Paragraph	Designation	Cooling or heating source	Air or substance to be cooled or heated
5.1.1	Direct system		
5.1.2.1	Indirect open spray system		
5.1.2.2	Double indirect open spray system		
5.1.2.3	Indirect closed system		
5.1.2.4	Indirect vented closed system		

Fig. 1 Refrigerating System Classification

TABLE 1 Refrigerant[a] and Amounts[b,e]

Refrigerant	Name	Chemical Formula	Quantity of Refrigerant per Occupied Space: Lb per 1000 ft³[a]	Vol. %	g/m³[c]
Group A1					
R-11	Trichlorofluoromethane	CCl_3F	1.6	0.4	25.
R-12	Dichlorodifluoromethane	CCl_2F_2	12	4.0	200.
R-13	Chlorotrifluoromethane	$CClF_3$	31	12	500.
R-13B1	Bromotrifluoromethane	$CBrF_3$	22	5.7	350.
R-14	Tetrafluoromethane (Carbon tetrafluoride)	CF_4	25	11	400.
R-22	Chlorodifluoromethane	$CHClF_2$	9.4	4.2	150.
R-113	Trichlorotrifluoroethane	CCl_2FCClF_2	1.9	0.4	300.
R-114	Dichlorotetrafluoroethane	$CClF_2CClF_2$	9.4	2.1	150.
R-115	Chloropentafluoroethane	$CClF_2CF_3$	38	9.4	600.
R-134a[f]	1,1,1,2-Tetrafluoroethane	CH_2FCF_3	16	6.0	250.
R-C318	Octafluorocyclobutane	C_4F_8	50	9.7	800.
R-400	R-12 and R-114	$CCl_2F_2/C_2Cl_2F_4$	d	d	d
R-500	R-12/152a (73.8/26.2)	CCl_2F_2/CH_3CHF_2	16	4.7	250.
R-502	R-22/115 (48.8/51.2)	$CHClF_2/CClF_2CF_3$	19	6.5	300.
R-503	R-23/13 (40.1/59.9)	$CHF_3/CClF_3$	25	11	400.
R-744	Carbon Dioxide	CO_2	5.7	5.0	900.
Group A2					
R-142b	1-Chloro-1,1,-Difluoroethane	CH_3CClF_2	3.7	1.4	60.
R-152a	1,1-Difluoroethane	CH_3CHF_2	1.2	0.7	20.
Group A3					
R-170	Ethane	C_2H_6	0.5	0.64	8.
R-290	Propane	C_3H_8	0.5	0.44	8.
R-600	Butane	C_4H_{10}	0.5	0.34	8.
R-600a	2-Methyl propane (Isobutane)	$CH(CH_3)_3$	0.5	0.34	8.
R-1150	Ethene (Ethylene)	C_2H_4	0.4	0.52	6.
R-1270	Propene (Propylene)	C_3H_6	0.4	0.34	6.
Group B1					
R-123[f]	2,2-Dichloro-1,1,1-Trifluoroethane	$CHCl_2CF_3$	0.004	0.001	.06
R-764	Sulfur Dioxide	SO_2	0.016	0.01	0.26
Group B2					
R-40	Chloromethane (Methyl Chloride)	CH_3Cl	1.3	1.0	21.
R-611	Methyl Formate	$HCOOCH_3$	0.78	0.5	12.
R-717	Ammonia	NH_3	0.022	0.05	.35

[a] The refrigerant safety groups in Table 1 are not part of ASHRAE Standard 15. The classifications shown are a partial list, for the convenience of the user, from ASHRAE Standard 34, which governs in the event of a difference. Because classifications are subject to revision as new data on refrigerants become available, the latest classification by Standard 34 shall be used.

[b] To be used only in conjunction with Section 7.

[c] To correct for height, H(feet), above sea level, multiply these values by $(1 - 2.42 \times 10^{-6}H)$. To correct for height, h(km), above sea level, multiply these values by $(1 - 7.94 \times 10^{-2}h)$.

[d] The quantity of each component shall comply with the limits set in Table 1 for the pure compound, and the total volume percent of all components shall not exceed 12 volume percent (see Appendix A).

[e] The basis of the table amounts is given as follows:

- Group A1 - 80 percent of the cardiac sensitization level for R-11, R-12, R-13B1, R-22, R-113, R-114, R-134a, R-500, and R-502. 100 percent of the IDLH (21) for R-744. Others are limited by levels where oxygen deprivation begins to occur.
- Group A2, A3 - Approximately 20 percent of LFL.
- Group B1 - 100 percent of IDLH for R-764, and 100 percent of the measure consistent with the TLV for R-123.
- Group B2, B3 - 100 percent of IDLH or 20 percent of LFL, whichever is lower.

[f] Toxicity classification is based on recommended exposure limits provided by chemical suppliers. This rating is provisional and will be reviewed when toxicological testing is completed.

[g] It shall be the responsibility of the owner to establish the refrigerant group for refrigerants used that are not classified in ASHRAE Standard 34.

TABLE 2 System Application Requirements[a]

Refrigerant Group	System Probability[b]	Occupancy		
		Institutional	Public Assm., Residential, Commercial	Industrial
A1	High	1	2	3
	Low	4	4	4
A2	High	5	5	3,6,8
	Low	7	7	7
A3	High	9	9	3,6,8
	Low	9	9	7
B1	High	1,6	2,6	3,6
	Low	4	4	4
B2	High	5,6	5,6	3,6,8
	Low	7	7	7
B3	High	9	9	3,6,8
	Low	9	9	7

[a] Numbers in the table under "Occupancy" refer to rules in Section 7.4

[b] See Section 5.2 for determining the System Probability.

6. Refrigerant Classification

6.1 Refrigerants are classified by ASHRAE Standard 34[3] into safety groups illustrated in the following matrix:

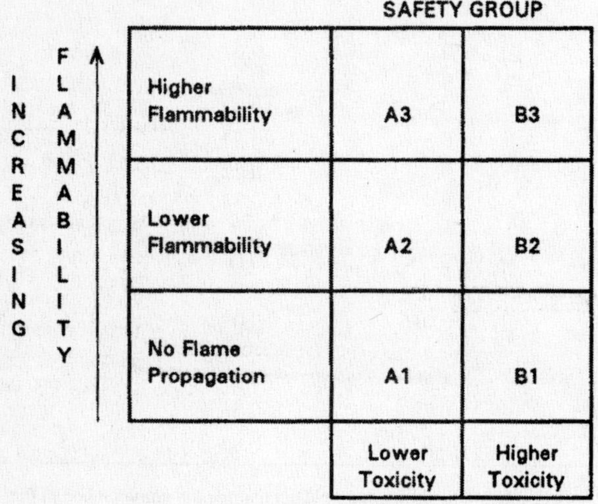

Single-component refrigerants and azeotropic blends so classified are listed in ASHRAE Standard 34 along with the criteria for classification. An abbreviated listing for the convenience of the user is also shown in Table 1.

6.2 Zeotropic blends are classified by worst case composition of fractionation as follows:

> For refrigerants that may change in flammability or toxicity, such as by fractionation of zeotropes, a dual rating, separated by a solidus (/), shall be provided. The first rating shall be the classification of the refrigerants as formulated. The second rating shall be the classification of the worst case composition of fractionation (see Appendix C for details).

7. Requirements For Refrigerant Use

7.1 System Selection. Refrigerating systems shall be applied in accordance with Table 2 and the requirements of Sections 7.2, 7.3, and 7.4.

To use Table 2, determine the occupancy class per Section 4, refrigerant group per ASHRAE Standard 34 (a partial list is given in Table 1 for the convenience of the user), and type of system per Section 5, then locate the rules that apply. When more than one rule exists, each is a limitation on the other.

7.2 General Restrictions—Nonindustrial Occupancy

7.2.1 Stairways and Exits. No portion of a refrigerating system shall be installed in or on a public stairway, stair landing, entrance, or exit.

7.2.2 Hallways and Lobbies. No portion of a refrigerating system shall interfere with free passage through public hallways, and a refrigerating system installed in a public hallway or lobby shall be limited to (a) unit systems containing not more than the quantities of Group A1 refrigerants specified in Table 1 or (b) sealed absorption systems as specified in Table 3.

7.2.3 Unventilated Spaces. When the refrigerant-containing parts of a system are located in one or more unventilated spaces, the volume of the smallest, enclosed occupied space, other than a machinery room, shall be used to determine the permissible quantity of refrigerant in the system. The purpose of this requirement is to ensure no ill effects (insufficient oxygen to support life, narcosis, or cardiac sensitization) to occupants in the event of a leakage of refrigerant.

TABLE 3[a] Maximum Permissible Quantities of Refrigerants for Use with Rule 5 (See 7.4)

	Maximum Pounds (kg) for Various Occupancies			
Type of Refrigeration System	**Institutional**	**Public**	**Residential**	**Commercial**
Sealed Absorption System				
In public hallways or lobbies	0(0)	0(0)	3.3(1.5)	3.3(1.5)
In adjacent outdoor locations	0(0)	0(0)	22(10)	22(10)
In other than public hallways or lobbies	0(0)	6.6(3)	6.6(3)	22(10)
Unit Systems				
In other than public hallways or lobbies	0(0)	0(0)	6.6(3)	22(10)

[a] Table 3 referenced in Table 2, Rule 5.

Where a building consists of several stories of unpartitioned space, such as a loft, the story having the smallest occupied space will be deemed to be the enclosed space.

7.2.4 Ventilated Spaces. When an evaporator or condenser is located in an air duct system, the volume of the smallest occupied space, or unpartitioned building story, served by the duct will determine the permissible quantity of refrigerant in the system. Except if airflow to any enclosed space cannot be reduced below one quarter of its maximum, the entire space served by the air duct system may be used to determine the permissible quantity of refrigerant in the system.

7.2.5 Plenums. When the space above a suspended ceiling is continuous and part of the air return system, this space may be included in calculating the volume of the enclosed space.

7.3 General Restrictions—Industrial Occupancy.

7.3.1 Safeguards. Means shall be taken to adequately safeguard piping, controls, and other refrigeration equipment to minimize possible accidental damage or rupture by external sources.

7.3.2 Electrical Classification. For the electrical classification of occupied spaces in which piping or other refrigeration equipment for Group A2, A3, B2, or B3 refrigerants is located, refer to Rule 8 in Section 7.4.

7.4 System Application Requirements.

7.4.1 Equipment Applied in a High-Probability System. In addition to the provisions of Section 2.4, equipment with refrigerant charge not exceeding 6.6 lb (3 kg) and listed (see Section 3, "Definitions") is deemed to meet the system application requirements when the equipment is installed in accordance with the listing specification.

7.4.2 General System Application Requirements. Except as permitted in 7.4.1, the following rules for system application requirements are applied as specified in Table 2, based on refrigerant group, system probability, and occupancy. These rules do not stand alone.

Blends that may fractionate to change in flammability or toxicity (see Section 6.2) are treated according to their worst case classification. For example, an A1/A2 blend would follow the rules for A2 refrigerants. The amount of blend allowed would correspond to the limit on the quantity of A2 refrigerant in the blend. The total amount of the blend is limited as in footnote d, Table 1.

Rules:

1. The refrigerant amount is limited to 50 percent of those listed in Table 1, except Rule 2 applies in kitchens, laboratories, and mortuaries. If any portion of a refrigerant system containing more than one pound of refrigerant (except R-744) is in a room with a flame-sustaining device, this device shall be provided with a hood to exhaust combustion products to the open air. Otherwise, Rules 5 and 6 shall be followed.
2. The refrigerant amount is limited as listed in Table 1.
3. The refrigerant amount is unlimited when
   (a) the area containing machinery is separated from the areas of the building not containing machinery by tight construction with tight-fitting doors;
   (b) free escape from the area is unhampered;
   (c) the number of persons in a machinery-containing space on any floor above the first floor (ground level or deck level) is equal to or less than one person per 100 ft^2 (9.3 m^2) of floor area or, if the number exceeds one person per 100 ft^2 (9.3 m^2), the machinery-containing space shall be provided with the required number of doors opening directly into approved building exits;[6]
   (d) detectors are located in areas where refrigerant vapor from a leak is likely to concentrate to provide an alarm at the following levels: Group

A1, below 19.5 percent volume oxygen; Groups A2 and A3, at levels listed in Table 1; and Groups B1, B2, and B3 (except ammonia), no higher than their TLV (or toxicity measure consistent therewith).

Otherwise, the rules for commercial occupancy apply.

4. When the quantity of refrigerant in the largest system exceeds Table 1 amounts, all refrigerant-containing parts, except piping and those parts outside the building, shall be installed in a machinery room per section 11.13.
5. Refrigerant amounts and types of systems are limited as shown in Table 3.
6. Applications involving air conditioning for human comfort are not allowed.
7. When the quantity of refrigerant in the largest system exceeds Table 1 amounts, all refrigerant-containing parts, except piping and those parts outside the building, shall be installed in a machinery room per 11.14 with limitations on refrigerant quantities as follows:
550 lb (250 kg)—Institutional
No limit except Rule 8—Public Assembly
No limit except Rule 8—Residential
No limit except Rule 8—Commercial
No limit except Rule 8—Industrial

Otherwise, Rule 5 applies to the amount of Group A2, A3, B2, or B3 refrigerant in the system.
8. When the quantity of refrigerant exceeds Table 1 amounts, all refrigerant-containing parts except piping, lowside components, condensers, and parts outside the building shall be installed in a machinery room per section 11.13.

In addition, refrigerants of Groups A2, A3, B2, and B3 shall meet the following requirements:
(a) The special machinery room requirements of 11.14 shall apply.
(b) Except for ammonia, amounts in excess of 1100 lb (500 kg) shall be approved by the authority having jurisdiction.
9. Use of these refrigerants is prohibited except in laboratories in commercial occupancies. Only unit systems containing not more than 6.6 lb (3 kg) of Group A3 or B3 refrigerant shall be used unless the laboratory is occupied by less than one person per 100 ft^2 (9.3 m^2) of floor area, in which case the requirements of industrial occupancies shall apply.

8. Design and Construction of Equipment Systems

8.1 Materials.

8.1.1 All materials used in the construction and installation of refrigerating systems shall be suitable for conveying the refrigerant used. Some refrigerants are corrosive to certain materials when moisture or air, or both, are present. No material shall be used that will deteriorate because of the refrigerant, the lubricant, or their combination in the presence of air or moisture to a degree that poses a safety hazard.

8.1.2 Aluminum, zinc, magnesium, or their alloys shall not be used in contact with methyl chloride. Magnesium alloys shall not be used in contact with any halogenated refrigerants.

8.1.3 Copper and its alloys shall not be used in contact with ammonia, except as a component of bronze alloys for bearings or other non-refrigerant-containing uses.

8.1.4 Aluminum and its alloys are suitable for use in ammonia systems.

8.2 Design Pressure.

8.2.1 Design pressures shall not be less than pressure arising under all maximum operating, standby, and shipping conditions. When selecting the design pressure, suitable allowance shall be provided for setting pressure-limiting devices and pressure-relief devices to avoid nuisance shutdowns and loss of refrigerant. Refer to ASME,[9] Section VIII, Division I, Appendix M for recommended guidelines.

Minimum design pressure shall not be less than 15 psig (103.4 kPa gage) and, except as noted in 8.2.2, 8.2.3, and 8.2.4, shall not be less than the saturation pressure (gage) corresponding to the following temperatures:

(a) Lowsides of all systems: + 80ºF (26.5ºC).
(b) Highsides of all water-cooled or evaporatively cooled systems: 30ºF (16.7ºC) higher than the ASHRAE summer 1 percent wet-bulb for the location as applicable, or 15ºF (8.3ºC) higher than the highest design leaving condensing water temperature for which the equipment is designed or 104ºF (40ºC), whichever is greatest.
(c) Highsides of all air-cooled systems: 30ºF (16.7ºC) higher than the highest ASHRAE summer 1 percent design dry-bulb for the location but not lower than 122ºF (50ºC).

8.2.1.1 The design pressure selected should exceed maximum pressures attained under any anticipated normal operating condition, including conditions created by reasonable fouling of heat exchange surfaces.

8.2.1.2 Standby conditions are intended to include all normal conditions that may be attained in the system when not operating. Selection of the design pressure for lowside components shall also consider pressure developed in the lowside of the system from equalization, or heating due to changes in ambient temperature, after the system has stopped.

8.2.1.3 The design pressure for both lowside and highside components that are shipped as part of a gas- or refrigerant-charged system shall be selected with consideration of internal pressures arising from exposure to maximum temperatures anticipated during the course of shipment.

8.2.2 The design pressure for either the highside or lowside need not exceed the critical pressure of the refrigerant unless such pressures are anticipated during operating, standby, or shipping conditions.

8.2.3 When part of a limited charge system is protected by a pressure-relief device, the design pressure of the part need not exceed the setting of the pressure-relief device.

8.2.4 When a compressor is used as a booster and discharges into the suction side of another compressor, the booster compressor shall be considered a part of the lowside.

8.2.5 Any components connected to pressure vessels and subject to the same pressure as the pressure vessel shall have a design pressure no less than the pressure vessel.

8.3 Refrigerant-Containing Pressure Vessels.

8.3.1 Inside Dimensions 6 Inches or Less These vessels have an inside diameter, width, height, or cross-sectional diagonal not exceeding 6 in. with no limitation on length of vessel or pressure.

8.3.1.1 Pressure vessels having inside dimensions of 6 in. (152 mm) or less shall be listed either individually or as part of an assembly by an approved, nationally recognized testing laboratory or shall meet the design, fabrication, and testing requirements of Section VIII of the *ASME Boiler and Pressure Vessel Code*,[9] except that such vessels having an internal or external design pressure of 15 psi (103.4 kPa gage) or less are exempted from this requirement. Pressure vessels having inside dimensions of 6 in. (152 mm) or less shall be protected by either a pressure-relief device or a fusible plug.

8.3.1.2 If a pressure-relief device is used to protect a pressure vessel having inside dimensions of 6 in. (152 mm) or less, the ultimate strength of the pressure vessel so protected shall be sufficient to withstand a pressure at least 3.0 times the design pressure.

8.3.1.3 If a fusible plug is used to protect a pressure vessel having an inside diameter of 6 in. (152 mm) or less, the ultimate strength of the pressure vessel so protected shall be sufficient to withstand a pressure 2.5 times the saturation pressure of the refrigerant used, corresponding to the temperature stamped on the fusible plug, or 2.5 times its critical pressure, whichever is less. Also see paragraphs 10.4.6, 10.4.7, 10.4.8, and 10.4.8.5 for size and length of discharge piping and for venting restrictions concerning fusible plugs.

8.3.2 Inside Dimensions Greater than 6 Inches. Pressure vessels having an inside diameter exceeding 6 in. (152 mm) and having an internal or external design pressure greater than 15 psig (103.4 kPa gage) shall comply with the rules of Section VIII of the *ASME Boiler and Pressure Vessel Code*[9] covering the requirements for design, fabrication, inspection, and testing during construction of unfired pressure vessels.

8.3.3 Pressure Vessels for 15 psi or Less. Pressure vessels having an internal or external design pressure of 15 psig (103.4 kPa gage) or less shall have an ultimate strength to withstand at least 3.0 times the design pressure and shall be tested with a pressure no less than 1.33 times their design pressure.

8.4 Refrigerant Piping, Valves, Fittings, and Related Parts

This section should be read together with the following paragraphs: 9.3, 10.1.3, 10.1.6, 10.4.8, 10.4.8.1, 10.4.8.5, 10.5, 11.10, 11.11, 11.12, 11.14(f), and 13.8.

8.4.1 All Refrigerants

8.4.1.1 Refrigerating piping, valves, fittings, and related parts having a maximum internal or external design pressure greater than 15 psig (103.4 kPa gage) shall be listed either individually or as part of an assembly or a system by an approved, nationally recognized laboratory or shall comply with the ASME code for refrigeration piping, B31.5,[10] where applicable.

8.4.1.2 The following minimum requirements apply for unprotected refrigerant-containing pipe or tubing:

(a) Copper tubing used for refrigerant piping shall conform to one of the following ASTM specifications: B88-89[11] types K or L or B280-88[12]. ASTM B68-86[23] and B75-86[24] tubing may also be used if the tube wall thickness meets or exceeds the requirements of ASTM B280-88[12] for the given outside diameter.

(b) Copper tube may be connected by brazed joints or by soldered joints. (For Groups A2, A3, B1, B2, and B3 refrigerants, see 8.4.2.2.)

8.4.2 All Refrigerants Except Group A1 and Ammonia

8.4.2.1 Rigid or flexible metal enclosures shall be provided for annealed copper tube erected on the premises, except that no enclosures shall be required for connections between a condensing unit and the nearest protected riser, provided such connections do not exceed 6 ft (1.83 m) in length.

8.4.2.2 Joints on refrigerant-containing copper tube that are made by the addition of filler metal shall be brazed.

8.5 Components Other Than Pressure Vessels and Piping.

8.5.1 Every pressure-containing component of a refrigerating system, other than pressure vessels, piping, pressure gages, and control mechanisms, shall be listed either individually or as part of a complete refrigerating system or a subassembly by an approved, nationally recognized testing laboratory or shall be designed, constructed, and assembled to have an ultimate strength sufficient to withstand three times the design pressure for which it is rated, except waterside components exempted from the rules of Section VIII of the *ASME Boiler and Pressure Vessel Code*[9] shall be designed, constructed, and assembled to have an ultimate strength sufficient to withstand 150 psig (1034 kPa) or two times the design pressure for which it is rated, whichever is greater.

8.5.2 Liquid level gage glass columns shall have automatic closing shut-off valves, and such glass columns shall be protected against damage. *Exception:* Liquid level gage glasses of the bull's eye or reflex type shall be exempted from these requirements.

8.5.3 When a pressure gage is permanently installed on the highside of a refrigerating system, its dial shall be graduated to at least 1.2 times the design pressure.

8.5.4 Liquid receivers, if used, or parts of a system designed to receive the refrigerant charge during pump-down shall have sufficient capacity to receive the pump-down charge. The liquid shall not occupy more than 90 percent of the volume when the temperature of the refrigerant is 90ºF (32ºC). *Note:* This does not require the receiver volume to contain the total system charge, only the amount being transferred. If the environmental temperature is expected to rise above 122ºF (50ºC), the designer shall consider the specific expansion characteristics of the refrigerant.

8.6 Service Provision. This paragraph should be read together with paragraphs 11.3, 11.4, and 11.5.

8.6.1 All serviceable components of refrigerating systems shall be safely accessible.

8.6.2 All systems shall have provisions to handle safely the refrigerant charge for service purposes. Properly located stop valves, liquid transfer valves, refrigerant storage tanks, and adequate venting for safe disposal may all be required for this purpose.

8.6.3 Systems containing more than 6.6 lb (3 kg) of refrigerant (except Group A1), other than systems utilizing nonpositive displacement compressors, shall have stop valves installed at the following locations:

(a) The suction inlet of each compressor, compressor unit, or condensing unit.
(b) The discharge of each compressor, compressor unit, or condensing unit.
(c) The outlet of each liquid receiver.

8.6.4 Systems containing more than 110 lb (50 kg) of refrigerant, other than systems using nonpositive displacement compressors, or systems having a pumpout receiver for the storage of the refrigerant charge, or self-contained systems, shall have stop valves installed at the following locations:

(a) The suction inlet of each compressor, compressor unit, or condensing unit.
(b) The discharge outlet of each compressor, compressor unit, or condensing unit.
(c) The inlet of each liquid receiver, except for self-contained systems or where the receiver is an integral part of the condenser or condensing unit.
(d) The outlet of each liquid receiver.
(e) The inlet and outlet of condensers when more than one condenser is used in parallel in the system.

8.6.5 Stop valves used with annealed copper tube or copper water tube of 0.875 in. (22 mm) outside diameter or smaller shall be securely mounted, independent of tubing fastening or supports.

8.6.6 Stop valves shall be suitably labeled if the components to and from which the valve regulates flow are not in view at the valve location. Labeling of the piping adjacent to the valve is sufficient to satisfy this requirement and should be accomplished in accordance with ANSI A13.1[22] or other industry-recognized guidelines. Numbers may be used to label the valves, provided a key to the numbers is located within sight of the valves and has letters at least 0.5 in. (12.7 mm) high.

8.7 Factory Tests.

8.7.1 All refrigerant-containing parts or unit systems shall be tested and proved tight by the manufacturer at not less than the design pressure for which they are rated. Pressure vessels shall be tested in accordance with 8.3 of this code.

8.7.2 The test pressure applied to the highside of each factory-assembled refrigerating system shall be at least equal to the design pressure of the highside. The test pressure applied to the lowside of each factory-assembled refrigerating system shall be at least equal to the design pressure of the lowside.

The test pressure on the complete unit may be conducted at the minimum lowside design pressure per 8.2 if final assembly connections are made per ASME/ANSI B31.5.[10] In this case, parts are to be individually tested by either the unit manufacturer or the manufacturer of the part at not less than the highside design pressure.

8.7.3 Units with a design pressure of 15 psig (103.4 kPa gage) or less shall be tested at a pressure not less than 1.33 times the design pressure and shall be proved leak tight at not less than the lowside design pressure.

8.8 Nameplate. Each unit system and each separate condensing unit, compressor, or compressor unit sold for field assembly in a refrigerating system shall carry a nameplate marked with the manufacturer's name, nationally registered trademark or trade name, identification number, the design pressures, and the refrigerant for which it is designed. The refrigerant shall be designated according to *ANSI/ASHRAE 34–1992, Number Designation and Safety Classification of Refrigerants.*[3]

9. PRESSURE-LIMITING DEVICES

9.1 When Required. Pressure-limiting devices shall be provided on all systems operating above atmospheric pressure, except that a pressure-limiting device may be omitted on any factory-sealed system containing less than 22 lb (10 kg) of Group A1 refrigerant that has been listed by an approved, nationally recognized testing laboratory and is so identified.

9.2 Setting. When required by 9.1, the maximum setting to which a pressure-limiting device may readily be set by use of the adjusting means provided shall not exceed the design pressure of the highside of a system that is not protected by a pressure-relief device or 90 percent of the setting of the pressure-relief device installed on the highside of a system, except as provided below. The pressure-limiting device shall stop the action of the pressure-imposing element at a pressure no higher than this maximum setting.

On systems using nonpositive displacement compressors, the pressure-limiting device may be set at the design pressure of the highside of the system provided the pressure-relief device is (1) located in the lowside and (2) subject to lowside pressure and (3) there is a permanent (unvalved) relief path between the highside and the lowside of the system.

9.3 Connection. Pressure-limiting devices, when required by 9.1, shall be connected between the pressure-imposing element and any stop valve on the discharge side with no intervening stop valves in the line leading to the pressure-limiting device.

10. PRESSURE-RELIEF PROTECTION

10.1 General Requirements.

10.1.1 Every refrigerating system shall be protected by a pressure-relief device or some other means designed to safely relieve pressure due to fire or other abnormal conditions.

10.1.2 All pressure vessels shall be protected in accordance with the requirements of 10.4.

10.1.3 A pressure-relief device to relieve hydrostatic pressure to another part of the system should be used on the portion of the liquid-containing parts of the system that can be isolated from the system during operation or service and that may be subjected to overpressure from hydrostatic expansion of the contained liquid due to temperature rise.

10.1.4 Evaporators located downstream, or upstream within 18 in. (460 mm), of a heating coil shall be fitted with a pressure-relief device discharging in accordance with the requirements of 10.4.8.1 or outside the building in accordance with the requirements of 10.4.8, except that such a relief valve shall not be required on self-contained or unit systems if the volume of the lowside of the system, which may be shut off by valves, is greater than the specific volume of the refrigerant at critical conditions of temperature and pressure, as determined by the following formula:

$V_1/[W_1 - (V_2 - V_1)/Vgt]$ shall be greater than Vgc

where

V_1 = lowside volume, ft^3 (m^3);
V_2 = total volume of system, ft^3 (m^3);
W_1 = total weight of refrigerant in system, lb (kg);
Vgt = specific volume of refrigerant vapor at 110°F (43.5°C), ft^3/lb (m^3/kg);
Vgc = specific volume at critical temperature and pressure, ft^3/lb (m^3/kg).

10.1.5 All pressure-relief devices shall be direct-pressure actuated. Each part of a refrigerating system that can be valved off and that contains one or more pressure vessels having internal diameters greater than 6 in. (152 mm) and containing liquid refrigerant shall be protected by a pressure-relief device.

10.1.6 Stop valves shall not be located between the pressure-relief device and the part or parts of the system protected thereby. A three-way valve, used in conjunction with the dual relief valve requirements of article 10.4.2.3, is not considered a stop valve.

When relief valves are connected to discharge to a common discharge header, as described in paragraph 10.4.8.4, an isolation valve may be installed in the discharge pipe between the relief valve and the common header. When such an isolation valve is installed, a locking device shall be installed to ensure the isolation valve is locked in the open position. This discharge isolation valve can be shut only if one of the following conditions exists:

(a) Parallel relief valves are installed, and the second relief valve is protecting the system and/or vessels.

(b) The system and/or vessels have been depressurized and are vented to atmosphere.

10.1.7 All pressure-relief devices shall be connected as nearly as practicable directly to the pressure vessel or other parts of the system protected thereby, above the liquid refrigerant level, and installed so that they are accessible for inspection and repair and so that they cannot be readily rendered inoperative.

Exception: Fusible plugs may be located above or below the liquid refrigerant level, except on the lowside.

10.1.8 The seats and discs of pressure-relief devices shall be constructed of suitable material to resist refrigerant corrosion or other chemical action caused by the refrigerant. Seats or discs of cast iron shall not be used. Seats and discs shall be limited in distortion, by pressure or other cause, to a set pressure change of not more than 5 percent in a span of five years.

10.2 Setting of Pressure-Relief Devices

10.2.1 Pressure-Relief Valve Setting. All pressure-relief valves shall start to function at a pressure not to exceed the design pressure of the parts of the system protected.

10.2.2 Rupture Member Setting. All rupture members used in lieu of, or in series with, a relief valve shall have a nominal rated rupture pressure not to exceed the design pressure of the parts of the system protected. The conditions of application shall conform to the requirements of paragraph UG-127 of Section VIII, Division 1, of the *ASME Boiler and Pressure Vessel Code*.[9] Rupture members installed ahead of relief valves need not be larger, but shall not be smaller, than the relief valve inlet.

10.3 Marking of Relief Devices and Fusible Plugs.

10.3.1 All pressure-relief valves for refrigerant-containing components shall be set and sealed by the manufacturer or an assembler as defined in paragraph UG-136(c)(4) of Section VIII, Division 1, of the *ASME Boiler and Pressure Vessel Code*.[9] Each pressure-relief valve shall be marked by the manufacturer or assembler with the data required in paragraph UG-129(a) of Section VIII, Division 1, of the *ASME Boiler and Pressure Vessel Code*, except relief valves for systems with design pressures of 15 psig (103.4 kPa gage) or less may be marked by the manufacturer with pressure-setting capacity.

10.3.2 Each rupture member for refrigerant pressure vessels shall be marked with the data required in paragraph UG-129(e) of Section VIII, Division 1, of the *ASME Boiler and Pressure Vessel Code*.

10.3.3 Fusible plugs shall be marked with the melting temperatures in °F (°C).

10.4 Pressure Vessel Protection.

10.4.1 Pressure vessels shall be provided with overpressure protection in accordance with rules of Section VIII, Division 1, of the *ASME Boiler and Pressure Vessel Code*,[9] with additional modifications as are necessary for control of refrigerants.

10.4.2 All pressure vessels containing liquid refrigerant, and which may be shut off by valves from other parts of a refrigerating system, shall be provided with overpressure protection. Pressure-relief devices or fusible plugs shall be sized per 10.4.5.

10.4.2.1 Pressure vessels with an internal gross volume of 3 ft^3 (0.085 m^3) or less may use a single pressure-relief device or a fusible plug.

10.4.2.2 Pressure vessels of more than 3 ft^3 (0.085 m^3) but less than 10 ft^3 (0.285 m^3) internal gross volume may use a single pressure-relief device but not a fusible plug.

10.4.2.3 Pressure vessels of 10 ft^3 (0.285 m^3) or more internal gross volume shall use a single rupture member or dual pressure-relief valves when discharging to the atmosphere. Dual pressure-relief valves shall be installed with a three-way valve to allow testing or repair.

A single relief valve may be used on pressure vessels of 10 ft^3 (0.285 m^3) or more internal gross volume, located on the lowside of the system, which have shut-off valves to isolate them from the rest of the refrigerating system, and when the system is designed to allow pumpdown of the refrigerant charge of the pressure vessel.

10.4.3 Pressure relief valves discharging into the lowside of the system: under the conditions permitted in 10.4.8.1, except as specified in 10.5, a single relief valve (not rupture member) of the required relieving capacity may be used on vessels of 10 ft^3 (0.283 m^3) or more.

10.4.4 Pressure-relief devices in parallel: on large vessels containing liquid refrigerant, the use of two or more pressure-relief devices or dual pressure-relief devices in parallel may be used to obtain the required capacity.

10.4.5 The minimum required discharge capacity of the pressure-relief device or fusible plug for each pressure vessel shall be determined by the following:

$$C = fDL$$

where

C = minimum required discharge capacity of the relief device in pounds of air per minute (kg/s),
D = outside diameter of vessel in feet (m),
L = length of vessel in feet (m),
f = factor dependent upon type of refrigerant.

Note: The values of *f* listed below do not apply if fuels are used within 20 ft (6.1 m) of the pressure vessel; the methods in API Recommended Practice 520[20] shall be used to size the pressure-relief device in this case.

Refrigerant	Value of *f*
When used on the lowside of *a limited-charge cascade system:*	
R-170, R-744, R-1150	1.0 (0.082)
R-13, R-13B1, R-503	2.0 (0.163)
R-14	2.5 (0.203)
Other applications:	
R-717	0.5 (0.041)
R-11, R-40, R-113, R-123, R-142b, R-152a, R-290, R-600, R-600a, R-611, R-764	1.0 (0.082)
R-12, R-22, R-114, R-134a, R-C318, R-500, R-1270	1.6 (0.163)
R-115, R-502	2.5 (0.203)

When one pressure-relief device or fusible plug is used to protect more than one pressure vessel, the required capacity shall be the sum of the capacities required for each pressure vessel.

10.4.6 The rated discharge capacity of a pressure-relief device expressed in pounds of air per minute (kilograms of air per second) shall be determined in accordance with paragraph UG-131, Section VIII, Division 1, of the *ASME Boiler and Pressure Vessel Code*.[9] All pipe and fittings between the pressure-relief valve and the parts of the system it protects shall have at least the area of the pressure-relief valve inlet.

10.4.7 The rated discharge capacity of a rupture member or fusible plug discharging to the atmosphere under critical flow conditions in pounds of air per minute (kg/s) shall be determined by the following formulas:

$$C = 0.8\,P_1 d^2 \qquad (C = 1.36 \times 10^{-6}\,P_1 d^2),$$
$$d = 1.12\,(C/P_1)^{0.5} \qquad (d = 857.5(C/P_1)^{0.5}),$$

where

C = rated discharge capacity in pounds of air per minute (kg/s),
d = smallest of the internal diameter of the inlet pipe, retaining flanges, fusible plug, and rupture member in inches (millimeters), where, for rupture members, P_1 = (rated pressure psig [kPa gage] × 1.10) + 14.7(101.33); for fusible plugs, P_1 = absolute saturation pressure corresponding to the stamped temperature melting point of the fusible plug or the critical pressure of the refrigerant used, whichever is smaller, psia (kPa).

10.4.8 Pressure-relief devices and fusible plugs on any system containing a Group A3 or B3 refrigerant, on any system containing more than 6.6 lb (3 kg) of a Group A2, B1, or B2 refrigerant, and on any system containing more than 110 lb (50 kg) of a Group A1 refrigerant shall discharge to the atmosphere at a location not less than 15 ft (4.57 m) above the adjoining ground level and not less than 20 ft (6.1 m) from any window, ventilation opening, or exit in any building. The discharge termination shall be fashioned in such a manner to prevent direct spray of discharged refrigerant on personnel in the vicinity and foreign material or debris from entering the discharge piping. Discharge piping connected to the discharge side of a fusible plug or rupture member shall have provisions to prevent plugging the pipe in the event the fusible plug or rupture member functions.

10.4.8.1 Pressure-relief devices may discharge into the lowside of the system and shall be of a type not affected by back pressure, provided the lowside is equipped with pressure-relief devices of equal relieving capacity. Such a lowside pressure-relief device shall be set in accordance with 10.2.1 and vented to the outside of the building in accordance with 10.4.8.

10.4.8.2 Optional Ammonia Discharge. Where ammonia is used, the preferred discharge is to atmosphere. An optional discharge may be into a tank of water that shall be used for no other purpose except ammonia absorption (see Appendix B for additional options). At least one gallon of fresh water shall be provided for each pound (1 m³ for each 120 kg) of ammonia in the system. The water used shall be prevented from freezing without the use of salt or chemicals. The tank shall be substantially constructed of not less than 1/8 in. (3.2 mm) or No. 11 U.S. gage iron or steel. No horizontal dimension of the tank shall be greater than one half the height. The tank shall have a hinged cover, or, if of the enclosed type, shall have a vent hole at the top. All pipe connections shall be through the top of the tank only. The discharge pipe from the pressure-relief valves shall discharge the ammonia in the center of the tank near the bottom. An indirect ammonia-water absorption unit system installed outdoors adjacent to a single-family residence is not required to comply with 10.4.8 provided the discharge is shielded and dispersed.

10.4.8.3 Optional Sulphur Dioxide Discharge. Where sulphur dioxide is used, the discharge may be into a tank of absorptive solution that shall be used for no other purpose except sulphur dioxide absorption. There shall be one gallon of standard dichromate solution equivalent to 2.5 lb sodium dichromate per gallon of water (300 g/L) for each pound of sulphur dioxide (8.3 L/kg) in the system. Solutions made with caustic soda or soda ash may be used in place of sodium dichromate provided the quantity and strength have the equivalent sulphur dioxide absorbing power. The tank shall be substantially constructed of not less than 1/8 in. (3.2 mm) or No. 11 U.S. gage iron or steel. The tank shall have a hinged cover or, if of the enclosed type, shall have a vent hole at the top. All pipe connections shall be through the top of the tank only. The discharge pipe from the pressure-relief valve shall discharge the sulphur dioxide in the center of the tank near the bottom.

10.4.8.4 The size of the discharge pipe from the pressure-relief device or fusible plug shall not be less than the outlet size of the pressure-relief device or fusible plug. Where outlets of two or more relief devices or fusible plugs are connected into a common line or header, the effect of back pressure that may be developed when more than one relief device or fusible plug operates must be considered. The sizing of any section of common discharge header downstream from each of the two or more relief devices or fusible plugs that may be reasonably expected to operate simultaneously shall be based on the sum of their outlet areas with due allowance for the pressure drop in all downstream sections.

10.4.8.5 The maximum length of the discharge piping permitted to be installed on the outlet of a pressure-relief device or fusible plug shall be determined as follows:

$$L = 9P^2d^5/16C_r^2$$
$$(L = 7 \times 10^{-13}P^2d^5/36Cr^2),$$

where

Cr = rated discharge capacity as stamped on the device by the manufacturer
in pounds of air per minute (kg/s),
d = internal diameter of pipe in inches (mm),
L = length of discharge pipe in feet (m).

For relief valves and rupture disks, P = (Rated pressure × 1.1) + 14.7 (101.33). For fusible plugs, P_1 = pressure as defined in 10.4.7.

See Table 4 for the results of computations using the relief valve formula.

10.5 Positive Displacement Compressor Protection. When required to be equipped with a stop valve in the discharge connection, every positive displacement compressor shall be equipped with a pressure-relief device of adequate size and pressure setting, as specified by the manufacturer, to prevent rupture of the compressor or any other component located between the compressor and the stop valve on the discharge side. The pressure-relief device shall discharge into the low-pressure side of the system or in accordance with 10.4.8.

TABLE 4 Length ("L" in Feet) of Discharge Piping for Pressure-Relief Devices of Various Discharge Capacities

Required Discharge Capacity C_r # Air/Min[c]	Standard wall pipe, pipe size in inches[b]						Standard wall pipe, pipe size in inches[b]					
	½	¾	1	1¼	1½	2	½	¾	1	1¼	1½	2
	Relief Valve Setting 150 psiga						*Relief Valve Setting 200 psiga*					
5	68	276	(d)				115	470	(d)			
10	17	69	231				29	118	394			
15	7	31	102				13	52	175			
20	4	17	58	226			7	29	98			
25	3	11	37	145			5	19	63	248		
30	2	8	26	100	218		3	13	44	172		
40		4	14	57	122		2	7	25	97	210	
50		3	9	36	78	274		5	16	62	134	
60		2	6	25	54	190		3	11	43	93	
70			5	18	40	140		2	8	32	68	238
80			4	14	31	105		2	6	24	52	182
90			3	11	24	84			5	19	41	144
100			2	9	20	68			4	15	33	117
125				6	12	44			2	10	21	75
150				4	9	30				7	15	52
175				3	6	22				5	11	38
200				2	5	17				4	8	29
	Relief Valve Setting 250 psiga						*Relief Valve Setting 300 psiga*					
5	176		(d)				248		(d)			
10	44	179					62	254				
15	20	80	267				28	114				
20	11	45	150				15	54	212			
25	7	29	96				10	41	136			
30	5	20	67	263			7	28	94			
40	3	11	37	147			4	16	53	208		
50	2	7	24	94	204		3	10	34	134		
60		5	17	66	142		2	7	24	93	200	
70		4	12	48	104			5	17	68	147	
80		3	9	37	80			4	13	52	113	
90		2	7	29	63	220		3	10	41	89	
100		2	6	24	51	178		2	8	33	72	252
125			4	15	33	114		2	5	21	46	162
150			3	11	23	79			4	15	32	112
175			2	8	17	58			3	11	24	82
200			2	6	13	44			2	8	18	63
	Relief Valve Setting 350 psiga						*Relief Valve Setting 400 psiga*					
5	335		(d)				433		(d)			
10	84	380					108	492				
15	37	169					48	219				
20	21	95	285				27	123	369			
25	13	61	183				17	79	236			
30	9	42	127				12	55	164			
40	5	24	71	281			7	31	92	364		
50	3	15	46	180			4	20	59	233		
60	2	11	32	125	270		3	14	41	162	349	
70	2	8	23	92	198		2	10	30	119	257	
80		6	18	70	152		2	8	23	91	197	
90		5	14	56	120			6	18	72	155	
100		4	11	45	97	339		5	15	58	126	439
125		2	7	29	62	217		3	9	37	81	281
150		2	5	20	43	151		2	7	26	56	195
175			4	15	32	111		2	5	19	41	143
200			3	11	24	85			4	15	31	110

[a] To convert psig to kPa gage, multiply psig by 6.895.

[b] To convert inches to millimetres, multiply inches by 25.4.

[c] To convert # air/min to kg air/sec, multiply # air/min by 7.559×10^{-3}.

[d] To convert feet to meters, multiply feet by 0.3048.

11. INSTALLATION REQUIREMENTS

11.1 Foundations. Foundations and supports for condensing units or compressor units shall be of substantial and noncombustible construction. Isolation materials such as rubber are permissible between the foundation and condensing or compressor units.

11.2 Guards. Moving machinery shall be guarded in accordance with approved safety standards.[13,14]

11.3 Safe Access. Reasonable access, including ladders, platforms, and clear space adequate for inspection and servicing of condensing units, compressors, condensers, and other machinery, shall be provided in accordance with approved safety standards.

11.4 Enclosures. Condensing units or compressor units with enclosures shall be readily accessible for servicing and inspection.

11.5 Water Connections. Water supply and discharge connections shall be made in accordance with approved safety and health standards.

Discharge water lines shall not be directly connected to the waste or sewer systems. The waste or discharge from such equipment shall be through an approved air gap and trap.

11.6 Illumination. Illumination adequate for inspection and servicing of condensing units or compressor units shall be provided.[15]

11.7 Electrical Safety. Electrical equipment and wiring shall be installed in accordance with approved safety standards.[7]

11.8 Gas Fuel Equipment. Gas fuel devices and equipment used with refrigerating systems shall be installed in accordance with approved safety standards.[16,17]

11.9 Air Duct Installation. Air duct systems of airconditioning equipment for human comfort using mechanical refrigeration shall be installed in accordance with approved safety standards.[18,19]

Air ducts passing through a machinery room shall be of tight construction and shall have no openings in such rooms.

11.10 Refrigerant Parts in Air Duct. Joints and all refrigerant-containing parts of a refrigerating system located in an air duct carrying conditioned air to and from an occupied space shall be constructed to withstand a temperature of 700°F (353.3°C) without leakage into the airstream.

11.11 Refrigerant Pipe Joint Inspection. Refrigerant pipe joints erected on the premises shall be exposed to view for visual inspection prior to being covered or enclosed.

11.12 Location of Refrigerant Piping.

11.12.1 Refrigerant piping crossing an open space that affords passageway in any building shall be not less than 7.25 ft (2.2 m) above the floor unless against the ceiling of such space as permitted by the local authority.

11.12.2 Passages shall not be obstructed by refrigerant piping. Refrigerant piping shall not be placed in any elevator, dumbwaiter, or other shaft containing a moving object or in any shaft that has openings to living quarters or to main exits. Refrigerant piping shall not be placed in exits, lobbies, or stairways, except that such refrigerant piping may pass across an exit if there are no joints in the section in the exit and provided nonferrous tubing of 1.12 in. (28.6 mm) outside diameter and smaller be contained in a rigid metal pipe.

11.12.3 Refrigerant piping shall not be installed vertically through floors from one story to another except as follows:

(a) It may be installed from the basement to the first floor, from the top floor to a machinery penthouse or to the roof, or between adjacent floors served by the refrigerating system.

(b) For the purpose of interconnecting separate pieces of equipment not located as described by 11.12.3(a) and excluding industrial occupancies, the piping may be carried in an approved, rigid and tight, continuous fire-resisting pipe duct or shaft having no openings into floors not served by the refrigerating system, or it may be carried on the outer wall of the building, provided it is not located in an air shaft, closed court, or similar spaces enclosed with the outer walls of the building. The pipe duct or shaft shall be vented to the outside or to the space served by the system.

(c) Piping of a direct system where refrigerant quantity is limited per the provisions of Section 7 need not be enclosed where it passes through space served by that system.

11.12.4 Refrigerant piping may be installed horizontally in closed floors or in open joist spaces. Piping installed in concrete floors shall be encased in pipe duct. All refrigerant piping shall be properly isolated and supported to prevent damaging vibration or corrosion.

11.13 Machinery Room, General Requirements.

11.13.1 When a refrigerating system is located indoors, a machinery room shall be provided when required by 7.4. Machinery rooms serve for accommodating refrigerating machinery but may also house other mechanical equipment. A machinery room shall be so dimensioned that all parts are easily accessible with adequate space for proper service, maintenance, and operations. There shall be clear head room of not less than 7.25 ft (2.2 m) below equipment situated over passageways.

11.13.2 Each refrigerating machinery room shall have a tight-fitting door or doors opening outward, self-closing if they open into the building, and adequate in number to ensure freedom for persons to escape in an emergency. There shall be no openings other than doors that will permit passage of escaping refrigerant to other parts of the building.

11.13.2.1 For Group A1 refrigerants, machinery rooms shall be equipped with an oxygen sensor to warn of oxygen levels below 19.5 volume percent since there is insufficient odor warning. The sensor shall be located in an area where refrigerant from a leak is likely to concentrate and shall actuate an alarm and start mechanical ventilation in accordance with 11.13.4.

11.13.2.2 For all other refrigerants, a refrigerant vapor detector shall be located in an area where refrigerant from a leak is likely to concentrate, and an alarm shall be employed. The alarm shall be actuated and the mechanical ventilation started in accordance with 11.13.4 at a value not greater than the corresponding TLV (or toxicity measure consistent therewith).

Exception: For ammonia, refer to 11.14(g).

11.13.2.3 Periodic tests of the detector(s), alarm(s), and mechanical ventilating system shall be performed in accordance with manufacturers' recommendations and/or local jurisdictional authority.

11.13.3 Machinery rooms shall be vented to the outdoors utilizing mechanical ventilation in accordance with paragraphs 11.13.4 and 11.13.7.

11.13.4 Mechanical ventilation referred to in paragraph 11.13.3 shall be by one or more power-driven fans capable of exhausting air from the machinery room at least in the amount given in the formula in paragraph 11.13.7. To obtain a reduced airflow for normal ventilation, multiple fans or multispeed fans may be used. The discharge of the air shall be to the outdoors in such a manner as not to cause inconvenience or danger. Provision shall be made for supply air to replace that being exhausted. Openings for supply air shall be positioned to avoid intake of exhaust air. Air supply and exhaust ducts to the machinery room shall serve no other area.

11.13.5 No open flames that use combustion air from the machinery room shall be installed where any refrigerant other than carbon dioxide is used. The use of matches, lighters, halide leak detectors, and similar devices shall not be considered a violation of this paragraph.

11.13.6 Access to the machinery room shall be restricted to authorized personnel.

11.13.7 The minimum mechanical ventilation required to exhaust a potential accumulation of refrigerant due to leaks or a rupture of the system shall be capable of removing air from the machinery room in the following quantity:

$$Q = 100 \times G^{0.5} \quad (Q = 70 \times G^{0.5})$$

where

Q = the airflow in cubic feet per minute (liters per second),

G = the mass of refrigerant in pounds (kilograms) in the largest system, any part of which is located in the machinery room.

A sufficient part of the mechanical ventilation shall be

(a) operated, when occupied, at least at 0.5 cfm per square foot (2.54 L/s per square meter) of machinery room area or 20 cfm per person (9.44 L/s) and

(b) operable, if necessary for operator comfort, at a volume required to maintain a maximum temperature rise of 18°F (10°C) based on all of the heat-producing machinery in the room.

When a refrigerating system is located outdoors more than 20 ft (6.1 m) from any building opening and is enclosed by a penthouse, lean-to, or other open structure, natural ventilation may be employed as an alternative to mechanical ventilation. The requirements for such natural ventilation are as follows:

The free-aperture cross section for the ventilation of the machinery room shall amount to at least

$$F = G^{0.5} \quad (F = 0.138G^{0.5})$$

where

F = the free opening area in square feet (square meters),

G = the mass of refrigerant in pounds (kilograms) in the largest system, any part of which is located in the machinery room.

Locations of the opening shall be with due regard for the relative density of the refrigerant to air.

Note: The minimum ventilation rates prescribed may not prevent temporary accumulations of flammable refrigerants above the LFL in the case of catastrophic leaks or ruptures. The designer may consider the provisions of NFPA 68[21] for venting of deflagrations in such cases.

11.14 Machinery Room, Special Requirements. In cases specified in Table 2, the machinery room shall meet the following special requirements in addition to those in 11.13:

(a) There shall be no flame-producing device or continuously operating hot surface over 800°F (427°C) permanently installed in the room.

(b) Any doors communicating with the building shall be approved, self-closing, tight-fitting fire doors.
(c) Walls, floor, and ceiling shall be tight and of noncombustible construction. Walls, floor, and ceiling separating the machinery room from other occupied spaces shall be of not less than one-hour fire-resistive construction.
(d) It shall have an exit door that opens directly to the outer air or through a vestibule equipped with self-closing, tight-fitting doors.
(e) Exterior openings, if present, shall not be under any fire escape or any open stairway.
(f) All pipes piercing the interior walls, ceiling, or floor of such rooms shall be tightly sealed to the walls, ceiling, or floor through which they pass.
(g) Ventilation in ammonia machinery rooms shall be either (1) run continuously or (2) equipped with a vapor detector that will automatically start the ventilation system and actuate an alarm at the lowest practical detection levels not exceeding 4 percent by volume, or (3) the machinery room shall conform to Class 1, Division 2, of the National Electrical Code.[7]
(h) When refrigerants of Groups A2, A3, B2 other than ammonia, and B3 are used, the machinery room shall conform to Class 1, Division 2, of the National Electrical Code.[7]
(i) Remote pilot control of the mechanical equipment in the machinery room shall be provided immediately outside the machinery room solely for the purpose of shutting down the equipment in an emergency. Ventilation fans shall be on a separate circuit and shall have a control switch located immediately outside the machinery room.

11.15 Manual Emergency Discharge of Refrigerant. Some mechanical codes and fire codes require manual emergency discharge or diffusion arrangements for refrigerants. While these provisions are neither recommended nor required by this standard, Appendix B has been included to aid in the safe accomplishment of this purpose when required.

11.16 Purge Discharge. The discharge of purge systems shall be governed by the same rules as pressure-relief devices and fusible plugs (see 10.4.8) and may be piped in conjunction with these devices.

Note: The reader is alerted that as of the date of this publication, there may be other pending non-safety regulations governing the release of refrigerants that are outside the scope of this standard.

12. FIELD PRESSURE TESTS

12.1 General.

12.1.1 Every refrigerant-containing part of every system that is erected on the premises, except compressors, condensers, evaporators, safety devices, pressure gages, control mechanisms, and systems that are factory-tested, shall be tested and proved tight after complete installation and before operation.

The highside and lowside of each system shall be tested and proved tight at not less than the lower of the design pressure or the setting of the pressure-relief device protecting the highside or lowside of the system, respectively, except as noted in 12.1.2.

12.1.2 Systems erected on the premises using Group A1 refrigerant and with copper tubing not exceeding 0.62 in. (16 mm) outside diameter may be tested by means of the refrigerant charged into the system at the saturated vapor pressure of the refrigerant at 68°F (20°C) minimum.

12.2 Test Medium. Oxygen or any combustible gas or combustible mixture of gases shall not be used within the system for testing.

The means used to build up the test pressure shall have either a pressure-limiting device or a pressure-reducing device with a pressure-relief device and a gage on the outlet side. The pressure-relief device shall be set above the test pressure but low enough to prevent permanent deformation of the system components.

12.3 Declaration. A dated declaration of test should be provided for all systems containing 55 lb (25 kg) or more of refrigerant. The declaration should give the name of the refrigerant and the field test pressure applied to the highside and the lowside of the system. The declaration of test should be signed by the installer, and if an inspector is present at the tests, the inspector should also sign the declaration. When requested, copies of this declaration shall be furnished to the authority having jurisdiction.

13. GENERAL REQUIREMENTS

13.1 Signs.

13.1.1 Installation Identification. Each refrigerating system erected on the premises shall be provided with an easily legible permanent sign, securely attached and easily accessible, indicating (a) the name and address of the installer, (b) the kind and initial charge of refrigerant, and (c) the field test pressure applied.

13.1.2 Controls and Piping Identification. Systems containing more than 110 lb (50 kg) of refrigerant shall be provided with durable signs having letters not less than 0.5 in. (12.7 mm) in height, designating

(a) valves or switches for controlling the refrigerant flow, the ventilation, and the refrigeration compressor(s), and

(b) the kind of refrigerant or secondary coolant contained in exposed piping outside the machinery room. Piping identification shall be in accord with *ANSI A13.1, Scheme for Identification of Piping Systems*,[22] or other industry-recognized guidelines. Legends indicating flow direction, function, temperature, or pressure may also be used in accord with accepted practice.

13.1.3 Changes in Refrigerant. When the kind of refrigerant is changed as provided in 13.2, there shall be new signs to identify the changes in accordance with 13.1.1 and 13.1.2.

13.2 Changing Refrigerant. A change in the type of refrigerant in a system shall not be made without the permission of the approving authority and the user, consultation with the manufacturers of the original equipment, and due observance of safety requirements.

13.3 Charging and Discharging Refrigerants. Refrigerant may be added to a system in a number of ways, depending primarily on the source of refrigerant supply. It may be charged into the low-pressure side of the system or at any point on the downstream side of the main liquid line stop valve when operating with said stop valve in the closed position. When delivered by bulk tanker with pump, charging is commonly done into the main high-pressure receiver. No service containers shall be left connected to a system except while charging or withdrawing refrigerant.

13.4 Withdrawal and Disposition of Refrigerants. Refrigerants withdrawn from refrigerating systems shall be transferred to approved containers only.[1] Except for discharge of pressure-relief devices and fusible plugs, incidental releases due to leaks, purging of noncondensibles, draining oil, and other routine operating or maintenance procedures, no refrigerant shall be discharged to the atmosphere or to locations such as a sewer, river, stream, lake, etc.

13.5 Containers. Containers used for refrigerants withdrawn from a refrigerating system shall be carefully weighed each time they are used for this purpose, and containers shall not be filled in excess of the permissible filling weight for such containers and such refrigerants as prescribed in the pertinent regulations of the Department of Transportation.[1]

13.6 Storing Refrigerant. Refrigerant stored in a machinery room shall not be more than 330 lb (150 kg) in addition to the charge in the system and the refrigerant stored in a permanently attached receiver and then only in approved storage containers.[1]

13.7 Self-Contained Breathing Apparatus. When a machinery room is required per the rules of 7.4, at least one approved self-contained breathing apparatus shall be provided outside of, but close to, the machinery room. The availability of a second self-contained breathing apparatus for backup is strongly recommended.

13.8 Maintenance. All refrigerating systems shall be maintained by the user in a clean condition, free from accumulations of oily dirt, waste, and other debris, and shall be kept readily accessible at all times.

All stop valves connecting refrigerant-containing parts to atmosphere during shipping, testing, operating, servicing, or standby conditions shall be capped, plugged, blanked, or locked closed when not in use.

13.9 Responsibility for Operation and Emergency Shutdown. It shall be the duty of the person in charge of the premises on which a refrigerating system containing more than 55 lb (25 kg) of refrigerant is installed to provide a schematic drawing or panel giving directions to the operation of the system at a location that is convenient to the operators of the equipment.

Emergency shutdown procedures, including precautions to be observed in case of a breakdown or leak, shall be displayed on a conspicuous card located as near as possible to the refrigerant compressor. These precautions shall address

(a) instructions for shutting down the system in case of emergency;

(b) the name, address, and day and night telephone numbers for obtaining service; and

(c) the name, address, and telephone number of the municipal inspection department having jurisdiction and instructions to notify said department immediately in case of emergency.

When a machinery room is used, the emergency procedures shall be posted outside the room, immediately adjacent to each door.

13.10 Calibration of Pressure Gages. Pressure gages should be checked for accuracy prior to test and immediately after every occasion of unusually high pressure, equal to full-scale reading either by comparison with master gages or by setting pointers as determined by a dead-weight pressure gage tester.

14. REFERENCES

1. U.S. Department of Transportation Code of Federal Regulations 49, TRANSPORTATION, Parts 100–199, "Regulations for Transportation of Explosive and other Dangerous Articles by Land and Water in Rail Freight Service and by Motor Vehicle (Highway) and Water, Including Specifications for Shipping Containers." Revised at least once each calendar year and issued as of October 1. U.S. Department of Transportation (DOT), Office of Hazardous Materials, Transportation, Washington, DC 20590.

2. *NIOSH Pocket Guide to Chemical Hazards* (1985), U.S. Department of Health and Human Services, Superintendent of Documents, U.S. Government Printing Office, Washington, DC 20402.

3. *ANSI/ASHRAE 34–1992, Designation and Safety Classification of Refrigerants*, American Society of Heating, Refrigerating, and Air-Conditioning Engineers, Inc., Atlanta, GA.

4. *ASTM D93–85, Standard Test Methods for Flash Point by Pensky-Martens Closed Tester*, American Society for Testing and Materials (ASTM), Philadelphia, PA 19103.

5. *1990–1991 Threshold Limit Values for Chemical Substances and Physical Agents and Biological Exposure Indices*, American Conference of Governmental and Industrial Hygienists, Cincinnati, OH.

6. ANSI/NFPA 101–1988, *Code for Safety to Life from Fire in Buildings and Structures,* National Fire Protection Association (NFPA), Boston, MA 02210.

7. ANSI/NFPA 70–1990, *National Electrical Code,* National Fire Protection Association (NFPA), Boston, MA 02210.

8. *ASHRAE Handbook—1989 Fundamentals,* Chapter 24, "Weather Data" (similar data are given in AFM 88–29, TM 5–785, and NAVFAC P–89, Departments of the Air Force, Army, and Navy, Superintendent of Documents, July 1978).

9. *ASME Boiler and Pressure Vessel Code,* Section VIII, Rules for Construction of Pressure Vessels, Division 1, 1989, with addenda, American Society of Mechanical Engineers (ASME), New York, NY 10017.

10. *ASME/ANSI B31.5–1987, Refrigeration Piping and Addendum B31.5A–1989,* American Society of Mechanical Engineers (ASME), New York, NY 10017.

11. *ANSI/ASTM B8--89, Standard Specification for Seamless Copper Water Tube,* American Society for Testing and Materials (ASTM), Philadelphia, PA 19103.

12. *ANSI/ASTM B280–88, Standard Specification for Seamless Copper Tube for Air Conditioning and Refrigeration Field Service,* American Society for Testing and Materials (ASTM), Philadelphia, PA 19103.

13. *ANSI/ASME B15.1–1984, Safety Code for Mechanical Power Transmission Apparatus and Addendum B15.1–A–1986,* American Society of Mechanical Engineers (ASME), New York, NY 10017.

14. *ANSI/UL 303–1987, Refrigeration and Air-Conditioning Condensing and Compressor Units,* Underwriters Laboratories Inc., Northbrook, IL 60062.

15. *ANSI/IES RP–7–1983, Practice for Industrial Lighting,* Illuminating Engineering Society of North America (IES), New York, NY 10017.

16. *NFPA Standard 54–1988 (ANSI Z223.1–1988), National Fuel Gas Code,* Nation Fire Protection Association (NFPA), Boston, MA 02210.

17. *ANSI/NFPA 37–1990, Standard for the Installation and Use of Stationary Combustion Engines and Gas Turbines,* National Fire Protection Association (NFPA), Boston, MA 02210.

18. *ANSI/NFPA 90A–1989, Standard for the Installation of Air Conditioning and Ventilating Systems,* National Fire Protection Association (NFPA), Boston, MA 02210.

19. *ANSI/NFPA 90B–1989, Standard for the Installation of Warm Air Heating and Air Conditioning Systems,* National Fire Protection Association (NFPA), Boston, MA 02210.

20. *API 520, Recommended Practice for the Sizing, Selection, and Installation of Pressure-Relieving Devices in Refineries*—Part I, Sizing and Selection, 5th ed., July 1990, American Petroleum Institute (API), Washington, DC 20037.

21. *NFPA 68–1988, Guide for Venting of Deflagrations,* National Fire Protection Association (NFPA), Quincy, MA 02269.

22. *ANSI A13.1–1981 (R1985), Scheme for the Identification of Piping Systems,* American Society of Mechanical Engineers (ASME), New York, NY 10017.

23. *ASTM B68–86, Standard Specification for Seamless Copper Tube, Bright Annealed,* American Society for Testing and Materials (ASTM), Philadelphia, PA 19103.

24. *ASTM B75–86, Standard Specification for Seamless Copper Tube,* American Society for Testing and Materials (ASTM), Philadelphia, PA 19103.

(This appendix is not part of this standard but is included for information purposes only.)

Appendix A

Calculation of the Maximum Allowable Concentration (Cm) of a Blend.

A1 For 100 lb of blend, determine the ideal gas volumes occupied by each component and by the blend at 70ºF and 1 atm.

$$387\ W_1 / (MW_1) = V_1 \quad V_T = V_1 + V_2 \ldots V_i$$

$$387\ W_2 / (MW_2) = V_2$$

–

–

–

$$387\ W_i / (MW_2) = V_i$$

Wi = weight (lb) of component *i* in 100 lb of blend,

MWi = molecular weight of component *i*,

Vi = volume (ft^3) of component *i* in 100 lb of blend at 70ºF and 1 atm pressure,

VT = volume (ft^3) of the blend at 70ºF and 1 atm pressure.

A2 Determine the dilution volume required for the 100 lb blend and each component therein.

$$V_1 / LV_1 = DV_1$$

–

–

–

$$V_i / LV_i = DV_i$$

$$V_T / LV_{max} = DV_T$$

LVi = (limiting volume percent from Table 1)/100,

DVi = dilution volume required for weight (*Wi*) of component *i*,

LVmax = the highest value of *LVi*.

A3 Determine the maximum allowable concentration (C_m) of a blend.

Cm = (100 lb/*DVmax*)1000,

Cm = the maximum allowable concentration of blend lb/1000 ft^3 (multiply this value by 0.016 to obtain *Dm* in kg/m^3),

DVmax = the largest of the values *DV1*, *DV2*, . . . *DVi*, *DVT*.

(This appendix is not part of this standard but is included for information purposes only.)

Appendix B

Guidelines for Emergency Discharge of Refrigerants

B1 Introduction

(a) Every precaution should be taken to prevent the accidental or deliberate discharge of refrigerants to the atmosphere, to the sewer, or into local lakes and rivers.

(b) Nevertheless, this appendix is provided to aid the design engineer where local codes require manual emergency discharge systems for refrigerants.

(c) It is permissible to use any departures suggested herein from provisions in the mandatory parts of this standard when granted by the jurisdictional authority.

B2 Emergency Discharge Lines

An emergency discharge pipeline, independent of any other lines, shall be connected above the liquid refrigerant level on the high-pressure side and, where required by local codes, on the low-pressure side of the system. The lines shall be pitched so as to drain to the system. These lines shall extend into an emergency refrigerant control box. This box shall be locked and identified with a permanent label reading "Emergency Refrigerant Control Box" with the name of the refrigerant in the system.

B3 Stop Valves

A readily accessible stop valve and a suitable pressure gage shall be installed on the discharge pipe within the emergency refrigerant control box. The gage shall be located ahead of the stop valve, and the valve shall have the same capacity as the discharge pipe it serves. A permanent label shall be attached to the valve, reading "High-Pressure Refrigerant Discharge Valve" or "Low-Pressure Refrigerant Discharge Valve" as appropriate.

B4 Sizing Valves and Lines

Determine the size of the discharge line and the stop valve from the required capacity per 10.4.5 and the length per 10.4.8.5.

B5 High- to Low-Pressure Valve

When both highside and lowside emergency discharge valves are located in a common box, a stop valve connecting them on the system side of the emergency discharge stop valves shall be provided in the box. The stop valve and line shall be the same size as the higher pressure line. This valve shall be labeled "High- to Low-Pressure Control Valve."

B6 Diffuser
The discharge line (B4) shall be vented to the atmosphere through a diffuser fitted to its upper extremity. The diffuser shall provide for mixing the refrigerant with air and shall have a rain cap or means to prevent water from easily entering the vent pipe.

B7 Sizing Headers and Diffusers
When more than one relief valve or emergency discharge line is connected to a common header or riser for discharge to the atmosphere, a diffuser shall be installed on the common riser. The area of the header or riser and the diffuser inlet shall be equal to the sum of the areas of all of the relief valve vent lines and emergency discharge lines feeding it.

B8 Location of Diffuser
The diffuser shall be located per 10.4.8 for discharge to the atmosphere.

B9 Provide Drip Legs
Adequately sized drip pockets for collecting moisture shall be installed on every emergency line beyond the emergency valve exposed to the atmosphere.

B10 Ammonia Diffusion Systems
Ammonia may be released from refrigerating systems to the atmosphere in the event of an emergency. If this is done by employees of the refrigerated facility, it may be subject to the reporting requirements of the Emergency Planning and Community Right-to-Know Act of 1986. In locations where atmospheric release may be hazardous due to the proximity of people or other premises, the diffuser shall be equipped with an automatic burner for reducing the discharge to nitrogen and water, or such emergency system shall discharge into a storage tank (per 10.4.8.2) or into a water mixer (B15) and retention tank (B13) or basin (B14).

B11 Ammonia Discharge Lines
For emergency discharge line connections to the system, the stop valves and control box shall be as described above.

B12 Ammonia Flares
Systems for reducing the ammonia to nitrogen and water by burning shall be approved by the jurisdictional authority.

B13 Water Tanks
Water tanks shall be as specified in 10.4.8.2.

B14 Basins
Retention basins shall meet the requirements as set forth by the fire chief in the local jurisdiction.

B15 Ammonia-Water Mixers
Ammonia-water mixers shall have the following components:

(a) Connection to a permanent water supply with a capacity as in (c).

(b) A fire department inlet hose connection to the diffuser adjacent to the Emergency Refrigeration Control Box.

(c) An engineered ammonia-water mixing chamber, sized to provide 2 gpm of water per lb/min of ammonia (17 L/s water per kg/s ammonia). The ammonia flow can be estimated at 77 percent of the equivalent airflow calculated for the discharge line from 10.4.5 and 10.4.8.5.

(d) Connection to an approved storage tank, basin, or drainage system by means of welded or flanged piping.

(e) Necessary control valves, check valves, and fittings.

B16 Design Responsibility
The design of the manual emergency discharging system and the components that comprise it, such as the diffusers for mixing refrigerants with air or water as well as the design of tanks and holding basins, is the responsibility of the engineer.

(This appendix is not part of this standard but is included for information purposes only.)

Appendix C

Worst Case Composition of Fractionation
Since fractionation can occur as the result of a system leak, both the fractionation of the blend remaining in the system and the composition of the blend leaking into the machinery room or equipment space shall be considered when determining "worst case composition." The phrase "worst case composition of fractionation" is to be defined as the composition, either as formulated or at a composition that occurs during fractionation, that

- for flammability results in the highest concentration of the flammable component(s) in either the vapor or liquid phase and
- for toxicity results in the highest concentration of the toxic component(s) in either the vapor or liquid phase.

The worst case composition for toxicity might not be the same as the worst case composition for flammability. Each parameter must be considered independently.

The toxicity of blends must be defined according to Appendix C of the ACGIH manual of Threshold Limit Values.[5] The basic formula is as follows:

$$TLV = \frac{1}{\frac{\text{mol frac A}}{TLV\,A} + \frac{\text{mol frac B}}{TLV\text{B}} + \frac{\text{mol frac C}}{TLV\,C} \text{ etc.}}$$

Appendix D

ASHRAE Safety Group Classifications

ASHRAE Standard ANSI/ASHRAE 34–1992 has reclassified refrigerants into safety groups consisting of two alphanumerical characters, such as A2 or B1, based on allowable exposure. The capital letter indicates toxicity, and the numeral indicates flammability.

Toxicity classifications consist of two classes, A and B, based on allowable exposure.

Class A signifies refrigerants for which toxicity has not been identified at concentrations less than or equal to 400 ppm, based on data used to determine threshold limit valve time weighted average (TLV-TWA) or consistent indices.

Class B signifies refrigerants for which there is evidence of toxicity at concentrations below 400 ppm, based on data used to determine TLV-TWA or consistent indices.

Flammability classifications assign refrigerants to one of three classes—1, 2, or 3—based on their flammability.

Class 1 signifies refrigerants that do not show flame propagation when tested in the air at 101 kpa (14.7 psia) and 18° Celsius (65° F).

Class 2 signifies refrigerants having a lower flammability limit (LFL) of more than 0.10 kg/m^3 (0.00625 lb/ft^3) at 21° Celsius and 1.1 kpa (70° F and 14.7 psia) and a heat of combustion of less than 19,000 kj/kg (8,1274 btu/lb). The heat of combustion is calculated assuming that combustion products are in the gas phase and in their most stable state.

Class 3 signifies refrigerants that are highly flammable, as defined by an LFL less than or equal to 0.10 kg/m^3 (0.0625 lb/ft^3) at 21° Celsius and 101 kpa (70° Fahrenheit and 14.7 psia) or a heat of combustion greater than or equal to 19,000 kj/kg (8.174 btu/lb).

ASHRAE Safety Groups

Increasing Flammability		Safety Group	
	Higher Flammability	A3	B3
	Lower Flammability	A2	B2
	No Flame Propagation	A1	B1
		Lower Toxicity	Higher Toxicity
		Increasing Toxicity	

Comparison of Safety Group Classifications

Refrigerant Number	Safety Group Old	Safety Group New
10	2	B1
11	1	A1
12	1	A1
13	1	A1
13B1	1	A1
14	1	A1
21	2	B1
22	1	A1
30	2	B2
40	2	B2
50	3a	A3
113	1	A1
114	1	A1
115	1	A1
123		B1
134a		A1
142b	3b	A2
152a	3b	A2
170	3a	A3
290	3a	A3
C318	1	A1
400	1	A1
500	1	A1
501	1	A1
502	1	A1
600	3a	A3
600a	3a	A3
611	2	B2
702		A3
704		A1
717	2	B2
718		A1
720		A1
728		A1
740		A1
744	1	A1
764	2	B1
1140		B3
1150	3a	A3
1270	3a	A3

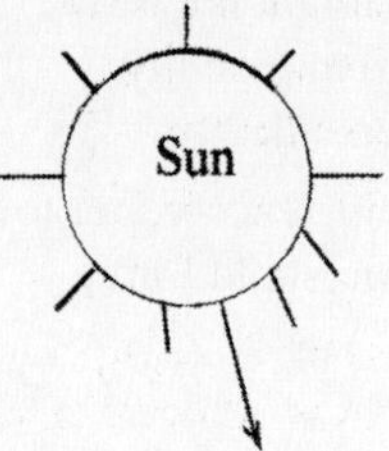

Ozone scattering Ultra Violet light with the Earth's atmosphere.

Ionosphere: 30 - 300 miles

Stratosphere: 7 to 30 miles

Here the ozone layer is formed, by the interaction of ultra violet radiation from the sun with molecular oxygen. Harmful UV radiation is absorbed during this formation process. ***Chlorine*** in the upper atmosphere reacts with formation process and diminishes, depletes, and destroys the ozone.

Troposphere: 7 miles about the Earth

This is where cloud form, and temperature decreases with rise in altitude

Typical question asked on a licensing exam:

As ultraviolet light collides with ozone molecules and chlorine molecules, it reacts to form

(A) chlorine dioxide.
(B) chlorine monoxide.
(C) ultraviolet radiation.
(D) cataracts radiation.

The correct answer is (B).

Chlorine in CFC and HCFC destroys ozone, forming chlorine monoxide: for each 1 percent of ozone depletion, results on 2 percent increased exposure to ultraviolet radiation.

Appendix E

Refrigerant Monitors: offers two important benefits in a refrigeration system: safety and refrigerant conservation.
Safety: deals with early warning of potentially hazardous situations in the Mechanical Equipment Room. Alarms should be designed to inform equipment room operators to take corrective action when necessary.
Refrigerant Conservation: deals with early warning of refrigerant loss, which costs the industry millions of dollars.
Refrigerant Monitors:

1. Should provide sensing capability down to one part per million.

2. Should have the ability to differentiate between various compounds. It should have the ability to selectively monitor for a specific refrigerant, which is the key in the elimination of nuisance alarms.
3. Must meet **ASHRAE-15R Mechanical Equipment Room Requirements** for **Class B1 refrigerants,** as well as any other refrigerants (Class A1) as desired.

Oxygen Deprivation Sensors: Whenever operating with toxic refrigerants, oxygen deprivation sensors should be installed, with an approved service mask for the operators, as emergency breathing apparatus. See Breathing Apparatus, Refrigeration Code C19–106.12.

SECTION II: NEW YORK CITY CODE

This section begins with the mechanical refrigeration requirements of the New York City Code, as edited by the author. Many refrigerant code questions have been taken from this section. Essential articles that may be on the City's written exam are emphasized. Supplemental reading is always advised to properly interpret the code.

To help you understand the subject matter, diagrams and tables are accompanied by their code interpretations.

Mechanical Refrigeration Sub-Article 1: Application Definitions

C19–96.0

This article shall be known and may be cited as the "refrigeration code."

C19–96.1: Scope

The application of this article is intended to govern the installation, operation, and inspection of every refrigerating system employing a fluid that is vaporized and is normally liquefied in its refrigerating cycle, when employed under the occupancy classifications listed in section C19–97.0. The provisions of this part are not intended to apply to the use of water or air as a refrigerant or to any system installed on or in railroad cars, vehicles, or vessels.

C19–96.2: Application

This article shall apply only to refrigerating systems installed subsequent to its adoption and to parts replaced or added to systems installed prior or subsequent to its adoption. In cases of practical difficulty or unnecessary hardship, the department may grant exceptions from the literal requirements of this article or permit the use of other devices or methods but only when equivalent protection is thereby secured.

C19–96.3: Definitions

1. **Absorption system:** a refrigerating system in which the gas evolved in the evaporator is taken up by an absorber.
2. **Absorber:** a part of the low side of an absorption system used for absorbing vapor refrigerant.
3. **Approved national recognized testing laboratory:** a laboratory acceptable to the department, which provides uniform testing and examination procedures under established standards; is properly organized, equipped, and qualified for testing; and has a follow-up inspection service of the current production of the listed products.
4. **Brazed joint:** a gas-tight joint obtained by the joining of metal parts with alloys that melt at temperatures higher than 1000° F but lower than the melting temperatures of the joined parts.
5. **Brine:** any liquid used for the transmission of heat without a change in its state, having a flash point above 150° Fahrenheit, determined by the Pensky-Martens Closed Cup Tester. Brine may be liquid, sweet water, salt water, or any other fluid that can be cooled.
6. **Code:** the local and state rules that govern the safe installation and service of systems and equipment for the purpose of safety of the public and trade personnel.
7. **Companion or block valve:** a valve in dual sections. Each section can be shut off to permit the connecting or disconnecting of a portion of a refrigeration system without loss of refrigerant charge or introduction of air into the system.
8. **Compressor:** a specific machine, with or without accessories, for compressing a given refrigerant vapor.
9. **Condenser:** a vessel or arrangement of pipe or tubing in which vaporized refrigerant is liquefied by the removal of heat.
10. **Condensing unit:** a refrigerating machine combination for a given refrigerant, consisting of one or more power-driven compressors, condensers, liquid receivers (when required), and the regularly furnished accessories.
11. **Container:** a cylinder for the transportation of refrigerant.
12. **Design working pressure:** the maximum allowable working pressure for which a specific part of a system is designed.
13. **Deluge ventilation:** water spray used where it may be extremely difficult to provide mechanical ventilation.

It is seen on old ammonia systems. Spray nozzles are placed over every piece of equipment, with a control valve located outside the engine-room space.

14. **Duct:** a tube, conduit, or shaft used for conveying or encasing purposes as specifically defined below:
    a. **Air duct:** a tube, conduit, or shaft used for conveying air (the air passages of self-contained systems are not to be constructed as air ducts.)
    b. **Pipe duct:** a tube, conduit, or shaft containing or used for encasing pipe.
    d. **Wire duct:** a tube, conduit, or shaft containing or used for encasing either moving or stationary wire, rope, etc.
15. **Evaporator:** that part of the system in which liquid refrigerant is vaporized to produce refrigeration.
16. **Expansion coil:** an evaporator constructed of pipe or tubing.
17. **Fire-resistant pipe duct:** a pipe duct that, if vertical, is enclosed as required for the class of building. If horizontal, a fire-resistant rating is not required, except that the duct enclosure shall be noncombustible.
18. **Fire-resistant shaft:** an enclosed shaft. The fire-resistant ratings required for shaft enclosures are given in C26–638.0.
19. **Fusible plug:** a fusible member with a predetermined temperature for the relief of pressure. (The plug may be placed on the condenser or receiver; it reacts to heat or temperature and melts at 280° F.)
20. **Generator:** any device equipped with a heating element that is used in the refrigerating system to increase the pressure of refrigerant in its gas or vapor state for the purpose of liquefying it.
21. **Hallway:** an enclosed hall or corridor leading to a stairway, fire tower, or other exit.
22. **High side:** the parts of a refrigerating system subject to condenser pressure.
23. **Humanly occupied space:** a space in which any human lives or is required to work or remain for continuous periods of two hours or more but, for the purposes of this article, excluding machinery rooms and walk-in coolers used primarily for refrigerated storage.
24. **Low side:** the parts of a refrigerating system subject to evaporator pressure.
25. **Machinery:** the refrigerating equipment forming a part of the refrigerating system, such as the compressor, condenser, generator, absorber, liquid receiver, connecting pipe, or evaporator.
26. **Machinery room:** a room containing a refrigerating system or systems and other mechanical equipment. It conforms to the following:
    a. It shall have a tight-fitting door or doors and no partitions or openings that permit the passage of escaping refrigerant to other parts of the building.
    b. It shall have means for ventilation in accordance with the provisions of section C19–100.7.
    c. It shall have emergency remote controls to stop the action of the refrigerant compressor. The controls shall be labeled, easily accessible, and located immediately outside the machinery room.
    d. If a mechanical means of ventilation is provided, emergency remote controls for such means shall be labeled, easily accessible, and located immediately outside the machinery room.
27. **Machinery room Class T:** a room having machinery, but no flame-producing apparatus permanently installed or operated, and conforming to the requirements of paragraph 26 of this section and adding to the following:
    a. Any doors communicating with the building shall be self-closing, tight-fitting fire doors.
    b. Wall, floors, and ceiling shall be tight and of not less than one-hour fire-resistant construction.
    c. It shall have an exit door that opens directly to the outer air or through a vestibule-type exit equipped with self-closing, tight-fitting doors.
    d. Exterior openings, if present, shall not be under any fire escape or any open stairway.
    e. All pipes piercing the interior wall, ceiling, or floor of such a room shall be tightly sealed to the walls, ceiling, or floor through which they pass.
    f. Mechanical means shall be provided for ventilation.
28. **Manufacturer:** the individual, company, or organization that affixes its name or nationally registered trademark or trade name to the refrigeration equipment concerned.
29. **Mechanical joint:** for the purpose of this article, a gas-tight joint obtained by the joining of metal parts through a positive-holding mechanical construction.
30. **Nonpositive displacement compressor:** a compressor in which increase in vapor pressure is attained without changing the internal volume of the compression chamber (example: centrifugal compressor).

31. **Positive displacement compressor:** a compressor in which increase in vapor pressure is attained by changing the internal volume of the compression chamber. (Reciprocating, rotary, and helical compressor are examples of positive displacement compressors.)
32. **Piping:** the pipe or tube mains for interconnecting the various parts of a refrigeration system.
33. **Pressure-imposing element:** any device or portion of the equipment used for the purpose of increasing the refrigerant vapor pressure (example: the generator in the absorption system).
34. **Pressure-limiting device:** a pressure-responsive mechanism designed to automatically stop the operation of the pressure-imposing element at a predetermined pressure (example: a high-pressure switch or high-pressure cut-out designed to stop the system at a predetermined pressure).
35. **Pressure-relief device:** a pressure-actuated valve or rupture member designed to automatically relieve excessive pressure (example: high-pressure relief valve, safety valve, rupture member, or frangible disc).
36. **Pressure-relief valve:** a pressure-actuated valve held closed by a spring or other means and designed to automatically relieve pressure in excess of its setting.
37. **Pressure vessel:** any refrigerant-containing receptacle of a refrigerating system, other than evaporators (where each separate section does not exceed 1/2 cubic foot of refrigerant containing volume), expansion coils, compressors, controls, headers, pipe, and pipe fittings.
38. **Receiver or liquid receiver:** a vessel on the high side permanently connected to a system by inlet and outlet pipes for storage of a liquid refrigerant.
39. **Refrigerant:** a substance used to produce refrigeration by its expansion or vaporization.
40. **Refrigerating system:** a combination of interconnecting, refrigerant-containing parts constituting one closed refrigerant circuit in which a refrigerant is circulated for the purpose of extracting heat.
    a. **Sealed absorption system:** a unit system for Group 2 refrigerants only, in which all refrigerant-containing parts are made tight by welding or brazing against refrigerant loss.
    b. **Self-contained system:** a complete factory-made and factory-tested system in a suitable frame or closure, which is fabricated and shipped in one or more sections and in which no refrigerant-containing parts are connected in the field other than by companion or block valves.
    c. **Unit system:** a self-contained system that has been assembled and tested prior to its installation and is installed without connecting any refrigerant-containing parts. A unit system may include factory-assembly companion or block valves.
    d. **Field-erected system:** a system other than a self-contained or unit system whose refrigerant-containing parts are assembled in the field with interconnecting piping fabricated and installed on the job site.
41. **Rupture member:** a device that ruptures at a predetermined pressure (example: rupture disk).
42. **Shaft:** an enclosed space for the transmission of light, air, material, or persons through one or more stories of a structure that connects a series of two or more openings in successive floors or floors and roof.
43. **Soldered joint:** a gas-tight joint obtained by the joining of metal parts with metallic mixtures or alloys that melt at temperatures below 1,000° F and above 400° F.
44. **Stop valve:** a wheel-operated shut-off for controlling the flow of refrigerant. A service valve is not a stop valve, because it does not have a wheel; it must be operated with a wrench or a key. A service valve is used only for installation, transportation, or repairs of equipment; a stop valve is used primarily for the operation of the equipment.
45. **Welded joint:** a gas-tight joint obtained by the joining of metal parts in the plastic or molten state.

Sub-article 2: Classifications

C19–97.0: Building classifications

Locations in premises governed by this article and in which refrigerating systems may be placed are grouped under building classifications by occupancy as follows:

1. **Public buildings:** structures or parts of structures having the following occupancy:
    a. **Institutional occupancy:** that portion of a building in which persons are confined to receive medical, charitable, educational, or other care or treatment or in which persons are held or detained by reason of public or civil duty or for correctional purposes, including, among other places, hospitals, asylums, sanitariums, police stations, jails, courthouses with cells, and similar occupancies.

b. **Public-assembly occupancy:** that portion of the premises in which persons congregate for civil, political, educational, religious, social, or recreational purposes, including, among other places, armories, assembly rooms, auditoriums, ballrooms, bath houses, bus terminals, broadcasting studios, churches, colleges, courthouses without cells, dance halls, cabarets, exhibition halls, fraternity halls, libraries, lodge rooms, mortuary chapels, museums, passenger depots, schools, skating rinks, subway stations, theaters, television and radio studios, and similar occupancies.

2. **Residence buildings:** structures or parts of structures in which sleeping accommodations are provided, except as may be classed as public buildings and including, among other places, clubhouses, convents, dormitories, hotels, lodging houses, apartments, studios, tenements, and similar occupancies.

3. **Commercial buildings:** structures or parts of structures that are not public buildings or residence buildings and that have the following occupancies:
   a. **Commercial occupancy:** that portion of a building used for the transaction of business, for the rendering of professional services, for manufacturing purposes, or for the performance of work or labor (except as included under paragraph (b), "industrial occupancy"), including, among other places, bake shops, fur storage facilities, laboratories, marketplaces, office buildings, professional buildings, restaurants, stores, catering establishments (except when used for public-assembly occupancy as described under lb of this section), and similar occupancies.
   b. **Industrial occupancy:** that portion of a building used for manufacturing, processing, or storage of materials or products, including, among other places, chemical, food, candy, and ice-cream factories, ice-making plants, meat-packing plants, refineries, perishable food warehouses, and similar occupancies—provided, however, that this occupancy classification shall apply only when the entire building is used by a single occupant.
   c. **Mixed occupancy:** a building occupied or used for different purposes in different parts. When the occupancies are cut off from the rest of the building by partitions, floors, and ceilings and protected by self-closing doors, the requirements for each type of occupancy shall apply to the portion of the building so used. For example, the cold-storage space in retail frozen-food lockers, hotels, and stores in buildings used by a single occupant should be classified under industrial occupancy, whereas other portions of the building should be classified under other occupancies. When the occupancies are not so separated, the occupancy carrying the more stringent requirements shall govern.

C19–97.1: Refrigerating systems by type
Refrigerating systems shall be divided into classes, descriptive of the method employed for extracting heat as follows:

Direct system: a system in which the evaporators are in direct contact with the material or space refrigerated or are located in air-circulating passages communicating with such spaces. It has an evaporator in the room or space to be cooled or a duct leading to the room or space to be cooled, with refrigerant in the evaporator.

Indirect system: a system in which a liquid, such as brine or water, is cooled by the refrigerant and circulated to the material or space refrigerated or is used to cool air so circulated. Indirect systems are distinguished by the type or method of application, as given in the following paragraphs:

a. **Indirect open-spray system:** a system in which a liquid, such as brine or water, is cooled by an evaporator located in an enclosure external to a cooling chamber and circulated to such cooling chamber and sprayed therein.
b. **Indirect closed-surface system:** a system in which a liquid, such as brine or water, is cooled by an evaporator located in an enclosure external to a cooling chamber and circulated to and through such cooling chamber in pipes or other closed circuits.
c. **Indirect-vented closed-surface system:** a system in which a liquid, such as brine or water, is cooled by an evaporator located in a vented enclosure external to a cooling chamber and circulated to and through such cooling chamber in pipes or other closed circuits.
d. **Double indirect-vented open-spray system:** a system in which a liquid, such as brine or water, is cooled by an evaporator located in a vented enclosure and circulated through a closed circuit to a second enclosure, where it cools another supply of a liquid, such as brine or water; this liquid in turn is circulated to a cooling chamber and is sprayed therein.

e. **Double (or secondary) refrigerant system:** a system in which an evaporative refrigerant is used in a secondary circuit. For the purpose of this article, each system enclosing a separate body of an evaporative refrigerant shall be considered a separate direct system.

C19–97.2: Refrigerants

Refrigerants are classified in accordance with their properties. For the purpose of this article, they are grouped as follows: those that are nontoxic, nonflammable, and nonirritating under normal conditions are placed in Group 1; those that are somewhat flammable, toxic, or irritating are placed in Group 2; and the hydrocarbons are placed in Group 3.

Refrigerants are cataloged by two different national organizations, the National Refrigeration Safety Code (NRSC) and the National Board of Fire Underwriters (NBFU). The NRSC catalogs all refrigerants into three groups:

Group One: Safest of the refrigerants

Group Two: Toxic and somewhat flammable refrigerants

Group Three: Flammable refrigerants

Name		Refrigerant number
Group I		
Trichloromonofluoromethane	(CFC)	R-11
Dichlorodifluoromethane	(CFC)	R-12
Tetrafluoromethane	(CFC)	R-14
Dichloromonofluoromethane	(CFC)	R-21
Monochlorodifluoromethane	(CFC)	R-22
Trichlorotrifluoroethane	(CFC)	R-113
Dichloroterafluoroethane	(CFC)	R-114
Azeotropes (R-12 and R-152a)	(CFC)	R-500
Azeotropes (R-22 and R-115)	(CFC)	R-502
Carbon dioxide		R-744
Group II		
Methyl chloride	R-40	
Ethyl chloride	R-160	
Methyl formate	R-611	
Sulphur dioxide (SO_2)	R-764	
Ammonia (NH_3)	R-717	
Dichloroethylene	R-1130	
Group III		
Ethane	R-170	
Propane	R-290	
Butane	R-600	
Isobutane	R-600a	
Ethylene	R-1150	

Chart courtesy of Modern Refrigeration and Air Conditioning, Goodheart-Willcox.

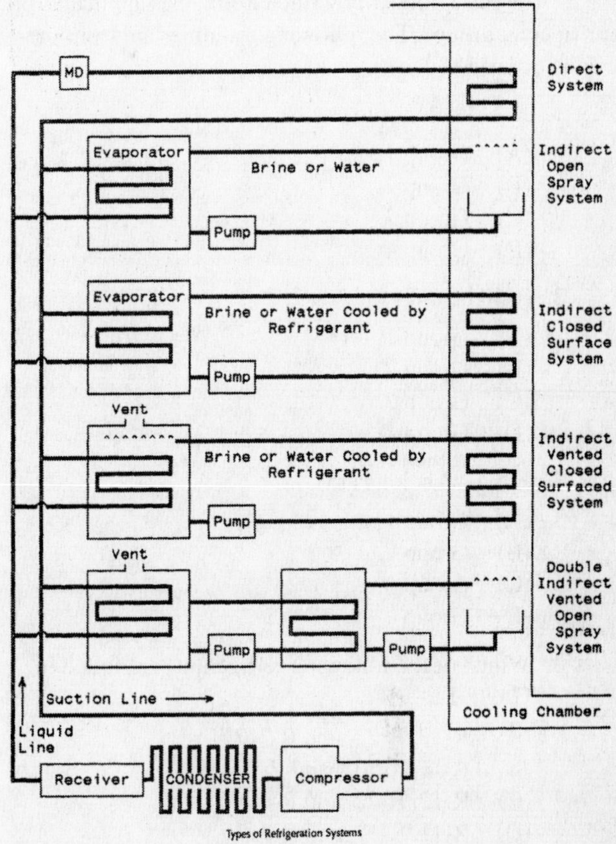

Fig. 17.1

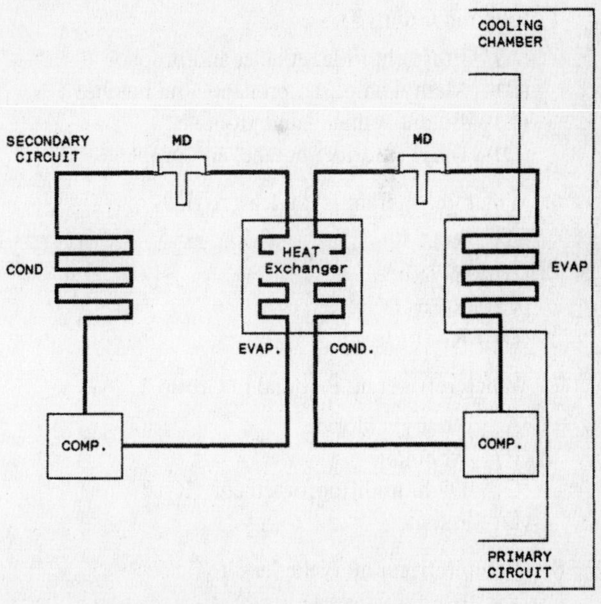

Fig. 17.2 Double Refrigerant System

ANSI/ASHRAE Standard 15–1978 classifies refrigerants into three groups according to flammability and toxicity. Group One refrigerants are the least hazardous; Group Three are the most hazardous.

The New York City written exam tests applicants on refrigerant groups. The following examples are from previous exams:

1. R-744 belongs to

(A) Group 1.
(B) Group 2.
(C) Group 3.
(D) Group 4.

2. R-40 belongs to

(A) Group 1.
(B) Group 2.
(C) Group 3.
(D) Group 4.

3. Ethylene belongs to

(A) Group 1.
(B) Group 2.
(C) Group 3.
(D) Group 4.

4. Which of the following refrigerants are found in Group 1?

(A) R-12, R-22, and R-717
(B) R-11, R-502, and R-744
(C) R-12, R-22, and R-611
(D) R-11, R-13, and R-717

5. Which of the following group of refrigerants are found in Group 3?

(A) Ethyl chloride, ethane, and propane
(B) Methyl chloride, propane, and butane
(C) Butane, ethane, and propane
(D) Ethyl chloride, butane, and propane

6. Which refrigerant is the least toxic?

(A) R-11
(B) R-717
(C) R-764
(D) R-40

7. Which refrigerant is found in Group 2?

(A) Methyl chloride
(B) Isobutane
(C) Dichlorodifluoromethane (R-12)
(D) Ethane

8. Which refrigerant is the least toxic?

(A) Propane
(B) Ammonia
(C) Methyl chloride
(D) R-113

9. Which refrigerant is widely used in centrifugal refrigeration compressors?

(A) R-12
(B) R-22
(C) R-113
(D) R-502

Answers:

1. A	4. B	7. A
2. B	5. C	8. D
3. C	6. A	9. C

ASHRAE Standard Designation of Refrigerants (ANSI/ASHRAE Standard 34–1978)

Name	Refrigerant Number
Halocarbon Compounds	
Carbontetrachloride	R-10
Trichloromonofluoromethane	R-11
Dichlorodifluoromethane	R-12
Tetrafluoromethane	R-14
Dichloromonofluoromethane	R-21
Monochlorodifluoromethane	R-22
Methylene chloride	R-30
Methyl chloride	R-40
Methyl fluoride	R-41
Trichlorotrifluoroethane	R-113
Dichloroterafluoroethane	R-114
Difluoroethane	R-152a
Ethyl chloride	R-160
Oxygen Compounds	
Methyl formate	R-611
Ethyl ether	R-610
Inorganic Compounds	
Hydrogen	R-702
Helium	R-704
Ammonia (NH3)	R-717
Water	R-718
Nitrogen	R-728
Oxygen	R-732
Carbon dioxide	R-744
Sulphur dioxide (SO_2)	R-764
Unsaturated Organic Compounds	
Dichloroethylene	R-1130
Chlorotrifluoroethylene	R-1113
Miscellaneous Organic Compounds	
Hydrocarbons	
Methane	R-50
Ethane	R-170
Propane	R-290
Butane	R-600
Isobutane	R-600a
Ethylene	R-1150
Propylene	R-1270
Azeotropes	
(R-12 and R-152a)	R-500
(R-22 and R-12)	R-501
(R-22 and R-115)	R-502

R-502 is an azeotropic mixture of R-22 and R-115. It is nonflammable, low in toxicity, and noncorrosive. Azeotrope refers to a stable mixture of refrigerants whose vapor and liquid phases retain identical compositions over a wide range of temperatures.

Underwriters Laboratories, Inc. have classified refrigerants according to their relative safety:

Group	Definitions	Examples
1	Gases or vapors that, in concentration of about 1/2 to 1 percent, for exposure durations of about 5 minutes, are lethal or produce serious injury	sulfur dioxide
2	Gases or vapors that, in concentrations of about 1/2 to 1 percent, for exposure durations of about 1/2 hour, are lethal or produce serious injury	ammonia, methyl bromide
3	Gases or vapors which, in concentrations of about 2 to 2-1/2 percent, for exposure durations of about 1 hour, are lethal or produce serious injury	carbon tetrachloride, chloroform, methyl formate
4	Gases or vapors that, in concentrations of about 2 to 2-1/2 percent, for exposure durations of about two hours, are lethal or produce serious injury	dichloroehylene, methyl chloride, ethyl bromide
Between 4 and 5	Gases or vapors classified as somewhat less toxic than those of Group 4 but somewhat more toxic thanthose of Group 5	methylene chloride, ethyl chloride, R-113
5a	Gases or vapors much lesstoxic than those of Group 4 but more toxic than those of Group 6	R-11, R-22, carbon dioxide
5b	Gases or vapors that available data classify as either Group 5a or Group 6	ethane, propane, butane
6	Gases or vapors that, in concentrations up to at least about 20 percent by volume, for exposure durations of about 2 hours, do not appear to produce injury	R-12, R-114, R-13B1

Relative Safety of Refrigerants

Refrigerant Number	Name	ANSI/ASHRAE 15–1978 safety code group	Underwriters Laboratories group classification	Explosive limits in air—percentage by volume
50	Methane	3	5b	4.9 to 15.0
14	Tetrafluoromethane	1	6	Nonflammable
1150	Ethylene	3	5b	3.0 to 25.0
744A	Nitrous oxide			Nonflammable
13	Chlorotrifluoromethane	1	6	Nonflammable
170	Ethane	3	5b	3.3 to 10.6
744	Carbon Dioxide	1	5	Nonflammable
13B1	Bromotrifluoromethane	1	6	Nonflammable
290	Propane	3	5b	2.3 to 7.3
502		1	5a	Nonflammable
22	Chlorodifluoromethane	1	5a	Nonflammable
717	Ammonia	2	2	16.0 to 25.0
500		1	5a	Nonflammable
152a	Difluoroethane			5.1 TO 17.1
12	Dichlorodifluoromethane	1	6	Nonflammable
505			5	Nonflammable
40	Methyl chloride	2	4	8.1 to 17.2
506			5	Nonflammable
600a	Isobutane	3	5b	1.8 to 8.4
764	Sulfur dioxide	2	1	Nonflammable
600	Butane	3	5	1.6 to 6.5
114	Dichlorotetrafluoroethane	1	6	Nonflammable
21	Dichlorofluoromethane	1	4-5	Nonflammable
160	Ethyl chloride	2	4a	3.7 to 12.0
11	Trichlorofluoromethane	1	5	Nonflammable
611	Methyl formate	2	3	4.5 to 20.0
30	Methylene chloride	1	4a	Nonflammable
113	Trichlorotrifluoroethane	1	4-5	Nonflammable
1130	Dichloroethylene	2	4	5.6 to 11.4

Chart courtesy ASHRAE Handbook, 1985 Fundamentals, Chapter 16, page 16–11.

Installation And Refrigerant Requirements

Group A: All Buildings and Occupancies other than Industrial Occupancy

C19–98.0: Public stairway, entrance, or exit
No refrigerating system shall be installed in or on a public stairway, entrance, or exit.

C19–98.1: Hallway or lobby
No refrigerating system shall obstruct a means of egress. No Group 2 refrigerant shall be permitted in hallways or lobbies of institutional or public assembly occupancies.

Refrigerating systems installed in a hallway or lobby shall be limited to

- **a.** unit systems containing not more than the quantities of a Group 1 refrigerant specified in the maximum permissible quantities of Group 1 refrigerants for Direct Systems Table, or
- **b.** sealed absorption systems containing not more than 3 pounds of Group 2 refrigerant when in residence buildings and commercial occupancies.

C19–98.2: Refrigerant piping through the floor
Refrigerant piping shall not be carried through floors except as follows:

- **a.** It may be carried from the basement to the first floor or from the top floor to a machinery penthouse or to the roof.
- **b.** For the purpose of connecting to a condenser on the roof, it may be carried through a rigid, continuous fire-resisting pipe duct or shaft having no openings on intermediate floors; or it may be carried on the exterior wall or open court of the building, in which case it shall be enclosed in a rigid and tight fire-resisting pipe duct and be so located as not to violate applicable provisions of zoning and building laws, regulations, and resolutions.
- **c.** In direct systems containing Group 1 refrigerants, the refrigerant piping may also be carried through floors, intermediate between the first floor and the top floor, provided it is enclosed in a rigid and tight continuous fire-resisting pipe duct or shaft where it passes through intermediate spaces not served by the system. The piping need not be enclosed where it passes through spaces served by the system. The pipe duct or shaft shall be vented to the outside or to a space served by the system and if vented to such space, the duct or shaft shall be sealed at the other end.

C19–98.3: Group 1 refrigerants

- **a.** In direct systems, the maximum permissible quantity of a Group 1 refrigerant is specified in the following table, except for institutional occupancies further limited by paragraph (b) of this section.

Table 1: Maximum Permissible Quantities of Group 1 Refrigerants of Direct Systems

Refrigerant		Maximum quantity in lb. per 1000 cu. ft. of humanly occupied space
Carbon dioxide		11
Dichlorodifluoromethane	(R-12)	31
Dichlorodifluoromethane and ethylidene fluoride		26
Dichloromethane (methylene chloride)		6
Dichloromonofluoromethane	(R-21)	13
Dichlorotetrafluoroethane	(R-114)	44
Monochlorodifluoromethane	(R-22)	22
Trichloromonofluoromethane	(R-11)	35
Trichlorotrifluoroethane	(R-113)	24

1. When the refrigerant-containing parts of a system are located in one or more enclosed spaces, the cubic content of the smallest enclosed humanly occupied space, other than the machinery room, shall be used to determine the permissible quantity of refrigerant in the system. Where a refrigerating system has evaporator coils serving individual stores of a building, the story having the smallest volume shall be used to determine the maximum quantity of a refrigerant in the entire system.
2. When the evaporator is located in an air duct system, the cubic content of the smallest humanly occupied enclosed space served by the air duct system shall be used to determine the permissible quantity of refrigerant in the system; however, if the air flow to two or more enclosed spaces served by the air duct system cannot be shut off or reduced below one quarter of its maximum, the total cubic contents of all such spaces may be used to determine the permissible quantity of refrigerant in the system.
3. The gas or liquid charge in a control device shall not be considered as refrigerant.

b. Direct systems in institutional occupancies shall be limited to unit systems each containing not more than 20 pounds of Group 1 refrigerants, except in kitchens, laboratories, and mortuaries.

c. In institutional and public assembly occupancies, direct expansion coils or evaporators used for air conditioning and located downstream from and in proximity to a heating coil, or located upstream within 18 inches of a heating coil, shall be fitted with a relief device discharging to the outside of the building as provided in section C19–104.9, except that such a relief device shall not be required on a unit or self-contained system.

d. Systems containing more than the quantity of a Group 1 refrigerant allowed in Table 1 shall be of the **indirect** type, with all refrigerant-containing parts (except parts mounted outside the building or piping connected to a condenser on the roof, as provided in section C19–98.2 b) installed in a machinery room used for no other purpose than for mechanical equipment.

e. No **open flame** or apparatus to produce an open flame shall be installed in a **machinery room** where any refrigerant other than carbon dioxide is used, unless the flame is enclosed and vented to the open air. The use of halide leak detectors, electric heating elements, and similar devices shall not be considered a violation of this paragraph.

f. In **institutional and public assembly occupancies**, when more than six pounds of a Group 1 refrigerant, other than carbon dioxide, are used in a system, any portion of which is in a room where there is an apparatus for producing an open flame, then such refrigerant shall be classed in Group 2, unless the flame-producing apparatus is provided with a hood and flue capable of removing the products of combustion to the open air. The use of halide leak detectors, electric heating elements, and similar devices shall not be considered a violation of this paragraph.

C19–98.4: Group 2 refrigerants

a. **Direct systems** containing Group 2 refrigerants shall not be used for air-conditioning for human comfort. For other applications of Group 2 refrigerants in a direct system, the permissible quantity of such refrigerants is shown in Table 2.

Table 2: Maximum permissible quantities of Group 2 refrigerants for direct systems, other than air-conditioning for human comfort

	Maximum pounds for various occupancies and buildings			
Type of refrigerating systems:	**Institutional**	**Public Assembly**	**Residence**	**Commercial**
Seal absorption systems				
a. In public hallways or lobbies	0	0	3	3
b. Other than public hallways, lobbies	0*	6	6	20
Self-contained or unit systems				
a. In public hallways or lobbies	0	0	0	0
b. Other than public hallways, lobbies	0	0*	6	20

*Six pounds allowed when installed in kitchens, laboratories, and mortuaries.

b. The maximum permissible quantity of Group 2 refrigerant in an indirect system is shown in Table 3. Such systems shall be of the following types:

1. **Institutional and public assembly occupancies:** Indirect-vented closed surface or double indirect-vented open spray.
2. **Residence building and commercial occupancies:** Indirect-vented closed surface, double indirect-vented open spray, or primary circuit of double refrigerant type.

c. Indirect systems using Group 2 refrigerants not in excess of the quantities shown in column 1 of Table 3 shall have all refrigerant-containing parts (excepting parts mounted outside the building or piping connected to a condenser on the roof, as provided in section C19–98.2 b) installed in a machinery room used for no other purpose than for mechanical equipment.

Table 3: Maximum permissible quantities of Group 2 refrigerants for indirect systems

Occupancy or building	Column 1 Machinery rooms Maximum lbs	Column 2 Class T machinery Room's maximum lbs.
Institutional	0	500 lbs.
Public assembly	0	1000 lbs.
Residence	300 lbs.	no limit
Commercial	600 lbs.	no limit

d. Indirect systems using Group 2 refrigerants containing more than the quantities shown in column 1 of Table 3 and not more than the quantities shown in column 2 of that table shall have all refrigerant-containing parts installed in a Class T machinery room.

e. Where a **machinery room** is required by this article to house a refrigerating system containing any Group 2 refrigerant other than sulphur dioxide, **no flame-producing device or hot surface** above 800° F shall be permitted in such room, and all **electrical equipment** in the room shall conform to the requirements of the hazardous locations provisions of the electrical code. The use of halide leak detectors and similar devices shall not be considered a violation of this paragraph.

C19–98.5: Group 3 refrigerants

Group 3 refrigerants shall not be used in residential buildings or in institutional, public assembly, or commercial occupancies, except in laboratories for commercial occupancies. Group 3 refrigerants in such laboratory installations shall be used only with the approval of the department.

Group B: Industrial Occupancies

C19–99.0: Industrial occupancies

There shall be no restriction on the quantity or kind of refrigerant used in an industrial occupancy, except as specified in section C19–99.1 and C19–100.6.

C19–99.1: Number of persons

When the number of persons in a refrigerated space, served by a direct system, on any floor above the first floor served by a direct system, on any floor above the first floor (ground level or deck level), exceeds one person per 300 square feet of floor area, the requirements of commercial occupancy shall apply.

Group C: Installation

C19–100.0: Foundations and support

When foundations and supports, other than vibration dampeners, for condensing units or compressor units are used, such foundations and supports shall be of incombustible construction.

C19–100.1: Clear space

In all installations, clear space adequate for inspection of condensing units or compressor units shall be provided.

C19–100.2

Condensing units or compressor units with enclosure shall be readily accessible for inspection.

C19–100.3

Refrigerant piping crossing an open space that affords passageway in any building shall be not less than 7 1/2 feet above the floor unless against the ceiling of such space.

C19–100.4

Passageways shall not be obstructed by refrigerant piping. Refrigerant piping shall not be placed in any elevator, dumbwaiter, or other shafts containing a moving object or in any closed shaft that has openings to living quarters or to stairways. Refrigerant piping shall not be placed in public hallways, lobbies, or stairways, although such refrigerant piping may pass across a public hallway if the section in the hallway is contained in a rigid metal pipe and is labeled in accordance with the provisions of C19–106.4.

C19–100.5: Open flames

When the quantity of flammable refrigerant in any one refrigerating system exceeds the amount given in the flammable refrigerants' table, for each 1,000 cubic feet of room volume in which the system or any part thereof is installed, no flame-producing device or hot surface above 800° F shall be permitted in such room and all electrical equipment in the room shall conform to the requirements of the hazardous locations provisions of the electrical code.

C19–100.6: Flammable refrigerants

Flammable refrigerants as listed in the following table shall not be used in a refrigerating system unless approved by the department. Use of such refrigerants shall in no case be approved unless applicant submits evidence, acceptable to the department, that no public hazard will be created thereby. No refrigerating system containing a Group 3 refrigerant shall be installed unless it conforms with the provisions of this code and with the additional conditions of approval specified by the department.

Flammable refrigerants

Name	Maximum quantity in lbs. per 1,000 cu. ft. of room volume
Butane	2-1/2
Ethane	2-1/2
Ethyl chloride	6
Ethylene	2
Isobutane	2-1/2
Methyl chloride	10
Methyl formate	7
Propane	2-1/2

C19–100.7: Machinery room ventilation requirements

a. Each refrigerating machinery room shall be provided with means for ventilation to the outer air. The amount of ventilation for refrigerant removal purposes shall be determined by the refrigerant content of the largest system in the machinery room.

b. Mechanical ventilation, when used, shall consist of one or more power-driven exhaust fans, which shall be capable of removing from the refrigerating machinery room the amount of air specified in the following table. The inlet to the fan(s) or air duct connection shall be located near the refrigerating equipment.

c. Where heavier-than-air refrigerants are used, the inlet shall be located near the floor. Where lighter-than-air refrigerants are used, the inlet shall be located near the ceiling. The outlet from the fan(s) or air duct connections shall terminate outside of the building and not within 10 feet of any intake or exhaust or any opening in an adjoining building. This outlet shall not be within 10 feet of any fire escape or exterior stair. Provisions shall be made for the intake of air to replace that being exhausted.

d. **Class T machinery rooms** in basements or sub-basements shall have, as specified in the following table, mechanical ventilation operating continuously when the system is in operation.

e. **Mechanical ventilation systems** for machinery rooms, when required, shall consist of inlet air ducts, exhaust blowers, and exhaust ducts, all of which shall be independent of any other building facilities.

The following chart lists minimum air duct areas and openings by weight in pounds of refrigerants used in a system; mechanical discharge of air, in cubic feet per minute; duct area required in square feet; and window or door area in square feet needed. Highlighted within the table are figures used in previous exams.

Minimum Air Duct Areas and Openings

Weight of refrigerant in system, by lbs.	Mechanical discharge of air, per cfm	Duct areas in sq. ft.	Window or door area in sq. ft.
up to: 20	150	1/4	4
50	250	1/3	6
100	400	1/2	10
150	550	2/3	12-1/2
200	680	2/3	14
250	800	1	15
300	900	1	17
400	1,100	1-1/4	20
500	1,275	1-1/4	22
600	1,450	1-1/2	24
700	1,630	1-1/2	26
800	1,800	2	28
900	1,950	2	30
1,000	2,050	2	31
1,250	2,250	2-1/4	33
1,500	2,500	2-1/4	37
1,750	2,700	2-1/4	38
2,000	2,900	2-1/4	40
2,500	3,300	2-1/2	43
3,000	3,700	3	48
4,000	4,600	3/4	55
5,000	5,500	4-1/2	62
6,000	6,300	5	68
7,000	7,200	5-1/2	74
8,000	8,000	5-3/4	80
9,000	8,700	6-1/4	85
10,000	9,500	6-1/2	90
12,000	10,900	7	100
14,000	12,200	7-1/2	109
16,000	13,300	7-3/4	118
18,000	14,300	8	125
20,000	15,200	8-1/4	130
25,000	17,000	8-3/4	140
30,000	18,200	9	145
35,000	19,400	9-1/4	150
40,000	20,500	9-1/2	155
45,000	21,500	9-3/4	160

This exam question was drawn from the chart above:

In cubic feet per minute, what amount of ventilation is required for a machinery room with 600 pounds of refrigerant?

(A) 1000 cfm
(B) 1450 cfm
(C) 1650 cfm
(D) 2650 cfm

The correct answer is (B).

Sub-Article 4: Refrigerant Piping, Valves, Fitting, and Related Parts

C19–101.1: Metal enclosures or pipe ducts for soft copper tubing

Rigid or flexible metal enclosures shall be provided for the mechanical protection of soft anneal copper tubing used for refrigerant piping erected on the premises and containing other than Group 1 refrigerants. No enclosures shall be required for connections between condensing unit and nearest riser box, provided such connections do not exceed 6 feet in length.

C19–101.2: Specific minimum requirements for refrigerant pipe and tubing

a. Standard wall steel or wrought-iron pipe may be used for design-working pressures not exceeding 300 psig, provided lap-welded, electric-resistance-welded, or seamless pipe is used for sizes 2 inches and larger, and extra-strong wall pipe is used for liquid lines sizes 1 1/2 inches and smaller.

b. Standard iron-pipe-size copper and red brass (not less than 80 percent copper) pipe and tubing may be used.

c. Standard water-tube-size hard copper tubing of types K or L may be used for refrigerant piping erected on the premises. Minimum wall thickness shall be as follows:

Standard water tube Inches	Wall thickness Type K inches	Wall thickness Type L inches
1/2	.049	.040
5/8	.049	.042
3/4	.065	.045
1	.065	.050
1-1/4	.065	.055
1-1/2	.072	.060
2	.083	.070
2-1/2	.095	.080
3	.109	.090
3-1/2	.120	.100
4	.134	.110
5	.160	.125
6	.192	.140
8	.271	.200
10	.338	.250
12	.405	.280

Copper tubing with outside diameters of 3/8 inch and 1/4 inch must have a minimum nominal wall thickness of not less than 0.032 inch and 0.030 inch, respectively.

d. Standard soft annealed copper tubing used for refrigerant piping erected on the premises shall not be used in sizes larger than 7/8 inch outside diameter (3/4 inch nominal). It shall have minimum nominal wall thickness, as follows:

Outside diameter in inches	Wall thickness in inches
1/4	.030
3/8	.032
1/2	.032
5/8	.035
3/4	.042
7/8	.045

e. Sweat joints on copper tubing used in refrigerating systems containing Group 2 or Group 3 refrigerants shall be brazed joints. Soldered joints shall not be used for such refrigerants.

C19–101.3: Joints and refrigerant-containing parts in air ducts

Joints and all refrigerant-containing parts of a refrigerating system located in an air duct of an air-conditioning system for human comfort shall be constructed to withstand, without leakage, a temperature of 100° F.

C19–101.4: Stop valves

1. All systems containing more than 50 pounds of Group 1 refrigerant or 6 pounds of Group 2 or 3 refrigerant, other than systems utilizing nonpositive displacement compressors operating at less than 15 psig, shall have stop valves installed at

a. each inlet of each compressor, compressor unit, or condensing unit;
b. each discharge outlet of each compressor, compressor unit, or condensing unit, and of each liquid receiver.

2. All systems containing 100 pounds or more of a refrigerant, other than systems utilizing nonpositive displacement compressors operating at less than 15 psig, shall have stop valves, in addition to those in paragraph 1 of this section, on each inlet of each liquid receiver and each branch liquid and suction line, except that none shall be required on the inlet of a receiver in a condensing unit nor on the inlet of a receiver that is an integral part of a condenser.
3. Stop valves used with soft annealed copper tubing or hard-drawn copper tubing 3/4 inch nominal size or smaller shall be securely mounted, independent of tubing fastenings or supports.
4. Stop valves shall be labeled in the same manner as prescribed in Section C19–106.4 for exposed piping.

C19–102.0: Equipment design and testing

a. Every part of a refrigerating system, with the exception of pressure gauges and control mechanisms, shall be designed, constructed, and assembled to be capable of withstanding a test pressure not less than the minimum refrigerant leak field test pressure (as specified in the Field Test Pressure Chart), without being stressed beyond one third of its ultimate strength.
b. Every refrigerant containing part of every system, including pressure gauges and control mechanisms but excluding field-erected piping and tubing, shall be tested and proven tight by the manufacturer. The test pressure applied to either the high side or low side of each refrigerating system shall be at least equal to the design working pressure of the pressure vessels on the high- or low-side of the system, respectively, but not less than the minimum refrigerant leak test pressure specified in the Field Test Pressure Chart. Any component connecting to said pressure vessel shall be of sufficient strength to conform to the design requirements of a section.
c. Equipment listed by an approved nationally recognized testing laboratory having a follow-up inspection service shall be deemed as meeting the intent of the requirements of this section.

C19–102.1: Materials

All materials used in the construction and installation of refrigerating systems shall be suitable for conveying the refrigerant used. No material shall be used that will deteriorate because of the refrigerant, the oil, or the combination of both.

C19–102.2

Aluminum, zinc, or magnesium shall not be used in contact with methyl chloride in a refrigerating system. Magnesium alloys shall not be used in contact with any Freon refrigerant. Copper and copper alloys shall not be used in contact with ammonia.

C19–102.3

Pressure-limiting devices shall be provided on all systems containing more than 20 pounds of refrigerant and operating above atmospheric pressure and on all water-cooled systems so constructed that the compressor or generator is capable of producing a pressure in excess of the test pressure, except in water-cooled unit systems containing not more than 3 pounds of Group 1 refrigerant, providing the operating pressure developed in the system with the water supply shut-off does not exceed the refrigerant leak test pressure or providing an overload device will stop the action of the compressor before the pressure exceeds the refrigerant leak field test pressure.

C19–102.4: Maximum setting

The maximum setting to which a pressure-limiting device may readily be set by use of the adjusting means provided shall not exceed 90 percent of the setting of the pressure relief device, 90 percent of the refrigerant leak field test pressure actually applied, or 90 percent of the design working pressure of the high side of the system, whichever is smallest. The maximum setting of a pressure-limiting device is the maximum point at which the device functions to stop the action of the pressure-imposing element. In computing this maximum setting on systems erected in the field and tested in accordance with Section C19–106.0, the minimum leak field test pressure may be utilized in lieu of the field test pressure actually applied.

C19–102.5: Connections

Pressure-limiting devices shall be connected with no intervening stop valves between the pressure-imposing element and any stop valve on the discharge side.

C19–102.6

Liquid-level gauge glasses, except those of the bull's-eye or reflex type, shall have manual and automatic closing shut-off valves, and such glasses shall be adequately protected against injury.

C19–102.7
The dial of a pressure gauge, when the gauge is permanently installed on the high side of a refrigerating system, shall be graduated up to approximately double the opening pressure but in no case less than 1.2 times the design working pressure.

C19–102.8
Pressure gauges shall be checked for accuracy prior to an air test and immediately after the occasion of unusually high pressure, either by comparison with master gauges or by setting the pointer as a deadweight pressure gauge tester.

Group A: Refrigerant-Containing Pressure Vessels

C19–103.0: Refrigerant-containing vessels exceeding 6 inches in diameter
Refrigerant-containing pressure vessels, except those having a maximum allowable internal or external working pressure 15 psig or less, irrespective of size, or having an inside diameter of 6 inches or less, irrespective of pressure, shall comply with the rules of Section VIII of the 1952 edition of the ASME Boiler and Pressure Vessel Code covering the requirements for the design, fabrication, and inspection during construction of unfired pressure vessels.

C19–103.3: Safety devices
All pressure vessels shall be equipped with safety devices in accordance with the requirements of Group C of this sub-article.

Group B: Relief Devices in General

C19–104.0: Devices required
Every refrigerating system shall be protected by a pressure-relief device so constructed that pressure due to fire conditions will be safely relieved by soldered joints, lead gaskets, fusible plugs, or other parts of the system.

C19–104.1: Stop valve location
No stop valve shall be located between any automatic pressure-relief device or fusible plug and the part or parts of the system protected thereby, except when the parallel relief devices required in Section C19–105.3 are so arranged that only one can be rendered inoperative at a time for testing or repair purposes.

C19–104.2: Devices, where connected
All pressure-relief devices shall be connected as near as practicable directly to the pressure vessel or other parts of the system protected thereby, above the liquid refrigerant level, and installed so that they are accessible for inspection and repair and so that they cannot be readily rendered inoperative. Fusible plugs may be located above or below the liquid refrigerant level.

C19–104.3: Seats and discs, construction
The seats and discs of pressure-relief devices shall be constructed of suitable material to resist refrigerant corrosion or other chemical action caused by the refrigerant. Seats or discs of cast iron shall not be used.

C19–104.4: Discharge capacity, relief valve
The rated discharge capacity of a pressure-relief valve for a refrigerant-containing vessel, expressed in pounds of air per minute, shall be determined at a pressure at the inlet of the relief valve equal to 110 percent of the valve setting in accordance with Paragraph Ug-131, Section VIII of the 1952 edition of the ASME Boiler and Pressure Vessel Code.

C19–104.5: Discharge capacity, rupture member
The rated discharge capacity of a rupture member or fusible plug in pounds of air per minute shall be determined by the following formulas:

$$C = 0.6\, P_1 d^2$$

$$\text{or}\quad d = 1.29\sqrt{\frac{C}{P_1}}$$

Equation 1

where C = minimum required discharge capacity, in pounds of air per minute
and d = minimum diameter of bore of fusible plug or internal diameter of inlet pipe to rupture member in inches.
for rupture member:

P1 = bursting pressure equal to design working pressure, except that for Section C19–105.10, the bursting pressure equals 1.20 times design working pressure, psig.

for fusible plugs:

P1 = saturated pressure, corresponding to the stamped temperature melting of the fusible plug or the critical pressure of the refrigerant used, whichever is smaller, psig.

C19–104.6: Devices, pressure-actuated
All pressure-relief devices (not fusible plugs) shall be directly pressure-actuated. A rupture disk is an example of a pressure-actuated relief device.

C19–104.7: Discharge pipe, size

a. The size of the discharge pipe from the pressure-relief device shall not be less than the size of the relief device outlet. The discharge from more than one relief device may be run into a common header, the area of which shall be not less than the sum of the areas of the pipes connected thereto.

b. The sizing of discharge piping permitted to be installed on the outlet of a relief valve, rupture member, or fusible plug shall be determined from the following table. For determinations not covered by the table, the following formula shall be used:

$$C = \frac{3 P d^{3/2}}{L^{1/2}}$$

or

$$d = \sqrt[5]{\frac{C^2 L}{9 P^2}}$$

Equation 2

where C = minimum required discharge capacity in pounds of air per minute, d = internal diameter of pipe in inches, L = length of discharge pipe in feet, and P = 0.25P1 (P1 is defined under Equation 1).

Length of Discharge Piping for Relief Valves or Rupture Members of Various Discharge Capacities

Equivalent length of discharge pipe in feet
Discharge capacity in pounds pf air per minute (C)
Standard wall iron pipes, sizes, inches

(L)	1/2	3/4	1	1-1/4	1-1/2	2	2-1/2	3
50	0.81	1.6	2.9	5.9	8.7	16.3	25.3	43.8
75	0.67	1.4	2.4	4.9	7.2	13.3	20.9	35.8
100	0.58	1.2	2.1	4.2	6.2	11.5	18.0	30.9
150	0.47	0.95	1.7	3.4	5.0	9.4	14.6	25.3
200	0.41	0.8	1.5	2.9	4.4	8.1	12.6	21.8
300	0.33	0.67	1.2	2.4	3.6	6.6	10.5	17.9
Relief device set at 50 psig (P1)								
50	1.6	3.3	5.9	11.9	17.4	32.5	50.6	87.6
75	1.3	2.7	4.9	9.7	14.3	26.5	41.8	71.5
100	1.2	2.3	4.2	8.4	12.3	23.0	36.0	61.7
150	0.94	1.9	3.5	6.9	10.0	18.7	29.2	50.6
200	0.81	1.6	2.9	5.9	8.7	16.3	25.3	43.7
300	0.66	1.3	2.5	4.9	7.1	13.3	21.0	35.7
Relief device set at 75 psig (P1)								
50	2.4	4.9	8.9	17.9	26.1	48.7	75.9	131.5
75	2.0	4.1	7.3	14.6	21.4	39.8	62.8	107.0
100	1.7	3.5	6.4	12.6	18.5	34.4	54.0	92.6
150	1.4	2.8	5.2	10.3	15.0	28.0	43.8	75.9
200	1.2	2.5	4.4	8.9	13.1	24.4	37.9	65.6
300	0.9	2.0	3.7	7.3	10.7	19.9	31.5	53.5
Relief device set at 100 psig (P1)								
50	3.2	6.6	11.9	23.8	34.8	65.0	101.2	175.2
75	2.7	5.4	9.7	19.4	28.6	53.0	83.6	143.0
100	2.3	4.6	8.5	16.8	24.6	45.9	72.0	123.6
150	1.9	3.8	6.9	13.7	20.0	37.4	58.4	101.2
200	1.6	3.3	5.9	11.9	17.5	32.5	50.6	87.6
300	1.3	2.7	4.9	9.7	14.2	26.5	42.0	1.4
Relief device set at 150 psig (P1)								
50	4.9	9.9	17.9	35.7	52.3	97.5	151.8	262.8
75	4.0	8.1	14.6	29.2	42.9	79.5	125.5	214.5
100	3.5	6.9	12.7	25.2	36.9	68.9	108.0	185.4
150	2.8	5.7	10.4	20.6	30.6	56.1	87.6	151.8
200	2.4	4.9	8.9	17.8	26.2	48.7	75.9	131.4
300	1.9	4.0	7.4	14.6	21.1	39.7	63.0	107.1
Relief device set at 200 psig (P1)								
50	6.5	13.2	23.8	47.6	69.7	130.0	202.4	350.4
75	5.3	10.8	19.4	38.9	57.2	106.0	167.2	286.0
100	4.6	9.2	16.9	33.6	49.2	91.8	144.0	247.2
150	3.8	7.6	13.8	27.4	40.0	74.8	116.8	202.4
200	3.2	6.5	11.8	23.8	34.9	64.9	101.2	175.2
300	2.6	5.3	9.8	19.4	28.4	52.9	84.0	142.8

C19–104.8: Pressure-relief devices for positive displacement compressors

Positive displacement compressors operating above 15 pounds per square inch gauge and having a displacement exceeding 50 cubic feet per minute shall be equipped by the manufacturer with a pressure-relief device to prevent rupture of the compressor. The device is located between the compressor and stop valve on the discharge side. The discharge from such relief device may be vented to the atmosphere or into the low-pressure side of the system.

C19–104.9: Discharge of pressure-relief devices and fusible plugs

On all systems containing more than 6 pounds of Group 2 or 3 refrigerant, discharge shall be to the outside of the building. On systems containing more than 100 pounds of Group 1 refrigerant, discharge of the pressure-relief device and fusible plugs shall be to the outside of the building. Discharge of Group 1 refrigerants to the outside of the building shall be not less than 12 feet above the grade level and the discharge shall be turned downward. Discharge of systems employing Group 2 or Group 3 shall be approved by the fire department.

C19–104.10: Pressure-relief devices discharging into the low side of the system

Pressure-relief devices may discharge into the low side of the system, provided the pressure-relief devices are of a type not appreciably affected by back pressures and provided the low side of the system is equipped with pressure-relief devices. Pressure relief devices on the low side of the system shall have sufficient capacity to protect the pressure vessels that are relieved into the low side of the system or to protect all pressure vessels on the low side of the system, whichever relieving capacity is the larger, as computed in Section C19–105.8.

C19–104.11: Sulphur dioxide discharge

Where sulphur dioxide is used, the discharge may be put into a tank of absorptive brine that shall be used for no purpose except sulphur dioxide absorption. There shall be one gallon of standard dichromate brine (2 1/2 pounds sodium dichromate per gallon of water) for each pound of sulphur dioxide in the system. The tank shall be substantially constructed of not less than 1/8 inch Number 11 U.S. gauge iron or steel. The tank shall have a hinged cover, or if of the enclosed type, shall have a vent hole at the top. All pipe connections shall be through the top of the tank only. The discharge pipe from the pressure relief valve shall discharge the sulphur dioxide in the center of the tank near the bottom.

Group C: Relief Device for Pressure Vessels

C19–105.0: General

The rules of this Group C are based upon those given in paragraphs UG–125 to UG–134, inclusive, of Section VIII of the 1952 edition of the ASME Boiler and Pressure Vessel Code, with such additional modifications as are necessary for control of refrigerants.

C19–105.1: Pressure vessels over 3 cubic feet

Each pressure vessel containing liquid refrigerant with internal gross volume exceeding 3 cubic feet, except as specified in Section C19–105.7, and that may be shut off by valves from all other parts of a refrigerating system shall be protected by a pressure-relief device having capacity computed in accordance with Section C 19–105.8.

C19–105.2: Pressure vessels over 3 cubic feet but under 10 cubic feet

Under conditions specified in Section C19–105.1, a single relief device (relief valve or rupture member) may be used on pressure vessels having less than 10 cubic feet gross volume.

C19–105.3: Pressure vessels over 10 cubic feet

Under the conditions specified in Section C19–105.1, a pressure-relief valve in parallel with rupture member or second pressure-relief valve shall be provided on pressure vessels having a gross volume of 10 cubic feet or over. Each pressure-relief valve or rupture member shall have capacity computed in accordance with Section C19–105.8.

Under conditions permitted in Section C19–104.10 governing discharge of relief valves in the low side of the system, a single relief valve (not rupture member) of the required relieving capacity may be used.

C19–105.4: Pressure vessels with gross volume of 3 cubic feet or less

Each pressure vessel having a gross volume of 3 cubic feet or less; containing liquid refrigerant, except as specified in Section C19–105.7; and that may be shut off by valves from other parts of a refrigerating system shall be protected by a pressure-relief device or fusible plug. A fusible plug is permitted only on the high side of a refrigerating system. Pressure vessels of less than 3 inches I. D. (Inside Diameter) are exempt from pressure-relief requirements.

C19–105.5: Relief valves on pressure vessels with gross volume of 3 cubic feet or less

If a relief valve or rupture member is used to protect a pressure vessel, the ultimate bursting pressure of the pressure vessel so protected shall be at least 2 1/2 times the pressure setting of the pressure relief valve or rupture member.

C19–105.6: Fusible plugs on pressure vessels with gross volume of 3 cubic feet or less

If a fusible plug is used, the ultimate bursting pressure of the pressure vessel so protected shall be at least 2 1/2 times the refrigerant saturation pressure, psig, corresponding to the stamped temperature on the fusible plug, or at least 2 1/2 times the critical pressure of the refrigerant used, whichever is smaller.

(*Author's note:* Whenever a question relating to fusible plugs is asked on the license exam, it is presumed that a predetermined temperature will burst them, not pressure.)

C19–105.7: Relief device for pressure vessels used as or as part of the evaporator
Pressure vessels having internal diameters greater than 6 inches, used as or as part of evaporators insulated or installed in insulated space, and that may be shut off by valves from all other parts of a refrigerating system shall be protected by a pressure-relief device in accordance with the provisions stated, except that the provisions of Section C19–105.3, requiring a second parallel relief device, shall not apply. Such pressure vessels having internal diameters of 6 inches or less are exempt from pressure-relief requirements.

C19–105.8: Required capacity
The minimum required rated discharge capacity of the pressure-relief device or fusible plug for a refrigerant-containing vessel shall be determined by the following formula:

$$C = fDL$$

where C = minimum required discharge capacity of the relief device in pounds of air per minute,

D = outside diameter of the vessel in feet, L = length of the vessel in feet, and f = factor dependent upon kind of refrigerant as follows:

Kind of refrigerant	Value of f
Ammonia	0.5
R-12	R-22
All other refrigerants	1.0

C19–105.9: Pressure-relief device setting
Except as permitted in Section C19–105.5, all pressure-relief devices shall be set to start functioning at a pressure not to exceed the design working pressure of the pressure vessel as determined by the manufacturer and stamped on the pressure vessel or system.

C19–105.10: Rupture member setting when used in parallel with relief valves
Rupture members used in parallel with pressure-relief valves on refrigerant-containing vessels shall function at a pressure not to exceed 20 percent above the design working pressure of the vessel.

Sub-article 6: Field Tests and Operating Precautions

C19–106.0: General
Every refrigerant-containing part of every system that is erected on the premises, except compressors, condensers, evaporators, safety devices, pressure gauges, and control mechanisms that are factory sealed, shall be tested and proved tight after complete installation and before operation, at not less than the minimum refrigerant-leak test pressures shown in the following table.

Systems erected on the premises using 20 pounds or less of Group 1 refrigerant may be tested by means of the refrigerant charged into the system at the saturated vapor pressure of the refrigerant at 70° F or more for the low side and during operation at normal working pressures for the high side.

Refrigerant name	Minimum refrigerant eak field test pressures: High side psig	Low side psig
Ammonia	300	150
Butane	95	50
Carbon dioxide	1500	1000
Dichlorodifluoromethane (R-12)	235	140
Dichlorodifluoromethane and Ethylidene	285	150
Dichloroethylene	30	30
Dichloromethane (C-1) Methylene chloride	30	30
Dichloromonofluoromethane (R-21)	70	40
Dichlorotetrafluoroethane (R-114)	50	50
Ethane (R-170)	1200	700
Ethyl chloride	60	50
Ethylene (R-1150)	1600	1200
Isobutane	130	70
Methyl chloride (R-40)	210	120
Methyl formate	50	50
Monochlorodifluoromethane (R-22)	300	150
Propane (R-290)	300	150
Sulphur Dioxide (R-764)	170	85
Trichloromonofluoromethane (R-11)	30	30
Trichlorotrifluoroethane (R-113)	30	30

C19–106.1: Test medium
No oxygen, air, or any combustible gas or combustible mixture of gases shall be used within the system for testing.

1. For refrigerants not listed in the table above, the test pressure for the high-pressure side shall not be less than the saturated vapor pressure of the refrigerant

at 150° F, while the test pressure for the low-pressure side shall be not less than the saturated vapor pressure of the refrigerant at 110° F. In no case shall the test pressure be less than 30 psig.

2. When a compressor is used as a booster to obtain a low pressure and discharge into the suction line of another system, the booster compressor is considered part of the low side, and values listed under the low-side column of the table above shall be used for both high and low sides of the booster compressor. A low-pressure stage compressor of the positive displacement type must have a pressure-relief valve.
3. In field-testing systems with nonpositive displacement compressors, the entire system shall be considered (for field-test purposes) as the low-side pressure.

(As amended by local law 65, effective October 30, 1958)

C19–106.2: Posting of tests

A date declaration of test shall be provided for all systems in which the prime mover or compressor is more than 15 horsepower or its equivalent in kilowatts where required by Section C19–106.0. The declaration shall be mounted in a frame protected by glass and posted in the machinery room, and it shall give the name of the refrigerant and the field refrigerant leak test pressure applied to the high and low sides of the system. The declaration of test shall be signed by the installer.

C19–106.3: Signs

Each refrigerating system erected on the premises shall be provided with an easily legible permanent sign securely attached and easily accessible, indicating thereon the name and address of the installer, the horsepower of the prime mover or compressor or the equivalent thereof in kilowatts, the kind and total number of pounds of refrigerant required in the system for normal operation, and the refrigerant-leak field test pressure applied. Each refrigerating system not erected on the premises and for which a permit is required under this article shall have stamped thereon the horsepower of the prime mover or compressor or the equivalent thereof in kilowatts and the kind and total pounds of refrigerant required in the system for normal operation or shall have affixed thereto a metal plate containing the same information. The stamp or plate shall be easily legible and placed in a readily accessible position.

C19–106.4: Metal signs for systems whose prime mover or compressor is 25 horsepower or more or the equivalent thereof in kilowatts

Systems whose prime mover or compressor is 25 horsepower or more or the equivalent thereof in kilowatts shall be provided with metal signs having letters not less than 1/2 inch in height designating the main stop valves to each vessel, main steam or electrical control, remote control switch, and pressure-limiting device. On all exposed high-pressure and low-pressure piping in each room where installed outside the machinery room shall be signs as specified above, with the name of the refrigerant and letters "HP" or "LP."

C19–106.5: New signs for changed refrigerant

When the kind of refrigerant is changed as provided in section C19–106.10 (substitution of refrigerant), there shall be a new sign of the same type in Section C19–106.4 indicating clearly that a substitution has been made and stating the same information for the new refrigerant as was required in the original.

C19–106.6: Nameplate

Each separately condensing unit or compressor sold for field assembly in a refrigerating system shall carry a nameplate marked with the manufacturer's name, nationally registered trademark or trade name, identification number, horsepower of the prime mover or compressor or the equivalent of such horsepower in kilowatts, and name of the refrigerant for which it is designed.

C19–106.7: Charging and discharging refrigerants

When refrigerant is added to a system, except a unit system requiring less than 6 pounds of refrigerant, it shall be charged on the low-pressure side of the system. Any point on the downstream side of the main liquid-line stop valve shall be considered part of the low-pressure side when operating with said stop valve in the closed position. No service container shall be left connected to a system, except while charging or withdrawing refrigerant.

C19–106.8

Refrigerants withdrawn from refrigerating systems shall be transferred to Interstate Commerce Commission-approved containers only. No refrigerant shall be discharged to a sewer except in emergency, and then only under the supervision of the department.

C19–106.9

Containers used for refrigerant withdrawn from a refrigerating system shall be carefully weighed each time they are used for this purpose, and the containers shall not be filled in excess of the permissible filing weight for such containers and such refrigerants as are prescribed in the pertinent regulations of the Interstate Commerce Commission and in no case more than 75 percent of the container capacity.

C19–106.10: Substitution of kind of refrigerant
Substitution of the kind of refrigerant in a system shall not be made without the permission of the department and due observance of safety requirements, including the following:

- **a.** the effects of the substituted refrigerant on materials in the system;
- **b.** the possibility of overloading the liquid receiver, which shall not be more than 80 percent full of liquid;
- **c.** the liability of exceeding motor horsepower, design working pressure, or any other element that would violate any of the provisions of this article;
- **d.** the proper size of refrigerant controls;
- **e.** the effect on the operation and setting of safety devices;
- **f.** the possible hazards created by mixture of the original and the substituted refrigerant; and
- **g.** effect of the classification of the refrigerant as provided in this code.

C19–106.11
Refrigerant stored in a machinery room shall be not more than 20 percent of the normal refrigerant charged nor more than 300 pounds of the refrigerant, in addition to the charge in the system and the refrigerant stored in a permanently attached receiver, and then only in Interstate Commerce Commission-approved storage containers.

C19–106.12: Breathing apparatus
One service mask shall be provided at a location convenient to the machinery room when an amount of a Group 2 refrigerant between 100 and 1,000 pounds, inclusive, is employed. If more than 1,000 pounds of a Group 2 refrigerant are employed, at least two such masks shall be provided. Only all service masks marked as approved by the Bureau of Mines of the United States Department of the Interior shall be used, and they shall be kept in a suitable cabinet immediately outside the machinery room or other appropriate accessible location. Since the 1990s, the Environmental Protection Agency (EPA) monitors safety regulations for HVAC systems in the United States.

C19–106.13: Maintenance
All refrigerating systems shall be maintained by the user in a clean condition, free from accumulations of oily dirt, waste, and other debris, and shall be kept readily accessible at all times.

C19–106.14: Emergency instructions
A refrigerating system whose prime mover or compressor is more than 15 horsepower or equivalent in kilowatts shall have a sign permanently fastened as near as practicable to the refrigerant compressor, giving instructions for the operation of the system, including precautions to be observed in case of a breakdown or leaks, as follows:

- **a.** Instructions for shutting down the system in case of emergency
- **b.** Name, address, and day and night telephone numbers for service
- **c.** Fire Department telephone number and instructions to notify said department immediately in case of an emergency
- **d.** Where such systems are installed in machinery rooms, instructions posted in a prominent place shall state that in case of emergency or refrigerant leakage, the machinery room shall be vacated promptly, the system shut down by means of the required remote controls located outside the machinery room, and the room ventilated.

Sub-article 7: Permits and Administration

C19–107.0: Permits

1. Except as otherwise provided in this article, it shall be unlawful to maintain or operate a refrigerating system without a permit.
2. Permits shall not be required for systems installed in the residence portion of any building; nor for any system installed in vehicles, vessels, or railroad cars; nor for any system employing water or air as a refrigerant; nor for any unit system having a compressor or prime mover of 1 horsepower or less and used for the purpose of human comfort cooling or for the chilling of drinking water in a freestanding self-contained water cooler.
3. Applications for permits shall be submitted to the department on department forms and shall be signed by the owner of the premises, his duly authorized representative, or the lessee seeking such permit. Plans or sketches showing machinery locations and pressure-relief devices shall be submitted when required by the Fire Department.

Ammonia Mixer
By law, ammonia mixer pressure is 50 psig. If a system contains up to 27,000 pounds of ammonia, one mixer is required. An additional mixer is required for each 27,000 pounds of ammonia or any portion of this amount.

The ammonia-line connection from the system can be taken from any point on the low side of the system. It can be connected from the outlet side of the system or from the outlet side of the expansion valve, up to the suction side of the compressor.

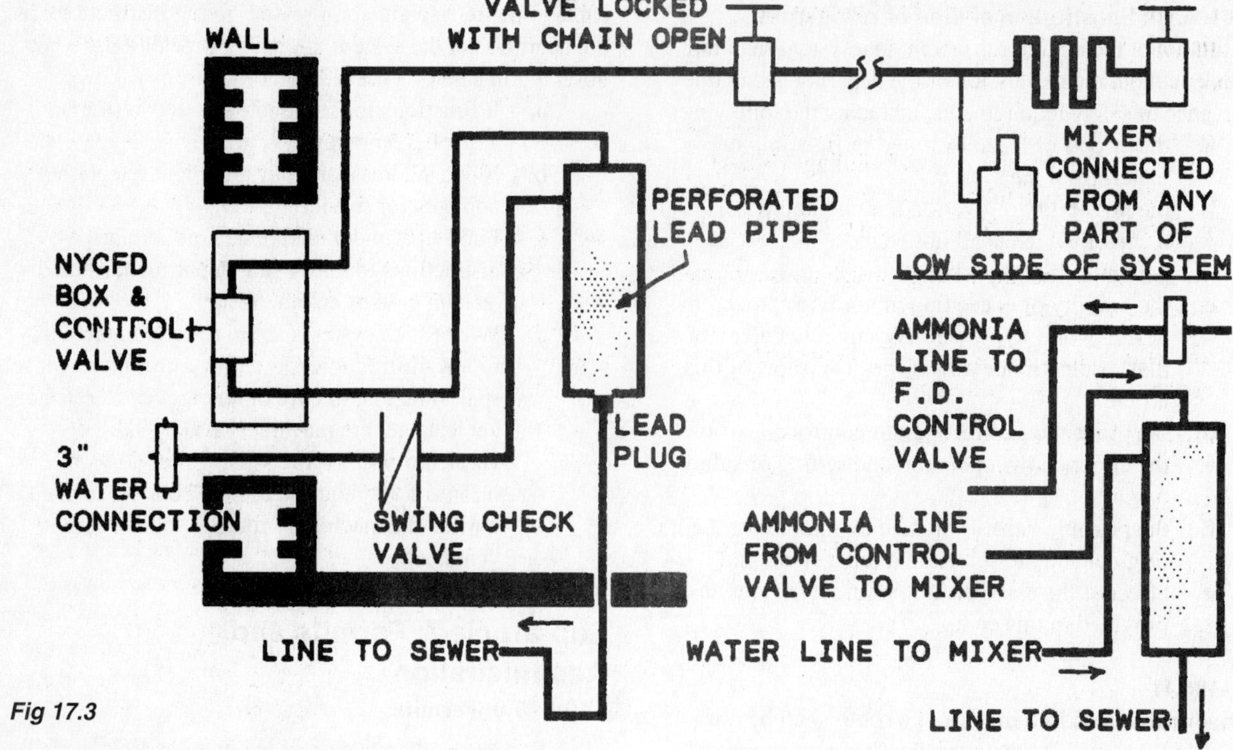

Fig 17.3

Reference standard RS13: list of referenced national standards for mechanical ventilation, air conditioning, and refrigeration systems.

ANSI-B9.1: American National Standard for mechanical refrigeration. Outlines specific requirements for the testing of pressure-relief valves.

ANSI B136.1/UL353: limit controls; revision November 1976, 1974.

ANSI-B57.1: compressed gas cylinder valve outlet and inlet connections code.

ANSI B60.1/ASHRAE 15: safety code for mechanical refrigeration, 1978. Mechanical refrigeration used with air duct systems shall be installed in accordance with nationally recognized safety practices and the ANSI/ASHRAE 15–1978 safety code for mechanical refrigeration.

ANSI-B70.1: American National Standard for refrigeration flare-type fittings. Outlines accurately all the dimensions required on refrigeration flare-type fittings.

ANSI B144.1/UL465: standard for central cooling air conditioners; revision May 1981, 1978.

ANSI Z263/UL 303: standard for refrigeration and air conditioning, condensing and compressor units; revision March 1982, 1980.

ANSI/NFIPA 90A: standard for the installation of air conditioning.

ANSI Z263/UL 207: standard for refrigerant-containing components and non-electrical accessories, 1982 913–82 BCR; local law 80–1973.

Article 5 (C26–1304.3) 27–786 refrigeration: Fire Department issues, operating permits, and qualifications for refrigeration.

New York State Environmental Protection Act, chapter 294, amendment 1990, effective January 1, 1992: prohibits intentional venting or release of CFC refrigerants during the service or repair of air conditioning equipment.

U.S. Clean Air Act of 1990, effective July 1, 1992: prohibits intentional venting of CFC and HCFC refrigerants during the service or repair of air-conditioning equipment. Title Seven of this act provides for fines and penalties up to $10,000 for violators and a bounty up to $25,000 for individuals reporting such violations. The bounty is paid by the violators.

Local Law 16–1984 and Ventilating Systems, as Modified 1981

1-1 Definitions

accepted: The Material and Equipment Acceptance Division of the Department of Buildings (MEA) considers a system to meet requirements of Building Code Sections C26–106.2 and C26–107.2.

air inlet: any opening through which air is removed from a space back to a system.

air outlet: any opening through which air is delivered to a space from a system.

air terminal unit: an appliance receiving, conditioning, and delivering air supplied through a duct system.

authority having jurisdiction: the Commissioner of the Department of Buildings or his or her designee.

blower: a fan used to force air under pressure into an area.

duct: a conduit for conveying air.

duct system: a continuous passageway for the transmission or air that, in addition to ducts, may include duct fittings, dampers, plenums, fans, and accessory air-handling equipment.

fan: a blower or exhaust fan comprising blades or runners and housing or casing.

fire damper: a device, installed in an air distribution system, designed to close automatically upon detection of heat, to interrupt migratory air flow, and to restrict the passage of flame. A combination fire and smoke damper shall meet the requirements of both.

fire-resistance rating: the time, in minutes or hours, that materials or assemblies have withstood a fire exposure, as established by the test procedures of NFIPA 251–1979, Standard Methods of Fire Tests of Building Construction and Materials.

New York State Environmental Protection Act, Chapter 294 Amendment

The New York State Department of Environmental Conservation drafted regulations to implement Chapter 294, a law passed in 1990. Regulations are consistent with Clean Air Act dates established for recovering and recycling CFCs from motor vehicle air-conditioning systems, stationary air-conditioning, and refrigeration equipment subject to the law. Motor vehicle repair shops are required to state whether they intend to service air-conditioning systems within the next two years.

Since January 1, 1992, Chapter 294 has required that no CFCs shall knowingly be vented into the atmosphere or otherwise be improperly disposed of during the repair or servicing of refrigeration systems but instead shall to the greatest extent possible be captured for recycling. Refrigeration systems shall include refrigerators used in retail stores, cold-storage warehouse refrigeration systems, and air-conditioning systems in large buildings commonly referred to as chillers.

Captured CFC refrigerants must be recycled to a uniform level of quality, such as that specified by the Air Conditioning and Refrigeration Institute's Standard 700 "Specification for Fluorocarbon Refrigerants."

Since January 1, 1991, persons repairing or servicing motor vehicle air conditioners have been prohibited from knowingly venting CFCs into the atmosphere. The law requires that, to the greatest extent possible, such persons should capture and recycle the CFC compounds during servicing and repair of such air conditioners by properly using approved refrigerant recycling equipment. The law bans the use or sale of containers containing less than 20 pounds of CFCs, except to persons who use approved recycling equipment. It also bans nonessential products containing CFCs.

Since January 1, 1992, disposal of motor vehicle air conditioners by any means has been prohibited until the CFCs they contain are captured for recycling. Any local law, ordinance, rule, or regulation relating to sale, use, reuse, reclamation, or disposal of CFCs must be identical to or the same as the provisions of this law and the rules and regulations adopted under it.

Since January 1, 1992, the Clean Air Act has prohibited the sale or purchase of containers or packaging materials for which CFCs or HCFCs are used as a blowing agent, such as aerosol spray cans and nonessential items containing CFCs.

A 549—KELLEHER

Since January 1, 1992, it has been unlawful to operate on any public highway or street in the state any motor vehicle registered in New York state, manufactured or assembled after said date and designated as a 1993 or subsequent model, if the motor vehicle has an air-conditioning unit using any fluorocarbon as a coolant.

Energy Bill Amendment

On February 6, 1992, Senator Al Gore of Tennessee proposed an energy bill amendment to phase out chemicals that damage the ozone layer. The trend toward halting CFC manufacture is forcing many industries to redouble their efforts to find substitutes, while recycling those CFCs already in use.

U.S. Clean Air Act

On February 12, 1992, President Bush directed American manufacturers to end virtually all production of chemicals that destroy ozone by December 31, 1995. The policy was authorized under a provision of the 1990 U.S. Clean Air Act. The President's order affects a family of chlorine- and bromine-based chemicals widely used in American industry as solvents, refrigerants, fire retardants, and feedstocks for other chemicals. These chemicals are chlorofluorocarbons, halons, methyl chloroform, and carbon tetrachloride.

Effective January 1, 1994, the bill prohibits the sale or purchase of CFC-based room or window air-conditioning units and automobile air-conditioning units. On this date, the EPA Commissioner is authorized to issue rules and regulations to reduce or prohibit uses of HCFC–22 and HCFC–141(b) and to schedule the phased reduction in use, ending their use by the year 2000.

Effective January 1, 1995, no person may sell CFC-based refrigerators and freezers, cold-storage warehouse refrigeration and freezer systems, or air-conditioning systems.

Effective January 1, 2000, no person may sell or purchase any compounds of CFCs or HCFCs or any product containing these compounds.

SECTION III: PROPOSED REGULATIONS ON SECTION 608 OF THE CLEAN AIR ACT—REFRIGERANT RECYCLING AND THE PROHIBITION ON VENTING

Definitions

refrigerant recovery: removal of refrigerant from a system and storage of it in an external container with the lowest emissions possible. The Environmental Protection Agency recommends that a 95 percent minimum of refrigerant should be recovered during this procedure. The recovered refrigerant may not be used in another system, except as specified by the Air Conditioning and Refrigeration Institute (ARI).

refrigerant recycling: The process of cleaning a refrigerant of dirt and contaminates, such as oil, acid, foreign material, and noncondensables.

refrigerant reclamation: The reprocessing of refrigerant into a new product that can be reused in another system. The refrigerant may have to undergo a distillation process and chemical analysis. The reprocessed refrigerant is considered a new product but is sold as "reclaimed refrigerant."

Proposed Regulations

The following are the latest regulations proposed by the Environment Protection Agency on the recycling requirements of Section 608 of the Clean Air Act, including regulations proposed on December 10, 1992 (57 FR 58644) and effective July 1, 1992.

Under Section 608 of the Clean Air Act, EPA is proposing regulations that would

a. require service practices that maximize recycling of ozone-depleting compounds—both chlorofluorocarbons (CFCs) and hydrochlorofluorocarbons (HCFCs)—during the servicing and disposal of air-conditioning and refrigeration equipment;

b. set certification requirements for reclaimers and for recovery and recycling equipment; and

c. establish safe disposal requirements to ensure removal of refrigerants from goods that enter the waste stream with the charge intact. Examples of affected goods are motor vehicle air conditioners, home refrigerators, and room air conditioners.

The Prohibition on Venting

Effective July 1, 1992, Section 608 of the act prohibits individuals from knowingly venting ozone-depleting compounds used as refrigerants into the atmosphere while maintaining, servicing, repairing, or disposing air-conditioning or refrigeration equipment. Only three types of releases are permitted under the prohibition:

1. "De minimis" quantities of refrigerant released in the course of making good-faith attempts to recapture and recycle or safely dispose of refrigerant.
2. Refrigerants emitted in the course of normal operation of air-conditioning and refrigeration equipment (as opposed to during the maintenance, servicing, repair, or disposal of this equipment), such as from leaks and mechanical purging.
3. Mixtures of nitrogen and R-22 that are used as holding charges or as leak test gases, because in

these cases the ozone-depleting compound is not used as a refrigerant.

The Environmental Protection Agency recognizes that some common maintenance and repair procedures that are not associated with efforts to recover or recycle may release a small quantity of refrigerant. Such releases constitute violation of the prohibition on venting. However, the EPA will consider the circumstances of a refrigerant release, including the magnitude of the release and the availability of technology to control it, in determining whether or not to pursue an enforcement action.

Proposed Regulatory Requirements

Service Practice Requirements

Under the proposed regulation, technicians would be required to evacuate air conditioning and refrigeration equipment to established vacuum levels. If the technician's recovery or recycling equipment were manufactured any time up to six months after publication of the final rule, the air conditioning and refrigeration equipment would have to be evacuated to the levels described in Table 2. If the technician's recovery or recycling equipment were manufactured more than six months after the publication of the final rule, the air conditioning and refrigeration equipment would have to be evacuated to the levels described in Table 1.

Table 1 Proposed standards for recovery and recycling equipment manufactured more than six months after publication of the final rule (excluding small appliances)

Types of air-conditioning or refrigeration equipment with which recycling or recovery is to be used	Inches of vacuum that must be achieved by recovery or recycling equipment
High-pressure equipment with a charge of less than 50 pounds	10
High-pressure equipment with a charge of more than 50 pounds	20
Very high-pressure equipment (13,503)	0
Intermediate pressure equipment (114)	25
Low-pressure equipment	29

Under the proposal, recovery equipment intended for use by a technician on small appliances, such as household refrigerators, household freezers, and water coolers, must recover 80 to 90 percent of the refrigerant in the system.

EPA data indicate that most recovery and recycling equipment currently on the market can meet the standards described above. Under the proposal, self-built equipment would be grandfathered provided it met those standards.

The EPA is also proposing that refrigerant recovered and/or recycled could be returned to the same system or other systems owned by the same person without restriction. If refrigerant changed ownership, however, that refrigerant would have to be reclaimed; that is, it would have to be cleaned to the ARI 700 standard of purity and chemically analyzed to verify that it meets this standard.

In developing these regulations, the EPA has considered other options permitting limited off-site recycling. These options have not been proposed, as there is currently no guarantee that an individual recycling machine is capable of removing acids and moisture to ensure safe refrigerant reuse. In the future, a "clean-up" standard may be developed. If and when this occurs, the EPA will view off-site recycling with more confidence.

Equipment Certification

The EPA is proposing a certificate program for recovery and recycling equipment. Under the program, it would require testing of equipment manufactured more than six months after the final rule is published to ensure that it minimized refrigerant emissions during the recycling process. The EPA is proposing recovery efficiency standards that vary depending on the size and type of air-conditioning or refrigeration equipment being serviced. These standards are the same as those in Table 1.

Table 2 Proposed standards for the grandfathering of recovery and recycling equipment manufactured until six months after publication of the final rule (excluding equipment used with small applicances)

Type of air conditioning or refrigeration equipment with which recycling or recovery is to be used	Inches of vacuum that must be achieved by recovery or recycling equipment
High-pressure equipment with less than 50 pounds (R-12, R-22, R-500, R-502)	4
High-pressure equipment with a charge of more than 50 pounds	4
Equipment at intermediate or low pressure (R-11, R-113, R-114, R-123)	25

Grandfathering Provisions

Recycling or recovery equipment used to comply with the prohibition on venting does not have to meet any particular standards at this time. Technicians purchasing such equipment, however, may wish to consider the standards that it would have to meet in order to be grandfathered under the EPA's proposal. These standards, which would apply to all equipment manufactured until six months after the final rule is published, are described in Table 2.

Refrigerant Leaks and Purging

The EPA's proposal addresses refrigerant releases that take place during servicing and disposal of air-conditioning and refrigeration equipment, because such releases account for between 50 and 95 percent of total emissions over the lifetime of this equipment. Once the EPA issues final refrigerant recycling regulations, it will begin to focus on emissions of CFCs and HCFCs during normal operations of equipment, such as leaks and purging. Although the EPA recommends that technicians make every effort to repair leaks and utilize high-efficiency purges, technicians are not required to meet purge-efficiency or leak test requirements at this time.

Voluntary Technician Certification

The EPA plans to establish a voluntary technician certification program. It is considering establishing four types of certification:

1. Servicing household appliances
2. Servicing equipment containing less than 50 pounds of high-pressure refrigerant (R-12, 22, 500, 502)
3. Servicing equipment containing 50 pounds of high-pressure refrigerant
4. Servicing equipment using low- or intermediate-pressure refrigerants (R-11, 113, 114, 123)

Technicians wishing to become certified under the voluntary program would be required to pass an EPA-approved test.

Contractor and Reclaimer Certification

The EPA proposes to require contractor and reclaimer certification. Contractors would be required to have recovery or recycling equipment to perform on-site recovery or recycling. Reclaimers would be required to return refrigerant to the purity level specified in ARI-700 (an industry-set purity standard) and to verify this purity using the laboratory protocol set forth in the same standard.

Safe Disposal Requirements

Under the EPA's proposal, equipment that is typically dismantled on site before disposal (for example, retail food refrigeration, cold storage warehouse refrigeration, chillers, and industrial process refrigeration) would have to have the refrigerant removed and recovered in accordance with the EPA's requirements for servicing.

However, equipment that typically enters the waste stream with charge intact (for example, motor-vehicle air conditioners, household refrigerators, freezers, and window air conditioners) would be subject to special disposal requirements.

Under these requirements, the final person in the disposal chain (for example, a scrap-metal recycler or landfill owner) would be responsible for ensuring that refrigerant is recovered from equipment before the final disposal of the equipment. In addition, persons "upstream" can remove the refrigerant and provide documentation of its removal to the final person, if this is more cost-effective.

Hazardous Waste Disposal

If refrigerants are recycled or reclaimed, they are not considered hazardous under federal law. In addition, used oils contaminated with CFCs are not hazardous if

1. they are not mixed with other waste;
2. they are subject to CFC recycling or reclamation; and
3. they are not mixed with used oils from other sources.

Used oils that contain CFCs after the CFC reclamation procedure are, however, subject to specification limits for used oil fuels if these oils are destined for burning.

Enforcement

The EPA is responding to tips reporting venting. Under the Act, the EPA is authorized to assess fines of up to $25,000 per day per violation of the Act. In addition, the EPA may pay an award, not to exceed $10,000, to any person who furnishes information or services that lead to a criminal conviction or a judicial or administrative civil penalty assessed as a result of a violation of the Act. These dollar amounts are maximum figures and are not necessarily the amount that will be assessed or paid in all cases.

REFRIGERATION CODE LICENSE QUESTIONS

1. The amount of ventilation required for a machinery room with 1,500 pounds of refrigerant is
   (A) 2,050 cfm.
   (B) 2,650 cfm.
   (C) 2,500 cfm.
   (D) 3,000 cfm.

2. The amount of ammonia permitted in a Class T machinery room for a commercial building is
   (A) 300 lbs.
   (B) 1,000 lbs.
   (C) 500 lbs.
   (D) unlimited.

3. Refrigerant piping across a passageway in any building must not be less than which of the following heights above the floor?
   (A) 7′
   (B) 7′2″
   (C) 7′6″
   (D) 7′8″

4. There is a check valve in the water line, from the Fire Department box. Its purpose is
   (A) to stop the NH_3 from backing up into the fire engine pump and damaging the impeller.
   (B) to make sure that the water goes in only one direction.
   (C) to make sure that the ammonia mixes well with water.
   (D) to make sure that the city water is not contaminated.

5. The U.S. Clean Air Act of 1990 most nearly
   (A) recognizes that some common maintenance and repair procedures are not associated with recovery or recycling.
   (B) prohibits intentional venting or release of CFC or HCFC during the service or repair of air-conditioning equipment.
   (C) prohibits the sale or purchase of containers or package materials of CFC or HCFC and nonessential items containing CFC.
   (D) describes the process of cleaning a refrigerant of dirt and contaminants, such as oil, acid, and foreign material.

6. Soft copper tubing containing other than Group I refrigerants must
   (A) have straps every 10 feet.
   (B) have a rigid or flexible metal enclosure.
   (C) use approved clamps.
   (D) all of the above.

7. A screwed joint in refrigeration piping for pressure above 250 psig is permitted if the nominal pipe size is not more than
   (A) 1 1/4″
   (B) 1 3/4″
   (C) 2 1/4″
   (D) 3″

8. The maximum quantity and group of refrigerant for institutional occupancy (other than kitchen labs and mortuaries) in a direct-expansion unit system is
   (A) 10 lbs. Group 1.
   (B) 10 lbs. Group 2.
   (C) 20 lbs. Group 2.
   (D) 20 lbs. Group 1.

9. In a refrigeration system, cast-iron pipe may be used only with
   (A) nonvolatile brines.
   (B) volatile refrigerants.
   (C) flammable refrigerants.
   (D) toxic refrigerants.

10. Of the following piping materials, which is suitable for use with methyl chloride?
    (A) Magnesium
    (B) Zinc
    (C) Aluminum
    (D) Copper

11. Freons should never contact
    (A) magnesium.
    (B) copper.
    (C) cast iron.
    (D) aluminum.

12. Copper alloys should never contact
    (A) R-11
    (B) R-290
    (C) R-718
    (D) R-717

13. The maximum quantity of Group II refrigerants for an indirect system in an institutional building with a Class T machinery room is

(A) 500 lbs.
(B) 1,000 lbs.
(C) unlimited.
(D) 600 lbs.

14. The maximum permissible quantity of Group II refrigerants for an indirect system in a public assembly building with a Class T machinery room is

(A) 500 lbs.
(B) 1,000 lbs.
(C) unlimited.
(D) 600 lbs.

15. The maximum permissible quantity of Group II refrigerants for an indirect system in a residential building's machinery room is

(A) 300 lbs.
(B) 500 lbs.
(C) 600 lbs.
(D) 1,000 lbs.

16. The maximum permissible quantity of Group II refrigerants for an indirect system in a commercial building's Class T machinery room is

(A) unlimited.
(B) 500 lbs.
(C) 600 lbs.
(D) 1,000 lbs.

17. The liquid receiver must not be overloaded beyond what percentage of liquid refrigerant?

(A) 75 percent
(B) 80 percent
(C) 90 percent
(D) 100 percent

18. The minimum field leak test pressure for R-12 on the high-pressure side is

(A) 235 psig.
(B) 185 psig.
(C) 150 psig.
(D) 95 psig.

19. After repairing a refrigeration circuit, you pressurize it to test for leaks. Which of the following should not be used for pressurizing?

(A) Oxygen
(B) Nitrogen
(C) Carbon dioxide
(D) Refrigerant

20. In a booster refrigeration design serving a two-temperature load, the low-pressure compressor suction comes from the

(A) low-temperature load.
(B) high-temperature load.
(C) liquid and gas cooler.
(D) primary compressor discharge.

21. In charging a compression system with vapor, it is customary to charge into the

(A) discharge side of the compressor.
(B) discharge side of the condenser.
(C) suction side of the compressor.
(D) charging valve on the liquid line.

22. To minimize down-time with a Freon system while connecting a rigid copper pipe to a cast-iron pipe, you would

(A) electric weld.
(B) resistance weld.
(C) braze.
(D) soft solder.

23. A booster compressor should be

(A) on the high side.
(B) on the low side.
(C) for Freon-11 only.
(D) for CO_2 only.

24. The amount of refrigerant stored in a machine room must not exceed

(A) 20 percent of refrigerant charge in system nor more than 300 lbs.
(B) 25 percent of refrigerant charge in system nor more than 325 lbs.
(C) 30 percent of refrigerant charge in system nor more than 300 lbs.
(D) 35 percent of refrigerant charge in system nor more than 350 lbs.

25. When drawing refrigerant from a system into a container with a capacity of 80 lbs., you would infuse a maximum of

(A) 40 lbs.
(B) 20 lbs.
(C) 60 lbs.
(D) 80 lbs.

26. The setting of a fusible plug is

(A) 280° F.
(B) 300° F.
(C) 280 psig.
(D) 300 psig.

27. The minimum field leak-test pressure for piping on the high side of a methyl chloride system is

(A) 30 psig.
(B) 95 psig.
(C) 130 psig.
(D) 210 psig.

28. What is the minimum waiting time when testing refrigerant piping for leaks?

(A) 5 minutes
(B) 10 minutes
(C) 20 minutes
(D) 30 minutes

29. You have a refrigeration machine room using R-12. The system calls for vents on one or more power-driven fan units. The inlets for these vents are located

(A) near the floor, by the compressor.
(B) just below the ceiling in the center of the room.
(C) 6 feet above the floor on the wall, near the compressor.
(D) above the cylinder of the compressor.

30. Assume that a refrigeration system is normally charged with 150 pounds of refrigerant. The total refrigerant that can be stored in the machine room is

(A) 15 lbs.
(B) 30 lbs.
(C) 45 lbs.
(D) 60 lbs.

31. Of the following piping materials, which one cannot be used with methyl chloride?

(A) Cast iron and steel
(B) Copper or steel
(C) Aluminum or zinc
(D) Muntz or admiralty metal

32. If it is necessary to dump sulphur dioxide from a system, dump it into a tank containing

(A) 2 1/2 lbs. of carbonate brine.
(B) absorptive brine containing 2 1/2 lbs of sodium dichromate per gallon of water.
(C) absorptive sodium chloride brine.
(D) carbonate brine, then dump it into the sewer.

33. Brine piping is usually made of

(A) brass.
(B) stainless steel.
(C) standard-weight steel.
(D) copper.

34. Soft copper tubing used for refrigerant piping erected on premises and containing other than Group I refrigerant must be protected by

(A) supporting it by approved clamps.
(B) a rigid or flexible metal enclosure.
(C) limiting its length between supports to 10 feet.
(D) wrapping it with cotton tape throughout its length.

35. A fuse or circuit breaker in an air-conditioning system does not protect against

(A) short circuit.
(B) motor burnout.
(C) high temperature.
(D) all of the above.

36. To evacuate an SO_2 system, you would dump it into

(A) water.
(B) absorptive brine.
(C) calcium chloride.
(D) sodium chloride.

37. In a Freon refrigerating system in which all piping is made up of hard copper fittings and streamlined "wrought"-type fittings, the joints should be

(A) screwed.
(B) soldered or brazed.
(C) flanged with ground faces.
(D) flanged with lined rubber gaskets.

38. If any piece of equipment can be isolated as a separate unit,

(A) a gauge must be present.
(B) a safety valve must be installed.
(C) valves must be locked.
(D) the system must be able to run without it.

39. A 100-ton Freon plant must be equipped with

(A) a gauge glass on the receiver.
(B) purge lines on each piece of equipment.
(C) a remote-control shut-off switch outside the machine room.
(D) a cross bypass from high side to low side.

40. Why are there laws banning CFC and HCFC refrigerants?

(A) To make money from the refrigeration industry
(B) To replace toxic refrigerants in use
(C) To allow the consumer alternative refrigerants
(D) To protect the ozone layer in the atmosphere

41. Which of the following metals, when used with methyl chloride, would form a highly flammable gas, causing an explosion hazard?

(A) Copper
(B) Steel
(C) Aluminum
(D) Brass

42. All the following refrigerants have the same high and low minimum field-leak test pressure of 30 psi EXCEPT

(A) R-113.
(B) R-11.
(C) methylene chloride.
(D) ethyl chloride.

43. According to the provisions of the rule, a soldered joint is a gas-tight joint obtained by the joining of metals with metallic mixtures or alloys that melt at temperatures below

(A) 700° F and above 100° F.
(B) 800° F and above 200° F.
(C) 900° F and above 350° F.
(D) 1,000° F and above 400° F.

44. The minimum required rated discharge capacity of the pressure-relief device or fusible plug for a refrigerant-containing vessel is determined by the following formula: C = Fd1. What is "C" equal to?

(A) btu per minute
(B) Refrigerant pressure
(C) Air in pounds per minute
(D) Cubic feet per minute

45. A pressure or temperature response mechanism for automatically stopping the operation of the pressure-imposing element is the

(A) pressure-limiting device.
(B) pressure-relief valve.
(C) pressure-imposing device.
(D) pressure-relief device.

46. In a system containing 2,000 pounds of refrigerant, the mechanical air discharge from the engine room should be

(A) 2,500 cfm.
(B) 2,750 cfm.
(C) 2,900 cfm.
(D) 3,050 cfm.

47. If a system contains 900 pounds of Group 2 refrigerant, the number of breathing service masks required is

(A) one.
(B) two.
(C) three.
(D) four.

48. When used in parallel with a relief valve, rupture members

(A) operate at 30 percent of the designed working pressure.
(B) should not exceed 20 percent above the designed working pressure.
(C) operate at 10 percent above the designed working pressure.
(D) should not exceed 25 percent below the designed working pressure.

49. Which of the following refers to a Class "T" machine room?

(A) It must have a sealed room with no less than 2 hours of fire-proof construction.
(B) It must have a door opening into or under a fire escape.
(C) All pipes piercing the wall and ceiling should be tightly sealed with no less than 1 hour of resistance construction.
(D) All pipes must be sealed into the wall, ceiling, and floor.

50. The International Montreal Protocol called for the production of CFC to cease by the year

(A) 1992
(B) 1995
(C) 2000
(D) 2020

51. The International Montreal Protocol was signed in

(A) 1975
(B) 1987
(C) 1992
(D) 1995

52. Early evidence regarding ozone depletion due to CFCs and bromides led to the regulations of nonessential aerosols in 1978 by the

(A) Montreal Protocol.
(B) Molina-Rowland theory.
(C) Protocol in Copenhagen.
(D) Clean Air Act Mandate.

53. Of the following types of refrigerant emissions, which is NOT currently permitted by the EPA?

(A) De minimus quantities of CFC or HCFC refrigerants
(B) Knowingly venting, releasing, or disposing of CFC or HCFC refrigerants
(C) Refrigerants emitted in the course of normal operation of HVAC equipment
(D) Mixtures of nitrogen and R-22 used as holding charges or leak test gases

54. The De minimus clause of the Clean Air Act Amendments of 1990 refers to

(A) criminal penalties and prison terms against any person who knowingly releases refrigerants into the atmosphere.
(B) servicemen's minor loses associated with good faith attempts to recapture, recycle, or safely dispose of refrigerant.
(C) air conditioning appliances being equipped with servicing devices to facilitate the recapture of refrigerant during service and repair.
(D) the training of service personnel in recovery, reclaiming, and recycling of refrigerants.

55. Effective July 1, 1992, it is unlawful to knowingly vent, release, or dispose of CFCs and HCFCs during the repair, service, maintenance, or disposal of appliances or industrial process refrigeration equipment. Which of the following releases are permitted under the prohibition?

(A) De minimus quantities of refrigerants released in the course of making good faith attempts to recapture and recycle or safety dispose of refrigerant
(B) Refrigerants emitted in the course of normal operation of A/C and refrigeration equipment
(C) Mixtures of nitrogen and R-22 that are used as holding charges or as leak gases, because as in these cases, the ozone-depleting compound is not used as a refrigerant
(D) All of the above

56. The EPA is authorized to seek legal redress through the local, state, and U.S. District Courts that would impose heavy fines and/or imprisonment to those violating the Clean Air Act, enforcement Title VII. Which of the following is an EPA-imposed action against violators?

(A) Civil penalties of up to $25,000 per day, per violation of the Act.
(B) Awards up to $10,000 to persons furnishing information that leads to the conviction of a person violating provisions of the Act.
(C) A hearing called by the EPA for pursuing a violation less than $200,000 and less than 1 year old (administrative hearing).
(D) All of the above

57. Which of the following is an Administrative Order from the EPA to a Clean Air Act violator?

(A) An EPA communication order directing compliance of the Act or risk having their business closed down
(B) Notification of a violation letter from the EPA that documents a violation and places it on file
(C) A letter from the EPA to a suspended violator of the Act that charges a violation and requires additional information to the EPA from the accused party (Section 114 letter)
(D) All of the above

58. The EPA is authorized to seek legal redress through the local, state, and U.S. District Courts that would impose heavy fines and/or imprisonment to those violating the Clean Air Act, Enforcement Title VII. Which of the following are violations?

(A) Failing to report a substantial refrigerant release
(B) Falsifying documents
(C) Tampering with monitoring devices
(D) All of the above

59. According to EPA legislation and regulations, equipment and reclaimer certification,

(A) before opening a system for maintenance, evacuation to a system receiver or certified recovery or recycling machine is required.
(B) contractor ownership certification of recovery or recycling equipment is mandatory.
(C) refrigerant is not to change ownership until brought to purity standards.
(D) all of the above.

60. The main objective of the Clean Air Act is to **reduce** the production, use, and emissions of ozone-depleting substances. Substances affected are divided into two classifications. What is the difference between these classifications?

(A) Class I substances are non-toxic below 400 ppm, non-flammable.
(B) Class II substances are toxic above 400 ppm, highly flammable.
(C) Class I substances are CFC; Class II substances are HCFC.
(D) Class I substances are HCFC; Class II substances are CFC.

61. A technician or mechanic servicing small appliance equipment MUST have which of the following certifications?

(A) Small appliance Type I
(B) High pressure Type II
(C) Low pressure Type III
(D) Type I or Universal

62. Small appliances are

(A) units hermetically sealed with three pounds or less of refrigerant.
(B) units hermetically sealed with five pounds or less of refrigerant.
(C) units in which a refrigerant's boiling point is above 10 degrees Celsius at atmospheric pressure.
(D) refrigerator or window units with a refrigerant boiling point below –50 degrees Celsius at atmospheric pressure.

63. What is the procedure to reclaim a refrigerant that has been contaminated with another refrigerant?

(A) Separate and reclaim by distillation
(B) Separate by chemical recycling process
(C) Send refrigerants to an authorized facility for destruction
(D) Chemically mix refrigerants into an azeotropic blend

64. Refrigerant recovery is defined as

(A) removing the refrigerant from a system and storing it in an external container, with the lowest emissions possible.
(B) reprocessing a refrigerant into a new product that can be reused in another system.
(C) the process of cleaning a refrigerant of dirt and contaminates, such as oil, acid, foreign material, and noncondensibles.
(D) none of the above.

65. Air monitoring systems will sense

(A) HCFC-22 leaks.
(B) halogen leaks.
(C) oxygen deprivation.
(D) group 3 refrigerants.

66. Refrigerant recycling is defined as

(A) removing the refrigerant from a system and storing it in an external container, with the lowest emissions possible.
(B) the process of cleaning a refrigerant of dirt and contaminates, such as oil, acid, foreign material, and noncondensibles.
(C) reprocessing a refrigerant into a new product that can be reused in another system.
(D) all of the above.

67. The Active Method of recovery involves

(A) refrigerant removal by system pump-down into condenser.
(B) refrigerant recovery into system's receiver unit.
(C) refrigerant removal into a certified self-contained recovery unit.
(D) refrigerant reclaiming to an authorized facility.

68. Refrigerant should be *recovered* from a system

(A) as high-temperature, high-pressure gas.
(B) as low-temperature, low-pressure gas.
(C) as high-temperature, high-pressure liquid: high side of the system.
(D) from the discharge service valve of the compressor.

69. If contaminated refrigerant is removed from a storage tank, what is the recommended handling procedure?

(A) Reclaim the refrigerant at a reprocessing manufacturing facility.
(B) Dispose of or destroy the refrigerant
(C) Recover and recycle the refrigerant offsite
(D) Recover, recycle, and process the refrigerant onsite

70. According to Title 49 CFR Section 173.34(e), cylinders and tanks must be hydrostatically retested

(A) once every year by visual inspection.
(B) a minimum of once every 5 years.
(C) every six months.
(D) a minimum of once every 2 years.

71. Who is responsible in a plant to assure refrigerant cylinders are within the hydrostatic test dates?

(A) Operating engineer
(B) Plant manager
(C) Chief engineer
(D) Owner

72. Chlorine-based refrigerants without hydrogen are so stable that they do not breakdown in the lower atmosphere

(A) until 10 to 20 years after their release.
(B) until 20 to 40 years after their release.
(C) until 40 to 70 years after their release.
(D) even after 100 years or more after being released.

73. A cylinder is to be filled with refrigerant, and chances are that it may be exposed to temperatures of 130 degrees. What is the recommended fill rate?

(A) 40 percent
(B) 60 percent
(C) 80 percent
(D) 90 percent

74. Disposable cylinders

(A) are refilled only with qualified recovery equipment.
(B) meet D.O.T. specification 4BA-300.
(C) can be recycled with your scrap metal once used and punctured with valve open.
(D) are equipped with a safety relief device that is designed to relieve cylinder pressure at 400 psi.

75. D.O.T. 39 refrigerant cylinders are equipped with safety relief devices of which of the following types?

(A) Frangible disc, fusible plug
(B) Fusible plug, rupture disc
(C) Spring actuated relief valve, pressure relief valve
(D) Spring loaded relief, frangible disc

76. What color are recovery containers painted?

(A) It is yellow around the top, with the corresponding refrigerant color code along the side, and hood painted gold.
(B) The hood is painted yellow, and shoulder is painted gold, with the remaining body corresponding to the refrigerant color code.
(C) It is painted yellow on the shoulder and 12" down the side, with the remaining cylinder body corresponding to refrigerant color code, and the hood is painted gold.
(D) The body shall be painted gray, and the shoulder and cap shall be painted yellow.

77. DOT - 39 cylinder is

(A) disposable.
(B) refillable.
(C) reusable.
(D) used for recover.

78. The capacity of a disposable refrigerant cylinder ranges from

(A) 1 to 25 lbs.
(B) 1 to 30 lbs.
(C) 1 to 50 lbs.
(D) 1 to 60 lbs.

79. To determine the refrigerant type on air-conditioning equipment, the technician must

(A) read the equipment name plate.
(B) read the expansion valve plate.
(C) connect manifold gauges and compare the pressures.
(D) pump down the system and take samples.

80. According to ASHRAE Standard R15 (Safety Code for Mechanical Refrigeration), an Oxygen Deprivation Sensor can also be used as

(A) an atmospheric purger.
(B) a breathing apparatus.
(C) a refrigerating leak detector.
(D) mechanical ventilation.

81. A pressure regulator must be used with a fully charged nitrogen cylinder. A fully charged nitrogen cylinder possesses approximately

(A) 1000 psi.
(B) 1500 psi.
(C) 2000 psi.
(D) 2500 psi.

82. A safety pressure relief valve must be installed downstream of the nitrogen cylinder pressure regulator. What is the release pressure setting of the safety pressure relief valve?

(A) 125 psi
(B) 150 psi
(C) 280 psi
(D) 300 psi

83. After a system's charge has been recovered, it is pressurized with nitrogen to test for leaks. What is the maximum pressure used to leak test?

(A) 125 psi
(B) 150 psi
(C) 280 psi
(D) 300 psi

84. When leak checking a fully charged low pressure chiller,

(A) pressurize with nitrogen and R-22.
(B) pressurize with controlled hot water.
(C) pressurize with oxygen.
(D) none of the above.

85. Safety Group A2 signifies

(A) high flammability, high toxicity.
(B) lower flammability, lower toxicity.
(C) no flame propagation, low toxicity.
(D) no flame propagation, high toxicity.

86. Safety Group A3 signifies

(A) high flammability, high toxicity.
(B) lower flammability, lower toxicity.
(C) high flammability, low toxicity.
(D) no flame propagation, high toxicity.

87. Refrigerants for which there is evidence of toxicity at concentrations below 400 ppm that do not show flame propagation are

(A) lower flammability, lower toxicity.
(B) no flame propagation, low toxicity.
(C) high flammability, high toxicity.
(D) no flame propagation, high toxicity.

88. Safety Group A1 signifies

(A) high flammability, high toxicity.
(B) lower flammability, lower toxicity.
(C) no flame propagation, low toxicity.
(D) no flame propagation, high toxicity.

89. Which of the following refrigerants may be classified as A3 ?

(A) 600, 170, 290, 50
(B) 142b, 717, 611, 500
(C) 11, 12, 22, 30
(D) 113, 114, 123, 764

90. A refrigerant with low flammability and high toxicity may be classified as

(A) A1
(B) A3
(C) B2
(D) B3

91. Safety Group B1 signifies

(A) lower flammability, lower toxicity.
(B) no flame propagation, low toxicity.
(C) high flammability, high toxicity.
(D) no flame propagation, high toxicity.

92. The safest refrigerant group classification is

(A) A1
(B) B1
(C) A3
(D) B3

93. What is the operating pressure of HCFC-123 at 30 degrees F?

(A) 20.8 psi
(B) 20.8" Hg
(C) 23.7 psi
(D) 23.7"Hg

94. Which statement is true concerning Ternary Blends?

(A) Leak at faster rates than other refrigerants
(B) Leak at uneven amounts due to vapor pressures
(C) Leak at even rates
(D) Leak on the high side due to high pressure

95. Which refrigerant classification has the least depletion effect to the ozone?

Ozone Depletion Potential

(A) HCFC-123: .016
(B) CFC-12: .93
(C) MP-39: .03
(D) HP-80: .03

96. If all of the hydrogen atoms have been replaced in the base molecule by chlorine and fluorine, the refrigerant is said to be

(A) fully halogenated.
(B) partially halogenated.
(C) hydrochlorofluorocarbon.
(D) azeotropic.

97. Depletion of the ozone results in three types of skin cancer. Which of the following are the most common non-malignant type of skin cancer?

(A) Basal, squamous
(B) Malignant melanoma
(C) Cataracts
(D) Leishmaniasis

98. Refrigerant R-123 is classified by the EPA as a(n)

(A) toxic refrigerant.
(B) class I refrigerant.
(C) class II refrigerant.
(D) oxygen-depleting refrigerant.

Answers to Refrigeration License Code Questions

1. **The correct answer is (C).**
2. **The correct answer is (D).**
3. **The correct answer is (C).**
4. **The correct answer is (D).**
5. **The correct answer is (B).**
6. **The correct answer is (B).**
7. **The correct answer is (A).**
8. **The correct answer is (D).**
9. **The correct answer is (A).**
10. **The correct answer is (D).**
11. **The correct answer is (A).**
12. **The correct answer is (D).**
13. **The correct answer is (A).**
14. **The correct answer is (B).**
15. **The correct answer is (A).**
16. **The correct answer is (A).**
17. **The correct answer is (B).**
18. **The correct answer is (A).**
19. **The correct answer is (A).**
20. **The correct answer is (A).**
21. **The correct answer is (C).**
22. **The correct answer is (C).**
23. **The correct answer is (B).**
24. **The correct answer is (A).**
25. **The correct answer is (C).**
26. **The correct answer is (A).**
27. **The correct answer is (D).**
28. **The correct answer is (D).**
29. **The correct answer is (A).**
30. **The correct answer is (B).**
31. **The correct answer is (C).**
32. **The correct answer is (B).**
33. **The correct answer is (C).**
34. **The correct answer is (B).**
35. **The correct answer is (C).**
36. **The correct answer is (B).**
37. **The correct answer is (B).**
38. **The correct answer is (B).**
39. **The correct answer is (C).**
40. **The correct answer is (D).**
41. **The correct answer is (C).**
42. **The correct answer is (D).**
43. **The correct answer is (D).**
44. **The correct answer is (C).**
45. **The correct answer is (A).**
46. **The correct answer is (C).**
47. **The correct answer is (A).**
48. **The correct answer is (B).**
49. **The correct answer is (C).**
50. **The correct answer is (C).**
51. **The correct answer is (B).**
52. **The correct answer is (B).**
53. **The correct answer is (B).**
54. **The correct answer is (B).**
55. **The correct answer is (D).** Note that all three types of releases are permitted under the prohibition.
56. **The correct answer is (D).**
57. **The correct answer is (A).**
58. **The correct answer is (D).** Note that violation affects administrative, manufacturing, distribution, and user levels.
59. **The correct answer is (D).**
60. **The correct answer is (C).**
61. **The correct answer is (D).**
62. **The correct answer is (B).**
63. **The correct answer is (C).**
64. **The correct answer is (A).**
65. **The correct answer is (C).**
66. **The correct answer is (B.**
67. **The correct answer is (C).**

68. **The correct answer is (C).**

69. **The correct answer is (A).**

70. **The correct answer is (B).**

71. **The correct answer is (D).**

72. **The correct answer is (D).**

73. **The correct answer is (B).**

74. **The correct answer is (C).**

75. **The correct answer is (D).**

76. **The correct answer is (D).**

77. **The correct answer is (A).**

78. **The correct answer is (B).**

79. **The correct answer is (A).**

80. **The correct answer is (C).**

81. **The correct answer is (D).**

82. **The correct answer is (B).**

83. **The correct answer is (A).** Pressure regulators on nitrogen cylinders

84. **The correct answer is (B).**

85. **The correct answer is (B).**

86. **The correct answer is (C).**

87. **The correct answer is (D).**

88. **The correct answer is (C).**

89. **The correct answer is (A).**

90. **The correct answer is (C).**

91. **The correct answer is (D).**

92. **The correct answer is (A).**

93. **The correct answer is (B).** Note that R-123 is a low-pressure refrigerant.

94. **The correct answer is (B).** Cover blends (ternary or binary) that require synthetic lubricants such as alkylbenzene or ester oil

95. **The correct answer is (A).**

96. **The correct answer is (A). Malignant Melanoma**: less common, yet a more harmful type of skin cancer that affects 25,000 people per year, resulting in about 5,000 deaths. **Cataracts**: clouds that form on the lens of the eye, causing about 18,000 cases annually, due to ozone depletion. **Leishmaniasis and Herpes Simplex**: parasitic diseases that weaken the body's immune system.

97. **The correct answer is (A).**

98. **The correct answer is (C).** Class I refrigerants are listed as CFC refrigerants; Class II refrigerants are listed as HCFC refrigerants

Chapter 18

WRITTEN EXAM REVIEW

PRACTICE TEST 1

1. Assuming all other conditions remain constant, a decrease in evaporator load causes
   (A) high head pressure.
   (B) low suction pressure.
   (C) high suction pressure.
   (D) loss of oil pressure.

2. In a flooded evaporator using an accumulator and float valve, flash gas
   (A) passes directly into the evaporator.
   (B) passes directly into the suction line.
   (C) does not occur.
   (D) stays in the receiver.

3. The oil trap on a refrigeration system is on the
   (A) discharge line, as far from the compressor as possible.
   (B) suction line, close to the evaporator.
   (C) liquid line, between the receiver and evaporator.
   (D) discharge line, as close to the compressor as allowed.

4. What controls the operation of a high-side float?
   (A) The condenser
   (B) The evaporator
   (C) The condenser and receiver
   (D) The evaporator and condenser

5. When suction pressure decreases, compressor capacity
   (A) increases.
   (B) decreases.
   (C) rises.
   (D) slightly increases.

6. Cooling-tower water should be maintained at a pH near
   (A) 4
   (B) 6
   (C) 7.8
   (D) 10

7. The subcooling effect of the liquid refrigerant just before the expansion valve causes increased
   (A) horsepower.
   (B) refrigeration effect.
   (C) expansion valve capacity.
   (D) refrigerant flow.

8. Subcooling the liquid refrigerant just before the expansion valve results in an increase in
   (A) horsepower.
   (B) refrigeration effect.
   (C) expansion valve capacity.
   (D) refrigerant flow.

9. What percentage of oil travels with the refrigerant?
   (A) 10 percent
   (B) 20 percent
   (C) 25 percent
   (D) 33 percent

10. Any water present in the refrigerant side of a Freon refrigerating system causes a
    (A) clogged oil trap.
    (B) frozen discharge valve.
    (C) clogged scale trap.
    (D) frozen expansion valve.

11. When heated, R-12 changes to
    (A) hydrochloric acid.
    (B) phosgene gas.
    (C) carbonic acid.
    (D) chlorine gas.

12. In an absorption system, the medium normally used to vaporize refrigerant and increase its temperature is
    (A) water.
    (B) propane.
    (C) ethylene.
    (D) steam.

13. Which does not increase the capacity of a water-cooled condenser?

(A) Increasing the water flow
(B) Reducing the water flow
(C) Decreasing the ambient temperature
(D) None of the above

14. When energizing a solenoid valve (to close the valve), its position will be

(A) normally closed.
(B) dual opening.
(C) normally open.
(D) none of the above.

15. A valve that does not restrict flow is the

(A) automatic expansion valve.
(C) low-side float valve.
(B) capillary tube.
(D) solenoid valve.

16. The oil separator is located on the

(A) suction, as close to the compressor as possible.
(B) suction line, as far from the compressor as possible.
(C) discharge line, as close to the compressor as possible.
(D) discharge line, as far from the compressor as possible.

17. When we say a refrigerant is anhydrous, we mean

(A) water is present.
(B) it is aqua ammonia.
(C) water is absent.
(D) it has ammonia.

18. The primary purpose of a purger in a Freon system is the removal of

(A) water.
(B) air.
(C) noncondensables.
(D) oil.

19. Operating a Freon air-conditioning unit with the filters clogged is likely to result in

(A) liquid refrigerant entering the compressor.
(B) excessive temperature in the liquid line to the expansion valve.
(C) low suction pressure.
(D) high suction pressure.

20. A refrigerant overcharge would

(A) increase head pressure.
(B) decrease head pressure.
(C) decrease suction-side pressure.
(D) decrease discharge-side pressure.

21. On the most common three-phase, four-wire service, the voltage between any phase and neutral should be

(A) 105 volts.
(B) 120 volts.
(C) 208 volts.
(D) 220 volts.

22. Which of the following statements about brine is most correct?

(A) CO_2 decreases the corrosive action of brines.
(B) Acidic brine does not attack ferrous metals.
(C) Alkaline brine does not attack zinc.
(D) pH should be slightly alkaline at 7.8.

23. Which desiccant is NOT used in refrigeration?

(A) Drierite
(B) Activated alumina
(C) Calcium chloride
(D) Soda lime

24. In an efficiently operating induced-draft cooling tower, the leaving water temperature is

(A) 10° F higher than entering temperature.
(B) between dry-bulb and wet-bulb temperature.
(C) at the dewpoint temperature.
(D) at the dry-bulb temperature.

25. A reciprocating refrigeration compressor is controlled in response to the water temperature leaving the water chiller. If the thermostat used for compressor control did not have a wide enough differential, the probable result would be

(A) inadequate time for oil to return to the compressor.
(B) stop on high-pressure cutout.
(C) stop on low-pressure cutout.
(D) a very long operating cycle.

26. Which does NOT remove acid from refrigerant?

(A) Calcium oxide
(B) Activated alumina
(C) Calcium chloride
(D) Silica gel

27. Which desiccant CANNOT be used with an R-40 system?

(A) Drierite
(B) Calcium chloride
(C) Activated alumina
(D) Silica gel

28. The substance commonly used to dry methyl chloride refrigerant is

(A) activated alumina.
(B) calcium sulphate.
(C) sodium chloride.
(D) muriatic acid.

29. To operate two evaporators at different temperatures in a compression system with only one compressor, install a back-pressure valve in the

(A) suction line of the low-temperature evaporator.
(B) suction line of the high-temperature evaporator.
(C) common suction line.
(D) common discharge line.

30. At a given temperature, the ratio of actual atmospheric vapor pressure to saturation pressure is called

(A) relative humidity.
(B) humidifying effect.
(C) partial pressure.
(D) refrigeration effect.

31. Assuming all other conditions remain the same in a refrigerating plant, which statement about operating characteristics is most correct?

(A) As load decreases, low-side pressure falls; suction pressure is affected first.
(B) As head pressure rises, plant capacity increases; condenser pressure is affected first.
(C) As low-side pressure falls, compressor capacity increases.
(D) Low-side pressure is not affected by the load change.

32. In reciprocating compressors using the slash system of lubrication, oil foaming is most likely to occur when

(A) pressure suddenly increases.
(B) the oil has a high moisture content.
(C) inferior grades of oil are used.
(D) pressure suddenly decreases.

33. What does HCFC refrigerant stand for?

(A) Hydrochlorofluorocarbon
(B) Hychlorotrifluoroethane
(C) Hyclorofluorocarbon
(D) Hychloromonofluorocarbon

34. Which motor-protection device resets itself automatically after cooling to a safe temperature?

(A) The dual-element fuse
(B) The circuit breaker
(C) The thermal protector
(D) The fusetron cartridge fuse

35. You are testing for leaks in newly repaired refrigeration circuits. Which substance should NOT be used to develop pressure in the circuits?

(A) Nitrogen
(B) Oxygen
(C) Carbon dioxide
(D) Refrigerant

36. A refrigerant cylinder has an 80-pound capacity. How many pounds of refrigerant can you store in it?

(A) 20
(B) 40
(C) 60
(D) 80

37. If the belts were installed too tightly in a V-belt driven compressor, the

(A) motor will run normally.
(B) motor will overheat.
(C) compressor head pressure will increase.
(D) compressor suction pressure will increase.

38. When a refrigerant such as R-12 passes through the TXV, pressure and temperature drop due to

(A) refrigerant evaporation.
(B) oil logging.
(C) system overcharging.
(D) flash gas.

39. A dryer is generally installed with other equipment in a commercial Freon compressor system. The recommended location for this dryer is on the

(A) high-pressure line between condenser and receiver.
(B) suction line between evaporator and compressor.
(C) discharge line between compressor and condenser.
(D) liquid line between receiver and expansion valve.

40. When comparing a brine with a pH of 10 to one with a pH of 8, its alkalinity is

(A) 2 times greater.
(B) 50 times greater.
(C) 10 times greater.
(D) 100 times greater.

41. The units of vacuum on a compound pressure gauge are read in inches of

(A) air pressure.
(B) water.
(C) ammonia.
(D) mercury.

42. When charging a compression system with vapor, charge into the

(A) discharge side of the compressor.
(B) discharge side of the condenser.
(C) suction side of the compressor.
(D) charging valve on the liquid line.

43. To produce the desired evaporator temperature, power input is reduced by keeping head pressure

(A) as low as possible and suction pressure as low as needed.
(B) as high as possible and suction pressure as high as needed.
(C) as low as possible and suction pressure as high as needed.
(D) as high as possible and suction pressure as low as needed.

44. Cast-iron pipe may be used only with

(A) nonvolatile brines.
(B) flammable refrigerants.
(C) volatile brines.
(D) toxic refrigerants.

45. Reciprocating compressor unloaders usually unload the compressor by

(A) keeping the discharge valves open.
(B) keeping the suction valves open.
(C) keeping the discharge valves closed.
(D) increasing compressor speed.

46. The gas from a reciprocating compressor is

(A) superheated.
(B) 100 percent dry, supersaturated.
(C) supercooled.
(D) supersaturated.

47. A sample of water taken from a cooling tower has a pH of 7.8. It is

(A) slightly acid.
(B) neither acid or alkaline.
(C) slightly alkaline.
(D) highly alkaline.

48. A sudden decrease in condenser cooling water in a compression-type plant would result in

(A) low discharge pressure.
(B) reduced compressor speed.
(C) high discharge pressure.
(D) unloading the compressor.

49. Heat transfer takes place by

(A) evaporation, conduction, and condensation.
(B) radiation, conduction, and convection.
(C) condensation, evaporation, and radiation.
(D) sublimation, evaporation, and convection.

50. 600,000 btu per hour equals how many tons of refrigeration?

(A) 300
(B) 3,000
(C) 500
(D) 50

51. Absolute zero is

(A) –459° F.
(B) –273° F.
(C) –100° F.
(D) 0° F.

52. You are using an automatic expansion valve. Where would you hook up the thermal bulb to the cooling coil?

(A) At the beginning
(B) In the middle
(C) At the end
(D) None of the above

53. Superheat is heat added

(A) to change liquid to vapor.
(B) to increase pressure.
(C) after liquid has been changed to vapor.
(D) to raise water temperature.

54. A 10-ton refrigeration unit has a capacity of

(A) 2,000 btu per minute.
(B) 12,000 btu per hour.
(C) 20,000 btu per minute.
(D) 144,000 btu per day.

55. "The best and fastest way to charge an air conditioner is to apply an open flame to the tank of refrigerant." This statement is

(A) true.
(B) sometimes true.
(C) false.
(D) none of the above.

Answers to Practice Test 1

1. **The correct answer is (B).**
2. **The correct answer is (B).**
3. **The correct answer is (A).**
4. **The correct answer is (C).**
5. **The correct answer is (B).**
6. **The correct answer is (C).**
7. **The correct answer is (B).**
8. **The correct answer is (B).**
9. **The correct answer is (A).**
10. **The correct answer is (D).**
11. **The correct answer is (B).**
12. **The correct answer is (D).**
13. **The correct answer is (C).**
14. **The correct answer is (C).**
15. **The correct answer is (D).**
16. **The correct answer is (D).**
17. **The correct answer is (C).**
18. **The correct answer is (C).** A purger removes water, air, and noncondensables.
19. **The correct answer is (C).**
20. **The correct answer is (A).**
21. **The correct answer is (B).**
22. **The correct answer is (D).**
23. **The correct answer is (D).**
24. **The correct answer is (B).** It also may be some temperature between the prevailing dry- and wet-bulb temperature.
25. **The correct answer is (A).**
26. **The correct answer is (C).**
27. **The correct answer is (B).**
28. **The correct answer is (A).**
29. **The correct answer is (B).**
30. **The correct answer is (A).**
31. **The correct answer is (A).**
32. **The correct answer is (D).**
33. **The correct answer is (A).**
34. **The correct answer is (C).**
35. **The correct answer is (B).**
36. **The correct answer is (C).**
37. **The correct answer is (B).**
38. **The correct answer is (A).**
39. **The correct answer is (D).**
40. **The correct answer is (D).**
41. **The correct answer is (D).**
42. **The correct answer is (C).**
43. **The correct answer is (C).**
44. **The correct answer is (A).**
45. **The correct answer is (B).**
46. **The correct answer is (A).**
47. **The correct answer is (C).**
48. **The correct answer is (C).**
49. **The correct answer is (B).**
50. **The correct answer is (D).** 600,000 + 12,000 = 50
51. **The correct answer is (A).**
52. **The correct answer is (D).**
53. **The correct answer is (C).**
54. **The correct answer is (A).** 10 × 200 btu = 2,000 btu/min.
55. **The correct answer is (C).**

PRACTICE TEST 2

1. Which of the following statements is incorrect?
   (A) A service valve is a key-operated shut-off valve used during shipment, installation, and repairs.
   (B) Brine is a liquid cooled by refrigeration and used for the transmission of heat.
   (C) A fusible plug has a set-temperature fusible member to relieve pressure.
   (D) A rupture member automatically ruptures at a predetermined temperature.

2. The reading on a gauge in a refrigeration system is 10 inches of mercury vacuum. The pressure expressed in psia is
   (A) 6.4
   (B) 9.8
   (C) 10
   (D) 11

3. Oil in a refrigeration system should
   (A) have a high pour point.
   (B) have a low flash point.
   (C) have a high viscosity.
   (D) not contain moisture.

4. The setting of a fusible plug is
   (A) 280° F.
   (B) 300° F.
   (C) 380° F.
   (D) 300 psig.

5. Oil foaming in a refrigeration compressor is caused by
   (A) very high flash-point temperature of oil.
   (B) very low pour-point temperature of oil.
   (C) very low acidity of oil.
   (D) high solubility of refrigerant in oil.

6. The use of screwed joints for systems with refrigerant pressure above 250 psi is permitted, provided that the pipe is not more than
   (A) 3 inches.
   (B) 2 inches.
   (C) 2 1/2 inches.
   (D) 1 1/4 inches.

7. On a wet compression system, discharge gas is
   (A) saturated.
   (B) supersaturated.
   (C) subcooled.
   (D) superheated.

8. The eutectic point of calcium brine is
   (A) –59.8° F with a hydrometer reading of 1.29 specific gravity.
   (B) –59.9° F with a hydrometer reading of 1.17 specific gravity.
   (C) –6° F with a hydrometer reading of 1.29 specific gravity.
   (D) –6° F with a hydrometer reading of 1.17 specific gravity.

9. Suction pipes are insulated to
   (A) absorb moisture.
   (B) reduce vibration.
   (C) prevent loss of refrigeration.
   (D) increase oil circulation.

10. What indicates a leaking ammonia refrigerant cylinder?
    (A) A hissing sound
    (B) A gurgling sound
    (C) Fog or mist in the vicinity
    (D) Frost around the hole

11. Which refrigerants are in Group 2?
    (A) SO_2, R-40, R-717
    (B) SO_2, methane, R-717
    (C) Ethane, propane, R-11
    (D) R-40, propane, R-717

12. Freon-12 is similar to methyl chloride as a refrigerant because
    (A) they have the same chemical properties.
    (B) their cost is identical.
    (C) their vapor densities are practically equal.
    (D) both are miscible with lubricating oil.

13. The refrigerant least miscible in oil is
    (A) CO_2
    (B) R-12
    (C) R-40
    (D) R-141

14. Which refrigerant is the least toxic?
    (A) Propane
    (B) Ammonia
    (C) Methyl chloride
    (D) R-113

15. Of the following, the most desirable Freon gas for a centrifugal machine is
    (A) R-11
    (B) R-12
    (C) R-500
    (D) R-717

16. Which refrigerant has the highest refrigeration effect when operating at standard ton conditions of 5° F evaporating temperature and 86° condensing temperature?

(A) R-21
(B) R-22
(C) R-113
(D) R-12

17. A specific test for CO_2 in condenser water is bromthymol blue. If CO_2 is present, the sample turns

(A) green.
(B) purple.
(C) white.
(D) yellow.

18. Which refrigerant has the least refrigeration effect when operating at 86° F condensing temperature and 5° F evaporating temperature?

(A) R-113
(B) R-22
(C) R-21
(D) R-12

19. Which Freon refrigerant has the highest refrigeration effect in btu per pound?

(A) R-11
(B) R-12
(C) R-113
(D) R-114

20. The head pressure in a receiver holding R-12 is 135 psig. What is the liquid temperature in the receiver?

(A) 135° F
(B) 98° F
(C) 110° F
(D) 86° F

21. A 200-ton air-conditioning plant has two Freon compressors. Neither compressor is equipped with bypass solenoids. At least four-step capacity is desired. What type of drive should be selected?

(A) Repulsion-induction motor
(B) Wound-rotor induction motor
(C) Synchronous motor
(D) Capacitor motor

22. In an operating evaporator, the oil stays on top of which refrigerant?

(A) R-12
(B) R-717
(C) R-20
(D) R-744

23. A brine used at –25° F may not contain

(A) calcium chloride.
(B) ethylene glycol.
(C) sodium chloride.
(D) alcohol.

24. Thermostatic expansion valves control the amount of superheat within

(A) 1 to 3°.
(B) 7 to 10°.
(C) 10 to 15°.
(D) 15 to 20°.

25. Reversing a three-phase, 60-cycle induction motor should be done by

(A) changing any two leads to the rotor.
(B) reversing the field connections.
(C) reversing the starting winding connections.
(D) interchanging two of the power leads.

26. The instrument that indicates air velocity directly when used in air conditioning duct flow measurements is the

(A) anemometer.
(B) manometer.
(C) psychrometer.
(D) humidifier.

27. On a compression-type refrigeration plant, a synchronous motor

(A) can be used as a multispeed compressor drive.
(B) can be used as a variable-speed compressor drive.
(C) can be used as a constant-speed compressor drive.
(D) cannot be used as a compressor drive.

28. The normal gauge color for pressure is

(A) red for pressure.
(B) black for superheat pressure.
(C) black for pressure.
(D) black for saturated pressure.

29. On an R-12 reciprocating compressor that has been shut down for the purpose of adding oil, the oil is

(A) pumped into the service valve in the high-pressure liquid line.
(B) pumped into the service valve on the crankcase.
(C) sucked into the suction service valve.
(D) pumped into the discharge service valve.

30. Which device automatically resets itself?

(A) The fusetron
(B) The fusestat
(C) The circuit breaker
(D) The thermal protector

31. Which fluid is recommended to be used with a swab when cleaning the interior of refrigerant copper tubing?

(A) Sodium hydroxide
(B) Refrigerant 11
(C) Carbon tetrachloride
(D) Ammonia

32. Anhydrous ammonia is

(A) a mixture of ammonia and water.
(B) 29 percent aqua ammonia.
(C) 59 percent aqua ammonia.
(D) ammonia without any water present.

33. In an ammonia compression system, if the compressor operates with the suction valve closed and the discharge valve open,

(A) less purging is required.
(B) noncondensables will enter the system.
(C) more refrigerant charge is required.
(D) less refrigerant charge is required.

34. A refrigeration system has an electrically operated valve. The operating current is

(A) 6 volts AC or DC.
(B) 12 volts AC or DC.
(C) 18 volts.
(D) 24 volts AC or DC.

35. As a general rule, the condensers and receivers of industrial refrigeration systems should be filled to a maximum of

(A) 80 percent of total volume.
(B) 85 percent of total volume.
(C) 90 percent of total volume.
(D) 95 percent of total volume.

36. ASHRAE 34–1992 classifies refrigerant safety groups by two alphanumeric characters. What do the characters signify?

(A) Letters A and B signify refrigerant toxicity based on allowable exposure.
(B) Numbers 1, 2, and 3 indicate refrigerant flammability ranges.
(C) Classification 1 indicates refrigerant does not show flame propagation.
(D) All of the above

37. Compute the rpm of a single-acting air compressor, given S (stroke) = 9 inches and piston speed in feet per minute = 300:

Formula: $\frac{2 \times S \times \text{rpm}}{12}$

(A) 200 rpm
(B) 100 rpm
(C) 400 rpm
(D) 300 rpm

38. A halide torch is used in a refrigeration plant to

(A) solder piping.
(B) light up the equipment.
(C) test for ammonia leaks.
(D) test for Freon leaks.

39. The low-pressure side of the system is between the

(A) compressor and the king valve.
(B) evaporator outlet and the compressor.
(C) expansion valve and the compressor.
(D) suction stop valve and the discharge stop valve.

40. Which is most nearly the velocity of air in an air-conditioning duct, given rate of flow = 340 cfm and duct area = 4.5 sq. ft.?

Formula: $V = Q \div \lambda$

(A) 68 ft./min.
(B) 36 ft./min.
(C) 94 ft./min.
(D) 76 ft./min.

41. A machine operating at 10 tons produces

(A) approximately 10 tons of ice per day.
(B) more than 10 tons of ice per day.
(C) exactly 10 tons of ice per day.
(D) less than 10 tons of ice per day.

42. The booster compressor of a two-stage refrigeration system is located between the

(A) main compressor and the condenser.
(B) intercooler and the main compressor.
(C) condenser and the metering device.
(D) evaporator and the intercooler.

43. Carron oil, used to treat skin burns, is a mixture of

(A) lanolin and vinegar.
(B) sulphur dioxide and water.
(C) linseed oil and lime water.
(D) Vaseline and picric acid.

44. The amount of sodium chromate that may be added to 1,000 cubic feet of sodium chloride brine solution for corrosion protection is approximately

(A) 50 lbs.
(B) 75 lbs.
(C) 100 lbs.
(D) 200 lbs.

45. An R-22 refrigeration system contains a moisture indicator, which indicates moisture by

(A) changing color.
(B) setting off an alarm.
(C) popping up.
(D) opening a bypass valve.

46. The units of vacuum on a compound pressure gauge are read in inches of

(A) air.
(B) water.
(C) centimeter.
(D) mercury.

47. When evacuating a R-22 refrigeration system, connect the vacuum pump to

(A) the high-side of the system.
(B) the low-side of the system.
(C) both the high and low sides of the system.
(D) the top and bottom of the system receiver.

48. The New York State Environmental Protection Act, Chapter 294, and the U.S. Clean Air Act of 1990 are similar in that they

(A) regulate the shipment of explosives, including liquefied compressed gases.
(B) prohibit intentional venting or release of CFC refrigerants.
(C) permit oxygen deprivation sensors to be used as refrigerant leak detectors.
(D) none of the above.

49. Which of the following conditions can cause high discharge pressure?

(A) A condenser that is too small
(B) Overcharge of liquid refrigerant
(C) Insufficient cooling water
(D) All of the above

50. Electric expansion valves are operated or controlled by

(A) 6 volts AC or DC.
(B) 18 volts AC or DC.
(C) 12 volts AC or DC.
(D) 24 volts AC.

51. Blank-off pressure, used to rate vacuum pumps for evacuating refrigeration systems, is

(A) pressure cutout limit.
(B) the vacuum pump start-up pressure.
(C) the pressure needed to overcome system pressure.
(D) the pressure at which gases stop flowing from the system to the pump.

52. An R-12 refrigeration system utilizes a TXV valve with a direct expansion type evaporator. According to recommended practice, the superheat is best determined by subtracting the

(A) inlet absolute temperature at the evaporator, from the outlet.
(B) saturation temperature of the refrigerant to the remote bulb, from the measured temperature at the remote bulb.
(C) outlet temperature at the evaporator from the temperature of the refrigerated space.
(D) saturation temperature of the refrigerant at the remote bulb from the inlet temperature of the evaporator.

53. The lubricant used with HFC refrigerants such as R-134a is

(A) Alkylbenzene.
(B) PAG.
(C) Polyolester.
(D) Mineral.

54. Hydrochlorofluorocarbons may be classified as having a

(A) high ozone depletion potential.
(B) very low ozone depletion potential.
(C) high global warming potential.
(D) threshold limit value refrigerant.

55. Two-way, normally closed, direct-acting pilot solenoid valves are generally NOT used with which of the following components?

(A) A large piston-type, spring-loaded expansion valve
(B) An evaporator pressure regulator to provide either shut-off service or pressure pilot selector
(C) Four-way refrigerant switching valves on heat pump systems
(D) A cylinder unloading mechanism for compressor capacity reduction

56. The water flowing in a vertical shell and tube condenser makes

(A) a single pass.
(B) a double pass.
(C) a triple pass.
(D) no pass—since water is in the shell.

57. If a high side is operating at 100 psig, what is the high side full-scale deflection read on the gauge?

(A) 100 psig
(B) 110 psig
(C) 120 psig
(D) 150 psig

58. Side outlet dryers used on systems using R-22, R-12, and R-500 refrigerants are generally located

(A) in the liquid line, mounted vertically with the flange on top.
(B) in the liquid line, mounted horizontally or vertically with the flange on the bottom.
(C) between the evaporator and the compressor, mounted horizontally with the flange on the top.
(D) just after the expansion valve, mounted vertically with the flange on top.

59. When a smoke detector that is installed in the duct of an air distribution system that consists of 2500 cubic feet per minute detects a smoke condition, what action should be followed?

(A) The system should remain on line while the operator checks the cause of the smoke detector's activation.
(B) The compressor of the air conditioning system should be turned off.
(C) The air distribution fans must be run at maximum capacity, in order to vent the smoke as quickly as possible.
(D) The air distribution fans must be automatically shut down.

60. What is the compression ratio of an ammonia system, which is functioning at standard operating conditions, with a suction pressure of 24.27 psig and head pressure of 169.2 psig?

(A) 2.5 to 1
(B) 6.9 to 1
(C) 17.2 to 1
(D) 202 to 1

Answers to Practice Test 2

1. **The correct answer is (D).**
2. **The correct answer is (C).**
3. **The correct answer is (D).**
4. **The correct answer is (A).**
5. **The correct answer is (D).**
6. **The correct answer is (D).**
7. **The correct answer is (A).**
8. **The correct answer is (A).**
9. **The correct answer is (C).**
10. **The correct answer is (A).**
11. **The correct answer is (A).**
12. **The correct answer is (C).**
13. **The correct answer is (A).**
14. **The correct answer is (D).**
15. **The correct answer is (A).**
16. **The correct answer is (A).**
17. **The correct answer is (D).**
18. **The correct answer is (D).**
19. **The correct answer is (A).**
20. **The correct answer is (C).**
21. **The correct answer is (B).**
22. **The correct answer is (D).**
23. **The correct answer is (C).**
24. **The correct answer is (A).** TXV expansion valve controls superheat within a range of 1 to 3° F variation. The normal superheat setting is 7 to 10° F.
25. **The correct answer is (D).**
26. **The correct answer is (A).**
27. **The correct answer is (C).**
28. **The correct answer is (C).**
29. **The correct answer is (B).**
30. **The correct answer is (D).**
31. **The correct answer is (B).**
32. **The correct answer is (D).**
33. **The correct answer is (B).** Noncondensables will enter the compressor and then be drawn into the system.
34. **The correct answer is (D).**
35. **The correct answer is (B).**
36. **The correct answer is (D).**
37. **The correct answer is (A).**

$$\text{Piston speed} = \frac{2 \times S \times \text{rpm}}{12}$$
$$300 = \frac{2 \times 9 \times \text{rpm}}{12}$$
$$(12)\ 300 = \frac{2 \times 9 \times \text{rpm}\ (12)}{12}$$
$$3600 = 18\ \text{rpm}$$
$$\frac{3600}{18} = \frac{18\ \text{rpm}}{18}$$
$$200 = \text{rpm}$$

38. **The correct answer is (D).**
39. **The correct answer is (C).**
40. **The correct answer is (D).**
    $V = Q \div \lambda$
    $V = 340 \div 4.5 = 75.5$
41. **The correct answer is (D).**
42. **The correct answer is (D).**
43. **The correct answer is (C).**
44. **The correct answer is (D).** Note: If it was calcium chloride brine, the amount added for the same question would be 100 pounds.
45. **The correct answer is (A).**
46. **The correct answer is (D).**
47. **The correct answer is (C).**
48. **The correct answer is (B).**
49. **The correct answer is (D).**
50. **The correct answer is (D).**
51. **The correct answer is (D).**
52. **The correct answer is (B).**
53. **The correct answer is (C).**
54. **The correct answer is (B).**
55. **The correct answer is (D).**
56. **The correct answer is (A).** Water flows from the top of the condenser down the swirls, to the bottom of the condenser.
57. **The correct answer is (C).** Code specifies high side full-scale deflection to be 20 percent greater than the high side operating pressure.
58. **The correct answer is (B).**
59. **The correct answer is (D).**
60. **The correct answer is (B).** Solution: $169.2 \div 24.27 = 6.97$

PRACTICE TEST 3

1. Which does not restrict the flow of liquid refrigerant?
   (A) The automatic expansion valve
   (B) The thermostatic expansion valve
   (C) The solenoid valve
   (D) The capillary tube

2. Two or three eliminators are sometimes used in large shell-and-tube coolers to
   (A) obtain dry suction gas from the coolers.
   (B) purge air or foul gas before it enters the suction line.
   (C) remove any oil from the suction gas.
   (D) eliminate the need for an economizer.

3. In many Freon compression systems, the liquid line and suction line contact one another because
   (A) only half as many pipe hangers are required.
   (B) this makes a neater-looking insulation job.
   (C) the refrigerating effect is somewhat increased per pound of refrigerant pumped.
   (D) there is less likelihood of the evaporators becoming oil-logged.

4. A standard-angle-pattern packed-globe valve for ammonia service is double-seated so
   (A) it won't leak much under normal operating conditions.
   (B) it can be easily repacked without taking the plant out of service.
   (C) the packing alone serves as extra insurance that the valve won't leak during plant operation.
   (D) the pressure drop through the valve is moderate under normal operating conditions.

5. On which tachometer do you mark the rotating object with reflecting tape?
   (A) The electronic tachometer (stroboscope)
   (B) The digital photo tachometer
   (C) The centrifugal-type tachometer
   (D) The chronometric tachometer

6. Gaskets used with ammonia-flanged fittings are made of
   (A) rubber.
   (B) neoprene.
   (C) lead.
   (D) asbestos and copper.

7. An external-equalized expansion valve with a sensing bulb
   (A) eliminates the effect of pressure drop through the coil.
   (B) prevents the thermostatic valve from becoming oil-logged.
   (C) permits the use of different types of refrigerants in the system.
   (D) eliminates superheat adjustments.

8. The faces of an ammonia oval-flanged (two-bolt) fitting are usually
   (A) flat-faced.
   (B) raised-faced.
   (C) tongue and groove.
   (D) serrated.

9. In an ammonia refrigerating plant, a ground-joint union would most likely be found in the
   (A) purge line.
   (B) relief valve discharge.
   (C) bypass line around the expansion valve.
   (D) starting bypass on the compressor.

10. Which of the following is a disadvantage of the flooded system?
    (A) A large refrigerant charge is needed.
    (B) Heat transmission in the evaporator is reduced.
    (C) Wet vapor enters the compressor.
    (D) The refrigerant picks up less heat per pound.

11. An oil separator is used in the discharge line of a Freon refrigeration system to
    (A) lubricate the solenoid.
    (B) return oil to the compressor crankcase.
    (C) provide oil for the unloaders.
    (D) remove noncondensable gas from the oil.

12. As the specific gravity of calcium chloride brine increases,
    (A) specific heat increases and then decreases.
    (B) density decreases.
    (C) freezing point increases.
    (D) freezing point decreases.

13. A cooler is 72 inches in diameter and 35 feet long. Its gross volume is about
    (A) 750 cu. ft.
    (B) 850 cu. ft.
    (C) 1,000 cu. ft.
    (D) 1,100 cu. ft.

14. The main function of a thermostatic expansion valve is to

(A) control suction pressure.
(B) modulate refrigerant flow.
(C) vary compressor running time.
(D) completely change liquid refrigerant into dry, saturated vapor.

15. The instrument that indicates air velocity directly when used in air-conditioning duct flow measurement is the

(A) psychrometer.
(B) anemometer.
(C) manometer.
(D) humidifier.

16. The minimum field leak test pressure for the high side of a methyl chloride refrigeration system is

(A) 30 psig.
(B) 95 psig.
(C) 130 psig.
(D) 210 psig.

17. It is customary to charge a compression refrigeration system with vapor to the

(A) discharge side of the compressor.
(B) discharge side of the condenser.
(C) suction side of the compressor.
(D) charging valve in the liquid line.

18. In an automatically operated, flooded shell-and-tube cooler, an electric float switch is used primarily to

(A) control the flow of brine into the tubes.
(B) control the flow of refrigerant into the shell.
(C) purge oil from the cooler.
(D) purge noncondensable gas from the cooler.

19. A refrigerating system operates at 100 psi in the high side. The dial of the pressure gauge permanently installed in the high side should have a minimum full-scale reading of

(A) 100 psi.
(B) 110 psi.
(C) 115 psi.
(D) 120 psi.

20. Which distributor does NOT require an external equalizer valve?

(A) Manifold type
(B) Centrifugal type
(C) Venturi type
(D) Pressure-drop type

21. The blank-off pressure is commonly used to rate

(A) refrigeration compressors.
(B) vacuum pumps.
(C) air-cooled condensers.
(D) metering devices.

22. The performance of a condenser in a chilled-water refrigeration system can best be determined by the

(A) compressor capacity rating.
(B) size of the refrigerant device.
(C) amount of subcooling.
(D) refrigerant effect of the cooling coil.

23. Refrigeration systems A and B each absorb 400 btu per minute. The suction temperature of system A is 5° F, and the suction temperature of system B is 10° F. Which of the following statements is correct?

(A) Both systems A and B are operating at 1 ton.
(B) Both systems A and B are operating at 2 tons.
(C) System A is operating at 1 ton, and system B is operating at 2 tons.
(D) System A is operating at 2 tons, and system B is operating at 1 ton.

24. Which refrigerant is R-718?

(A) Ammonia
(B) Methyl chloride
(C) Water
(D) Propane

25. To clean scale deposits from a shell-and-coil condenser, you should use a

(A) special nylon brush.
(B) wire brush and scraper.
(C) solution of inhibited hydrochloric acid.
(D) weak caustic soda solution.

26. The index of performance of a refrigeration system is the

(A) refrigeration performance factor.
(B) coefficient of performance.
(C) efficiency.
(D) pressure ratio.

27. The boiling point of R-22 at atmospheric pressure is about

(A) –40° F.
(B) –10° F.
(C) 10° F.
(D) 40° F.

28. "Anhydrous" means the

(A) presence of ammonia.
(B) presence of water.
(C) absence of Freon.
(D) absence of water.

29. Which is the main reason why some cooling towers have a constant water bleed-off?

(A) To prevent the build-up of solids in the tower water
(B) To dispose of some hot water for cooling purposes
(C) To eliminate the need for chemical treatment and save money
(D) To remove all noncondensables

30. To vary the capacity of an absorption-type refrigeration plant from 50 percent to 100 percent of rated load, you should

(A) charge more refrigerant into the system and reset the expansion valve.
(B) open the purge valve and reset the expansion valve.
(C) increase the flow of condenser water and reset the expansion valve.
(D) increase the flow of steam to the generator and reset the expansion valve.

31. The principal difference between a lithium bromide water absorption cycle and an ammonia water absorption cycle is the

(A) thermodynamic cycle.
(B) pressure range of the cycle.
(C) type of evaporator used in the system.
(D) control of the generator and absorber in the system.

32. The force exerted on a 4" piston with a cylinder pressure of 90 psi is

(A) 1,140 lbs.
(B) 1,200 lbs.
(C) 1,224 lbs.
(D) 1,256 lbs.

33. If the evaporator in a compression system becomes oil logged, the direct result is

(A) decrease in head pressure.
(B) increase in head pressure.
(C) loss of refrigerating effect.
(D) increase in suction pressure.

34. Which is an auxiliary apparatus in a conventional absorption system?

(A) The generator
(B) The absorber
(C) The analyzer
(D) The evaporator

35. Which statement is most accurate about the use of metals in refrigerating systems?

(A) Aluminum should not contact any Freon refrigerants.
(B) Magnesium alloys can contact R-22.
(C) Ammonia cannot contact copper.
(D) Magnesium can contact methyl chloride.

36. The reading on a gauge in a refrigeration system is 10 inches of mercury vacuum. The pressure expressed in absolute is about

(A) 14.70 psia.
(B) 11.8 psia.
(C) 9.8 psia.
(D) 6.4 psia.

37. Which piping material can be used with methyl chloride systems?

(A) Zinc
(B) Magnesium
(C) Aluminum
(D) Copper

38. In relation to suction pressure, oil pressure in a modem compressor should be

(A) 60 to 90 pounds higher.
(B) 30 to 90 pounds higher.
(C) 15 to 30 pounds higher.
(D) none of the above (both pressures should be the same).

39. A cylinder containing activated alumina in the high side of a Freon system

(A) drys the refrigerant.
(B) prevents oil carryover.
(C) acts as a very fine strainer.
(D) regenerates the refrigerant.

40. Pressure relief valves on a reciprocating compressor handling R-12 are normally set

(A) higher than that of the high-pressure cutout.
(B) equal to that of the high pressure cutout.
(C) below that of the high pressure cutout.
(D) at twice the oil pressure.

41. Which refrigerant is widely used in centrifugal compressors?

(A) R-12
(B) R-22
(C) R-113
(D) R-502

42. If silica gel picks up moisture before being replaced as a drier in a refrigeration system, it may be reactivated by heating to about

(A) 100° F.
(B) 450° F.
(C) 800° F.
(D) 1150° F.

43. According to both the New York City and ASHRAE codes, if an R-717 refrigeration machine room calls for ducts on one or more power-driven units, where should the inlet for these ducts be located?

(A) On the floor near the compressor
(B) Six feet above the floor by the compressor
(C) Near the ceiling of the engine room
(D) Above the cylinder of the compressor

44. The most correct statement about the compression ratio of a reciprocating compressor is

(A) it remains constant under all operating conditions.
(B) it varies according to operating conditions.
(C) it equals the ratio of gauge suction pressure to gauge discharge pressure.
(D) it equals the saturated discharge temperature divided by the saturated suction temperature.

45. An evaporator absorbs heat from air or brine because liquid refrigerant entering the evaporator

(A) has a lower temperature than the air or brine.
(B) has a higher temperature than the air or brine.
(C) boils to a low-pressure gas.
(D) boils to a high-pressure gas.

46. Which is a chemical property of refrigerant lubricating oil?

(A) Refrigerant resistance
(B) Volatility
(C) Solubility of water in the oil
(D) Wax separation

47. If electricity costs 15 cents per kilowatt hour, the cost per hour to operate a 45-horsepower motor with an efficiency of 85 percent is about

(A) $3.00
(B) $4.00
(C) $5.00
(D) $6.00

48. The rated discharge capacity of a rupture member discharging to atmosphere under critical flow conditions in pounds of air per minute is given by the formula $C = 0.8\ p^1\ D^2$. Given that C = 1.2 pounds per minute and p1 = 24 psia, the valve of D (diameter of the rupture disc) is about

(A) .165 inches.
(B) .185 inches.
(C) .220 inches.
(D) .250 inches.

49. A three-phase, 40-HP induction motor operating at 440 volts, 50 hertz has 8 poles. Calculate the revolutions per minute.

(A) 1,800 rpm
(B) 1,200 rpm
(C) 900 rpm
(D) 750 rpm

Answers to Practice Test 3

1. **The correct answer is (C).**
2. **The correct answer is (A).**
3. **The correct answer is (C).**
4. **The correct answer is (B).**
5. **The correct answer is (B).**
6. **The correct answer is (C).**
7. **The correct answer is (A).**
8. **The correct answer is (C).**
9. **The correct answer is (B).**
10. **The correct answer is (A).**
11. **The correct answer is (B).**
12. **The correct answer is (C).**
13. **The correct answer is (C).** The volume is 989.604. The closest choice to this answer is (C), 1,000.
14. **The correct answer is (B).**
15. **The correct answer is (B).**
16. **The correct answer is (D).** Low side = 120 psi
17. **The correct answer is (C).**
18. **The correct answer is (B).**
19. **The correct answer is (D).** The gauge limit should be 20 percent above the highest system operating pressure.
20. **The correct answer is (A).**
21. **The correct answer is (B).**
22. **The correct answer is (C).**
23. **The correct answer is (B).** Given 1 minute per ton, A system and B system are absorbing 400 tons of refrigeration. 400 + 200 = 2 tons of refrigeration per minute.
24. **The correct answer is (C).**
25. **The correct answer is (D).**
26. **The correct answer is (B).**
27. **The correct answer is (A).**
28. **The correct answer is (D).**
29. **The correct answer is (A).**
30. **The correct answer is (D).**
31. **The correct answer is (B).**
32. **The correct answer is (A).** Total force = $\pi R^2 \times$ pressure

    3.14 (2)(2)(90)

    12.56(90)

    1130.4
33. **The correct answer is (C).**
34. **The correct answer is (C).**
35. **The correct answer is (C).**
36. **The correct answer is (C).** $\frac{30-10}{2} = 10$
37. **The correct answer is (D).**
38. **The correct answer is (C).**
39. **The correct answer is (A).**
40. **The correct answer is (A).**
41. **The correct answer is (C).**
42. **The correct answer is (B).**
43. **The correct answer is (C).**
44. **The correct answer is (B).**
45. **The correct answer is (A).**
46. **The correct answer is (B).**
47. **The correct answer is (D).**
48. **The correct answer is (D).**
49. **The correct answer is (D).**

PRACTICE TEST 4

1. A pressure or temperature response mechanism for automatically stopping the operation of the pressure-imposing element is a
   (A) pressure-imposing device.
   (B) pressure-limiting device.
   (C) pressure-relief device.
   (D) pressure-relief valve.

2. In a properly operating system, flash gas is most likely to form in the
   (A) condenser.
   (B) evaporator.
   (C) receiver.
   (D) compressor.

3. Which refrigerant operates at a head pressure of 50 psig?
   (A) Carbon dioxide
   (B) Sulphur dioxide
   (C) Methyl chloride
   (D) Nitrous oxide

4. Which does NOT cause high head pressure in a comfort-cooling system?
   (A) Insufficient condenser water
   (B) Overcharge
   (C) Refrigerant gas in the liquid line
   (D) An undersized condenser

5. The temperature of refrigerant leaving the intercooler of a two-stage system is most likely to be
   (A) the cooling water temperature.
   (B) near evaporator temperature.
   (C) 120° F.
   (D) 60° F.

6. In a flooded shell-and-tube brine cooler, the brine is usually pumped
   (A) alternately through the tubes and the shell.
   (B) through the tubes.
   (C) through the tubes and the shell.
   (D) through the shell.

7. In a centrifugal compressor, oiling is required
   (A) only at the shaft end bearings.
   (B) at the shaft end bearing and the rotor.
   (C) at the shaft end bearing, rotor, and stage separators.
   (D) at the shaft end bearing and stage separators.

8. A direct expansion (bare) coil evaporator is used to maintain a meat storage space at 28 to 30° F. The last coil has no frost. It can be said that this
   (A) condition is acceptable to maintain a high plant efficiency.
   (B) is a direct indication of air in the system.
   (C) indicates moisture in the refrigerant.
   (D) is a direct indication that the coil is being starved.

9. Sodium chloride is not used when the temperature is
   (A) –20° F.
   (B) 10° F.
   (C) 5° F.
   (D) 0° F.

10. Which indicates a two-stage system?
    (A) Two identical pistons
    (B) An intercooler
    (C) An aftercooler
    (D) Suction and discharge on both sides of the piston

11. To defrost a low-temperature, direct-expansion evaporator quickly,
    (A) open the cold-storage door and let frost melt off.
    (B) circulate heated brine through the coil.
    (C) take a snow chisel and scrape frost off.
    (D) send hot gas to the coil.

12. An oiling system in a large centrifugal system should consist of at least
    (A) reservoir, oil heater, and filter.
    (B) reservoir, centrifuge, and filter.
    (C) reservoir, pump, and distribution lines.
    (D) pump, filter, and centrifuge.

13. Which of the following is suitable material for use in the conveying of R-22?
    (A) Magnesium
    (B) Copper
    (C) Cast iron
    (D) Aluminum

14. A constant-pressure expansion valve is operating under a fluctuating load. Under a heavy load, this valve will
    (A) starve the evaporator.
    (B) starve, then flood, the evaporator.
    (C) flood the evaporator.
    (D) increase suction pressure.

15. The accumulator is generally between the

(A) evaporator and compressor.
(B) compressor and condenser.
(C) receiver and expansion valve.
(D) metering device and evaporator.

16. What kind of metering device would be used in a flooded evaporator system?

(A) Low-side float
(B) Thermostatic expansion valve
(C) Hand expansion valve
(D) High-side float

17. In an ammonia absorption system, the counterflow heat exchanger would be located between the

(A) compressor and receiver.
(B) generator and rectifier.
(C) generator and absorber.
(D) rectifier and absorber.

18. The suction pressure of an ammonia system must be adjusted to maintain

(A) 5° F evaporator temperature.
(B) 5 psig in the evaporator.
(C) an evaporator temperature below that of the material being cooled.
(D) an evaporator temperature equal to that of the material being cooled.

19. Assume that a refrigeration system is normally charged with 150 pounds of refrigerant. According to code, how much refrigerant could be stored in the machine room?

(A) 60 lbs.
(B) 45 lbs.
(C) 30 lbs.
(D) 15 lbs.

20. Freon compressors sometimes have magnetic cylinder bypass valves. These valves primarily

(A) protect the compressor from liquid slugs.
(B) allow operation at different capacities.
(C) equalize working pressures in all cylinders.
(D) return oil from the cylinders to the crankcase.

21. Which system cools a home in the summer and heats it in the winter?

(A) Heat pump
(B) Absorption
(C) Thermostat with remote bulb
(D) Differential

22. If a dirty cooling tower is started in a reverse cycle system, what is likely to clog?

(A) The check valves
(B) The evaporator
(C) The four-way valve
(D) The condenser

23. In a reverse-cycle system, what changes the flow of refrigerant vapor when the system switches from heating to cooling?

(A) The compressor
(B) The four-way valve
(C) The differential control
(D) The check valves

24. Many gauges in refrigeration work have black and red scales on the face. What is true about these scales?

(A) Red indicates pressure.
(B) Black indicates saturation temperature.
(C) Red indicates superheat temperature.
(D) Black indicates pressure.

25. The capillary line of a thermostatic expansion valve with an external equalizer is ruptured, and the charge is lost from the thermal bulb. The expansion valve will

(A) remain fully open.
(B) be operated by the external equalizer.
(C) hunt constantly.
(D) remain fully closed.

26. If the capacity of a refrigeration plant increases,

(A) head pressure and horsepower increase.
(B) horsepower increases and suction pressure decreases.
(C) compression ratio and horsepower decrease.
(D) volumetric efficiency decreases and horsepower increases.

27. In an ammonia refrigerating plant, calcium chloride is used as an indirect cooling agent in an ice field. A leak occurs and the brine becomes partially saturated with ammonia. After fixing the leak, you

(A) dump all of this brine and make a new batch.
(B) pump the brine through the plant condensers and test for ammonia; if none is present, reuse the brine.
(C) treat the brine with Nesslers solution, then reuse it.
(D) treat the brine with sulfur, then reuse it.

28. The remote bulb of a thermostatic expansion valve 7/8" and larger should be installed

(A) on the suction line, upstream of the equalizer line.
(B) on the suction line, at the 4 or 8 o'clock position.
(C) on the suction line, on a horizontal run.
(D) all of the above.

29. Thermal expansion valves are generally rated at stated suction temperatures in

(A) tons of refrigerating effect.
(B) pounds per minute of refrigerant pumped.
(C) pounds per hour of refrigerant pumped.
(D) cubic feet per minute of refrigerant pumped.

30. A refrigerating plant has a single compressor serving two evaporators. One operates at 40° F and the other at 20° F. A back pressure, or two-temperature, valve should be installed in the

(A) low-temperature suction line.
(B) high-temperature suction line.
(C) low-pressure suction line.
(D) liquid line to the high-temperature coil.

31. "Swirls" direct water through the tubes of what kind of condenser?

(A) Horizontal tube-and-shell condenser
(B) Double-pipe condenser
(C) Evaporative condenser
(D) Vertical shell-and-tube condenser

32. Which of the following new refrigerants was designed for centrifugal applications?

(A) HCFC-123
(B) HCFC-124
(C) HCFC-125
(D) HCFC-152a

33. Refrigeration systems A and B each absorb 336,000 btu per hour. The suction temperature of system A is 15° F, and the suction temperature of system B is 25° F. Both systems are operating at

(A) 28 tons.
(B) 1,680 tons.
(C) 1.7 tons.
(D) 168 tons.

34. Which expansion valve can be located in any ambient temperature and used for any application from 50° F to –40° F?

(A) Gas-charge type
(B) Vapor cross-charge type
(C) Liquid-charge type
(D) Liquid cross-charge type

35. Which vacuum-indicating instrument is recommended for measuring pressures in the range of 1,000 microns or less?

(A) The compound gauge
(B) The U-tube manometer
(C) The electronic vacuum gauge
(D) The wet-bulb-type vacuum indicator

36. To automatically control the operation of a compressor from suction pressure, a system should have a(n)

(A) thermostat in the room to be cooled.
(B) pressurestat with the control line connected to the low side of the system.
(C) pressurestat with the control line connected to the top of the receiver shell.
(D) aquastat with the bulb set in the water line from the condensers.

37. In a comfort-cooling installation of a Freon compression plant, an overcharge of refrigerant would most likely result in

(A) an increase in high-side pressure when operating.
(B) a decrease in high-side pressure when operating.
(C) normal operation.
(D) a decrease in the horsepower per ton of refrigerating effect.

38. Freon is similar to methyl chloride as a refrigerant because

(A) they have the same chemical properties.
(B) their cost is identical.
(C) their vapor densities are practically equal.
(D) both are miscible with lubricating oil.

39. A central air-conditioning plant is used to cool a residential building. The ratio of horsepower to tonnage of refrigeration is

(A) 1
(B) 2.5
(C) 3
(D) 3.5

40. Which statement is correct?

(A) A spray pond and an evaporative condenser operate exactly alike.
(B) A spray pond requires recirculation of a secondary body of ocean or bay water.
(C) A closed-type cooling tower depends on stack effect for circulation of air.
(D) An evaporative condenser depends upon the vaporization of spray water for economical operation.

41. A sudden reduction in the supply of condenser cooling water in a compression system usually results in

(A) a decrease in head pressure.
(B) unloading of the compressor.
(C) an increase in head pressure.
(D) a decrease in compressor speed.

42. A compressor has a volumetric efficiency of 72 percent when operating at its design speed of 300 rpm. If the speed is increased to 500 rpm, volumetric efficiency

(A) decreases.
(B) increases and remains higher as long as it is run at the higher speed.
(C) remains at 72 percent.
(D) increases for the first 24 hours of operation at the higher speed, then decreases.

43. A stuffing box lantern is

(A) made of metal with oil circulating through it.
(B) made of rubber and surrounded by packing.
(C) prevented from spreading by the packing.
(D) made of metal with the oil sleeve and oil supply not opposite each other.

44. The capacity of a reciprocating compressor decreases as the

(A) suction pressure increases.
(B) volumetric efficiency increases.
(C) compression ratio increases.
(D) discharge pressure decreases.

45. A finned-tube evaporator is operating efficiently when it is

(A) totally frosted.
(B) partially frosted.
(C) wet.
(D) dry.

46. In an evaporator that chills brine, the greatest cooling effect on the brine results from the

(A) boiling of low-pressure liquid.
(B) heat absorption by the flashed gas.
(C) transfer of heat to the low-pressure gas.
(D) low temperature of the refrigerant entering the expansion valve.

47. Which of the following refrigerants has the lowest solubility with lubricating oil?

(A) Carbon dioxide
(B) R-12
(C) Genetron 141
(D) Methyl chloride

48. The rated discharge capacity of the pressure-relief device or fusible plug for a refrigerant-containing vessel is determined by the formula C = Fd1. "C" equals

(A) btu per minute.
(B) refrigerant pressure.
(C) air in pounds per minute.
(D) cubic feet per minute.

49. Which of the following refers to a Class T machine room?

(A) It must have a door opening into or under a fire escape.
(B) All pipes must be sealed into the wall, ceiling, and floor, constructed to resist fire for over 2 hours.
(C) It must be a sealed room constructed to resist fire for no less than 2 hours.
(D) All pipes piercing the wall and ceiling should be tightly sealed and constructed to resist fire for no less than 1 hour.

50. One of the most common fan motors used for condensers and evaporators is the

(A) repulsion-start induction motor.
(B) capacitor-start induction motor.
(C) squirrel cage.
(D) synchronous motor.

Answers to Practice Test 4

1. **The correct answer is (B).** (at a predetermined pressure)
2. **The correct answer is (B).**
3. **The correct answer is (B).**
4. **The correct answer is (C).**
5. **The correct answer is (B).**
6. **The correct answer is (B).**
7. **The correct answer is (A).**
8. **The correct answer is (D).**
9. **The correct answer is (A).** Sodium chloride freezes at –6°F.
10. **The correct answer is (B).**
11. **The correct answer is (D).**
12. **The correct answer is (C).**
13. **The correct answer is (B).**
14. **The correct answer is (A).**
15. **The correct answer is (A).**
16. **The correct answer is (A).**
17. **The correct answer is (C).**
18. **The correct answer is (C).**
19. **The correct answer is (C).**
20. **The correct answer is (B).**
21. **The correct answer is (A).**
22. **The correct answer is (C).**
23. **The correct answer is (B).**
24. **The correct answer is (D).** Black scale indicates pressure; red scale indicates temperature.
25. **The correct answer is (D).**
26. **The correct answer is (C).**
27. **The correct answer is (A).**
28. **The correct answer is (B).** (suction line 7/8″ and larger)
29. **The correct answer is (A).**
30. **The correct answer is (B).**
31. **The correct answer is (D).**
32. **The correct answer is (A).**
33. **The correct answer is (A).**
34. **The correct answer is (B).**
35. **The correct answer is (C).**
36. **The correct answer is (B).**
37. **The correct answer is (A).**
38. **The correct answer is (C).**
39. **The correct answer is (A).**
40. **The correct answer is (D).**
41. **The correct answer is (C).**
42. **The correct answer is (B).**
43. **The correct answer is (A).**
44. **The correct answer is (C).**
45. **The correct answer is (C).**
46. **The correct answer is (A).**
47. **The correct answer is (A).**
48. **The correct answer is (C).**
49. **The correct answer is (D).**
50. **The correct answer is (C).**

PRACTICE TEST 5

1. The suction pressure of any refrigeration system is adjusted
   (A) to an evaporator temperature below that of the material being cooled.
   (B) to an evaporator temperature equal to that of the material being cooled.
   (C) to a pressure above atmospheric at all times.
   (D) none of the above.

2. Where would the muffler be placed in a reciprocating system?
   (A) Between the receiver and condenser
   (B) Between the evaporator and condenser
   (C) Between the compressor and evaporative condenser
   (D) Between the evaporator and compressor

3. The TXV is controlled by
   (A) coil temperature.
   (B) the difference in gas temperature and the temperature corresponding to the gas pressure.
   (C) the difference in gas pressure and the pressure corresponding to the gas temperature.
   (D) coil pressure.

4. Assuming all other conditions remain constant, a decrease in evaporator load causes
   (A) higher head pressure.
   (B) lower suction pressure.
   (C) higher suction pressure.
   (D) lower oil pressure.

5. In a flooded evaporator using an accumulator and float valve, flash gas
   (A) passes directly into the evaporator.
   (B) passes directly into the suction line.
   (C) does not occur.
   (D) stays in the receiver.

6. The feeler bulb of a TXV would be located
   (A) before the evaporator.
   (B) after the evaporator.
   (C) midway along the evaporator.
   (D) before the liquid seal.

7. The oil trap on a refrigeration system is located
   (A) on the discharge line, as far from the compressor as possible.
   (B) on the suction line, close to the evaporator.
   (C) on the liquid line, between the receiver and evaporator.
   (D) none of the above.

8. What controls the operation of a high-side float?
   (A) The condenser
   (B) The evaporator
   (C) The condenser and receiver
   (D) The evaporator and condenser

9. When suction pressure decreases, compressor capacity
   (A) increases.
   (B) decreases.
   (C) slightly decreases.
   (D) slightly increases.

10. The three operating pressures of the TXV valve are
    (A) evaporator pressure, spring pressure, and suction pressure.
    (B) evaporator pressure, bulb pressure, and condenser pressure.
    (C) evaporator pressure, spring pressure, and discharge pressure.
    (D) evaporator pressure, spring pressure, and bulb pressure.

11. The suction pressure in a refrigerating system is 15″ Hg. Converted to absolute, this pressure, in pounds per square inch, is
    (A) 30 psia.
    (B) 16 psia.
    (C) 8 psia.
    (D) 2 psia.

12. When the low-side pressure of an ammonia refrigeration plant is 15 psig, what is the corresponding evaporator temperature?
    (A) 15 degrees
    (B) –15 degrees
    (C) –10 degrees
    (D) 0 degrees

13. The speed of an 8-pole synchronous motor rated at 40 HP, 440 volts, and 60 hertz is
    (A) 480 rpm.
    (B) 900 rpm.
    (C) 1,800 rpm.
    (D) 7,200 rpm.

14. How much refrigerant may be stored in a machine room if the system contains 125 lbs.?
    (A) 25 lbs.
    (B) 35 lbs.
    (C) 45 lbs.
    (D) 55 lbs.

15. What would it cost to run a 10 hp motor, operating at 85 percent efficiency, for 1 hour at 8 cents per kilowatt hour?

(A) $.50
(B) $.70
(C) $1.00
(D) $1.20

16. At 1,000 psig, the total head pressure on a piston 3 inches in diameter is

(A) 3,104 lbs.
(B) 5,065 lbs.
(C) 7,065 lbs.
(D) 8,104 lbs.

17. The amount of refrigerant stored in a machine room should not be more than

(A) 20 percent of refrigerant charge in system nor more than 300 lbs.
(B) 25 percent of refrigerant charge in system nor more than 325 lbs.
(C) 30 percent of refrigerant charge in system nor more than 300 lbs.
(D) 35 percent of refrigerant charge in system nor more than 350 lbs.

18. A lithium bromide water absorption system is used to produce chilled water. The lowest possible water temperature leaving the evaporator is

(A) 31° F.
(B) 33° F.
(C) 35° F.
(D) 38° F.

19. The dielectric strength of a refrigerant oil is

(A) the temperature at which it ceases to flow.
(B) the strength of its acidic pH.
(C) a measure of resistance to the passage of electric current.
(D) a measure of velocity of refrigerant flow through piping.

20. One ton of refrigerant equals

(A) 3.3 btu per minute.
(B) 288 btu per minute.
(C) 200 btu per minute.
(D) 7.48 btu per minute.

21. Sixty gallons of water are to be cooled from 80° F to 40° F, with no spare capacity. This requires a machine rated at

(A) 85 tons.
(B) 100 tons.
(C) 55 tons.
(D) 75 tons.

22. Is there an ideal treatment for all cooling water systems?

(A) Yes—sodium-dichromate
(B) No—treatment is determined by size and type of system
(C) Yes—sodium bichromate
(D) None of the above

23. Which two types of brines are used as secondary refrigerants?

(A) Sulfur chloride and sodium chloride
(B) Sodium chloride and calcium chloride
(C) Calcium chloride and ethyl chloride
(D) Sulfur chloride and calcium chloride

24. The ventilation required for a machinery room containing 1,500 pounds of refrigerant is

(A) 2,500 cfm.
(B) 2,650 cfm.
(C) 1,500 cfm.
(D) 1,450 cfm.

25. According to code, how many service masks (breathing apparatus) should be in a machinery room using 950 pounds of a Group 2 refrigerant?

(A) One
(B) Two
(C) Three
(D) Four

26. The mechanical ventilation of a machinery room using R-22 consists of one or more power exhaust fans with the inlet

(A) near the floor by the A/C unit.
(B) 6 inches from the ceiling.
(C) above the A/C unit.
(D) none of the above.

27. Machinery rooms with Group 1 refrigerant should be equipped with vapor alarms to warn of oxygen levels below

(A) 10 percent volume.
(B) 20 percent volume.
(C) 30 percent volume.
(D) 40 percent volume.

28. The maximum permissible quantity of a Group 2 refrigerant indirect system in an Class T machinery room of a public assembly building is

(A) 500 lbs.
(B) 1,000 lbs.
(C) 300 lbs.
(D) unlimited.

29. The maximum temperature of a system is 78° Celsius. What is the equivalent on the Fahrenheit scale?

(A) 125° F
(B) 155.4° F
(C) 172.4° F
(D) 179.4° F

30. The high-side test pressure is the same for which refrigerants?

(A) Ammonia, R-22
(B) R-11, R-22
(C) R-11, R-12
(D) CO_2, NH_3

31. The low-side test pressure is the same for which refrigerants?

(A) R-11, R-22
(B) R-11, methylene chloride
(C) Methyl chloride, methylene chloride
(D) R-11, R-12

32. Which metal is NOT used in a methyl chloride system?

(A) Aluminum
(B) Carbon steel
(C) Cast iron
(D) Lead

33. Copper alloys should NOT contact

(A) magnesium.
(B) methylene chloride.
(C) ammonia.
(D) Freon.

34. How much oxygen is permissible for system testing?

(A) 20 lbs.
(B) 35 lbs.
(C) There is no limit.
(D) It is not allowed.

35. Where should you charge less than 6 pounds of refrigerant into a system?

(A) Any point downstream of the liquid line
(B) On the low side of the system
(C) On the high side of the system
(D) The discharge service valve

36. If a direct expansion system used in an air-conditioning system for human comfort contains Group 2 refrigerants,

(A) the permissible quantity is 10 pounds.
(B) the permissible quantity is 20 pounds.
(C) it is permitted only in residential buildings.
(D) it is not permissible.

37. The temperature on a system is 110° Celsius. What is the Fahrenheit equivalent?

(A) 230° F
(B) 245° F
(C) 255° F
(D) 220° F

38. Raising head pressure raises discharge temperature and causes

(A) a decrease of power per ton of refrigeration.
(B) more power to be needed per ton of refrigeration.
(C) less power to be needed per ton of refrigeration.
(D) horsepower to decrease.

39. When suction pressure decreases, compressor capacity

(A) decreases.
(B) increases.
(C) increases slightly.
(D) stays the same.

40. Carbonate deposits from brine on ice cans can be controlled to a great extent by

(A) adding sodium dichromate to brine.
(B) adding calcium chloride to brine.
(C) increasing the pH to 8 for awhile.
(D) decreasing the pH to slightly under 7 for a while.

41. A good chemical characteristic of a refrigerant is

(A) the ability to mix readily with oil.
(B) stability.
(C) the ability to change easily from liquid to vapor and back to liquid.
(D) wax content.

42. At what temperature will the safety thermostat in a chiller stop the compressor?

(A) 3° F
(B) 32° F
(C) 35° F
(D) 38° F

43. You are using an atmospheric condenser. The entering water temperature is 80° F. The leaving water temperature should be about

(A) 70° F.
(B) 80° F.
(C) 90° F.
(D) 100° F.

44. An evaporative condenser

(A) works the same as a spray pond.
(B) evaporates some water.
(C) uses the outside atmosphere to reject the heat.
(D) all of the above.

45. The purpose of pre-cooling air in an ice-making plant is to

(A) reduce plant capacity.
(B) increase plant capacity.
(C) prevent ice from melting.
(D) prevent freezing of air lines.

46. The suction strainer of a condenser water pump is clogged. This is likely to result in

(A) loss of oil from the crankcase.
(B) high head pressure in the compressor.
(C) low head pressure in the compressor.
(D) low suction pressure in the compressor.

47. The ratio of actual pressure of vapor in the atmosphere to its saturation pressure is called

(A) refrigeration effect.
(B) psychrometric effect.
(C) relative humidity.
(D) humidifying effect.

48. An ammonia compressor is running at 20 psi suction and 165 psi head. If the suction pressure drops to 0 psi and everything else remains the same, tonnage

(A) decreases and horsepower decreases.
(B) increases and horsepower increases.
(C) increases and horsepower decreases.
(D) decreases and horsepower increases.

49. According to New York City code, a soldered joint is a gas-tight joint obtained by joining metals with metallic mixtures or alloys that melt at temperatures

(A) below 1,500° F and above 350° F.
(B) below 1,000° F and above 400° F.
(C) below 900° F and above 250° F.
(D) below 800° F and above 200° F.

50. Rupture members, when used in parallel with a relief valve, operate

(A) at 10 percent above the designed working pressure.
(B) at 30 percent of the designed working pressure.
(C) not to exceed 20 percent above the designed working pressure.
(D) no less than 25 percent below the designed working pressure.

51. The manometer measures

(A) pressure of vapors and gases.
(B) the difference in absolute temperature.
(C) relative humidity.
(D) dew point.

52. In a system containing 2,000 pounds of refrigerant, the mechanical air discharge from the engine room should be

(A) 2,500 cu. ft./min.
(B) 2,700 cu. ft./min.
(C) 2,800 cu. ft./min.
(D) 2,900 cu. ft./min.

53. The scale trap is located between the

(A) compressor and condenser.
(B) condenser and receiver.
(C) receiver and evaporator.
(D) compressor and evaporator.

54. In the evaporator in which brine is being chilled, the greatest cooling effect is caused by the

(A) temperature of refrigerant entering the expansion valve.
(B) transfer of heat to the low-pressure gas.
(C) heat absorption of the flash gas.
(D) effect of boiling of low-pressure liquid.

55. In an air-conditioning system equipped with a Freon compressor, it is noted that the air cooling coil is always wet. It can be correctly stated that

(A) coil surface temperature is below the leaving air dew point temperature.
(B) coil surface temperature is above the leaving air wet bulb temperature.
(C) coil is not working efficiently, otherwise it would be frosted.
(D) low side temperature is too high to permit coil to operate.

56. According to recommended practice, to clean a shell and coil condenser of scale deposits, an operator would use a

(A) specially made nylon brush.
(B) combination wire brush and scraper.
(C) solution of inhibited hydrochloric acid.
(D) weak caustic soda solution.

57. What color are recovery cylinders painted?

(A) They are yellow around the top, with the corresponding refrigerant color code along the side, and the hood is painted gold.
(B) The hood is painted yellow and the shoulder gold, with the remaining body corresponding to the refrigerant color code.
(C) The shoulder and 10" down the side are painted gold, with the remaining cylinder body corresponding to refrigerant color code, and the hood is painted yellow.
(D) They are gray, with the shoulder painted yellow.

58. Which of the following is NOT true concerning recovery and recycling equipment for refrigerant?

(A) Recycling cleans deficient refrigerant of contaminants.
(B) Improves oil logged refrigerant by straining and filtering oil from the refrigerant
(C) System isolates and separates different refrigerant mixtures.
(D) Serviceman performing recovery and recycling of refrigerant assumes liability

59. Which of the following is correct regarding refillable cylinder discharge pressures?

(A) 100 lb. cylinder with designed pressure of 302 psi
(B) Set to discharge from 1.5 to 2.0 times the designed pressure
(C) 500 psi designed pressure for 1000 lbs. cylinder
(D) 2.0 to 3.5 times the designed pressure

60. Refillable cylinders are protected from over-pressurization with

(A) 1/4" NPT rupture disc, sized to rupture at 600 psi.
(B) spring type relief valve, used with 1000 lb. cylinders.
(C) spring actuated relief valve, set to discharge at 1.5 to 2.0 times the design pressure.
(D) all of the above.

61. Effective July 1, 1992, Section 608 of the Clean Air Act prohibits individuals from knowingly venting ozone-depleting chemicals into the atmosphere. Of the following which type of refrigerant release is NOT permitted?

(A) De minimis quantities of refrigerant release
(B) Refrigerant emitted in the course of normal operation
(C) System HCFC-22 vented along with nitrogen, during the course of leak testing
(D) Small releases of refrigerant that result from purging hoses or from connecting or disconnecting hoses to charge service appliances

62. According to the 1990 Clean Air Act, De minimus releases associated with good-faith attempts to recapture and recycle refrigerant shall not be subject to the prohibition set forth. Of the following, concerning the De minimus, which reverses this ruling?

(A) July 1, 1992: a serviceman who even inadvertently releases a refrigerant into the atmosphere would be a violation.
(B) November 1995: the above prohibition will apply irrespective of whether or not the release was intentional.
(C) November 1997: set date on reversal of De minimus ruling, associated with minor loses of refrigerant during servicing.
(D) June 1996: criminal penalties and prison terms will be imposed on any person who claims the De minimus clause.

Answers to Practice Test 5

1. **The correct answer is (A).**
2. **The correct answer is (C).**
3. **The correct answer is (B).**
4. **The correct answer is (B).**
5. **The correct answer is (B).**
6. **The correct answer is (B).**
7. **The correct answer is (A).**
8. **The correct answer is (C).**
9. **The correct answer is (B).**
10. **The correct answer is (D).**
11. **The correct answer is (C).**
12. **The correct answer is (D).**
13. **The correct answer is (B).**
14. **The correct answer is (A).**
15. **The correct answer is (B).**
16. **The correct answer is (C).**

    Total pressure = $\pi R^2 \times$ Force

    3.14(1.5)(1.5)(1000) = 7065 pounds
17. **The correct answer is (A).**
18. **The correct answer is (D).**
19. **The correct answer is (C).**
20. **The correct answer is (C).**
21. **The correct answer is (B).**

    1 gallon of water = 8.33 pounds

    60 gallons of water = 8.33 × 60 = 499.8 pounds

    Q = MSh(Th – T1) = 499.8(1) (80 – 40)

    499.8(40) = 19992 btu

    19992 btu ÷ 200 btu (1 ton) = 99.96 tons
22. **The correct answer is (B).**
23. **The correct answer is (B).**
24. **The correct answer is (A).**
25. **The correct answer is (A).**
26. **The correct answer is (A).**
27. **The correct answer is (B).**
28. **The correct answer is (B).**
29. **The correct answer is (C).**
30. **The correct answer is (A).**
31. **The correct answer is (B).**
32. **The correct answer is (A).**
33. **The correct answer is (C).**
34. **The correct answer is (D).**
35. **The correct answer is (B).**
36. **The correct answer is (D).**
37. **The correct answer is (A).**
38. **The correct answer is (B).**
39. **The correct answer is (A).**
40. **The correct answer is (D).**
41. **The correct answer is (B).**
42. **The correct answer is (D).**
43. **The correct answer is (C).**
44. **The correct answer is (D).**
45. **The correct answer is (D).**
46. **The correct answer is (B).**
47. **The correct answer is (C).**
48. **The correct answer is (D).**
49. **The correct answer is (B).**
50. **The correct answer is (C).**
51. **The correct answer is (A).**
52. **The correct answer is (D).**
53. **The correct answer is (D).**
54. **The correct answer is (D).**
55. **The correct answer is (A).**
56. **The correct answer is (D).**
57. **The correct answer is (D).**
58. **The correct answer is (C).**
59. **The correct answer is (B).**
60. **The correct answer is (D).**
61. **The correct answer is (C).**
62. **The correct answer is (B).**

PRACTICE TEST 6

1. The evaporator in a refrigeration system
   (A) converts low-pressure liquid to high-pressure gas.
   (B) absorbs heat into the refrigeration system.
   (C) absorbs heat into the refrigerant by the principle of latent heat of fusion.
   (D) converts high-pressure gas to low-pressure liquid.

2. The internal equalizer in a TXV
   (A) consists of a line connecting the evaporator outlet to the underside of the diaphragm.
   (B) provides a closing force based on the pressure of the refrigerant vapor at the evaporator outlet.
   (C) consists of a line connecting the valve outlet to the evaporator outlet.
   (D) provides a closing force based on the pressure of the refrigerant vapor at the evaporator inlet.

3. A liquid cooler is sometimes installed in a Freon compression system. The result is generally a(n)
   (A) increase in refrigeration effect per pound of refrigerant pumped.
   (B) decrease in suction gas temperature.
   (C) increase in compressor displacement.
   (D) decrease in liquid-line friction loss.

4. A suction gauge on a refrigeration system reads 15″ Hg absolute. The absolute pressure in pounds per square inch absolute is
   (A) 15
   (B) 8
   (C) 25
   (D) 12

5. With superheat set on a TXV, an increase in the refrigeration load results in a(n)
   (A) increase in charge pressure.
   (B) initial decrease in superheat.
   (C) decrease in charge pressure.
   (D) increase in spring tension.

6. What does a high superheat indicate?
   (A) A flooded evaporator
   (B) Low refrigerant-specific heat entering the compressor
   (C) A starved evaporator
   (D) None of the above

7. What does a low superheat indicate?
   (A) High refrigerant-specific heat entering the compressor
   (B) A starved evaporator
   (C) A refrigerant has just turned to vapor
   (D) A flooded evaporator

8. You are adding oil to the crankcase of an R-12 reciprocating compressor after shutting it down. The oil should be
   (A) pumped into a service valve on the compressor discharge.
   (B) sucked into a service valve on the suction side of the compressor.
   (C) pumped into a service valve on the compressor crankcase.
   (D) pumped into a service valve at the top of the liquid line.

9. The TXV meters refrigerant to the evaporator according to changes on the
   (A) discharge pressure only.
   (B) condenser temperature only.
   (C) hot gas defrost temperature.
   (D) load placed on the evaporator.

10. 

    On a refrigeration plan drawing, this symbol represents a(n)
   (A) water-cooled condenser.
   (B) evaporative condenser.
   (C) cooling tower.
   (D) cascade condenser.

11. What is used to defrost the ice from a medium-temperature evaporator?
   (A) An ice pick
   (B) A halide torch
   (C) An electric defrost
   (D) Ambient temperature

12. In an evaporator in which brine is being chilled, the greatest cooling effect on the brine results from the
   (A) heat absorption by the flash gas.
   (B) low temperature of the refrigerant entering the expansion valve.
   (C) effect of boiling low-pressure liquid.
   (D) transfer of heat to the low-pressure gas.

13. During system operations, refrigerant in the evaporator

(A) boils and changes state from liquid to gas.
(B) absorbs heat while changing state from gas to liquid.
(C) boils and changes state from gas to liquid.
(D) none of the above.

14. An R-12 system is accidentally charged with R-22. The probable result is a(n)

(A) overheated evaporator.
(B) clogged distributor.
(C) overloaded compressor motor.
(D) damaged expansion valve.

15. A system uses a thermostatic expansion valve. The capillary line on the remote bulb breaks, and the charge is lost. The valve

(A) operates erratically.
(B) remains open.
(C) closes, then opens.
(D) shuts off completely.

16. The evaporator absorbs heat from air or brine because the refrigerant entering the evaporator

(A) is at a higher temperature than the air or brine.
(B) is at a lower temperature than the air or brine.
(C) boils off as low-pressure gas.
(D) boils off as high-pressure gas.

17. If a refrigeration system does not respond to the adjustment of the expansion valve, it may be due to

(A) noncondensable gases in the system.
(B) excessive motor speed.
(C) an oil-logged coil or evaporator.
(D) insufficient condenser water.

18. Which would NOT cause noisy operation of a reciprocating compressor?

(A) Lack of oil
(B) Flash gas in the line after the expansion valve
(C) Loose drive coupling
(D) A dry or scored seal

19. What determines the pressure on the low-pressure side of the system?

(A) Amount of load on the system
(B) Compressor capacity
(C) Evaporator capacity
(D) Latent heat of vaporization

20. Double-seated valves are commonly used in ammonia plants to

(A) increase plant efficiency.
(B) repair leaks on the low side while the system operates.
(C) repair leaks on the high side while the system operates.
(D) facilitate valve repacking without shutting down the system.

21. An ammonia plant rated at 10 tons produces

(A) slightly more than 10 tons of ice.
(B) slightly less than 10 tons of ice.
(C) 20 tons of ice.
(D) exactly 10 tons of ice.

22. Which of the following refrigerants are in Group 2?

(A) Sulphur dioxide, ethyl chloride, and ammonia
(B) CO_2, ammonia, and methyl chloride
(C) Butane, ethane, and propane
(D) Ammonia, methyl formate, and isobutane

23. What is a typical superheat for a refrigeration system evaporator?

(A) 3 to 5° F outlet difference
(B) 10° F outlet difference
(C) 15° F outlet differences
(D) 15 to 20° F outlet difference

24. The three forces on the diaphragm of a TXV can be expressed as

(A) spring pressure opposes evaporator pressure plus charge pressure.
(B) evaporator pressure plus spring pressure opposes charge pressure.
(C) evaporator pressure opposes spring pressure.
(D) charge pressure plus spring pressure opposes evaporator pressure.

25. Convert 14 psia to psig.

(A) 15″ Hg psig
(B) 5″ Hg psig
(C) 2″ Hg psig
(D) 29 lbs. psig

26. What happens to suction pressure when evaporator load increases?

(A) Suction pressure increases; horsepower decreases.
(B) Suction pressure decreases; horsepower increases.
(C) Suction pressure remains unchanged; temperature increases.
(D) Suction pressure increases; system tonnage decreases.

27. A system is charged with 150 pounds of refrigerant. How many pounds does the New York City code allow to be stored in the machinery room?

(A) 15 lbs.
(B) 20 lbs.
(C) 30 lbs.
(D) 150 lbs.

28. In a comfort-cooling system using a thermostatic expansion valve, the remote bulb is clamped to the center of the evaporator. Most likely,

(A) there is no cooling effect.
(B) air is properly cooled.
(C) the refrigerant suction line is excessively superheated.
(D) the refrigerant suction line is saturated.

29. A medium-temperature refrigeration device operates within what temperature range?

(A) 45 to 60° F
(B) 5 to –20° F
(C) 30 to 45° F
(D) 10 to 25° F

30. A low-temperature refrigeration device operates within what temperature range?

(A) 10 to 25° F
(B) 5 to –20° F
(C) 30 to 45° F
(D) 144 btu to 180 btu

31. The auxiliary apparatus in a conventional absorption system is called the

(A) absorber.
(B) evaporator.
(C) generator.
(D) analyzer.

32. Refrigerant recovery is

(A) cleaning a refrigerant of dirt and contaminates, such as oil, acid, foreign material, and noncondensables.
(B) removing refrigerant from a system and storing it in an external container with the lowest emissions possible.
(C) reprocessing refrigerant into a new product that can be reused in another system.
(D) storing refrigerant in a receiver or storage tank during winter maintenance.

33. We must recover, recycle, and reclaim refrigerants because of

(A) the U.S. Clean Air Act of 1990 and the New York State Environmental Protection Act, Chapter 294, Amendment 1990.
(B) ASHRAE Standard 15–1992, "Safety Code of Mechanical Refrigeration."
(C) New York Local Law 16–1992.
(D) none of the above.

34. Refrigerant recycling is

(A) removing excess refrigerant from a system and storing it for reuse.
(B) removing refrigerant and storing it in a receiver or tank during winter maintenance.
(C) cleaning refrigerant of dirt and contaminates, such as oil, acid, foreign material, and noncondensables.
(D) reprocessing refrigerant into a new product that can be used in a new system.

35. You are charging the low side of a system with a 25-pound cylinder of R-12. To charge quickly, you should

(A) wrap an electric resistance heater around the cylinder.
(B) turn the cylinder upside down and shake it gently.
(C) stand the cylinder upright in a bucket of warm water.
(D) heat the bottom of the cylinder with a propane torch.

36. Refrigerant reclaiming is

(A) reprocessing refrigerant into a new product that can be reused in another system.
(B) chemically analyzing and distilling refrigerant.
(C) selling reprocessed refrigerant as "reclaimed refrigerant."
(D) all of the above.

37. Assuming all other pressures remain constant, increasing the spring tension on the TXV causes

(A) no change in superheat.
(B) increased superheat.
(C) desuperheating of the TXV.
(D) decreased superheat.

38. The remote bulb of which the thermostatic expansion valve operates in a temperature range of –20° F to 40° F is the

(A) gas charge type.
(B) liquid charge type.
(C) liquid cross-charge type.
(D) gas cross-charge type.

39. The bypass control is commonly used on large, automatically operated reciprocating compressors with two or more cylinders. The bypass control

(A) ensures proper lubrication.
(B) ensures smooth refrigerant flow.
(C) varies compressor capacity.
(D) reduces friction loss in the liquid or suction line.

40. If the specific heat of glass is .196, how many btu are needed to raise the temperature of 10 pounds of glass from 50° F to 70° F?

(A) 40.2
(B) 39.2
(C) 59.2
(D) 36.2

41. The external remote bulb of a thermostatic expansion valve is to be attached to a one-inch O.D. suction line. The bulb should be placed

(A) on top of the suction line.
(B) at a 90-degree angle from the top of the suction line.
(C) on the bottom of the suction line.
(D) at a 45-degree angle below the midpoint of the suction line.

42. A TXV is shipped from the factory with a superheated static setting of 3° F. The field setting will be most nearly

(A) 4 to 8° F.
(B) 7 to 11° F.
(C) 12 to 18° F.
(D) 16 to 20° F superheat.

43. A Freon system uses an evaporative condenser. In this type of condenser,

(A) refrigerant sprays over water-filled tubes.
(B) water sprays over and air blows over refrigerant-filled tubes.
(C) air blows over water-filled tubes.
(D) water and refrigerant spray over tubes.

44. The result of overcharging a Freon compression system is usually

(A) low suction pressure.
(B) high head pressure.
(C) normal system operation.
(D) a decrease in horsepower per ton of refrigeration.

45. An air-conditioning system has three compressors. Each compressor can operate at either 50 percent or 100 percent of capacity. The maximum number of different operating capacities in this system is

(A) three.
(B) four.
(C) five.
(D) six.

46. The main purpose of an external equalizer line with a TXV is to

(A) permit a cross liquid-feed power assembly to be used.
(B) eliminate the effect of a pressure drop in the coil.
(C) permit use of a different type of refrigerant.
(D) prevent the diaphragm from being clogged.

47. What would indicate a restriction (such as dirt or scale) in the liquid line?

(A) An exceptionally warm expansion valve
(B) The liquid line would feel hot up to the expansion valve.
(C) Frost immediately before the restriction
(D) Frost immediately after the restriction

48. You are checking leaks in a system containing a halocarbon refrigerant. Your electronic leak detector indicates a leak by a(n)

(A) flashing light in the probe.
(B) swinging pointer on the indicator dial.
(C) increased number of clicks per minute.
(D) buzzing sound.

49. The difference between a rotary and helical compressor is

(A) rotary is positive displacement; helical is negative displacement.
(B) rotary ranges up to 5 tons; helical ranges between 100 and 700 tons.
(C) rotary has screws; helical has a sliding vane.
(D) rotary has male and female rotors; helical has a sliding vane.

50. The two or three rows of eliminators in a flooded shell-and-tube cooler

(A) ensure the passage of dry suction vapor.
(B) remove noncondensable gases.
(C) prevent oil carryover.
(D) eliminate economizer use.

51. When the piston is at the bottom of the stroke in a single-acting V-type reciprocating compressor, the

(A) suction and discharge valves are open.
(B) suction valve is closed and the discharge valve is closed.
(C) discharge valve is open and the suction valve is closed.
(D) discharge valve is closed and the suction valve is open.

52. A meat storage plant uses a direct expansion refrigeration system. The cooling coil is fitted with baffles to

(A) collect drip and aid circulation.
(B) retard frost.
(C) collect dirt.
(D) prevent food contamination.

53. What does nonpositive displacement mean?

(A) As the piston moves up, it traps and compresses gas, then ejects it from the compressor.
(B) Vapor pressure in the compressor increases, although the internal volume of the compressor chamber does not change.
(C) The compression ratio varies as much as 10-to-1 in a two-stage compressor.
(D) The compression ratio varies as much as 10-to-1 in a one-stage compressor.

54. The compressor oil check valve (between the crankcase and the motor housing)

(A) keeps the valve open during normal operation.
(B) keeps the valve closed during shutdown while gradually relieving the crankcase of excess pressure.
(C) keeps the valve closed during start-up.
(D) all of the above.

55. 60° F equals

(A) 32° C.
(B) 18° C.
(C) 21° C.
(D) 15° C.

56. Two charges commonly used in TXV power elements are

(A) *liquid charge* (different refrigerant from that used in the system) and *cross charge* (same refrigerant as that used in the system).
(B) *liquid charge* (same refrigerant as that used in the system) and *gas charge* (different refrigerant from that used in the system).
(C) *gas charge* (same refrigerant as that used in the system) and *cross charge* (different refrigerant from that used in the system).
(D) *liquid charge* (different refrigerant from that used in the system) and *gas charge* (same refrigerant as that used in the system).

57. The TXV external equalizer normally consists of a

(A) passageway between the valve outlet and the underside of the diaphragm.
(B) line connecting the valve outlet to the evaporator outlet.
(C) passageway between the valve inlet and valve outlet.
(D) line connecting the evaporator outlet to the underside of the diaphragm.

58. A condenser's water-circulating pump is belt-driven by an electric motor with an adjustable pitch motor sheave. This sheave

(A) permits adjustment of pump speed.
(B) prevents overload and/or burnout of the pump and motor.
(C) prevents excessive wear on the belt and motor shaft bearings.
(D) facilitates belt replacement.

59. The fastest way to remove frost from a direct-expansion finned-tube evaporator is to

(A) send hot gas through the coil.
(B) scrape off frost.
(C) wash with warm water.
(D) shut down and let frost melt.

60. To change the direction of rotation of a 440-volt, 3-phase induction motor,

(A) reverse lines to start winding.
(B) interchange any two power leads.
(C) replace any two wires to the rotor.
(D) remove any two power leads.

61. You want to change refrigerants in a Freon-12 plant using a reciprocating single-acting compressor. Which refrigerant requires the smallest amount of change to the system?

(A) Carbon dioxide
(B) Ammonia
(C) Methyl chloride
(D) Aqua ammonia

62. Fuses and circuit breakers do NOT protect electric motors from

(A) short circuiting.
(B) motor burnout.
(C) overload.
(D) overheating.

63. Which is NOT commonly used to cool and dehumidify equipment?

(A) Calcium chloride
(B) Activated alumina
(C) Sodium zeolite
(D) Silica gel

64. Soft copper tubing that is used for refrigerant piping, erected on premises, containing other than Group 1 refrigerant must be protected by

(A) supporting it by approved clamps.
(B) limiting its length between supports up to 10 feet.
(C) a rigid or flexible metal enclosure.
(D) wrapping it with insulation tape throughout its length.

65. When the piston is at top center of the cylinder in a double-acting reciprocating compressor, all suction valves are

(A) open and all discharge valves are closed.
(B) closed and all discharge valves are closed.
(C) closed and all discharge valves are open.
(D) open and all discharge valves are open.

66. A Freon-12 refrigeration system is fitted with thermal expansion valves. The valves are rated in

(A) pounds per minute.
(B) superheat setting.
(C) tons of refrigeration.
(D) cubic feet per minute.

67. An ammonia plant has a suction pressure of 15 psig. Its temperature is

(A) –40° F.
(B) –28° F.
(C) 5° F.
(D) 0° F.

68. Which are undesirable refrigerant characteristics?

(A) Being nonflammable and nontoxic
(B) High latent heat and low boiling point
(C) High critical temperature and low freezing point
(D) Low critical temperature and high freezing point

69. In a high-side float refrigeration system, frost on the suction line indicates

(A) the system is overcharged with refrigerant.
(B) the system needs refrigerant recharging.
(C) the suction line is leaking.
(D) noncondensables have entered the system.

70. An indicator diagram

(A) can be used to check valves in a reciprocating compressor.
(B) indicates a brine solution.
(C) measures amperage drawn by an electric motor.
(E) increases overall plant efficiency.

Answers to Practice Test 6

1. **The correct answer is (B).**
2. **The correct answer is (D).**
3. **The correct answer is (A).**
4. **The correct answer is (B).** It is 7.5.
5. **The correct answer is (A).**
6. **The correct answer is (C).**
7. **The correct answer is (D).**
8. **The correct answer is (C).**
9. **The correct answer is (D).**
10. **The correct answer is (B).**
11. **The correct answer is (D).**
12. **The correct answer is (C).**
13. **The correct answer is (A).**
14. **The correct answer is (C).**
15. **The correct answer is (D).**
16. **The correct answer is (B).**
17. **The correct answer is (C).**
18. **The correct answer is (B).**
19. **The correct answer is (A).**
20. **The correct answer is (D).**
21. **The correct answer is (B).**
22. **The correct answer is (A).**
23. **The correct answer is (B).**
24. **The correct answer is (B).**
25. **The correct answer is (C).** 14 – 15 = 1 × 2 = 2" Hg psig
26. **The correct answer is (A) .**
27. **The correct answer is (C).** See code C19-106.11: 150 × 20% = 30 lbs.
28. **The correct answer is (C).**
29. **The correct answer is (C).**
30. **The correct answer is (B).**
31. **The correct answer is (D).**
32. **The correct answer is (B).**
33. **The correct answer is (A).**
34. **The correct answer is (C).**
35. **The correct answer is (C).**
36. **The correct answer is (D).**
37. **The correct answer is (B).**
38. **The correct answer is (B).**
39. **The correct answer is (C).**
40. **The correct answer is (B).** $Q = MSH (T_H - T_L)$
41. **The correct answer is (D).**
42. **The correct answer is (B).**
43. **The correct answer is (B).**
44. **The correct answer is (B).**
45. **The correct answer is (D).**
46. **The correct answer is (B).**
47. **The correct answer is (D).**
48. **The correct answer is (C).**
49. **The correct answer is (B).**
50. **The correct answer is (A).**
51. **The correct answer is (B).**
52. **The correct answer is (A).**
53. **The correct answer is (B).**
54. **The correct answer is (D).**
55. **The correct answer is (D).**
56. **The correct answer is (C).**
57. **The correct answer is (D).**
58. **The correct answer is (C).**
59. **The correct answer is (A).**
60. **The correct answer is (B).**
61. **The correct answer is (C).**
62. **The correct answer is (D).**
63. **The correct answer is (A).**
64. **The correct answer is (C).**
65. **The correct answer is (B).**
66. **The correct answer is (C).**
67. **The correct answer is (D).**
68. **The correct answer is (D).**
69. **The correct answer is (A).**
70. **The correct answer is (A).**

Chapter 19

PRACTICAL EXAM REVIEW

To the instructor:

This chapter is divided into three sections covering the ACME model HMCW, Carrier 17M, and Trane Centravac systems.

First, review the theory and principles of refrigeration and air conditioning. Your students must express themselves as refrigeration engineers, and that requires a strong foundation in refrigeration principles. Repeated drilling is essential because students must be able to verbally explain themselves in engineering terms. They must be able to describe a refrigeration system using the appropriate terminology.

Candidates must take the practical exam confidently. A weekly quiz and review will prepare students for the differences and similarities in refrigeration systems. Question-and-answer sessions with diagrams and visual aids will train students to respond to the terminology.

Advise students that the weekly quiz is used for review purposes only. Quizzes indicate what is important and can be used for reference. Stress to the students that the practical is a safety test.

To the student:

Bring a flashlight to the practical exam. It will help you see gauges and components in dark areas of the engine room. The flashlight can also be used as a pointer when discussing refrigerant flow.

Wear work clothes and boots to the practical. You must play the role of a watch engineer, and sneakers and jeans don't cut it with the examiners.

When answering questions, never try to impress the examiners with what you know. Just answer the question. Don't let the examiners confuse you. If you answer a question and are asked, "Are you sure?", stick to your guns. More often than not, your first answer is correct. If you don't know the answer, tell the examiners you don't know. Most of the time they will give you clues.

The objective is to demonstrate that you are ready to operate a refrigeration plant in a safe and professional manner. *If you fail one safety question on the practical exam, you fail the entire exam.*

Be confident. A successful career in refrigeration may be at hand after you pass the practical.

DEFINITIONS

Sump pumps (SP) drain water from the engine room in an emergency. These four electric pumps are at the center of the room.

Steam-driven sump pumps (SDS) are emergency backup pumps. If water shorts out the electric pumps, the steam-driven sump pumps will continue removing water from the engine room.

Condenser water pumps are centrifugal pumps. On top of the pump is an abrasive strainer that removes scale and dirt before the water cools the mechanical seal. On the suction side of the pump is a globe valve and a strainer. On the discharge side, a check valve prevents backflow of water during shutdown.

Chill water pumps are in another room and are not part of the practical.

PART I: ACME MODEL HMCW REVIEW

The ACME practical focuses on two racks of ACME direct-expansion refrigeration systems. There is one evaporator on each rack. Within the evaporator are three independent coils, one for each compressor. R-22 circulates in the tubes, cooling water in the shells. The evaporator uses a predetermined amount of refrigerant to cool the secondary refrigerant (water) in the shell.

The racks have multicylinder reciprocating compressors. These suction-cooled, hermetic motor compressors operate at 1750 rpm. Each rack consists of two V-type compressors and one W-type compressor. There are two cylinders in the V compressor with four pistons and three cylinders in the W compressor with six pistons. Each of the V-type compressors contains 40 pounds of R-22 in its cycle. The W-type contains 42 pounds of R-22 in its cycle.

Additional standard features on each compressor:

1. Each piston has a capacity of approximately 5 tons of refrigeration.

2. Each compressor acts independently and has its own condenser, thermostatic expansion valve, and direct expansion coil within the main evaporator. (There are no connections between the coils for different compressors.)

3. Each compressor has a magnetic solenoid unloader used to start and reduce the capacity of the compressor.

4. The compressor crankcase heater is ON during system shutdown, OFF during system operations.

5. An automatic, reversible direct-drive oil pump supplies oil under pressure to the connecting rods and main bearings.

6. The compressor has suction and discharge gauges.

A three-step thermostat on the chilled water return controls the operation of each compressor in sequence. As chilled water temperature drops, the first step of the thermostat is reached. This opens the circuit to the first compressor's liquid-line solenoid valve, which closes the valve. The compressor continues to pump down until its low-pressure cutoff setting is reached. The first compressor then shuts down. If the chilled water temperature continues to fall, the second step of the thermostat is reached, and the second compressor shuts down. If the chilled water temperature continues to fall, the third compressor shuts down in a similar manner.

A muffler between the compressor and the condenser eliminates pulsations, or high-frequency sound waves, from the compressor.

Each rack has three condensers and three compressors. They have removable heads for tube cleaning during the off-season. The condensers are of the shell-and-tube type. Water from the cooling tower on the roof flows through the tubes and refrigerant through the shells. The flow of condenser cooling water is controlled by the head pressure.

A PENN water-regulating valve on the condenser outlet has a bellows connected directly to the high side. Any increase in high-side pressure causes the valve to open, allowing more cooling tower water into the condenser.

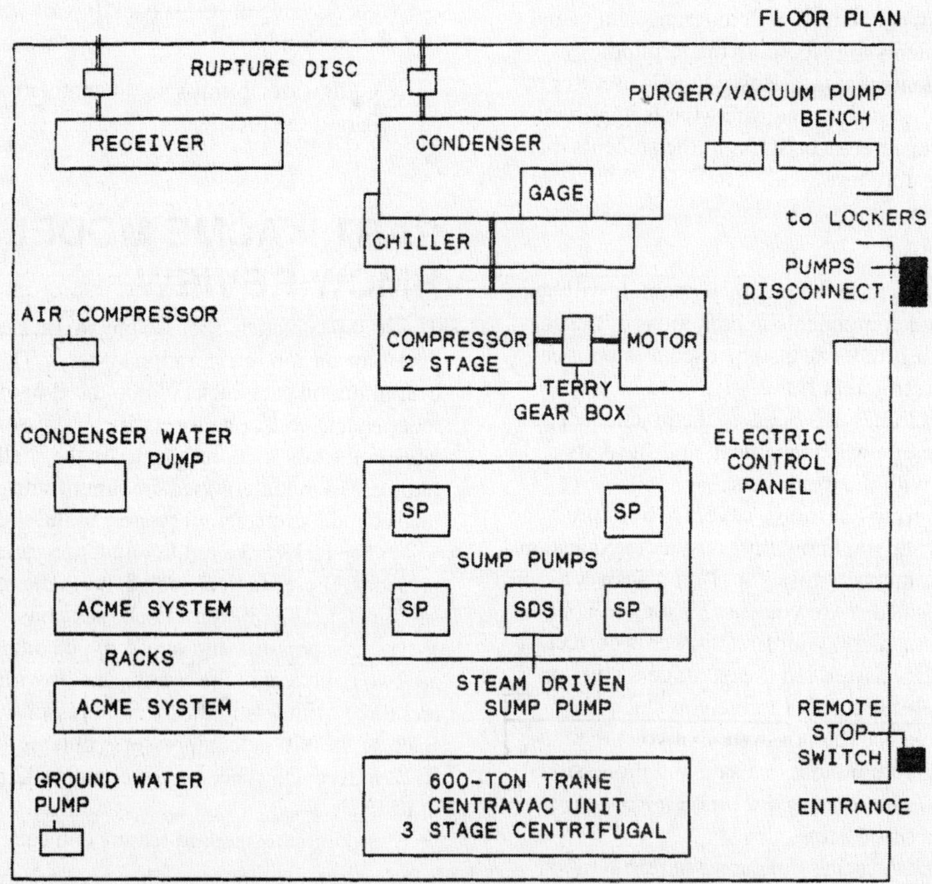

Fig. 19.1

The high-side connection of the water-regulating valve is a flared fitting connected to a purge service valve. The purge valve has two service ports. The Penn water-regulating valve flared fitting can be connected to either one. The valve senses the high-pressure changes at the flared fitting and regulates the water flow at the condenser.

Notice that water enters the condenser at one end and exits at the opposite end. This is an odd-pass condenser. If asked about the number of passes in the design, just answer, "Water passes an odd number of times through the condenser."

As the high-pressure/high-temperature liquid refrigerant exits the condenser, it flows through the liquid-line service valve. The valve is normally back-seated to allow refrigerant flow during operations. It is front-seated for manual pumpdown operations.

After the liquid-line service valve is a filter drier, which removes moisture and solid particles from the liquid line.

The filter drier is followed by a normally closed solenoid valve. This valve is energized by a three-step thermostat on the chilled-water return. When energized, the solenoid valve opens, allowing refrigerant to flow through the liquid line.

The sight glass on the liquid line allows monitoring of refrigerant flow during startup and operation. It is a simple glass port. Bubbles in the port indicate a shortage of refrigerant, or a restriction. The filter-drier is normally upstream of the sight glass.

Each unit has a thermostatic expansion valve with an external equalizer connected to the suction line. The equalizer line is physically connected into the system so the low-side pressure can operate the TXV at a pressure equal to the pressure of the sensing bulb.

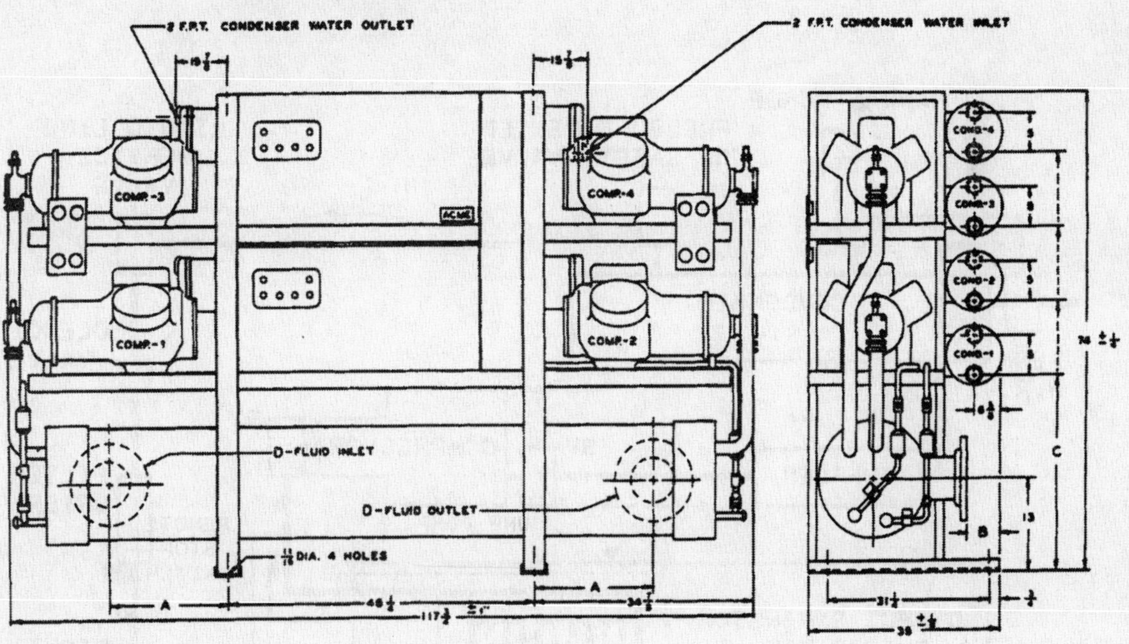

Fig. 19.2 Model HMCW
Illustration and diagram courtesy ACME Industries, Inc.

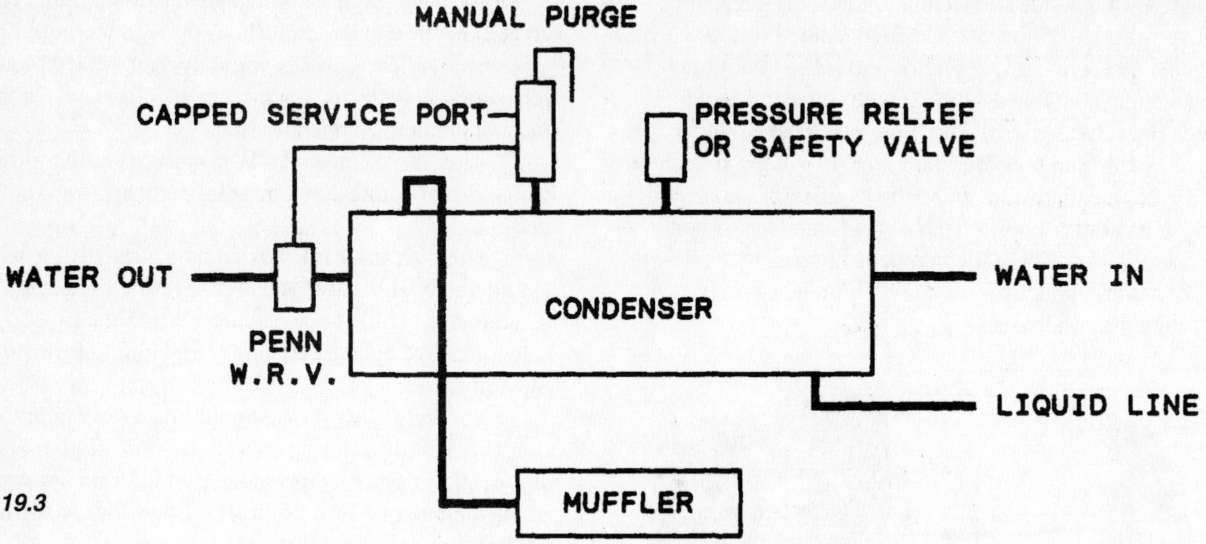

MANUAL PURGE
CAPPED SERVICE PORT
PRESSURE RELIEF
OR SAFETY VALVE
WATER OUT
WATER IN
CONDENSER
PENN
W.R.V.
LIQUID LINE
MUFFLER

Fig. 19.3

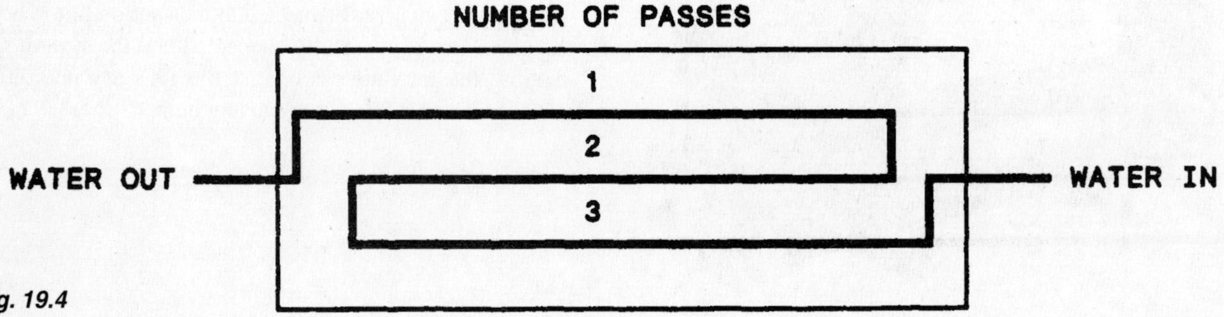

NUMBER OF PASSES
1
2
3
WATER OUT
WATER IN

Fig. 19.4

MANUAL PURGE
PRESSURE RELIEF
OR SAFETY VALVE
LIQUID LINE
SERVICE
VALVE
CONDENSER
PENN
W.R.V.
SOLENOID
VALVE
SV
COMPRESSOR
SV
MUFFLER
FILTER
DRIER
DIRECT EXPANSION
EVAPORATOR
(3 CIRCUITS)
SIGHT
GLASS
TXV

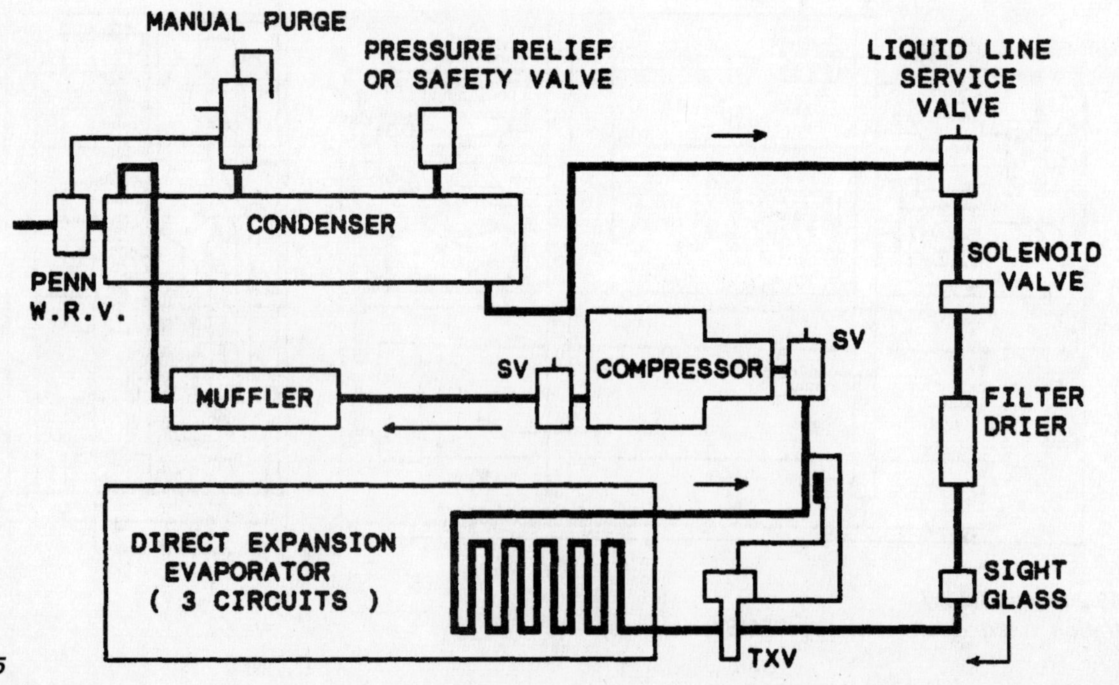

Fig. 19.5

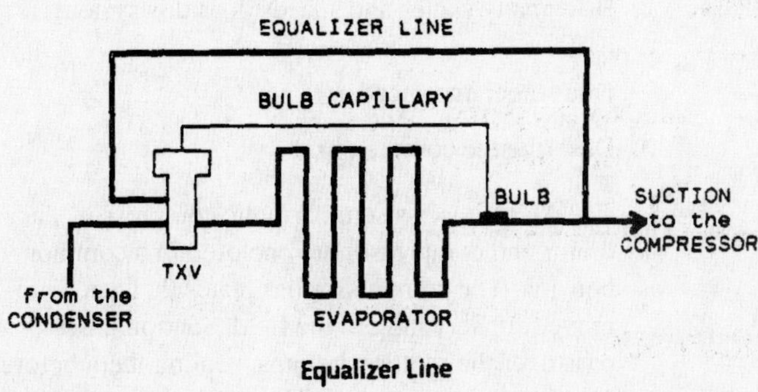

Fig. 19.6

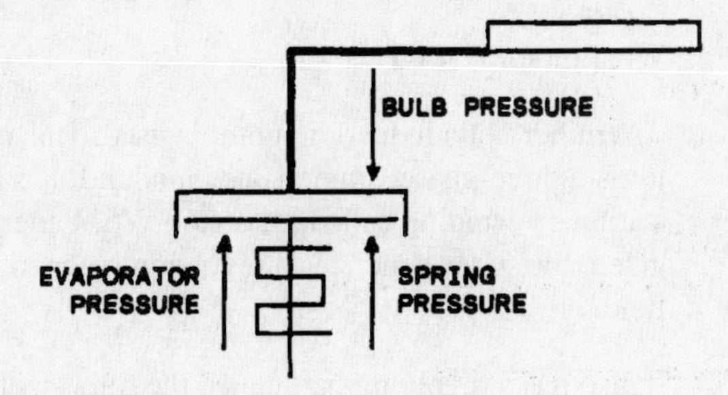

Fig. 19.7

At the exam site, the equalizer line may be installed upstream of the bulb. In the field, it may be connected downstream or upstream of the bulb, depending on the application.

The temperature-sensing bulb is clamped to the suction line to meter refrigerant to the evaporator by opening or closing the TXV. As the load in the building increases, refrigerant in the evaporator boils off, increasing the superheat temperature at the evaporator outlet. The increase in temperature causes the bulb's charge to expand, exerting more pressure up the capillary tube to the TXV power element. A diaphragm within the power element is forced down by the increase in pressure, causing the valve needle to open. A decrease in load reduces the superheat at the evaporator outlet, causing the TXV to close.

As bulb pressure overcomes evaporator and spring pressure, the valve opens. If evaporator or spring pressure overcomes bulb pressure, the valve closes. Anywhere in the middle is balanced or equilibrium operation; the valve throttles between the open and closed positions.

Charging on the Low Side of the System

Figure 19.8 shows a manifold gauge after it has been properly connected.

To monitor the manifold gauge while charging gas into the system, the suction and discharge service valves may be placed in the front-seated, back-seated, or cracked-off-the-back-seat positions.

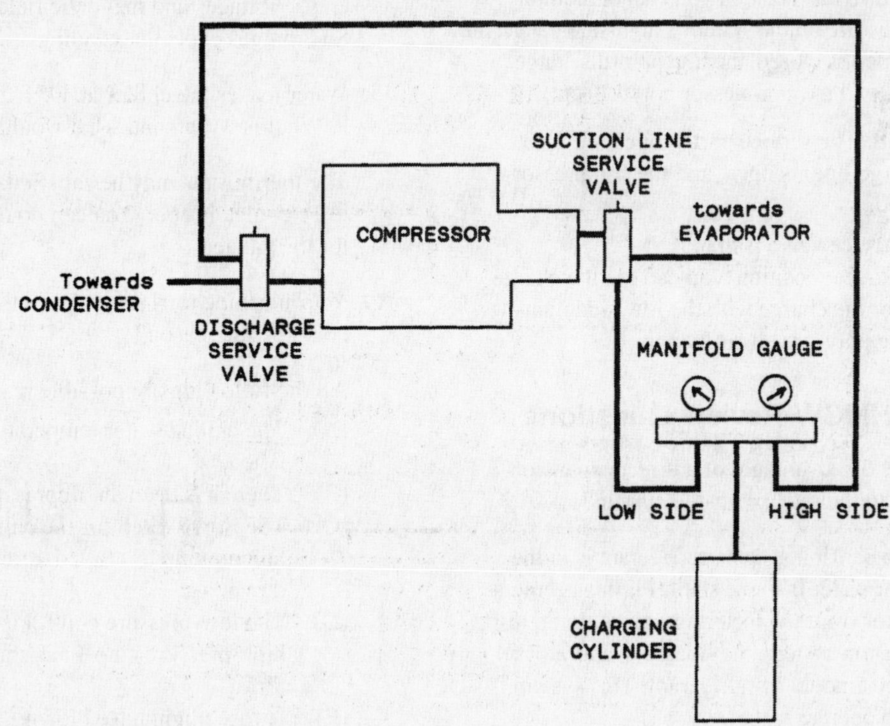

Fig. 19.8

Suction Service Valve Positions

1. **Cracked-off-the-back-seat:** During normal operations the valve is in this postion, with all three ports open. Attached to the service port of the valve is a "tee" fitting, which allows the system's low-side gauge to be connected with an additional service port capped. This allows the operator to monitor low-side pressure. It also enables gas charging without disconnecting the system's low-side gauge. Before charging on the suction service port, back-seat the valve.
2. **Back-seated:** Suction pressure cannot be monitored in this position. The service port is closed, the line port (suction line) is open, and the compressor port is open.
3. **Front-seated:** This position is used for servicing operations. The service port is open, the line port is closed, and the compressor port is open.

Discharge Service Valve Positions

1. **Cracked-off-the-back-seat:** During normal operations the valve is in this postion, with all three ports open. Attached to the service port of the valve is a "tee" fitting, which allows the system's high-side gauge to be connected with an additional service port capped. This allows the operator to monitor high-side pressure.
2. **Back-seated:** In this position you cannot monitor discharge pressure on the system's high-side gauge. The service port is closed, the line port (discharge line) is open, and the compressor port is open.
3. **Front-seated:** The service port is open, the line port (discharge line) is open, and the compressor port is closed.

When the suction service valve is in the cracked-off-the-back-seat position, you can top the charge with gas and monitor the charge with the low-side manifold gauge. All three ports are slightly open.

ACME Model HMCW Review Questions

1. What are the disadvantages of a direct expansion system and an indirect expansion system?

In a direct expansion system, refrigerant is in the coil. Brine or water is in the shell. Flash gas enters the evaporator from the metering device. In an indirect expansion system, the floated evaporator requires a large amount of refrigerant. This system is expensive to operate.

2. How many stages and speeds does this system have?

One stage; one speed.

3. Describe the compressor.

The ACME uses a semihermetic compressor. The motor and compressor are enclosed in a common housing. The compressor has plates that can be removed for servicing in the field. Suction gases pass over the motor windings, cooling them before entering the compressor. The crankshaft converts the circular motion of the motor to reciprocating (up and down) motion.

4. What motor is used?

A semihermetic induction motor is used. This motor is a three-phase, single-speed model. It has a stationary winding called the stator. When energized, the stator generates a revolving magnetic field.

It also has a revolving part called the rotor, with bearings that support the rotor shaft. The rotor is a laminated cylinder with heavy copper bars for windings. The copper bars are connected at each end by copper or brass rings.

The rotating magnetic field generated in the stator cuts through the copper bars in the rotor and generates voltages and magnetic fields in the rotor. Suction gas cools the windings.

5. Water leaves the chiller at 44° F and returns at 46° F. What is wrong and what would you do?

The thermostats may be satisfied; that is, the area to be cooled is cool. You can do nothing but monitor the gauges.

6. Your machine runs for an hour, then stops. What could be the reason?

All the following are possible reasons:

(A) The chilled water temperature has been satisfied.
(B) There has been an oil pressure failure.
(C) The flow switch for the chilled water circulating pump has failed, or the pump has shut down.
(D) The low-pressure control or the high-pressure cutoff has shut the machine down.
(E) A fuse might have blown.

7. Identify the automatic water-regulating valve and describe how it works.

It is located at the condenser cooling water outlet. The valve controls the flow of condenser water based on refrigerant pressure. This water-regulating valve has a line connected to the purge valve. It is activated automatically by high pressure. The valve opens when head pressure rises. As pressure drops, the valve closes. The valve stops water flow when the machine is shut down.

8. How do you change the speed of this machine?

It is driven by an induction motor. The speed cannot be changed.

9. The ACME has unloaders. What is their purpose? How are they activated?

The cylinder unloaders are used to assist the compressor on startup. They are also used to reduce the capacity of the compressor. Each compressor has only one unloader, located on one of the compressor cylinder heads. When the unloader is activated, the suction valve stays open. Unloaders are activated at startup, allowing the compressor to start without a load. Unloaders relieve the starting torque on the compressor. A temperature-sensing bulb on the chilled water return line activates the unloader. If the load drops during operation, the return chilled water temperature decreases. As it continues to decrease, the pumpdown sequence is started by the three-step thermostat; this de-energizes a solenoid valve on the liquid line.

10. You just put another compressor on line. What will happen to brine pressure?

Nothing. The compressor affects brine temperature, not brine pressure.

11. What would happen if you ran a reciprocating compressor with the suction valve closed and the discharge valve open?

Noncondensable gases would enter the compressor.

12. Why should you touch the crankcase cover before starting the system?

The oil heater should be ON when the system is OFF. If it is not warm, you must turn the heaters on before startup.

13. The liquid line service valve is closed. Why? What is the technical term for the closed position?

It is closed to pump down the system. "Front-seated position" is the technical term used.

14. What are the components of the pumpdown system? How does it work?

The components are the solenoid valve in the liquid line, the thermostat, and the low-pressure control. When the liquid-line service valve is closed and the compressor is jumped electrically, the compressor will run until all the refrigerant is in the receiver. Pumpdown is normally done for maintenance and repairs, or during winter shutdown.

15. What would happen if there were a small amount of dirt in the return-line solenoid?

The system would short-cycle; that is, the compressors would repeatedly restart.

16. Where are the oil heaters?

They are at the bottom of the compressor crankcase.

17. On shutdown, do high and low pressures equalize?

No. The solenoid valve closes the liquid ine, separating the high and low sides.

18. At what pressure does the relief valve pop?

It doesn't pop, it *blows*, at 300 psi condenser pressure. It reseats itself if the pressure drops below 300 psi.

19. What controls the operation of each compressor sequence?

The three-step thermostat on the chilled-water line does this, assuming all three compressors are operating. The steps are as follows:

(A) As chilled-water temperature drops, the thermostat opens the circuit to the first liquid-line solenoid valve, which closes the valve. The compressor continues pumping down until the setting of the low-pressure cut-off is reached.

(B) If chilled-water temperature continues to fall, the chilled-water thermostat temperature is reached, and the second compressor shuts down.

(C) If the load continues to drop, the third compressor shuts down.

20. There are two colors on the compound gauge. What do they mean?

Red: temperature
Black: pressure

21. You notice the condenser pressure is too high. How would you troubleshoot?

(A) Check the condenser water pump and its circuit breaker and/or fuses.
(B) Check purger operation (relief valve).
(C) Check for any closed valves in the water circuit.
(D) Check the cooling tower fan for proper operation.
(E) Check that the tower makeup water valve is not stuck shut.
(F) Determine whether the water-box division plates are damaged, causing water bypass.
(G) Examine condenser tubes and clean if necessary.

22. Where are the refrigerant and water in the evaporator?

In a direct-expansion evaporator, refrigerant is in the coil and brine or water is in the shell.

23. What are the cut-in and cut-out points of high- and low-pressure controls?

High-pressure control: Cuts in at 235 psi, cuts out at 270 psi.

Low-pressure control: Cuts in at 60 psi, cuts out below 55 psi.

24. Can the Acme system operate at 40 psi?

No. It could freeze up and crack the tubes.

25. What are the system operating pressures?

Suction pressure = 60 psi
Head pressure = 200 psi

26. Give some temperature/pressure ratios for the Acme:

R-22 Pressure		Fahrenheit temperature
270 psi	=	123°
235 psi	=	113°
210 psi	=	105°
200 psi	=	103°
60 psi	=	33°
55 psi	=	30°

27. Where in the Acme system is the fusible plug?

The system does *not* have a fusible plug. It has a pressure-relief valve set for 300 psi. This valve is located on top of the condenser. If there were a fire in the engine room, or if system pressure exceeded 300 psi, the pressure-relief valve would blow the refrigerant out of the system.

28. What is the temperature of refrigerant in the suction line?

It is 38 to 48° F, 10° superheat after refrigerant is vaporized.

29. Where is the chiller-water flow switch?

On the chill-water outlet.

30. What instrument do you use to check for water in the system?

You use the moisture indicator in the sight glass. A green color in the middle of this instrument indicates dryness. A yellowish-red color indicates moisture.

31. If a refrigerant is 38° F, what is the brine temperature?

It is 48° F. (Rule of thumb: Add 10° to the refrigerant temperature to get the brine temperature.)

32. If suction pressure increased to 100 psi, what would happen?

Warm water would be produced. Normal suction pressure is 60 psi.

33. What would happen if the water supply to the condenser were cut off?

The system would shut down, or cut out, at 270 psi.

34. What is the purpose of the muffler, and where is it?

It is on the discharge line. It eliminates gas pulsations, noise, and vibrations.

35. What do bubbles in the sight glass indicate?

The system is short of refrigerant. Bubbles travel toward the evaporator due to compressor suction. Bubbles also may indicate a restriction in the liquid line.

36. The discharge service valve is on the discharge side of the compressor. What position is this valve in, and how do you charge liquid into it? (Safety question)

It is cracked off the back seat, because the high-pressure gauge is connected to it. The discharge service valve is front-seated when part of the system is isolated during repairs. The discharge service valve is *not* used for charging.

37. What is the purpose of the TXV?

It meters the refrigerant into the evaporator according to changes in refrigeration load. It also controls the superheat, insuring that 100 percent gas enters the compressor through the suction line.

38. Describe the evaporator's function.

As liquid refrigerant enters the evaporator coils, its pressure drops to the pressure inside the evaporator, due to the difference in water (brine) temperature. Once the liquid refrigerant reaches its latent heat of vaporization, it starts to boil. As liquid refrigerant passes through the evaporator coil, it continues absorbing heat and vaporizing. The absorption of heat by the vaporizing refrigerant produces cooling. Put more simply, the evaporator absorbs heat into the refrigerant from the secondary refrigerant, or brine.

39. What is the function of the compressor?

It removes or draws low-pressure gas from the chiller through the suction line and compresses it to a high-pressure gas.

40. The condenser is an odd-pass (horizontal shell-and-tube) type. How does water flow through it?

Cooling water enters through the bottom at one end and exits through the top at the opposite end. The Penn water-regulating valve is also found at the condenser cooling water outlet and regulates the water flow according to condenser pressure.

41. Where does the external equalizer on the TXV get its pressure?

It gets its pressure from the suction side of the evaporator.

42. What happens if the TXV gets clogged?

It closes.

43. What happens if the TXV equalizer line breaks?

The first indication of a break is high suction pressure. Once refrigerant is discharged into the atmosphere, refrigeration will stop.

44. The TXV has snow on the valve. What does that indicate?

Moisture in the refrigerant has frozen at the TXV orifice.

45. What is the function of the condenser?

The condenser converts high-pressure refrigerant gas from the compressor to a high-pressure liquid. While the refrigerant is changing state, it releases the latent heat of vaporization. In other words, it removes heat from the refrigerant to the condenser cooling water.

46. What are the two parts on top of the condenser?

They are the pressure relief valve and the purge valve. The purge valve is connected to the Penn water-regulating valve.

47. You notice refrigerant blowing out of the pressure relief valve. How do you reset it or shut it down?

You do nothing. It resets itself; it is only blowing off excess pressure.

48. If this machine has a pressure cut-off of 270 psi, is it close to blowing the refrigerant out of the system?

No. Pressure would have to exceed 300 psi to blow the refrigerant out of the system.

49. What will occur in event of oil-pressure failure?

The oil safety switch will shut down the compressor.

50. Describe the three positions on the suction-line service valve.

(A) *Backseated:* line port open, compressor port open, service port closed.

(B) *Frontseated:* service and compressor ports open, line port closed.

(C) *Cracked:* all three ports open.

51. Normally, in what position is the liquid-line service valve?

It is normally in the backseated position.

52. How would you add 10 lbs. of refrigerant into the Acme system?

Weigh the cylinder while charging into the liquid line service valve. You can top off the charge into the suction-line service valve.

53. On shutdown, do the system's pressures equalize?

No, because the solenoid valve separates the high and low sides.

54. How does the solenoid valve in the liquid line operate?

It is electrically controlled by a three-step thermostat on the compressor circuit. It is a normally closed (N.C.) solenoid. When energized, the solenoid opens the liquid line, allowing refrigerant flow. When the system shuts down, the valve closes and stops refrigerant flow.

55. Where is the unloader located?

An unloader is located on top of the compressor cylinder head. There are three compressors on a rack, with one unloader for each compressor.

56. How does the TXV operate?

The thermostatic expansion valve meters refrigerant to the evaporator using a thermal sensing bulb. When the bulb senses the superheated suction line, the pressurized gas or liquid within the sensing element expands. The pressurized gas then passes through a capillary tube to the valve, where it expands a metal diaphragm. This diaphragm pushes on a needle inside the TXV, opening the valve. The opened TXV valve allows liquid refrigerant into the evaporator.

57. How does the equalizer line on the TXV work?

It enables the low-side pressure operating the valve to equal the pressure of the sensing bulb. This compensates for any pressure drop through the evaporator while the compressor is running. The equalizer joins the suction line at the evaporator outlet to the underside of the TXV. It is located downstream or upstream of the bulb, depending on the application.

58. In what position is the purge valve on the condenser, and why?

The purge valve is in the cracked-off the backseat position, because it is connected to the Penn water regulating flare fitting, which senses high pressure.

59. In the condenser, where is the refrigerant and where is the brine? Refrigerant is in the shell and brine is in the tubes.

60. What is the pressure in the R-22 cylinder at 70° F?

121 psi

61. At what pressure would the compressor cut out?

Below 55 psi

62. What is the oil pressure for this system?

It is 30 to 50 psi above suction pressure. Suction pressure is 60 psi.

63. What would happen if the water supply to the condenser were stopped during operation?

The system would cut out at 270 psi.

64. How do you charge the Acme system with gas?

(A) Wear your goggles for safety.
(B) Charge at the suction service valve at the compressor end of the suction line. The valve is normally in the cracked position.
(C) Before connecting the charging hose, backseat the suction service valve.
(D) The charging cylinder has a red and blue valve. Connect the hose to the blue service port to charge with gas.
(E) Connect the other side of the hose to the charging port of the suction service valve.
(F) Bleed the hose from the cylinder to the charging port. Then tighten the connection at the suction service valve.
(G) Now you're ready to charge. Crack the suction service valve to charge with gas. This tops off the charge to the correct operating pressure (60 psi low side).
(H) After low-side pressure is attained, backseat the suction service valve.
(I) Close the charging cylinder blue valve.
(J) Remove the hose.
(K) Place caps back on the suction service valve and the charging cylinder.
(L) Crack the suction service valve off the back seat one-half turn, until the gauge reads a steady suction pressure.

65. How do you charge the Acme system with liquid refrigerant?

(A) Wear your goggles for safety.
(B) Charge at the liquid line service valve. Place this valve in the back-seated position.
(C) Connect the charging hose from the charging cylinder to the charging port of this valve. Use the red stem on the charging cylinder to charge liquid refrigerant.
(D) Be sure to bleed any air from the line before tightening the connection.
(E) The low-pressure cutout must be reduced from 60 to 40 psi so the machine will not cut out during charging. The machine will then pump down without shutting off.
(F) The liquid-line service valve is moved from the back-seated to the front-seated position.
(G) Open the valve on the charging cylinder until the system pressure is about 60 pounds.
(H) Once 60 pounds is reached, back-seat the liquid-line service valve.
(I) Close the charging cylinder stem and shut down the Acme system.
(J) Reset the low-pressure cutout back to 60 psi.
(K) Turn the system back on and check your pressures.
(L) When the correct pressures are reached, remove the charging hose.

66. Describe the compressors on the Acme system:

Two "V" vertical, single-action reciprocating compressors.

One "W" vertical, single-action reciprocating compressor.

67. Describe the components inside the head of the Acme compressor:

Under each head are two cylinders with pistons and connecting rods attached to a crankshaft. Suction and discharge valve plates are above each piston.

68. What is the discharge temperature of the Acme system?

105° F

69. What do you do if your machine has high head pressure?

Check that the condenser pump is running. You can lower the head pressure by cleaning the condenser strainer. If the strainer is clean, and the head pressure continues to rise, check the cooling towers. A fuse may have blown, shutting down the cooling-tower fans. Make sure you have makeup water to the cooling tower.

70. If the temperature on the chilled-water return line is 40° F, what should be done?

The system should respond automatically. The thermostat sensor should signal the unloader to unload the compressor.

71. What three pressures act on the TXV?

Spring pressure, evaporator pressure, and bulb pressure.

72. When does the TXV open?

As the system load increases, low-pressure liquid in the evaporator boils more quickly. Superheat increases, affecting the TXV bulb on the suction line. The bulb pressure pushes harder on the top of the TXV diaphragm and overcomes the spring and evaporator pressure. The TXV opens.

73. Where is the TXV equalizer line connected to the system?

It is connected downstream or upstream of the sensing bulb.

74. What are the four major parts of a thermostatic expansion valve?

(A) Power assembly (connects to the sensing bulb)
(B) Guts, containing a spring under pressure
(C) Dome, housing the diaphragm
(D) Valve seat

75. How do you increase the superheat on a TXV?

Normally, there is a set screw on top of the TXV to adjust the spring pressure. Turn it clockwise to increase the superheat and counterclockwise to decrease it.

76. Describe a TXV in equilibrium on a system:

At the top of the TXV power assembly, a capillary tube is extended to the evaporator suction line. At the end of the capillary tube, a sensing bulb is attached to the suction line. Evaporator pressure enters at the bottom of the diaphragm. Spring pressure also pushes on the bottom of the diaphragm. As the bulb gas pressure increases due to rising superheat in the suction line, it presses on top of the diaphragm. When the pressure on top of the diaphragm equals the pressure on the bottom, the TXV is in equilibrium. Then refrigerant flows steadily into the evaporator.

77. Your brine pressure just dropped from 100 psi to 50 psi. What would you do first?

Put another pump on the line to prevent the brine coolers from freezing up due to the pressure drop. Then investigate the pressure drop-off.

78. How do you add oil to the Acme system?

(A) With the system off, front-seat the suction service valve.
(B) Start the system until it pumps down to two pounds. It will do this very quickly.
(C) Once the machine has reached two pounds, shut down the system and front-seat the discharge service valve.
(D) Turn the machine's circuit breaker off to prevent anyone from accidentally starting the system. Disconnect the fuses to the system.
(E) Open the seal of a new container of refrigerant oil. Do not use any leftover oil. This will prevent contaminated oil from entering the system.
(F) Pump out any air from the hand pump before connecting it to the compressor.
(G) Connect the hand pump between the crankcase oil service valve and the refrigerant oil container.
(H) Pump refrigerant oil into the compressor until the sight glass is half-full.
(I) Remove the hand pump from the compressor and tighten the oil service valve. Secure the cap on this valve.
(J) Back-seat the suction service valve.
(K) Crack the suction service valve off the back seat to register pressure on the system's low-side gauge.
(L) Back-seat the discharge service valve.
(M) Crack the discharge service valve off the back seat to register pressure on the system's high-side gauge.
(N) Reinstall the fuses into the system and turn the circuit breaker on.
(O) Start the system. Observe the oil sight glass and pressure gauges.

PART II: CARRIER 17M SYSTEM REVIEW

The Carrier 17M is a nonpositive displacement two-stage compressor, rated at 750 tons of refrigeration. It is driven by a wound-rotor induction motor. A Terry gear box with speed-increasing gears and self-aligning coupling drives the compressor. The system is charged with 2,200 pounds of R-11.

The shell-and-tube evaporator is also known as a chiller. This is an indirect system; refrigerant boils in the shell and chilled water is pumped through the tubes. The chiller has a rupture disc designed to burst at 15 psig. If the chiller experienced excessive pressure or temperature, the rupture disc would burst, routing the refrigerant charge into the atmosphere. A fire in the engine room, for example, would increase pressure in the evaporator from 15″ Hg to 15 psig, bursting the rupture disc. If a water tube broke in the evaporator or condenser, increased pressure could also rupture the disc.

Like the evaporator, the condenser is of the shell-and-tube type. High-pressure vapor from the compressor is discharged into the condenser, where it is cooled and returned to the liquid state. Liquid refrigerant leaves the condenser through the bottom connection and moves towards a metering device called the economizer.

The economizer is located on the evaporator shell at the opposite end from the suction connection. The economizer has two float valve chambers, as shown in figure 19.11.

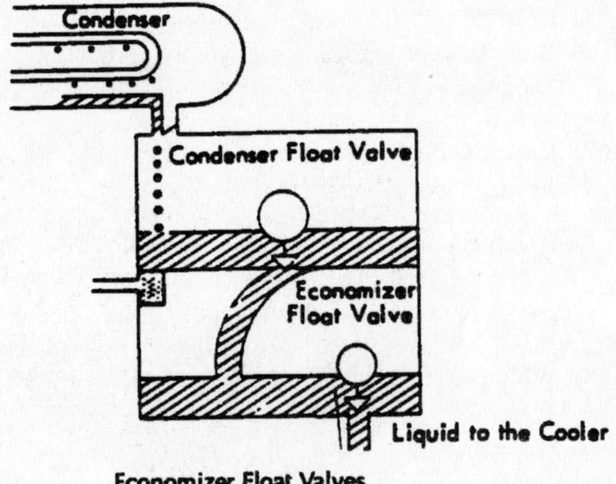

Fig. 19.10

The condenser float valve is contained in the upper chamber of the economizer. Refrigerant drains from the condenser and enters the lower chamber. As the valve restricts the flow of liquid refrigerant, some of it flashes and is precooled. The flashing refrigerant is drawn from the

Fig. 19.9 Carrier 17M Centrifugal Refrigeration System Courtesy Carrier Corporation.

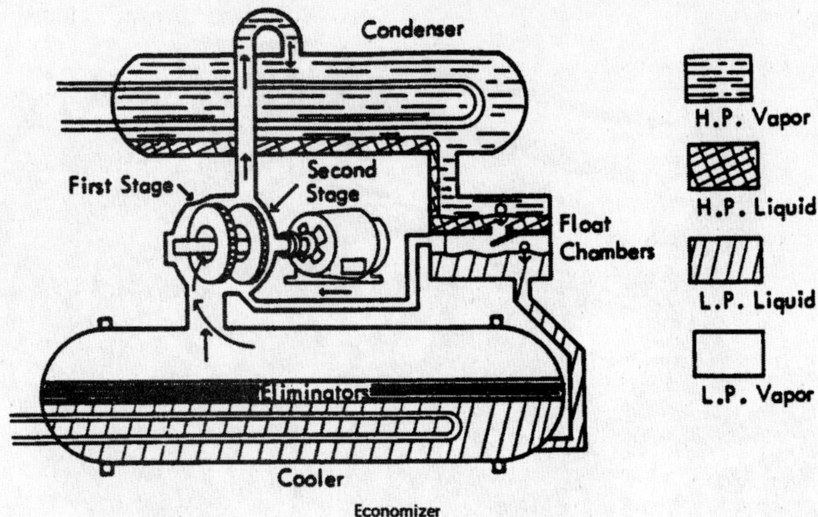

Fig. 19.11

top of the economizer float chamber back to the second stage of the compressor. Any liquid trying to leave with the flash gas is removed by eliminators on the inlet to the second stage. The remaining (cool) liquid refrigerant flows into the lower chamber. As the lower float valve rises, it opens a port to the cooler and returns liquid refrigerant to the evaporator. By drawing the flash gas into the second stage of the compressor, the economizer increases the evaporator's efficiency.

The Refrigerant Cycle

In the evaporator, the brine flowing through the tubes is warmer than the refrigerant in the shell surrounding the tubes. Heat from the brine is transferred to the refrigerant, which evaporates at a temperature in accordance with pressure in the cooler.

The evaporated refrigerant is sucked into the compressor and is partially compressed by the first-stage impeller. It then joins the gas stream from the economizer and enters the second-stage impeller. The economizer gas is compressed to only a portion of the pressure difference between the cooler and the condenser. Pumping flash gas back to the compressor increases cycle efficiency and saves horsepower.

The refrigerant discharged by the compressor condenses on the condenser tubes at a temperature above the condenser water temperature, thereby transferring the heat of condensation to the condenser water in the tubes. The liquefied refrigerant drains into the metering device's condenser float chamber. The rising refrigerant level in this chamber opens the float valve and allows the liquid to pass into the lower economizer chamber. As the evaporator pressure is lower than the economizer pressure, some of the liquid evaporates, passes through the remaining liquid to the compressor section, and cools the economizer liquid. This remaining liquid, also controlled by float valve action, makes up the refrigerant losses of the evaporator operation.

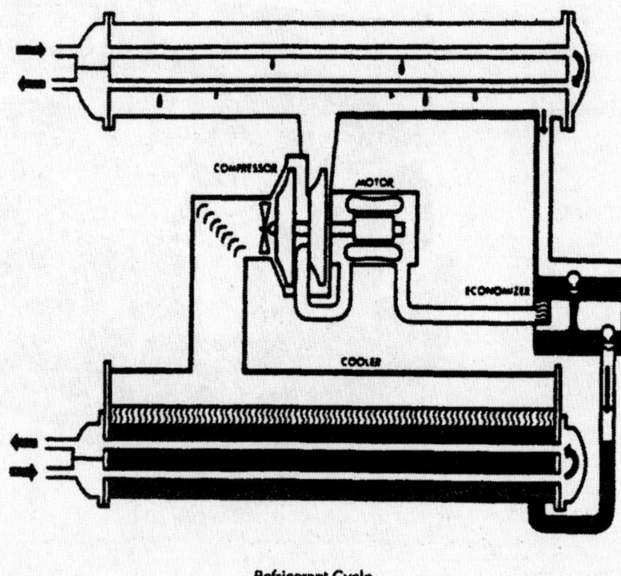

Fig. 19.12
Illustration courtesy Carrier Corporation.

The Gauge Panel

air indicator: a gauge with two pointers, above the panel.

(A) **red pointer:** shows total pressure in the condenser.

(B) **black pointer:** shows pressure of R-11 in a feeler bulb located in the top of the condenser.

When total pressure in the condenser (red pointer) exceeds the pressure of the feeler bulb (black pointer), the unit needs purging.

chilled water temperature controller: a safety control with a sensing bulb in the leaving chilled waterbox. It stops the compressor if the chilled water drops below the minimum temperature requirement, which prevents the evaporator tubes from freezing.

evaporator pressure gauge: a gauge with operating pressure of 15″ Hg.

condenser pressure gauge: a gauge with operating pressure of 5 psi.

differential pressure chilled water: a low-pressure cutout device.

oil pressure safety or control: a device that cuts out at 6 psi and cuts in at 12 psi.

refrigerant temperature controller: an additional protection against freezing. The control has a sensing bulb located in an expansion thermometer connection on the side of the cooler. It is field-set by the operating engineer to cut out slightly below the minimum design refrigerant temperature.

safety devices: The contacts of all protective devices are closed when machine operation is normal. The safety device contacts open and stop the compressor when any of the following occurs:

(A) high condenser pressure

(B) low compressor oil pressure

(C) Brine temperature below minimum temperature requirement.

(D) Low refrigerant temperature

All safety devices are wired in series. If one safety exceeds its limits (or fails), the machine shuts down.

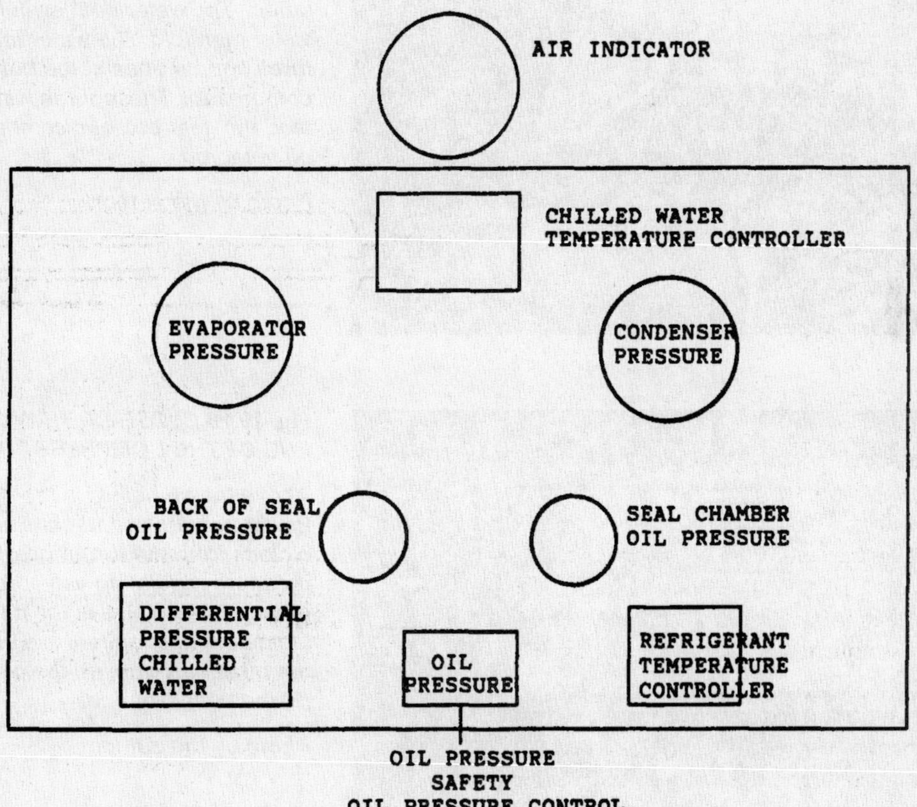

Gauge panel for the Carrier unit, located on the side of the condenser.

Fig. 19.13

Fig. 19.14 SEAL END OF THE COMPRESSOR

The system gauge panel, on the side of the condenser, is seen at the center of the picture. To the left of the gauge panel is the seal oil reservoir. Between the seal end of the compressor and the Terry gear box is the shaft coupling. The atmospheric oil chamber is shown bottom center.

Photo by the author.

Fig. 19.15 TRUST END OF THE COMPRESSOR

A water float switch, located in the water supply line, is electrically connected by Greenfield wiring to the oil heater. The oil heater is located inside the thrust-end oil sump. The water float switch line leads to a water manifold. The water manifold feeds to three copper lines at the bottom of the compressor. These three water cooling lines feed the gear box cooler, shaft seal, and the oil reservoir.

Photo by the author.

Fig. 19.16 CLOSE-UP VIEW OF THE THRUST END OF THE COMPRESSOR

Above the oil heater is the Kingsbury thrust-bearing round plate cover. At 4 o'clock from the thrust bearing is the oil pressure regulating valve. To the right of the oil regulating valve is the oil manifold. Inside the oil manifold are three lines: (1) the oil supply line, (2) the oil return line, and (3) the equalizer line.

Photo by the author.

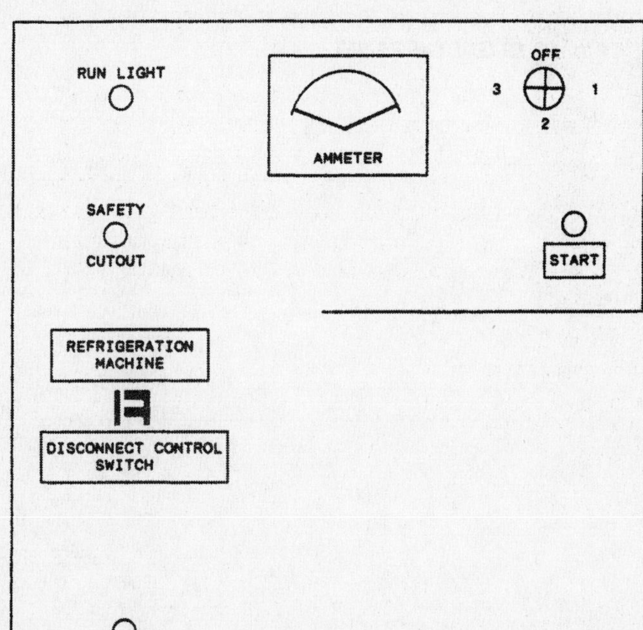

Fig. 19.17 GAUGE PANEL

The safety cutout button is pushed when the unit is started. If the unit shuts down on safety, or is stopped, the safety cutout button pops out.

The disconnect control switch prevents accidental starts during winter shutdown or maintenance operations (knife disconnect switch).

The start button starts the machine.

The run light is lit during system operations.

The four-pole switch on the upper right monitors the three-phase motor. Each phase should read approximately the same amount of current, indicating that the motor is balanced. If it is not, an electrician should check motor resistance.

The stop button stops the system.

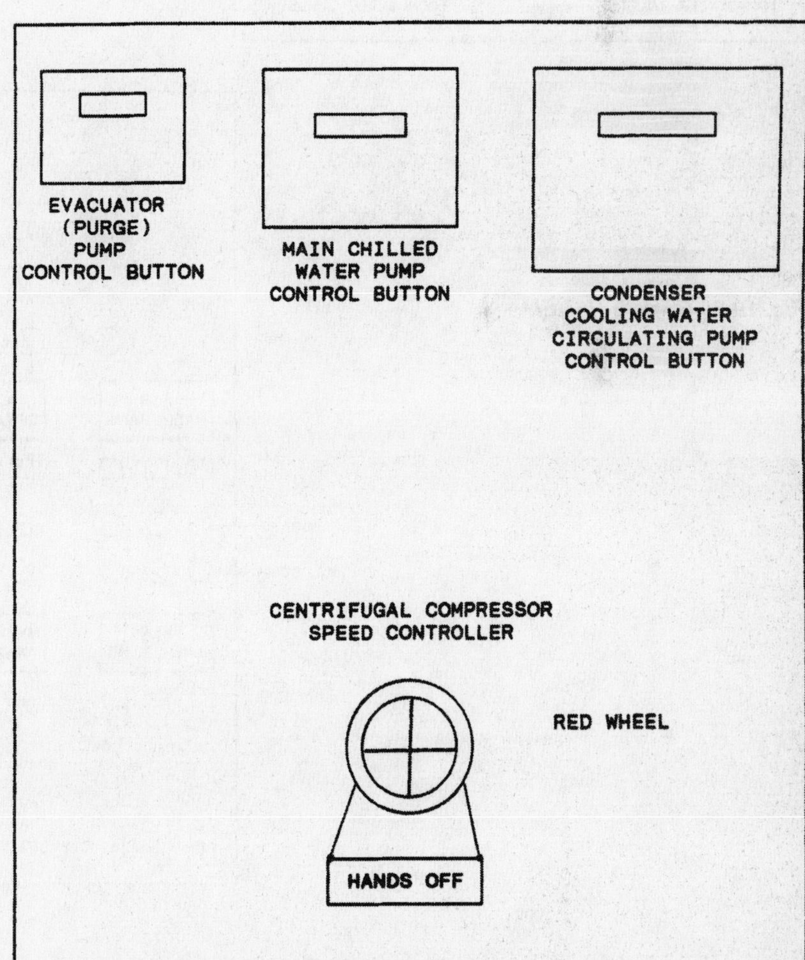

Fig. 19.18 GAUGE PANEL

The red wheel is the speed controller (rheostat). It must be in the lowest position when starting the unit. To increase output or reduce temperature of the brine being delivered by the system, increase the speed. To reduce output or raise temperature, reduce speed.

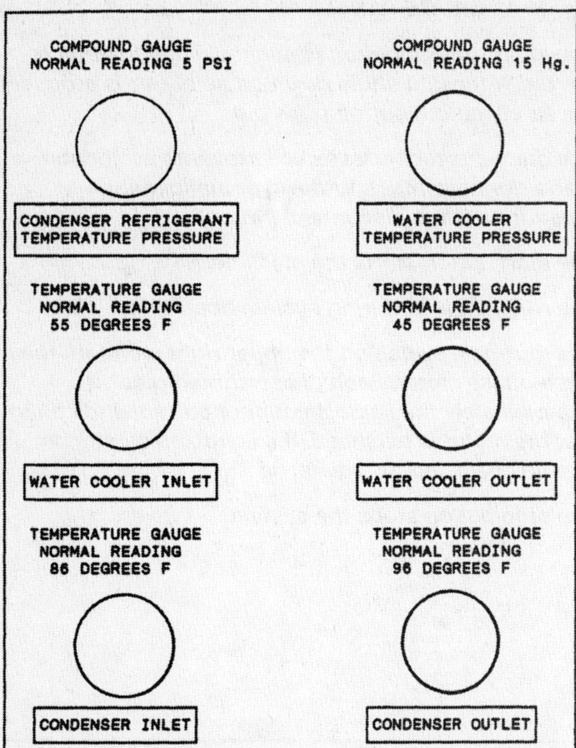

Fig. 19.19 GAUGE PANEL

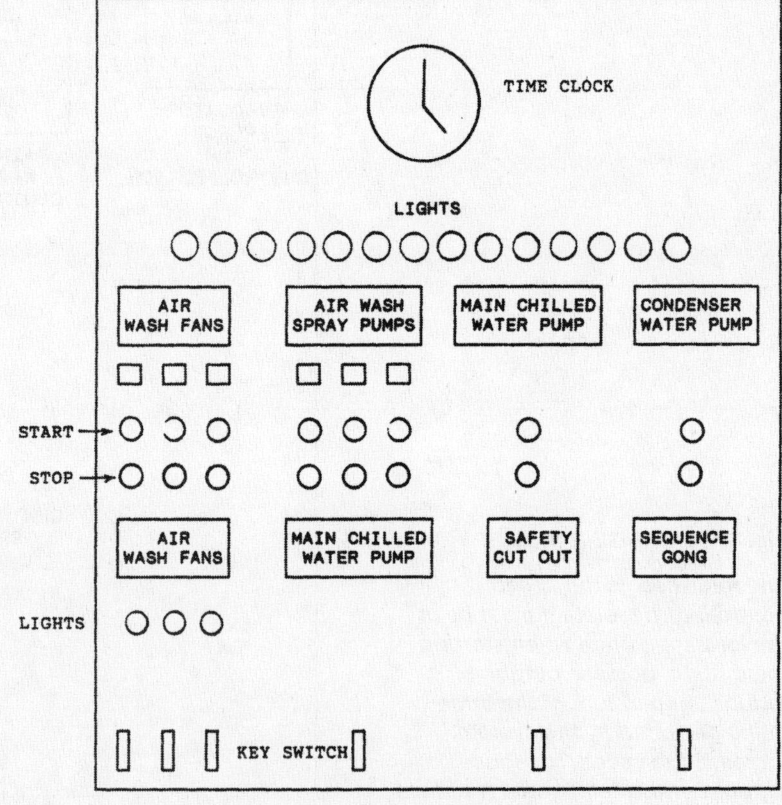

GAUGE PANEL

Fig. 19.20 GAUGE PANEL

The Oil Cycle

On startup, the compressor shaft rotation drives the oil pump drive gears (35) and starts the oil circulating to the thrust bearings (34). After passing through the thrust bearings, the oil divides into two lines. One line supplies oil through the strainer (1) to the oil pump drive gear, oil rings (27), and journal bearings (28). The other line carries oil to the seal end of the machine through the check valve or stop valve (11) and oil filter (9) and into the bellows seal (14).

The check valve opens when oil-pump pressure reaches approximately 8 psi at startup. During shutdown or when pressure is below 8 psi in the oil line, the check valve closes and the air vent (6) opens. This keeps a thin

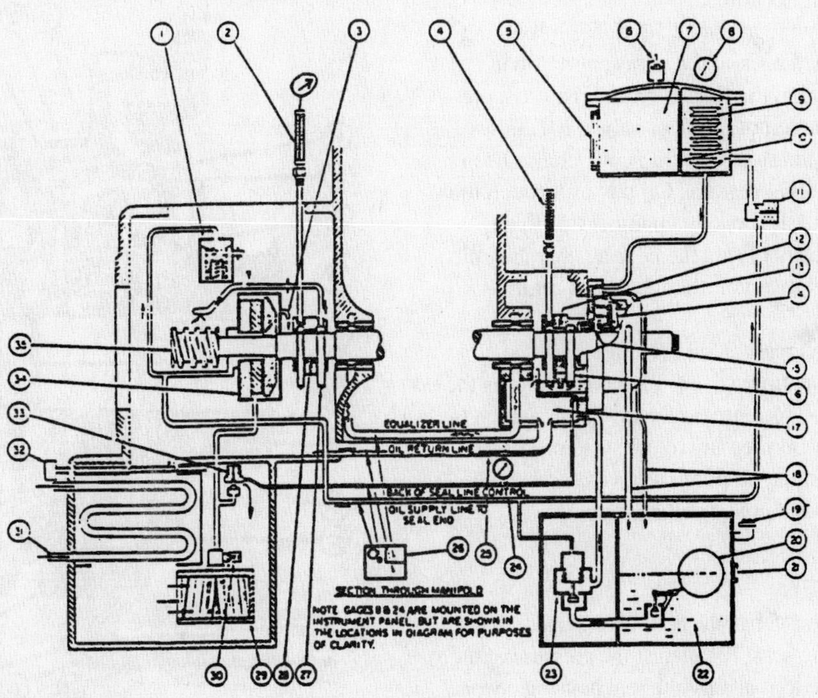

Fig. 19.21 OIL PIPING DIAGRAM

LEGEND

1. Oil strainer
2. Bearing thermometer
3. Overflow with orifice
4. Bearing thermometer
5. Sight glass for oil reservoir
6. Air vent and vacuum breaker
7. External seal oil reservoir
8. Seal pressure gauge for reservoir
9. Oil filter
10. Orifice
11. Stop valve or check valve
12. Shaft seal (drive end)
13. Seal housing cover
14. Bellows seal
15. Inner floating seal ring
16. Oil rings located in the seal housing
17. Bearing chamber
18. External and internal oil return lines to atmospheric chamber
19. Atmospheric oil chamber service filler plug
20. Atmospheric oil chamber float valve
21. Oil sight glass
22. Atmospheric oil chamber
23. Automatic oil stop valve
24. Back of seal oil pressure gauge
25. Oil return line (back of seal)
26. Oil manifold
27. Oil rings
28. Journal bearings—rear shaft bearings
29. Oil pump
30. Pressure relief valve
31. Oil cooler inlet
32. Oil heater
33. Oil pressure regulating valve
34. Thrust bearings
35. Oil pump drive gears

Courtesy Carrier Corporation Operations Manual.

film of oil on the bellows seal faces and ensures a tight seal. Refer to the section on the bellows seal for further information.

Bearing oil rings (16) bring oil from the bearing wells in the bearing chamber while the pressure is building up to 8 psi and before the check valve opens. Any excess oil on the shaft bearings during operation will collect in the bearing chamber and drop through the oil return line (25) to the oil pump chamber.

Oil that passes by the intermediate floating seal ring during operation is piped back to the atmospheric float chamber (22). As the oil in the float chamber rises to a predetermined level, the action of the float valve (20) allows the oil to pass through the stop valve (23), which has been opened by pump discharge pressure. Oil passes through the stop valve and back into the bearing chamber due to the vacuum inside the machine. From the bearing chamber, the oil flows back to the oil reservoir though the oil return line (25).

An increase or decrease in oil pressure from back-of-seal to the regulating valve (33) opens or closes the valve to allow excess oil to return to the oil pump, which in turn maintains a steady oil pressure in the system. The pressure relief valve (30) on the oil pump relieves excessively high pressure and avoids damage to the oil pump.

The Bellows Seal

When oil pressure reaches 5 psi, the bellows expands, moving the stationary sealing seat (12) against the pressure of the seal spring (14), until it stops against the seal housing cover (18) at point A. This movement opens a space between the faces of the sealing seat (12) and sealing ring (26).

From this groove, oil flows in two directions across the sealing seat and seal ring:

1. Oil flows across the outside diameter of the face of the stationary sealing seat (12) and into the cavity between the bellows assembly (31) and the compressor shaft. The oil then flows from this cavity into the atmosphere float chamber. The seal housing cover (18) has a water jacket that minimizes refrigerant loss from the oil by keeping the oil temperature down.
2. A small amount of oil also passes by the outer floating seal ring (9) and is returned to the atmosphere float chamber through the external connection. Oil entering the atmospheric float chamber is returned to the compressor through the float valve and stop valve. Since machine pressure is below atmospheric pressure during operation, oil passes through the stop valve and into the seal-end bearing (17). It then passes back to the main oil reservoir through the oil return line.

The stop valve is set to open at approximately 8 psi and is actuated by an oil pressure line taken from the main oil-pump discharge supply to the seal end. The stop valve opens immediately after the compressor has started. It also prevents refrigerant vapor from flowing out of the machine if the pressure rises above atmospheric during shutdown.

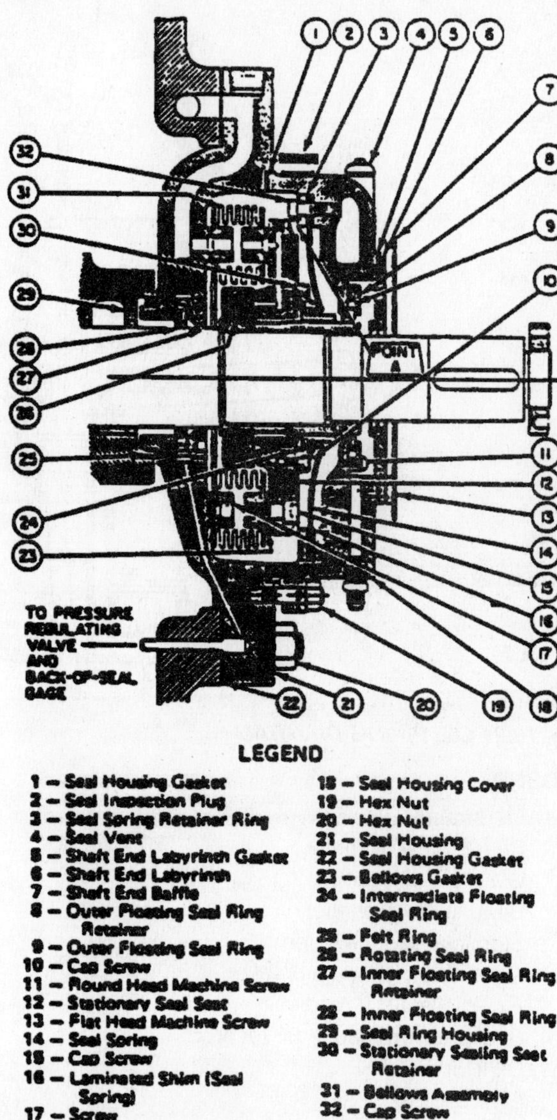

Fig. 19.22 Bellows Seal Assembly
Illustration courtesy Carrier Corporation.

The Cooling Water Manifold

The cooling water manifold is located below the thrust end of the compressor. It uses city water to cool the compressor's bearings and seals. The temperature of the bearings and seals is controlled by the supply of cooling

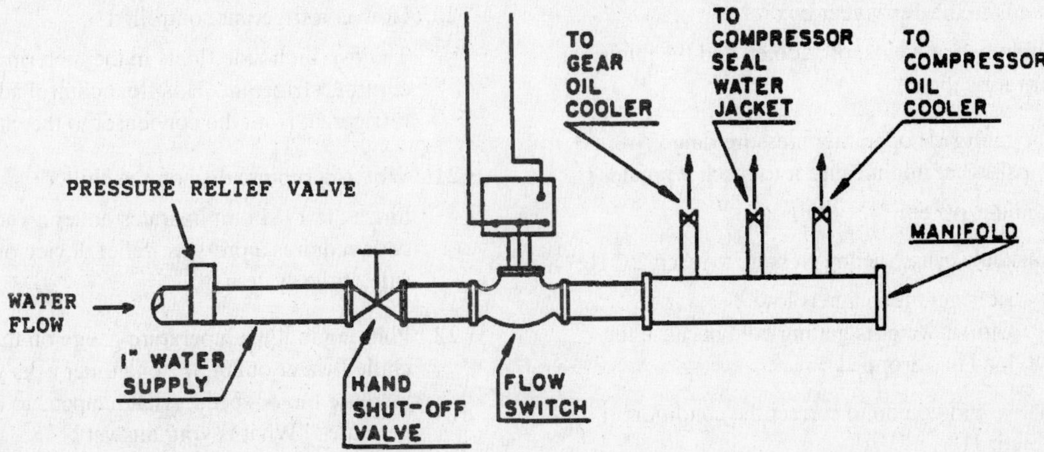

Fig. 19.23
Illustration courtesy Carrier Corporation.

water. Below is a description of the components connected to the cooling water manifold.

1. The pressure relief valve relieves any excess pressure from the water manifold to the three petcocks.
2. The hand shutoff valve is closed to stop the flow of water through the system while the system is shut down. Before the system is turned on, the hand shutoff valve is opened.
3. The flow switch, located on the water supply line, automatically turns the oil heater ON when the water supply is shut OFF by hand. It automatically turns OFF the oil heater when water flow is restored.
4. The cooling water manifold has three pet cocks:
   - **(A)** The first petcock is piped to the gearbox oil cooler at the thrust end of the compressor.
   - **(B)** The second petcock cools the shaft seal.
   - **(C)** The third petcock cools the oil reservoir.
5. After the supply water has circulated through the machine, it is dumped through a floor drain at the thrust end of the system.

Carrier 17M Review Questions

1. Does horsepower increase with motor speed?

   Yes.
2. What are the motor and compressor speeds?

   Motor: 1,750 rpm; compressor: 5,000 rpm.
3. How is the heater turned ON and OFF in the main oil reservoir?

   The flow switch, located inside the water manifold, turns the heater ON and OFF. When the machine is ON, the switch turns the heater OFF, and vice versa.
4. You have two gauges, one indicating it has 17″ Hg and the other 13″ Hg. Which has the higher pressure?

   13″ Hg
5. If pressure continues rising in the system, what happens?

   (A) The high-pressure cutout shuts down the machine.

   (B) If the high-pressure cutout fails, the rupture disc blows refrigerant out.
6. On the bottom of the evaporator is a line with a globe valve and plug at the end. What is the line for?

   It moves refrigerant from the evaporator to the storage receiver.
7. If you have 13″ Hg on the evaporator, what is wrong?

   You are producing warm water. You must increase the speed by turning the drum controller (the wheel that controls motor speed).
8. What type of chiller is used in the 17M centrifugal system?

   A flooded chiller.

9. What is in the Terry gear box?

Double helical gears, oil, cooler, and the pump for gear lubrication.

10. If the high-side operating pressure ranges from 3 to 5 psi, what might cause it to reach 9 pounds?

Air in the system.

11. What could cause suction pressure to reach 25″ Hg?

(A) Refrigerant charge is low.
(B) Chiller water is getting cold because the load has dropped.

12. What would you do to correct the condition in problem 11?

(A) Charge the machine with more refrigerant.
(B) Slow the machine down.
(C) Check the safety controls.

13. What are some of the safety devices on the Carrier 17M?

(A) Oil-pressure safety switch
(B) Rupture disc
(C) Chilled-water pressure differential switch
(D) High/low-pressure controls

14. What are the gauge glasses at each end of the motor for?

They indicate the oil level for bearing lubrication.

15. Where is the relief valve for the water pumps?

There is no relief valve. Pumps are centrifugal and cannot build up excess pressure even if the discharge is closed.

16. What could cause high pressure to blow the rupture disc?

A possible fire in the engine room.

17. What else could cause the rupture disc to blow?

Other possible causes are leaking condenser tubes and water pressure in the system.

18. How would you control the speed of the gears?

The gears cannot be adjusted. They are governed by motor speed.

19. What controls the capacity of this machine?

The variable wound-rotor AC induction motor controls capacity. It has nine speeds.

20. How is refrigerant controlled?

The two high-side floats in the metering device control refrigerant. This float control admits liquid refrigerant from the condenser to the chiller.

21. Why is a rupture disc on the chiller?

Since the 17M unit operates under a vacuum, the code requires a pressure-relief device on the low side of the system.

22. Pointing to the temperature gauge on the chiller's chilled water outlet, the examiner asks you, "If we increase motor speed, what happens to the temperature?" What is your answer?

The capacity of the machine increases and water temperature goes down.

23. If the high-pressure cutout is set at 15 psig, won't it rupture the disc?

No. It takes 15 psig in the evaporator to blow the rupture disc. Evaporator operating pressure is 15 inches of mercury vacuum.

24. Where do the oil manifold lines go?

(A) The oil supply line goes to the seal end.
(B) The oil return line goes between the seal end and thrust-end bearing chamber.
(C) The equalizer line equalizes the seal end labyrinth with the first-stage suction.

25. What is the purpose of the bellows seal?

(A) To prevent leakage of refrigerant gas to the atmosphere.
(B) To prevent seepage of air into the system.

26. What happens when the compound gauge reads 8″ Hg in the evaporator?

Warm water is produced. At 8″ Hg = 57° refrigerant temperature plus 6° to equal 63° chill water.

27. Give the operating evaporator refrigerant pressure and water temperature:

11 to 15″ Hg refrigerant; 40 to 45° F chilled water temperature.

28. What would cause the system to have 21″ Hg?

(A) Refrigerant shortage
(B) Strainer blockage; it may have to be blown down.

29. Which end of the compressor is for suction, and which is for discharge?

The thrust end is for suction; the seal end is for discharge.

30. What is the sight glass on the side of the chiller for?

It's used for checking refrigerant level.

31. How do you pressurize the machine and why?

This machine is pressurized with air or water during repairs, leak testing, or winter shutdown. It may be pressurized with the purger unit to move the refrigerant from the evaporator into the receiver. The evaporator is pressurized with hot water when testing for refrigerant leaks.

32. How do you know you have water in the system and how do you test for it?

When you start the system and purger, observe the water sight glass on the top of the purger. If water level rises in an hour, you have a water leak in the system. Take samples of water in a cup and test the water box, petcocks, etc., with a halide torch to track down the leak.

33. What is the pressure of the receiver tank in the engine room?

Pressure in the receiver corresponds to the ambient temperature in the engine room. You should know this because there might be no pressure gauge on the receiver.

34. What are some controls that are safety devices?

(A) The differential pressure-chilled water or chilled-water flow switch
(B) The oil pressure control
(C) The chilled water temperature controller
(D) The low refrigerant temperature safety

35. What is the air indicator gauge for, and how does it work?

It determines when the machine needs purging. A red pointer indicates total pressure in the condenser. A black pointer indicates the pressure of R-11 in a feeler bulb located in the top of the condenser. When the total pressure in the condenser exceeds refrigerant pressure in the feeler bulb, the system needs purging.

36. A compound gauge has two colors. What do they mean?

Red signifies temperature; black signifies pressure.

37. How does the oil safety switch work?

It is activated by pressure. A pressure reading at the oil pump discharge is the sum of the actual oil pressure plus suction pressure. If a lower pressure is sensed at the oil pump discharge, the oil safety switch shuts down the compressor. Oil pressure is never less than suction pressure. If the system's oil pressure does not come up within eight seconds, the system shuts down.

38. Where are the condenser water lines?

They are located on the thrust end of the condenser. The condenser water lines enter from the top of the condenser and exit from the bottom.

39. Where do the three copper lines from the water manifold go?

One goes to the gear-box oil cooler; another to the shaft seal; the last to the oil reservoir (oil sump) at the thrust end. Be aware that at the exam you must trace these lines and identify them.

40. Pointing to an orange R-11 drum, the examiner asks, "Can you charge the 17M machine with that?" What is your answer?

No, because you don't know whether or not the drum is uncontaminated. The color code on drums is not standard in the industry. You must see R-11 on it.

41. Where is the oil-pressure regulating valve, and what does it do?

This valve is located on the thrust end of the compressor, between the thrust-bearing cover and the oil sump cover housing the oil pump, heater, and oil water cooler, on the right.

42. Where are the refrigerant and water in the 17M?

Refrigerant is in the shell and water is in the tubes.

43. What is the purpose of the oil heater?

The oil heater evaporates refrigerant left in the oil sump so oil integrity and viscosity are maintained constant.

44. What are the high and low cut-in and cutout settings for the 17M?

The low-oil-pressure control cuts in at 12 psi and cuts out at 6 psi. The high-condenser-pressure control cuts in at 8 psig and cuts out at 15 psig.

45. When the 17M is shut down, what are the pressures for the condenser and evaporator?

The pressures range from two to three inches of mercury vacuum. This vacuum keeps refrigerant from leaking. If any air is sucked in, the purger can remove it.

46. What is the purpose of the abrasive strainer on the condenser water pump?

The strainer cleans water before it goes to the mechanical seal on the pump.

47. How does the vacuum breaker work on the Terry gear box?

It works like a check valve. It allows air into the Terry gear box when the system is off and closes when the system is on.

48. What type of oil is used on the 17M?

A good grade of machine oil is used.

49. What type of lubricant is used on the motor?

Grease is used. Look for grease fittings.

50. What type of lubricant is used on the pumps?

Machine oil is used. Look for open and closed caps.

51. What indicates the direction of water flow through the condenser water pump?

The check valve, on the discharge side of the pump, indicates this.

52. If you have 25″ Hg in the chiller, what is wrong?

Either the low-pressure cutout or the freezestat in the chiller has failed.

53. What kind of relief device is used on the 17M and why?

The ruptured disc is used. It is a metallic disc designed to break at a predetermined pressure. It is used because the 17M operates below atmospheric pressure.

54. Describe the 17M motor.

It is a four-pole, three-phase, 750 HP, 1,750 rpm, variable-speed induction motor.

55. Describe the 17M charging procedure.

(A) Wear your goggles while charging.

(B) Make up a 3/4″ nipple into a standard globe valve and close the valve. This connection is done at the charging drum.

(C) Remove the 3/4″ cap and plug on the refrigerant drum.

(D) Screw the valve with the nipple into the opening, turning it in far enough to push off the inside cap. Open the valve slightly for an indication that the cap is off.

(E) Elevate the drum in a horizontal position with a chain and hoist for proper support. Do this near the chiller charging valve and high enough to allow the refrigerant to flow as a liquid. The 3/4″ nipple and valve on the drum are connected at the evaporator charging valve. If charging gas, simply allow the refrigerant to be drawn in as a gas, with the drum resting on the floor.

(F) With a chain and hoist, rotate the drum so the valve is at the bottom.

(G) Use copper tubing with necessary fittings to connect the two valves, making all joints tight.

(H) Start the chilled water pump to circulate chilled water during the charging process.

(I) When the machine pressure reaches 18.5″ Hg vacuum or less, open drum and chiller charging valves and allow the machine vacuum to draw in liquid refrigerant.

(J) Open both valves and allow the refrigerant to be drawn in by the machine's vacuum.

(K) Check whether the drum is empty by shaking it slightly. When it is empty, close the evaporator charging valve.

(L) Close the valve on the charging drum. Disconnect the drum from the evaporator. Remove the drum valve for use with the next drum.

56. How does the drum controller work on the 17M?

The drum controller, or "big red wheel," adjusts external resistances to the motor. When all resistance is removed, the motor runs at full speed. The windings from panel to motor have nine resistance levels.

57. Describe the secondary drum controller:

It adjusts the amount of resistance in the slip-ring circuit of the motor, thus accelerating and regulating its speed. The 17M motor is a nine-speed wound-rotor induction motor.

58. If the brine temperature is abnormally low, what safety will stop the compressor?

The chill-water temperature control will stop the compressor.

59. If refrigerant temperature is too low, what safety device will shut down the compressor, and why?

The refrigerant temperature controller will shut down the compressor, probably due to low refrigerant charge.

60. On startup, your 17M has 5 psi oil pressure. What will happen, and why?

The oil-pressure safety will shut down the compressor, because within eight seconds of operation the machine must have at least 8 psi oil pressure.

61. How much oil pressure does the oil pressure regulator maintain to the back of the seal?

14 to 18 psig is maintained.

62. If refrigerant is 36° F, what is brine temperature?

42°. Rule of thumb: add 6° to refrigerant temperature to get brine temperature.

63. In the center of the engine room are five pumps. Describe their function.

(A) Four electric sump pumps are used to remove or drain ground water from the engine room.
(B) One pump is a steam-driven backup for the electric pumps, for emergency use only.

64. Describe the ammeter on the 17M control panel.

It is an instrument that measures electrical current in amperes. It is adjusted with a set screw in the middle.

65. What drives the oil pump on the 17M?

The main compressor shaft.

66. What are the main oil circuits for the 17M?

(A) Oil pump worm-gear drive
(B) Two-shaft bearings
(C) Thrust bearings
(D) Shaft seal

67. What device reacts to oil-pressure failure?

The oil safety switch reacts by shutting down the compressor.

68. The engine room you work in has a Type C fire extinguisher for putting out electrical fires. While you are on duty, the condenser pump motor suddenly starts burning. What is the first thing you should do?

Call the Fire Department.

69. How does the metering device operate on the 17M?

The economizer has two chambers with two high-side floats. It functions as follows:

(A) Liquid from the condenser falls into the upper valve chamber. This chamber has a float, called the condenser float.
(B) When this float rises, liquid enters the lower chamber, called the economizer chamber.
(C) As liquid enters the economizer, some flashes.
(D) This flashing vapor is drawn into the second stage of the centrifugal compressor.
(E) Liquid refrigerant left in the economizer enters the evaporator.
(F) Any liquid trying to leave with the flash gas is removed by the eliminators. They are on the inlet side of the flash gas connection to the second stage. The economizer increases the efficiency of the 17M.

70. What are the temperatures of primary components operating under a heavy load?

(A) entering chilled water: 55° F
(B) returning chilled water: 45° F
(C) condenser refrigerant: 90–100° F
(D) evaporator refrigerant: 15° Hg or 40° F

71. Describe the evaporator's water flow.

The evaporator has an odd-pass design. Secondary refrigerant (water) enters the evaporator shell at the thrust end and exits at the opposite side of the chiller, which is the motor end.

72. How do you reduce output or raise brine temperature?

You must reduce system speed by turning the drum controller ("big red wheel").

73. Low refrigerant or brine causes what kind of damage?

It may freeze evaporator tubes and cause them to burst.

74. What type of evaporator and condenser are used in the 17M?

It uses the horizontal tube-and-shell type.

75. If the 17M had low oil pressure and the safeties failed, what could result?

Low oil pressure will result in damage to the bearings and seals.

76. Describe the components and operation of the bellows seal.

When oil pressure is supplied to the bellows assembly during operation, the bellows expands, moving the seal against spring pressure. Between the seal seat and its rotating assembly is a space where oil forms a seal. On shutdown, the oil reservoir supplies oil to the bellows, preventing leaks.

77. If the 17M had high condenser pressure and the safeties did not function, what could happen?

Overloading of the compressor, gears, and motor could occur and result in condenser damage.

78. How do you check the two high-side floats for proper functioning?

Put your hand on the top and then on the bottom of the high-side floats. The economizer is located on the bottom of the floats and should be cooler than on the top.

79. What is the vacuum pump for?

It completely evacuates the system. It is used only after repairs have been made.

80. How can you count the stages in a centrifugal compressor?

Count the number of volutes (impeller housing).

81. What is the purpose of Kingsbury thrust bearings?

Kingsbury thrust bearings absorb thrust pressure. During system operation, axial thrust, caused by pressure differential across the impellers, pushes toward the suction end. The thrust pressure must be absorbed to keep the machine intact.

82. Describe the condenser water pump.

It is a centrifugal type pump driven by a 50-HP AC induction motor.

83. Describe the cycle of condenser water.

(A) Condenser water leaves the condenser from the bottom at the thrust end of the machine.
(B) Water then enters the condenser pump and is pumped up to the cooling tower, where 10 percent of the heat is to be removed.
(C) From the cooling tower, the water flows down, back to the engine room. The water enters the thrust end of the condenser from the top.

84. How would you get air into the 17M?

The evaporator and suction piping is under a vacuum. Air can be pulled into the system through the flanges or gaskets. Air may also be pulled in through the shaft end, if the seal is worn.

85. What indicates the presence of noncondensable gases in the system?

(A) The air indicator
(B) An increase in head pressure while water temperatures are normal

86. How is the purge unit activated? Briefly describe its operation.

(A) The stop valve opens on the suction line between the condenser and the purge compressor.
(B) The purge compressor is activated, raising mixed gas pressure to approximately 80 psig.
(C) High-pressure gases are discharged to purge the air-cooler condenser.
(D) The oil separator between the compressor and condenser returns oil to the purge compressor.
(E) High-pressure gases are liquefied in the condenser and discharged to the separator tank.
(F) At the separator tank, refrigerant drops to the bottom of the trap while water, lighter than R-11, floats on top of the trap. Noncondensable gases also remain on top.
(G) Water is drained out by a manual drain valve.
(H) When the refrigerant trap fills, a ball float rises, allowing refrigerant to flow back to the economizer.
(I) Noncondensable gases are automatically vented by an air relief valve.

87. How is refrigerant removed from the 17M during maintenance or repairs?

To remove the entire charge, the purger pressurizes the system with air, forcing the refrigerant into the receiver.

88. What is the procedure to store refrigerant in the receiver?

(A) Shut down the purger and the 17M.
(B) Connect the line between the refrigerant removal connection on the chiller to the receiver.
(C) Open the water drain valve.
(D) Close the valve on the purge suction and refrigerant return line to the condenser.
(E) Connect a hose between the water drain and the "T" in the refrigerant return line.
(F) Remove the plug from the "T" in the purge suction line.
(G) Open valves between the refrigerant removal connection and the receiver.
(H) Start the purge pump and allow pressure to develop in the system to at least 5 psig but no more than 8 psig.

89. What is the purpose of the vacuum pump, and how is it used?

The vacuum pump is used only to completely evacuate the 17M to check for leaks before returning refrigerant to the system.

(A) "Tee" the vacuum suction line into the purge suction unit.
(B) Close the valve at the purge suction line by the purge compressor.
(C) Open the stop valve from the condenser to the purge suction.
(D) Open the valve on the vacuum-pump suction line.
(E) Start the vacuum pump and observe the machine pressure.
(F) When the vacuum reaches 27″ Hg, stop the pump and close the valve on the vacuum-pump suction line.
(G) Observe system pressure for 24 hours.

90. How can you distinguish between the suction and discharge sides of any centrifugal water pump?

The suction side is usually larger than the discharge side, and the discharge side has a check valve immediately after the pump.

91. The centrifugal water-pump packing gland seal permits how much leakage from the pump?

It allows no more than 6 drops of water leakage per minute.

92. On a centrifugal water pump with a mechanical seal, how much leakage is permitted?

No water leakage is allowed. If the mechanical seal leaks, you must shut down the pump and replace the seal.

93. How is the 17M compressor cooled?

It is cooled by a combination of suction gas, oil, ambient temperature, and the economizer.

94. How do you add oil to the 17M system?

Good-grade machine oil can be poured into the seal-end sump. The thrust end is under a vacuum. To add oil into the thrust-end sump, you would have to pressurize the machine until you achieved positive pressure on the thrust end. When pressurizing the system, do not exceed 5 psi.

95. What are normal condenser water inlet and outlet temperatures under full load?

The inlet water temperature should be 86° F; the outlet water temperature should be 96° F.

96. What is the purpose of the pneumatic valve connected outside the system?

It controls the amount of chilled water entering the chiller coil. The temperature in the area being served by this air handler determines the setting of the pneumatic valve.

97. Where is the chiller sight glass?

It is off the bottom of the chiller on the left side of the evaporator (thrust-end side of the compressor).

98. Where is the thermometer, and what is it for?

It is located next to the sight glass and measures chiller-water temperature.

99. What does the impeller rpm depend on?

The speed of the impeller depends on the nine-speed drum controller setting. Due to the Terry gear-box configuration, its maximum speed may range up to 5,000 rpm.

100. What is the motor speed?

It is 1,750 rpm.

PART III: TRANE CENTRAVAC SYSTEM REVIEW

The basic components of the Trane model CVHE Centravac chiller are the evaporator, the three-stage compressor, the water-cooled condenser, the two-stage economizer, and related piping. Figure 19.25 shows the general assembly of a typical CVHE Centravac chiller.

The CVHE Refrigeration Cycle

Liquid refrigerant is distributed along the length of the evaporator and sprayed through orifices to uniformly coat each evaporator tube. The liquid refrigerant absorbs heat from the cooling-system water being circulated through the tubes and vaporizes. Refrigerant gas is drawn through the eliminators to remove any droplets of liquid refrigerant entrained in the gas.

The Centrifugal Three-Stage Compressor

The refrigerant gas is then drawn through the first-stage variable-inlet guide vanes into the first-stage impeller. The inlet vanes modulate the flow of gas to match capacity requirements. The vanes also prerotate the gas so it enters the impeller at an angle for maximum efficiency at all loads. Compressed discharge gas from the first stage flows through the fixed second-stage inlet vanes to the second-stage impeller. Here the refrigerant gas is again compressed and discharged through the third-stage variable guide vane and into the third-stage impeller. The third-stage impeller compresses the gas and discharges it to the condenser.

Baffles distribute the compressed gas evenly across the condenser tube bundle. Cooling-tower water circulating through the condenser tubes absorbs heat from the refrigerant, causing it to condense. The liquid refrigerant passes through an orifice into the two-stage economizer.

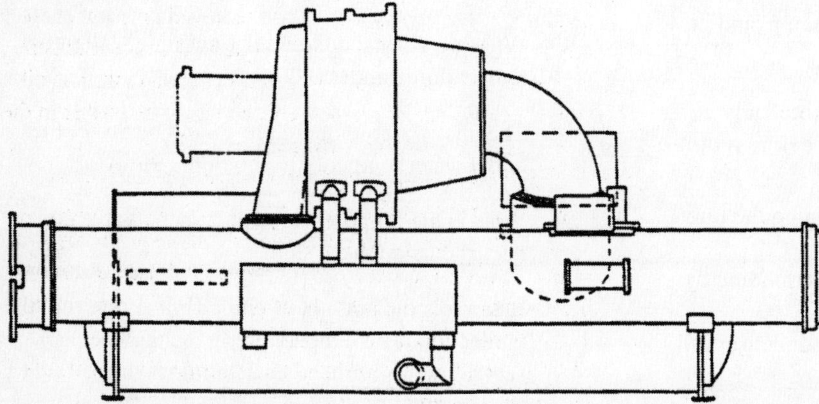

Fig. 19.24 LIQUID CHILLERS: CENTRIFUGAL DIRECT DRIVE CENTRAVAC: CVHE–M–1

MODELS CVHE 013 THROUGH CVHE 125

Illustration courtesy the Trane Company.

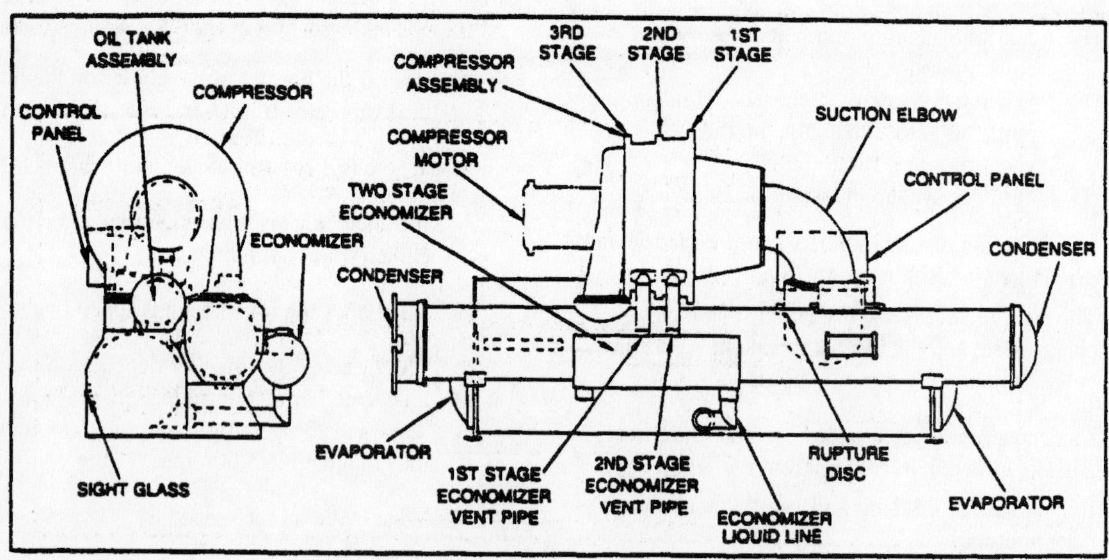

Fig. 19.25
Illustration courtesy the Trane Company.

The economizer reduces the refrigeration energy requirements by avoiding the necessity to pass all the gas through every stage of compression. Some liquid refrigerant flashes to gas as a result of the pressure drop across the orifice. This cools the remaining liquid refrigerant, and the flash gas is drawn directly from the first and second stages of the economizer into the third and second stages of the compressor, respectively. The remaining liquid flows through an additional orifice to the evaporator. Figure 19.26 shows how the dual-stage economizer functions.

Liquid refrigerant from the condenser passes through Orifice A into Chamber A. This area's pressure equals the pressure between the second- and third-stage impellers. As a result, some of the liquid flashes to gas and is drawn directly into the third-stage impeller. The remaining liquid refrigerant passes through Orifice B into Chamber B, where the pressure equals the pressure between the first- and second-stage impellers. Again, liquid refrigerant that flashes to gas is drawn directly into the second-stage impeller. The remaining liquid flows through Orifice C to the evaporator.

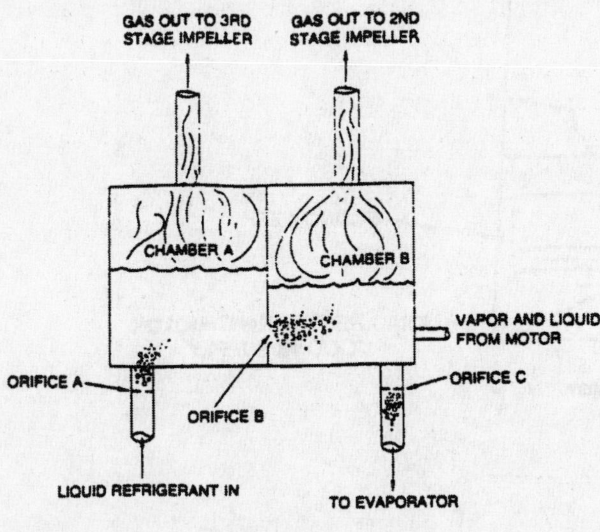

Fig. 19.26
Illustration courtesy the Trane Company.

Some units have an optional single-stage economizer. They function like two-stage economizers, except all refrigerant gas is discharged to the third-stage impeller.

The Compressor Lubrication System

Figure 19.28 is a diagram of the CVHE compressor lubrication system, which oils the motor bearings.

Oil is pumped from the oil tank by a pump and motor inside the oil tank. The oil passes through the oil-pressure regulating valve, which maintains the net oil pressure at approximately 15 psig. The oil is then filtered, sent to the compressor motor bearings, and returned to the oil tank. The oil return lines have sight glasses. Oil flow must be visible in the sight glass whenever the oil pump is energized.

For proper lubrication and to prevent refrigerant from condensing in the tank, one 1,000-watt oil-tank heater is fastened to the outlet side of the tank. In response to the oil temperature control, the heater is energized to maintain the oil tank at 140 to 145° F when the chiller is not running.

The oil tank is vented to the compressor suction elbow to remove any refrigerant from the oil tank. A drain from the first-stage suction cover to the oil tank allows any oil trapped in the suction cover area to return to the oil tank.

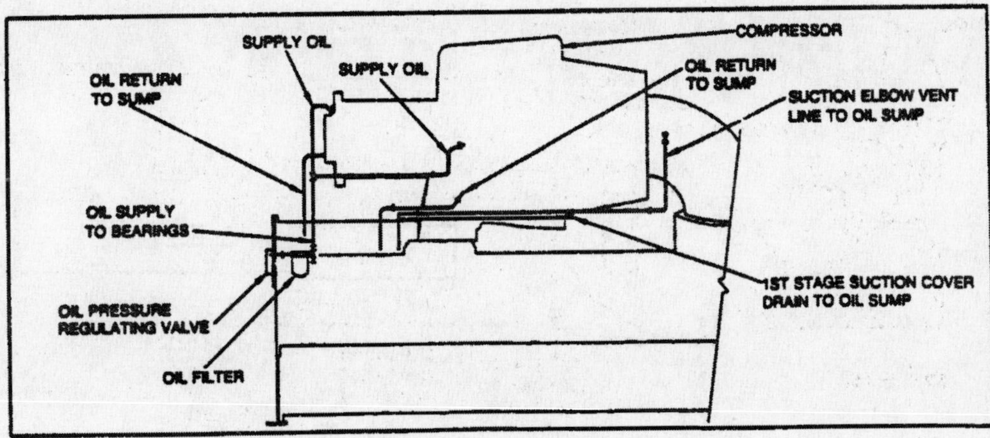

Fig. 19.27
Illustration courtesy the Trane Company.

The Motor Cooling System

The Centravac motor is cooled with refrigerant, as shown in figure 19.28.

Liquid refrigerant flows from the condenser sump to the bottom of the compressor motor. The refrigerant enters the motor chamber, where some of it flashes, since the chamber is at low-side economizer pressure. The gas flows around the rotor and stator; liquid refrigerant flows through a slot in the stator lamination. The refrigerant cools the motor and then flows from the motor chamber through a drain in each end to the evaporator. The pressure difference between condenser and economizer (low side) maintains a flow of refrigerant through the motor at all times.

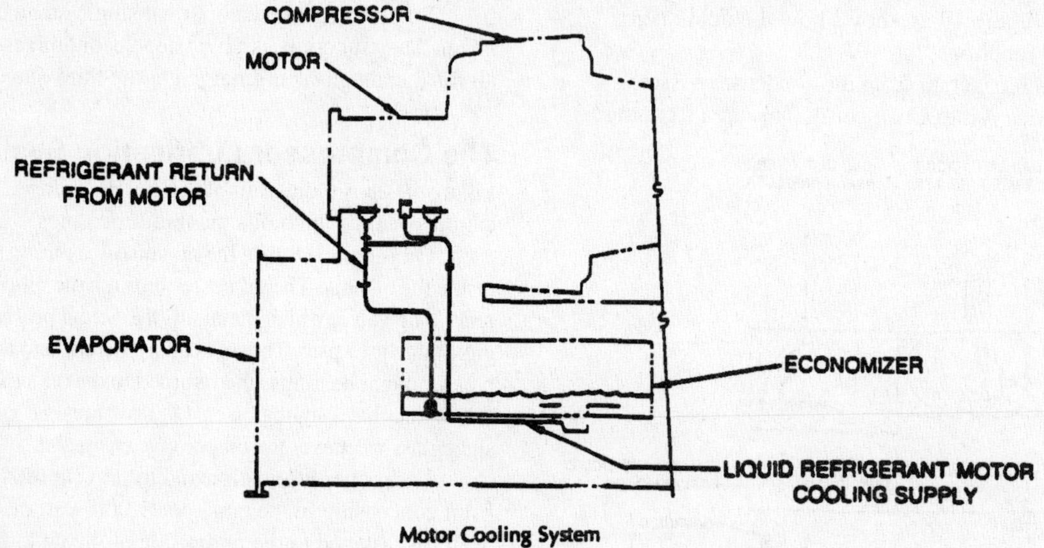

Fig. 19.28
Illustration courtesy the Trane Company.

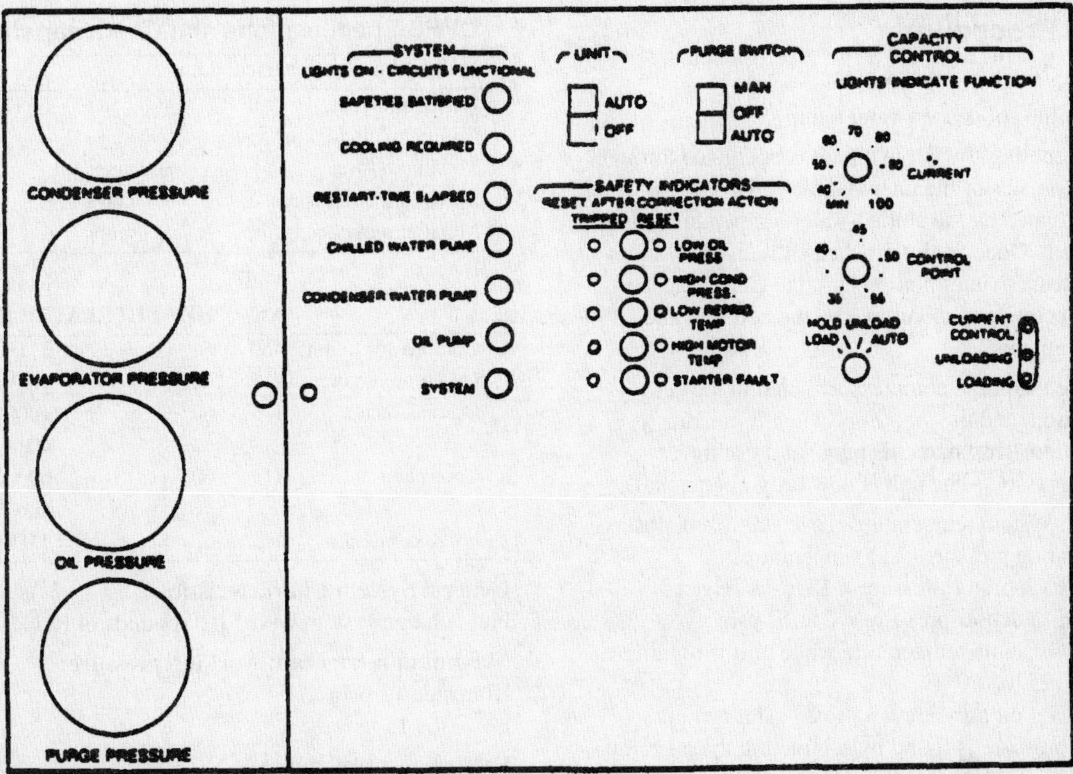

Fig. 19.29 Model CVHE Centravac Control Panel
Illustration courtesy the Trane Company.

The Control System

The Centravac model CVHE is capable of continuous capacity modulation from 100 percent to 10 percent of full load at design conditions. This is achieved through the electronic control panel.

The Control Panel

All safety operating controls are housed in the Centravac control panel. Panel functions are divided into four categories, as indicated by the external panel layout.

1. Pressure gauges show only condenser, evaporator, lubricating-oil, and purge-drum pressures.
2. System-sequence status lights perform an important diagnostic function. A series of seven lights shows the progress of the starting sequence. As each of the seven circuit-interlocks is verified, its pilot light goes on. The cause of an aborted start can be determined by observing the pilot lights to see where the sequence stopped.
3. Five fault-trip indicators display the status of each safety-cutout control.

Startup Precautions

Before proceeding, make a few checks to ensure a trouble-free startup.

1. The pneumatic system should be under 20 psi.
2. Lubricating oil should be visible in the oil-sump sight glass.
3. To prepare the purge system for operation, switch the purge heater on about 30 minutes before startup. This allows the oil separator to warm up enough to eliminate refrigerant from the purge compressor oil.
4. Check that the demand limiter switch setting has not been disturbed. The demand limit charge is based on the highest rate of power consumption that occurred during any continuous 15-minute interval within that particular billing period. The demand limiter should be set at a capacity that was found satisfactory for that period and remain at that setting throughout the month.

Startup Procedure

1. Start the chilled-water pump.
2. Start the condenser-water pump.
3. The cooling-tower fan circuit is energized through the contacts of the pneumatic-electric switch, which is actuated by the chilled-water temperature control system. Once the interlocked chilled- and condenser-water pumps start, the Centravac starts. Its operation is monitored by the control panel instruments.
4. Place the purge compressor switch in the auto position, and the oil pump switch in the run position. This starts the purge and Centravac compressors. The unit is now fully operational.
5. After system temperatures have stabilized, observe operating pressures and temperatures.
   (A) Evaporator pressure = 12 to 18″ Hg
   (B) Condenser pressure = 2 to 12 psig
   (C) Oil sump temperature while unit is running = 125 to 150° F
   (D) Net oil pressure = 18 to 20 psig. Net oil pressure is found by subtracting the oil sump (evaporator) pressure from the oil-pressure gauge reading.
6. Observe the lubricating oil-sump and oil-cooler thermometers.
   (A) Oil cooler = 110° F
   (B) Oil sump = 140-145° F
7. From this point, the machine operates automatically.

Shutdown Procedure

If the system is to be removed from service with a load still on the machine, stop it by turning the oil-pump switch off.

After the compressor has coasted down and stopped, the chilled-water pumps are stopped with the stop button on the chilled-water pump pushbutton station.

The pumps and compressor are not turned off at the same time, because during compressor coast-down, some refrigeration continues to take place in the evaporator. If the evaporator water flow is stopped during coast-down, the water in the evaporator tubes could freeze.

If required, open the electrical disconnects supplying the compressor and pump motors. Keep the control-power disconnect closed during shutdown to energize the compressor oil-pump heater.

The sump heater should be operated continuously to prevent refrigerant from condensing in the sump and dissolving in the oil.

CVHE Specifications and Characteristics

Unit and motor electrical data

Rated voltage:	460 volts	60 HZ	3 PH
Minimum circuit ampacity:	500 amps		
Maximum fuse:	800 amps		
Maximum circuit breaker:	800 amps		
Maximum overload trip:	421 amps		

	Volts-AC	**HZ**	**PH**	**RLA**	**Max LRAY**	**Max LRAD**
Compressor motor:	460	60	3	394	711	2216
Oil pump motor:	115	60	1		4.9 fla	
Oil tank heater:	115	60	1		1000 watts	
Control circuit:	115	60	1		60 va max	
Purge comp mtr:	115	60	1		5.0 fla	

General System Characteristics
Field charge system with 1,020 pounds of R-11.

Maximum refrigerant working pressure:
High side 15 psig
Low side 15 psig

Factory test pressures:
High side 45 psig
Low side 45 psig

Field leak test pressure:
8 psig maximum

Unit service literature:
Installation Manual CVHE-M-5
Operation/Maintenance Manual CVHE-IN-6

Wiring diagram numbers:
Schematic pg1: X39470520010
Schematic pg2: X39470487010
Field wiring: X39470501010
Alternate stator wiring: X39470503010

The Heat Recovery Cycle (Optional)

Heat recovery is the salvaging of heat that is normally rejected to the atmosphere through the cooling tower and putting it to use. For example, a high-rise office building may require simultaneous heating and cooling during the winter months. With a heat recovery cycle, heat removed from the cooling load can be transferred to areas requiring it. Keep in mind that heat recovery is possible only when a cooling load is available as a heat source.

To provide heat recovery, a heat-recovery condenser is added to the unit. Though physically identical to a standard condenser, the heat-recovery condenser is piped into a heating circuit, not the cooling tower.

During the heat-recovery cycle, the unit operates as usual, except that the cooling-load heat is rejected to the heating-water circuit rather than the cooling-tower water circuit. When hot water is required, the heating water circuit pumps are energized. Water is circulated through the heat-recovery (or auxiliary) condenser-tube bundle, where it absorbs cooling-load heat from the compressed refrigerant gas. The heated water is then used to supply building comfort heating.

Refrigerant Charging

The refrigerant charging procedure for the Trane is listed below.

1. If water is present in the tubes, either break machine vacuum with refrigerant vapor or circulate water to avoid tube damage.
2. Always use refrigerant-compatible hoses or copper tubing with self-sealing connections or shut-off valves.
3. Transfer the refrigerant using one of the following techniques (listed in order of decreasing preference):
   - **(A)** An approved Trane low-pressure refrigerant recovery/recycle unit
   - **(B)** The available pressure differential
   - **(C)** Gravity. Use a return-vent line to refrigerant drums to equalize.
   - **(D)** A mechanical gear pump with compatible seals, or a magnetically driven pump
4. When charging from new drums, use a fitting designed for use with a 3/4-inch center drum bung of 2-inch bung, as shown in the illustration below.
5. Do not use dry nitrogen to push refrigerant into the chiller, as in the past. This will contaminate the charge and require excessive purging, which will result in unnecessary refrigerant release.
6. Weigh in the proper charge.
7. Use a recovery/recycle unit or vacuum pump to evacuate hoses; discharge outdoors.

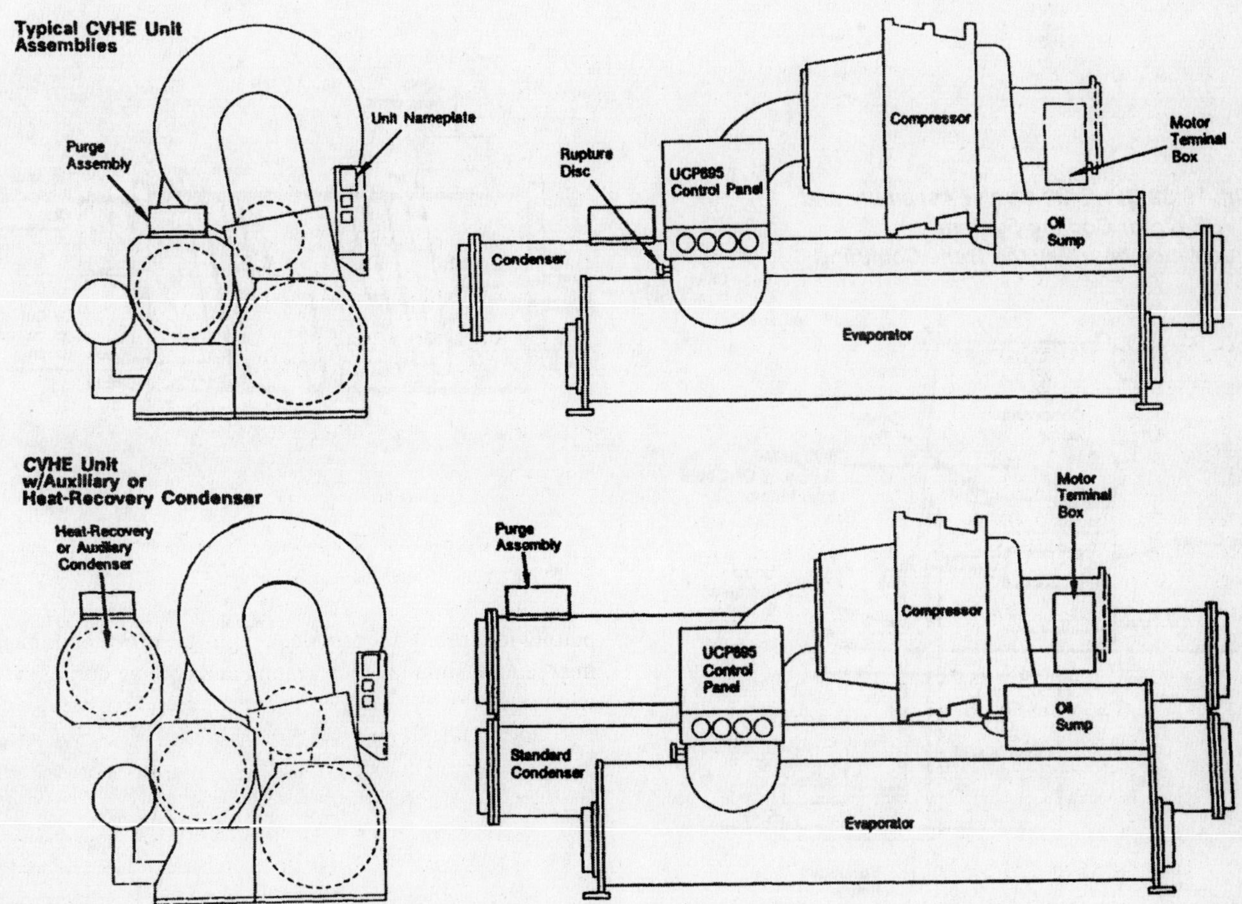

Fig. 19.30
Illustration courtesy the Trane Company.

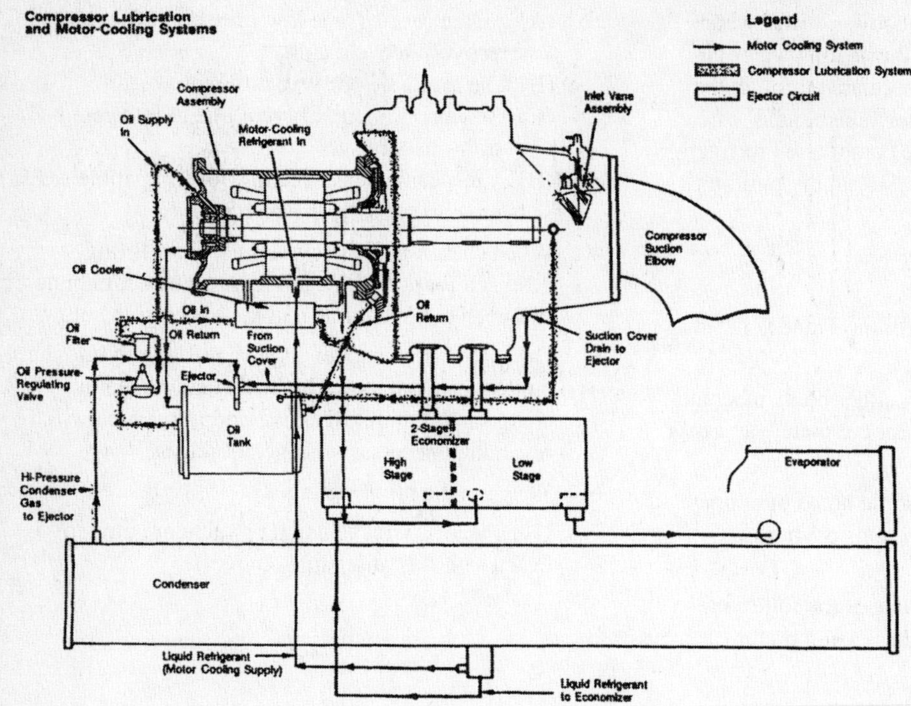

Fig. 19.31
Illustration courtesy the Trane Company.

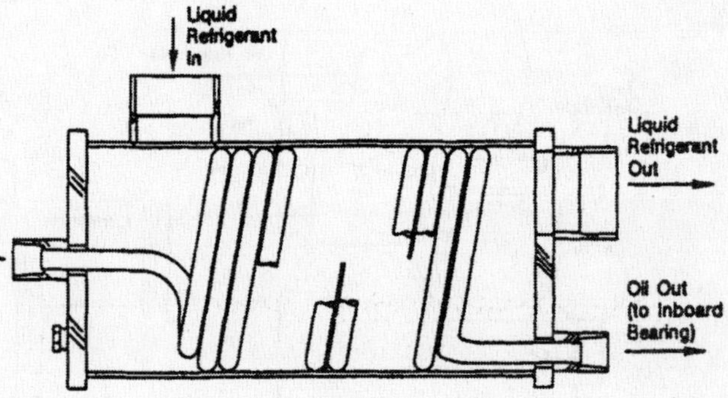

Fig. 19.32 CVHE Oil Cooler Assembly and CVHE Motor Cooling System
Illustration courtesy the Trane Company.

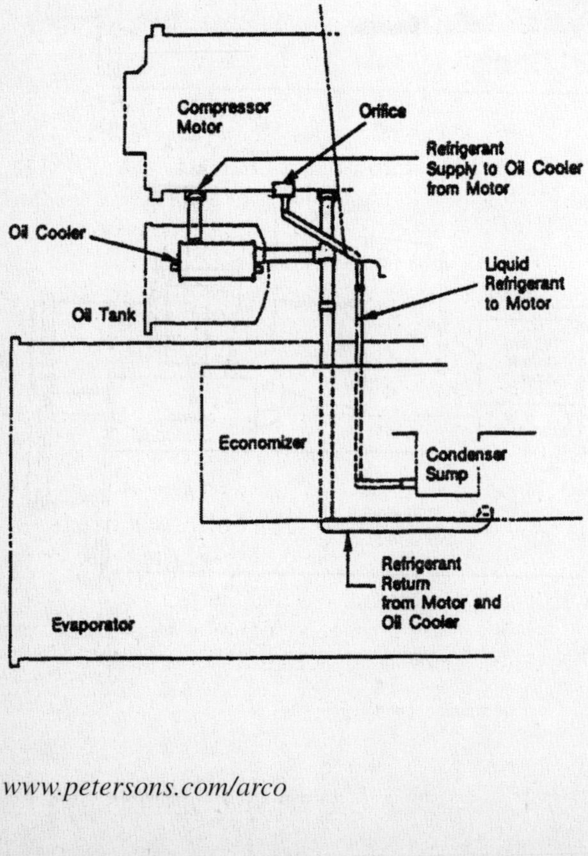

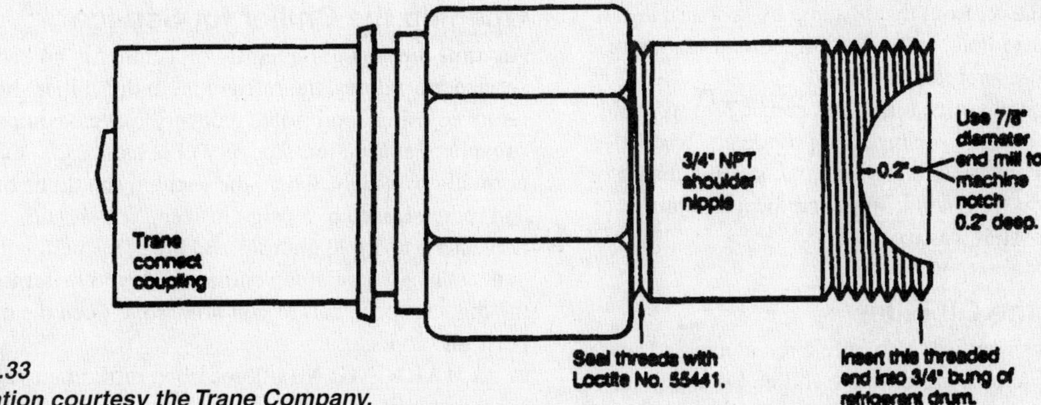

Fig. 19.33
Illustration courtesy the Trane Company.

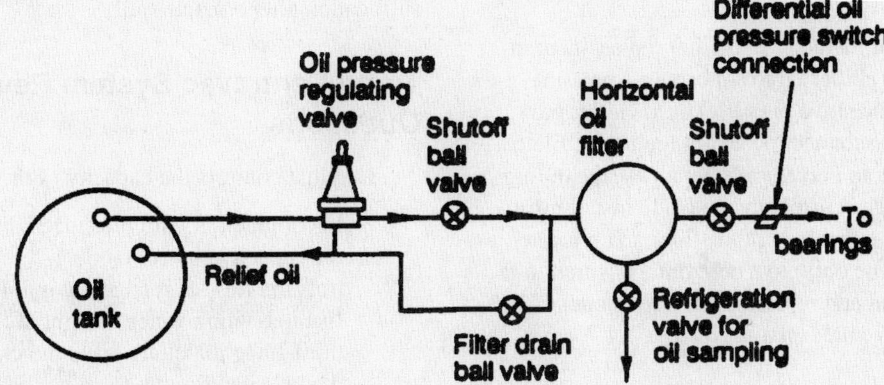

Fig. 19.34
Illustration courtesy the Trane Company.

Handling Refrigerant During Maintenance and Service

In the past, venting refrigerant to the outside atmosphere and/or equipment room was common during many service procedures. Today this is strictly prohibited.

Current editions of the operation and maintenance literature for Trane centrifugal chillers describe certain procedures that are no longer entirely appropriate. These procedures should be modified as described below.

Purge Tank Water Removal

Part of the chiller weekly maintenance program is inspection for and removal of water from the purge unit. The present procedure allows water and other noncondensables to be discharged from the purge tank blowoff valve on older-style purgers into the equipment room.

Do not vent refrigerant from the purger into the equipment room! Instead, once the purge tank is pressurized, connect an approved refrigerant containment vessel to the valve and discharge the water and refrigerant from the purge tank into the vessel.

Chiller Lubrication System Compressor Oil Change

Previously, part of the chiller's recommended maintenance program included an annual oil change. Today, rather than change oil automatically every year, an oil analysis program is recommended that you determine the necessity for changing oil. This reduces the chiller's overall lifetime oil consumption and minimizes refrigerant emissions. A drain fitting should be installed in the oil line after the oil filter for obtaining oil samples.

Oil Change Procedure

When oil analysis indicates the need to change compressor oil, use the following procedure for removing oil:

1. Draw oil from the chiller through the oil charging valve on the chiller oil sump (refer to previous illustration) into an approved, evacuated tank, or
2. Pump the oil from the chiller through the oil charging valve into an air-tight resealable container, using a magnetically driven auxiliary pump.

Forcing the oil from the oil sump by pressurizing the chiller (for example, by raising chiller temperature or adding nitrogen) is not recommended.

Refrigerant dissolved in the oil can be removed and returned to the chiller by using an appropriate deep-vacuum recovery unit and heating/agitating the oil container. Follow all federal, state, and local regulations regarding disposal of waste oil.

Replacing the Oil Filter

Oil-filter replacement was also once a recommended annual maintenance procedure for the chiller. Filter replacement is currently recommended at each oil change. More frequent replacement is recommended only if low oil pressure prevents unit startup, or if erratic oil pressure is experienced during chiller operation.

The traditional method of oil-filter replacement involved bringing the chiller up to atmospheric pressure (the unit is under a negative pressure) or, if chiller pressure was positive, disconnecting and plugging the filter inlet and outlet lines to prevent refrigerant escape during filter replacement. The current method is to install refrigerant ball valves on either side of the filter and relocate the filter (spin-on type only) to a horizontal position to facilitate filter removal and replacement. Late-model CVHE and CVHF units have the isolation valves factory-installed.

Oil Filter Replacement Procedure

1. Run the oil pump for 2 to 3 minutes to insure that the oil filter is warmed to oil-sump temperature.
2. Close the shutoff valves before and after the filter and open the filter drain valve. Drain time can be reduced by momentarily opening the oil-sampling drain valve.
3. Allow the filter to drain. Remove the filter and replace into a resealable container. Follow all federal, state, and local regulations regarding filter disposal.

Purge Service

Purge service instructions in the chiller maintenance literature contain procedures that recommend disassembly of the purge system while it is still pressurized with refrigerant. This should not be done! The purge system must be valved off and evacuated before disassembly for service.

Opening the Chiller for Service

Anytime the vacuum integrity of a chiller is broken for service procedures, the refrigerant in the chiller should be removed using appropriate recovery/recycle equipment capable of evacuation/recovery of at least 2,000 microns, normally overnight. Then, the vacuum should be broken and repressurized to 5 psig nitrogen. You should reevacuate to 1,000 microns and break vacuum with nitrogen again. All available ventilation should be turned on to the highest speed before you proceed to open the unit and perform service.

WARNING: All fluorocarbon refrigerant vapors are three to five times heavier than air. Leaking vapors collect and concentrate in confined spaces or low spots. Fluorocarbon refrigerants displace the air, posing a risk to suffocation after a major spill.

Trane Centravac System Review Questions

1. What controls the capacity of the Trane?

   In conjunction with the current limiter control and the capacity control module, the vane motor controls the flow of refrigerant into the compressor. Its modulating vanes in front of the first-stage and third-stage impellers open and close according to the load conditions.

2. What are the operating temperature/pressures of the Centravac?

   High-side (condenser) pressure = 2 to 10 psi

   Low-side (evaporator) pressure = 15" Hg (vacuum)

   Oil pressure = 10 to 12 pounds
   Purge pressure = 2 1/2 to 5 pounds

   If purge pressure increases to 10 psi, check the sight glass on the purger. Water may have to be drained.

3. Why have a hot gas bypass on a centrifugal machine?

   If the system is running on a summer day at 55 to 60° F outdoor temperature, it is essentially running without a load. Since the building is not calling for air conditioning, the system stops and start often. The hot gas bypass idles the system without shutting it down, whenever the 40° F set-point temperature is met. Although the machine continues running, it saves energy while idling. Motor startup requires a large amount of electricity.

4. List ten items that can be found in the specifications section of the CVHE service guide.

   (A) General information
   (B) Operations guide
   (C) Installation instructions
   (D) Startup procedures
   (E) Maintenance information
   (F) Troubleshooting guide
   (G) Analysis guide
   (H) Controls guide
   (I) Repair, replacement, and overhaul instructions
   (J) Service bulletins

5. Why is the rupture disc used on this machine?

   By code, a rupture disc is needed on a system that operates below atmospheric pressure and is installed on the low side.

6. How many stages does the Trane Centravac have, and how can you tell?

   It has three stages. You can determine the number of stages on a centrifugal machine by counting the volutes.

7. Which digit of the CVHE model number denotes the design sequence?

   The tenth digit.

8. Why should the Centravac system maintain a minimum of two pounds head pressure?

   The system's head pressure should always be maintained at a positive pressure with a minimum of two pounds. If there is no head pressure, or if it falls into negative pressure, the system can experience oil problems during operation. Normally the cooling-tower temperature should be maintained at approximately 85° return water temperature. This will provide at least two to five pounds head pressure. The cooling tower thermostat controlling the fans should be adjusted to provide the 85" return water.

9. Does increased refrigerant gas density in the evaporator cause a rise in compressor motor amperage?

   Yes.

10. Does the economizer reduce the energy required by the compressor motor to pump refrigerant?

    Yes.

11. Is the oil pump located outside the oil sump?

    No.

12. Does the oil heater help boil refrigerant from oil?

    Yes.

13. What is the speed of the 60-cycle Centravac compressor motor used on a CVHE or CVHB machine?

    The speed is 3,600 rpm.

14. Can Centravac motors be either refrigerant-cooled or water-cooled, depending on motor type?

    Yes. Machines that are 20 years old or older are water-cooled; newer machines are refrigerant-cooled.

15. If the motor overheats, will a circuit breaker in the control panel trip?

    Yes. Motor overheating generally trips a safety on the control panel.

16. What are the four major sections of the control panel? Which section is of most help in troubleshooting?

    The four major sections are lights, breakers, gauges, and controls. The lights are most helpful in troubleshooting.

17. What two readings are needed to determine net oil pressure?

    The oil pressure and evaporator pressure readings are needed.

18. What are the four causes of oil loss on a refrigerant-cooled motor?

    (A) Internal oil leaks
    (B) Cold condenser water
    (C) High-pressure oil leak in sump
    (D) Low load

Author's note: HCFC-123 is the refrigerant used in upgraded Trane machines.

19. What are the operating pressures of HCFC-123?

Temperature in degrees F		Vapor pressure in psig
–100	*	29.9
–90	*	29.8
–80	*	29.7
–70	*	29.6
–60	*	29.5
–50	*	29.2
–40	*	28.9
–30	*	28.5
–20	*	27.8
–10	*	27.0
0	*	26.0
10	*	24.7
20	*	23.0
30	*	20.8
40	*	18.2
50	*	15.0
60	*	11.2
70	*	6.6
80	*	1.1
90	2.6	
100	6.3	
110	10.5	
120	15.4	
130	21.0	
140	27.3	
150	34.5	
160	42.5	
170	51.5	
180	61.4	
190	72.5	
200	84.7	
210	98.1	
220	112.8	
230	128.9	
240	146.3	
250	165.3	
260	185.8	
270	207.9	
280	231.8	
290	257.5	
300	285.0	

** Figures are shown in inches of mercury vacuum. Chart courtesy SUVA DuPont Pocket Reference Guide.*

20. Has the HCFC-123 compatibility issue been resolved?

HCFC-123 is compatible with traditional lubricating oils, but not with seals, "O" rings, and gaskets. To resolve this problem, an alternative compatible refrigerant oil is installed in the upgraded system with HCFC-123.

21. What is the availability of HCFC-123?

DuPont opened plants in Maitland, Ontario and Corpus Christi, Texas in 1991. This refrigerant is available through local distribution channels.

22. What equipment changes are needed to use HCFC-123 in an R-11 system?

(A) Replace the existing purger with a purifier purger. The purifier purger is a high-efficiency purge system that can reduce CFC refrigerant loss during normal purge operation by up to 90 percent. It can operate with the chiller off. The purifier purger logs the air ejected from the chiller, which helps the operator determine air leaks.

(B) Replace the orifice to the metering device.

(C) Overhaul the motor; install new gaskets, seals, and "O" rings.

(D) Replace chiller and condenser head gaskets.

(E) Replace compressor impeller seals and gaskets.

(F) Replace refrigerant oil with oil that is HCFC-123-compatible.

(G) place oil filters.

23. Define the emergency exposure limit (EEL). What is the EEL for HCFC-123?

The EEL is an inhalation exposure limit for emergency situations in which chemicals are accidentally spilled or released. The EEL specifies brief durations and concentrations from which escape is feasible without escape-impairing or irreversible effects on a person's health. The EEL is applicable only to emergencies. Reoccurrence is rarely expected in a person's lifetime. The EEL for HCFC-123 is 1,000 parts per million (ppm) for up to one hour or 2,500 ppm for up to one minute.

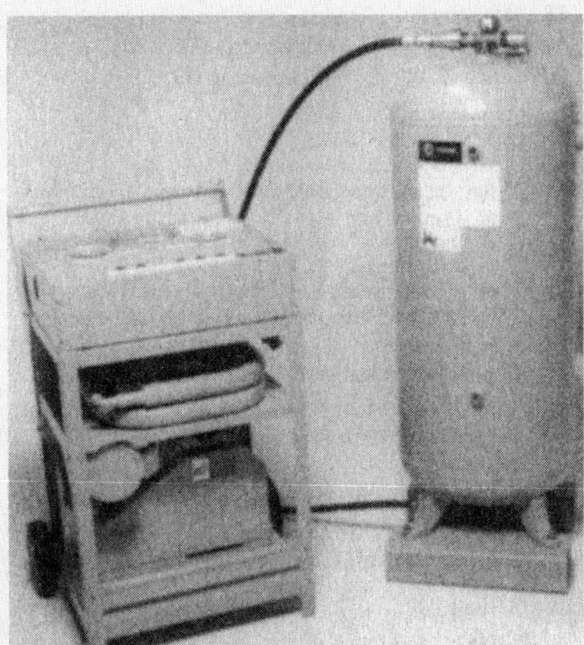

Fig. 19.35
Evacupac photo courtesy the Trane Company.

24. What is the allowable exposure limit (AEL) of HCFC-123, and how was it determined?

The Program for Alternative Fluorocarbon Toxicity (PAFT) performed an inhalation toxicity test on rats over a two-year period. The results indicated that the animals lived longer but suffered a higher incidence of benign pancreatic tumors. Due to these findings, DuPont reduced the allowable exposure limit (AEL) of HCFC-123 from 100 parts ppm to 10 ppm

The AEL is the concentration to which a worker can be exposed for eight hours per day, 40 hours per week, for 50 or more years, without experiencing harmful effects. This rating was designed for workers who may be continually exposed to the refrigerant. A typical chiller plant operator rarely spends more than one hour per day in an engine room and consequently enjoys an enhanced margin of safety.

25. What is the greatest danger posed by any halogen refrigerant?

Halogen refrigerants pose an acute threat of asphyxiation. All halogen refrigerants are heavier than air and displace oxygen in an enclosed space. A significant refrigerant leak in an engine room can cause a person to drown in refrigerant, in a way similar to drowning in water.

26. What is the advantage of installing a run-time meter on a purger unit?

Installing a run-time meter on a purger unit displays and records purger operation in minutes. This shows whether or not a machine is "tight". If a purger runs over five minutes per day, the system is a "leaker." If it runs less than one minute per day, the chiller is a very "tight" machine.

Trane offers an optional refrigerant monitor for refrigerant conservation and operator safety. The refrigerant monitor, installed in a compressor room, provides an early warning of refrigerant loss. This can help limit exposure of maintenance personnel to HCFC-123. The monitor employs an infrared sensor with sensing capability of one ppm. It is also able to differentiate between various compounds.

27. How does Trane comply with the 1990 Federal Clean Air Act, which forbids the venting of controlled refrigerants to the atmosphere?

To reduce refrigerant loss during service operations, Trane offers the Evacupac. It is a portable system that can recover and recycle low-pressure CFC-11, CFC-113, and HCFC-123 refrigerants with virtually no refrigerant escape to the environment. The Evacupac's modular design allows a single operator to transport and set up the system, even in hard-to-manuever equipment rooms. This is an important zero-emissions tool.

The industry offers other portable recovery and recycling systems for different refrigeration systems. All operators and owners must understand that saving refrigerant is the law of the land.

28. When charging R-11 in a centrifugal system's floated chiller, how does an operating engineer determine when enough vapor has entered the system before he can charge with liquid refrigerant?

When the chiller's pressure guage is approximately 16" Hg vacuum the refrigerant's saturation temperature is 36° F.

29. What is the significance of charging a low pressure centrifugal system with liquid refrigerant under a 29" Hg vacuum?

The water flowing through the tubes of the chiller will freeze.

30. The chiller of a centrifugal system, using refrigerant HCFC-123 requires internal repairs to the tube bundle. After recovering liquid refrigerant from the system, what must the operating engineer do before opening the chiller for repairs?

He must recover the remaining refrigerant vapor in the system.

31. What is the pressure of HCFC-123 at 32° F?

20.8 inches of Mercury.

32. During winter maintenance, what is the recommended method used to pressurizing a low pressure centrifugal chiller?

By adding controlled hot water to the chiller's water box.

33. After a system has been evacuated and repairs have been made, what is the recommended method of pressurizing a low pressure centrifugal chiller?

A low pressure chiller is pressurized with nitrogen to test for leaks.

34. A low pressure chiller is to be pressurized with nitrogen. What is the significance if the pressure exceeds 10 psi in the chiller?

If the pressure exceeds 10 psi and reaches 15 psi, the system's rupture disc will break.

35. A mechanic has completed repairs on a HCFC low pressure chiller. To properly leak test the chiller, what component must be installed downstream of the nitrogen cylinder, and why?

A fully charged nitrogen cylinder contains approximately 2500 psi. A pressure regulating valve can be used to provide a very slow flow of nitrogen into the system.

36. At what temperature should refrigerant be charged as vapor into a low pressure chiller in order to raise the saturation temperature?

above 32° F?

37. Standard procedure used to charge a low pressure chiller is

(A) Circulate chill water through the evaporator
(B) Begin charging in the vapor phase
(C) Do not add liquid refrigerant into the system until it has reached the saturation temperature of 32° F.

38. Why does the Trane CentraVac use a purge unit to remove noncondensable gases?

Because low pressure chillers operate below atmospheric pressure.

39. What are the operating pressures for a Trane CentraVac using refrigerant HCFC-123?

3 – 7 psi condenser pressure; 18" Hg evaporator pressure

40. What are the High/Low safety pressure cutouts?

Low Pressure Control cutout = 20" Hg
High Pressure Control cutout = 15 pounds

41. What refrigerant does the Trane Purifier Purger utilize?

Refrigerant HFC-134a

42. What are the cut-in and cut-out temperatures utilized to start and stop the purge tank compressor, in order to remove noncondensable gases?

Temperature control sensor is activated at
18°F—Pumpout compressor turns "ON."
22°F—Pumpout compressor turns "OFF."

43. At what pressure does the rupture disk blow out system pressure?

15 pounds

44. At what pressure can you start to charge the system with refrigerant?

18" Hg

45. At what temperature is the freezestat set to shut down the compressor?

38 degrees F

46. What are the oil pressures of the system?

18 – 22 psi

47. How much oil pressure is regulated to the bearings of the system?

18 – 22 psi

48. What pressure is the oil safety switch set to cut-out?

9 psi

NOTES